MW01156823

AMERICA'S COMMUNAL UTOPIAS

AMERICA'S
COMMUNAL
UTOPIAS

EDITED BY DONALD E. PITZER

FOREWORD BY PAUL S. BOYER

The University of North Carolina Press | Chapel Hill and London

The paper in this book meets the guidelines for permanence and
durability of the Committee on Production Guidelines for Book
Longevity of the Council on Library Resources.

Library of Congress Cataloging-in-Publication Data
America's communal utopias / edited by Donald E. Pitzer ;
foreword by Paul S. Boyer.
p. cm.   Includes bibliographical references and index.
ISBN 0-8078-2299-X (cloth : alk. paper)
ISBN 0-8078-4609-0 (pbk. : alk. paper)
1. Collective settlements—United States—History.
2. Communitarianism—United States.   I. Pitzer, Donald E.
HX653.A63   1997   96-10889
335'.9'0973—dc20   CIP

02 01 00 99 98   6 5 4 3 2

TO THE MEMORY OF ARTHUR E. BESTOR JR.,
DEAN OF AMERICAN COMMUNAL SCHOLARS

CONTENTS

FOREWORD

America's Communal Utopias, a welcome and much-needed book, brings into sharp focus a hitherto ill-mapped stretch of American social-history terrain. In some respects, of course, fragments of the story told here are already well known. As long ago as 1944, after all, Alice Felt Tyler published her engaging and readable account of many of these groups—along with much else—in a popular work called *Freedom's Ferment: Phases of American Social History from the Colonial Period to the Outbreak of the Civil War*. Most Americans probably know something about the Shakers; many have visited restored Shaker settlements or admired reproductions of Shaker furniture. Thanks to the composer Aaron Copland, the Shaker song "The Gift to Be Simple" has become almost as familiar—not to say clichéd—as the dour farm couple immortalized by Grant Wood in *American Gothic*.

Many, too, have heard of John Humphrey Noyes and his Oneida community, around which swirl titillating (and wildly distorted) tales of sexual experimentation and "free love." The word "phalanstery" echoes dimly in the penumbra of some Americans' cultural awareness. Brook Farm is remembered, too, for its connections with Ralph Waldo Emerson, Margaret Fuller, and Nathaniel Hawthorne. The Amana Colonies of Iowa are a major tourist attraction, their name preserved in a line of appliances found in many American homes. Historians and antiquarians keep alive the memory of Robert Owen and his utopian New Harmony venture in Indiana. In more recent times, "hippie" communes and various communal ventures loosely linked to the amorphous New Age movement have attracted attention—sometimes admiring, often puzzled and disapproving.

In short, when the American communal tradition is remembered at all, it tends to be in a confusing and disjointed fashion, as free-floating bits of cultural ephemera. Isolated communities or movements are rarely seen as

ix

comprising a distinctive historical phenomenon whose ideological underpinnings, organizational strategies, and complex interconnections can be studied systematically and traced over time. Though in recent years insightful studies of specific movements have appeared, interest in the hundreds of utopian communities that dot the American past (and present) has in general flourished more among antiquarians and local-history buffs (who deserve high praise for preserving endangered sites and saving crumbling records) than among social historians.

Apart from the tendency toward fragmented rather than comprehensive attention, other reasons for the paucity of serious scholarly consideration of these communal ventures might be suggested. Is not the "communal" impulse vaguely unpatriotic? Have not Americans from time immemorial, as Alexis de Tocqueville and many others tell us, prided themselves on their individualism, preferring the open road, the remote log cabin, or at most the isolated nuclear family, to the constraints of more complex social organizations? When Huck Finn takes off alone for "the territory" at the end of Mark Twain's novel, is he not acting out an impulse buried deep in the American breast? This aspect of the national mythology has perhaps also stood in the way of Americans' fully coming to terms with the communal strand of their history. Even the word itself, with its unsettling similarity to "communism," has heightened the sense that this is a vaguely alien phenomenon, best confined to the periphery of American social history and Americans' sense of national identity.

Marxist and radical historians, meanwhile, have dismissed these communal experiments as the definitive example of romantic "Utopian" socialism, the dreamy movement whose only historical interest lies in its role as the forerunner of its revolutionary, "scientific," and allegedly non-Utopian successor, Marxian socialism. Labor historians have tended to emulate Norman J. Ware, who as long ago as 1924, in *The Industrial Worker, 1840–1860*, viewed the utopian communities, especially those modeled on the ideas of the French visionary Charles Fourier, as a middle-class diversion from the serious business of trade-union organization and working-class consciousness raising.

For a variety of reasons, then, American utopian communities have not fared well at the hands of historians. Arthur Bestor made a promising interpretive beginning in the early 1950s, but his work found few successors.[1] Textbook references tend to be superficial, treating these movements (if at all) in a catch-all chapter on "antebellum reform" and evaluating them in bland terms reminiscent of Alice Felt Tyler's patriotic conclusion in 1944 that while these communities failed, their ideals nevertheless entered "the mainstream of

American life . . . , contributing their share to the democratic philosophy of the New World."

In reality, of course, these often marginalized and patronized movements arose from basic human needs and impulses. All human populations, including Americans, display the tendency to come together in extended social groups. Indeed, as Donald Pitzer reminds us in his introduction, the communal impulse seems encoded in the genetic makeup of nearly all life-forms. The much-celebrated, much-vilified "American individualism," while it no doubt offers one key to understanding the national character, has always been balanced by a powerful affiliative drive drawing men and women into religious congregations, fraternal lodges, ethnic organizations, sports clubs, reform groups, mutual-improvement juntas, professional societies, civic associations—and communal ventures. As Michael Fellman noted in his 1973 work *The Unbounded Frame: Freedom and Community in Nineteenth-Century American Utopianism*, the tension between freedom and individualism, on the one hand, and social commitment and submission to true authority, on the other, is a central dynamic in American history. In one sense, indeed, the intentionally formed communities examined in *America's Communal Utopias* merely represent a particularly strong manifestation of a much more pervasive social process.

The communitarian impulse can hardly be claimed as uniquely American. Few things are. Indeed, the ideological and social antecedents of many of the groups considered in this volume lay in Europe. But American society, with its comparative lack of hierarchy, freedom from the weight of tradition, and openness to social innovation, has historically provided a particularly congenial environment in which communal experimentation could flourish.

From the days of the Puritans to the latest California commune, the impulse to form highly cohesive communities knit together by a common ideology and a shared vision of social harmony has been a constant in American history. While communalism enjoyed its greatest efflorescence in the 1820–50 era (with a second wave in the post-1960 years), it has never been absent from the American experience.

Yet, surprisingly, American historians have had difficulty making sense of the nation's utopian tradition—a difficulty mirrored in the profession as a whole. As Frank E. Manuel wrote in 1965 of the many Utopian communities that have arisen in the history of the West, "Their full collective story has not yet been told, despite the availability of individual accounts." When this movement found its historian, he concluded, assessments of its significance would surely be amended in important respects.[2] The three decades that have elapsed since Manuel wrote these words have seen the publication of a number of monographic studies and histories of specific movements—some of them excellent[3]—but the comprehensive work that he envisioned remains unwritten.

The historians who have collaborated on *America's Communal Utopias*, many of whom are active in the Communal Studies Association, have taken a major step toward filling this gap in the historical literature. The work represents a significant advance in viewing this phase of American social history comprehensively and highlighting its central contours.

The scholars represented here respect the uniqueness and rich diversity of the various communities and movements they examine, but they are also sensitive to the continuities and commonalities that come into focus as one looks at these movements broadly rather than in isolation. In these essays on many different utopian communities and movements, one can recognize both their individual differences and their family resemblance.

The essays also illustrate the chameleon-like adaptability of the communal impulse. Over a span of three centuries, this mode of social organization has served the needs of German Pietist sects, millenarian visionaries immersed in Bible prophecy, religious perfectionists, sexual reformers, secular ideologists searching for alternatives to the emerging urban-industrial order, and a host of spiritual seekers from theosophists to devotees of various Eastern gurus. Taken together, these histories add up to a rich tapestry of American social experimentation.

America's Communal Utopias moves beyond earlier studies in the breadth of its coverage, including not only the comparatively well known communities rooted in the German Pietist or English dissenting traditions, but also communities founded by Roman Catholic monastics, impoverished Jewish immigrants, and destitute African Americans coping with the Great Depression. Further, as Donald Pitzer notes in his introduction, the work challenges the dismissive "forerunner" interpretive model and the simplistic "success/ failure" dichotomy of some earlier studies. The social historians represented here assess these movements on their own terms and view them from a developmental perspective in which communalism may be embraced by a group for a period of time and then yield to another mode of social organization.

This is not by any means a ramble down some arcane byway of American social history. These communities tell us much about the culture that spawned them and the time periods in which they arose. These efforts to devise radical new forms of social organization illuminate the fears and issues of their day. While these ventures attracted relatively few active participants, and while from one perspective they seem on the margins of American society, the concerns they addressed and the goals they sought resonated far more widely.

The men and women who planned these communities, and the thousands who joined them, are at last beginning to find their place in American history. The contributors to *America's Communal Utopias* have made a major contribution to this process.

Paul S. Boyer

Notes

1. Arthur E. Bestor Jr., *Backwoods Utopias: The Sectarian Origins and the Owenite Phase of Communitarian Socialism in America, 1663–1829* (Philadelphia: University of Pennsylvania Press, 1950) and "Patent Office Models of the Good Society: Some Relationships between Social Reform and Westward Expansion," *American Historical Review* 58 (1952): 505–26. For further discussion of the historiography of American utopian communities, see Paul Boyer, "A Joyful Noyes: Reassessing America's Utopian Tradition," *Reviews in American History*, March 1975, pp. 25–30, and "Association Forever: A New Look at the Fourier Movement," *Reviews in American History*, March 1992, pp. 35–40.

2. Frank E. Manuel, ed., *Utopias and Utopian Thought* (Boston: Houghton Mifflin, 1966), p. xiii.

3. See, for example, *The Utopian Alternative: Fourierism in Nineteenth-Century America* (Ithaca: Cornell University Press, 1991), by Carl J. Guarneri, also a contributor to this volume.

This book has two purposes. The first is to make available to students and general readers the stories of America's historic communal utopias in clear and concise form based on the latest scholarship. The second is to present communal utopias from the perspective of "developmental communalism." This developmental approach places communal groups in the broader context of the movements and historic circumstances that create, change, and sometimes destroy them.

Public and scholarly interest in communal utopias increased dramatically in the decades after the sunburst of communes founded by the youth movement of the 1960s. The creation of thousands of communal havens to escape the Establishment and to build Utopia raised pressing questions about the benefits and dangers of living communally. Most of these could be answered best by an examination of the historical record. Therefore, historians and scholars from a wider variety of other academic disciplines than ever before became attracted to the study of utopian communalism. These students of communalism have enjoyed greater access to historical documentation and to information from practicing communitarians than any previous generation of researchers. They have used these advantages to produce new analyses of the many forms, purposes, and results of communal usage from ancient times to the present.

This anthology became possible, if not imperative, as a product of the burgeoning of such recent scholarship. The growth of knowledge reached a critical mass by the 1990s through the interchange of ideas occurring in publications, networks, and meetings. Three organizations arose after 1975 to facilitate the sharing of communal and utopian information by means of conferences, journals, and newsletters: the National Historic Communal Societies Association (NHCSA) (begun in 1975 and renamed the Communal Studies Association [CSA] in 1990), the Society for Utopian Studies (1976), and the

International Communal Studies Association (ICSA) (1985). The NHCSA/CSA grew out of the first annual Historic Communal Societies Conference in New Harmony, Indiana, in November 1974. This meeting was sponsored by the history department of Indiana State University in Evansville (now the University of Southern Indiana [USI]), which had granted me a leave of absence the previous spring. During this leave, I visited numerous historic and contemporary communal sites in the United States and Europe and made the contacts from which the New Harmony meeting became possible. It was my privilege to represent the university and New Harmony on the conference planning committee with others who became active in the NHCSA: Ronald Nelson of Bishop Hill, Illinois; Karen Platz-Hunt-Adams of Bethel, Missouri; and Daniel Reibel of Old Economy Village in Ambridge, Pennsylvania. The second annual Historic Communal Societies Conference that met in November 1975 in the restored Shaker Village at Pleasant Hill, Kentucky, witnessed the formal organization of the NHCSA. By 1976 the Center for Communal Studies, for which I was named director, was established by Indiana State University in Evansville (USI) as NHCSA headquarters, a clearinghouse for information and an archival repository. In the meantime, interaction of scholars on communal themes progressed on other fronts. Sociologist Ruth Shonle Cavan, who attended the meeting at which the NHCSA was founded, had organized a Conference on Communes: Historical and Contemporary the previous April at Northern Illinois University. She guest edited the papers from that gathering in the *International Review of Modern Sociology* 6 (Spring 1976).

In 1976 another professional organization, the Society for Utopian Studies, sprang from a meeting called by history professor Merritt Abrash at Rensselaer Polytechnic Institute. He and English professor Arthur O. Lewis of Pennsylvania State University were leading founders. Several of us who attended the early utopian and communal meetings took the opportunity to begin the ICSA in 1985 during the International Conference on Kibbutz and Communes directed by historian Yaacov Oved at Yad Tabenkin in Efal, Israel. Elected executive director of the ICSA headquartered at Yad Tabenkin, Professor Oved has organized triennial conferences in Scotland, the United States, and Israel. Also important in bringing together communal scholars from various disciplines was political scientist Charles Redenius of Pennsylvania State University at Erie. In the 1980s he introduced a track of sessions on utopianism and communitarianism at the annual meetings of the Popular Culture Association.

Developmental communalism, the theoretical framework for the essays in this book, grew from provocative seeds of thought sown by Madeline Roemig during a 1981 conference at the Inspirationist Amana Colonies in Iowa. After my paper "Phases of American Communalism," Roemig, a community descendant, asked why I had indicated that the Amanas no longer fit into communal history after 1932 when the Inspirationists abandoned strict community of goods. In essence, she said, "We are still a community. We still share common concerns. We still care deeply for one another. We still practice the faith of our religious movement. We still worship together. We still have an Amana Society."

At that moment my mind was not open to the developmental process she understood by experience. I could not then conceive that in the seven Amana villages I was witnessing the postcommunal phase of a living religious movement. After its German origin in the eighteenth century and migration to the United States in the nineteenth, the Inspirationist movement had adopted common property in 1843 to satisfy specific needs. After nearly a century, in 1932 its members had just as consciously decided to abandon their imitation of first-century Christian communism in order to adjust to new circumstances. They were realistically permitting their movement to continue its developmental process in other organizational forms. Perhaps unwittingly, they were following the pattern of structural adjustment seen when the early Christians themselves, as well as the later Moravians, Mormons, and others, stopped requiring the sharing of property. The Inspirationists had shown the vitality of innovative decision making that I would later term "developmental communalism."

In 1983 my first visit to the Jewish communes known as kibbutz in Israel began to help me clarify the developmental process at work within movements that chose to organize communally in response to needs. Before me stood communal settlements that served as Jewish sanctuaries begun since early in this century by the socialist Zionist movement that helped secure an independent Israel by 1948. I began to understand that movements sometimes find communal, cooperative, and collective organizational structures attractive during a formative stage for the strength, solidarity, and security they offer while the group reaches hopefully toward an ultimate secular or religious objective. Yet in 1983 I found kibbutzim in different stages of development. Some were just forming while others were pondering whether they had fulfilled their basic national purpose and could now abandon the disciplines of communal living even though they treasured kibbutz fellowship, equality, and other benefits. I wondered whether the larger Zionist movement was still viable as a driving inspiration or had lost its identity to the communal form and communal objectives of its own creation, the kibbutz. Could the two now be separated? Had communal living become an end in itself, maybe the new objective? If the last were true, I was concerned whether the kibbutz faced the withering trend that had beset the movements that sacrificed their identities to the communal and other disciplines they had adopted in an early stage of development. The Shakers, Harmonists, Zoarites, Keilites, and Janssonists came readily to mind.

Coincidentally, Madeline Roemig of Amana and I both attended the 1985 International Conference on Kibbutz and Communes at the Yad Tabenkin in Israel. After a session in which she spoke about the Amana Colonies, she fielded a standard question: "Why did the Amana Colonies fail?" As she had done for me in 1981, Roemig quickly explained that the Amana Colonies had not failed. They were still functioning communities, and their Inspirationist religious movement was still very much alive. By that time I already had become convinced enough of the validity of the developmental communalism concept to mention it in an earlier meeting of the NHCSA. Now, when I introduced the idea following Roemig's comments, I discovered that this developmental approach seemed to open new avenues of understanding and to stimulate significant interest.

Developmental communalism as described in the introduction and illustrated in the essays of this book builds on these early insights as supported by subsequent investigation and the refinements provided by the shared wisdom and critical comments of academic colleagues and current communitarians. In its present form, developmental communalism rests on three assumptions. First, communal living is a generic social mechanism available in all ages to all peoples, governments, and movements. Second, communal structuring usually is adopted in an early stage of development (or during a crisis) because of the security, solidarity, and ease of experimentation it promises. Third, communal arrangements that are not adjusted over time to changing realities or abandoned altogether for organizational strategies more compatible with long-range objectives may contribute to the decline or demise of the original movements, governments, or peoples that chose them. In actuality, then, developmental communalism suggests that double jeopardy may confront all communal utopias. If movements that found them eventually make needed adjustments away from communal living, the communes dissolve. If movements embrace communal living as a "permanent" structure or tenet of faith, the resulting rigidity of discipline may cause the stagnation or death of the movements themselves and, thus, their communal units.

The understanding and encouragement of many colleagues and communitarians assisted me in formulating the developmental interpretation. My close associate in the NHCSA/CSA and Center for Communal Studies, sociologist Charles Petranek, encouraged me to pursue my earliest conceptions of a developmental hypothesis regarding communal groups and would not let me quit until I researched the idea further and stated it publicly. My late friend Charles Redenius gave me the opportunity to present my first paper completely devoted to developmental communalism at the Popular Culture Association meeting in Atlanta in 1986. Several contributors to this book and I have discussed examples of developmentalism in communal history on panels at NHCSA/CSA conferences and at one meeting of its Pacific Coast Chapter. Dennis Hardy and Lorna Davidson permitted me to test the developmental concept with a broader audience in an address to a plenary session at the ICSA meeting at the University of Edinburgh in 1988 and published it as "Developmental Communalism: An Alternative Approach to Communal Studies" in their *Utopian Thought and Communal Experience* (1989).

I am particularly grateful for the theoretical observations of Jonathan Andelson, Albert Bates, Joe Peterson, Don Janzen, Timothy Miller, Michael Cummings, Elizabeth Schoenfelder, Allen Butcher, Dan Questenberry, Yaacov Oved, Carol Jean Rogalski, Marjorie Jones, Thomas Askew, Jon Wagner, Mildred Gordon, and Robert Brown. Kibbutz members and scholars at meetings at Yad Tabenkin, Harvard University, and New Lanark, Scotland, shared their critical perspectives. To the contributors to this book who ventured to test developmental communalism against the experience of the movements about which they know best, I express special appreciation. Beyond all the exposure, critiques, and testing, however, any errors and gaps that remain in the developmental communalism approach remain my own.

The possibility of editing this volume derived from opportunities for which I am grateful. As the first president of the NHCSA in 1975 and 1976 and its executive director from 1977 to 1993, I was privileged to become acquainted with the people, places, and resources essential to producing such an anthology. The consistent, enthusiastic support of administrators of the University of Southern Indiana for my historical research and direction of annual conferences expressed itself in the creation of the Center for Communal Studies as a base of operation under my direction in the history department and School of Liberal Arts. Especially helpful have been Social Science Division Chair Daniel Miller, School of Liberal Arts Dean James Blevins, Academic Vice-President Robert Reid, and Presidents David L. Rice and H. Ray Hoops. USI archivist emerita Josephine Mirabella Elliott, the predominant inspiration for my work, has been a storehouse of ready information on her beloved New Harmony. Current archivist Gina Walker has tirelessly pursued needed references. A USI faculty research grant relieved many expenses in producing the manuscript. The authors themselves gave unsparingly of their time and expertise to summarize their understandings of the history and development of the utopian movements and communal initiatives in which they are specialists, while generously agreeing that virtually all the proceeds will accrue to the CSA. My special thanks go to Jonathan Andelson and Lawrence Foster for tendering seminal suggestions on textual form and content throughout the project. Donald Janzen, Timothy Miller, and the late Lawrence Anderson contributed freely from their own research to the appendix listing of communal utopias founded by 1965. Geoph Kozeny, Dan Questenberry, Laird Schaub, Harvey Baker, and other members of the Fellowship for Intentional Community (FIC) shared their extensive knowledge of contemporary intentional communities. The FIC itself permitted me to guest edit its Winter 1985 *Communities: Journal of Cooperation* as a survey of historic communal groups in essays by several of the authors featured in the current anthology.

Since this volume is addressed particularly to students and general readers, I found it useful to have the comments of the students in my communal history seminar, who read most of these essays in early drafts. I am especially grateful to Leigh Ann Chamness, my graduate student who collaborated with me in preparing Karl J. R. Arndt's essay for publication after his death. In the Center for Communal Studies and School of Liberal Arts offices, Mary Hayden oversaw the constant flow of drafts and proofread copy while Kim Reddington, Cheril Griswold, and Mary Jane Schenk assisted with word processing.

Professor Paul Boyer of the Institute for Research in the Humanities at the University of Wisconsin gave invaluable support and counsel from the inception of the project and contributed the foreword. Barbara Hanrahan, Sian Hunter White, David Perry, and Ron Maner of the University of North Carolina Press kindly encouraged and wisely guided the editorial and production efforts. Stephanie Wenzel expertly copyedited the manuscript. My wife, Mariann, graciously endured yet another of my academic ventures while our daughter and son, Tonja and Don, volunteered their usual unbiased criticism of my writing.

The authors affectionately dedicate this work to the memory of distinguished historian Arthur E. Bestor Jr. In 1950 he set the standard for scholarship in the communal field with his *Backwoods Utopias: The Sectarian Origins and the Owenite Phase of Communitarian Socialism in America, 1663–1829.* Although his main focus later moved away from communitarianism, Professor Bestor encouraged the communal studies of others and endorsed the work of the NHCSA. He participated in NHCSA/CSA meetings in Aurora, Oregon, and Tacoma, Washington. In 1988 Professor Bestor returned to New Harmony to give the address commemorating the 150th anniversary of the founding of the Workingmen's Institute Library, where he had cataloged much of the Owenite collection during his communal research in the 1940s.

On May 14, 1988, he received an honorary doctorate from the University of Southern Indiana in recognition of his scholarly achievements. It was my privilege to read the citation honoring Dr. Bestor on that occasion and on that of his receipt of the Distinguished Scholar Award of the Communal Studies Association during its Aurora, Oregon, conference in 1991. The opening era of communal scholarship ended with the death of Arthur Bestor at his home in Seattle on December 13, 1994. With this anthology we open the next era in his honor.

Center for Communal Studies
University of Southern Indiana
April 1996

AMERICA'S COMMUNAL UTOPIAS

Those who occupy its peaceful dwellings [at New Harmony, Indiana], are so closely united by the endearing ties of friendship, confidence and love, that one heart beats in all, and their common industry provides for all.
GEORGE RAPP, *Thoughts on the Destiny of Man*, 1824

It is of all truths the most important, that the character of man is formed FOR—not BY himself.
ROBERT OWEN, *The Crisis*, 1833

DONALD E. PITZER

Introduction

Communal sharing is as old as the earliest known fossils of living things on earth and as new as electronic communities in cyberspace. More than 3 billion years ago, stromatolite bacteria formed colonies to protect all but those on their exteriors from deadly ultraviolet sunlight. "This may have been a potent early impetus for a communal way of life," according to Carl Sagan in *Shadows of Forgotten Ancestors*. "Some died that others might live. . . . We glimpse the earliest lifeforms on Earth and the first message conveyed is not of Nature red in tooth and claw, but of a Nature of cooperation and harmony."

In the dim recesses of the past as human beings began to develop, they also discovered the security, solidarity, and survival offered by cooperative and communal organization. Bands, kinship groups, and tribes, then and now, display certain features of community of goods and shared responsibilities. In their formative stages and during crises, many religious, social, and political movements have chosen the benefits and discipline of tight-knit communal cooperation. Essenes and the early Christians lived communally. Social reformers have urged building self-contained communities. Governments sometimes have encouraged or forced citizens to live communally, as in Soviet collective farms, New Deal homesteads, and Maoist Peoples Communes.

Since the youth movement and hippie communes beginning in the 1960s, communal sharing has burgeoned into new forms to serve new purposes. Traditional communes of common property or joint-stock agreements have been outnumbered by cooperatives, collectives, and land trusts. Intentionally formed communities now satisfy needs not only for religious commitment and social reform, but also for alternative lifestyles, cohousing, private

3

schooling, medical care, and retirement opportunities. Most recently, electronic communities have emerged as individuals with common interests communicate with, fraternize with, and assist one another on computer online networks.

Like communal sharing, utopian dreaming has ancient origins and modern applications. Early Western civilization imagined paradise and the ideal state in the Hebrew account of the Garden of Eden, Plato's *Republic* of the fourth century B.C., and the Zoroastrian and Christian conceptions of a transcendent heaven of splendor. In 1516 Thomas More coined from one of two Greek words, *Outopia* (no place) or *Eutopia* (the good place), the ambiguous term *Utopia* as the title for his now-famous book. Before and since the Protestant Reformation, Christian sects have anxiously awaited the peace and plenty to follow an imminent second coming of Christ. America itself beckoned like a utopia to such millennialist sectarians and to a myriad of secular dreamers. Meanwhile in England, Sir Francis Bacon's *The New Atlantis* offered a vision of a scientific promised land in 1627, and James Harrington's *Commonwealth of Oceana*, printed in 1656, explained how political control could be balanced ideally among monarchical, aristocratic, and popular factions. Utopian socialists in eighteenth-century Europe imagined ways to alleviate the human hardships that accompanied the Industrial Revolution. Their plans for rebuilding society inspired movements led by generations of socialists and communitarian socialists. In the United States the perfect system labeled "Nationalism" by Edward Bellamy in his influential 1888 novel *Looking Backward: 2000–1887* was Socialism under a more palatable name. American Theosophists by the late nineteenth century and many counterculture youth during the Vietnam War era drew upon Eastern thought for their ideal models of society and enlightenment.

From the perverted, private utopias conceived in the minds of Stalin, Franco, Hitler, Mussolini, Mao, Hussein, and others sprang the *dystopias* of our century in the ugly forms of imperialism, war, racism, and the Holocaust. Alarmed by such nightmares and the growing nuclear threat, "New Utopians" appeared in America. Since the 1980s their New Age movement has called for personal and planetary transformation. They champion cooperation, human values, common sense, holistic health, consensus decision making, and worldwide networking for peace. By the 1990s virtual reality through computer imaging was being declared the ultimate frontier for human social experimentation by one of its pioneers, Jaron Lanier. In the artificial cyberspace of this revolutionary technology, he claims, our species has its first opportunity to create entirely new environments and interactions for good or ill—utopia or dystopia.

DONALD E. PITZER

When utopian dreams and communal sharing combine, they produce communal utopias, the intriguing social phenomenon discussed in this book. In this type of close-knit community much or all property is shared communally. Members join voluntarily and live in rural settlements or urban housing partly isolated and insulated from the general society. They share an ideology and lifestyle while attempting to implement the group's ideals. As microcosms, they form unique and instructive social laboratories.

Communal utopias formed by the religious and social movements examined in this volume are often described by a host of rather confusing terms. You will meet their "communists" and "communitarians" in "communes," "communal societies," "utopian communities," "millennial sects," "socialist phalanxes," "monasteries," and "cults." Regardless of the names used to describe and deride them, communal utopias have been a perennial topic of fascination for generations of Americans—both scholars and the general public. Until recently, however, much of this popular interest has been relatively unsophisticated, sensationalistic, or sentimentalized. Communal experimenters have often been portrayed simply as colorful "freaks," psychological misfits outside the "mainstream" who inevitably "failed" because they allegedly were out of step with American life and values. Although some sensitive scholarship has appeared, communitarians have more commonly been presented as if they were primitive natives in some exotic foreign culture or mindless actors in a circus side show. Even the early Marxists, whose communistic efforts often have been misleadingly equated with those of the communitarians, criticized such groups as visionary and impractical "utopian socialists" only frustrating the coming revolution of the proletariat. Seldom have the efforts of those who chose the communal way been judged on their own merits, from the point of view of what *they* were trying to accomplish and how well they succeeded from their *own* perspectives. Seldom have such groups been considered effectively as an important element in the larger American social and cultural context of which they were a part.

This book reflects the new thrust of scholarly interest in alternative communal living that has emerged during the past three decades. This new scholarship continues to convey the lively and colorful character of American utopian communal experimentation. But it also goes beyond this surface level to look more closely at what these groups themselves were trying to do, how they went about doing it, and how well they achieved their goals before, during, and sometimes after a communal stage. The dynamic developmental process at work within their founding movements rather than merely a static snapshot of their communal days has been the major focus of these newest studies. This new scholarship also has emphasized the relationship of alternative communal experiments to the larger fabric of American society. Precisely because tightly organized intentional communities frequently exaggerate characteristic American values or carry particular concerns to their extreme logical conclusion, they may more vividly highlight issues easily overlooked when studying more conventional movements. In particular, utopian communal experiments suggest new perspectives on the distinctive character of American religion, ethnicity, and social reform, as well as on our particular sense of national mission.

The roots of self-conscious communal experimentation in America go back to the early days of English colonial settlement. Both the Pilgrims who settled Plymouth Colony in 1620 and the Puritans who started their "Bible Commonwealth" in Massachusetts in 1630 expressed many concerns that continued to influence later American immigrants' efforts to create cohesive communal societies. As a survival technique, the Calvinist Pilgrims of Plymouth accepted the discipline of community of property from 1620 to 1623. The Puritan effort to set up a "City upon a Hill" that would serve as a model for the transformation of both English and American society has been particularly influential and studied by scholars. The Puritan village, which historian Kenneth Lockridge characterized as an example of "Christian closed corporate utopian community," and the larger Bible Commonwealth of which it was a part, served, in the words of historian Perry Miller, as an "ideal laboratory" through which the process of social change can more readily be studied than in larger and more complex social contexts. Despite the original "declension" and loss of a sense of the intensity of the original Puritan vision of their ideal society, the idealism of these early formative experiments has continued to influence the development of America's distinctive sense of mission. Although this book contains no essays on the heavily studied Pilgrims and Puritans, who developed more readily beyond their communal sharing phase than some later groups, their experience nevertheless set an important precedent for later communal experiments assessed in this volume.

Closely connected with such early efforts to create planned societies in America was the millennial religious emphasis associated with the Judeo-Christian tradition of a coming Messiah. Millennialism, the idea that Christ, the Christian Messiah, will come a second time and reign on earth during a thousand-year "Millennium" of peace and redemption, abundance and wealth, justice and happiness, is one of the most potent ideas in Western civilization. The primary sources of millennialism come from biblical prophecies, especially those of Daniel, chapter 2, and Revelation, chapter 20, and statements in the Gospels about Jesus' return to establish a kingdom of heaven on earth. Of special significance for those religious movements seeking to recapture the faith and social structure of early Christianity is the passage from Acts 2:44–45, which states, "And all who believed were together and had all things in common; and they sold their possessions and goods and distributed them to all, as any had need." The fact that millennial and communal passages can be interpreted in a variety of ways has encouraged a proliferation of blueprints for the ideal society by those who are convinced that a corrupt existing system will eventually be replaced by a new and more just order under divine guidance. Eventually many of these millenarian religious hopes also came to influence secular social reformers, such as Robert Owen, in their parallel efforts at achieving a more equitable social order.

Let us look briefly at the different communitarian experiments discussed in this book and some of their unique stories. European immigrants who followed the Pilgrims and Puritans to colonial America and who chose to be even more fully and lastingly communal also had millenarian religious roots. The earliest of these were the ill-fated Dutch Mennonites of Plockhoy's Commonwealth, founded in 1663 by Pieter Plockhoy and completely destroyed the next year as the English captured the Dutch settlement on the Delaware River, possibly selling some of the communal settlers into slavery. Several decades later Jean de Labadie, "the second Calvin," founded a community, like several he had already started in Europe, at Bohemia Manor in Pennsylvania. Thinking Christ would descend from the skies in 1694 and that they would never die, forty celibate male scholars from Europe calling themselves The Woman in the Wilderness, created an engrossing community near Germantown, Pennsylvania. The Ephrata Cloister of the Seventh Day Baptists, now an inviting historic restoration in Lancaster County, thrived for decades after 1735, known for its calligraphy, manuscript illumination, and choral music. And the Moravian Brethren, the first Protestant denomination, following Jan Hus, who had been martyred in 1415, and later Count Nicholas Zinzendorf, developed a successful plan for settling their converts in America by means of communal "congregation towns" organized temporarily under a "general economy." Known for their music, schools, and painting, extensive Moravian towns can still be seen at Bethlehem, Pennsylvania, and Old Salem in present-day Winston-Salem, North Carolina.

The best-known religious movement to espouse communal living as a tenet of faith in nineteenth-century America was the group popularly known as the Shakers. Originating in a small revivalistic English sect that its leader, Ann Lee, led to America in 1774, the Shakers by the 1830s had attracted some 4,000 members to more than sixty celibate community units called "families" in nearly twenty different agricultural settlements from Maine to Indiana. Controversial in the nineteenth century because of their lively religious services, requirement of celibacy, and veneration of Ann Lee, the movement survives after more than 200 years in one small community at Sabbathday Lake, Maine. Many know the Shakers today because of the prominent role they accorded women; the simplicity of their furniture, textiles, and other products; and their original songs such as "Simple Gifts."

Among the many immigrant groups of Germanic and North European origins who turned to the security of communal economies in illustrious and long-lived communities in America, this book focuses on four: the Harmonists, the Inspirationists, the Janssonists, and the Hutterites. Patriarchal Pietist George Rapp came to America in 1803 followed by more than 1,000 disciples awaiting the cosmic Harmony to follow Christ's return. As members of the celibate Harmony Society, they built Harmony and Economy (now Ambridge), Pennsylvania, and New Harmony, Indiana, where guides still bring their dreams, music, and crafts to life. Often still mistaken for Amish, the residents of the seven closely welded Amana villages in Iowa are Inspirationists, a separate German sect led for a time, like the Shakers, by a woman of special spiritual gifts, Barbara Heinemann. In 1932, nearly a century after adopting community of goods out of necessity in New York, the Inspirationists sought to preserve the vitality of their movement by returning to the freedom of private ownership. The famous Amana brand of refrigerators is one result. A third communal group from Europe highlighted here are the Swedish Separatists who followed the controversial Pietist Eric Jansson to their communal haven in Bishop Hill, Illinois, where they nearly froze upon arrival in 1846 and later saw their leader murdered by a disgruntled convert in 1850. The thriving Swedish town survived Jansson's death in communal form for more than a decade. Visitors now enjoy its lingering Swedish flavor, faithfully restored buildings, and famous paintings of Olof Krans memorializing the Bishop Hill colony and its citizens.

Today the most numerous and economically successful of all the Germanic immigrant communitarians in America, the Hutterites, trace the roots of their Anabaptist movement to 1528 in the Austrian province of Tyrol. One of their earliest leaders, Jacob Hutter, was burned at the stake in 1536 in a martyrdom later suffered by thousands of Hutterites. Following the first-century Christian example, these pacifists united in communal *bruderhofs* for their own protection against persecution in several European countries. In 1874 800 fled to the Dakota Territory from Russia. Four hundred of these chose to continue their tradition of community of goods and now have branched into some 400 Hutterite colonies with 40,000 residents spread across the western United States and Canada. Hutterites are closely related religiously to the Amish, who nevertheless found the secret of building their sect on the spirit

8

of community without demanding community of property. Further, where the Amish use modern technology very selectively, the Hutterites enthusiastically embrace the latest devices from complex farm machinery to fax machines. A few areas of the United States and Canada have passed laws limiting Hutterite acquisition of land because of the opposition of commercial farmers who have difficulty competing with them. The Hutterites share this challenge with the Amish as well as the threat of erosion from within presented by the influx of secular culture.

Two millennial groups that originated in America also engaged in some of the most controversial and interesting communal experimentation. The largest and most successful of all the millennial movements that have had a strong communal emphasis is the Church of Jesus Christ of Latter-day Saints, better known as Mormons. Although the rapidly growing Mormon community is the fifth largest denomination in the United States today, with some 9 million members worldwide, when begun by Joseph Smith in the 1820s and 1830s the group was violently attacked because of its distinctive theology, binding communal commitments, and practice of polygamy—all of which were important components in its successful colonization of Utah and adjacent areas of the Great Basin during the last half of the nineteenth century. Far smaller, but even more unorthodox, were the Perfectionists of John Humphrey Noyes at the Oneida Community in New York. For more than thirty years they practiced a form of birth control, a group marriage misleadingly described as "free love," and, eventually, a unique eugenic experiment. Public reaction to such radicalism forced Noyes to flee into Canada, while his perfectionists reorganized in 1880 as a joint-stock corporation that still produces the well-known Oneida silverware.

In addition to the religious millenarian groups, three important secular communitarian efforts of the nineteenth century are assessed in this volume. Robert Owen, the wealthy cotton manufacturer who set up his model factory town at New Lanark, Scotland, dreamed of a New Moral World based on education, science, and the communal living he learned from the Shakers and Harmonists. He organized an influential but short-lived community at New Harmony, Indiana, during the mid-1820s that inspired twenty socialistic communities elsewhere in the United States and Britain. In the early 1840s, American followers of the reclusive French social theorist Charles Fourier began the formation of dozens of generally short-lived, joint-stock communities called "phalanxes" devoted to ameliorating problems suffered by rapidly industrializing America in the wake of the panic of 1837. And in the late 1840s, Etienne Cabet, the French social reformer and author of the utopian novel *Voyage en Icarie*, came to America to plant a series of Icarian communities that expanded for nearly fifty years from Texas and Illinois to Missouri, Iowa, and California.

Almost all previous studies of communitarians in America, influenced by the white Anglo-Saxon Protestant biases that have pervaded American scholarship until recently, have ignored the role of the numerous Roman Catholic, Jewish, and African American communal associations of the nineteenth and twentieth centuries. The essay on Roman Catholic monasticism in America provides, for the first time in a book of this type, a synoptic overview of the Catholic religious orders, encompassing hundreds of thousands of individuals carrying on in America the rich traditions of more than 1,500 years of organized Roman Catholic monasticism. Now struggling mightily in their own developmental process to prove the ability of their celibate orders to overcome the odds of an aging membership and a dearth of novices, these Catholic communitarians have founded and served schools, hospitals, and churches whose immense impact on American history are beyond calculation.

A similar overview analysis demonstrates how the communal method was used to settle Jewish immigrants in more than eighty farming colonies founded from 1820 to 1938. The ideals of this collective effort suggest much about the impulses that later gave rise to the use of communal kibbutz by the Zionist movement to settle thousands of immigrant Jews in Palestine to help achieve an independent state of Israel. Although communal settlements were also used in America to assist hundreds of former slaves into the life of freedom, as at Frances Wright's Nashoba community near Memphis, Tennessee, the essay devoted to African American use of communalism deals with the Peace Mission Movement of Father Divine in this century. The religious movement he founded has challenged America to live up to its egalitarian ideals and has offered insight into how Americans of varied ethnicity have united their efforts in a single movement combining religion, community, and social uplift to help solve the problems of urban, industrial America.

In the late nineteenth and early twentieth centuries the focus of much of America's communal utopian experimentation shifted to California, Oregon, and Washington, where all manner of religious and social causes found a sympathetic hearing. Two essays in this book concentrate on movements that introduced utopian communalism along the Pacific coast. One details the proliferation of communities founded by disgruntled socialists, communists, and labor unionists in California. At Kaweah Cooperative Commonwealth, where they had the giant redwood they dubbed the "Karl Marx Tree," now known as the "General Sherman Tree," they labored bravely against impossible conditions to found a utopia based on lumber production. Outside Los

Angeles, socialists under Job Harriman set up Llano del Rio, one of the largest and most family-oriented communes, boasting the earliest Montessori school in California. The essay on Theosophical communities illustrates the impact of the first wave of Eastern mysticism in America by the late nineteenth century as a precursor of the widespread effects it would have on the youth movement in its counterculture communal experimentation after the mid-1960s. One wing of Theosophy, led by humanitarian Katherine Tingley, created at Point Loma near San Diego the most culturally oriented collective group of its day. It emphasized music, education for Cuban orphans, and plays in its own Greek amphitheater that still overlooks the Pacific shore as a physical monument to the Theosophical utopian dream.

As seemingly bizarre to outsiders as any modern flying saucer group led by a channeler was the Koreshan Unity founded by a medical doctor, Cyrus Reed Teed, who experienced an "illumination" proclaiming him the new messiah in 1869. Although in no way related to David Koresh's Branch Davidians who were assaulted in 1993 by agents of the federal government at Waco, Texas, both Teed and Vernon Howell adopted the Hebrew form of "Cyrus" as a new name—Teed becoming simply "Koresh." Teed's Koreshans combined a complex hollow-earth cosmology with feminist and environmental concerns that would resonate with many today. The "immortal" Koresh died in 1908, but his faithful endured for decades at his lovely communal estate in Estero, Florida, now preserved as Koreshan State Park with the movement's archives in the adjacent headquarters of the Koreshan Unity Foundation.

Any book such as *America's Communal Utopias* inevitably must be selective. For a variety of reasons, many groups worthy of consideration have been omitted from this volume. One example would be tribal Native Americans, either during the early days of European contact or in modern, New Age-influenced incarnations. Another omission is additional Germanic groups that began Zoar, Ohio; Bethel, Missouri; and Aurora, Oregon, which possess excellent historic sites but whose inclusion would have overloaded the Germanic component of the book. In other instances important movements and their communal expressions were omitted because the leading scholars found it impossible to contribute an original essay at this time. We hope that future editions of this study will include some of these critical missing analyses and others worthy of consideration.

The most significant omission for many of our readers is one made deliberately. No communitarian experiments founded since 1965 are included. Although several contributors to this volume first became interested in communitarianism in response to the proliferation of communal experimentation by the youth movement, the past thirty years of communal experimentation in

America are simply too rich, fluid, and close to us to allow for a brief survey that would do justice to the most recent past. Even though the absolute number of communities appears to have declined from an estimated 10,000 or more in the late 1960s and early 1970s to 2,000 or so now, the 1995 *Communities Directory* describes more than 500 groups in North America. This list could be doubled or tripled easily because it only includes 11 of the 400 Hutterite colonies and none of the numerous Roman Catholic monastic communities. If interest warrants, *America's Communal Utopias* may be supplemented eventually by a follow-up volume covering the most recent decades of communal development.

How does this volume differ from previous analyses of communal experimentation in America? Most importantly, each essay in this study is written by one of the foremost scholars familiar with the primary sources of each group and able to interpret the founding movement's significance to a larger popular audience. In addition, photographs bring the uniqueness of each group to life, brief chronologies aid in quickly understanding the story of each movement, and authoritative reading lists with each essay open doors for further exploration. Also, the most complete list of American communal utopias ever printed appears in the appendix. It has been compiled under my direction at the Center for Communal Studies at the University of Southern Indiana during the past twenty years from all available printed sources, from the contributors to this anthology, and from many other scholars of the Communal Studies Association and International Communal Studies Association.

Finally, this book is significantly different from all such previous studies because its essays offer a new approach to the subject that takes into account the dynamic quality of communal utopias. We call this approach "developmental communalism" as explained in my "Developmental Communalism: An Alternative Approach to Communal Studies," published in 1989 in *Utopian Thought and Communal Experience*, edited by Dennis Hardy and Lorna Davidson. Developmental communalism examines whole movements and how they change over time, from their idealistic origins to their communal stages, and beyond. Anything but static, as the term *utopian* immediately implied to earlier writers, the communes of the most vital historic and current movements are creatively engaged in a developmental process that both precedes and may extend well after their communal phase. Thus, our essays clearly depict how and why certain movements chose the discipline of communal living to survive or to implement a utopian plan and why certain of them later moved beyond the close fellowship and collective strength of a communal period into other ways of organizing that proved better for their movement's development.

Our essays include the following communitarians who found ways to develop beyond their communal stage: Ephrata Baptists, Moravians, Owenites, Mormons, Fourierists, Amana Inspirationists, Theosophists, Jewish immigrants, and disciples of Father Divine. We also examine the present state of the Roman Catholic religious orders and the Hutterite *bruderhofs* that are being weighed now in the balance of the developmental communal process that will determine the future of their movements and their communal way of life.

The developmental approach also offers escape from the unfortunate "success-failure" pattern of earlier studies, which only considered communal groups "successful" if they maintained their communal bonds for a long time. Rosabeth Moss Kanter and other writers used twenty-five years as a yardstick. Ironically, some of the groups considered the most "successful" in terms of communal longevity are seen from the newer, developmental point of view to have helped doom their larger founding movements by making a lifetime commitment to community of property a rigid membership requirement and, in many cases, a tenet of faith. In this category, essays here treat the Shakers, the Harmonists, the Zoarites, the Oneidans, the Janssonists, and the Koreshans.

In this volume we see the developmental process posing a double jeopardy threat to communal longevity. The movements that make needed adjustments away from their communal stage abandon their communes. The movements that become locked into their communal discipline often stagnate, killing their movements and their communes. Therefore, regardless of their time in existence, we prefer to evaluate the success of communal utopias in terms of how well they achieve their own objectives, service the needs of their own members, and influence the general society, as suggested by Jon Wagner in his "Success in Intentional Communities" (*Communal Societies*, 1985).

In our examination of the colorful and sometimes tragic stories of the religious and secular movements that produced America's most noted communal utopias, we find real human beings struggling with real human problems and trying to realize hopes and dreams common to us all. We find in their brave, sometimes foolhardy, efforts to bring new, more creative solutions to bear on the universal condition of humanity a serious challenge to take their communal experiments seriously and to be no less innovative than they in our own world today.

DONALD F. DURNBAUGH

Communitarian Societies
in Colonial America

lthough many claim "rugged individualism" as the original hallmark
of American character, any careful student of the development of
the American nation will note the early and continued presence
of communal values. Roman Catholic friars organized their Indian converts into mission villages; Anglican and Puritan settlers established
commonwealths. The classic text of seventeenth-century New England was
John Winthrop's "Modell of Christian Charity," written and delivered in 1630
on the vessel *Arbella* as it plowed through the waves toward the New World.
Winthrop granted that God places humans in different estates, some rich and
some poor, yet held there are times when Christians "must sell all and give to
the poore, as they did in the Apostles times . . . [and] must give beyond theire
abillity, as they of Macedonia." To save their faith, he urged his companions,
"wee must be knitt together in this worke as one man, wee must entertaine
each other in brotherly Affeccion, wee must be willing to abridge our selves of
our superfluities for the supply of others necessities."[1]

It would be possible to select comparable, if less eloquent, quotations from
the foundational documents of the American heritage. At the very heart of the
American experience was firm dedication to communal values. Of particular
interest, moreover, are those societies for which true community meant more
than willingness to give in cases of need. For significant portions of their histories these societies believed that total sharing of goods was required for true
community. They practiced common ownership of property, common production of goods, and common use of all things. Their unusual lifestyles and
commitments often brought them into tension with the larger society, which,

14

nevertheless, gave at least grudging acknowledgment to their cultural and economic achievements. Such societies have been given various names, such as *utopias* or *communes*; scholars describe them as *communitarian*. However designated, they form an important chapter in the story of the American people.[2]

Common to these early communal bodies was rootage in religious dissent in Europe. They were shaped by the reforming movements of Anabaptism (sixteenth century) and Radical Pietism (seventeenth century). Although having different historical initiation and development, both opposed the religious establishment and its coercive state backing. Both stressed religious liberty, intense spirituality, and rigorous ethical standards. Many were imbued with millenarian beliefs, that is, expecting the imminent second coming of Jesus Christ. These unorthodox convictions led to persecution, making migration to the free lands of North America an appealing option. When the newly constituted American colonies sought settlers, many of these dissenters were among the early waves of migration. A substantial minority of these religious radicals chose to live together communally.[3]

Valley of the Swans

A fascinating figure in early communitarianism was Pieter Cornelius Plockhoy van Zierikzee (ca. 1620–ca. 1700), who was active in his native Holland, in England, and in colonial America. Of Dutch Mennonite parentage, he was first noticed in the 1640s as a leader of a Collegiant circle in Amsterdam. The Collegiants formed a loosely organized but influential religious fellowship of Socinian (Unitarian) outlook, who attracted liberal-minded members from different church bodies. They reacted against the harsh confessionalism of seventeenth-century Dutch religious life and hoped for increased contacts and agreement across denominational lines.[4]

By 1658 Plockhoy was in England with the hope that the victorious Puritan commonwealth could provide a setting for his reforming ideas. He spoke with the lord protector, Oliver Cromwell (1599–1658), and was able to interest highly placed Englishmen in his plans. These he popularized through several publications, including *The Way to the Peace and Settlement of These Nations Fully Discovered* (three editions, 1659–1660) and *A Way Propounded to Make the Poor in These and Other Nations Happy* (1659). These treatises contained strong criticism of the social and economic problems then prevalent in the British Isles; they also presented rather complete and practical plans for reorganized commonwealths, with room for the unemployed, craftspeople, and investors. Skill and experience would be pooled, but private property preserved. Several attempts to realize Plockhoy's plans were made in London, Bristol, and Ireland. The overthrow of the protectorate and the restoration of the Stuart monarchy in 1660, however, foiled the successful elaboration of the schemes.[5]

Plockhoy then returned to Holland, where he set about securing government aid for a colony in the New Netherlands. The Dutch West India Company, chartered in 1621, had successfully planted settlements on the North American seaboard. New Amsterdam (later New York) was the center of its holdings, which extended southward past the Delaware valley, with jurisdiction of the latter section given to the city fathers in Amsterdam. In order to exploit their colonial territory, the Amsterdam burghers were eager to find Dutch citizens willing to migrate to the New World. Wealthy patroons had dominated early Dutch settlement, but in 1640 the *Freedoms and Exemptions* statute provided possibilities of land grants for smaller entrepreneurs such as Plockhoy.

In June 1662 Plockhoy signed a contract with the Amsterdam authorities, who promised land and substantial advance funding for twenty-five Mennonite settlers. In turn, they agreed to reside along the Delaware and "to work at farming, fishing, handicrafts, etc., and to be as diligent as possible." Despite the contract's language, by which the settlers agreed to "depart by the first ship or ships to the aforesaid colony," Plockhoy delayed emigration for nearly one year. He hoped to attract a total of 100 colonists to provide better financing and more security, again using the press in his attempt to gain adherents (*A Brief and Concise Plan* [1662]). Failing in this, he departed the Netherlands in May 1663 on the vessel *St. Jacob*, which dropped "41 souls with their baggage and farm utensils" on the Delaware shores in late July.[6] Very little is known about the progress of the settlement, located at a site known variously as the Valley of the Swans (Zwaanendael) or Horekill, near the present town of Lewes. Given Plockhoy's careful planning and the financial backing of the Amsterdamers, it might have been reasonably assumed that the colony would flourish, but larger events intruded.

In 1664 the English took over the Dutch colonies in North America in the generally bloodless Anglo-Dutch War. The Horekill settlement was crushed when Admiral Robert Carr of the English navy seized Dutch holdings along the Delaware. In September, according to the laconic account, Carr "destroyed the Quaking society of Plockhoy to a naile." History has not recorded the result for the displaced colonists; some may have been sold into slavery in Virginia. Plockhoy emerged briefly from obscurity in 1682–83 when he took possession of property in Lewes and declared allegiance to England. In 1695

DONALD F. DURNBAUGH

Plockhoy and his wife were granted public assistance in Germantown, north of Philadelphia; the old, blind, and indigent Plockhoy was last mentioned in a will dated 1700, when he was given a bequest.[7]

Despite the failure of the Delaware venture, it has been recognized as the first American utopian settlement; in addition, it was the first colony to ban slavery officially by its foundational governing charter. In 1913 a plaque was raised in Zierikzee commemorating Plockhoy as a "pioneer of Christian civilization in America." Several scholars have noted his priority in the rise of utopian socialism generally and claimed that he was the real father of the modern cooperative movement.[8]

Bohemia Manor

Not far from the abortive Plockhoy colony was the longer-lived Labadist community in what is now Cecil County, Maryland. As with other colonial communes, this also had European roots. Bohemia Manor was planted in 1683–84 by a large and active religious community with several continental locations, especially at Wieuwerd, West Friesland. Maryland was chosen as a site after an earlier Labadist venture (1680–88) in the Western hemisphere in Dutch-owned Surinam, South America; this failed because of the tropical climate and unstable political conditions.[9]

The term "Labadist" derives from an outstandingly gifted religious leader, Jean de Labadie (1610–74), called a "second Calvin." Born into an aristocratic family in Bourg, France, he was ordained by the Society of Jesus following philosophical studies. Labadie became a secular (community) priest in 1639, after being released from his Jesuit vows, and won acclaim in Paris for his rhetorical skill and theological acuteness. He lost favor, however, in the church because of increasingly radical views and became a Protestant in 1650. Forced from several parishes in France by Catholic authorities, he spent several years in Geneva in a special pastorate. He then was called to the Netherlands, where he embarked on a thorough reform of the Dutch Reformed Church, only to be suspended by a synod in 1668 for his separatist views.[10]

The religious beliefs of Labadie were an amalgam of Jansenism, Calvinism, and mysticism. Jansenism was a Puritan-type reform movement within seventeenth-century Catholicism. It emphasized in Augustinian fashion the importance of divine grace because of human sinfulness and the need for believers to pursue lives of utter dedication and devotion. The natural impulses of the body were considered evil; hence, they must be strictly bridled. The elect experienced grace, thus allowing them to mortify the flesh and to withdraw from the distractions and sinful pleasures of the world. The inner light given by God could be depended upon for guidance; it was to be nourished by periods of silence and fasting. Continual interior prayer, as described by the mystical writers, was sought. Believers could evidence repentance and new birth by leading holy lives.[11]

Despite his official suspension, Labadie refused to cease his religious activities and gathered a community about him, first at Veere and then at Amsterdam. Members of his house-church held their goods in common. It was during this period that he attracted prominent figures as converts; especially famous was Anna Maria van Schurman (1607–78), considered to be the most erudite woman of her century.[12] In 1670 Labadie accepted the invitation of Princess Elizabeth of the Palatinate to move with some fifty followers to Herford in Westphalia. When pressure from the imperial diet came upon them there, the community moved in 1672 to Altona (near Hamburg), under the tolerant jurisdiction of the Danish crown. It was there that Labadie died in 1674. His followers then returned to the Netherlands, settling on a noble estate in Wieuwerd, West Friesland. The Labadist society there gave up full community of goods in 1692 and was dissolved in 1732 following the death of its last spiritual leader.

Earlier, in 1679–80, two Labadist agents, Jasper Danckaerts (1639–1702) and Pieter Sluyter (1645–1722), were sent under assumed names to North America to find a place for settlement. After arrival in New York, they were directed to the Bohemia Manor land grant in Maryland at the head of the Chesapeake Bay, where they eventually secured title to 3,750 acres. With this success in hand they went back to West Friesland, returning in 1683 with other Labadists to take possession of the site, which they soon developed as an active colony.[13]

Members of the society—numbering perhaps 100—were noted for an extremely ascetic lifestyle. Dress was plain and food designedly meager. If a particular foodstuff was especially distasteful to members, as a discipline it was made a steady diet. Fires for comfort were forbidden in the dwelling areas, even in bitterly cold weather. Labadists toiled on the fields of corn, tobacco, flax, and hemp or tended cattle. Handicrafts featured the manufacture of linen. Those who joined the community, whether rich or poor, put all of their possessions into the common stock; if they left the community, they forfeited all that they had brought. Men and women were largely kept separate, although marriage was not completely banned. Members confessed sins in public assemblies. Quakerlike worship services featured long periods of si-

DONALD F. DURNBAUGH

lence, broken by devotional admonitions or expositions of scripture by spiritually gifted leaders.

Contemporaries noted the similarities of the Labadist beliefs and practices to those of the Religious Society of Friends; there were, in fact, many contacts between the two groups. Quaker leaders (including George Keith, Robert Barclay, and William Penn) visited the Labadists in the Netherlands and in Westphalia to seek union, but without success. Nevertheless, so alike were the two bodies that the Labadists were often called "Quakers" by their opponents. A traveling Quaker leader, Samuel Bownas (1676–1753), described in his journal a meal at Bohemia Manor as being consumed in silence; members prayed silently as individuals, beginning and ending as the spirit moved each one. They removed their hats when praying, donning them again to eat. When he questioned his guide about this practice, he was told that "they held it unlawful to pray till they felt some inward motion for the same; and that secret prayer was more acceptable than to utter words."[14]

Some accounts have it that Pieter Sluyter, the leader at Bohemia Manor, was a tyrant, living a comfortable life and even keeping slaves. It is known that when communal property holding was partially abandoned in 1698, Sluyter received a large and advantageous settlement and became a rich man before his death in 1722. By 1727 the community had been disbanded.

Society of the Woman in the Wilderness

Germantown, the place of refuge for the aged Plockhoy, won early prominence in the history of communitarianism as the home of the Contented of the God-Loving Soul or Chapter of Perfection, known more popularly as the Society of the Woman in the Wilderness; the latter name was taken from the harbinger of the millennium cited in the New Testament (Revelation 12:6).[15] Some forty scholars from Europe arrived there in 1694, led by the youthful Johannes Kelpius (1673–ca. 1708), the Latinized form of the original name "Kelp." The group had originally been gathered in Europe by the brilliant Johann Jakob Zimmermann (1644–93), noted for his achievements in theology, astronomy, and mathematics and for his attachment to the views of the theosophist Jakob Boehme (1575–1624). Zimmermann's career as a pastor in Württemberg ended in 1685 because of his prediction of the imminent advent of Christ's kingdom and his criticism of the corrupt state of the church. Because of these unorthodox views, during the next years Zimmermann was unable to stay long in one place despite his many gifts, although he was briefly a professor at Heidelberg.[16]

At one point Zimmermann calculated that the millennium would begin in 1694; seekers should gather in the wilderness (that is, in North America) to await the divine coming. In 1693 he summoned his followers (primarily scholars) to Rotterdam for the trip to Pennsylvania, in which undertaking he was aided by the good offices of the Quaker merchant and scholar Benjamin Furly (1636–1714). One event he had not taken into his reckoning—his own death—occurred shortly before the company was scheduled to embark on the voyage. Nevertheless, the group decided to continue and named the twenty-year-old Kelpius, of their number, as their new leader.[17]

A native of Transylvania, Kelpius had at age sixteen taken a master's degree at the University of Altdorf and had then published several scholarly works. His travel diary to Pennsylvania has been preserved; the pertinent excerpt for the departure from Europe read, "On the 7th of Jan[uary 1694], I . . . resolved upon going to America, my companions being: Henry Bernhard Cöster, Daniel Falkner, Daniel Lutke, John Seelig, Ludwig Bidermann, as well as about 40 other companions, some of whom were numbered and others convicted by God, in Germany . . . in the preceeding year, [and] resolved upon that voyage."[18]

Of these companions, those who became the best known were Heinrich Bernhard Köster, Daniel Falckner, and Johann Gottfried Seelig. Köster (1662–1749) founded another community (Irenia or the True Church of Brotherly Love) about 1697 after leaving Kelpius's society; he was a gifted if polemical leader among Lutherans and dissident Quakers in Pennsylvania before returning to Germany in 1699. There he lived in many different places for the next five decades, active as a diplomat, linguist, teacher, and evangelist, calling himself the "Angel of Philadelphia with the seven seals." Although never ordained, Falckner (1666–ca. 1741) became one of the pioneer Lutheran pastors in North America. After 1700 he was the land agent for the Frankfurt Land Company, organized by a band of Pietists from among the circle of Phillip Jakob Spener, a leader among German Pietism. Seelig (1668–1745), who remained faithful to the religious quest of Kelpius's group for the longest time, died as a hermit near Germantown, leaving a number of mystical hymns.[19]

After departing from Rotterdam, the Kelpius-led party stayed for six months in England, where they were in intimate contact with the followers of Boehme, known there as the Philadelphian Society. The leading figures were Jane Leade (1624–1704) and John Pordage (1608–88); the writings of both were popular on the Continent.[20] When the company of savants arrived in Philadelphia in late June 1694, they secured land along a ridge near the Wissahickon Creek in what is now Fairmount Park. They lived in caves and later

DONALD F. DURNBAUGH

erected a large building for their meetings. Their organization could be called semimonastic after the pattern of the early Christian hermits in Egypt.[21]

The first impressions of the freedom of their new home were positive; they also suggest the pattern of life adopted by members of the group. The author (perhaps Seelig) of an account of the sometimes difficult Atlantic crossing and early days in Pennsylvania wrote, "What pleases me here most is that one can be peasant, scholar, priest, and nobleman all at the same time without interference, which of all modes of living has been found to be the best and most satisfactory since patriarchial times. To be a peasant and nothing else is a sort of cattle-life; to be a scholar and nothing else, such as in Europe, is a morbid and self-indulgent existence; to be a priest and nothing else ties life to blunders and responsibilities; to be a nobleman and nothing else makes [one] godless and riotous."[22]

The group embarked on a regulated program of private study and meditation; received opinion has it that they spent long hours studying ancient manuscripts and scanning the sky, eager for the first portents of the final days of humankind. At any rate, Kelpius and his colleagues were not completely isolated from society. They created a school for the neighborhood children, held public worship services, occasionally visited other religious gatherings, and practiced medicine. It is unlikely, despite claims to the contrary, that they were part of the secretive Rosicrucian fraternity. It is known that they were well-read intellectuals, gifted in many aspects of art, science, and literature. The best-known products of their pens were mystical hymns and a devotional treatise, *A Method of Prayer*, by Kelpius, first published in English in 1761 and republished as recently as 1951.[23]

The "good, grey" poet John Greenleaf Whittier (1807–92) caught the tenor of the life of Kelpius and his colleagues in several stanzas of his poem "The Pennsylvania Pilgrim." He called Kelpius the "maddest of good men," who read Daniel, John, and Boehme's "Morning-Redness, through the Stone of Wisdom, vouchsafed to his eyes alone." (This was a reference to Jakob Boehme's principal work *Aurora*.) Kelpius, according to Whittier, "saw the visions man shall see no more till the great angel, striding seas and shore, shall bid all flesh await, on land or ships, the morning trump of the Apocalypse, shattering the heavens before the dread eclipse."[24]

There was gradual slippage of membership from the society, as members became active in local affairs; some newcomers joined the group, such as the mystic Conrad Matthäi and the physician Christopher Witt, but the modest influx was insufficient to counter the number of those who left. Kelpius died about 1708, and with his death the loose community expired as well. It is said that Seelig declined to assume leadership, preferring his life as a hermit. The celibate chroniclers of Ephrata, who referred respectfully to Kelpius, described the dispersal with special distaste for those who married: "After their leader died the tempter found occasion to scatter them, as those who had been most zealous against marrying now betook themselves to women again, which brought such shame on the solitary state that the few who still held to it dared not open their mouths for shame."[25] Nevertheless, a handful (in particular Seelig and Matthäi) remained faithful to their millennial expectations and theosophist rule. With their deaths, the mystical community remained simply a poignant memory, to be referred to in plaques for park visitors or as gothic background in novels such as *Paul Ardenheim, the Monk of Wissahickon* (1848) by George Lippard.[26]

Ephrata Cloister

Before its complete dissolution, the Labadist colony at Bohemia Manor received a visit in 1721 by the future leader of the most noted (and notorious) communitarian society of the American colonial period. This was Conrad Beissel (1691–1768), the founder of the Ephrata Cloister. Beissel was one of the most complex personalities of eighteenth-century America; appraisals of his character and achievements differed widely in his day and since. To some a religious genius, to others a hypocritical and dissolute tyrant, Beissel was called by a biographer a "mystic and martinet."[27]

Beissel was a native of Eberbach on the Neckar River in the Electoral Palatinate. Born after the death of his father, he soon lost his mother as well. He came into contact with Pietists in Heidelberg during his travels as a journeyman baker and lost a promising position there because of his adherence to the Pietist circle. He associated for a time with both the Schwarzenau Brethren (currently known as the Church of the Brethren) and the Inspirationists (currently, the Amana Society) in the counties of Wittgenstein and Marienborn; these isolated territories offered relative tolerance to dissidents in early eighteenth-century Germany.

Hearing of the mystics on the Wissahickon led by Johannes Kelpius, Beissel decided in 1720 to join them, not realizing that they had already been dispersed for some time. After arrival in Germantown, he spent some time with Peter Becker (1687–1758), first minister of the Schwarzenau Brethren in America, to learn the weaving trade. He then found some friends willing to live with him in the backcountry as isolated religious seekers. When a Brethren-led revival effort reached that area in 1724, Beissel reluctantly accepted baptism from his friend Peter Becker, although his spiritual pride at first kept him from it. Beissel eventually reasoned that Jesus Christ had de-

DONALD F. DURNBAUGH

The restored Saal (chapel) and Saron (sisters' house) of the Ephrata Cloister in Ephrata, Pennsylvania, built in 1741 and 1743, are rare surviving American examples of medieval Germanic architectural style. (Photograph by Donald Janzen)

meaned himself to accept baptism from John the Baptist, and that was sufficient precedent for him.[28]

For several years Beissel was part of the Brethren movement, but strains soon became evident. Convinced of his superior spiritual insights, he insisted that followers accept his views on the virtue of celibacy, Saturday as the true Sabbath, and dietary laws from the Old Testament. The central issue was the conviction that his views were direct revelations from heaven, supplanting the scriptures. The basic source document for Beissel, the Ephrata chronicle (*Chronicon Ephratense*), described his preaching practices: "He conducted all meetings . . . with astonishing strength of spirit, and used so little reflection over it, that even in the beginning he was not suffered to use a Bible; so that the testimony in its delivery might not be weakened by written knowledge. He began his discourse with closed eyes, before a large crowd of hearers; and when he opened his eyes again . . . most of them were gone, not being able to endure the Spirit's keenness." His opponents found other reasons to explain the disappearance of the audience.[29]

Thus differentiated, a group of Beissel adherents became increasingly critical of the mainline Brethren, who, in turn, began to criticize the talented but imperious mystic. Despite many attempts at reconciliation, the inevitable schism took place in 1728. Beissel dramatized the rupture by having himself baptized backward, thus "giving back" the baptism of the Brethren (which had taken place in their customary threefold forward action); he was then baptized once again in the multiple forward mode.

To the amazement of his followers, many of whom had built cabins near his residence, in the dead of winter of early 1732 Beissel abruptly left the Conestoga area where he had lived since 1721. He settled farther inland in a desolate spot along the Cocalico Brook. Before long, his adherents followed his example, so that by late 1732 the Ephrata Cloister could be said to have taken form. Gradually, monastic fellowships of sisters and brothers were established on a celibate basis (the "Solitary Sisters" and "Solitary Brethren"); to these was added a third grouping (the "Householders"), composed of those adherents who lived in family groupings. Some householding couples lived together but refrained from marital relations.[30]

These arrangements reflected a key teaching of Beissel, absorbed from the theosophical writings of Boehme and his popularizer, Johann Georg Gichtel (1638–1710), that the faithful must renounce sexual activity to achieve the highest level of spiritual attainment. Farther down the ladder came those men and women who lived together chastely, followed by those who bore children in Christian wedlock, and finally those of the world who pursued sexual pleasures.

Life at the cloister followed the traditions of monastic life. Members accepted a highly ordered regimen of meditation, work, and worship, including lengthy nighttime meetings. In the beginning, when great efforts were made to construct large buildings to accommodate the growing number of converts, Ephrata members allowed themselves as little as three hours of sleep each night. They used wooden benches for beds, blocks of wood as pillows. Food was limited. It was common for members to hitch themselves to a wooden plow to break ground. Older members and those who were ill were allowed some limited comforts, including meat in their diet. Not surprisingly, observers commenting on Ephrata residents at this time noted their emaciated bodies.

Early members wore plain dress along the lines of the Mennonites, but before long a monastic habit evolved, following the style of the Capuchin order. Members discarded their former names, taking new names for the cloistered life. Celibate men received the tonsure. Suspicious neighbors believed those at Ephrata to have converted to Catholicism, and there were even accusations that they were spies for the French military forces.

DONALD F. DURNBAUGH

The unusual developments at Ephrata soon became widely known, and it later became customary for travelers in Pennsylvania, including highly placed personages, to make the side-trip to visit the institution. Many of these visitors wrote down their impressions; it is possible to gain some idea of the outer life of Ephrata from their comments. Most observers praised their dedication but questioned the severity of their deprivations.[31]

Ephrata is best known for its cultural accomplishments in calligraphy, manuscript illumination, and choral music. The sisters attained great proficiency in drafting, rubricating, and illustrating *Fraktur*, achieving true master works in hymnals and collections of spiritual essays. This delicate artistry conveys to this day something of the intense spirit of austerity and devotion of the Ephrata faithful.

Beissel's treatise on music is said to be the first ever written in North America. Skilled in the playing of the violin, Beissel developed his own theories of music, using "master" and "servant" notes. These ideas were later picked up by the famed German writer Thomas Mann (1875–1955), whose novel *Doktor Faustus* (1948) portrays Beissel's musical conceptions in great detail. Beissel demanded especially strict preparation from his singers, including an even more meager diet than usual at the cloister along with untold hours of practice. The result was outstanding. Visitors speak of the near-angelic quality of the singing. A cultivated Anglican divine who heard the Ephrata singers in 1771, long after Beissel's death when the standard of music had declined, had this description:

> The music had little or no air or melody; but consisted of simple, long notes, combined with the richest harmony. . . . The performers sat with their heads reclined, their countenances solemn and dejected, their faces pale and emaciated from their manner of living, their clothing exceedingly white and quite picturesque, and their music such as thrilled to the very soul. I almost began to think myself in the world of spirits, and the objects before me were ethereal. In short, the impression of this scene made upon my mind continued strong for many days, and I believe, will never be wholly obliterated.

Ephrata choir members claimed that "the angels themselves when they sang at Christ's birth had to make use of our rules."[32]

After 1745 Ephrata was also famed for its printing. Their earlier publications had been given to the Franklin and Bradford presses in Philadelphia or to the press of Christopher Sauer in Germantown. But there were problems. Neither of the Philadelphia presses possessed the gothic typeface favored by the Germans for their books; Sauer (1695–1758) was a religious separatist and therefore critical of all religious organizations. When he detected a tendency in Ephrata writings to deify Beissel, he angrily called this to their attention and refused to print anything to which he could not agree in conscience. Skeptics speculated that Sauer was recalcitrant because his wife had left him and their young son to join the Ephrata movement, where she served as leader of the women members. (She eventually returned, but not until the son was an adult.)

Some ninety book productions issued from the Ephrata press before 1794, when it was rented to private entrepreneurs. Several unusually demanding publications came from Ephrata, including the huge *Martyrs Mirror*, translated into German from the Dutch and printed for the Mennonites in 1748–49. It is conceded to be the largest single publication known to American printing history during the colonial period. Of more importance for the historical record is the *Chronicon Ephratense* (1786), compiled by "Lamech and Agrippa," possibly Peter Miller and Jacob Gast. Although written with the bias of justifying the community and the genius of Conrad Beissel's leadership, it is a dependable source for the religious events of the period. Today, rare imprints from the Ephrata press are avidly sought by public and private collectors, with prices soaring into the thousands of dollars.

Life at Ephrata was often turbulent, as the unpredictable Beissel kept the community off balance with suggestions and demands. He withstood a serious attempt by the gifted Eckerlin brothers to wrest control from his hands. Under the guidance of Israel Eckerlin, acting as prior, Ephrata experienced a boom of construction and economic advance. Mills of several kinds, farming operations, orchards, and fields became so productive that extensive commercial connections were established in Philadelphia to sell Ephrata's products. Beissel managed to win back leadership initiative, leaving the Eckerlins little alternative but to depart the society. They traveled to the distant hinterlands of Virginia, creating a mini-Ephrata in the wilderness, before they fell victim to a French-led Indian raid; this resulted in the capture of two of the brothers. Both died in France, where their captors had taken them.[33]

Ephrata or its adherents spun off other daughter colonies. These included Antietam in Franklin County (founded in 1752), Bermudian Creek in York County (1758), and smaller settlements at Stony Creek in Somerset County, in the Shenandoah valley of Virginia, and in the Carolinas. The most important, however, was Snow Hill, formed as a commune by the Snowberger family in 1798 in Franklin County, Pennsylvania, from the remnants of the Antietam settlement. Although the Ephrata Cloister itself met its legal end in 1814, when the Society of Seventh Day Baptists was incorporated, single sis-

DONALD F. DURNBAUGH

ters still lived in the remaining buildings for many years. The daughter colony, Snow Hill, flourished as a community until 1889. The last sister died in 1894; the last brother, in 1895. Families, however, were also present, thus continuing the German Seventh Day Baptist Church. Of this branch, perhaps 150 members exist today, most belonging to a sabbatarian congregation near New Enterprise in central Pennsylvania.[34]

Moravian Brethren

In 1742 Count Nicholas Ludwig von Zinzendorf (1700–1760), head of the Renewed Moravian Church, came to Pennsylvania and attempted to mold all of its religious groups into a united fellowship, the Congregation of God in the Spirit, through a series of synods. In the early meetings, representatives of the Ephrata society took part. One of the questions posed for ecumenical discussion was, "Do Moravians place too much importance on marriage and the Ephrata people too little?" Despite this obvious difference, Count Zinzendorf hoped that he could make common cause with the famous Ephrata Cloister and, as an inducement, even adopted (for a time) the seventh-day Sabbath for his movement. He visited Ephrata personally, only to be rebuffed by the leader, Beissel, who may have feared that his own leadership might be overshadowed by the talented and articulate Moravian bishop. Ironically, the upshot of Zinzendorf's ecumenical efforts in Pennsylvania was heightened denominational division and doctrinal disputes. Members at Ephrata themselves composed and published lengthy critiques of the Moravians. Christopher Sauer, for his part, shifted critical attention from Ephrata, the better to attack the Moravians in his newspaper.[35]

The roots of the Moravian movement stretch beyond the Protestant Reformation. The year 1467 is often used as a beginning date, although the story begins earlier in the fifteenth century with the reform movement of Jan Hus, executed in 1415 as a heretic at the Council of Constance. A radical wing of the Hussite movement, with ties to the yet-earlier Waldensians, wanted to reform the church in root and branches. Its chief spokesman was Peter Chelčický, a self-educated yeoman, whose treatise *The Net of Faith* (ca. 1440) attacked the "unholy" alliance of pope and emperor.[36]

The Unity of Czech Brethren, as the movement came to be known, had won widespread support by the late fifteenth century. As burghers and even nobility joined the Brethren, some compromise of their sharp church-state dualism seemed necessary; it had, therefore, become a modified reforming body by the time of the Lutheran reformation (1517), making possible considerable cooperation with the mainline Protestant reformers. The Unity was nearly crushed in the Catholic Counter-Reformation of the seventeenth century, managing to cling to existence only with exiles such as the great educator J. A. Comenius (1592–1670) and, secretly, with a few families within Moravia. Some members of this latter "Hidden Seed" sought refuge in 1722 on the estates of Count Zinzendorf in Saxony; this led in 1727 to renewal under his direction as the Reorganized Moravian Church. The new settlement for the Moravian refugees and the large number of Pietists who joined them was called *Herrnhut* (the watch of the Lord) and became the world center of the vigorous movement.[37]

Like Ephrata members, Moravians were praised for their musical accomplishments. Unlike Ephrata, this featured instrumental as well as choral music. Talented Moravian musicians brought their tradition of playing and singing to the New World, where they passed it on to each new generation. Besides their contributions with brass and string ensembles, Moravians also developed skills in organ playing and construction; especially noted was the work of David Tannenberg. Moravian church music holds a respected role in the tradition of American musicology.[38]

In economic matters, the course of development of the Moravian colonies was exemplary. With conscientious workers, careful administrators, and spiritual encouragement, Moravians soon made a name for themselves for their well-built and tidy settlements, bountiful fields, well-kept livestock, and modern farming methods. They early won urban markets for their produce and prospered. Education was a matter of careful attention and also soon enjoyed such a favorable reputation that the gentry sent their young men and women to the Moravians for polite learning.

As decades came and went, political and military tensions brought considerable strain to the still largely pacifist Moravians; pressures also grew for changes in the strictly controlled economic system. Some of the handcrafters wanted more independence in meeting consumer demands and also in keeping profits. Dissatisfaction also increased with the "choir" system, a pattern of organization covering all age and gender groups. The nuclear family as observed outside the colonies seemed ever more attractive to the communal Moravians.

Finally, in 1762, the "General Economy" at Bethlehem, their center, was dropped; the church kept control of some farms and the tavern. The land on which the industries and businesses were located was retained on lease to the individuals who ran them. This was a major change, but it had been foreseen. The total community of labor had never been understood as a permanent arrangement; rather, it was the most efficient way to establish newcomers in a frontier situation. Similar changes took place at other colonies—Lititz,

DONALD F. DURNBAUGH

The half-timbered Moravian Single Brothers House of Salem (now Winston-Salem), North Carolina, which dates to 1769, served as the residence of the men who produced many of the commercial goods of the community. (Photograph by Donald Pitzer)

Communitarian Societies in Colonial America

Nazareth, Salem, and Bethabara (the latter two in North Carolina). Still, it was not until 1845 that Bethlehem ceased to be guided in its town affairs by religious leaders, changing in that year its status from that of a church village to that of a borough. The Moravian settlements continued as centers of a small but active denomination.[39]

Summary

Valley of the Swans, Bohemia Manor, Society of the Woman in the Wilderness, Ephrata Cloister, Moravian colonies—all were fascinating expressions of religious communitarian outlook. Their communal existence has long since disappeared, though some of the outward fabric remains. The Moravian Church still uses many of its handsome colonial structures. The Commonwealth of Pennsylvania has restored the Ephrata Cloister, now a favorite object of tourism; the main building and the meetinghouse of Ephrata's daughter colony at Snow Hill still stand, as does the Great House of the Labadists.

Moreover, the spirit of these devoted communitarians lives on in artifacts, such as beautifully illuminated manuscripts. Scholars return to the pages describing their histories; their uniqueness speaks across the years. Peter Miller, successor to Conrad Beissel as Ephrata's leader, once pondered the fate of his community, concluding, "And, if as [Beissel] maintains God has promised him, a seed of his labors is to remain until the second advent of Jesus Christ, this does not mean the Settlement of the Solitary shall stand so long; although they are just as well entitled to this as any congregation of Christ on earth."[40]

Chronology

1467   The Unity of Czech Brethren (Unitas Fratrum) is formed.
1658   P. C. Plockhoy attempts to found commonwealths in England.
1663   Valley of the Swans colony is established on Delaware River.
1664   Valley of the Swans colony is destroyed by English forces.
1668   Labadie establishes communal house in Amsterdam.
1674   Labadist colony is established in Wieuwerd, West Friesland.
1683   Labadist colony is established at Bohemia Manor, Maryland.
1694   Society of the Woman in the Wilderness is founded near Germantown.
1708   Society of the Woman in the Wilderness is dissolved.
1720   Conrad Beissel arrives in Pennsylvania.
1722   Moravian refugees settle at Herrnhut, Saxony.
1727   Renewed Moravian Church is organized.
1728   Beissel faction breaks away from the Germantown Brethren.
1732   Ephrata Cloister is formed.
1742   Count Zinzendorf travels to North America.

1745	Ephrata organizes a printing press.
1748	Ephrata publishes Mennonite *Martyrs Mirror*.
1762	General Economy is terminated in Moravian colonies.
1786	Ephrata chronicle (*Chronicon Ephratense*) is published.
1814	Snow Hill builds community house.
1814	Religious Society of Seventh Day Baptists is incorporated.
1835	Snow Hill receives state charter.
1845	Bethlehem loses status as church village, becomes a borough.
1895	Last of monastic brothers at Snow Hill dies.
1939	Commonwealth of Pennsylvania acquires Ephrata as historic site.

Notes

1. John Winthrop, "A Modell of Christian Charity," *Winthrop Papers* (Boston: Massachusetts Historical Society, 1931), 2:292–95, excerpts of which were published in Conrad Cherry, ed., *God's New Israel: Religious Interpretations of American Destiny* (Englewood Cliffs, N.J.: Prentice-Hall, 1971), 39–42.

2. The classic study is Arthur Bestor Jr., *Backwoods Utopias: The Sectarian Origins and the Owenite Phase of Communitarian Socialism in America, 1663–1829*, 2d enl. ed. (Philadelphia: University of Pennsylvania Press, 1970), although space given to the earlier, religiously oriented communities is limited. A recent comprehensive treatment is Yaacov Oved, *Two Hundred Years of American Communes* (New Brunswick, N.J.: Transaction, 1988). See also Mark Holloway, *Heavens on Earth: Utopian Communities in America, 1680–1980*, 2d ed. (New York: Dover, 1966); Donald F. Durnbaugh, "Work and Hope: The Spirituality of the Radical Pietist Communitarians," *Church History* 39 (1970): 72–90; Delburn Carpenter, *The Radical Pietists: Celibate Communal Societies Established in the United States before 1820* (New York: AMS Press, 1975); David S. Lovejoy, *Religious Enthusiasm in the New World: Heresy to Revolution* (Cambridge, Mass.: Harvard University Press, 1985), 154–77; Clarke Garrett, *Spirit Possession and Popular Religion: From the Camisards to the Shakers* (Baltimore: Johns Hopkins University Press, 1987); and Trevor J. Saxby, *Pilgrims of a Common Life: Christian Community of Goods through the Centuries* (Scottdale, Pa.: Herald, 1987).

For biographies of communal leaders and brief information on societies, see Robert S. Fogarty, *Dictionary of American Communal and Utopian History* (Westport, Conn.: Greenwood, 1980). Literature before 1932 is found in Emil Meynen, ed., *Bibliography on German Settlements in Colonial North America* (Leipzig: Otto Harrossowitz, 1937), reprinted as *Bibliography on the Colonial Germans of North America* (Baltimore: Genealogical Pub. Co., 1982). Useful, if not complete, bibliographies are provided in Philip N. Dare, ed., *American Communes to 1860: A Bibliography* (New York: Garland, 1990).

3. An overview of the dissenting tradition is given in Donald F. Durnbaugh, *The Believers' Church: The History and Character of Radical Protestantism* (New York: Macmillan, 1968; reprint, Scottdale, Pa.: Herald, 1985). For more information on Anabaptism and Pietism, see J. Denny Weaver, *Becoming Anabaptist: The Origin and Significance of Sixteenth-Century Anabaptism* (Scottdale, Pa.: Herald, 1987); Cornelius J. Dyck, *An Introduction to Mennonite History*, 3d ed. (Scottdale, Pa.: Herald, 1993); and Dale W. Brown, *Understanding Pietism* (Grand Rapids, Mich.: Eerdmans, 1978). An early section of Bestor's *Backwoods Utopias*, 20–22, discusses the European background of the "communitive sects."

4. There are two authoritative monographs: Leland Harder and Marvin Harder, *Plockhoy from Zurik-zee: The Study of a Dutch Reformer in Puritan England and Colonial America* (Newton, Kans.: [Mennonite] Board of Education and Publication, 1951), and Jean Séguy,

Utopie Coopérative et Oecuménisme: Pieter Cornelisz Plockhoy van Zurik-Zee, 1620–1700 (Paris: Mouton, 1968); both include Plockhoy's writings. Also helpful are Irwin B. Horst, "Pieter Cornelisz Plockhoy: An Apostle of the Collegiants," *Mennonite Quarterly Review* 23 (1949): 161–85, and W. H. G. Armytage, *Heavens Below: Utopian Experiments in England, 1560–1960* (London: Routledge and Kegan Paul, 1961), 9, 29.

5. Harder and Harder, *Plockhoy*, 25–47, 108–73; Donald F. Durnbaugh, ed., *Every Need Supplied: Mutual Aid and Christian Community in the Free Churches, 1525–1675* (Philadelphia: Temple University Press, 1974), 149–55.

6. Harder and Harder, *Plockhoy*, 49–71.

7. Leland Harder, "Plockhoy and His Settlement at Zwaanendael, 1663," *Delaware History* 3 (1949): 138–54, 186–99, and "Pioneer of Christian Civilization in America," *Mennonite Life* 4 (January 1949): 41–45, 49; Friedrich Nieper, *Die ersten deutschen Auswanderer von Krefeld nach Pennsylvanien* (Neukirchen/Moers: Erziehungsverein, 1940), 101, 104; Richard B. MacMaster, *Land, Piety, Peoplehood: The Establishment of Mennonite Communities in America, 1663–1790* (Scottdale, Pa.: Herald, 1985), 31–33, 42, 49.

8. Harder and Harder, *Plockhoy*, 72–78.

9. The most complete study is still Bartlett B. James, *The Labadist Colony in Maryland*, Johns Hopkins University Studies in Historical and Political Science, 17. no. 6 (Baltimore: 1899; reprint, New York: AMS Press, 1978). See also Ernest J. Green, "The Labadists of Colonial Maryland, 1683–1722," *Communal Societies* 8 (1988): 104–21, and George A. Leakin, "Labadists of Bohemia Manor," *Maryland Historical Magazine* 2 (1906): 337–45.

10. A recent biography of Labadie is Trevor J. Saxby, *The Quest for the New Jerusalem: Jean de Labadie and the Labadists, 1610–1744* (Dordrecht: Nijhoff, 1987), taken from a Ph.D. dissertation, Oxford University, 1984; a useful study of Labadie is included in C. David Ensign, "Radical German Pietism, c.1675–c.1760" (Ph.D. diss., Boston University, 1955), 64–75.

11. F. Ernest Stoeffler, *The Rise of Evangelical Pietism* (Leiden: E. J. Brill, 1965), 162–69.

12. U. C. Birch, *Anna van Schurman: Artist, Scholar, Saint* (London: Longmans, Green, 1909); Joyce Irwin, "Anna Maria van Schurman: From Feminism to Pietism," *Church History* 46 (1977): 48–62.

13. Bartlett B. James and J. Franklin Jameson, eds., *Journal of Jasper Danckaerts, 1679–1680* (New York: Scribner's, 1913), in the series Original Narratives of Early American History (reprint, New York: Barnes & Noble, 1952).

14. William I. Hull, *William Penn and the Dutch Quaker Migration to Pennsylvania*, Swarthmore College Monographs on Quaker History, 2 (Philadelphia: Swarthmore College, 1935; reprint, Baltimore: Genealogical Pub. Co., 1970), 1–19; Mary Maples Dunn and Richard S. Dunn, eds., *The Papers of William Penn* (Philadelphia: University of Pennsylvania Press, 1981), 215–19, 412, 415, 440–41, 473–79, 503, 507; *The Life and Travels of Samuel Bownas* (London: William Dunlap, 1795), quoted in Hull, *William Penn* (1935), 18–19. The life and ministry of Bownas are described in Rufus Jones, *The Later Periods of Quakerism* (London: Macmillan, 1921; reprint, Westport, Conn.: Greenwood, 1970), 7–10).

15. The most recent study is Willard M. Martin, "Johannes Kelpius and Johann Gottfried Seelig: Mystics and Hymnists on the Wissahickon" (Ph.D. diss., Pennsylvania State University, 1973), which supersedes the extensive early study by Julius F. Sachse, *The German Pietists of Provincial Pennsylvania, 1694–1708* (Philadelphia: The author, 1895; reprint, New York: AMS Press, 1970). See also Elizabeth W. Fisher, "'Prophecies and Revelations': German Cabbalists in Early Pennsylvania," *Pennsylvania Magazine of History and Biography* 109 (1985): 299–333; Klaus Deppermann, "Pennsylvanien als Asyl des frühen deutschen

Pietismus," *Pietismus und Neuzeit* 10 (1984): 190–212; Ernest L. Lashlee, "Johannes Kelpius and His Woman in the Wilderness," in *Glaube, Geist, Geschichte: Festschrift für Ernst Benz*, ed. G. Müller and W. Zeller (Leiden: E. J. Brill, 1967), 327–38; Ernst Benz, *Die protestantische Thebais* (Wiesbaden: Franz Steiner, 1963); E. Gordon Alderfer, "Johannes Kelpius and the Spiritual Ferment of the Seventeenth Century," *American-German Review* 17 (August 1951): 3–6; Andrew Steinmetz, "Kelpius: The Hermit of the Wissahickon," *American-German Review* 7 (August 1941): 7–12.

16. On Zimmermann, see Heinrich Hermelink, *Geschichte der evangelischen Kirche in Württemberg von der Reformation bis zur Gegenwart* (Stuttgart: R. Wunderlich, 1949), 182–83; Hartmut Lehmann, *Pietismus und weltliche Ordnung in Württemberg vom 17. bis zum 20. Jahrhundert* (Stuttgart: W. Kohlhammer, 1969), 31–32; and Hermann Boehmer, *Geschichte der Stadt Bietigheim an der Enz* (Stuttgart: W. Kohlhammer, 1956); his writings are listed in Gottfried Mälzer, *Die Werke der württembergischen Pietisten des 17. und 18. Jahrhunderts* (Berlin: de Gruyter, 1972), 398–404. The best recent study of Jakob Boehme is Andrew Weeks, *Boehme: An Intellectual Biography of the Seventeenth-Century Philosopher and Mystic* (Albany: State University of New York Press, 1991).

17. Hull, *William Penn* (1935), 337–39; William I. Hull, *Benjamin Furly and Quakerism in Rotterdam*, Swarthmore College Monographs on Quaker History, 5 (Lancaster, Pa.: Swarthmore College, 1941).

18. Julius F. Sachse, ed., *The Diarium of Johannes Kelpius*, Proceedings of the Pennsylvania-German Society, 25 (Lancaster, Pa.: Pennsylvania-German Society, 1917); another account suggests that there were about twenty in the party.

19. On Köster, see Alfred J. Vagts, *Deutsch-Amerikanische Rückwanderung* (Heidelberg: Carl Winter, 1960), 64, based on Joh. Chr. Adelung, *Geschichte der menschlichen Narrheit* (Leipzig: Weygandsche Buchhandlung, 1785), esp. 5:86. On Falckner, see Julius F. Sachse, ed., *Curiuese Nachricht von Pensylvania in Norden-America*, Proceedings of the Pennsylvania-German Society, 14 (Lancaster, Pa.: Pennsylvania-German Society, 1905). On Seelig, see Martin, "Kelpius and Seelig," and Oswald Seidensticker, "Johann Gottfried Seelig and the Hymnbook of the Hermits of the Wissahickon," *Pennsylvania Magazine of History and Biography* 25 (1901): 336–40. For information on the three leaders, see also Sachse, *German Pietists*, 251–340, and Martin, "Kelpius and Seelig," 10–18.

20. Nils Thune, *The Behmenists and the Philadelphians* (Uppsala: Almqvist and Wiksell, 1948); Serge Hutin, *Les Disciples anglais de Jacob Boehme aux XVIIe et XVIIIe siècles* (Paris: Editions Denoël, 1960), 119; and Hans-Jürgen Schrader, *Literaturproduktion und Büchermarkt des radikalen Pietismus* (Göttingen: Vandenhoeck & Ruprecht, 1989), 63–73.

21. Francis Burke Brandt, *The Wissahickon Valley within the City of Philadelphia* (Philadelphia: Corn Exchange National Bank, 1927), 84–95.

22. Oswald Seidensticker, "The Hermits of the Wissahickon," *Pennsylvania Magazine of History and Biography* 11 (1887): 427–41.

23. E. Gordon Alderfer, ed., *A Method of Prayer* (New York: Harper and Bros., 1951). For a recent evaluation of Kelpius's writing, see Harold Jantz, "German-American Literature: Some Further Perspectives," in *America and the Germans: An Assessment of a Three-Hundred-Year History*, ed. Frank Trommler and Joseph McVeigh (Philadelphia: University of Pennsylvania Press, 1985), 283–93. See also Robert Bornemann, *Five Hymns from the Hymnbook of Magister Johannes Kelpius* (Philadelphia: Fortress, 1976), and Jon Butler, "Magic, Astrology, and the Early American Religious Heritage, 1600–1760," *American Historical Review* 84 (1979): 317–46.

24. John Greenleaf Whittier, *The Pennsylvania Pilgrim and Other Poems* (Boston: James R. Osgood, 1872), 33–34.

25. Lamech and Agrippa [pseud.], *Chronicon Ephratense: A History of the Community of*

Seventh Day Baptists at Ephrata, Lancaster County, Penn'a, trans. J. Max Hark (Lancaster, Pa.: S. H. Zahn, 1889), 14–15.

26. Carsten E. Seecamp, "The Chapter of Perfection: A Neglected Influence on George Lippard," *Pennsylvania Magazine of History and Biography* 94 (1970): 192–212.

27. Walter C. Klein, *Johann Conrad Beissel, Mystic and Martinet* (Philadelphia: University of Pennsylvania Press, 1941; reprint, Philadelphia: Porcupine Press, 1972); see also Guy T. Hollyday and Christoph E. Schweitzer, "The Present Status of Conrad Beissel / Ephrata Research," *Monatshefte* 68 (1976): 171–78.

28. Documents on the early relationships between Beissel and the Brethren, followed by increasing strain and eventual rupture, are given in Donald F. Durnbaugh, ed., *The Brethren in Colonial America* (Elgin, Ill.: Brethren, 1967), 63–89.

29. Lamech and Agrippa, *Chronicon Ephratense*, 31; Jobie E. Riley, "The Rhetoric of the German Speaking Pulpit in Eighteenth-Century Pennsylvania," *Journal of the Lancaster County Historical Society* 81 (1977): 138–59.

30. The most recent study is E. G[ordon] Alderfer, *The Ephrata Commune: An Early American Counterculture* (Pittsburgh: University of Pittsburgh Press, 1985), based on a rather complete survey of secondary literature. The older monograph, long considered standard, was Julius F. Sachse, *The German Sectarians of Pennsylvania, 1708–1800: A Critical and Legendary History of the Ephrata Cloister and the Dunkers*, 2 vols. (Philadelphia: The author, 1899–1900; reprint, New York: AMS Press, 1971). Earlier references, along with a listing of Ephrata imprints, are found in Eugene E. Doll and Anneliese M. Funke, comps., *The Ephrata Cloisters: An Annotated Bibliography* (Philadelphia: Carl Schurz Memorial Foundation, 1944), 9–36.

31. A useful anthology of descriptions of Ephrata is Felix Reichmann and Eugene E. Doll, eds., *Ephrata As Seen by Contemporaries*, Pennsylvania German Folklore Society, 17 (Allentown, Pa.: Pennsylvania German Folklore Society, 1953); see also the recent volume, Peter C. Erb, ed., *Johann Conrad Beissel and the Ephrata Community: Mystical and Historical Texts* (Lewistown, N.Y.: Edwin Mellen, 1985).

32. Thomas Mann, *Doktor Faustus . . .*, trans. H. T. Lowe-Porter (New York: Knopf, 1948); Jacob Duché, *Caspipina's Letters* (Bath and London: 1777), esp. 79, reprinted in Reichmann and Doll, *Contemporaries*, 101–2; Hans Theodore David, "Hymns and Music of the Pennsylvania Seventh-Day Baptists," *American-German Review* 9 (June 1943): 4–6, 36; Russell P. Getz, "Music in the Ephrata Cloister," *Communal Societies* 2 (1982): 27–38; Betty Jean Martin, "The Ephrata Cloister and Its Music, 1732–1785: The Cultural, Religious, and Bibliographical Background" (Ph.D. diss., University of Maryland, 1974).

33. Klaus Wust, *The Saint-Adventurers of the Virginia Frontier* (Edinburgh, Va.: Shenandoah History Pub., 1977).

34. Charles W. Treher, *Snow Hill Cloister*, Publications of the Pennsylvania-German Society, 2 (Allentown, Pa.: Pennsylvania-German Society, 1968).

35. John R. Weinlick, *Count Zinzendorf* (New York: Abingdon, 1956), and A. J. Lewis, *Zinzendorf, the Ecumenical Pioneer: A Study in the Moravian Contribution to Christian Mission and Unity* (Philadelphia: Westminster, 1962).

36. Murray L. Wagner, *Peter Chelčický: A Radical Separatist in Hussite Bohemia* (Scottdale, Pa.: Herald, 1983).

37. The standard denominational history is J[ohn] Taylor Hamilton and Kenneth G. Hamilton, *History of the Moravian Church: The Renewed Unitas Fratrum, 1722–1957* (Bethlehem, Pa.: Moravian Church in America, 1967); see also Heinz Renkewitz, ed., *Die Brüder-Unität*, Die Kirchen der Welt, 5 (Stuttgart: Evangelisches Verlagswerk, 1967). Some of the extensive archival records of the Moravians are in print; see especially Adelaide L. Fries and Kenneth G. Hamilton, eds., *Records of the Moravians in North Carolina* (Raleigh: North

Carolina Historical Commission, 1922–69); see also William H. Schwarze and Samuel H. Gapp, eds., *A History of the Beginning of Moravian Work in America* (Bethlehem, Pa.: Archives of the Moravian Church, [1955]), and Kenneth G. Hamilton, ed., *The Bethlehem Diary*, vol. 1, *1742–1761* (Bethlehem, Pa.: Archives of the Moravian Church, 1971).

38. Jeannine S. Ingram, "Music in American Moravian Communities: Transplanted Traditions in Indigenous Practices," *Communal Societies* 2 (1982): 39–51; Raymond J. Brunner, *"That Ingenious Business": Pennsylvania German Organ Builders*, Pennsylvania German Publications, vol. 24 (Birdsboro, Pa.: Pennsylvania German Society, 1990).

39. Jacob John Sessler, *Communal Pietism among Early American Moravians* (New York: Henry Holt, 1933; reprint, New York: AMS Press, 1970); Gillian Lindt Gollin, *Moravians in Two Worlds* (New York: Columbia University Press, 1967); Beverly Prior Smaby, *The Transformation of Moravian Bethlehem: From Communal Mission to Family Economy* (Philadelphia: University of Pennsylvania Press, 1988); and Daniel B. Thorp, *The Moravian Community in Colonial North Carolina: Pluralism on the Southern Frontier* (Knoxville: University of Tennessee Press, 1989).

40. Lamech and Agrippa, *Chronicon Ephratense* (1786), 286–87.

Selected Bibliography

P. C. Plockhoy and the Valley of the Swans

Harder, Leland, and Marvin Harder. *Plockhoy from Zurik-zee: The Study of a Dutch Reformer in Puritan England and Colonial America*. Newton, Kans.: [Mennonite] Board of Education and Publication, 1952. Includes sources.

Plockhoy, P. C. "An Invitation to the Society of Little Commonwealth." In *Every Need Supplied: Mutual Aid and Christian Community in the Free Churches, 1525–1675*, edited by Donald F. Durnbaugh, 143–55. Philadelphia: Temple University Press, 1974.

Jean de Labadie and Bohemia Manor

Greene, Ernest J. "The Labadists of Colonial Maryland, 1683–1722." *Communal Societies* 8 (1988): 104–21.

Saxby, Trevor J. *The Quest for the New Jerusalem: Jean de Labadie and the Labadists, 1610–1740*. Dordrecht: Nijhoff, 1987.

Stoeffler, F. Ernest. *The Rise of Evangelical Pietism*. Leiden: E. J. Brill, 1965, 162–69.

Johannes Kelpius and the Society of the Woman in the Wilderness

Bornemann, Robert. *Five Hymns from the Hymnbook of Magister Johannes Kelpius*. Philadelphia: Fortress, 1976.

Martin, Willard M. "Johannes Kelpius and Johann Gottfried Seelig: Mystics and Hymnists on the Wissahickon." Ph.D. diss., Pennsylvania State University, 1973.

Sachse, Julius F. *The German Pietists of Provincial Pennsylvania, 1694–1708* (Philadelphia: The author, 1895).

Conrad Beissel and the Ephrata Community

Alderfer, E. G. *The Ephrata Commune: An Early American Counterculture*. Pittsburgh: University of Pittsburgh Press, 1985.

Erb, Peter C., ed. *Johann Conrad Beissel and the Ephrata Community: Mystical and Historical Texts*. Lewistown, N.Y.: Edwin Mellen, 1985. Studies in American Religion, 14.

Wust, Klaus. *The Saint-Adventurers of the Virginia Frontier*. Edinburgh, Va.: Shenandoah History Pub., 1977.

Count Zinzendorf and the Moravians

Gollin, Gillian Lindt, *Moravians in Two Worlds*. New York: Columbia University Press, 1967.

Lewis, A. J. *Zinzendorf, the Ecumenical Pioneer: A Study in the Moravian Contribution to Christian Mission and Unity*. Philadelphia: Westminster, 1962.

Smaby, Beverly Prior. *The Transformation of Moravian Bethlehem: From Communal Mission to Family Economy*. Philadelphia: University of Pennsylvania Press, 1988.

General Reading

Durnbaugh, Donald F. *The Believers' Church: The History and Character of Radical Protestantism*. Scottdale, Pa.: Herald, 1985.

Erb, Peter C., ed. *Pietists: Selected Writings*. New York: Paulist Press, 1983.

Oved, Yaacov. *Two Hundred Years of American Communes*. New Brunswick, N.J.: Transaction, 1988.

Film

(Moravian) *First Fruits*. 1982. Gateway Films, Box A, Lansdale, PA 19446.

PRISCILLA J. BREWER

The Shakers of Mother Ann Lee

With fewer than a dozen members surviving at this writing, the United Society of Believers in Christ's Second Appearing (commonly called Shakers) exerts an influence on modern America out of all proportion to its size. Books on such popular Shaker topics as furniture, cooking, music, textiles, herbs, and baskets proliferate. Increased scholarly attention in the last twenty-five years has resulted in the publication of more than twenty major studies of the sect. Prominent museums have hosted Shaker exhibitions, public television stations across the country have aired documentaries about the Believers, and eager antique dealers and collectors have flocked to auctions hoping to acquire authentic Shaker artifacts for ever-escalating prices. Yet the story of Shaker development is too little understood. Shaker contributions to the growth of communal alternatives to the dominant culture deserve greater attention.

The Shakers were remarkable primarily because they were successful, a characteristic that makes them appealing to achievement-oriented Americans today. Widely recognized as one of America's most successful communal sects, the Shakers, after arriving in the colonies in 1774 with only nine members, boasted close to 4,000 adherents by 1850.[1] During a history that has already spanned more than 200 years, at least 20,000 Americans have lived part of their lives as Shakers.[2] In the nineteenth century, eighteen separate communities flourished from Kentucky to Maine, and carefully produced Shaker sales items such as garden seeds and wooden ware earned them many admirers among non-Believers. Reformers such as Robert Owen and Bronson

Alcott and philosophers such as Ralph Waldo Emerson found in the Shaker experience lessons of far broader application.

The significance of the Shakers' story transcends both their achievements and their likely demise. Like many other eighteenth-century Americans, the Believers were revolutionaries, but not in the commonly understood sense. Following the lead of their founder, an unlettered English mystic named Ann Lee (1736–84), the early Shakers decided that the world was incurably diseased with sin and burdened by its consequences: war, poverty, greed, and lust. To overcome these conditions and to enable men and women to live in a proper relationship to one another and to God, the Shakers set out to rebuild society from its foundation. Four tenets came to comprise the core of Shaker ideology: celibacy, communalism, confession of sin, and separation from the outside world. By vigorously adhering to these principles, Shaker converts believed they could become perfect.

Although perfectionism attracted many American evangelical Christians in the early national period, the Shakers were among the few to embody this concept in concrete social and economic forms. Beginning in the 1770s, the Shakers created a new society in which men and women were spiritually equal and in which members lived to serve God, not themselves. This is the Shaker story most worth telling.

The influence of Ann Lee on thousands of dissatisfied American evangelicals suggests that individuals can significantly affect the historical process. Born on or about February 29, 1736, into a poor blacksmith's family in the slums of Manchester, England, Ann demonstrated spiritual gifts from an early age. Her concern for morality, especially with regard to sexual behavior, was particularly marked. She received no formal schooling and worked in a textile mill in her early teens. Around 1750 she learned of the teachings of George Whitefield, the stirring evangelist who preached the necessity of a fundamental "new birth" for Christians who hoped to be saved. Possibly as a result of Whitefield's influence, Lee became increasingly discontented with the Anglican Church and concerned about the morass of social and moral problems she saw multiplying around her.[3]

Continuing to pray for divine guidance in her search for remedies for the human condition, Lee came into contact about 1758 with James and Jane Wardley, leaders of a group of radical religious "seekers." Evidence suggests that the Wardleys borrowed a number of concepts from the Quakers, including pacifism and the rejection of religious ritual, sacraments, and ordained clergy. They were also apparently influenced by a small band of French charismatics called "Prophets," several of whom had fled to the Manchester area after the 1689 revocation of the Edict of Nantes sparked persecution of

PRISCILLA J. BREWER

A Shaker "laboring," or community worship meeting, at New Lebanon, New York, drawn by a "Worldly" spectator. This set pattern "dance" characterized Shaker worship from the 1790s to the 1880s. (Hancock Shaker Village, Pittsfield, Massachusetts)

Protestants in Roman Catholic France.[4] Like the Prophets, members of the Wardley group surrendered themselves freely to the operation of the spirit. They spoke in unknown tongues, shouted, and shook violently, leading observers to call them derisively "Shaking Quakers." These religious radicals were convinced that the end of the world was near. "Mother Jane" Wardley urged her followers to "amend your lives. Repent. For the kingdom of God is at hand. The new heaven and the new earth prophesied of old is about to come. . . . And when Christ appears again, and the true church rises in full and transcendant [sic] glory, then all anti-Christian denominations—the priests, the church, the pope—will be swept away."[5]

Ann Lee found these principles and practices exceedingly congenial. Personal circumstances cemented her relationship to the Wardley group. In January 1762, perhaps as a result of pressure from relatives who had witnessed her spiritual odyssey with growing concern, Lee married Abraham Stanley, a blacksmith. During the next four years she bore four children, none of whom survived early childhood. Convinced that the death of her children was a judgment from God for indulging in "concupiscence" against the dictates of her conscience, Ann became increasingly troubled about the influence of lust on human relationships. Her guilt and remorse gradually led her to the conviction that the purification of the soul required "a full mortification of the body," a regimen based on chastity and celibacy.[6]

After the death of her children, Lee became more active within the Wardley group. She was periodically imprisoned for breaking the Sabbath, a circumstance that raised her in the estimation of fellow members, who viewed her as a victim of religious persecution. The pivotal event in early Shaker history occurred in 1770 during one of Lee's periods of incarceration. She later testified that Christ had appeared to her in a series of visions and vividly described the origins of human misery. Adam and Eve, Lee explained, had indulged in the "original sin" of sexual intercourse not to procreate but to satisfy their lust. Abstinence from sex was necessary to purify and perfect human nature and to eliminate all of the world's evils. Lee delivered this revelation with new authority, reporting, "I feel the blood of Christ running through my soul and body! I feel him present with me, as sensibly as I feel my hands together. . . . It is not I that speak. It is Christ who dwells in me."[7] Lee's disciples recognized the truth of her visions and acknowledged her mandate. Henceforth Lee was called "Mother Ann," the female completion of the Christ spirit. Her followers determined to live new lives of virgin purity in a millennial kingdom of peace and perfection.

In 1772 Mother Ann announced that she had seen in a vision the "place that had been prepared" for the faithful in America.[8] Two years later she and eight other Believers (including her husband) sailed from Liverpool to establish the new Eden. After landing in New York City on August 6, 1774, the Shakers endured severe hardship. Mother Ann added to the group's support by working as a washerwoman, but her marriage disintegrated. Then, in 1775, the Believers purchased a tract of wilderness land in Niskeyuna, some eight miles northwest of Albany, a purchase financed by a relatively well-to-do English convert named John Hocknell. The following fall Mother Ann moved her tiny band of adherents to the new site.

Constantly struggling to provide subsistence, the early Shakers informally practiced communal sharing of goods and services, more out of necessity than religious conviction. They persevered in the effort to accumulate a surplus of provisions to enable them to welcome the hordes of converts visions had promised. More than three years passed before progress on this front materialized, but Mother Ann refused to become disheartened. She counseled her followers, "O my dear children, hold fast, and be not discouraged. God has not sent us into this land in vain; but he has sent us to bring the gospel to this nation, who are deeply lost in sin; and there are great numbers who will embrace it, and the time draws nigh."[9]

Mother Ann's confidence was fully justified. The religious, social, and economic climate in the northern states in the late 1770s proved ideal for the rapid spread of Shakerism. Postrevolutionary political instability, concern over commerce and currency, and a general atmosphere of cultural upheaval fostered religious revivalism throughout New England and New York. Many evangelical Christians, particularly Baptists and Methodists, were disillusioned by squabbles over doctrine and the noticeable decline in religious fervor. Some anticipated that America, miraculously successful in defeating the mighty British Empire, would prove the site of the long-awaited millennium, Christ's thousand-year reign on earth.[10]

When word reached New Light Baptists in New Lebanon, New York (near the Massachusetts border), in 1780 that a small group of Shaking Quakers some forty miles west believed the millennium had already begun, excitement pervaded the community. Having endured periodic draining cycles of revivalism that had failed to produce any concrete, permanent changes in their lives, these evangelical Christians had been waiting for such news for years. Their minister, Joseph Meacham Jr. (1742–96), dispatched an associate, Calvin Harlow, to Niskeyuna to meet Mother Ann and the "Elders" and question them about their beliefs. He was particularly impressed by the Shakers' practical Christianity, as he later explained: "The Church . . . held the property which they had there as a Joint Interest. . . . So the doctrine implied plainly . . . that those who went to see the Church, that were able to support ourselves, it was our duty to do it, or give as much as we received, and those that were able to do more, it was their duty to give more. . . . For if none were to do more than support themselves, the poor could not have an equal privilege of the gospel with the rich."[11]

Harlow returned to New Lebanon convinced that the Shakers had solved the puzzle of salvation. After a similar visit, Meacham concurred. He confessed his sins and was accepted as a convert. Many members of his congregation followed him into the new church, providing an important nucleus of faith, energy, and property. Meacham himself, whom Mother Ann called her "first born son in America," rapidly demonstrated the spiritual and temporal abilities that would help ensure the group's survival after its founder's death.[12]

In the ten years between her arrival in the colonies and her death in 1784, Mother Ann initiated a process of religious development that continues today. Because the Shakers believed in continuous revelation from the "Spirit World," their doctrine and social structure never became fixed. Yet Mother Ann established a core of tenets that persist, primarily chastity and communalism. By putting these principles into daily practice, Shakers believed they could create a perfect society characterized by peace, brotherhood, and purity.

This vision survived Lee's death because its appeal transcended the personality of a single leader. James Whittaker (1751–87), an early English convert, assumed the mantle of leadership in 1784 and supervised the beginnings of institutionalized Shakerism. During the next three years Whittaker moved the sect's spiritual and administrative center from Niskeyuna to New Lebanon, New York, where the first Shaker meetinghouse was built in 1786. He also continued Mother Ann's tradition of a traveling ministry, journeying to New Hampshire and Maine in 1785–86 to lay the foundations of Shaker expansion in northern New England. Perhaps most important, Whittaker forcefully enunciated the Shaker principle of communalism. In 1782 he scolded convert Josiah Talcott of Hancock, Massachusetts, for indolence, saying, "You have Land enough to maintain three families or more, well improved." The following winter Father James issued a more general injunction, telling all members, "The time is come for you to give up yourselves and your all to God—your substance, your temporal property—to possess as though you possessed not." [13]

After Whittaker's death, leadership passed to Mother Ann's American-born converts. Joseph Meacham was accepted as the sect's spiritual "Father" in 1787. He soon appointed Lucy Wright (1760–1821), who had been Mother Ann's most capable assistant at Niskeyuna, to share the duties of the lead ministry so that the spiritual equality of the sexes might be mirrored in the society's organizational structure. Under Meacham and Wright's joint administration, Shaker ideology was formalized as the Believers accepted the principle of unquestioning obedience to anointed leaders. Led by visions, Meacham directed worship away from the free-flowing but often individualized and chaotic "back manner." Instead he favored large "laboring" (dancing) meetings and small "union" (discussion) meetings to foster proper relationships between members. [14]

Father Joseph also authored the first in a long series of Shaker theological publications, *A Concise Statement of the Principles of the Only True Church* (1790). In this treatise he described the Shaker version of Christian history comprised of four divine dispensations to men: first to Abraham, then to Moses, then to Christ, and, finally, to Ann Lee. Rejecting the divinity of Christ, the Shakers viewed Jesus and Mother Ann as human vessels into which God had sent the "Christ Spirit" to show men and women the path to salvation. God, too, possessed a dual nature: the male principle of "Father Power" and the female principle of "Holy Mother Wisdom." The message

PRISCILLA J. BREWER

brought hope. In contrast to Calvinists who accepted the selectivity of predestined salvation, the Shakers believed, as Meacham declared, "that God was no respecter of persons but willing that all should come to the knowledge of the truth, and be saved."[15]

Father Joseph's forte was social organization. Under his direction Believers in several areas were invited to "gather" into communities physically and ideologically separated from the outside world. Members at New Lebanon, most notably David Darrow, donated land on which the model community could take shape. Here Father Joseph divided the Shakers into three groups: a Senior or Church Order for adults who had completely severed their economic and familial ties to the "World," a Junior Order for members less advanced in spiritual understanding and still entangled in Worldly responsibilities, and a special order for the elderly and infirm. By 1800 a fourth Gathering or Novitiate Order had been established for converts fresh from the World.

To reduce the risk that Believers might be tempted by the desire for economic gain, Meacham separated temporal and spiritual leadership at New Lebanon in the late 1780s. He appointed David Darrow and Ruth Farrington as elder and eldress to supervise the spiritual growth of Church Order members but assigned the task of economic management to his brother, David. Deacons such as David Meacham were instructed to "give all members of the Church an equal privilege, according to their abilities, to do good, as well as an equal privilege to receive according to their needs."[16] Because most converts to Shakerism possessed only modest estates, this system made it possible for leaders to maximize limited resources.

Following the practices introduced by Meacham at New Lebanon, Believers throughout New England and eastern New York began to form their own communities. Between 1787 and Meacham's death in 1796 ten additional villages were "gathered into gospel order": Watervliet (formerly Niskeyuna), New York (1787); Hancock, Massachusetts (1790); Enfield, Connecticut (1790); Harvard, Massachusetts (1791); Tyringham, Massachusetts (1792); Canterbury, New Hampshire (1792); Shirley, Massachusetts (1793); Enfield, New Hampshire (1793); Alfred, Maine (1793); and Sabbathday Lake, Maine (1794). Each community was divided into "Families" of approximately thirty to one hundred members that were grouped into "Orders" representing different levels of commitment to the faith. Within each Family, elders and eldresses superintended spiritual development, deacons and deaconesses managed temporal activities, and trustees handled business transactions with the outside world. Communities were themselves organized into "Bishoprics" under the leadership of a ministry of two elders and two eldresses that reported directly to the lead ministry at New Lebanon.

At every level men and women shared spiritual and temporal authority, but spheres of activity were sharply divided along gender lines. Brethren were responsible for constructing and maintaining community buildings; planting, tending, and harvesting crops; caring for livestock; and industries such as metalworking and woodworking. Sisters produced, mended, and cleaned textiles; preserved and prepared food; and manufactured sales items such as candy, dolls, and sewing notions. Both men and women treated the sick, physicians caring only for members of the same sex whenever possible.

Brethren and sisters also shared responsibility for the instruction and supervision of children. As outlined in the society's first written covenant, signed at New Lebanon in 1795, minors could not be admitted to full membership. Shaker leaders believed children did not have the maturity to understand the full requirements of Shakerism. Moreover, they did not have the legal right to surrender their property to the society. Yet children quickly became an important part of the Shaker world. Families commonly joined the society as units, husbands and wives agreeing to live as brothers and sisters, with children cared for and educated communally. After 1810, minors were more often brought into the society by single parents or indentured to trustees by guardians who declined to join the sect. All of these children received the opportunity to become full members upon reaching adulthood.

The social structure developed under Joseph Meacham's guidance proved resilient. After Meacham's death in 1796, Mother Lucy Wright governed the society for twenty-five years, the most stable period in its history. Membership grew as continuing revivalism in the World, together with the sect's increasing prosperity and proven success, attracted substantial numbers of converts, many of them adults. Numbering 1,373 members in 1800, the population of the eastern communities rose to 2,316 by 1830, an increase of nearly 70 percent.[17] Selective proselytization and a publication program that produced five works of theology and history in a single decade drew many eager inquirers to Shaker villages.

The most successful of these efforts began in 1805, when Mother Lucy, intrigued by reports of massive revivals sweeping the western frontier, dispatched Brothers Issachar Bates, Benjamin Youngs, and John Meacham there to spread the Shaker gospel. Their mission resulted in the establishment of seven new communities: Union Village, Ohio (1806); Watervliet, Ohio (1806); Pleasant Hill, Kentucky (1806); South Union, Kentucky (1807); West Union, Indiana (1810); North Union, Ohio (1822); and Whitewater, Ohio (1824). The Shakers also founded a new community at Sodus Bay in western New York in 1826.

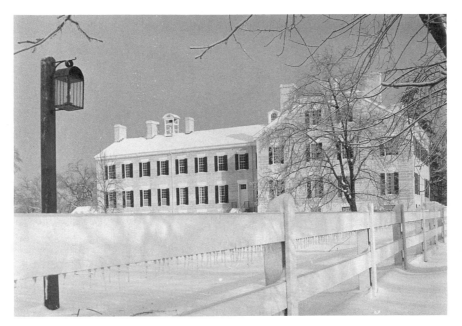

As the most impressive structure built in the western Shaker settlements, the stone Centre Family Dwelling House at Pleasant Hill, Kentucky, contained forty rooms and took ten years of labor to complete in 1834. (Photograph by Donald Janzen)

During this tremendous geographic expansion, the Shakers increased their efforts to bring their gospel to the attention of the "World's People." *The Testimony of Christ's Second Appearing*, the best-known and most extensive work of Shaker theology, was published in 1808. Written by Brothers Benjamin Youngs and Calvin Green, *The Testimony* detailed key dissident developments in Christian history from Adam and Eve to Mother Ann and firmly established the millennial nature of the Shaker faith. A number of readers in the World became convinced of the truth of the Shaker story and converted, leading Brother Calvin Reed to call the book "a bait to catch . . . good Gospel fish."[18]

Despite these developments, serious difficulties loomed. Demographic shifts after 1810 undermined the Society's spiritual health. The proportion of unconverted young members increased while the proportion of middle-aged members, who served as the sect's leaders and role models, declined.[19] Young people who had never experienced the purifying crucible of a religious revival began to exhibit inappropriate behavior. As early as 1807 Mother Lucy chastised a group of young members for "vain jesting, joking, [and] obscene & filthy communication."[20]

Tension emerged over economic issues as well. Young members rarely brought substantial property into the sect when they joined, a situation that strained resources and engendered some grumbling on the part of older Believers. Mother Lucy had to remind her followers, "If a man has labored and acquired an interest and then consecrates it . . . he does but give up all. The young who have nothing; and consecrate their time and talents . . . it may be said with equal propriety that they give up all."[21]

In the midst of their greatest success some Shakers succumbed to materialism. A significant number of converts joined the society as much for the guarantee of temporal security as for the promise of salvation. In 1817 the lead ministry regretfully observed that the society "could have a great many *loaf Believers* in this distressing time (especially children) if we were willing to take them—doubtless we could have enough to fill all our buildings and consume all our provisions, and by that time they would be willing to go somewhere else."[22] Even among Shakers who chose to remain in the faith, Mother Lucy noted a distressing increase in "worldly sense," commenting in 1815 that "the sense seems so drowned in temporal things that there can be but little desire for the gifts of God. . . . I sometimes feel that I would be thankful with all my heart if the sense was so that it could be satisfied with less . . . of this world's treasures."[23]

Some leaders argued that these developments necessitated the compilation of Shaker regulations, but Mother Lucy resisted this step because it might compromise the ability of future leaders to alter rules as dictated by continuing revelation. After Wright's death in 1821, however, the lead ministry that succeeded her agreed that Shaker rules should be codified for the benefit of new and young members. Accordingly, Brother Freegift Wells of Watervliet, New York, assembled all the regulations that could be recalled from the administrations of various leaders and organized them under headings such as "Separation of the Sexes" and "Orders on uniformity in certain acts of behavior." Every Family received a copy of these "Millennial Laws" to read aloud during worship meetings.

Unfortunately these precautions did not prevent a further decline in commitment and an increase in the number of behavior problems. More young members chose to leave the sect to pursue individual freedom in the World. Brother Isaac Youngs of New Lebanon, one of many worried by this trend, asked in 1837, "What in the name of reason does it mean that so many are going off nowadays???!!! Is there none of the younger part that will abide & be good for something—are we indeed unable to raise any children or youth among us?"[24] William Sims Bainbridge has concluded that Youngs's fears were justified. "Defection," he observed, "seems to have been the rule for

PRISCILLA J. BREWER

younger members."[25] In some instances relations between the sexes became far more intimate than Shaker ideology allowed. A number of brethren and sisters fell in love and left the sect to marry. Two cases of fornication even came to light, one at Shirley in 1832 and another at New Lebanon in 1835.[26] The members involved were, of course, required to leave the sect.

As behavior deteriorated and the apostasy rate rose, the level of internal dissension heightened. Beginning in the mid-1830s, Believers divided over vegetarianism. Some members (most of them young) adopted the recommendations of dietary reformer Sylvester Graham, who advocated a meatless, fiber-rich diet to control, among other things, sexual impulses in the young. But many older Believers were reluctant to abandon their rich and varied table fare, particularly to obey the dictates of a reformer from the corrupt World. Arguments on the issue continued for decades.[27] An 1841 "gift" (inspired communication) directing all Believers to abandon the use of tea, coffee, and pork did little to defuse the situation. Shaker "union" suffered a serious blow, as an unknown scribe lamented in the New Lebanon Elders' *Confidential Journal*, "It is evident that a division of sentiment and feeling has produced more loss than everything else put together."[28]

During the 1830s the Shakers suffered difficulties unparalleled in the society's previous history. Many members agreed that the time for spiritual renewal was at hand. Those young members who had never experienced the searing epiphany brought about by revivalistic enthusiasm finally received their opportunity. In the winter of 1837–38 residents in the Girls' Order at Watervliet, New York, suddenly began receiving visions and messages from the Spirit World. The excitement spread quickly to other communities and involved Shakers of all ages and levels of commitment. Leaders were delighted by the increased zeal they witnessed. In 1838 the lead ministry reported, "It is truly a wonderful day. . . . Numbers who have been spiritually dead for many years, have been raised to life, and are now living souls in the house of God."[29]

The revival, called "Mother's Work" because so many of the inspired messages originated with the spirit of Mother Ann, lasted into the mid-1840s, but its effects were not universally beneficial.[30] Some young Shakers experienced conversions and many older Believers rekindled their commitment to the faith, but the revival could not solve the sect's fundamental problems of how to regulate economic and ideological contacts with the World and how to attract and retain young members. Liberalizing trends in religion, social thought, and aesthetics in the outside world crept insidiously into the society, an influence conservative Believers abhorred. Brother Isaac Youngs was one of those concerned, remarking in 1860, "It is a day of great improvements in the world, a day of much free thinking and freedom of investigation, every man may judge for himself, &c. and this spirit, where there is so much freedom as now unavoidably exists between Believers and the world, insinuates itself powerfully among Believers, which is very injurious to their advancement in the gospel."[31]

Throughout the middle of the nineteenth century the Shaker apostasy rate remained high. Fewer adults joined the sect, and those who did often came for economic rather than spiritual reasons. Even Worldly movements such as Millerism and Spiritualism, to which Shaker leaders looked hopefully for signs of "ingathering," induced few people to join the sect.[32] Children brought into the communities failed to make up for the diminished number of adult converts. Of the 678 children under age sixteen raised at the New Lebanon Church Family between 1787 and 1900, for example, only 121 (17.8 percent) died in the faith. Two hundred and fifty-seven (37.9 percent) chose to sign the covenant and later left, while a nearly equal number (255, or 37.6 percent) were taken away by relatives. Only one of the 197 youngsters admitted after 1860 permanently converted after reaching adulthood. Children in this Family had a less than one in five chance of living out their lives as Shakers, a proportion that declined precipitously as the nineteenth century progressed.[33]

Faced with these apparently insurmountable problems, those Believers who remained faithful struggled to find in their ideology and social structure elements that might still attract converts from the secularizing, industrializing World. Progressive members such as Elder Frederick W. Evans of New Lebanon strove to convince Shakers and "World's People" alike that the society still had important work to do. He declared in 1869, "The Shaker Order is the source and medium of spiritual religious light to the world; the fountain of progressive ideas."[34] To spread these "progressive ideas," Evans and his supporters started a periodical called The Shaker (1871–99), which met with considerable success among reformers in the World.

But Evans's emphasis on Shaker socialism, which he felt provided a valuable example to a world beset by the social and economic dislocations attendant upon rapid industrialization, alienated many conservative members. Championed by Elder Hervey Eads of South Union, Kentucky, these Believers resisted attempts to dilute Shakerism's evangelical Christian core by adding what they sneeringly called a "new dress to Mother Ann's gospel."[35] The division between progressive and conservative leaders bewildered many rank-and-file members and prevented the forging of a healthy new consensus regarding the role of the United Society in late nineteenth-century America.

Sister Martha Burger (1853–1926) at New Lebanon, New York, tending the Shaker community's "Fancy Goods Store." Despite internal opposition, most villages opened such souvenir shops beginning in the mid-nineteenth century to cater to a growing tourist trade. Visitors could purchase postcards, candy, pin cushions, dolls, feather dusters, pen wipers, and sewing baskets, most manufactured by Shaker sisters. (Shaker Museum and Library, Old Chatham, New York)

As a result of these trends, Shaker membership plummeted. After reaching a peak of 3,842 in 1850, the society had only 1,849 members in 1880, 855 in 1900, and 92 in 1936.[36] Reluctantly, society leaders decided to begin closing communities, selling assets, and consolidating membership. Tyringham was the first village to close in 1875, followed by North Union (1889), Groveland (successor of Sodus Bay, New York; 1895), Whitewater (1907), Watervliet, Ohio (1910), and Pleasant Hill (1910). In 1922 South Union, the last Shaker community in the Midwest, closed its doors. By 1961 only two villages remained, both in northern New England. Today, only the community at Sabbathday Lake, Maine, remains active.

A controversial ministry decision in 1965 closed the sect to new members, sparking considerable controversy both within and outside the society. But interest in Shaker ideology, history, and, especially, material culture has grown dramatically in recent years.[37] Before her death, Mother Ann prophesied that Shakerism would experience a revival after membership had fallen to five. Opinion is divided as to whether this will be a revival of influence or actual numbers. Yet the few surviving Believers maintain their way of life, supported by the knowledge that, as Brother Philemon Stewart of New

Lebanon phrased it in 1871, "God's true work will never run out, tho' Zion's present Organizations will be mostly scattered and broken—yet a Remnant will be preserved who will willingly obey God's full requirements according to the day and age in which they live."[38]

Chronology

1736	Ann Lee, founder of the United Society of Believers in Christ's Second Appearing, is born in Manchester, England.
ca. 1758	Disenchanted with England's established Anglican Church, Ann Lee becomes a member of a group of religious "seekers" led by James and Jane Wardley.
1762–66	Ann Lee marries Abraham Stanley and subsequently bears four children, none of whom survives.
1770	Ann Lee receives a vision in which Christ explains that the root of human sin is lust and the only remedy is a life of celibacy. Members of the Wardley group accept the truth of this vision and begin to prepare for the establishment of a millennial kingdom guided by the revelations of Lee, now called "Mother Ann."
1772	Mother Ann receives a vision of a Shaker home in America.
1774	Mother Ann and eight followers arrive in New York City to search for the promised new Eden.
1776	The small group of so-called Shaking Quakers leaves New York City for their new home in Niskeyuna, near Albany.
1780	After enduring a disappointing revival, groups of "New Lights" from western New England and eastern New York learn of Mother Ann and her teachings, visit Niskeyuna, and convert to the faith.
1784	Mother Ann dies and is succeeded by Father James Whittaker, an early English convert, who moves the center of the Shaker church from Niskeyuna to New Lebanon, N.Y.
1787	Father James dies and is succeeded by Father Joseph Meacham, who elevates Mother Lucy Wright to share supreme authority with him. Shakers throughout New England and New York begin to "gather into order."
1787–94	Believers organize eleven communities in New York, Massachusetts, Connecticut, New Hampshire, and Maine under the leadership of bishopric ministries appointed by Father Joseph and Mother Lucy.
1790	Joseph Meacham's *A Concise Statement of the Principles of the Only True Church* is published anonymously in Bennington, Vt.
1795	The first written Shaker covenant is signed at New Lebanon, outlining members' responsibilities, including a provision for donation of property to the society.
1796	Father Joseph dies and is succeeded by Mother Lucy Wright.
1799	As interest in the World increases, Mother Lucy directs the establishment of a Gathering Order for adult converts at New Lebanon.
1800	Federal census lists 1,373 Shakers.
1805	Three Shaker brethren embark on a missionary tour of the western frontier that results in the establishment of seven new communities in Ohio, Kentucky, and Indiana.

PRISCILLA J. BREWER

1808	*The Testimony of Christ's Second Appearing,* by Brothers Benjamin Youngs and Calvin Green, is published in Lebanon, Ohio.
1816	Brother Rufus Bishop's *Testimonies of the Life, Character, Revelations and Doctrines of Our ever Blessed Mother Ann Lee* is published in Hancock, Mass.
1821	Mother Lucy dies and is succeeded by four leaders at New Lebanon: Elders Ebenezer and Rufus Bishop and Eldresses Ruth Landon and Asenath Clark. The "Millennial Laws," the first codification of Shaker rules, is assembled and dispatched to all Shaker Families.
1822	Mary Dyer, an apostate from the Enfield, N.H., community, publishes a vituperative account of her experience with the Shakers: *A Portraiture of Shakerism.*
1823	*A Summary View of the Millennial Church,* by Brothers Calvin Green and Seth Wells, is published in Albany, N.Y.
1826	The final Shaker community to experience lasting success is established at Sodus Bay in western New York. Ten years later, the community is moved to Groveland, N.Y.
1820s	As apostasy rates rise, particularly among young brethren, many communities are forced to begin hiring "World's People" as laborers.
1835–41	Debate over Sylvester Graham's ideas about dietary reform divides Believers in many villages. A spiritual direction in 1841 requires members to abstain from tea, coffee, and pork.
1837–44	Active period of the revival called "Mother's Work" increases zeal and commitment among some members but fails to solve long-standing problems.
1850	Federal census reports the peak documented Shaker membership: 3,842 Believers in eighteen villages.
1853	Hervey Elkins, an apostate from the Enfield, N.H., community, publishes a sympathetic but poignant account of his life as a Believer: *Fifteen Years in the Senior Order of Shakers.*
ca. 1855	In spite of the objections of some members, the rule requiring partial vegetarianism is rescinded.
1860	Federal census reports a Shaker membership of 3,489.
1871–99	*The Shaker,* a periodical published by progressive members, attempts to convince Believers and sympathetic outsiders that Shaker social ideology provides the key to many of the world's problems.
1875	The community at Tyringham, Mass., is closed due to declining membership and prosperity.
1880	Federal census lists 1,849 Shakers.
1889–1910	Five more communities are closed.
1893	Elder Frederick W. Evans, the society's most vocal progressive member, dies.
1900	Federal census reports a Shaker membership of 855.
1904	The United Society's last major public statement appears: *Shakerism: Its Meaning and Message,* by Sisters Anna White and Leila S. Taylor.
1912–60	Nine more communities are closed.
1933	Edward Deming Andrews's first book, *The Community Industries of the Shakers,* is published in connection with the first major exhibition of Shaker artifacts, marking the beginning of serious scholarly interest in the United Society.

1936	Shaker membership falls to ninety-two.
1961	The society's last elder, Delmer Wilson, dies at Sabbathday Lake, Me. Only the Sabbathday Lake and Canterbury, N.H., communities remain.
1965	Amid controversy, the lead ministry closes the society's covenant to new members.
1988	Eldress Gertrude Soule dies at Canterbury.
1990	The last Shaker eldress, Bertha Lindsay, dies at Canterbury.
1992	The last Shaker at Canterbury, Sister Ethel Hudson, dies.
1996	Fewer than a dozen Shakers live at the last Shaker community, Sabbathday Lake.

Notes

1. William Sims Bainbridge, "The Decline of the Shakers: Evidence from the United States Census," *Communal Societies* 4 (1984): 22. Bainbridge counted 3,842 Shakers in the 1850 federal census.

2. Priscilla J. Brewer, *Shaker Communities, Shaker Lives* (Hanover, N.H.: University Press of New England, 1986), 203.

3. Edward Deming Andrews, *The People Called Shakers* (1953; reprint, New York: Dover, 1963), 3–7.

4. Clarke Garrett, *Spirit Possession and Popular Religion: From the Camisards to the Shakers* (Baltimore: Johns Hopkins University Press, 1987), 141–42; Stephen J. Stein, *The Shaker Experience in America: A History of the United Society of Believers* (New Haven: Yale University Press, 1992), 5–6.

5. Quoted by Andrews, *People Called Shakers*, 6.

6. Ibid., 7–8.

7. Quoted by Stephen A. Marini, *Radical Sects of Revolutionary New England* (Cambridge, Mass.: Harvard University Press, 1982), 76.

8. Quoted by ibid., 77.

9. Quoted by Andrews, *People Called Shakers*, 17.

10. This is the central argument of Nathan O. Hatch, *The Sacred Cause of Liberty: Republican Thought and the Millennium in Revolutionary New England* (New Haven: Yale University Press, 1977).

11. Quoted by Andrews, *People Called Shakers*, 48–49.

12. Quoted by Rufus Bishop and Seth Y. Wells, eds., *Testimonies of the Life, Character, Revelations and Doctrines of Mother Ann Lee and the Elders With Her*, 2d ed. (Albany, N.Y.: Weed, Parsons, 1888), 181.

13. Quoted by Andrews, *People Called Shakers*, 48.

14. For an account of these developments, see Brewer, *Shaker Communities*, 16, 21, 52–53.

15. [Joseph Meacham], *A Concise Statement of the Principles of the Only True Church, according to the Gospel of the Present Appearance of Christ. As Held to and Practiced upon by the True Followers of the Living Saviour, at New Lebanon, &c. Together with a Letter from James Whittaker, Minister of the Gospel in this Day of Christ's Second Appearing—to his Natural Relations in England* (Bennington, Vt.: Haswell & Russell, 1790), 14.

16. Letter of Joseph Meacham to David Meacham, in Rufus Bishop, comp., *A Collection of the Writings of Father Joseph Meacham Respecting Church Order and Government* (New Lebanon, N.Y.: 1850), 33. Manuscript in Western Reserve Historical Society Shaker Collection, Cleveland, Ohio, VII B 59 (cited hereafter as WRHS).

17. Statistics are taken from the 1800 and 1830 federal census reports. Because tabulations for Grafton County, New Hampshire (where the Enfield community was located), are missing from federal records, the 1820 population figure of 1,956 is incomplete. See Brewer, *Shaker Communities*, 215.

18. Calvin Reed, "Autobiography" (New Lebanon, N.Y., n.d.), WRHS VI B 29, 121.

19. See Brewer, *Shaker Communities*, 207–8.

20. Quoted by John Warner, "A Short Account of the birth, character, and ministration of Father Eleazer and Mother Hannah" (Harvard, Mass., 1824), WRHS VI B 7, 18.

21. Quoted by ibid., 20.

22. Letter of Ministry New Lebanon to Ministry Union Village, February 22, 1817, WRHS IV A 33.

23. Quoted by Calvin Green, "Biographic Memoir of the Life, Character & Important Events in the Ministration of Mother Lucy Wright" (New Lebanon, N.Y., 1861), WRHS VI B 27, 88–94.

24. Isaac N. Youngs, *Personal Journal* (New Lebanon, N.Y.: 1837–57), March 24, 1837. Manuscript at the Shaker Museum, Old Chatham, N.Y., #10,509.

25. Bainbridge, "Decline of the Shakers," 26.

26. See Brewer, *Shaker Communities*, 93–95.

27. See ibid., 106–12.

28. Philemon Stewart and Daniel Crosman, *A Confidential Journal Kept in the Elders' Lot* (New Lebanon, N.Y.: 1842–81), WRHS V B 136, Sept. 21, 1847.

29. Letter of Ministry New Lebanon to Ministry South Union, June 20, 1838, WRHS IV B 36.

30. For a fuller account, see Brewer, *Shaker Communities*, 115–35, and Andrews, *People Called Shakers*, 152–76. The rich heritage of Shaker songs and "gift" drawings, many of which originated during Mother's Work, is discussed in Daniel W. Patterson, *The Shaker Spiritual* (Princeton: Princeton University Press, 1979), and Patterson, *Gift Drawing and Gift Song* (Sabbathday Lake, Maine: United Society of Shakers, 1983).

31. Isaac N. Youngs, *A Concise View of the Church of God and of Christ on Earth Having its foundation in the faith of Christ's first and Second Appearing* (New Lebanon, N.Y.: 1856–60). Manuscript in Edward Deming Andrews Memorial Shaker Collection, Henry Francis DuPont Winterthur Museum, Winterthur, Del., #861, 509 (cited hereafter as Andrews Collection).

32. See Brewer, *Shaker Communities*, 150–55.

33. See ibid., 213–14.

34. Frederick W. Evans, *Autobiography of a Shaker and Revelation of the Apocalypse*, 2d ed. (1888; reprint, Philadelphia: Porcupine Press, 1972), x.

35. Freegift Wells, "Testimonies, Predictions and Remarks" (Watervliet, N.Y., 1865), WRHS VI B 51, 22.

36. Bainbridge, "Decline of the Shakers," and Bainbridge, "Shaker Demographics, 1840–1900: An Example of the Use of U.S. Census Enumeration Schedules," *Journal for the Scientific Study of Religion* 21 (1982): 355. The population figure for 1936 is cited in Henri Desroche, *The American Shakers: From Neo-Christianity to Presocialism* (Amherst: University of Massachusetts Press, 1971), 129.

37. For a detailed description of these developments, see Stein, *Shaker Experience*, 370–409.

38. Philemon Stewart, *A Brief Weekly Journal* (New Lebanon, N.Y.: 1870–74), Andrews Collection, #850, Sept. 6, 1873.

Selected Bibliography

Primary Sources

Bishop, Rufus, and Seth Y. Wells, eds. *Testimonies of the Life, Character, Revelations and Doctrines of Mother Ann Lee and the Elders With Her.* 2d ed. Albany, N.Y.: Weed, Parsons, 1888.

Brown, Thomas. *An Account of the People Called Shakers: Their Faith, Doctrines and Practice, Exemplified in the Life, Conversations, and Experience of the Author during the Time he Belonged to the Society, to Which is Affixed a History of Their Rise and Progress to the Present Day.* Troy, N.Y.: Parker & Bliss, 1812.

Dyer, Mary. *A Portraiture of Shakerism.* Concord, N.H.: The author, 1822.

Elkins, Hervey. *Fifteen Years in the Senior Order of Shakers: A Narration of the Facts Concerning That Singular People.* Hanover, N.H.: Dartmouth Press, 1853.

Evans, Frederick W. *Autobiography of a Shaker and Revelation of the Apocalypse.* 2d ed. 1888. Reprint, Philadelphia: Porcupine Press, 1972.

Green, Calvin, and Seth Y. Wells. *A Summary View of the Millennial Church or United Society of Believers, Commonly Called Shakers, Comprising the Rise, Progress and Practical Order of the Society Together with the General Principles of their Faith and Testimony.* Albany, N.Y.: Packard & Van Benthuysen, 1823.

Lamson, David. *Two Years' Experience Among the Shakers: Being a Description of the Manners and Customs of That People; the Nature and Policy of Their Government; Their Marvellous Intercourse with the Spiritual World; the Object and Uses of Confession, Their Inquisition; in Short, a Condensed View of Shakerism.* West Boylston, Mass.: The author, 1848.

[Meacham, Joseph]. *A Concise Statement of the Principles of the Only True Church, according to the Gospel of the Present Appearance of Christ. As Held to and Practiced upon by the True Followers of the Living Saviour, at New Lebanon, &c. Together with a Letter from James Whittaker, Minister of the Gospel in this Day of Christ's Second Appearing—to his Natural Relations in England.* Bennington, Vt.: Haswell & Russell, 1790.

Wells, Seth Y., and Calvin Green. *Testimonies Concerning the Character and Ministry of Mother Ann Lee and the First Witnesses of the Gospel of Christ's Second Appearing; Given by Some of the Aged Brethren and Sisters of the United Society.* Albany, N.Y.: Packard & Van Benthuysen, 1827.

White, Anna, and Leila S. Taylor. *Shakerism: Its Meaning and Message.* Columbus, Ohio: Fred J. Heer, 1904.

Youngs, Benjamin S., and Calvin Green. *The Testimony of Christ's Second Appearing.* 2d ed. Albany, N.Y.: E. & E. Hosford, 1810.

Secondary Sources

Andrews, Edward Deming. *The Community Industries of the Shakers.* Albany: University of the State of New York, 1933.

———. *The People Called Shakers.* 1953. Reprint, New York: Dover, 1963.

Bainbridge, William Sims. "The Decline of the Shakers: Evidence from the United States Census." *Communal Societies* 4 (1984): 19–34.

———. "Shaker Demographics, 1840–1900: An Example of the Use of U.S. Census Enumeration Schedules." *Journal for the Scientific Study of Religion* 21 (1982): 352–65.

Brewer, Priscilla J. "'Numbers Are Not the Thing for Us to Glory In': Demographic Perspectives on the Decline of the Shakers." *Communal Societies* 7 (1987): 25–35.

———. *Shaker Communities, Shaker Lives.* Hanover, N.H.: University Press of New England, 1986.

PRISCILLA J. BREWER

————. "'Tho' of the Weaker Sex': A Reassessment of Gender Equality among the Shakers." *Signs* 17 (1992): 609–35.

Burns, Deborah E. *Shaker Cities of Peace, Love, and Union: A History of the Hancock Bishopric*. Hanover, N.H.: University Press of New England, 1993.

Campbell, D'Ann. "Women's Life in Utopia: The Shaker Experiment in Sexual Equality Reappraised, 1810–1860." *New England Quarterly* 51 (1978): 23–38.

Deignan, Kathleen. *Christ Spirit: The Eschatology of Shaker Christianity*. Metuchen, N.J.: Scarecrow Press, 1992.

Desroche, Henri. *The American Shakers: From Neo-Christianity to Presocialism*. Translated and edited by John K. Savacool. 1955. Reprint, Amherst: University of Massachusetts Press, 1971.

Emlen, Robert P. *Shaker Village Views*. Hanover, N.H.: University Press of New England, 1987.

Filley, Dorothy M. *Recapturing Wisdom's Valley: The Watervliet Shaker Heritage*. Albany, N.Y.: Albany Institute of History and Art, 1975.

Foster, Lawrence. *Religion and Sexuality: Three American Communal Experiments of the Nineteenth Century*. New York: Oxford University Press, 1981.

Garrett, Clarke. *Spirit Possession and Popular Religion: From the Camisards to the Shakers*. Baltimore: Johns Hopkins University Press, 1987.

Gidley, Mick, ed. *Locating the Shakers: Cultural Origins and Legacies of an American Religious Movement*. Exeter: University of Exeter Press, 1990.

Grant, Jerry V., and Douglas R. Allen. *Shaker Furniture Makers*. Hanover, N.H.: University Press of New England, 1989.

Hayden, Dolores. *Seven American Utopias: The Architecture of Communitarian Socialism, 1790–1975*. Cambridge, Mass.: MIT Press, 1976.

Horgan, Edward R. *The Shaker Holy Land: A Community Portrait*. Harvard, Mass.: Harvard Common Press, 1982.

Humez, Jean, ed. *Gifts of Power: The Writings of Rebecca Jackson, Black Visionary, Shaker Eldress*. Amherst: University of Massachusetts Press, 1981.

————. *Mother's First-Born Daughters: Early Shaker Writings on Women and Religion*. Bloomington: Indiana University Press, 1993.

Kern, Louis J. *An Ordered Love: Sex Roles and Sexuality in Victorian Utopias—the Shakers, the Mormons, and the Oneida Community*. Chapel Hill: University of North Carolina Press, 1981.

Kitch, Sally L. *Chaste Liberation: Celibacy and Female Cultural Status*. Urbana: University of Illinois Press, 1989.

Marini, Stephen A. *Radical Sects of Revolutionary New England*. Cambridge, Mass.: Harvard University Press, 1982.

Melcher, Marguerite. *The Shaker Adventure*. Princeton: Princeton University Press, 1941.

Morse, Flo. *The Shakers and the World's People*. New York: Dodd, Mead, 1980.

Neal, Julia. *By Their Fruits: The Story of Shakerism in South Union, Kentucky*. Chapel Hill: University of North Carolina Press, 1947.

Patterson, Daniel W. *Gift Drawing and Gift Song*. Sabbathday Lake, Maine: United Society of Shakers, 1983.

————. *The Shaker Spiritual*. Princeton: Princeton University Press, 1979.

Piercy, Caroline B. *The Valley of God's Pleasure: A Saga of the North Union Shaker Community*. New York: Stratford House, 1951.

Procter-Smith, Marjorie. *Women in Shaker Community and Worship: A Feminist Analysis of the Uses of Religious Symbolism*. Lewiston, Maine: Edwin Mellen, 1985.

Promey, Sally M. *Spiritual Spectacles: Vision and Image in Mid-Nineteenth-Century Shakerism*. Bloomington: Indiana University Press, 1993.

Richmond, Mary L. *Shaker Literature: A Bibliography*. 2 vols. Hanover, N.H.: University Press of New England, 1977.

Rourke, Constance. "The Shakers." In *Roots of American Culture and Other Essays*, edited by Van Wyck Brooks, 195–237. New York: Harcourt, Brace, 1942.

Sasson, Diane. *The Shaker Spiritual Narrative*. Knoxville: University of Tennessee Press, 1983.

Sprigg, June. *By Shaker Hands*. New York: Knopf, 1975.

———. *Shaker Design*. New York: Norton, 1986.

Stein, Stephen J. *The Shaker Experience in America: A History of the United Society of Believers*. New Haven: Yale University Press, 1992.

———, ed. *Letters from a Young Shaker: William S. Byrd at Pleasant Hill*. Lexington: University Press of Kentucky, 1985.

Whitworth, John M. *God's Blueprints: A Sociological Study of Three Utopian Sects*. London: Routledge and Kegan Paul, 1975.

PRISCILLA J. BREWER

KARL J. R. ARNDT

George Rapp's Harmony Society

I am a prophet, and I am called to be one."

George Rapp made this shocking statement in 1791 to the civil affairs official in Maulbronn, Germany, who promptly had him imprisoned for two days and threatened with exile if he did not cease preaching. To the great consternation of church and state authorities, this mere peasant from Iptingen had become the outspoken leader of several thousand Separatists in the southern German duchy of Württemberg.[1]

The Separatists who left the established Evangelical Lutheran Church to follow George Rapp were by no means the first or the only such group in Württemberg's troubled history. Economic and political problems began in the area during the era of world exploration, when the development of the German provinces fell behind that of Western Europe. Württemberg's locale, which included Stuttgart, made it especially vulnerable to all European military activities. The Thirty Years' War (1618–48) had a disastrous effect on the region that lasted well into the eighteenth century. Under the corrupt rule of Duke Karl Eugen (1737–93), who lived a licentious life at the expense of his subjects, government offices were bought and sold. The suffering German peasantry turned to the church for comfort, only to be met with cold formality and the intellectualism of the university-trained clergy. Disaffected, some emigrated while others turned to Pietism. Pietism stressed heartfelt conversion from sin, personal communication with God, and the pursuit of Christian perfection. Some Pietists wanted only to reform the state Lutheran church, while others desired a complete break with what they considered to be a hopelessly corrupt institution.

Into this disquiet Johann Georg Rapp was born on November 1, 1757, the second of five children in the family of Hans Adam Rapp, a farmer, and Rosina Berger Rapp. In 1771 George was confirmed in the Lutheran Church and also lost his father. George had learned vine dressing from his father, and he adopted weaving as his trade. After a period as a journeyman weaver, he married Christina Benzinger of Pfiolzheim in early 1783 and settled in his birthplace of Iptingen, a small village northwest of Stuttgart. Late that same year a son, Johannes, was born to the couple; a daughter, Rosina, followed in 1786.

By his own admission Rapp's religious conduct while a journeyman weaver had been improper. His mother suggested that he cease attending church until his behavior improved, which he did. It was then, however, that he felt filled with the spirit of Christ and became convinced that the established church, the clergy, and rituals were unnecessary to individual salvation and communication with God. Years of spiritual unrest followed for young Rapp. At first vacillating in his commitment to God, he finally found strength to follow the path he felt God had set for him.

Rapp officially broke with the church in 1785 when he was called before the Iptingen Church Council to explain his absence from services. By this time he had a small band of local followers with whom to begin his sectarian movement. They immediately caused trouble themselves by keeping their children out of the Lutheran-dominated school and refusing to have them baptized in the church. Rapp and his disciples made statements that were considered blasphemous. They claimed that the local pastor was not a servant of God, the parishioners were hypocrites, and communion as administered in the church was an idolatrous sacrifice. They objected to baptism, confirmation, and communion because those rites had lost their original meaning and become only empty formalities.

In Württemberg at that time civil and religious affairs were so closely intertwined that Rapp's words and actions posed a threat to government and civil order. The first of many official investigations of his Separatists took place in 1787. Fourteen of them, including George and Christina Rapp, were questioned. The results of this investigation were not reported to the higher civil and religious authorities until 1790. In 1791 those authorities recommended that Rapp be imprisoned and threatened with exile.

Rapp's brief incarceration did nothing to change his ideas and only strengthened the resolve of his 3,000 to 4,000 followers to practice their beliefs. The Württemberg Synod recommended that Rapp be exiled, but Duke Karl Eugen and his advisory council refused to allow it and urged greater toleration. While the mid-1790s saw relaxation of enforcement against the Sep-

KARL J. R. ARNDT

George Rapp was a commanding figure who reportedly stood nearly six feet tall. This painting, one of only two known images of the Harmonist leader, depicts him as he appeared about 1830, wearing his warm undercap. (Courtesy of The Pennsylvania Historical and Museum Commission, Old Economy Archives, Ambridge, Pennsylvania)

aratists, there were other tensions. Duke Karl Eugen died after a rule of fifty-six years and was replaced in rapid succession by Ludwig Eugen and Friedrich Eugen, each of whom ruled only two years. Military activities and preparations for war accelerated in response to France's increasing aggression. Travel was restricted, and in 1794 George Rapp's Separatists appealed to the duke for military exemption.

By 1798 George Rapp and his Separatist movement were required to submit a written statement of faith to the Reform Legislature of Württemberg. Known to be against the strong influence of the state church, the Reform Legislature intended to give the Separatists a hearing and, possibly, legal status. Unfortunately the new and politically ambitious duke of Württemberg, Frederich II, let his military concerns overshadow all else. He dissolved the Reform Legislature in 1799 before it was able to consider the Separatist issue. Immediately the situation began to deteriorate for Rapp and his faithful.

In their 1798 Articles of Faith, Rapp's Separatists indicated their belief in the Christian Church as established by the Apostles. They believed communion should be administered only to the righteous. They opposed infant baptism, confirmation, governmental oaths, and military service. These articles of the early movement make no mention of three tenets that later held central importance for Rapp's Harmony Society in America: community of goods, millennialism, and abstinence from sex. These tenets were, however, being practiced in their formative stages in the 1790s. George Rapp and his wife had observed chastity since 1785, and in 1791 Special Superintendent Klemm, who was investigating Rapp's congregation, reported that the Separatists considered all sexual intercourse, even in marriage, to be a mortal sin. Adopting a chaste, even celibate life was part of the Separatist attempt at Christian perfection, and Rapp justified it with certain biblical passages and with the writings of seventeenth-century German mystic Jakob Boehme. From Boehme Rapp took the idea that Adam, created in God's image, was a "biune" creature who originally possessed no sex organs but contained both male and female elements. The Fall of Man occurred when the female element separated, resulting in alienation from God and a loss of universal harmony. By ceasing sexual relations, the Separatists sought to return to Adam's pure, Godlike state before the Fall and thus to help effect the return of cosmic harmony. These concepts helped motivate the outright adoption of chastity for all members of Rapp's congregation in 1807.

Rapp, like the leaders of the Moravians, Seventh Day Baptists, and Shakers, was influenced by the description of first-century Christian communal practices in Acts 2 and 4. *Christianopolis*, written in nearby Vaihingen during the Thirty Years' War, also helped convince Rapp of the feasibility of communal living. This book by seventeenth-century German social reformer Johann Valentin Andreae described an imaginary communal Christian republic. To capture the advantages of sharing resources, Rapp's Separatists began keeping a common purse by the late 1790s, a fund used for minor expenses and assisting poorer believers.

Rapp's millennialism also became evident in the formative years of his movement in Württemberg. Inspired by writings of his contemporary philosopher Johann Herder as well as by German mystic Johannes Tauler and Swedish theologian Emanuel Swedenborg, Rapp began to preach the imminent second coming of Christ. As can be seen from his pastoral letters, Rapp had, by the late 1790s, become very concerned with correlating the biblical prophecies in Daniel and Revelation with the disturbing historical events of his own time. He regarded the rise of Napoleon as especially significant.

In Württemberg Rapp's millennialist views were considered a threat. Separatist literature was confiscated. One particularly significant millennial work reported to be a favorite of the Separatists was *Güldene Rose* (The golden rose) by Christoph Schutz. The association of the golden rose with Christ's reign on earth springs from Martin Luther's translation of Micah 4:8: "And Thou, o Tower Eder, a stronghold of the Daughter of Zion, Thy Golden Rose shall come, the former dominion, the Kingdom of the Daughter of Jerusalem." The golden rose during Martin Luther's time was a mark of great distinction bestowed by the pope on kings in recognition of special achievements in behalf of the kingdom of Christ on earth. Micah 4:8 asserted that the center of government would again return to Jerusalem. By this allusion in his translation, Martin Luther suggested that though Jerusalem was presently weak and neglected, it would be awarded the golden rose, the most coveted prize in Christendom, because the Messiah would return there. Rapp's followers used Luther's translation of the Bible and found this particular passage especially important. In America they made the golden rose their religious symbol and trademark.[2]

After forming a distinct sectarian movement about 1785, Rapp's Separatists grew rapidly in numbers and influence. By 1802 10,000 to 12,000 actively believed Rapp's teachings. The Württemberg government, however, had also grown in power, and a confrontation loomed inevitable. Rapp's activities became a cause for serious political concern. Many feared a renewal of the Peasant War of 1525. After preaching to an overwhelming crowd in the disturbed area of Knittlingen in 1803, Rapp was called to Maulbronn for another investigation.

For some time Rapp had entertained thoughts of emigrating, possibly to French Louisiana or to Russia, where a few Rappites did later seek refuge. His concern over the dangerous turn of events throughout Europe, as well as his perceptive belief that his group would be the losers in a confrontation with the Württemberg government, brought about his final decision. There was also spiritual justification for emigration. Rapp had come to see his congregation as the embodiment of the Sunwoman of Revelation 12:6 who "fled into the wilderness, where she hath a place prepared of God." He came to view America as the land of millennial promise where his congregation must flee.

In the summer of 1803 George Rapp left for America to seek a location on which his congregation could settle. He was accompanied by Dr. Frederick Conrad Haller, who soon broke with Rapp to establish his own colony at Blooming Grove, Pennsylvania; his son, Johannes, a certified surveyor; and Dr. Christopher Mueller (Johann Christoph Müller), a multitalented man who played an important role in the group's later history. Twenty years younger than Rapp, Mueller probably had a university degree. Mueller and George Rapp were friends as early as 1801, when Rapp wrote a letter to Mueller, who was then an apothecary in Feuerbach. Mueller's usefulness to Rapp in America proceeded both from his knowledge of medicine and his command of English. Due to Mueller's extensive knowledge, Rapp had him in mind as a schoolteacher even before Rapp's followers had arrived in America or formed a community.

Rapp left Württemberg just in time. Late in 1803 stricter regulations regarding Separatists were enacted. Some of Rapp's followers were briefly imprisoned. Meetings were broken up, and some who wished to emigrate had their property confiscated and thus were forced to depart for America penniless. Rapp had left his congregation in the care of a man named Frederick Reichert. Known as a stonemason and architect, Frederick left his native Endersbach in 1798 to move into the home of George and Christina Rapp at Iptingen. He was given charge of the common treasury of the Separatists and made responsible for coordinating their emigration beginning in 1804.

Once in America, the members of Rapp's advance party dispersed, searching for land and the means to obtain it. They first intended to settle on government land in Ohio. Rapp wished to purchase 40,000 acres there but needed time to raise funds. For this he appealed personally to President Thomas Jefferson, who responded sympathetically but explained that congressional action was necessary. By this time it was the summer of 1804, and the first shipload of Rapp's followers had arrived in Philadelphia on July 4. Unable to delay his acquisition of land any longer, Rapp selected a site in December 1804. The location, soon to be called Harmony (Harmonie), lay on Connoquenessing Creek in Butler County, Pennsylvania, thirty miles north of Pittsburgh. From the time of their arrival in the summer and fall of 1804 until shelter could be erected on Connoquenessing Creek in the spring of 1805, Rapp's followers were somewhat scattered, and many were in dire financial straits. Threatened by starvation in Philadelphia, the group was saved only by donations from local citizens and by the generosity of merchant Godfrey Haga, who extended them credit.

February 15, 1805, is considered the official founding date of George Rapp's Harmony Society, since the original Articles of Association carry that date. By signing the articles, about 500 charter members of the Harmony Society first officially became communal, agreeing to surrender all their property and possessions to the common treasury. Further, they submitted to the rules and regulations of the society and relinquished all claim to reimbursement should they leave. In return George Rapp and the Harmony Society were bound to provide them with all physical needs in times of sickness and health, access to all educational and religious benefits of the society, and a cash donation or return of property if members left in an orderly manner.[3]

Communal living was adopted partly out of necessity. Rapp's fledgling movement was in need of the economic security and social solidarity offered by community of goods. Many families were poor or had been forced to leave their possessions behind. An organized community meant that Rapp's congregation could work together to clear land, plant crops, build houses, and establish industries. There were ideological reasons for the communal way as well; Rapp had been moving in this direction for years. By 1805 he apparently wanted to institute communal sharing as an essential, permanent feature of his religious sect by a written commitment that he looked upon as irreversible. In 1807 the society submitted its articles to the Pennsylvania legislature as part of a request for incorporation. Early in 1808 the articles were rejected as hostile to the state constitution because they did not make provision for return of property to dissenting members. A clause providing for return of property or a cash donation was added, possibly reluctantly, for Rapp was known for his evasion on this issue. Much later, in 1836, he coerced the members into declaring that clause invalid.

During this period of transition in which Rapp led the most committed members of his religious movement into the discipline of community of goods, he also alienated a good number of his followers. Like half of the Hutterites who migrated from Russia in 1874 and chose individual farming (as "Prairieleut") rather than joining the Bon Homme or other Hutterite *bruderhofs* in South Dakota, many Rappite immigrants never took up residence in Harmony, or they left once they witnessed the increasingly communal direction of Rapp's preaching.

Those who arrived aboard the *Margaret* at Philadelphia in 1804 found a leader in Haller, who had accompanied Rapp to America in 1803. This group founded the community of Blooming Grove near Germantown in Lycoming

County, Pennsylvania. At Harmony, until January 1805, the idea of an association for mutual assistance but based on private property was prevalent. At that time at least 1,300 acres of land in Butler County were held by individual Harmonists. But on January 14, 1805, in a "final reckoning" these landowners had their debits and credits balanced and their land turned over to "George Rapp and Associates." However, the imitation of first-century Christian communism was not readily accepted, and much praying and preaching were required to convince the faithful to sign the communal articles in February 1805. The 500 or so who signed this agreement did not include the Rappites who had remained at Bull Creek in Columbiana County, Ohio, purchasing individual farms and thinking that their fellow millennialists would eventually settle there. Many of these Ohio Rappites and others who decided to leave Harmony as it became a communal village had already placed funds in Rapp's common treasury. Those who sued to recover their investment strained the limited resources of the Harmony Society in a difficult stage of its development.

The new communal town of Harmony grew slowly at first, as the group was relatively poor and intended its stay in Pennsylvania to be temporary. Rapp expected hundreds more of his faithful to arrive from Germany. Harmony's location did not permit expansion or allow for the isolation his peculiar sect required. Also, the climate was unsuitable for the grape cultivation so important to German culture. Rapp still hoped that Congress would grant him special conditions for a purchase of government lands in Ohio, but in 1806 the Harmonist petition was defeated in the House of Representatives. Building went forward at an advanced pace after that.

Ten years after their first land purchases, members of the Harmony Society enjoyed a modest prosperity in their neat, attractive town. They had planted orchards, vineyards, and fields of grain and now tended fine merino sheep. They operated several mills, a brewery, and a tannery and manufactured woolen cloth. Their first exports in 1807 were grain and whiskey. The Harmony Inn accommodated visitors, and the general store supplied the community members. Each family had its own house—most were of log—on a quarter-acre lot, and most kept their own cows, pigs, and chickens and tended their own gardens. All other needs were provided for them. Each family had accounts with the store and with the various tradesmen, and took whatever they needed. If anyone appeared extravagant he or she might be called upon by George Rapp for an explanation.

Cultural pursuits were not neglected. A school was conducted in the upper level of the woolen factory, and a small brass band was formed that played on religious occasions and sometimes for visitors. Religious services were held

KARL J. R. ARNDT

twice on Sunday and once in midweek in the brick church on the town square. Although their children were being taught English and German in the school, most adult Harmonists spoke only their native Swabian German dialect. None but a few society leaders and business agents journeyed outside the town. The Harmonists became American citizens. They celebrated the independence day of their new country on July 4, the date when the first group of Harmonists had arrived in America in 1804. They paid their taxes and assessments in place of military duty but otherwise wished to separate themselves from the world.

George Rapp was accepted as the spiritual as well as organizational head of the society. After 1809 his followers began to address him as "Father." In addition to preaching sermons, he heard their confessions, led prayers and religious discussions, and advised them in spiritual matters. Rapp also knew much about agriculture and manufacturing—especially the manufacture of cloth—and was involved in all details of daily life in Harmony. The fact that his congregation never exceeded about 800 allowed him an intimacy with them. His charisma and hold over his congregation should not be underestimated.

One man integral to the society's increasing prosperity was Frederick Reichert. A member of Rapp's household, he had been officially adopted by George Rapp in 1805 and became Frederick Rapp. Skilled in masonry, architecture, town planning, drafting, and accounting, Frederick assumed the position of the society's business manager. He developed a reputation for honest dealing and was highly regarded in the outside business world. A man with many interests, he composed hymns and sculpted figures of Sophia, the embodiment of wisdom, in Harmony and of the golden rose in New Harmony. He collected rare "curiosities" and tended to the spiritual affairs of the community in Father Rapp's absence.

In 1807–8 the Harmony Society experienced a religious revival. Just when the economically trying times began to ease, a great excitement gripped the society. This was caused by world events—a series of natural catastrophes and the clash of arms in Napoleonic Europe—that George Rapp interpreted as signs of the last days prior to the second coming of Christ. As a trustee of the society later explained, "It was realized that the true imitation of Christ demanded more than natural man suspected or believed. This realization led to a confession of sins, to regret and penance, and to a more serious conviction to lead a pure life. This had a strong effect on old and young and convinced us that we should live a life of self-denial and discipline."[4] Thus the Harmonists decided to forsake the use of tobacco and to adopt a chaste or celibate life. Those already married would remain together but would cease sexual relations. All further marriages were discouraged. The last for many years was that of George Rapp's son, Johannes, to Johanna Diem in November 1807. Harmonist celibacy became internationally known and was chided by Lord Byron in canto 15 of *Don Juan*.

Christopher Mueller, who served as physician and schoolteacher at this time, was also among the last to marry in the Harmony Society. He and his wife had a son in 1806 who died a few days after birth; another child, a daughter, was born in July 1808 but also survived only a few days. A month later a daughter was born to Johannes and Johanna Rapp. This child, named Gertrude, was destined to become one of the most committed and best known of all Harmonists. Just before her fourth birthday Gertrude lost her father, who probably died as a result of an injury sustained while hoisting grain (although the ugly rumor spread that he died after a forced castration by his own father).[5] The Harmonists buried nearly all their dead in plain, unmarked graves, but Johannes Rapp's grave was graced by a tombstone provided by sympathetic neighbors from outside Harmony. The stone, with its golden rose marking, can still be viewed in the Harmonist cemetery at Harmony.

After the death of Johannes, Gertrude and her mother moved into the George Rapp household where, no doubt, Gertrude was spoiled by her grandparents as well as by her Aunt Rosina and her Uncle Frederick. Christopher Mueller was also destined to play an important role in her life. Great care was taken with Gertrude's education. Thus Mueller, as schoolteacher and society scholar, spent a good deal of time with her. Each filled a void in the life of the other; she had lost a father, and he a daughter.

George Rapp intended the location on Connoquenessing Creek to be temporary. By 1814 he felt the time had come to move west. The Harmonists found land to their liking in the Indiana Territory along the banks of the navigable Wabash River, fifteen miles over land and sixty miles upstream from the Ohio. They eventually purchased 30,000 acres there, some of it on the Illinois side, allowing them control of a several-mile stretch of the Wabash. In the summer of 1814 an advance party under the leadership of John L. Baker left the old Harmony to carve a new Harmony out of the Indiana wilderness, where they could continue to await the millennium. In the swampy lowland and muggy climate, malaria struck the group immediately. Work came to a virtual standstill as many began to die. The situation became critical when Baker himself, responsible for purchasing land and obtaining supplies, became ill. About 120 Harmonists eventually died at Harmony on the Wabash over the next two years until swamps could be drained and living conditions improved.[6]

The restored Harmonist Community House Number 2, with adjoining kitchen, was built in New Harmony, Indiana, in 1822. Four such massive brick structures were erected to house young people of both sexes and families fragmented by malaria. (Photograph by Donald Janzen)

Once Father and Frederick Rapp arrived and the sickness subsided, building went forward at a remarkable pace. The Harmonists called their second town both Harmony and the new Harmony. Families first lived in log cabins, but later these were replaced with spacious, two-story homes of frame and brick like those they had built in Pennsylvania. By 1818 the Rapp family resided in a large brick mansion, described as "by far the best in Indiana."[7]

Over the course of their decade in Indiana, the Harmonists constructed other fine brick buildings, including a tavern, a granary, mills, and four large community houses. A detailed map of New Harmony, drawn by young Harmonist artist Wallrath Weingartner, has allowed historians and preservationists to determine not only the location but also the physical appearance of the original town's structures. Perhaps the most impressive piece of architecture was their cruciform church built in 1822. The roof was supported by twenty-eight huge columns turned from the large black walnut trees of the Indiana forest and was topped by a balcony where their band sometimes performed.

William Hebert, an English traveler, said of the church, "I could scarcely imagine myself to be in the woods of Indiana . . . while pacing the long resounding aisles, and surveying the stately colonnades of this church."[8] The north door of the church was especially significant and reveals the continuing Harmonist concern with the coming millennium. The stone lintel of the door, designed and sculpted by Frederick Rapp, featured the golden rose symbol, the date 1822, and the biblical reference Micah 4:8. According to George Rapp's millennial calculations, the year 1822 began the era of the golden rose.[9]

This golden rose, such a potent millennial symbol for the Harmonists, had a very different meaning to the outside world with which they conducted business. The Harmonists used the golden rose as a trademark on their products, and it soon became synonymous with quality goods. In addition to their agricultural surplus, the Harmonists sold a wide variety of products such as rope, shoes, leather goods, and pottery. They were especially renowned for their superior whiskey and fine woolen, linen, and cotton cloth. In addition to their store in New Harmony, which did a brisk business on the frontier, they had stores and trusted agents in cities near and far. During the decade from 1814 to 1824 they traded with twenty-two states and ten foreign countries.

Neighboring backwoodsmen needed the Harmonists. New Harmony was the only place for miles around where they could purchase supplies, have their grain ground, or tend to their banking needs. Some, such as the English settlers in Albion, Illinois, were impressed with the neat, orderly community of New Harmony and its pious inhabitants. But others, like those midwesterners who would attack the communal and polygamous Mormons, felt threatened by Harmonist prosperity, control of the river, political power through group unity, and strange practices such as celibacy.[10] Relations with distrustful neighbors reached a low point in 1820 when violence erupted in the streets of New Harmony. Nine outsiders were charged with rioting, and Frederick Rapp and Harmonist innkeeper Frederick Eckensberger were accused of assault. In a humorous letter, one Indiana resident even appealed to the general assembly to outlaw celibacy in the Harmony Society, "as there is many young Girls of Ex[c]elent Conduct and Beheavour in [H]armony And many young men of Good parts . . . it is shurly not Right that those who are man & wife should not Enjoy [each] other as such [just to] please the old gentleman."[11]

The Harmonists made no small contribution to politics and government when the new state of Indiana was created in 1816. Frederick Rapp served as a delegate to the first constitutional convention in Corydon and helped to

KARL J. R. ARNDT

select the site for a permanent state capital in Indianapolis. By serving on the militia committee at the convention, pacifist Frederick Rapp saw to it that the Indiana constitution permitted conscientious objectors to pay a fine in lieu of bearing arms. The Harmonists had experienced trouble in Pennsylvania when several of their members were drafted for service in the War of 1812 but refused to comply. They did not intend to have such trouble again. The Harmonists also showed their support for the new state by loaning the government $5,000. Many office seekers cultivated the political clout of 800 like-minded Germans who would vote in a block. The group was continuously courted by candidates for Indiana governor and the legislature.

Though Harmonist relations with the outside world were often less than cordial, their relations with other religious communal groups were warm and friendly. Themselves influenced by the example of the Ephrata Cloister in Pennsylvania, the Harmonists set an example for many groups such as the German Zoarites of Ohio. Contact and exchange with the Shakers at West Union north of Vincennes was especially frequent. In fact the two groups considered the possibility of a merger in 1816. Over the decades Harmonists gave generous financial assistance to the Zoarites, the Mormons, and the Hutterites and were solicited by the Koreshans of Cyrus Teed. When Rappite followers could not produce certain items themselves, they preferred to buy from other religious communal groups. In later years, when they ceased producing their own cloth, the Harmonists purchased this commodity from the communal Inspirationists of Amana, Iowa.

Unrest within the society first became noticeable at New Harmony. An influx of new emigrants from Württemberg in 1817–18 caused tension. Many were not as committed to a life of Christian perfection as the original congregation, and George Rapp found it expedient to perform several marriages. In 1818 the Book of Debts, containing the record of members' contributions upon joining, was ceremoniously burned on the anniversary of the society's founding. This made it more difficult for members to lay claim to their property should they decide to leave, and it kept their children from knowing exactly what their parents had contributed. More explicit, individualized agreements were drawn up in 1821, which omitted the earlier section on the return of property to withdrawing members. George Rapp was gradually making it more difficult for anyone to withdraw and was guaranteeing financial security for the society by not allowing departing members to claim any of the society's growing wealth. Nevertheless, this bold attempt to tighten control would help undermine Rapp's leadership and divide his Harmony Society in the decade ahead. Intentionally, he was closing the door on compromise in the face of disgruntled members and the rising generation.

The standardization of clothing in the society was part of an attempt to discourage pride and to ensure equality among all members through uniformity. The turn-of-the-century German peasant style of clothing was not adapted to fashions of the day. Women wore high-waisted gowns in a variety of colors, modesty scarves, aprons, and prayer caps or straw hats when outdoors. Men wore plain dark frock coats or surtouts, trousers, vests, and broad-brimmed hats. Like the dress of the Amish and the Hutterites, Harmonist clothing was plain; no ornamentation was permitted. Though some thought the Harmonist appearance unattractive, others found the German peasant style picturesque and charming.

Increasing prosperity gave the Harmonists the funds and time to upgrade their educational system and pursue literary, cultural, and musical activities. Keeping their children away from school in their German homeland had been due to their objection to Lutheran indoctrination and exposure to corrupting influences rather than lack of interest in education. On the contrary, in the one book he wrote, George Rapp stated that "the proper education of Youth is of the greatest importance to the prosperity of any plan, for the melioration of mankind." [12]

The Harmonists modeled their own schools after the vernacular schools of Württemberg and the schools of utopian literature, especially Andreae's *Christianopolis*. Classes were conducted Monday through Saturday mornings, three days in German and three in English. Boys and girls ages six through fourteen were taught the intellectual disciplines as well as vocational trades. Christopher Mueller had been headmaster of the school in Harmony since 1805. Although sometimes assisted by other members of the society, especially innkeeper and composer Frederick Eckensberger, Mueller was the primary teacher at least through 1826. Instruction included reading, spelling, mathematics, English, German grammar, singing, religious studies, French, geography, ancient and modern history, natural history, physics, and chemistry. The variety of these subjects indicates the broad range of Harmonist interests and of Mueller's knowledge. As was standard European practice, at age fourteen boys were apprenticed in the trades and girls were taught the traditional feminine occupations of housework, sewing, spinning, and weaving. The Harmonist educational system served nearly 100 children during the New Harmony years, children of members born before the adoption of celibacy, offspring of new members, and apprentices and indentured servants. [13]

Gertrude Rapp, who passed the majority of her childhood in Indiana, was a credit to Mueller's abilities and to the society's educational system. Great care was taken with her education and upbringing. At age seven she went with her Aunt Rosina to learn English at the Shaker village of West Union. The only female instrumentalist in the society, she played the pianoforte and also sang in the girls' quartet. She made sketches and paintings as well as wax flowers. Later, at age twenty, she became manager of the Harmonist silk industry, which won awards for the quality of its products. Even as a teenager Gertrude served as society hostess and conversed engagingly with visitors of distinction. Mueller lavished attention on her, purchasing music especially for her, presenting her with beautiful drawings, and spending hours preparing handwritten music books and a watercolor certificate of musical achievement as gifts for her.

When members reached adulthood, they found an array of educational and cultural activities available. The store was stocked with books on many subjects, and the society subscribed to several newspapers. Religious discussions, literary competitions, and concerts took place in the village. By the 1820s the German Harmonists had access to a 360-volume library—truly an anomaly on the Indiana frontier, where most of the general population could not read, write, or find education.

In 1824 the society acquired a printing press, of which Christopher Mueller was given responsibility. Typically Harmonist, when Mueller first printed a sample of the press's work on a single sheet of paper, the statement he chose referred to the significance of the press in the millennium: "In the future when the decree goes out from Zion, the press will unquestionably be an important and valuable tool."

The most significant book to come from the Harmonist press was *Gedanken uber die Bestimung des Menschen, besonders in Hinsicht der gegenwartingen Ziet* (Thoughts on the destiny of man, particularly with reference to the present times) by George Rapp. Perhaps the earliest book of philosophy printed in Indiana, this small volume presented Rapp's religious and social theories, taken largely from the works of Johann Herder. In one passage Rapp caught the essence of communal living at its best in describing New Harmony as a community "where those who occupy its peaceful dwellings are so closely united by endearing ties of friendship, confidence and love, that one heart beats in all, and their common industry provides for all. Here, the members kindly assist each other, in difficulty and danger, and share with each other, the enjoyments, and the misfortunes of life; one lives in the breast of another, and forgets himself; all their undertakings are influenced by a social spirit, glowing with noble energy, and generous feeling, and pressing forward to the haven of their mutual prosperity."[14] The German edition of *Thoughts* appeared in 1824, and the English edition in 1825. Displeased with the English translation, which had been prepared by Mueller and Frederick Rapp, George refused to have it circulated, thereby denying English-speaking Americans a clearer understanding of the heart of his millennial movement.

The results of a prose and poetry competition among members at New Harmony resulted in the publication of *Feurige Kohlen* (Fiery coals).[15] Published in 1826, this collection of verses and short essays remains largely untranslated but reveals the spiritual and temporal emotions of a cross-section of ordinary Harmonists. As might be expected, many of the pieces express millennial hope: "People of Harmony, you should be content with the present age, for a better future is near at hand. In that distant time to come, the entire earth will bloom, as a garden of God; the ennobled and improved man shall live in peace with his brothers; lambs shall feed with wolves, and babies play with young lions; and freedom, truth, justice, love and goodness will be commonplace on the beautiful earth."[16]

Music was part of the school curriculum at Harmony, Pennsylvania, but by the Indiana period it had become a separate activity directed by Christopher Mueller. Music served religious and social functions in the Harmonist community. Choral and instrumental performances helped foster group cohesion, provided a means of personal expression, and were a constructive form of recreation for the society's young people. The music program began to blossom in New Harmony with the purchase of several instruments, including a piano; formation of an orchestra that sometimes performed for outsiders; and publication of the society's first hymnbook in 1820, titled *Harmonisches Gesangbuch, Theils Von andern Authoren, Theils neu Verfasst* (Harmony songbook written by early and modern authors). The Harmonists even considered purchasing an organ for their cruciform church that would have cost over $7,000 in the 1820s. As music director, Mueller arranged pieces for performance by the orchestra, ordered supplies, selected programs for concerts, directed practice sessions, gave instrumental and vocal lessons, and prepared musical publications. He also composed hymns. Many, such as "Durch Zerfallne Kirchen Fenster" (Through fallen church windows), became Harmonist favorites.[17]

Gardening was another favorite pastime of the Harmonists. In the European Baroque tradition, all Harmonist towns had a labyrinth composed of flowering shrubs, vines, and trees, with a small shrine in the center. In addition to recreation, the labyrinths stimulated meditation, perhaps upon themes such as the twisting paths one must follow before reaching the ideal of harmony. Formal gardens, a botanical garden, and a greenhouse on rollers for covering and uncovering citrus trees and other plants not native to Indiana could all be found in New Harmony.

George Rapp's house in the Harmonists' third town of Economy (now Ambridge), Pennsylvania, was built in 1826. It was adorned by their symbolic garden of paradise, which included fruit trees, a botanical garden, and a pond and grotto, and it was filled with fine examples of American decorative arts. By 1831 their church, with its hour-hand clock in the steeple, stood across the street. Rapp died in his bedroom in 1847 at age 89, still expecting to lead his followers into the millennium upon Christ's return. (Photograph by Donald Janzen)

Having built such a lovely and functional town of 180 buildings, established industries, cleared fields, and won leisure time for pursuit of cultural activities, the Harmonists might have chosen to stay in Indiana forever. But in 1824 George Rapp decided to sell New Harmony and move back to Pennsylvania. Though Rapp tried to justify the move by quoting scripture to tell his congregation it was time for the Sunwoman of Revelation to again flee into the wilderness, there were several practical reasons for the move. Less land was needed than Rapp originally had anticipated, as improved conditions for religious dissenters in the German provinces resulted in fewer emigrants than expected. New Harmony was far from the eastern markets where Harmonist products were sold, and the frontier economy was unstable. There were problems with neighbors. The group felt isolated from others of their cultural background. Malaria was still a threat. Rapp also seemed to believe that moving and building a new town every ten years was an effective way to keep the discipline and spirit of his sectarian movement alive. He was keenly aware that restlessness while awaiting the millennium could seriously undermine his leadership.

The Harmonist exodus from New Harmony began in 1824. In January 1825 they sold their famous communal village, called "that Wonder of the West," to British social reformer Robert Owen, who conducted his own socialistic community there from 1825 to 1827. The Harmonists moved to a location on the Ohio River in Beaver County, Pennsylvania, ten miles north of Pittsburgh. There they began to build a new town, which they called Economy. This new name referred to the new perfect world order (the "Divine Economy") they expected to come. But the term "Economy" also reflected their increasing concern with industry in their new location. Special pride was reserved for their silk industry. In the 1830s and 1840s many in America hoped that silk production would develop into an important part of the economy. Even before they left Indiana, the Harmonists had been doing research on sericulture and began to experiment as soon as they settled in Economy. As a result they soon became known throughout America, and even abroad, for their superior, award-winning silk.

The Harmonists continued to attain high standards in their cultural activities. At Economy, Mueller established a museum of natural history. This collection was later dispersed, but Old Economy Village still uses the museum rooms for exhibits and plans to restore the Harmonist museum.[18] Mueller also turned his attention increasingly to upgrading the music program. In 1827 the society hired W. C. Peters, a professional Pittsburgh musician, to give musical instruction. Under Mueller's direction and with Peters's help, the orchestra began to perform increasingly sophisticated pieces by European masters, such as portions of Mozart's *The Marriage of Figaro*.[19]

Economy began to take on the atmosphere of an eighteenth-century court, and Christopher Mueller was the man largely responsible. George Rapp regarded the increasing emphasis on music and the arts with ambivalence, however, believing that individual expression, scholarly pursuits, and cultivation of the mind must not be out of proportion with other aspects of life. No Harmonist had ever been permitted to make music more than an avocation. Tensions between Mueller and Rapp began to surface, coming to a head in 1831 when Rapp locked the music room without Mueller's knowledge and suspended all musical performance for a month. The refined, well-mannered Mueller was incensed to the point of violence.[20]

Other conflicts were also beginning to tear the fabric of Rapp's Harmony Society. It is true that rifts surfaced among the Harmonists in Indiana, but compared with what happened in Economy, the New Harmony years were an

KARL J. R. ARNDT

idyllic interlude. The problems began in 1826 and 1827 when Rapp had new articles of association drafted by lawyers outside the society and required all members to sign in the presence of witnesses. Opposition to these articles mounted, and many members withdrew rather than sign. Although detailed causes of the uproar are unclear, apparently some members felt that George and Frederick Rapp had become dishonest and intended to cheat them. There had been lawsuits against the society from its earliest days, but after 1826 confrontations became particularly ugly. Former Harmonists made scurrilous accusations. Some went so far as to submit a petition to the Pennsylvania legislature requesting an investigation of the Harmony Society itself.

The issue of celibacy had caused periodic dissension, but after 1826 the conflict amplified. Those who did not adhere to a life of sexual abstinence were at first tolerated. But as the years passed, they began to be forced out of the community. A few who ran away to be married were later readmitted, according to the whim of Father Rapp. This inconsistency caused much dissatisfaction, but a major uproar occurred over one particularly beautiful young woman named Hildegard Mutschler, who had been born in the society in 1806. After Father Rapp's close personal involvement with her from 1826 to 1829, even the most loyal members could not ignore his unfairness, inconsistency, and hypocrisy.

In 1827 Father Rapp outraged Frederick Rapp and others when he made Hildegard his laboratory assistant in his alchemy experiments. After moving to Economy, the Harmonist leader had become obsessed with finding the "Philosopher's Stone," which would turn base metals into gold. In the discovery of this magical substance, the Harmonists believed they would have the key for transforming sickness into health, old age into youth, and earthly life into supernatural existence. In the early nineteenth century the existence and pursuit of the Philosopher's Stone were taken very seriously by many in both Europe and America. This belief later drove wedges between Rapp and scores of his disciples, causing permanent grief to followers like Mueller. The outrage over Hildegard's participation in Rapp's experimentation was aroused because only the pure in spirit were thought fit to participate. Father Rapp refused to see Hildegard as the lying, deceitful girl others held her to be. She gradually took Frederick's place as Father Rapp's confidant and constant companion. There was much suspicion about the exact nature of their relationship. When Hildegard eloped in 1829 with another society member, Father Rapp, in contrast to his usual contempt for seceders, actively sought her return. He then readmitted her and her husband despite their disregard of the chastity rule, and Hildegard bore several children.

At Economy the Harmonist prophet had predicted that on September 15,

1829, the age of "the 3½ times of the Sun-woman" described in Revelation 12:6 would end and a new age begin. Understandably, a state of gloom pervaded the town when the long-awaited date passed uneventfully. Then, on September 24, an impressive letter arrived from Germany, announcing the great day for which the Harmony Society had been waiting. Not only did the letter seem miraculously timed, but its writer also demonstrated knowledge about the Harmony Society, speaking of the significance of specific events in its history and referring to passages from Revelation very familiar to the Harmonists. In reply the Harmonist leaders reported that "you can scarcely imagine what an impression your letter made upon the souls and hearts of the homesick when it was read in the meeting. Everyone here is taking new courage and inspiration in the expectation of the opening of the Kingdom of Jesus Christ. Most of the brethren wept for joy over the statements of the Lord."[21]

The author of the letter called himself the "Lion of Judah" who had been promised to the world in Revelation 5:9. In reality he was Bernhard Mueller, the illegitimate son of Baron Dalberg of Aschaffenberg, Germany. Bernhard Mueller had become convinced, though reluctantly, that he himself was the reincarnated Messiah who would lead the world in the millennium. Thus in 1829 he sent letters to all monarchs and ecclesiastical leaders that they were to read and have printed so that all the faithful would know the time had come to gather in America, where they would escape the great destruction to be visited upon Europe prior to the Christ's return. One of these letters was sent to the Harmony Society and was quite impressive because its author had studied travelers' accounts and spoke so knowledgeably of Rapp's congregation. Bernhard Mueller's letters caused quite a sensation in the German states. He was placed under house arrest, and it became expedient for him to leave the country. Thus he departed for America with the intention of going to Economy, since he had received a favorable reply letter from the Harmonists.

During the two years that elapsed between the arrival of Mueller's letter and his coming to Economy, Rapp curiously enough preached that the Lion of Judah was the Anointed One who would lead the Harmonists into the new age. Rapp's congregation was in a state of great expectation by the time the Lion of Judah arrived in America in 1831 and adopted the name Count de Leon. Father Rapp proudly presented him to the Harmony Society congregation at Economy on October 18, 1831. Reportedly a charismatic figure with a Christlike appearance, he impressed many members (among them Christopher Mueller) with his claim to have found the Philosopher's Stone. He was accompanied by an aide, Dr. John G. Goentgen, and several European families of high social standing. All were housed at Economy as welcome guests.

KARL J. R. ARNDT

However, it was not long before the count and George Rapp were disappointed with each other. Rapp decided that the count was not, after all, the man to lead his Harmonists into the millennium, and the count was dismayed by the dissatisfaction he sensed among Harmony Society members. The two millennialists also disagreed over the issue of celibacy. The count maintained that all forms of crucifixion of the flesh would cease under the new order.

In early 1832 Count de Leon and his retinue realized they were no longer welcome when Frederick presented them with a charge for room and board. Originally the count had not come to undermine George Rapp's leadership or to take over Economy; he intended to establish his own colony, although he hoped for affiliation with the Harmonists. It seems that he would have withdrawn peaceably once he ascertained Rapp's attitude, except for the fact that the already dissatisfied members of the society begged for his help. This element, fully one-third of the society, declared themselves the "true Harmonists." All others, they claimed, were seceders who had departed from the society's original purpose. Declaring the count their temporary head, this group of some 175 organized a democratic form of government that deposed the Rapps as leaders. They asserted that they did not wish to destroy the society but wanted to maintain it as originally founded.

To counter this the remaining majority of the society drafted a document expressing complete confidence in George and Frederick Rapp and their desire for them to continue as society leaders. They, too, established a pseudo-democratic form of government consisting of a council of twelve elders to be elected annually by vote of all male members of the society. Two factions now existed, each with its own governing body, each claiming that it represented the true Harmonists. For nearly two months they lived in Economy together and tried to carry on community life until the dispute could be resolved.

The dissenters complained that Rapp claimed to be God and thought himself above the Commandments. They claimed that the 1826–27 Articles of Association were signed under duress as a "premeditated fraud" intended only to "get absolute possession of our property." They asserted that, although withdrawal from the Harmony Society was theoretically possible, George Rapp had made it extremely difficult by refusing to let them learn English, by not allowing them knowledge of "the liberal institutions of our [adopted] country," and by refusing to give departing members their former fortunes or any funds on which to begin anew.[22] An agreement between the two factions was reached in March 1832. About 175 dissenters agreed to leave Economy at once and to relinquish all claim to Harmony Society property in exchange for their household possessions and the sum of $105,000. They withdrew to nearby Phillipsburg, Pennsylvania, where under Count de Leon's leadership they established the communally organized New Philadelphia Society. Nevertheless, tensions continued between the two groups. A propaganda battle took place in the press, and the count's followers rioted in the streets of Economy on one occasion.

The deep bitterness typical of the Harmonist attitude toward dissenting members is illustrated by the experience of their beloved physician, schoolmaster, and music director, Christopher Mueller. Unable to endure George Rapp's despotism any longer, Mueller departed with the count. It must have been an agonizing decision, for he had devoted thirty years of his life to the society. Leaving Gertrude Rapp, his friend and former pupil, was most difficult of all. After he had been gone a few weeks, he wrote her a letter expressing his hope that they might remain friends. Gertrude, ever loyal to the Harmony Society, sent him a vicious reply likening him to Satan. Similar to the Amish practice of shunning, the Harmonists were not permitted even to shake hands with former members. When Christopher Mueller encountered a Harmony Society business agent in Bridgewater, Pennsylvania, he offered his hand "as an old friend and dear acquaintance" but was coldly rebuffed.[23]

Christopher Mueller, like his fellow seceders, had based his faith in the Count de Leon on his claim to have the Philosopher's Stone and, like many of the others, soon suffered great disillusionment. The count squandered their funds on further alchemistic endeavors but failed to produce the stone. A little more than a year after the schism, the New Philadelphia Society dissolved. By then Mueller and a score of other former Harmonists had so lost confidence in the count that they did not accompany him when he departed for Louisiana. But others became part of the count's Grand Ecore communal settlement in Natchitoches Parish from 1834 until his death in 1836. These faithful then founded a final community named Germantown under the leadership of the count's trusted Dr. John Goentgen, near Minden in Webster Parish, which lasted until 1871. Still other Harmonists who had left Economy with the count in 1832 fell under the spell of a charismatic German immigrant preacher, Dr. William Keil, who claimed miraculous powers from a book written in blood. These "Keilites," freed from Harmonist celibacy and inflexible communal legalism, established the more tolerant communal colonies of Bethel, with its three out-colonies of Elim, Hebron, and Mamri (1844–80), and Ninevah (1850–78) in Shelby and Adair Counties in Missouri; Willapa (1853–55), near Willapa Bay in the present state of Washington; and Aurora (1856–81), south of Portland, Oregon.[24]

Though the Harmony Society officially endured for seventy-four years after the 1832 schism, the Count de Leon affair marked the beginning of the end. The schism was a turning point at which George Rapp chose an uncompromising path that would lead to his utopian society's extinction. Christopher Mueller was not a typical seceder; most were members of a second generation, born into the society, whose parents had joined the Separatists in Germany. Many were young people who, if allowed to marry as they wished, could have ensured the continuation of Rapp's sectarian movement. They had not chosen communal life, celibacy, or the leadership of George Rapp. Their push for democratic government just before the schism reflected their need to have a voice in the course of their lives. Suspicion of George Rapp's dishonesty became intense, and members wanted a fair leader accountable to the membership. By his inflexibility on the issues of celibacy, return of property to departing members, and democratic government, George Rapp failed to make necessary adjustments for a rising generation, a developmental matter that confronts all religious movements.

Tragedy struck the Harmony Society in the form of Frederick Rapp's death at age fifty-nine in 1834. No single person could fill the enormous gap created by the loss of Frederick's faithful service. But business with the outside continued to be conducted efficiently by several trusted agents, especially Romelius L. Baker. The Harmony Society was by now quite well known and received many applications for membership. Many people wished to join for economic rather than spiritual reasons. After the schism Rapp decided not to accept any new members, other than those children already within the society as they came of age and perhaps a few very close relatives of current members. Barring the expected second coming of Christ, the Harmonist leader was slowly sealing the fate of his religious sect in any developmental sense. In 1836 members signed a statement declaring Article VI of the Articles of Association invalid. This was the controversial requirement providing for return of property to departing members. In order to free the society from economic uncertainty and to be prepared for the millennium, George Rapp by 1845 had collected half a million dollars in gold and silver coins, which he kept hidden in a vault under his bedroom. The panic of 1837 had convinced him, again, that the millennium was near.

Nonetheless, Father Rapp died without leading his congregation into the promised Kingdom of God on Earth. After an illness of three weeks, he died in his own bed at age eighty-nine on August 7, 1847. His dying words indicated that he greeted his own death with the disbelief of a true believer in his own millennial teaching: "If I did not so fully believe, that the Lord has designed me to place our Society before his presence in the land of Canaan, I would consider this my last."[25] One might think that the devoted members of the society would be crushed by such a blow, but they pressed onward. As Gertrude wrote to her friend Marie Wilson, "We must submit to the decrees of an all ruling Providence, which measures and weighs all our days and destinies. Therefore the Will of God be done."[26]

After Rapp's death, 288 members renewed their pledge to the society by signing new articles of agreement. A board of nine elders was established to govern the society, two of these nine also serving as trustees to deal with outside affairs. The first trustees were Rapp's close friends Jacob Henrici and R. L. Baker. Henrici had joined the society in 1826 at Economy. Born in 1804 in Rhenish Bavaria, he felt divinely inspired to come to America and join the Harmony Society. At Economy he served as schoolteacher, assisted with the music program, and became a trusted business agent. Jacob quickly endeared himself to Father Rapp and seems to have fallen in love with Rapp's granddaughter Gertrude. Legend has it that she returned his feelings, though the two never gave in to the temptation to violate the vow of celibacy.

The transition to a new form of government was not particularly smooth. Henrici, George Rapp's successor in spiritual matters, was like his uncompromising predecessor in many ways. He wanted all decisions to rest ultimately with him. Accused of "despotic behavior" by members and other elders, Henrici resigned as minister and moved out of the Rapp house in 1848, only to move back in and resume his position a few months later.

The twenty years between George Rapp's death and that of R. L. Baker in 1868 saw a great increase in society wealth. The aging Harmonists adjusted their communal economic base from agriculture to industry and investment capitalism as the industrial revolution gained momentum in the United States after the mid-nineteenth century. They became pioneers in the emerging American oil industry and participants in the railroad building boom after the Civil War. As their profits accumulated, they continued their long-standing tradition of contributing to charitable causes and kindred religious sects. Before and during the years of Henrici's direction, the society generously aided the German Zoarites in Ohio, the Inspirationists in their seven Iowa Amana colonies, and the Shakers of Indiana and Kentucky. Harmonist interest in millennially related events in Palestine made them supporters of the Temple Society in the Holy Land, an organization dedicated to rebuilding the Jerusalem Temple in preparation for the second advent of Christ. Rapp's millennialists finally went so far as to purchase land in Haifa, thus anticipating the Zionist movement that would also employ communal methods in the form of kibbutzim.

As the Harmony Society's wealth increased, however, its numbers diminished. Because celibacy continued to be insisted upon and new members were not recruited, the sect accepted its fate of dying out unless Christ returned.

KARL J. R. ARNDT

Hiring outside labor, renting farms, and closing factories became necessary. Only 140 members, most of them elderly, remained in 1868. In that year Jonathan Lenz, one of the last children born into the society before the adoption of celibacy, took R. L. Baker's place as Henrici's cotrustee.

The wealth of the Harmony Society had become common knowledge, and there was much speculation on, and interest in, what would happen to it once it became apparent that the society was destined for extinction. Though repeatedly pressed to make provision for disposal of their property, the Harmonist leadership refused, believing that it would be a sacrilege to dissolve the society or make a will to transfer property to an individual or nonreligious owner. In case the society should become extinct before the arrival of the millennium, Henrici thought it "highly probable that the State of Pennsylvania would be glad to employ our savings as an aid in the payment of her heavy debt."[27]

As long as original Harmony Society members Gertrude Rapp and Jonathan Lenz were alive, people without religious motives were kept from joining the society. But when both died in the winter of 1889–90, the rush to acquire Harmonist gold began. Within days several new members were admitted, among them John Duss. Duss had been educated in the society, where his mother was a hired worker. Within six months Duss managed to have himself appointed junior trustee. As soon as Henrici died in 1892, Duss secured absolute power. As aging members died, Duss paid others to leave and forced still others out of the society. Soon he began liquidating society property for his own personal use. Duss used society funds to employ excellent accountants and lawyers, who succeeded in having the society's nonpersonal and indivisible property declared private and divisible, thereby making it the sole personal property of Duss. The Harmony Society was dissolved in 1916, with its real property reverting to the state of Pennsylvania. Not, however, before Duss, a musician, had squandered millions of the Harmonist fortune on personal publicity and national tours for an orchestra of which he was maestro. On one occasion alone in 1903 he spent $100,000 to transform Madison Square Garden into a watery replica of Venice for one summer's performances by New York's Metropolitan Opera.

The seeds of the Harmony Society's demise were sown with its founding. In 1805, communalism was adopted out of necessity and for ideological reasons in a time of religious fervor. But as years passed, the Harmony Society became quite wealthy, rendering the communal way unnecessary for survival. Dissatisfaction increased when the millennium failed to arrive and a rising generation demanded a voice in the course of their lives. Members had banded together voluntarily in Germany, but if commitment to a group is not reversible, then membership ceases to be voluntary. Rapp resisted making communalism reversible by not allowing dissenting members to claim any share of the society's wealth that they had helped accumulate or to reclaim any property they had brought with them. Legally Rapp made provision for dissenters when forced to do so but did his best to circumvent the issue. Repeatedly he met the just demands of the Harmony Society membership with a rigid and uncompromising attitude. Perhaps by moving his faithful to a new location every ten years he postponed the inevitable crisis until 1832. The schism was the turning point at which change and adaptation were necessary for the continuation of the movement. Rapp's refusal to address the need for new communal or other organizational forms in a developmental process caused him to miss the opportunity that could have permitted a vastly different future for his millennialist sect. Nevertheless, the Harmony Society had a strong influence on other religious and nonsectarian movements that chose the communal way, from the Shakers and Zoarites to the Owenites and Hutterites. Rapp's Harmonists contributed to the formation of the state of Indiana, helped open the American West, and influenced the growth of the United States economy.

Despite the sordid conditions surrounding its dissolution, the outstanding legacy of the Harmony Society lives on in the three towns its members carved out of the wilderness. Thanks to organized preservation, restoration, and public interpretation efforts at historic Harmony, New Harmony, and Economy, the Harmonists' legacy may still be witnessed in their church buildings, cemeteries, private dwellings, communal dormitories, wine cellars, granaries, workshops, and re-created gardens. Sometimes one stumbles upon an especially poignant reminder of the former Harmonist presence, such as the words written in German under a staircase in Community House Number 2 in New Harmony. A Harmonist leaving Indiana inscribed, "On the 24th day of May, 1824, we have departed. Lord, with Thy great help and goodness, in body and soul protect us."

The Harmonists also speak to the modern world through their copious written records, most in their native Swabian German. Their correspondence, sermons, poetry, prose, and official documents offer limitless opportunities for research to those patient enough to attempt translation. Often the experiences and emotions of the everyday Harmonist come through, such as in this segment of an ode penned at New Harmony. Unknowingly its author presented us with a fitting epitaph for his or her beloved Harmony Society and its unrealized utopian dream:

A little sweet flower blossomed on the meadow,
lifted joyously by its delicate stalk. The fragrance
from its open chalice filled the air near and far.
Happily I gave my heart to the little flower. I
tended it throughout the long, delightful day. And were
the moon high in the heavens, I would still be there,
waiting and caring for it.
I once bid it good night and returned as soon I
awoke. I sought it everywhere, but my little flower had
ceased to be.
Earth you sad, friendly, fearsome one, return me to your
protecting womb. All that I live for, all that I have aspired to,
seems devoid of compassion. My life, my suffering, my pain and joy
repose in you.
Earth you hostile, comforting, kind one, shelter
me in your redeeming embrace![28]

Chronology

1757	George Rapp is born Johann Georg Rapp in Iptingen, near Stuttgart, in the German province of Württemberg on November 1.
1783	George Rapp marries Christina Benzinger. Two children are born—Johannes in 1783 and Rosina in 1786—before the couple forsake sexual relations.
1785	Rapp's Separatist movement begins with his declaration of faith and official break with the Evangelical Lutheran Church.
1798	Rapp and other Separatists present their Articles of Faith to the Württemberg legislature.
1800	Rapp's Separatist disciples number as many as 20,000.
1803	Rapp and a small advance party begin emigration to the United States.
1804–5	Rapp's followers begin arriving in America on July 4, 1804, purchase land in Butler County, Pa., and begin building their first town of Harmony.
1805	On February 15 the Harmony Society is organized communally under the Articles of Association.
1807–8	Celibacy/chastity is adopted; tobacco and "luxuries" are given up.
1814–15	Harmonists move to the Indiana Territory to build their second Harmony (New Harmony) on the Wabash River.
1816	Frederick Rapp participates in the Indiana constitutional convention.
1818	Book of Debts—recording contributions of each member upon joining—is burned.
1824	Rapp's philosophy is printed on the Harmony Society press as *Thoughts on the Destiny of Man*, and Harmonists begin moving to their third town site of Economy, on the Ohio River north of Pittsburgh.
1825	Harmonists sell New Harmony to Robert Owen of New Lanark, Scotland, for about $150,000.

1826–29	Over seventy members withdraw from Economy in protest over new articles of association, Rapp's sterner attitude toward celibacy, and Rapp's involvement with Hildegard Mutschler.
1832	Schism occurs; 176 members leave with the Count de Leon (Bernhard Mueller) to establish the New Philadelphia Society at Phillipsburg, Pa. Schismatics later found other communal villages of Grand Ecore and Germantown, La.; Bethel, Mo.; and Aurora, Oreg.
1847	George Rapp dies on August 7.
1848–68	Romelius L. Baker serves as head trustee.
1868–92	Jacob Henrici serves as head trustee.
1892–1905	John S. Duss family trusteeship.
1905	Harmony Society is formally dissolved.
1916	Harmony Society assets revert to the state of Pennsylvania.

Notes

Professor Arndt's essay is printed posthumously. He wrote a first draft. The editor is grateful to his own graduate student and former coordinator of education and research at Historic New Harmony, Leigh Ann Chamness, for her assistance in the preparation of the published version.

1. Unless otherwise indicated, this narrative is based on the following monographs and documentary histories of Karl J. R. Arndt: *George Rapp's Harmony Society, 1785–1847* (Rutherford, N.J.: Fairleigh Dickinson University Press, 1972); *George Rapp's Successors and Material Heirs, 1847–1916* (Rutherford, N.J.: Fairleigh Dickinson University Press, 1971); *George Rapp's Separatists, 1700–1803: The German Prelude to Rapp's American Harmony Society* (Worcester, Mass.: Harmonie Society Press, 1980); *Harmonie on the Connoquenessing, 1803–1815: George Rapp's First American Harmony* (Worcester, Mass.: Harmonie Society Press, 1980); *A Documentary History of the Indiana Decade of the Harmony Society, 1814–1824*, vol. 1, *1814–1819*, and vol. 2, *1820–1824* (Indianapolis: Indiana Historical Society, 1975, 1978); *Harmony on the Wabash in Transition to Rapp's Divine Economy on the Ohio and Owen's New Moral World at New Harmony on the Wabash, 1824–1826* (Worcester, Mass.: Harmonie Society Press, 1982); *Economy on the Ohio, 1826–1834: George Rapp's Third American Harmony* (Worcester, Mass.: Harmonie Society Press, 1984); *George Rapp's Years of Glory: Economy on the Ohio, 1832–1847* (New York: Peter Lang, 1987); and *George Rapp's Re-established Harmony Society: Letters and Documents of the Baker-Henrici Trusteeship, 1848–1868* (New York: Peter Lang, 1993). Dr. Gerhard Friesen is finishing Dr. Arndt's documentary history of the Harmony Society for the years 1868 to 1916.

2. Karl J. R. Arndt, "Luther's Golden Rose at New Harmony, Indiana," *Concordia Historical Institute Quarterly* 49 (Fall 1976): 112–22.

3. Although the Harmony Society was founded on February 15, 1805, the legally valid articles must have been prepared later and backdated for various reasons. The signatures on the document have always been an enigma, as many who signed had not yet arrived in America by the date indicated, and Johannes Rapp's signature is not found on the articles although he was certainly a member of the congregation until his death in 1812. Additionally, the original articles contain a clause providing for the return of property to withdrawing members, but this clause could not have been included until after 1808, when the Pennsylvania legislature rejected the articles because they did not include such a clause. A

Harmonist who later withdrew from the society claimed that the articles were drawn up specifically for a lawsuit that took place in the early 1820s. See Arndt, *Harmonie on the Connoquenessing*, 80–82.

4. Arndt, *George Rapp's Harmony Society*, 97.

5. Arndt, *Harmonie on the Connoquenessing*, 271, and Aaron Williams, *Harmony Society at Economy, Pennsylvania, Founded by George Rapp, A.D. 1805* (Pittsburgh: W. S. Haven, 1966), 32.

6. John W. Larner Jr., "Nails and Sundrie Medicines: Town Planning and Public Health in the Harmony Society, 1805–1840," *Western Pennsylvania Historical Magazine* 45 (1962): 225.

7. Elias P. Fordham, *Personal Narrative of Travels in Virginia, Maryland, Pennsylvania, Ohio, Indiana, Kentucky: and of a Residence in the Illinois Territory: 1817–1818*, ed. F. A. Ogg (Cleveland: Arthur H. Clark, 1906), 207. This mansion, which stood on the square, burned in 1844 and was rebuilt in the late 1840s. William Maclure and others occupied it in the early nineteenth century. In 1991 the mansion was restored by Kenneth Dale Owen, Robert Owen's great-great-grandson.

8. William Hebert, *A Visit to the Colony of Harmony in Indiana, in the United States of America* (London: Plummer and Brewis, 1824). Reprinted in H. Lindley, *Indiana As seen by Early Travellers* (Indianapolis: Indiana Historical Commission, 1916), 335.

9. When the 1822 Harmonist brick church was torn down in 1874, the golden rose door was saved and incorporated into two school buildings that subsequently stood on the site. The second of these was razed in 1989. A memorial park now occupies the site, with a replica of the golden rose door resting on the location of the original.

10. Lucy Jayne Botscharow-Kamau, "Neighbors: Harmony and Conflict on the Indiana Frontier," *Journal of the Early Republic* 11 (Winter 1991): 507–29.

11. Arndt, *Documentary History of the Indiana Decade*, 1:578.

12. George Rapp, *Thoughts on the Destiny of Man, Particularly with Reference to the Present Times* (New Harmony, Ind.: Harmonie Society Press, 1824), 95.

13. Donald E. Pitzer, "Education in Utopia: The New Harmony Experience," in *Indiana Historical Society Lectures, 1976–1977: The History of Education in the Middle West*, by Donald E. Pitzer and Timothy L. Smith (Indianapolis: Indiana Historical Society, 1978), 77–78, 82–90.

14. Rapp, *Thoughts on the Destiny of Man*, 66.

15. *Feurige Kohlen der aufsteigenden Liebesflammen in Lustspiel der Weisheit* (Fiery coals in the ascending flames of lust for the elusive Sophia) (Economy, Pa.: Harmonie Society Press, 1826).

16. Ibid., 229.

17. A detailed treatment of the Harmony Society music program can be found in Richard D. Wetzel, *Frontier Musicians on the Connoquenessing, Wabash, and Ohio: A History of the Music and Musicians of George Rapp's Harmony Society, 1805–1906* (Athens: Ohio University Press, 1976).

18. Donald E. Pitzer, "The Original Boatload of Knowledge down the Ohio River: William Maclure's and Robert Owen's Transfer of Science and Education to the Midwest, 1825–1826," *Ohio Journal of Science* 89 (December 1989): 134.

19. Richard D. Wetzel, "J. C. Mueller and W. C. Peters at Economy: A Reappraisal," *Communal Societies* 3 (1983): 159.

20. Evidence for the growing tensions caused by the music program can be found in Christopher Mueller's "Memorandum Buch des Music Bandes der Oekonomie" (Memorandum book of the band of Economy), which he kept from 1828 to 1831. A synopsis and

commentary on the book can be found in a series of articles by Karl J. R. Arndt and Richard D. Wetzel, "Harmonist Music and Pittsburgh Musicians in Early Economy," *Western Pennsylvania Historical Magazine* 43 (1971).

21. Quoted in Arndt, *George Rapp's Harmony Society*, 443.

22. Ibid., 485–88.

23. Arndt, *George Rapp's Years of Glory*, 572–73.

24. Historic restoration and interpretive programs are maintained in Bethel, Missouri, and Aurora, Oregon.

25. Arndt, *George Rapp's Harmony Society*, 599.

26. Arndt, *George Rapp's Years of Glory*, 1099–1100.

27. Arndt, *George Rapp's Harmony Society*, 605.

28. *Feurige Kohlen*, 284–85.

Selected Bibliography

Arndt, Karl J. R. *A Documentary History of the Indiana Decade of the Harmony Society, 1814–1824*. Vol. 1, *1814–1819*, and vol. 2, *1820–1824*. Indianapolis: Indiana Historical Society, 1975, 1978.

———. *Economy on the Ohio, 1826–1834: George Rapp's Third American Harmony*. Worcester, Mass.: Harmonie Society Press, 1984.

———. *George Rapp's Disciples, Pioneers, and Heirs: A Register of the Harmonists in America*. Edited by Donald E. Pitzer and Leigh Ann Chamness. Evansville: University of Southern Indiana Press, 1994.

———. *George Rapp's Harmony Society, 1785–1847*. Rutherford, N.J.: Fairleigh Dickinson University Press, 1972.

———. *George Rapp's Re-established Harmony Society: Letters and Documents of the Baker-Henrici Trusteeship, 1848–1868*. New York: Peter Lang, 1993.

———. *George Rapp's Separatists, 1700–1803: The German Prelude to Rapp's American Harmony Society*. Worcester, Mass.: Harmonie Society Press, 1980.

———. *George Rapp's Successors and Material Heirs, 1847–1916*. Rutherford, N.J.: Fairleigh Dickinson University Press, 1971.

———. *George Rapp's Years of Glory: Economy on the Ohio, 1834–1847*. New York: Peter Lang, 1987.

———. *Harmonie on the Connoquenessing, 1803–1815: George Rapp's First American Harmony*. Worcester, Mass.: Harmonie Society Press, 1980.

———. *Harmony on the Wabash in Transition to Rapp's Divine Economy on the Ohio and Owen's New Moral World at New Harmony on the Wabash, 1824–1826*. Worcester, Mass.: Harmonie Society Press, 1982.

Arndt, Karl J. R., and Richard D. Wetzel. "Harmonist Music and Pittsburgh Musicians in Early Economy." *Western Pennsylvania Historical Magazine* 54 (1971): 2–4.

Bole, John A. *The Harmony Society: A Chapter in German American Culture History*. Philadelphia: American Germanica Press, 1904.

Feurige Kohlen der aufsteigenden Liebesflammen in Lustspiel der Weisheit. Economy, Pa.: Harmonie Society Press, 1826.

Kring, Hilda A. *The Harmonists: A Folk-Cultural Approach*. Metuchen, N.J.: Scarecrow Press, 1973.

Larner, John W. Jr. "Nails and Sundrie Medicines: Town Planning and Public Health in the Harmony Society, 1805–1840." *Western Pennsylvania Historical Magazine* 45 (1962): 115–38.

Pitzer, Donald. "Education in Utopia: The New Harmony Experience." In *Indiana Historical Society Lectures, 1976–1977: The History of Education in the Middle West*, by Donald E. Pitzer and Timothy L. Smith, 77–78, 82–90. Indianapolis: Indiana Historical Society, 1978.

Pitzer, Donald, and Josephine Elliott. "New Harmony's First Utopians, 1814–1824." *Indiana Magazine of History* 75 (September 1979): 225–300.

Rapp, George. *Thoughts on the Destiny of Man, Particularly with Reference to the Present Times*. New Harmony, Ind.: Harmonie Society Press, 1824.

Wetzel, Richard D. *Frontier Musicians on the Connoquenessing, Wabash, and Ohio: A History of the Music and Musicians of George Rapp's Harmony Society, 1805–1906*. Athens: Ohio University Press, 1976.

———. "J. C. Mueller and W. C. Peters at Economy: A Reappraisal." *Communal Societies* 3 (1983): 158–74.

Williams, Aaron. *Harmony Society at Economy, Pennsylvania, Founded by George Rapp, A.D. 1805*. Pittsburgh: W. S. Haven, 1866.

DONALD E. PITZER

The New Moral World of Robert Owen and New Harmony

The first issue of *The New-Harmony Gazette* appeared in America's earliest socialistic utopian community on October 1, 1825.[1] It featured not only founder Robert Owen's introductory address and "The Constitution of the Preliminary Society of New Harmony" but also "Song No. 1" for the children.

> Ah, soon will come the glorious day,
>   Inscribed on Mercy's brow,
> When truth shall rend the veil away
>   That blinds the nations now.
>
> When earth no more in anxious fear
>   And misery shall sigh:
> And pain shall cease, and every tear
>   Be wiped from every eye.
>
> The race of man shall wisdom learn,
>   And error cease to reign:
> The charms of innocence return,
>   And all be new again.
>
> The fount of life will then be quaffed
>   In peace by all that come;
> And every wind that blows shall waft
>   Some wandering mortal home.[2]

Gazette coeditor William Pelham wrote and printed these simple, millennial-sounding lines for a purpose. When sung to the familiar tune of "Auld Lang Syne" they were to rivet in the minds of the rising generation the benefits to come in Robert Owen's vision of the New Moral World: peace and plenty, truth and happiness.[3] Every Owenite in New Harmony believed the new social order could be realized by creating a superior character in each individual from birth and that the means were readily available to human hands. Loving care and a liberal education within the protective environment of socialistic communities of equality would lead inevitably to rational mental independence and universal human bliss.

Robert Owen's own character was molded as the sixth of seven children in a working-class family in Newtown, Wales.[4] He was born on May 14, 1771, just five years before Britain's American colonies dared revolt against King George III in the name of "the pursuit of happiness," which became the ultimate objective of Owen's own utopian crusade. His mother was a farmer's daughter. His father was variously an ironmonger, saddler, storekeeper, and postal worker. Like most poor children caught in the early social distress of the Industrial Revolution, the young Owen faced but two options after his tenth birthday. He could enter the factory labor force or seek an apprenticeship. At ten he ended his formal education and moved to London, where his brother helped him become the apprentice of Mr. McGuffog, a prominent Scottish clothing fabric and dry goods merchant in Stamford, England.

McGuffog's home and store gave direction to the thought and career of his apprentice. By his own testimony, Owen received kind treatment and averaged five hours a day reading books from his master's library.[5] During this time he gradually relinquished the Christian faith he had learned at home. In its place came a rational and eclectic approach to ethics and morality with an abiding skepticism of the motives and doctrines of organized religion. After 1817, when Owen the social reformer began expressing these unorthodox views in public attacks on the abuses of the clergy and the injustices of marriage as tied to religion, he discovered this drew far more criticism, and did more damage to his appeal, than all his radical economic theories and community-building schemes. In America he was widely castigated after using his speech in New Harmony on July 4, 1826, the fiftieth anniversary of the Declaration of Independence, to make his own "Declaration of Mental Independence." He praised the American Revolution as the first opportunity to use political power to attack the "Trinity" of evils: "PRIVATE, OR INDIVIDUAL PROPERTY—ABSURD AND IRRATIONAL SYSTEMS OF RELIGION—AND MARRIAGE, FOUNDED ON INDIVIDUAL PROPERTY COMBINED WITH SOME ONE OF THESE IR-

RATIONAL SYSTEMS OF RELIGION."[6] Many unfairly branded him and his movement atheistic. Yet Owen, like other rationalists of his time, reasoned "that there is an external or an internal cause of all existences, by the fact of their existence; [and] that this all-pervading cause of motion and change in the universe, is that Incomprehensible Power, which the nations of the world have called God."[7] Eventually Owen proposed a universal "Rational Religion" within a Rational System of Society based on the idea that "truth is nature, and nature God; that God is truth, and truth is God."[8]

Just as machines and steam power were revolutionizing textile manufacturing, Owen left McGuffog's store in about 1787 with a thorough knowledge of textiles and their market potential. Then he went off to seek his fortune in Manchester, the center of England's emerging textile industry. The very industrial system from which he would acquire his wealth was also creating the social degradation that later touched his heart and fueled his social reform movement. Both Owen and his socialist contemporary in Paris, Charles Fourier, attributed the increasingly aggravated problems of society to both industrialization and the French Revolution. Coincidentally in 1774, just over a decade before Owen's arrival in Manchester, Ann Lee had escaped this same city's dehumanizing factories and religious constraints by emigrating to America with her small band of adventist Shakers. By 1816, when Owen first learned of the successful communal settlements of her religious movement, he had already used the factory town of New Lanark, Scotland, as the initial model for his projected ideal communities. Nevertheless, after he satisfied himself that the Shakers were achieving goals he prized (such as social discipline, breaking down family ties to serve the common good, and becoming self-sufficient through agriculture and high-quality handicrafts and fair dealing), in 1817 he gladly began to point to Shaker villages as proof that communal organization could mold character and solve basic economic and social problems.[9]

By his twentieth birthday the young capitalist of Manchester had turned borrowed money into a spinning machinery business and already managed the large Chorlton Twist Company. Then, in 1799, Owen made the decision that set the future course of his business and reform careers. With Manchester partners, he purchased the famous cotton-spinning mills of David Dale at New Lanark, Scotland, and assumed its management. Dale and Richard Arkwright, inventor of the water frame spinning machine, took advantage of the water power below the Falls of Clyde about midway between Glasgow and Edinburgh to complete the first massive stone mill in 1785 that grew into one of Britain's largest cotton manufacturing villages. Dale attracted 1,500 work-

DONALD E. PITZER

ers to this remote factory town in the scenic but narrowly confining valley of the Clyde River by adding row houses and schools.

In this company town Owen discovered a bride, an industrial fortune, and a ready-made laboratory for his social experiments. His hopes for both business profits and the eventual realization of the New Moral World rested on effective social controls and character formation. The New Lanark labor community itself, as a model factory town, provided the prototype for the decision he announced in 1816 to make the building of planned communities a means for implementing his campaign on behalf of the poor and working classes. He further explained that creating whole communities could also benefit the middle and upper classes, not only of Britain and the United States but of the entire world. British Owenite historian John F. C. Harrison has concluded that "the model factory was the germ of Owen's communitarianism." In fact, he raises the question of "whether Owen would have become a communitarian [at all] had he not been a cotton spinner." In any case, Harrison finds it clear that "the idea of the factory colony or community was closely associated with the early machine textile industry, which not only pioneered the technological changes of the first Industrial Revolution but also developed new forms of social organization."[10] Yet the impossible burden that the task of building entire new communities would lay on Owen's social reform movement seems only to have dawned on him years later as one after another proved unworkable. In the 1810s and early 1820s, however, his growing familiarity with the flourishing communities of the Shaker, Harmonist, and Moravian movements in America further convinced him to pursue the elaborate communal method.

The year in which Robert Owen purchased David Dale's spinning mills he also married Dale's daughter, Ann Caroline. Contrary to his own growing animosity to established religion, which he equated with oppressive superstition, Owen discovered his wife steeped in her father's Protestant fundamentalism and millennialism. He disdained the belief in the second coming of Christ to effect a better world that so possessed his wife and much of the churchgoing public in Britain. Yet after 1817 he incorporated a secular form of millennialism into his own reform propaganda and often quoted biblical passages to reinforce his arguments.[11] During his entire career he seems never to have missed an opportunity to turn an idea that had caught the popular imagination into a reason to believe in the truth of his own crusade, from millennialism and spiritualism to phrenology. Ann and Robert grew apart over religious and other matters. Their separation became complete when, in midlife, Robert left for America in 1824 to begin the community-building phase of his utopian ventures. The reformer did not even attend Ann's funeral in 1831 although he was in England when she died.

However, at least five of their eight children actively embraced their father's visionary humanitarianism. These capable individuals filled a particularly vital place as loyal practitioners and articulate exponents of their father's ideas in America. William Owen accompanied his father to New Harmony in 1824. Although only twenty-two years old, he and Owen's Scottish disciple Donald Macdonald became the initial managers of this first Owenite community while the elder Owen took a propagandizing tour. Eldest son Robert Dale Owen arrived in New Harmony in January 1826 with Philadelphia scientists and educators aboard the keelboat his father dubbed the "Boatload of Knowledge." David Dale Owen and Richard Owen came in January 1828, and their sister Jane Dale Owen arrived in 1833 after her mother's death. This involvement of Owen's children is of special importance. Owen and the Owenite communities of the 1820s came upon the American scene too early to receive the direct support that the leaders and organizations of the liberal political, labor, and social reform movements born in the Jacksonian era sometimes gave to the Fourierists and other communitarian socialists in the 1840s. Owen's own family members extended the effective life of Owenism in America by the developmental process of translating their father's utopian dreams into the crusades for women's rights, birth control, tax-supported public schools, and freedom for the slaves after the first wave of Owenite energy for community building abated in 1829.

In pursuit of the industrial fortune that made him one of Britain's wealthiest entrepreneurs by the 1810s, Owen became captivated by the idea of a science of society. His interest was driven by a desire akin to that of other contemporary milltown managers and owners, a good number of whom initiated projects for improvement among their own mill workers. Owen knew that factory production and village management depended on the health, well-being, and discipline of his poor villagers. In 1811 they numbered 2,206, of whom 1,360, mostly women and children, worked in the mills.[12] Thus he was drawn to methods promising social and behavioral control within the context of a community of workers about whose physical care and intellectual and cultural improvement he felt genuine concern. Determined to maximize his control while ensuring a contented, efficient workforce, Owen invented a "silent monitor," started an infant school, and opened his Institution for the Formation of Character. The monitor, a three-inch block of wood painted a different color on each side—black, blue, yellow and white—hung by each work station in the mills for Owen and all to see. The color on display indi-

This engraving of Matilda Heming's drawing of Robert Owen, published
in December 1823, captures the vigorous young manager of the New Lanark
mills on the eve of his utopian venture in communal living at New Harmony,
Indiana. (From John F. C. Harrison, *Quest for the New Moral World* [1969];
original in the Robert Owen Museum, Newton, Wales.)

cated each employee's performance the previous day as rated by a foreman
and recorded in a "book of character."[13]

Owen came to view education as central to socialization. He extended
David Dale's earlier schools for children ages six to ten downward to include
infants and upward to provide lifelong learning for adults. After 1809, for a

small fee, parents could place children as young as one year old in the new infant school. This not only freed mothers for the factory like modern day-care centers, but it also contributed to Owen's larger purpose of replacing initial negative family influence with a positive environment for instilling desired values and fashioning superior character. In effect, the infant school permitted the community to replace the family in matters of personal development and social control. The pioneering techniques Owen conceived for his infant and day schools soon aroused wide interest. Thousands of visitors from Europe and America inspected them. Nearly three decades before Friedrich Froebel began his kindergarten for German youngsters, Owen insisted that loving kindness with no contrived rewards or punishments permeate the New Lanark school system.

After 1813 Owen's new London partners, especially Quaker philanthropist William Allen and well-known utilitarian Jeremy Bentham, insisted on introducing the popular method of Englishman Joseph Lancaster that held promise of literacy and knowledge for all. As used in New Lanark and as far away as the Shaker and Harmonist communities in America, this Lancastrian system simply designated students as monitors to teach other students what they themselves had learned by rote. However, Owen refused to let instruction dominate. Instead, he wanted textbooks used sparingly. Students learned mostly by doing, in a style akin to that used in the school of Johann Heinrich Pestalozzi in Switzerland. Pestalozzi's approach to education appealed greatly to both Owen and William Maclure, the wealthy Scot dry goods merchant turned geologist and social reformer whom Owen later attracted as his philanthropic financial partner in the purchase of New Harmony. Owen sent all four of his own sons to the progressive school of Philip Emanuel von Fellenberg in Hofwyl, Switzerland. Maclure funded Pestalozzian schools in Paris, Spain, and Philadelphia before he and his protégée, Marie Fretageot, assumed responsibility for the Pestalozzian schools in New Harmony. Children in both New Lanark and New Harmony learned through play, conversation, singing, dancing, and military-style marching. The playground took on as much importance as the classroom. Huge maps and giant pictures of animals graced the walls of one room in the New Lanark school where geography was taught by a game. Owen required teachers to consider the needs and maturation levels of their charges and to tailor their methods accordingly.[14]

The New Lanark educational system was complete when Owen opened his Institution for the Formation of Character in 1816. The name itself boldly proclaimed the comprehensive purpose of his entire program of education. This single institution combined under one roof his infant and day schools and introduced educational, social, and cultural activities for adults. Lectures,

DONALD E. PITZER

discussions, and debates treated subjects from natural science to ancient history. Now the older residents became part of the captive audience in Owen's company town. Every event designed for them lent itself to adult education, recreation, or indoctrination in Owen's emerging utopian theories.

When the effectiveness of these methods of social control became apparent, Robert Owen gained a reputation for efficient, benevolent factory management. He soon distinguished himself beyond his fellow industrialists, even the socially conscious ones such as David Dale who tried similar progressive policies regarding wages, working hours, and education. Owen's keen sensitivity to the plight of poor workers injected a moral dimension into his thinking about poverty and riches existing side by side in the industrial age. He recognized and freely admitted that the increase of wealth in society as well as for himself during the Napoleonic era was not created by his or others' advanced managerial skills, but rather by the productivity of new machinery. He argued that if human beings were organized and serviced as carefully as the machines they operated, all employers would profit. But regardless of their profit or loss, standing as he did in the liberal vanguard as a socialist (a term coined by London Owenites in 1827),[15] Owen accepted the social responsibility of owners and managers to the working classes. His willingness to criticize selfishness itself placed him outside the circle of other cotton spinners and beyond the ideas of classical economists such as Adam Smith. It placed him closer to the socialist economic theories of David Ricardo. Owen also broke out of the mold of other business leaders when, beginning in 1812, he became a public propagandist for utopian radicalism. His speeches and writings were aimed initially at securing like-minded New Lanark partners and labor legislation, then developed into vehicles for finding philanthropic industrialists like himself to erect model industrial villages for both social improvement and personal profit.[16]

Equal to Owen's benevolence ranked his aggressive paternalism that aroused conflicts in New Lanark and New Harmony. In New Lanark he instituted curfews, random body searches to prevent theft, and fines for drunkenness or for having children out of wedlock. He established committees for house inspections somewhat like Henry Ford did much later in Detroit. Enraged women who called these inspectors the "Bug Hunters" and "military police" often refused to open their doors. Although Owen cast himself in the role of chief advocate for the interests of the masses, he never considered them his equal. He spoke with condescending certainty about the brutal ignorance and stupidity of the common people and equated the need to make them happy with the desire to make them docile.[17] In 1816, the year after he announced that community building rather than legislation would be the preferred method for his social movement, he firmly asserted that he did not wish "to have the opinions of the ill-trained and uninformed on any of the measures intended for their relief and amelioration. No! On such subjects, until they shall be instructed in better habits, and made rationally intelligent, their advice can be of no value."[18]

In New Harmony he unwittingly helped sink his flagship project of communitarian socialism by finding it all too easy to regard the majority of its 800 to 900 American farmer and mechanic volunteers as he had the poor, submissive residents of his milltown in Scotland. On April 27, 1825, he officially opened New Harmony for community life to all who would accept his generous offer to make it their home on an economic arrangement yet to be determined. But he bluntly announced to those gathered in the former Harmonist brick church that "as no other individual has had the same experience as myself in the practice of the system about to be introduced, I must for some time, partially take the lead in its direction."[19] Reflecting on the grave difficulties a manager turned philanthropist confronted in administrating a community filled mostly with a random lot of freedom-loving, backwoods Americans, his partner, Maclure, later observed that Owen had failed to recognize that "the materials in this country are not the same as the cotton spinners at New Lanark, nor does the advice of a patron go so far."[20] As events later proved, even in liberal New Harmony Owen's nagging paternalistic bent and entrepreneurial orientation, along with the irritations produced by trying to mix the community's lower and upper classes, blocked any complete implementation of the egalitarianism and community of property that he at times advocated after 1824. Neither he nor his wealthy partner found it in their nature to turn over their New Harmony property to the otherwise communitarian citizenry any more than Owen would have given his milltown to the laborers of New Lanark. Thus, in accord with Owen's earliest community plans, New Harmony can be described best as a philanthropic project of two Scottish businessmen turned social reformers.

However, in Owen's broader scheme for worldwide reform, New Harmony represented merely a temporary springboard to the entirely new towns he proposed. These were to be built on a grand scale according to designs he had engraved and printed as early as 1817.[21] By 1825 he had a six-foot-square architectural model displayed in New York, in Rembrandt Peale's museum in Philadelphia, and in the White House, where John Quincy Adams was president.[22] In Robert Owen's mind, the economic, social, and cultural benefits of the New Moral World could only be fully realized in the idyllic environment of these Agricultural and Manufacturing Villages of Unity and Mutual Cooperation. Each village was to feature a gigantic structure built in the form of

DONALD E. PITZER

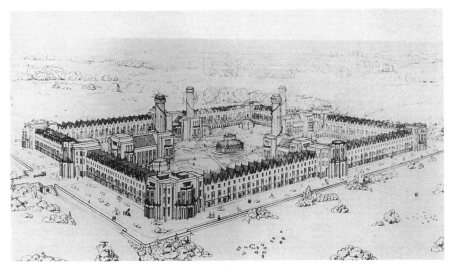

Robert Owen's New Moral World was to be realized in ideal Agricultural and Manufacturing Villages of Unity and Mutual Co-operation projected to dot the international landscape. Owen displayed a six-foot-square model in New York, Philadelphia, and the White House in 1825. Owenites fired bricks to build the first such village south of New Harmony, but construction never began. (From *Description of an Architectural Model from a Design by Stedman Whitwell . . .* , 1830.)

a quadrangle or parallelogram 1,000 feet on a side and set on a plot of about thirty-three acres with outlying mills, factories, and farmlands. These resembled Fourier's phalansteries and phalanxes although the two socialists did not borrow this idea from each other. Dwellings resembling the row houses of New Lanark formed the walls enclosing the quadrangle, offering housing with gas lighting and hot and cold running water for 2,000 residents. Everything imaginable was to be included for their comfort and enlightenment, from kitchens, dining halls, baths, laundries, and stores to schools, a library, a museum, botanic gardens, gymnasiums, music rooms, and dance and lecture halls. When noted German American writer Charles Sealsfield (Karl Postl) discovered Owen's design during his visit to Indiana, he reported that "a plan was shown and sold to us, according to which a new building of colossal dimensions is projected; and if Mr. Owen's means should not fall short of his good will, this edifice would certainly exhibit the most magnificent piece of architecture in the Union, [only] the Capitol at Washington excepted. This palace, when finished, is to receive his community [from New Harmony]."[23] Owen promised the citizens of New Harmony that the first utopian town-in-a-garden would soon be theirs to enjoy when constructed three miles to the south "on the high lands of Harmony from 2 to 4 miles from the [Wabash] river and its island of which the occupants will have a beautiful and interesting view."[24]

This new, quadrangular town, rather than New Harmony, was to be the showplace to be replicated. The actual implementation of Owen's vision would take place there. Only then would the New Moral World become a local and, over time, a global reality, much as Fourier envisioned exactly 2,985,984 of his joint-stock phalanxes covering the earth and revolutionizing the world order. Owen foresaw giant quadrangles with their fields, factories, and mills dotting every countryside, providing their citizens with every necessity of life. Acting in perfect concert for their mutual prosperity, sharing their superior products on the basis of need rather than profit, these communities were to achieve abundance for all and thus the disappearance of private property and social inequality. As the Great Truth of character formation ultimately triumphed along with these communitarian developments, all humanity would attain happiness along with a regenerated spirit. The Old Immoral World would give way to the New Moral World. In Owen's words,

> This second creation or regeneration of man will bring forth in him new combinations of his natural faculties, qualities, and powers which will imbue him with a new spirit, and create in him new feelings, thoughts, and conduct, the reverse of those which have been hitherto produced. . . . This re-created or new-formed man will be enabled easily to subdue the earth, and make it an ever-varying paradise, the fit abode of highly intellectual moral beings, each of whom, for all practical purposes, will be the free possessor and delighted enjoyer of its whole extent; and that joy will be increased a thousand-fold, because all his fellow-beings will equally enjoy it with him.[25]

Under these ideal conditions, Owen came to believe that the average life span would be extended to as many as 140 years.[26] Even the experience of terminal illness and death would lose the terror and grief it held during the individual isolation of the Old Immoral World. Instead, as Owen imagined,

> In these happy villages of unity, when disease or death assail their victim, every aid is near; all the assistance that skill, kindness, and sincere affection can invent, aided by every convenience and comfort, are at hand. The intelligent resigned sufferer waits the result with cheerful patience . . . and, when death attacks him, he submits to a conqueror who he knew from childhood was irresistible, and whom for a moment he never feared! . . . The survivors . . . have consolation in the certain

knowledge that within their own immediate circle they have many, many others remaining; and around them on all sides, as far as the eye can reach, or imagination extend, thousands on thousands, in strict, intimate, and close union, are ready and willing to offer them aid and consolation. . . . Here may it be truly said, "O death, where is thy sting? O grave, where is thy victory?"[27]

Driven by their hope for such an idealistic future, William Pelham noted, the New Harmony Owenites fired 240,000 bricks in their first summer of 1825 in a field adjacent to the proposed site, where a few broken ones can still be found. In August 1825 Pelham wrote optimistically to his son that "in 2 *years*, the contemplated new village will be ready for the reception of members."[28] However, the New Harmony experiment itself collapsed a few months before Pelham's targeted date. None of the proposed structures rose from the waiting bricks. And no other Owenite community came even this close to beginning the grandiose quadrangle with its illusive promise of realizing the New Moral World.

Although Robert Owen always asserted that all of his lofty ideas were original, born of his own experience and intuition, his approach to the social problems of the industrial age did not originate in an intellectual vacuum. His thoughts and actions clearly identify him with the Enlightenment rationalism of the late eighteenth and early nineteenth centuries that expressed concern over the social effects of industrialization and called for social planning to improve living conditions and even to perfect human character. Owen's voracious reading at McGuffog's, his association in the 1790s with the Literary and Philosophical Society in Manchester, and his membership in the Glasgow Literary and Commercial Society after 1800 gave him opportunities to begin absorbing these modern concepts. During his quarter-century at New Lanark he became acquainted with noted social theorists William Godwin, Jeremy Bentham, and James Mill. His private conversations with them and his reading of their published works affected Owen's thinking, as did the writings of Jean Jacques Rousseau and other Enlightenment figures. He borrowed directly from some of them. Perhaps the most obvious influence is Godwin's *An Enquiry concerning Political Justice* (1793). It is reflected in Owen's *A New View of Society*, the first printed summary of his ideas in 1813. However, where Godwin's new social order called for justice, equality, and freedom for the individual, Owen stressed the achievement of human happiness, which not only promised fulfillment in body, mind, and spirit but also implied making everyone manageable.[29] One London critic, William Hazlitt, took offense at Owen's calling his view of society "new." He insisted that "it is as old as the *Political Justice* of Mr. Godwin, as the Oceana of [James] Harrington, as the *Utopia* of Sir Thomas More, as the *Republic* of Plato."[30]

Owen and his movement were also closely associated with the earliest attempts to place the understanding and control of the individual and society on a scientific footing. He became friends with several professors at the University of Glasgow and the University of Edinburgh who were among the Scottish moral philosophers and political economists seeking bases for the scientific study of man and society that emerged as the behavioral sciences. Many Owenite converts who thought deeply about solutions for the problems of industrial society gained their first interest in behavioral science from Owen's impassioned call for a science of society.[31] Behaviorism composed the core of the Great Truth of the ages that Owen naively claimed as his own personal revelation. He referred to this Great Truth as the Messiah. He believed it had come to mankind through him, and he expressed it as one simple concept that drove his entire system of logic: "It is of all truths the most important, that the character of man is formed FOR—not BY himself."[32] Therefore, on a broad scale Owen claimed that "any general character, from the best to the worst, from the most ignorant to the most enlightened, may be given to any community, even to the world at large, by the application of proper means; which means are to a great extent at the command and under the control of those who have influence in the affairs of men."[33]

This theme dominated Owen's thought and schemes from 1813, when he subtitled *A New View of Society* "Essays on the Principle of the Formation of Human Character," to his last summary of his theories in their final form in *The Book of the Moral World*, a collection of essays he wrote between 1836 and 1844. Becoming an Owenite cliché laden with implications from the Enlightenment, social science, and environmental determinism, this assumption of the ability to improve individuals, communities, and the world by intentionally forming character underlay all of Owen's plans. Everything else he tried—in education, legislation, secular millennialism, philanthropy, and building whole villages of unity and mutual cooperation—was a means to this end.

Owen's partners fired him from his managerial position over the New Lanark mills in 1812. If this had not occurred, he might never have started writing the propaganda that marked the beginning of a distinct, nonsectarian Owenite movement with character formation as its fundamental principle and improvement of conditions of the poor, the unemployed, and the working classes as its practical goal.[34] His original partners having grown weary of his expensive educational projects, he was forced to seek the genuine reform

DONALD E. PITZER

advocates, including Jeremy Bentham, with whom he repurchased the mills and regained his managerial position in 1813. During months of scouting for partners in London, Owen used his first anonymous pamphlet, *Statement Regarding the New Lanark Establishment* (1812), to begin defining his theories, achievements, and plans. From that time forward he looked increasingly outward from his New Lanark base to achieve reforms of national and, eventually, international proportions.

With the eager encouragement of his new business associates, Owen began the developmental process by which he hoped to make his reforms effective in New Lanark and beyond. He proclaimed the solutions already found in his own small, self-contained mill community capable of solving the universal problems of poverty, unemployment, and ignorance in industrial society. Yet he tried gradual reform before adopting the laborious and expensive communal method of creating whole communities. As historian Arthur Bestor observes,

> The communitarian tendencies that marked Owen's activity at New Lanark were born of local circumstances rather than deliberate choice. Whether he would develop, in the national arena, a communitarian or a legislative (that is to say, a gradual) program was an open question. His first proposals were neither decisively the one nor the other. *A New View of Society* [1813] described at length his various proceedings at New Lanark and suggested, by unmistakable inference, that one path to reform might well be the imitation of them in other small-scale experiments. On the other hand, the final essay was entitled "The Principles of the Former Essays Applied to Government," and therein Owen advocated national programs of education and public works.[35]

When Owen opted first for the legislative route, it became clear that Owenism in its earliest years was *not* (and actually never became) a "communal movement." Community building never replaced character formation and the achievement of human happiness as the utopian commitment of the Owenite movement. As founding model communities became important to Owenites after 1816, these safe havens for character development and standard of living improvement always remained for them the means to an end, like legislation, education, science, and technology, not ends in themselves.

This helps explain why Owenism remained viable during, between, and following its waves of communal usage from 1825 to the 1860s in America and Britain, unlike certain other well-known movements. Shakers, Harmonists, Zoarites, and Janssonists eventually sacrificed the souls, if not the very existence, of their original movements to inflexible communal and other disciplines. Perhaps to this day the best-kept secret of the appeal and developmental vitality of the Owenite movement is that, although living in ideal communities became the centerpiece of Owenite methodology, no one ever felt required to start or live in a cooperative village in order to be an Owenite or to embrace Owenite socialism. The great majority of Owen's followers, in fact, never entered any of the nineteen American or nine British Owenite or Owenite-influenced communities. Furthermore, since Owenism never succeeded in forming communities in the number, size, or geographic scope called for to reform even a single county—let alone a nation or the world— no true Owenite ever considered the movement a failure. This does not discount the fact that Owen himself conceived of the formation of character taking place at both the individual and community levels, that eventually "the community, or Village of Cooperation, was the central institution of Owenism," or that "the largest practical commitment of the Owenite movement, measured by the amount of time, effort and capital involved, was to community building."[36]

However, Bestor confirms that "in his next important move [in 1815] Owen leaned definitely toward legislative, not communitarian, means."[37] At that time the cotton manufacturer began directing his energies toward convincing Parliament to enact nationally some features of his own enlightened factory management. These included forbidding child labor under age ten, requiring four years of schooling before child employment, restricting work to ten and a half hours per day for children under eighteen, and, yes, ensuring compliance by hiring government inspectors. Yet Owen was soon frustrated with the snail's pace of legislative reform. Not until 1819 did he see any act passed. Then it came with dishearteningly reduced provisions. Only the Factory Act of 1833, long after he had forsaken lobbying Parliament, came close to his recommendations. Even when he appealed to his industrialist friends to voluntarily adopt more humane standards in their own plants and villages, he was discouraged with the negative response.

Therefore, he finally turned to the community-building alternative.[38] He felt this promised more immediate, complete, and salutary results than gradual reform or assistance to individuals separately. Also, it would cancel, he thought, any repeat of violent revolution such as had shaken France. The master of New Lanark dramatically announced this new direction for the next phase of Owenism at the opening of his Institution for the Formation of Character on New Year's Day 1816. From that day until his death in 1858, his ever-changing proposals on the nature and application of his community plan passed through three distinct stages, eventually coming full circle to match his early class consciousness and paternalism.[39] In the first stage

(1816–24) he held conservatively to strict division of the social classes in separate communities funded by the government, industrialists, aristocratic philanthropists, or if all else failed, workers themselves. To Owen's chagrin, no viable communities were begun during this period.[40]

In the second stage (1824–29), which began with Owen's coming to America and the founding of New Harmony and other experimental communities, he made radical statements in support of common property and equality among community members. These ideals became stamped erroneously in many minds then and since as the only "real" Owenism. For Owen they represented his concessions in word to the social leveling process he saw around him in American society. He sensed the egalitarian waves from Jeffersonian and Jacksonian democracy, the Second Great Awakening, and the perpetual frontier moving across the American landscape. As early as the 1810s, Owen the milltown owner and paternalistic philanthropist came under strong influence by the community of property example of American sectarian communalists, especially the Harmony Society from whom he purchased New Harmony in January 1825 and the sixteen thriving Shaker settlements. However, Owen's suggestions of a future age without private property found roots in his belief that surplus production would eventually supply everyone with the necessities of life in abundance. He did not believe or advocate that anyone should be forced to relinquish private property through coercion or violence as in Marxist theory—a point on which Marx and Engels never forgave him.

As early as 1820 Owen stated the heart of his economic theories in his *Report to the County of Lanark*. He argued that since manual labor is the source of all wealth, laborers can properly claim their fair share (and some later Owenites such as William Thompson asserted this share to be the entirety of production in ideal communities). Owen foresaw in planned agricultural and manufacturing villages of cooperation such surplus that "each may be freely permitted to receive from the general store of the community whatever they may require."[41] Although he always held that both communal property and social equality were contingent on unlimited production, Owen and Owenism were pushed to advocate these ideals publicly during this period partly because of the writings of the movement's three main economic theorists in Britain: William Thompson, John Gray, and Thomas Hodgskin.[42] In reality, as long as the Old Immoral World endured in the general society, Owen's words in support of social and economic equality went far beyond his will or ability to implement them, even in a "community of equality" of his own making.

Robert Owen entered the final stage of his communitarian proposals in

1836. This came only after an interlude in which in some respects he became more radical by associating closely with the working classes for the first time in his life. In England between 1829 and 1835 he helped them initiate their own cooperative and trade union movements. The radicalism he learned during that time crept into his own movement as a denunciation of bankers, merchants, civilian professionals, military leaders, and the entire aristocracy as useless perpetrators of the harmful prevailing social system.[43] Otherwise he retreated into the more conservative posture of his 1816–24 period of justifying class divisions, paternalism, and philanthropic funding for communities. Perhaps the genius of communitarian Owenism lies in this very flexibility. Bestor suggests,

> The phrases by which he referred to his plans—a "new moral world," a "rational system of society"—were without economic content. His communities were designed to bring such a moral or rational society into being, and their economic organization was merely a subordinate part of the mechanism—a means, not an end. On secondary matters Owen never felt it necessary to commit himself, permanently and explicitly. To consult expedience in adapting means to ends, to modify subordinate details as need arose, was his normal procedure. Inconsistencies in economic detail were a natural consequence of his pragmatic approach.[44]

At first Owen called for self-sufficient communities of 500 to 1,500 residents to benefit only paupers and the greatly expanding ranks of the unemployed at the close of the Napoleonic wars, bringing to mind the New Deal homesteads of the 1930s in America.[45] Then, in 1817, he published the writings that committed his movement to a well-defined communitarian program for the much broader, even utopian, purpose of reorganizing the entire society for the emancipation of mankind. His expanded plan prescribed three new levels of communities above those for paupers and the unemployed. These, known as Villages of Unity and Mutual Co-operation, provided for separate communities to accommodate the unpropertied working class, the propertied working class, and wealthy aristocrats. The aristocrats, joined together in Voluntary and Independent Associations, must own property worth 1,000 to 20,000 pounds sterling. In his native Britain, before coming to New Harmony, Owen did not advocate any leveling process in present society or even placing individuals from different classes in the same village. Had he kept to this segregated plan, he might have spared New Harmony from the class conflicts that helped destroy its social fabric. In Britain he knew there could be nothing in his propaganda to frighten the upper class to whose interest in profit and philanthropy he addressed his appeal for support in establishing a first model village there. He even went so far as to propose with an elaborate chart that at least 140 different classifications of villages could be provided to house only those citizens who were comfortable with those of their own social class, religious sect, and political party.[46] In 1818 he personally handed the diplomats at the Congress of Aix-la-Chapelle copies of his scheme in three languages. In 1822 and 1823 he made speaking tours to Ireland. He persisted in laying his village plan before committees of Parliament until, in May 1824, his best friend in Parliament, Sir William de Crespigny, respectfully requested that he not bring up the matter again. In fact, though, no government, philanthropist, or industrialist stepped forward with any funding to test his plan. The one projected village at Motherwell near Glasgow never got beyond the talking stage. Owen knew that it would take double his fortune of about $250,000 to buy the 700 acres of unimproved land he had considered as a community site in Scotland. By contrast, he and William Maclure would pay a total of only about $135,000 for the complete town of New Harmony with its adjoining 20,000 acres.[47]

For these and other reasons, the frustrated reformer jumped at a chance to test his theories far away in America by means of his own philanthropy. The opportunity came in the summer of 1824 when Richard Flower, cofounder of the English settlement of Albion, Illinois, up the Wabash from Harmonist New Harmony, arrived in New Lanark. As an agent for the Harmony Society of George Rapp, he was trying to sell their second communal town, known as both Harmony (Harmonie) and New Harmony (Neu Harmonie). Owen found that personal, business, and managerial problems in New Lanark made it remarkably easy for him to phase out those responsibilities in order to devote all his time to his new social reform career. His marriage was contentious. His pious business partners were so upset with his public stand against established religion and a report that he had banned the Bible from New Lanark that they forced him to revise his prized school program and threatened to relieve him from his directorship of the mills. Even his normally congenial relations with his own employees were in disarray. He had seized the assets of their own benefit fund and frequently absented himself from his milltown as a general wage controversy swept the cotton industry of Scotland. The very scope and uniqueness of his New Lanark reforms came into question when an outbreak of typhoid fever suggested that Owen had overblown his claims for hygiene and housing in the village. Two books appeared claiming that social conditions in some other milltowns, including one at Catrine, at least equaled those instituted by Owen in New Lanark.[48]

When Owen, at age fifty-three, sailed from Liverpool for America in October 1824, he tried to break completely from his New Lanark problems. He did not return until 1827 and by 1829 had sold all his interests there, living from a modest annuity during the rest of his long life. Enroute to the United States he fixed his sights on inspecting and buying a second ready-made town. On the Indiana frontier he imagined he could begin a new community process to achieve the happiness for the entire human race that he could not find even for himself in his first experiment in New Lanark. Mercifully perhaps, his utopian vision blinded him from realizing how inadequately his New Lanark experience had prepared him for administrating the first model community for his social movement, a movement that now entered its applied communitarian stage that would last in an array of experimental villages from 1825 to 1863.[49]

As the British prophet of communitarian socialism stepped ashore in New York on November 4, 1824, he entered a vigorous, young republic that never ceased to inspire and confound him. Liberal Jeffersonian and Jacksonian trends were carrying Americans toward democracy and egalitarianism, while Owen harbored doubts about electoral processes and equality. Americans were still enjoying a period known as the "Era of Good Feelings." The sections of the nation and the political factions that split so bitterly during the War of 1812 with Britain mended relations after the nation signed the Treaty of Ghent late in 1814 and the conservative Federalist Party died. President James Monroe, who invited Owen to the White House on November 27, had been so universally favored for reelection in 1820 that he received all but one of the votes of the electoral college. The presidential election the month Owen arrived involved four major contenders, all campaigning under the same Republican Party banner. In the first American election in which the actual voters (men with and without property) instead of the state legislators chose most of the electors for the electoral college, Owen indulged his penchant for being near public figures. He met candidates John Quincy Adams, who won in a House of Representatives runoff, and General Andrew Jackson, whose championing of the interests of farmers, laborers, and small entrepreneurs brought him and his new Democratic Party to power in the next election in 1828.[50] During this time of domestic tranquility and an economic downturn from 1819 to 1824 that signaled the beginning of modern business cycles, Americans began to return to their interest in ways to improve their lives and to bring their institutions into line with their ideals.[51] Many reform crusades competed for the attention of the American conscience. Voices were raised for temperance, peace, education, the poor, the handicapped, the insane, the slaves, and the rights of women and laborers.[52] But before they could be heard in this early nineteenth-century enactment of the periodic American reform drama, Owen stood at center stage with a unique opportunity to recite

DONALD E. PITZER

and demonstrate a panacea calculated to transform the human character and condition in a planned community environment.

The extent to which Owen as the "Social Father" met this challenge defines the degree to which communitarian socialism in Owenite form affected the direction of American social history. With only a limited knowledge of American society, he exploited certain advantages as the exponent of the first non-sectarian community scheme in America. Unfortunately, in at least three respects he carried his least productive approaches to reform in Europe into the quite different American arena, where they became injurious to his movement. Unnecessary criticism, wasted time, and communal dysfunction resulted. First, Owen continued to indulge in the same pleasure in attacking established religion that had driven away even his reform-minded business partners. Seemingly oblivious to the religious freedom and separation of church and state secured for the new nation during the American revolutionary era, he chose to attack the faith of others rather than to assert his religious privilege of gaining a legitimate following for his own unorthodox rational religion. In this regard he repeated the anachronism of the German Separatist immigrants who began settling Zoar, Ohio, in 1817. When they drew up their communal Articles of Association in 1819, they named themselves the Society of Separatists of Zoar regardless of the fact that Ohio had never had an established church. As we have seen, Owen's 1826 Fourth of July speech in New Harmony emphasized his tendency to fight rearguard actions with ghosts from past times and places. Instead of extolling the blessings of American religious toleration or using the occasion to enumerate the advantages of rationalism, he could only blast organized religion.

In 1828, a year after New Harmony ceased to be an Owenite community, its apostle of rationalism continued baiting the Christian clergy. From New Orleans he issued a general challenge for a clergyman to defend the merits of religion in an open debate. The sharp-witted Alexander Campbell, later a co-founder of the Disciples of Christ Church, accepted the challenge. Capacity crowds of 1,200 attended fifteen public sessions in Cincinnati in April 1829. Owen courteously presented his Twelve Laws to disprove Christianity and tried "to Prove That the Principles of All Religions Are Erroneous, and That Their Practice Is Injurious to the Human Race."[53] At the conclusion only four people stood to indicate they found Owen's arguments convincing. Christians interpreted this as an encouraging sign from a region of the country not particularly known for its piety. Owen, knowing that all of his American and British communities begun in the 1820s already had passed out of existence, took the result as a cue to return to England. There, from 1829 to 1834, his adaptive reform movement sought "a fresh approach, using new institutions and agencies."[54] Owen did not return to the United States until 1844. By that time a new generation of reformers had sparked a revival of interest in his communitarian socialism, but not in his religious radicalism.

A second front on which Owen found that events in America had passed him by occurred in the unsuspected area of his dogged attachment to rationalist Enlightenment concepts regarding a science of society. This connection both gained and lost his movement devotees in the United States. His appeal to familiar Enlightenment themes placed him in the American tradition of Benjamin Franklin, John Adams, Thomas Jefferson, Thomas Paine, Joel Barlow, and Elihu Palmer. This helped attract a few leading persons to New Harmony, such as William Maclure, teacher Paul Brown, and feminist Frances Wright, who already adhered to natural rights, environmental determinism, deism, and the rights of women. However, Owen's appeal to Enlightenment thought proved to be a liability when attempting to attract independent Jeffersonian farmers. They had shelved deism and adopted the revivalism and evangelicalism that flowed from the powerful emotions of the camp meetings of the Second Great Awakening on the frontier since the turn of the century. This same revival of religion brought the Shakers to Kentucky, Ohio, and Indiana. Thus, as Harrison concludes, "When contemporaries charged Owenites with infidelity the condemnation implied that they were not only godless but also out of date."[55]

Owen's third difficulty in America was related to the second. Whenever he had to choose whether to direct his message to the upper or lower classes, he chose the upper as he always had in Britain. He continued to believe, although all his European experience indicated the contrary, that the wealthy and politically powerful would bless his designs with their philanthropy and legislation. Although between 1824 and 1829 he laid his plans before many individual legislators and twice in speeches in the Hall of Representatives in the Capitol, he neither requested nor received any specific legislation or funding. If William Maclure, by then the "Father of American Geology," had not become his investment partner in New Harmony and brought scientists and educators there at his own expense from Philadelphia, Owen's attention to potential philanthropists would have paid no dividends either. Yet Owen's first three and one-half weeks in America before heading west on November 28 to inspect New Harmony can only be described as a triumphal entry. Few other visitors to the United States have experienced such a grand reception. In New York, Philadelphia, and Washington, D.C., his reputation as one of Britain's wealthiest industrialists and the benevolent manager of the New Lanark mills won him invitations not only from President Monroe, Secretary of State Adams, John C. Calhoun, and other congressmen, but also to dinners where

DONALD E. PITZER

notable industrialists, aristocrats, and state officials welcomed him and heard his message. Jeremiah Thompson, who started the first line of transatlantic packets, held a dinner in Owen's honor attended by mercantile and shipping magnates. Dinner invitations came from the New York governor, Joseph Yates, and governor-elect, DeWitt Clinton.[56]

Upper-class reformers and intellectuals in New York and Philadelphia, part of a small but growing band of Owen enthusiasts, received him as the practical guide to a new moral age. The New York Society for Promoting Communities welcomed him the day he arrived in America. This organization, founded in 1820, had printed parts of his *A New View of Society* in 1822 along with John Melish's account of the Harmony Society. Such groups already concerned about social justice and anxious to imitate Harmonist and Shaker communal success in nonsectarian forms found in Owen's systematic theory and charismatic leadership the final ingredients needed to inspire communal experimentation patterned after his, Charles Fourier's, Etienne Cabet's, and others' schemes in the next three decades.[57] Owen's ideas had filtered through since 1817 in comments on his writings by major British reviews. An Owenite society soon formed in Philadelphia after segments of his *A New View of Society* made their American debut that same year in the town's Jeffersonian newspaper, *Aurora*. Members of this society, such as former druggist John Speakman and mineralogist Dr. Gerard Troost, also belonged to the Academy of Natural Sciences of Philadelphia, of which geologist-reformer William Maclure was president. Scientists and educators from these two organizations and from Maclure's Pestalozzian school whom Owen first met at this time became the most important members from the educated class in America to take up residence in New Harmony.

Madame Marie Duclos Fretageot, assistant in Maclure's school in Paris, brought an account of Owen's educational ideas with her when she came to direct Maclure's Philadelphia school in 1821. She apparently introduced academy scientists to the educational and communitarian sides of Owenism. Speakman, Troost, and other academy members projected a community by the fall of 1823 but, after meeting the magnetic Mr. Owen, decided to join his grander effort in New Harmony. Maclure showed some interest in the educational implications of a Philadelphia community project and had been favorably impressed by his visit with Owen in New Lanark in the summer of 1824. Nevertheless, it took the optimistic urging of Fretageot and a personal visit from Owen in Philadelphia in November 1825 to convince the wealthy former merchant that the New Harmony venture held enough promise to warrant the commitment of his considerable financial, educational, and scientific resources.[58] In the winter of 1825–26 Maclure and Owen would lead a Boatload of Knowledge from Pittsburgh to New Harmony on the Ohio and Wabash Rivers. Aboard the keelboat commissioned by Maclure as the *Philanthropist* were Philadelphia's finest Pestalozzian educators Marie Fretageot and William S. Phiquepal and elite naturalists Thomas Say and Charles-Alexandre Lesueur from the academy.[59]

Not until 1825 when he needed recruits from the ranks of the working classes to populate his experimental community in the backwoods did Robert Owen, this cultivator of America's most influential leaders, find himself compelled to turn his attention toward its common people. Only then, if ever, did he start to appreciate the power beginning to accumulate in their hands. He never seems to have pondered why, in their revolutionary overthrow of British royalty, the Americans rejected both nobility and aristocratic privilege with the denial of all use of hereditary titles. He never came to grips with the fact that Jeffersonian and Jacksonian democracy were bestowing voting, officeholding, and economic rights on adult, white, propertyless males. He seems never to have perceived the depths of the leveling process in religion sparked by the Second Great Awakening after 1795 that continued to affect the upland southerners and backwoodsmen who joined New Harmony. The more aristocratic Calvinistic doctrine that only a small number of "the elect" would be saved melted from the fiery emotion of the frontier camp meetings into the more egalitarian concept of "whosoever will may be saved." In this way the same equalizing of social rank and accumulation of political and economic power in the hands of the masses of people implied by Jeffersonian, and especially Jacksonian, democracy found expression in the very essence of religion on the American frontier. Owen, his communitarian plan, and his animosity toward religion were ambushed in the backcountry by this rising importance of the common people in America. In New Harmony he discovered he could not create a community of equality that implied imposing the cultural and living standards of eastern seaboard reformers, educators, and scientists of "the better sort" on the western farmers, mechanics, laborers, and artisans of "the common sort."[60] His early nightmares about mixing individuals of differing class, sect, and party in the same utopian village came true. Disdain for others grew at both ends of New Harmony's social ladder. Sarah Pears, among those who migrated from Philadelphia, exclaimed, "Oh, if you could see some of the rough uncouth creatures here, I think you would find it hard to look on them in the light of brothers and sisters. . . . I am sure I cannot in sincerity look upon these as equals."[61]

Yet in refusing to assume a position of deference, insignificance, or inferiority, the working classes in New Harmony, unlike those in New Lanark, held the key to the very survival of Owen's experiment. The farmers and mechanics, who objected to the lower exchange values placed on their labors at the communal store, harbored a resentment that must be calculated into the division and collapse of the Owenite community.[62] They preferred their own common music, dances, foods, drink, table manners, courting rituals, and speech to the sophisticated standards set for them by Owen, Maclure, and their eastern colleagues. In an act of near defiance the commoners even refused to don the official dress of New Harmony, considering it "uppity."[63] Owen miscalculated his need for the consent of the common people as the foundation for his communal experiment as badly as the aristocratic Federalist Party, which died in 1820, had misjudged its need for political support from the common man in an emerging democracy.

Vital lessons from American communitarian experience also evaded Owen's notice. This is true despite his long acquaintance with the use of communal arrangements by sectarian movements on these shores, and even though he paused twice during his whirlwind tour of the east for his first exposure to functioning utopian villages. He spent several hours with the Shakers at Niskayuna (Watervliet) near Albany, New York, on November 11, 1824, and stayed overnight with the Harmonists at their partly built third town of Economy north of Pittsburgh on the Ohio River on December 4 and 5.[64] If the British factory town had provided the prototype for Owen's idea of building entire new communities to redeem the working classes and shape human character, the economic success of the communally organized settlements of the Shakers of Ann Lee and the Harmonists of George Rapp supplied the proof that such communities could be practical. For a decade Owen had monitored their progress through reports from America. By 1815 he knew of Rapp's German radical Pietistic sect, the Harmony Society from Württemberg, that after 1804 had built Harmony in Beaver County, Pennsylvania, and had moved in 1814 to erect a "New Harmony" in the Northwest Territory on the Wabash River.[65] In 1816 the Philadelphia Quaker W. S. Warder gave Owen direct information on the Shakers that he printed in 1817 as *A Brief Sketch of the Religious Society of People Called Shakers*. Owen's Edinburgh friend George Courtauld kept him informed about both Harmonist progress and the rapid western expansion of the Shaker faith and communities. By 1820 the secular reformer of New Lanark was corresponding directly with the sectarian Father Rapp concerning the operation of his sizable community efforts.[66]

Before coming to America Robert Owen recognized that the cohesive force binding the Harmonist and Shaker communities together consisted of radical religious doctrines and peculiar practices, such as celibacy, that he condemned. Nonetheless, he overlooked the historical clue regarding the high level of commitment necessary to establish and maintain any voluntary community based on the discipline of sharing goods in common.[67] Sectarian leaders could call on the scriptural example of the early Christians using community of property (if only temporarily as a survival technique: Acts 2:44, 45, and 4:32–35) and insist that believers' salvation depended on their obedience to divinely ordained, authoritarian leadership. Owen did not have these advantages. In his advocacy of enlightenment, rationalism, and freedom of thought he missed the point that these desired elements could militate against a unified community unless members became strongly committed to a larger, well-defined, and well-understood central purpose. In New Harmony he neither screened the incoming residents nor ensured their commitment to his nebulous utopian dream by systematic indoctrination. He placed his faith in a progressive educational program to instruct the rising generation in the principles of the New Moral World. However, while he spent all but seven months of the two years New Harmony endured as an Owenite village preaching his utopian gospel elsewhere, the town suffered from rancorous debates that produced seven reorganizations and numerous desertions and divisions.

At Niskayuna and Economy Owen, his second son, William, and traveling companion Donald Macdonald viewed two separate religious movements well into the process of developmental communalism. The secular Owenite movement was just entering this process. Owen's attraction to the generic social mechanism of communal structuring sprang from its nonviolent, experimental, and utopian promise. By the time he visited the Shakers and Harmonists, he already had worked out educational, social, and even architectural plans for his ideal Agricultural and Manufacturing Villages of Unity and Mutual Co-operation. By contrast, the Shakers, Harmonists, Moravians, Hutterites, and other sectarians had been driven to the communal method first out of necessity for survival rather than by utopian preplanning of model communities. They combined their assets and labor and, by trial and error, found ways to make their vows to live communally work. Ann Lee had, in fact, died three years before her disciples first resorted to communalism in 1787 at New Lebanon, New York, the same year Niskayuna was founded. George Rapp, with whom Owen discussed the workings of his communal society and the prospects for the formation of character at Economy, had led his immigrant disciples into communal living in 1805 to save the group from being dispersed to seek individual employment.

By the time Owen visited the disciples of Ann Lee and Father Rapp, communal sharing was no longer a necessity for their economic survival, but its discipline had become a tenet of faith that was beginning to cause the desertions and schisms that helped sap the lifeblood from their very movements.

DONALD E. PITZER

Owen never permitted the communal method, which he witnessed in full operation at Niskayuna and Economy, to strangle his own movement. As he sailed down the icy Ohio River after visiting Economy to inspect New Harmony for his own experiment, he also departed from the sectarian example in this respect. In Indiana he might be frustrated by having his educational and social plans only partly realized, his intentions for economic sharing within the community left mostly undefined, and his grand architectural design for a model town unbuilt. Yet he would keep his system flexible and refuse to become a doctrinaire communitarian to the detriment of his broader social reform goals. Only the most radical individuals he attracted to his utopian village advocated complete communism like that of the Shakers and the Harmonists. Paul Brown became the most vocal and caustic critic of Owen's aristocratic paternalism and helped ruin any chance of harmony in New Harmony.[68] Owen never converted his socialistic town into a commune despite his own attacks on private property.

When the mill owner from Scotland reached New Harmony on December 17, 1824, he had virtually made up his mind to purchase the ready-made town. In a scant eighteen days he inspected the village and visited the nearby English settlement of Morris Birkbeck in Albion, Illinois, across the Wabash. Then, on January 3, 1825, he and Frederick Rapp, George's adopted son, made the $135,000 deal. Already famous as a Harmonist communal village, New Harmony rapidly overflowed with the new residents attracted by Owen's open invitation to join without any membership requirements. Its 180 buildings included dwellings and community houses for 800 people, two churches, four mills, numerous shops, a textile factory, a tanyard, distilleries, and a brewery. These plus vineyards, orchards, and 2,000 acres under cultivation would do just fine as Owen's staging area for a "preliminary society"— the one to be moved into the ideal quadrangular town Owen promised to build on his 20,000-acre estate where the New Moral World would be fully realized. By April he had optimistically declared, "The United States but particularly the States west of the Allegheny Mountains have been prepared in the most remarkable manner for the New System. The principle of union and cooperation . . . is now universally admitted to be far superior to the individual selfish system and all seem prepared . . . to give up the latter and adopt the former. In fact the whole of this country is ready to commence a new empire upon the principle of public property and to discard private property."[69]

The Owenites did not totally abandon private property or revolutionize human nature in their two-and-a-half-year communal experiment in New Harmony. However, they did start enough progressive and New Moral World enterprises in education, science, and communal experimentation to affect positively American cultural, economic, and social history and to raise a monument to Owen, Maclure, and Fretageot. Owen knew that recruiting educators, scientists, and cultured individuals was critical to executing his utopian plan. He announced with delight in his first New Harmony speech on January 12, 1826, that those about to arrive on the keelboat *Philanthropist* represented "more *learning* than ever was before contained in a boat," not "Latin and Greek & other languages but real substantial knowledge."[70] Known as the Boatload of Knowledge from that day on, it was laden with Pestalozzian teachers, physical scientists, musicians, and artists with their patron, Maclure.[71] It was "in truth one of the significant intellectual migrations of history. It represented the transfer to New Harmony—farther west than any existing American college—of a group of educational and scientific enterprises that had been notable features of the cultural life of Philadelphia."[72] Along with Pestalozzian instructors such as Joseph and Eloisa Buss Neef and scientists such as John Speakman and Gerard Troost who preceded or followed them, the boatloaders (including Maclure, Lesueur, Say, Fretageot, and Phiquepal) made frontier New Harmony an educational and scientific center for decades.

Owen's first speech in New Harmony also indicated that the boatload included "some of the ablest instructors of youth that c[oul]d be found in the U.S. or perhaps in the world." Residents concluded that "in [New] Harmony there will be the best Library & the best School in the United States."[73] An infant school, higher school, and School of Industry, complemented by lectures, libraries, and museums for adults, came close to proving them right. Maclure organized and directed this unprecedented educational program with a passion for education reform as deep as Owen's. Soon, however, their differing educational and social philosophies led to the disruption of the utopian communal experiment. Until then the Neefs, Fretageot, and Phiquepal supervised the three schools. Conchologist Thomas Say, editor of the *Disseminator*, served as a consultant for Fretageot, who directed the system during Maclure's long absences.[74] When Maclure left permanently in 1828 after the socialistic arrangements dissolved, Marie Fretageot oversaw the schools with Maclure's letters, mostly from Europe and Mexico, for guidance until her own departure in 1831.[75]

The school for infants ages two to five replicated Owen's in New Lanark. It may have been the earliest in the United States. As a boarding school it housed more than 100 children in the former Harmonist Community House No. 2, fulfilling Owen's plan of shielding them from the unwanted negative influence of their parents and families. Attempting a combination of Owenite

DONALD E. PITZER

and Pestalozzian methods, Marie Fretageot and Eloisa Buss Neef taught them to share communally, live humanely, and think freely.[76]

The higher school for six- to twelve-year-olds reflected Maclure's and Owen's conviction that children should be given mostly practical rather than classical instruction. Classes concentrated on mathematics, science, mechanics, language, writing, art, music, and gymnastics. All the scientists gave classroom instruction as well as public lectures for adults on mineralogy, chemistry, zoology, and natural history. Joseph Neef was the higher school principal and his children, Victor and Louisa, teachers. Early in 1826 Maclure advertised the higher and industrial schools in Benjamin Silliman's *American Journal of Science and Arts*, attracting students from as far away as New York and Philadelphia.

The School of Industry introduced the trade school to the United States.[77] This implemented Maclure's idea that each child should learn a useful trade. In a daily "co-op" arrangement more than eighty students from the higher school, nearly all boys, gained occupational skills. William Phiquepal taught printing, and John Beal, another boatloader, instructed in carpentry. Other craftsmen gave instruction in everything from farming, woodturning, blacksmithing, shoemaking, and hatmaking to taxidermy, joining, and wheelwrighting. Although the community professed gender equality, girls studied only the traditional homemaking arts of sewing, cooking, dressmaking, and millinery as taught by women of New Harmony. Maclure planned for the sale of products from the industrial school to pay for all the town's educational programs as well as the $100 annual fees of students from outside. Although this goal was never reached, the higher school and School of Industry did fulfill his dream of linking teaching to research and publication. New Harmony students, perhaps like no others in early America, studied with working scholars whose groundbreaking research they helped publish as the curriculum focused increasingly on drawing, engraving, and printing. By 1840, when the School of Industry closed, they had helped make 1,300 copperplates and printed works of New Harmony and other scientists in the vanguard of ichthyology, conchology, and geology.[78] They also assisted in the production of Maclure's periodical *The Disseminator of Useful Knowledge*, published in town from 1828 to 1841, and his *Opinions on Various Subjects* from 1831 to 1838.

Ironically, controversy over the nature of instruction flawed the New Harmony educational system and helped to destroy the community.[79] Owen wanted ideological indoctrination resulting in the formation of character. This implied uniformity imposed on passive children within a controlled communal setting. Maclure stressed involving children in the learning process and developing their critical intelligence in a freer environment compatible with society at large. With Maclure in charge of New Harmony's schools and adult education, the program naturally emphasized his, rather than Owen's, philosophy of education and social reform.[80] Maclure thought all peoples divided into two classes, productive laborers and nonproductive governors. Knowledge, he argued, separates the two, giving power and property to a few. To equalize power and property, he advocated setting working people free through ready access to progressive schools and free public libraries. Enamored of the Pestalozzian method of teaching by experiences aimed at students' level of maturation, Maclure visited Pestalozzi's institute at Yverdon, Switzerland, six times after 1805. He funded Pestalozzian schools in Paris and Spain, brought Joseph Neef from Paris to start the first American school of this type near Philadelphia in 1809, and made Pestalozzian methods paramount in the New Harmony schools. Bitterness over educational and economic arrangements marked the deteriorating relationship of Owen and Maclure. Owen publicly blamed Maclure at a town meeting in August 1826 for the fact that their experiment had failed to gel its disparate members into a harmonious community.[81] He charged that Maclure had not given the children of all parents equal access to all the educators and had defeated the communitarian goals by granting children a creative role in classes rather than just immersing them in the concepts of the New Moral World. Education, which Owen had praised as the centerpiece of New Harmony in his first speech to the residents in 1825, became his main reason to explain its collapse in his last address on May 6, 1827. He laid all the problems at the feet of Maclure and the teachers he had earlier praised. To Owen's mind, "If the schools had been in full operation, upon the very superior plan which I had been led to expect, so as to convince the parents . . . of the benefits which their children would immediately derive from the system, it would have been, I think, practicable, . . . to have succeeded in amalgamating the whole into a Community."[82]

Actually, New Harmony's school system and the libraries created from Maclure's interest in making knowledge accessible to men who worked with their hands became the longest-lasting social institutions created by the Owenite community. One hundred sixty workingmen's libraries, 144 in Indiana and 16 in Illinois, eventually received $500 each from assets set aside in Maclure's will for this purpose.[83] His assistance in forming the New Harmony Workingmen's Institute in 1838 made it the model for those founded after his death in 1840. The Workingmen's Institute, the only one of the 160 to survive to the present, is a living link to the historic utopian community, a treasure trove of Owenite archival material and Indiana's oldest continuously functioning library. Taken together the Maclure libraries stimulated the intellectual development of Indiana and southern Illinois, provided the basic collections for later libraries, initiated the tradition of a free public library system, and set a precedent for the Carnegie libraries of the twentieth century.[84] Furthermore, the statewide system of tuition-free public schools mandated in Indiana's second constitution in 1851 bore the imprint of Maclure's and Owen's concerns for an educated public. Owen's son Robert Dale, deeply affected by his New Harmony experience, insisted on this provision as a framer of the new constitution and later helped initiate it as a state legislator.

The scientific emphasis that Maclure, Say, Lesueur, and others brought to New Harmony made the village a focus of research in the natural sciences in community days and for decades thereafter. Geology, in which Maclure was then the most noted authority in America, became the chief focus. Dutch geologist Gerard Troost both taught and explored. Owen's sons David Dale and Richard were immediately attracted to this exciting field when they arrived in 1828. Geological research was in the first stages of challenging the older religious and scientific concepts about the age of the earth and of revealing the subsurface resources that promised to bring the industrial age to the United States. In 1837 David Dale did the first state-commissioned geological survey of Indiana and was appointed geologist by the federal government.[85] New Harmony became the base of regional surveys for the government from 1837 to 1856, long before the organization of the United States Geological Survey in 1876. David Dale led one geological expedition that surveyed the present lands of Iowa, Wisconsin, Minnesota, and northern Illinois to identify valuable mineral deposits before the government sold any public domain. The geological training and work of David Dale, his brother Richard, and others attracted to Maclure's hub in New Harmony opened the Midwest to industrialization. David Dale became state geologist for Kentucky from 1854 to 1857, for Arkansas from 1857 to 1859, and for Indiana from 1859 until he died in 1860. Richard Owen succeeded David Dale as Indiana state geologist, became a professor of natural science at Indiana University from 1864 to 1879, and was selected first president of Purdue University. Edward T. Cox, a student in the New Harmony schools of Maclure and Owen, became Indiana state geologist from 1868 until 1880. The five-story Harmonist granary and David Dale Owen laboratory, still prominent features in New Harmony, served as museums, laboratories, and lecture halls. The importance of these research facilities and their use for public instruction was not lost on Robert Dale Owen, who later played a major role in shaping the purpose of the Smithsonian Institution in Washington, D.C. As a member of the House of Representatives, he worked diligently to achieve the congressional action in 1846 that created the Smithsonian as a free, national museum to benefit the entire citizenry.

Finally, New Harmony itself became a monument to its founders as the first socialistic community in America. Its feats and flaws affected nonsectarian communal utopias ever after. Flaws in the communal fabric plagued New Harmony from beginning to end. It suffered from failing to screen members. It prided itself on inviting everyone of all classes to join, then found their harmonious union impossible. Hypocritically, it barred African Americans, although, to many, it became a symbol for human rights, racial equality, and an end to slavery. Frances Wright, one of the most outspoken women on behalf of emancipation and women's rights in the nineteenth century, devoted her New Harmony Fourth of July address in 1828 to an attack on slavery.[86] Two years earlier she had become a pioneer among those who employed the communal method to free, protect, and benefit thousands of slaves in at least eighteen settlements before the Civil War.[87] Her community of Nashoba, near Memphis, Tennessee, operated from 1826 to 1830 in the cause of freedom and racial equality.[88] Robert Dale Owen, whose activism and government service helped enhance New Harmony's liberal reputation, urged President Lincoln to issue his Emancipation Proclamation. In 1862 Robert Dale's letters to Lincoln, Secretary of War Edwin M. Stanton, and Secretary of the Treasury Salmon P. Chase urging emancipation as a war measure to bring peace were widely circulated in the press.[89]

Although New Harmony also became a symbol for equality of the sexes, its women found not only new freedoms but also increased demands on their timeworn domestic services. All women in Owen's village were promised equality of social and civil rights, but life could be best for single young women who came to attend school or to escape conditions back home. New Harmony offered weekly dances and concerts attended by liberal and interesting young men. Hannah Fisher Price, although married, testified that "there are many youth of both sexes that are very happy in the variety of each other."[90] Single women could find menial tasks in kitchens and barns fair trade-offs for such opportunities. Many married women in New Harmony and other Owenite communities, especially those from working-class backgrounds, also may have felt that their lot was bettered by the move, although they left little written record. However, married women from cultured families in the east and those who accompanied husbands seeking a new start in life often felt betrayed by false promises of equality that brought them mostly demeaning labor.[91] Owen rejected the idea of property in people, including spouses and offspring. Yet the traditional view of gender roles seemed to permeate the thinking of New Harmony's male leaders. Domestic chores became

DONALD E. PITZER

the exclusive and expected duty of women despite the guarantee of equal rights in New Harmony's reorganization as the Community of Equality in 1826. Married women often came to be thought of as "community wives" who "belonged" to the community. Therefore their obligations to their own households stretched into tiresome cooking, sewing, and cleaning for the entire village. Since one objective of Owen's communal egalitarianism was to have the community assume many of the functions of the home, women also were in jeopardy of losing their one, time-honored sphere of influence. These circumstances and the outright rebellion of certain wives may suggest that the promise of gender equality was broken, resulting in "the creation of a 'woman problem' that consumed the Owenite communities and helped to lead to their early demises."[92]

Yet New Harmony and its Owenites established a solid record in the vanguard of advocating women's rights. The leading feminist of the day, Frances Wright, found Owen's community a welcome place for repeated visits. As noted earlier, New Harmony adopted an official costume for women. Loose-fitting, ankle-length pantaloons under a knee-length or longer skirt gave increased freedom of movement.[93] This style was so radical it drew public criticism then and decades later when it appeared again on Amelia Bloomer and the women of communal Oneida. The *Illinois Gazette*, printed at nearby Shawnee-Town, jibbed,

> In beauty there's something to hide and reveal,
> There's a thing which we decency call;
> The old system ladies display a great deal,
> But the new system ladies—show all.[94]

In the community system, Owen promised personal happiness in which the fear, frustration, and sexual tyranny of the private family would cease. The ideal society would provide a wider selection of potential mates, early marriage, an end to unwanted pregnancies, and divorce for unhappy unions. Owen was involved in the birth control movement in Britain as early as 1823, and his son Robert Dale published a pioneering tract in New York in 1830 titled *Moral Physiology*.[95] Owen's denunciation of traditional marriage in his New Harmony Fourth of July address in 1826 and the community's sanction of divorce and remarriage elicited untrue charges of sexual infidelity. One newspaper wrote that "it would be no breach of charity, to class them all with whores and whoremongers, nor to say that the whole group will constitute one great brothel."[96]

If, despite the ways New Harmony stood for gender equality, discontent among its married women contributed to its downfall, Owen's failures in community building contributed much more. The utopian dreamer failed in areas crucial to all long-lasting communal societies. He did not unite all members in an inspiring purpose, clearly define or enforce members' financial commitment, develop a self-sustaining economic base, or institute a stable form of governance. Owen, the propagandizer for the New Moral World, never consistently assumed the practical role of Owen the on-site, charismatic leader and manager at New Harmony. He left his son William and others in charge as both he and Maclure traveled nearly as many months as they stayed in town during its two years as a planned community. Owen waited for more than a year after purchasing the town to define the financial obligations of residents beyond his first offer that they could live in the former Harmonist buildings and receive supplies from the community store if they donated their labor. In the meantime many who quickly overflowed the town's dwellings proved to be unskilled or simply freeloaders. Unlike George Rapp, whose devoted disciples built New Harmony and made it prosper in the wilderness, Owen failed to motivate his diverse followers sufficiently to make the former Harmonist fields and factories profitable, despite real efforts on his part. He introduced "labor notes" based on hours worked as a medium of exchange. This "time money" approach did little to improve production, but it deeply impressed resident Josiah Warren, who later began the time store cooperative movement and started its individualistic (rather than socialistic) communities of Equity and Utopia in Ohio and Modern Times in New York (see Appendix). Owen also revived his New Lanark "silent monitor" device. Superintendents made weekly reports that could be used in public meetings to identify those who worked least.[97] In reality, Owen's philanthropic underwriting of the New Harmony experiment at a cost of some $200,000 of his $250,000 fortune may have done most to kill worker initiative.[98]

Added to these problems, Owen could not solve the riddle of bringing his unruly flock together under a single governing instrument for more than a few months. Disagreements with his partner as well as public meetings permitting freedom of speech and open discussion, so prized by the community, often led to acrimonious debates and frequent reorganizations. Seven different arrangements were devised to govern Owenite New Harmony during its brief two-year existence. It was unified in the Preliminary Society beginning in May 1825, then in a Community of Equality during January and February of 1826. Thereafter, small groups, such as Macluria (made up of farmers) and Feiba-Peveli (composed of English settlers from Illinois), began splitting off under arrangements to use New Harmony land. In May 1826 the most important splintering occurred when Maclure, who wished to distance himself from Owen, recommended that separate, cooperating communities be

Robert Owen introduced labor notes, or "time money," as a medium of exchange in a failed attempt to motivate laborers in New Harmony. Josiah Warren, who opened a Time Store in New Harmony, later used such labor notes in his more individualistic communities of Equity and Utopia in Ohio and Modern Times in New York. (From Donald F. Carmony and Josephine M. Elliott, "New Harmony, Indiana: Robert Owen's Seedbed for Utopia," *Indiana Magazine of History* 76 [Sept. 1980]: 235.)

formed based on occupations. Maclure then organized his teachers and scientists in a group called the Education Society, while others set up an Agricultural and Pastoral Society and a Mechanic and Manufacturing Society. Relations among these three were never too harmonious; but they were coordinated by a Board of Union, and each paid only for the property it actually used.[99] Owen advocated self-government in Owenite communities, but his suspicion of elections and electioneering amounted to an avoidance of the democratic process. In 1820 he had recommended that governance be carried out "by a committee, composed of all the members of the association between certain ages—for instance, of those between thirty-five and forty-five."[100] The residents of Macluria and Feiba-Peveli used Owen's system. They set up councils of the five eldest members under age sixty-five and under fifty-five, respectively.[101]

Divisions within New Harmony mirrored the deteriorating relationship between Owen and Maclure. When the two sued each other in May 1827 over debts incurred in their financial partnership, Robert Owen's effort to create a working model of the New Moral World, so eloquently praised in William Pelham's "Song No. 1" for the children less than two years before, came to an end.[102] By 1830 twelve of the thirteen other Owenite settlements formed in the 1820s in America and Britain had also dissolved. The Owenites had exhausted the first of their two waves of interest in using the demanding communal method for reform. Many Americans saw these failures, and especially that of Owen's own New Harmony, as proof that only highly disciplined sectarian groups such as the Shakers and the Harmonists could make communalism work. Owenism as a reform movement was far from dead, however. Many other Americans and Britons, especially of the working classes, were willing to listen to its liberal agenda as presented from platforms and presses and carried into effect in conjunction with political parties, labor unions, cooperatives, and legislatures. As New Harmony and Nashoba ceased to be centers of communal activity, Robert Dale Owen and Frances Wright moved to New York to carry forward the reform crusade. They converted *The New-Harmony Gazette* into *The Free Enquirer* and lectured in their Hall of Science for women's rights, secularism, and free public boarding schools under the guardianship of the state.[103]

Arthur Bestor describes the developmental process that was taking Owenism beyond its early communal phase in this way: "The activities of the free enquirers in New York form no real part of the history of communitarianism. They represent, in fact, a translation of Owenite social radicalism from the language of communitarian experiment into the different language of gradual reform." Significantly, as he points out, "This transfer is important in the history of the other [American reform] movements, for into many of them it infused certain elements from Owen's wide-ranging view of society."[104] John F. C. Harrison notes, "The Owenites at this stage did not abandon their communitarian goals, but there was, not surprisingly, some disillusionment with the methods which had been employed to realize the new moral world. A fresh approach, using new institutions and agencies, seemed to be called for, and the initiative did not need to be confined to the benevolent Mr. Owen."[105] Owenites' attempts to align themselves with emerging workingmen's organizations after 1829 proved far more successful in Britain than in America. Although the free enquirers captured segments of the Working Men's Party of New York on behalf of their public education scheme, this first working-class political movement in America dissolved after the election of 1830. The American Owenites were left without effective institutions to give them leverage before the economic recession of the 1840s helped produce a general communitarian revival in 1843.[106] In Britain, however, rapidly growing working-class institutions became the new agencies through which Owenism sought its objectives. Showing its customary flexibility, "In its attempt to capture the working-class movement [in Britain] Owenism developed along new lines, adapting itself to the demands and interests of artisan leaders."[107]

In total, Owenism and Owenite influence accounted for twenty-nine communities, mostly attempted in two waves during the 1820s and 1840s. Nineteen of these were in the United States, one was in Canada, and nine were in

England, Scotland, Ireland, and Wales. They began with New Harmony in 1825 and ended when Josiah Warren closed his Modern Times settlement on Long Island in 1863. Spread over nearly four decades, these communal utopias introduced progressive educational methods and fostered freedom of thought and scientific inquiry. They decried organized religion as superstitious tyranny, dissolved unhappy marriages, and altered family life with infant schooling and communal child care. In varying degrees at different times and places they set aside private property and discrimination by class, sex, and race. Owen himself gave mixed signals about economic and social equality, never reconciling his own innate paternalism with the ideal of egalitarianism. Beyond benevolent paternalism, education, legislation, and communalism, Owen and his followers alertly responded with new methods and new catchwords as circumstances changed or as the popular imagination became captivated by potent concepts, such as millennialism. Attempting to build whole communities placed a burden on the movement, but Owenites never risked their prime objective of raising the cultural and living standards of the poor and working classes by a total fixation on communalism or any other single reform method. Both within their experimental communities and by propaganda, public meetings, workers' organizations, cooperatives, and political activism in society at large, Owenites helped effect progressive reform. In the United States, tax-supported public schools for both girls and boys, public libraries and museums, women's rights, birth control, liberalization of divorce laws, and freedom for slaves composed part of the Owenite agenda. In Britain, workers' cooperatives and trade unions originated in Owenite activity.

Ten years after Owen died in his hometown of Newtown, Wales, on November 17, 1858, English observer Harriet Martineau wrote that "his peculiar faculties so far fell in with the popular need that he effected much for the progress of society, and has been the cause of many things which will never go by his name."[108] Twenty years following Owen's death, Friedrich Engels, the critic of Owenite utopian and communitarian socialism as a frustration of the coming revolution of the proletariat, conceded that "all social movements, all real advance made in England in the interests of the working class were associated with Owen's name."[109] Today, with numerous Owenite reforms featured in modern society, Owen and Owenism excite continued interest. Robert Owen associations exist in Great Britain and Japan. The famous milltown of New Lanark, Scotland, where Owen began his social experiments, and the village of New Harmony, Indiana, where he and William Maclure sponsored the most prominent Owenite communal venture in America, both flourish as historic restorations with public interpretive programs.

Chronology

1771   Robert Owen is born in Newtown, Montgomeryshire, Wales, on May 14.

1781   Owen's schooling ends and apprenticeship begins.

1790   Owen becomes partner/manager of Chorlton Twist Company, Manchester, England.

1799   Owen and partners acquire mills of David Dale in New Lanark, Scotland. Owen becomes mill manager and marries Dale's daughter, Ann Caroline.

ca. 1810   Owen begins projects of social control and social welfare and infant and adult education in New Lanark.

1812   Owenite movement begins in Owen's propaganda campaign seeking new, reform-minded business partners who will support his educational plans for character formation at New Lanark.

1813   Owen repurchases New Lanark mills with partners interested in his reforms, including Jeremy Bentham, and writes first summary of his theories as *A New View of Society*.

1813–16   Owenism at first unsuccessfully seeks legislative solutions to working-class problems.

1816   Owen starts Institution for the Formation of Character in New Lanark.

1817   Owen first publicly turns from legislative reform to community building as a method his movement will employ to assist the poor and reform society.

1818   Owen corresponds with Shakers and Harmonists about practicality of communal living and visits them when he arrives in America in 1824.

1825   Owen purchases New Harmony, Ind., from Harmony Society of George Rapp on January 3.

Mar. 1825   Frances Wright, antislavery and women's rights advocate, learns communalism from Harmonists who had not yet left New Harmony and gets encouragement from George Flower of Albion, Ill., to use communal living as the means to free slaves in what later becomes her Nashoba community near Memphis, Tenn. (1826–30).

May 1825   Preliminary Society formed in New Harmony as the first of seven Owenite communities founded in America in 1825–26. Between 1825 and the 1860s nineteen Owenite or Owenite-influenced communities exist in the United States, one in Canada, and nine in Britain.

Jan. 1826   "Boatload of Knowledge" brings to New Harmony Owen's partner and geologist William Maclure, Pestalozzian educators Marie Duclos Fretageot and Phiquepal d'Arusmont, naturalists Thomas Say and Charles-Alexandre Lesueur, and Owen's eldest son, Robert Dale Owen.

1826   New Harmony reorganizes four times, once as a Community of Equality, and Owen designates land to permit its disgruntled farmers and English members from Illinois to form two subdivisions named Macluria and Feiba-Peveli.

1827   Owenite New Harmony collapses in April after seven reorganizations in two years fail to solve its internal strife and economic problems. Owen leaves in 1827, but Owenism continues as a social reform movement in America and Britain.

1828   Owen seeks land for a community in Mexico without success.

1828–35   Owenite movement takes literary form in *The Free Enquirer*, edited by Robert Dale Owen and Frances Wright in New York. Former New Harmony residents work with labor and political organizations for tax-supported

               DONALD E. PITZER

1828–41	public schools, public libraries, women's rights, birth control, freedom for slaves, and liberalization of divorce laws.
1828–41	*The Disseminator of Useful Knowledge* is printed in New Harmony as an organ of William Maclure's reform theories.
1829	Owen publicly debates the merits of religion with the Reverend Alexander Campbell in Cincinnati, Ohio.
1834	Owen influences Etienne Cabet in London before Cabet writes *Voyage en Icarie* in 1840.
1836–44	Owen summarizes his social theories in *The Book of the New Moral World*.
1838	Maclure helps create the New Harmony Workingmen's Institute as the first of 160 free libraries he funded in Indiana and Illinois.
1841–42	A revival of Owenism in America is expressed in *The Herald of the New Moral World and Millennial Harbinger* and formation of new communities.
1844	Owen visits communal groups in America during renewed interest in his ideas.
1847	Etienne Cabet confers with Owen in London before first Icarians leave for Texas.
1857–58	Owen publishes his autobiography, *The Life of Robert Owen*, in two volumes.
1858	Owen dies in his birthplace of Newtown, Wales, on November 17.

The Owenite movement continued in America as agitation for women's rights, public education, and emancipation of slaves, and in Britain as the beginnings of the cooperative and trade union movements.

Notes

1. As the socialistic, nonsectarian Owenite movement entered its communal phase, New Harmony became the first of no fewer than nineteen communities its adherents attempted in America, ten avowedly Owenite and the others strongly influenced by Owenite ideas. Nine Owenite communities followed in Britain, the last ending in 1855. See list in Appendix and in Arthur Bestor Jr., *Backwoods Utopias: The Sectarian Origins and the Owenite Phase of Communitarian Socialism in America, 1663–1829* (Philadelphia: University of Pennsylvania Press, 1950; 2d enl. ed., 1970), 235–43. Also see John F. C. Harrison, *Quest for the New Moral World: Robert Owen and the Owenites in Britain and America* (New York: Scribner's, 1969), 163. At least one known nonsectarian group used collective living in the United States before the Owenites of New Harmony. William Bullard led a few families in organizing a joint-stock arrangement akin to the Fourierist plan and known as The Union to settle on land north of present Potsdam in St. Lawrence County, New York, from 1804 to 1810. See Samuel W. Durant and Henry Peirce, *History of St. Lawrence County, New York* (Philadelphia: L. H. Everts, 1878), 238–39.

2. *New-Harmony Gazette*, October 1, 1825, 1, 8. New Harmony was also referred to as Harmony at that time.

3. The best and final summary of Owen's utopian thought and plans appeared in his *Book of the New Moral World* (London: Home Colonization Society, 1836–44; reprint, New York: Augustus M. Kelley, 1970), and as vol. 3 of the first comprehensive edition of all Owen's major writings in Gregory Claeys, ed., *The Works of Robert Owen*, 4 vols. (London: Pickering and Chatto, 1993).

4. The only narrative source for Owen's early life is his own two-volume *The Life of Robert Owen. Written by Himself. With Selections From His Writings and Correspondence*

(London: Effingham Wilson, 1857–58; reprint, New York: Augustus M. Kelley, 1967). The standard biographies are Frank Podmore, *Robert Owen, a Biography* (London: Allen and Unwin, 1906, 1923); G. D. H. Cole, *The Life of Robert Owen*, 2d ed. (New York: Macmillan, 1930); and Margaret Cole, *Robert Owen of New Lanark, 1771–1858* (London: Batchworth, 1953).

5. Owen, *Life of Robert Owen*, 1:13.

6. As printed in the *New-Harmony Gazette*, July 12, 1826, and reprinted in Donald E. Pitzer and Josephine M. Elliott, *New Harmony's Fourth of July Tradition* (New Harmony, Ind.: Raintree, 1976), 9–13.

7. Owen, *Book of the New Moral World*, pt. 4, 1.

8. Ibid., pt. 1, 69–70; pt. 4, 1–62.

9. *A Brief Sketch of the Religious Society of People Called Shakers* (1817), as described in 1816 to Owen by Philadelphia Quaker W. S. Warder and reprinted in Owen, *Life of Robert Owen*, 1:145–54; Harrison, *Quest for the New Moral World*, 99, 100.

10. Harrison, *Quest for the New Moral World*, 52.

11. See John F. C. Harrison, "Robert Owen's Quest for the New Moral World in America," and Robert G. Clouse, "Robert Owen and the Millennialist Tradition," in *Robert Owen's American Legacy*, ed. Donald E. Pitzer (Indianapolis: Indiana Historical Society, 1972), 33, 42–55.

12. Harrison, *Quest for the New Moral World*, 159.

13. The most extensive treatments of Owen's New Lanark reforms and the resulting occasional trouble with workers and residents appear in Ian Donnachie and George Hewitt, *Historic New Lanark: The Dale and Owen Industrial Community since 1785* (Edinburgh: University of Edinburgh Press, 1993); Anne Taylor, *Visions of Harmony: A Study in Nineteenth-Century Millenarianism* (New York: Oxford University Press, 1987); Bestor, *Backwoods Utopias*; and Harrison, *Quest for the New Moral World*.

14. Donnachie and Hewitt, *Historic New Lanark*, 97–107.

15. Arthur E. Bestor Jr., "The Evolution of the Socialist Vocabulary," *Journal of the History of Ideas* 9 (June 1948): 277.

16. Bestor, *Backwoods Utopias*, 64–66.

17. Donnachie and Hewitt, *Historic New Lanark*, 71; Harrison, *Quest for the New Moral World*, 37, 41, 49, 50, 63, 68, 75, 76, 135; Taylor, *Visions of Harmony*, 65, 66.

18. "Fourth Letter," September 6, 1817, in Owen, *Life of Robert Owen*, 1:119, 120.

19. "Address . . . on Wednesday, the 27th April, 1825, in the Hall of New-Harmony," *New-Harmony Gazette*, October 1, 1825.

20. William Maclure to Marie Fretageot, Louisville, Ky., September 25, 1826, quoted in Arthur Bestor Jr., ed., *Education and Reform at New Harmony*, Indiana Historical Society Publications, vol. 15 (Indianapolis: Indiana Historical Society, 1948), 371. In his *America's Utopian Experiments: Communal Havens from Long-Wave Crises* (Hanover, N.H.: University Press of New England, 1992), 56–58, Brian J. L. Berry argues that working-class Americans were drawn to Owenite communities during a primary economic trough in the 1820s and a "deflationary depression" in the 1840s.

21. See the drawing of the proposed Agricultural and Manufacturing Villages of Unity and Mutual Co-operation in Owen's third edition of his *A New View of Society* (London: n.p., 1817). Stedman Whitwell's drawing and description of a scale model are in *Description of an Architectural Model from a design by Stedman Whitwell, Esq. for a Community upon a Principle of United Interests as Advocated by Robert Owen, Esq.* (London: Hurst Chance, 1830; reprinted in Kenneth E. Carpenter, advisory ed., *Cooperative Communities: Plans and Descriptions* (New York: Arno, 1972). See also the illustration and narrative on Owen's

model village in Donald F. Carmony and Josephine M. Elliott, "New Harmony, Indiana: Robert Owen's Seedbed for Utopia," *Indiana Magazine of History* 76 (September 1980): 200–202.

22. Bestor, *Backwoods Utopias*, 129.

23. Charles Sealsfield, *The Americans As They Are* (London: Hurst, Chance, 1827), 66–71, as quoted in Harlow Lindley, ed., *Indiana As Seen by Early Travelers*, Indiana Historical Collections, vol. 3 (Indianapolis: Indiana Historical Society, 1916), 528.

24. As reported in the Washington *National Intelligencer*, December 6, 1825.

25. Owen, *Book of the New Moral World*, pt. 1, 74–76.

26. *Millennial Gazette*, January 1, 1857, 18.

27. Owen, *Life of Robert Owen*, 1:114.

28. "Letters to William Creese Pelham, 1825 and 1826," in Lindley, *Indiana As Seen by Early Travelers*, 365, 376, 394. Donald Macdonald mentioned passing the site chosen "because it is a flat space of from 400 to 500 yards square with the ground falling away on every side. It is a convenient distance from Harmony, and has excellent timber on it." See Caroline Dale Snedeker, ed., *The Diaries of Donald Macdonald, 1824–1826* (Indianapolis: Indiana Historical Society, 1942; reprint, New York: Augustus M. Kelley, 1973), 294–95. A disappointed member, Thomas Pears, later asked, "Where have the square palaces been built . . . ? Where are the gardens?" See Thomas Clinton Pears Jr., ed., *New Harmony, an Adventure in Happiness: Papers of Thomas and Sarah Pears*, Indiana Historical Society Publications, vol. 11 (Indianapolis: Indiana Historical Society, 1933).

29. Taylor, *Visions of Harmony*, 64; Harrison, *Quest for the New Moral World*, 4, 64, 78–85.

30. Quoted in Taylor, *Visions of Harmony*, 65.

31. Harrison, *Quest for the New Moral World*, 80. See also Merle Curti's assessment of the origins and nature of Owen's thought in his "Robert Owen in American Thought," in Pitzer, *Robert Owen's American Legacy*, 56–67.

32. Robert Owen and Robert Dale Owen, eds., *The Crisis* (London: n.p., 1833), title page. He repeated this idea in many forms beginning at least as early as 1814 in the third essay of his *New View of Society*, in which he wrote "that the character of man, is, without a single exception, always formed for him." In "A New Year's Gift To The World, For 1858," the year he died, Owen emphatically reaffirmed that he alone, as a near-Messianic figure, had been given both the grand insight and the gifts to bring it to reality: "But these combined qualities, so essential for this task, have been given to me,—forced upon me by a creating power, in a manner most mysterious, and to this hour undetected by all the faculties yet given to humanity, except by the visible creation of the universe. Thus gifted, without my knowledge or consent, and therefore without the possibility of individual merit, I continue to use these gifts, as I am impelled to do, with the view to change falsehood into truth, and evil into good." Printed in Owen, *Life of Robert Owen*, 1:vi.

33. *New View of Society*, 16. Here Owen also notes that children "can be trained to acquire any language, sentiments, belief, or any bodily habits and manners, not contrary to human nature."

34. Bestor, *Backwoods Utopias*, 67.

35. Ibid., 68.

36. Harrison, *Quest for the New Moral World*, 163. Bestor notes that Owen did claim that his programs at New Lanark "'effected a complete change in the general character of the village,'" and thus proposed the axiom "'Any character, from the best to the worst, from the most ignorant to the most enlightened, may be given to any community, even to the world at large.'" Quoted in Bestor, *Backwoods Utopias*, 67. On the workings of the develop-

mental process in the Owenite movement, see Donald E. Pitzer, "Developmental Communalism: An Alternative Approach to Communal Studies," in *Utopian Thought and Communal Experience*, ed. Dennis Hardy and Lorna Davidson (Enfield, England: Middlesex Polytechnic, 1989), 73–74.

37. Bestor, *Backwoods Utopias*, 68.

38. Robert Dale Owen, Robert's eldest son who sometimes managed the mills in his father's absence, supported his father's shift to a communitarian plan and argued that it would work where earlier methods had failed; see the preface to his *An Outline of the System of Education at New Lanark* (Glasgow: n.p., 1824), reprinted in *Owenism and the Working Class: 1821–1834*, in the series *British Labour Struggles before 1850* (Salem, N.H.: Ayer, 1972).

39. See the discussion in Bestor, *Backwoods Utopias*, 69–93, and Harrison, *Quest for the New Moral World*, 11–63, 195–97.

40. A group of London printers did form the Cooperative and Economical Society that operated a semicommunal arrangement for twenty-one families between 1821 and 1823 at Spa Fields in England, but funds sought by the British and Foreign Philanthropic Society to begin a community at Motherwell in Lanarkshire, Scotland, never materialized. See Harrison, *Quest for the New Moral World*, 168, 169.

41. *Report to the County of Lanark* (May 1, 1820), in Owen, *Life of Robert Owen*, 1:302.

42. Published in 1824 and 1825, the following works by these three men, all of whom were influenced by Owen, deeply affected the radical impression of Owenism in America as well as in Britain. Owen distributed copies of Thompson's *Inquiry into the Principles of the Distribution of Wealth* when he arrived in America in 1824. Gray's *Lecture on Human Happiness*, as published in the *New-Harmony Gazette* and reprinted in Philadelphia in 1826, became widely accepted in America as a statement of the egalitarianism and common property of Owenism, although Gray freely admitted that he offered plans "altogether different from those proposed by Mr. Owen" (71). Hodgskin's *Labour Defended against the Claims of Capital* had fewer American readers. The effect of the ideas of these men on Owen can be seen in Owen's denunciation of private property in his July 4, 1826, speech in New Harmony and his *Lectures on an Entire New State of Society*, printed in London in 1830, in which he used the term "Science of Society" for his newest route to reform and staunchly opposed in his utopian dream any private property, commercial competition, or inequality of rank or condition. William Godwin and David Ricardo argued for a radical Ricardian socialist stance to the left of that of Owen.

43. Owen, *Book of the New Moral World*, pt. 5, 16, 17, 27–29.

44. Bestor, *Backwoods Utopias*, 78.

45. Owen's ideal population for a planned community never dropped below 500, but he later indicated that as many as 2,000 to 3,000 might be accommodated. See his *Book of the New Moral World*, pt. 6, 85. On the New Deal homesteads, see Paul K. Conkin, *Tomorrow a New World: The New Deal Community Program* (Ithaca, N.Y.: Cornell University Press, 1959).

46. Owen, *Life of Robert Owen*, 1:128–32.

47. Bestor, *Backwoods Utopias*, 102, 103. Harrison, *Quest for the New Moral World*, 164, sets the sale price at $125,000 and Owen's additional expenses at about $75,000, making the New Harmony effort consume some $200,000 of Owen's $250,000 fortune.

48. Bestor, *Backwoods Utopias*, 102; Donnachie and Hewitt, *Historic New Lanark*, 135, 136; Harrison, *Quest for the New Moral World*, 163; Taylor, *Visions of Harmony*, 74, 75.

49. Owenite community building concentrated mostly in two waves in the 1820s and 1840s, from the opening of New Harmony in 1825 to the closing of Josiah Warren's Modern Times settlement in New York in 1863.

50. Owen met and laid his plans before every man who became president from John Adams to Andrew Jackson.

51. Brian J. L. Berry interprets the founding of Owenite communities in America in two waves, one in the 1820s and one in the 1840s, as evidence of a connection between economic hardship and community building during those periods. See his *America's Utopian Experiments*, 56–63, and Michael Barkun, "Communal Societies as Cyclical Phenomena," *Communal Societies* 4 (1984): 35–48.

52. See Alice Felt Tyler, *Freedom's Ferment: Phases of American Social History from the Colonial Period to the Outbreak of the Civil War* (Minneapolis: University of Minnesota Press, 1944, and later editions).

53. Robert Owen, *Robert Owen's Opening Speech, etc.* (Cincinnati, Ohio: Published for Robert Owen, 1829), title page; Earl Irvin West, "Early Cincinnati's 'Unprecedented Spectacle,'" *Ohio History* 79 (Winter 1970): 4–17.

54. Harrison, *Quest for the New Moral World*, 195. From the viewpoint of the developmental flexibility of Owenism it is significant that Harrison should suggest here that

> the year 1829 marked a turning point in the history of the Owenite movement. . . . The Owenites at this stage did not abandon their communitarian goals, but there was, not surprisingly, some disillusionment with the methods which had been employed to realize the new moral world. A fresh approach, using new institutions and agencies, seemed to be called for, and the initiative did not need to be confined to the benevolent Mr Owen—whose fortune was in any case no longer available for philanthropic enterprises after the investment in New Harmony. Until 1829 Owen had largely dominated the movement on both sides of the Atlantic, but thereafter his pecuniary influence was reduced and orthodox Owenism had to meet the challenge of alternative interpretations of doctrine and practice. Owen was by no means insensitive to these changes, and for the next five years (1829–34) his thinking was more radical than either before or later.

55. Ibid., 87.

56. A description of the important people whom Owen met in the first weeks he was in America appears in Bestor, *Backwoods Utopias*, 104–9.

57. Ibid., 95–98.

58. Ibid., 100, 108, 153–58.

59. Robert Dale Owen recorded in his journal the daily events of this migration of intellectuals into the backcountry; see Josephine M. Elliott, ed., *To Holland and to New Harmony: Robert Dale Owen's Travel Journal, 1825–1826*, Indiana Historical Society Publications, vol. 23 (Indianapolis: Indiana Historical Society, 1969), 235–64, and Donald E. Pitzer, "The Original Boatload of Knowledge down the Ohio River: William Maclure's and Robert Owen's Transfer of Science and Education to the Midwest, 1825–1826," *Ohio Journal of Science* 89 (December 1989): 128–42. On Thomas Say, see Patricia Tyson Stroud, *Thomas Say: New World Naturalist* (Philadelphia: University of Pennsylvania Press, 1992).

60. The nature and implications of the social structure of Owenite New Harmony are analyzed in Lucy Jayne Botscharow, "Disharmony in Utopia: Social Categories in Robert Owen's New Harmony," *Communal Societies* 9 (1989), 76–90. The separation and sometimes animosity between the classes gave the community an impersonal character that resident Paul Brown noted as "void of all intimacy regarding each other's feelings, views and situation, including often their names." See Paul Brown, *Twelve Months in New Harmony; Presenting a Faithful Account of the Principal Occurrences which Have Taken Place there within That Period; Interspersed with Remarks* (Cincinnati, Ohio, 1827; reprint, Philadelphia: Porcupine Press, 1972), 33.

61. Pears, *New Harmony*, 60.

62. Botscharow, "Disharmony in Utopia," 89, 90.

63. The costume for women was much like that later used at John Humphrey Noyes's Oneida community and the "Bloomer" advocated by feminist Amelia Bloomer. It gave women freedom of movement with loose-fitting pants down to their ankles covered by a knee-length or longer dress. See sketches printed in Josephine M. Elliott, *Partnership for Posterity: The Correspondence of William Maclure and Marie Duclos Fretageot, 1820–1833* (Indianapolis: Indiana Historical Society, 1994), 455, 584.

64. For descriptions of these visits, see Snedeker, *Diaries of Donald Macdonald*, 186–91, 228–32.

65. John Melish's account of the Harmonists appeared in William Allen's London *Philanthropist* in 1815.

66. George Flower, *History of the English Settlement in Edwards County, Illinois, founded in 1817 and 1818 by Morris Birkbeck and George Flower*, ed. E. B. Washburne (Chicago: Fergus Printing Co., 1882), 372–73, and Harrison, *Quest for the New Moral World*, 53, 54.

67. Religious orders in Europe displayed this. On the importance of commitment mechanisms to the maintenance of communal groups over time, see Rosabeth M. Kanter, *Commitment and Community: Communes and Utopias in Sociological Perspective* (Cambridge, Mass.: Harvard University Press, 1972).

68. Brown summarized his complaints in *Twelve Months in New Harmony*. As a communal and egalitarian purist, Brown argued that Owenites should epitomize complete community of goods and equality of persons in contrast to the Fourierists, who only proposed joint-stock-type capitalistic phalanxes based on social and economic inequalities. Other residents complained that New Harmony was too collectivistic. Josiah Warren, an anarchist at heart, advocated greater individualism. He later founded the time store cooperative movement with his communities of Equity and Utopia in Ohio and Modern Times in New York preserving individual freedom while paying members equally for the time they spent in actual production of goods and services (see Appendix). Warren borrowed the concept of "labor-time" as a medium of exchange and the labor note as "time money" from Robert Owen and New Harmony.

69. Manuscript letter, R. Owen to William Allen, April 21, 1825, Owen Papers, Manchester Co-operative Union, Manchester, England, as quoted in Harrison, *Quest for the New Moral World*, 55.

70. William Pelham to his son, January 13, 1826, "Pelham Letters," in Lindley, *Indiana*, 405.

71. Sarah Pears to Mrs. Benjamin Bakewell, March 10, 1826, in Pears, *New Harmony*, 71; Elliott, *To Holland and to New Harmony*, 233–68; and Pitzer, "Original Boatload of Knowledge," 128–42.

72. Bestor, *Backwoods Utopias*, 133.

73. William Pelham to his son, February 9, 1826, "Pelham Letters," in Lindley, *Indiana*, 411.

74. For details on the life and work of Say, see Stroud, *Thomas Say*.

75. See Elliott, *Partnership for Posterity*, and Bestor, *Education and Reform*.

76. On Owenite and Pestalozzian education, see Bestor, *Backwoods Utopias*; Carmony and Elliott, "New Harmony, Indiana"; Gerald Lee Gutek, *Joseph Neef: The Americanization of Pestalozzianism* (University: University of Alabama Press, 1978); Gerald Gutek, *Pestalozzi and Education* (New York: Random House, 1968); and Donald E. Pitzer, "Education in Utopia: The New Harmony Experience," in *Indiana Historical Society Lectures, 1976–1977: The History of Education in the Middle West*, by Donald E. Pitzer and Timothy L. Smith (Indianapolis: Indiana Historical Society, 1978), 74–101.

77. The Rensselaer [Polytechnic] Institute opened in 1824 but stressed technology rather than trades.

78. These works included parts of Charles-Alexandre Lesueur's proposed *American Ichthyology*; Thomas Say's *Descriptions of Some New Terrestrial and Fluviatile Shells of North America*, serialized in Maclure's *Disseminator* from 1829 to 1831; Say's landmark *American Conchology* in 7 vols. (1830–38), with superb engravings done in color from drawings by Say's wife, Lucy Sistare Say; and a new edition of François Andre Michaux's *North American Silva* that appeared in 1841.

79. See Charles Burgess, "A House Divided: Robert Owen and William Maclure at New Harmony," *Journal of the Midwest History of Education Society* 3 (1975): 110–21; Paul R. Bernard, "Irreconcilable Opinions: The Social and Educational Theories of Robert Owen and William Maclure," *Journal of the Early Republic* 8 (Spring 1988): 21–44; and Pitzer, "Education in Utopia," 93–98.

80. For Maclure's social philosophy and reform theories, see his *Opinions on Various Subjects, Dedicated to the Industrious Producers*, 3 vols. (New Harmony, Ind.: Printed at the School Press, 1831–38), and the introductions in John S. Doskey, ed., *The European Journals of William Maclure* (Philadelphia: American Philosophical Society, 1988), and Elliott, *Partnership for Posterity*. Also see Maclure's articles in *The Disseminator of Useful Knowledge*, printed in New Harmony after 1828.

81. The best summary of this ending scenario to Owenite New Harmony is in Bestor, *Backwoods Utopias*, 191–201.

82. *New-Harmony Gazette*, May 9, 1827.

83. Elliott, *Partnership for Posterity*, 13, 14, 833. See also the discussion and listing of the Maclure-funded libraries in Josephine M. Elliott, "William Maclure: Patron Saint of Indiana Libraries," based on her paper presented to the Communal Studies Conference, New Harmony, Ind., October 16, 1993.

84. Elliott, *Partnership for Posterity*, 13, 14.

85. W. B. Hendrickson, *David Dale Owen: Pioneer Geologist of the Middle West*, Indiana Historical Collections, vol. 27 (Indianapolis: Indiana Historical Society, 1943).

86. *New-Harmony Gazette*, July 9, 1828. See Celia Morris Eckhardt, *Fanny Wright: Rebel in America* (Cambridge, Mass.: Harvard University Press, 1984).

87. Some 3,000 to 5,000 slaves were freed and trained in communal settings in the four decades before the Civil War. See William H. Pease and Jane H. Pease, *Black Utopia: Negro Communal Experiments in America* (Madison: State Historical Society of Wisconsin, 1963), 4.

88. On Nashoba and how it, like Owen's New Harmony, was based on its founder's idea that the economically successful community system of the Harmony Society could be used to effect secular reform, see Eckhardt, *Fanny Wright*, 89–95, 108–34, and Bestor, *Backwoods Utopias*, 49, 114, 218–26.

89. See the New York *Evening Post*, August 8 and November 22, 1862, and the New York *Daily Tribune*, October 23, 1862. Robert Dale Owen also published *Emancipation Is Peace* (New York: Loyal Publication Society, no. 22, n.d.).

90. Hannah Fisher Price to Joseph Warner, March 10, 1826, Fisher-Warner Papers, Friends Historical Library, Swarthmore College, Swarthmore, Pa.

91. See the evidence and arguments from a late twentieth-century women's rights perspective in Carol A. Kolmerten, *Women in Utopia: The Ideology of Gender in the American Owenite Communities* (Bloomington: Indiana University Press, 1990); Kolmerten, "Voices from New Harmony: The Letters of Hannah Fisher Price and Helen Gregoroffsky Fisher," *Communal Societies* 12 (1992): 113–28; and Kolmerten, "Women's Experiences in the American Owenite Communities," in *Women in Spiritual and Communitarian Societies in the*

United States, ed. Wendy Chmielewski, Louis J. Kern, and Marlyn Klee-Hartzell (Syracuse, N.Y.: Syracuse University Press, 1993), 38–51. See also Jill Harsin, "Housework and Utopia: Women and the Owenite Communities," in *Women in Search of Utopia*, ed. Ruby Rohrich and Elaine H. Baruch (New York: Schocken, 1984), 76–80.

92. Kolmerten, *Women in Utopia*, 90; Kolmerten, "Women's Experiences," 39; Kolmerten, "Voices from New Harmony," 114.

93. See the sketches in Elliott, *Partnership for Posterity*, 455, 584.

94. The Shawnee-Town *Illinois Gazette*, July 12, 1826, 330, quoted in Bestor, *Backwoods Utopias*, 222.

95. See Harrison, *Quest for the New Moral World*, 61, 62, 253 n. An indication of how radical *Moral Physiology* was in 1830 can be gained by the fact that Edward Truelove stood trial in England in 1878 for reprinting it and served four months in jail (253 n). Robert Dale also proved his devotion to the interests of women when, as a drafter of the 1851 Indiana Constitution, he was instrumental in securing a provision for property rights for married women. The Minerva Society is another indication of the strong emphasis on intellectual and social opportunities for women in New Harmony. In 1859 it was founded as an early women's literary society in the home of Constance Fauntleroy, daughter of Jane Dale Owen Fauntleroy (Owen's only daughter to come to America).

96. Indianapolis *Indiana Journal*, November 14, 1826, 3; Bestor, *Backwoods Utopias*, 222–23.

97. *New-Harmony Gazette*, October 1, 1825, and February 15, 1826. See the analysis of Owenism and New Harmony in Edward K. Spann, *Brotherly Tomorrows: Movements for a Cooperative Society in America, 1820–1920* (New York: Columbia University Press, 1989), 17–49.

98. Bestor, *Backwoods Utopias*, 180, 181. Owen's effort in March 1826 to have the community assume the cost of some of the land resulted in further disagreement, disillusionment, and reorganization (181–82).

99. Ibid., 170–201; Carmony and Elliott, "New Harmony, Indiana," 175–76.

100. *Report to the County of Lanark* (1821), in Owen, *Life of Robert Owen*, 1:301. See also Lyman Tower Sargent, "Robert Owen as a Political Theorist" (paper presented to the International Communal Studies Association meeting in New Lanark, Scotland, July 19, 1988; copy in archives of the Center for Communal Studies, University of Southern Indiana, Evansville).

101. *New-Harmony Gazette*, March 29, April 12, 1826, 209, 225; Bestor, *Backwoods Utopias*, 64.

102. Bestor, *Backwoods Utopias*, 197, 198; Carmony and Elliott, "New Harmony, Indiana," 176–79.

103. Bestor, *Backwoods Utopias*, 226; and Harrison, *Quest for the New Moral World*, 196.

104. Bestor, *Backwoods Utopias*, 226, 227. He goes on to explain, "In engrafting, for example, the 'state guardianship' plan of education upon the political program of the workingmen, the free enquirers carried over into the labor movement and into politics the old communitarian ideal of a school where children would be separated from the pernicious influences of existing society by being boarded and clothed together at the common expense, raised in an atmosphere of perfect equality, trained in both manual and intellectual skills, and graduated at last as citizens capable of remaking the institutions of the old immoral world" (227). See also John R. Commons, ed., *History of Labour in the United States* (New York: Macmillan, 1918; reprint, New York: Augustus M. Kelley, 1966), 1:231–84.

105. Harrison, *Quest for the New Moral World*, 195.

106. Ibid., 196. See Berry, *America's Utopian Experiments*, 22, 58, on the possible effects of economic fluctuations on the formation of Owenite communities.

107. Harrison, *Quest for the New Moral World*, 196.

108. Harriet Martineau, *Biographical Sketches, 1852–1875* (London: Macmillan, 1877), 307.

109. Friedrich Engels, *Anti-Duhring: Herr Eugen Duhring's Revolution in Science* (1878; reprint, Chicago: C. H. Kerr, 1935), 296, 297.

Selected Bibliography

Bestor, Arthur, Jr. *Backwoods Utopias: The Sectarian Origins and the Owenite Phase of Communitarian Socialism in America, 1663–1829*. Philadelphia: University of Pennsylvania Press, 1950. 2d enl. ed., 1970.

Carmony, Donald F., and Josephine M. Elliott. "New Harmony, Indiana: Robert Owen's Seedbed for Utopia." Special ed. of *Indiana Magazine of History* 76 (September 1980): 161–261.

Claeys, Gregory, ed. *The Works of Robert Owen*. London: Pickering and Chatto, 1993.

Cole, G. D. H. *The Life of Robert Owen*. 2d ed. New York: Macmillan, 1930.

Cole, Margaret. *Robert Owen of New Lanark, 1771–1858*. London: Batchworth, 1953.

Donnachie, Ian, and George Hewitt. *Historic New Lanark: The Dale and Owen Industrial Community since 1785*. Edinburgh: University of Edinburgh Press, 1993.

Eckhardt, Celia Morris. *Fanny Wright: Rebel in America*. Cambridge, Mass.: Harvard University Press, 1984.

Elliott, Josephine M. *Partnership for Posterity: The Correspondence of William Maclure and Marie Duclos Fretageot, 1820–1833*. Indianapolis: Indiana Historical Society, 1994.

Gutek, Gerald Lee. *Joseph Neef: The Americanization of Pestalozzianism*. University: University of Alabama Press, 1978.

Harrison, John F. C. *Quest for the New Moral World: Robert Owen and the Owenites in Britain and America*. New York: Scribner's, 1969.

Kolmerten, Carol A. *Women in Utopia: The Ideology of Gender in the American Owenite Communities*. Bloomington: Indiana University Press, 1990.

Leopold, Richard W. *Robert Dale Owen*. Cambridge, Mass.: Harvard University Press, 1940.

Morton, A. L. *The Life and Ideas of Robert Owen*. New York: International, 1969.

Owen, Robert. *The Book of the New Moral World*. London: Home Colonization Society, 1842–44. Reprint, New York: Augustus M. Kelley, 1970.

———. *Life of Robert Owen. Written By Himself. With Selections From His Writings and Correspondence*. 2 vols. London: Effingham Wilson, 1857–58. Reprint, New York: Augustus M. Kelley, 1967.

Pitzer, Donald E. "Education in Utopia: The New Harmony Experience." In *Indiana Historical Society Lectures, 1976–1977: The History of Education in the Middle West*, by Donald E. Pitzer and Timothy L. Smith, 74–101. Indianapolis: Indiana Historical Society, 1978.

———, ed. *Robert Owen's American Legacy*. Indianapolis: Indiana Historical Society, 1972.

Podmore, Frank. *Robert Owen, a Biography*. 2 vols. London: Allen and Unwin, 1906.

Taylor, Anne. *Visions of Harmony: A Study in Nineteenth-Century Millenarianism*. New York: Oxford University Press, 1987.

Films and Videos

New Harmony: An Example and a Beacon. 1971. 16mm film produced by the Indiana University Audio Visual Center, Bloomington, Ind.

The New Harmony Experience. 1978. 16mm film produced by Historic New Harmony, Inc., New Harmony, Ind. For this and other videos on New Harmony, write Historic New Harmony, New Harmony, IN 47631.

DONALD E. PITZER

DEAN L. MAY

One Heart and Mind

Communal Life and Values
among the Mormons

I n 1885 members of the United Order of Orderville, a Mormon commune in Utah, were advised by church leaders to abandon their enterprise. Their clerk later wrote that the leaders' counsel had

caused many of the people of the Order to shed tears of sorrow. . . . They felt that to turn everything they possessed into the United Order . . . and offer themselves wholy [sic] to the service of the Lord in Temporal as well as in Spiritual things, and be of one heart and mind . . . was more than any cooperative institutions in the land. . . . They felt that the property was the Lord's . . . that dividends belonged to the Lord for the benefit of all the people of the Order and not for Individual gain. And that the rich and poor should be equal in all things. . . . If one individual had more intelligence than another that is his reward, not that he should go well dressed and fed while the one with less intelligence should go ragged and hungry.[1]

Francis L. Porter, the clerk of the Orderville company, here poignantly gave expression to the values that shaped Mormonism from its earliest days and remain at its core today. Mormon communalism was a natural outgrowth of Joseph Smith's strong reaction against what he saw as excessive pluralism and individualism in a society where old ideas of community were being rent by what Robert N. Bellah called a "flood of geographical, demographic, and economic expansion."[2] Communalism was a prominent part of Smith's doctrines

135

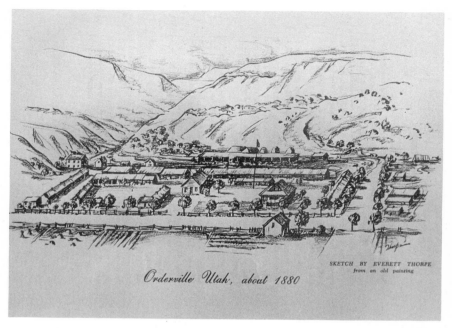

SKETCH BY EVERETT THORPE
from an old painting

Orderville Utah, about 1880

Orderville, Utah, shown about 1880 while it was still organized communally.
This sketch was made from an old painting by Everett Thorpe. (Courtesy of
Church Archives, Church of Jesus Christ of Latter-day Saints)

in the early 1830s. And it became integral to the Mormon character through
historical experience, long affecting the Mormon people whether or not they
were living under a communal order.

Smith first expressed his communal values as an economic program in
1831, less than a year after his new church was founded, in what has since
been called the Law of Consecration and Stewardship. Smith's successor,
Brigham Young, tried to implement its principles in the United Order movement of the 1870s and 1880s. Again, during the 1930s, in response to the
Great Depression, Mormon leaders drew on their communal values in founding and sustaining the Church Welfare Plan, an effort to provide for the poor
through a wide-ranging system of community-owned producers' cooperatives, a program that has continued to the present.

At no time did all Mormons live under the regimen of an economic communal order. Yet the recurrent efforts by the official church over the last 150
years to realize some form of economic cooperation bespeak an underlying
value system that cannot escape the initial direction given it by Joseph Smith.
Whether in a commune or out of it, communalism is at the heart of Mormonism, as Francis Porter well understood.

DEAN L. MAY

The Mormon movement began as an integrative force in the life of young Joseph Smith and his family.[3] His 1838 account of the founding of Mormonism begins with a listing of each family member. He remembered the upstate New York region to which the Smiths had moved from New England in 1816 as a place of "unusual excitement on the subject of religion," his mother, a sister, and two brothers converting to the Presbyterians, he being inclined toward the Methodists, and his father remaining an unreconstructed free-thinker. Smith described the religious enthusiasm of the region as a "war of words and tumult of opinions" that caused him great anxiety, asking himself, "What is to be done? Who of all these parties are right; or are they all wrong together? If any one of them be right which is it, and how shall I know it?"[4]

In the midst of this anxiety his prayers led to a powerful epiphany that, with subsequent revelations and visitations from heavenly messengers, culminated in his founding in 1830 the Church of Jesus Christ of Latter-day Saints (its members called Mormons, after the Book of Mormon, published that same year). Smith's religion included teachings that appealed to many Americans of the early republic. The young prophet's followers believed the Book of Mormon to be an inspired translation of the sacred history of three groups of middle eastern peoples who migrated to America under divine direction prior to 600 B.C. The apogee of their history was a visit to them by Christ, shortly after his resurrection. Thus the Book of Mormon complemented the traditional Christian canon with scriptures produced in an American setting.

Moreover, Smith had the audacity to teach that God had chosen him, a Vermont-born farm boy, to be one of the most important prophets of all ages. Through him was to be restored both the priesthood and teachings of Christ's primitive church. The latter-day restoration of pure Christianity was to draw together the central truths of all previous revelatory epochs or gospel dispensations, beginning with Adam. Smith's belief that he was to accomplish "the restitution of all things" led by the 1840s to the introduction of "celestial" or plural marriage (polygamy), following Old Testament patriarchs, and to temple ceremonies deemed essential to the salvation of both the living and, through sacraments performed by proxy for them in the temples, the dead. All of world history hinged on the success of the Latter-day Saints in making the "restored gospel" effective in their lives. They were obligated to "gather out" the elect and use the restored teachings in preparing a covenant people to greet Christ at his second coming, helping to usher in the millennium.

Especially urgent was the need to combat the great sin of Smith's generation, which was, as recorded in one of Smith's key revelations, that "every man walketh in his own way, and after the image of his own God." God's voice sternly warned Smith's followers in early 1831 that "if ye are not one ye

Joseph Smith Jr., founder of the Church of Jesus Christ of Latter-day Saints, who proclaimed the communal Law of Consecration and Stewardship in 1831. An unknown artist made this portrait during the time Smith led the Mormons at Nauvoo, Illinois, after 1839 and before he and his brother, Hyrum, were murdered in the Carthage jail in 1844. (Courtesy of the Library-Archives, Reorganized Church of Jesus Christ of Latter Day Saints, The Auditorium, Independence, Missouri. Reproduction by RLDS Graphic Design Commission.)

are not mine." "Let all things be done in order," he commanded in a revelation received later that year.[5] Smith's own family, including his other-minded father, became united in support of the young man's prophetic claims. Thus family unity and societal unity became principal preoccupations of early Mormonism, arising in part from Smith's reaction to the divisiveness he saw in his own family and in the society about him. No doubt the pool of early converts included many who, like Smith, sought haven from an increasingly disorderly society.

This bias in favor of the unity and order essential to a communal society was extended to temporal affairs through Smith's reading of Christian scriptures. In the Acts of the Apostles (4:32) he read of primitive Christians who "had all things common." Such accounts could by themselves have led Smith, devoted as he was to restoring the primitive church, to some form of communalism, as they had Christian dissenters since at least the sixteenth century, including Smith's contemporaries George Rapp and John Humphrey Noyes.

But the canon unique to the Mormons reinforced the New Testament vision of the perfect godly society. After Christ's visit to pre-Columbian Americans, as described in the Book of Mormon, the faithful lived for a time as a society where "they had all things common among them; therefore there were not rich and poor, bond and free, but they were all made free, and partakers of the heavenly gift." Perhaps more importantly, Smith, in December 1830, received a revelation recounting the deeds of the Old Testament prophet Enoch, in which Enoch's ideal city of Zion is described. "And the Lord called his people Zion, because they were of one heart and one mind, and dwelt in righteousness; and there was no poor among them."[6]

This account entered powerfully into Smith's consciousness. He at times used "Enoch" as a code name for himself. He named the city he intended to found in Missouri "Zion," and the scriptures he produced became filled with admonitions to build up and establish Zion, which Mormons understood to be a perfected people as well as a holy city. Prior to his acquaintance with these scriptures Smith had desired to build an enclave of unity and order in a highly individualistic and fragmented society. The scriptural accounts offered concrete models and put him under injunction to follow them if his self-proclaimed mission to "restore all things" were to be realized.

At that point events moved Smith to consider directly by what means he would accomplish among his followers a communal life. In the summer of 1830 Mormon missionaries working in the recently settled Western Reserve area of Ohio converted the whole congregation of Sidney Rigdon, an able minister in Alexander Campbell's Disciples of Christ movement. The Disciples were thoroughgoing Christian primitivists. Some, following the New Testament, and perhaps inspired by a Shaker colony in nearby Cleveland, had already formed a communal society called "the Family." However, the experiment had occasioned more dissension than good will among its members. The group, now converted to Mormonism, was anxious to have the prophet put them on a proper communal course.

Fleeing from persecution in upstate New York and northeastern Pennsylvania, Smith and his earliest followers moved to Ohio during the winter of 1830–31. On February 9, some ten days after his arrival, the prophet revealed the long-awaited "Law of the Church," a document that in prescribing the rules of governing the church and the moral principles by which members should live outlined a communal economic order since known as Consecration and Stewardship. Essentially the system attempted to equalize standards of living while preserving significant elements of individualism, including individual entrepreneurial responsibility, separate family dwellings, and to a considerable extent, the exercise of personal tastes and preferences.[7]

Efforts to implement Consecration and Stewardship in Ohio were unsuccessful, largely because a principal contributor reneged on his Consecration of land. But by the summer of 1831 Joseph Smith had announced that the latter-day city of Zion would be built in Jackson County, Missouri, then on the frontier, just east of present-day Kansas City. Communicants began to move west that summer and, as they arrived in Zion, came under the pastoral care of Edward Partridge, bishop of Zion.

As administered by Bishop Partridge, Consecration and Stewardship required faithful converts to make two solemn commitments relating to their secular lives: Consecration, or the giving of their possessions to God or his visible agent on earth, the church, and Stewardship, or performing all earthly endeavor as a service to God. The church would thus own all property, its disposition being the responsibility of the bishop as its agent. But the principle of Stewardship reserved *management* of property to the individual member, subject only to periodic review by the bishop. Prices and wages were to be determined by the market, not centrally administered; however, the bishop did have control of the allocation of capital. Partridge welcomed new arrivals with two printed forms that attempted in formal legal language to implement Consecration and Stewardship.

The first was a deed of Consecration (gift). In it the member gave to Edward Partridge, as representative of the church, an itemized list of his earthly possessions. One, for example, is Benjamin Eames's grant of "sundry articles of furniture valued fourteen dollars twenty-five cents,—also two beds, bed-

DEAN L. MAY

ding and extra clothing valued thirty-two dollars seventy-five cents,—also sundry farming utensils valued ten dollars seventy-five cents,—also one yoke of cattle and one cow valued thirty-eight dollars."

The deed specified that the Consecration was to be used for building Zion and caring for the poor. Eames bound himself and his heirs to release all right and interest to the property, and the bishop promised to use the property for the purposes stated and to turn it over to his successor should he leave office for any reason. This was all accomplished on the left half of a large printed form. Having signed the document, the member stood bereft of worldly possessions, giving literal meaning to the biblical decree that "the earth is the Lord's, and the fullness thereof; the world, and they that dwell therein."[8]

But that was only half of the agreement. The right half of the document was a deed of Stewardship (lease). In it the same personal possessions were given back to the steward as a life lease, together with land and materials sufficient to make a living at his chosen profession—in the case of Benjamin Eames, as a farmer. The household head agreed to pay civil taxes and each year to consecrate to the bishop any surplus above what he deemed necessary for the "support and comfort" of his family, an amount apparently to be agreed on during an annual negotiation with the bishop. The bishop, for his part, promised to care for the family out of church funds in case of the member's disability or call to full-time church service. The wife succeeded to the stewardship in the event of her husband's death; but should both parents die, it remained in the family only until the children came of age, when the stewardship then reverted to the church. Presumably at that time the children would receive stewardships of their own.[9]

Consecration and Stewardship was practiced in Missouri between 1831 and 1833. The bishop received Consecrations and issued Stewardships to new arrivals—artisans as well as farmers. Essential enterprises—mills, blacksmith shops, stores, and a printing press—were established under the system. There was, however, no ordered plan for the physical layout of the community. The incoming settlers distributed themselves among several hamlets in the area, building separate homes on their lands.

Smith, still living in Ohio, tried to impose order by sending in 1833 the Plat of the City of Zion, an ambitious plan for a mile-square city of 15,000 to 20,000 inhabitants with a central complex of twenty-four temples to serve as educational and religious centers. Half-acre lots were to be laid out in a rectangular grid of ten-acre blocks, with streets oriented toward the cardinal points of the compass. Citizens were to build brick or stone homes on town lots and commute to fields on the outskirts. When the population filled the platted site, a new settlement was to be made elsewhere, "and so fill up the world in these last days, and let every man live in the city, for this is the city of Zion."[10]

Except for the dedication of a temple site, the plan was not begun before the Saints (as the Mormons called themselves) were forced to flee the area. The surviving records indicate that the bishop was constantly concerned that the new Consecrations and the annual Consecrations of established members were not generating a surplus sufficient to support such an ambitious plan. Brigham Young recalled that many Saints were notably reluctant to consecrate: "I never knew a man . . . who had a dollar of surplus property. No matter how much one might have he wanted all he had for himself, for his children, his grandchildren, and so forth." Nonetheless, Partridge continued to acquire land, and the settlements grew. One of the participants, Parley P. Pratt, remembered that despite problems, "There was a spirit of peace and union, and love and good will manifested. . . . Peace and plenty had crowned their labors and the wilderness became a fruitful field, and the solitary place began to bud and blossom as the rose."[11]

By the summer of 1833 the Mormons numbered some 1,200, about one-third of the county population. Threatened perhaps more by the Saints' cohesiveness than by their numbers, the non-Mormon majority in July raided Mormon settlements and demanded that they leave the county. In October they forcibly drove the Mormons north, across the Missouri River, into Clay County. From there the Saints eventually moved northeast to Caldwell County and, in 1838, were driven from Missouri into Illinois. Through these searing experiences they developed a profound distrust of non-Mormons that turned them inward, reinforcing Smith's doctrinal insistence on unity within their community. There came to exist for them two social worlds: that of the Saints as a latter-day Israel, gathered from the nations; and that of all others, whom they called "Gentiles." In their world resided trust, openness, peace, and love; in the Gentile world resided suspicion, betrayal, hate, and fear. The elements for an enduring communal society were in place, whether or not the Mormons again attempted communal living.[12]

They did not do so during Joseph Smith's lifetime. In 1839 they founded the city of Nauvoo, northeast of Missouri on the Illinois side of the Mississippi River. Under liberal charter, the city was carefully planned and laid out, with significant church-directed public activities, including an ambitious temple, a store and guest home, an embryonic university, and a city militia. Swept along in a vortex of rapid population growth, doctrinal change, legal harassment, and political activity, Smith encouraged only episodic and limited cooperative enterprises. Consecration and Stewardship became more narrowly and precisely defined as a tithe of one's possessions on entering the church and an annual tithe of their "increase" after that time.[13] Yet the language and the sentiments that were a part of the Consecration and Stewardship system remained. The high point of solemn temple ceremonies introduced in Nauvoo was the taking of a Consecration covenant. Church assignments, including the many involved with secular matters, were called "Stewardships," retaining all the implications of the term as used in Missouri: limited tenure, individual responsibility to "magnify" the calling, periodic accounting to higher church officials, and consideration of all such assignments sacred callings from God.

Perhaps even more importantly the Missouri period remained in the Mormon consciousness as a utopian moment in their collective past that one day must be reclaimed in preparation for Christ's return. Generations of Mormons have hoped for the day when they will one day return to Missouri, build a temple on the site dedicated there, and complete the city of Zion with all its appurtenances, including living the law of Consecration and Stewardship. Mormon folklore is replete with stories of the faithful who kept a team and wagon ready in Utah for years in anticipation of the expected call to return to Zion. A Mormon hymn, originally written in the 1830s to praise Zion, remains a favorite among many:

> This earth was once a garden place,
> With all her glories common,
> And men did live a holy race,
> And worship Jesus face to face,
> In Adam-ondi-Ahman.
> . . . .
>
> Hosanna to such days to come,
> The Saviour's second coming,
> When all the earth in glorious bloom
> Affords the Saints a holy home,
> Like Adam-ondi-Ahman.

Smith's successor, Brigham Young, at the end of carefully detailed instructions concerning his burial in Utah, insisted they be followed to the letter, "but if I should live to go back with the Church in Jackson County, [Missouri] I wish to be buried there."[14] Though the time in Jackson County was short, the Mormon millennial vision developed there—including Consecration and Stewardship—and has been communicated to subsequent generations as well as to millions of converts. Besides providing the vocabulary and terms of everyday church governance, the vision has remained since that time both a burden and a promise, forming a communal bedrock to which church leaders have periodically returned in times of crisis.

In 1844 Joseph Smith and his brother Hyrum were killed by an armed mob while in jail awaiting trial on charges stemming from Joseph's order as mayor to destroy an opposition press in Nauvoo. Leadership of the main body of Mormons fell upon Brigham Young, president of the Twelve Apostles. In attempting to keep the Mormon movement from disintegrating, Young sought advice and assistance not only from fellow members of the apostolic quorum but also from the Council of Fifty, a select group of loyal men chosen by Smith shortly before his death to help govern during the impending millennial rule of the Saints.[15] Yet many Latter-day Saints, while accepting Young's authority as president of the apostles, looked elsewhere for a successor to the prophet. Several competing claimants to Smith's mantle attracted followers, but in 1853 a substantial number who had not moved west formed the Reorganized Church of Jesus Christ of Latter Day Saints. They ultimately established their headquarters in Independence, Missouri, and recognized the prophet's son, Joseph Smith III, as his father's successor.[16]

Most of the Nauvoo Saints chose to follow Young to the West. Brigham Young was a self-educated, Vermont-born painter and glazier, highly intelligent, a natural leader, and utterly devoted to Smith's religious and social vision. In the face of mounting opposition from non-Mormons in Illinois, he made plans to transport some 15,000 Nauvoo Mormons to the Far West and build a new gathering place there. In the early spring of 1846 the migration began. Carefully organized and carried out as a communal effort, it remained his principal preoccupation through 1852, when the last of those still residing in temporary settlements near Council Bluffs and Omaha were brought to Utah.[17]

In Utah Young and his flock were isolated by some 800 miles of unsettled territory in all directions. Faced with the responsibility of providing the economic as well as the religious needs of an immigration averaging some 3,000 a year for the next four decades, church leaders further narrowed traditional distinctions between secular and religious pursuits. A church-sponsored perpetual immigration company not only advanced funds to the poor but required the church to create an elaborate structure of agents to oversee the travel of those "gathering to Zion." Ironmaking became as sacred a Stewardship as temple service; colonizing, as much a religious obligation as seeking out converts.

DEAN L. MAY

Mormon leader Brigham Young at the time he launched the United
Order Movement in Utah in the 1870s. (Courtesy of Church Archives,
Church of Jesus Christ of Latter-day Saints)

Communal Life and Values among the Mormons

Yet with all this Brigham Young remained fully committed to carrying out Joseph Smith's unfinished agenda. In the mid-1850s, during a time of serious crop failures and extravagant religious revivalism, Young encouraged what seems almost a spontaneous movement on the part of Mormons to consecrate all their property to the church. A form document to accomplish this was distributed among the church members, and nearly half of all household heads listed their possessions and presented the forms to county recorders and church officials. Perhaps disappointed that more of his flock did not consecrate, Young did not take actual possession of any of the property or issue Stewardships. In any case, he soon became preoccupied with the Utah war of 1857–58. That conflict resulted in his being replaced as governor of Utah Territory by a non-Mormon, and in the establishment of a military post some forty miles from Salt Lake City. Few Consecrations were made after 1858.

Young remained convinced, however, that the Saints should move in the direction of economic cooperation, confirming their spiritual commitment through their willingness to participate in church-sponsored enterprise. The tithing system brought under his control substantial amounts of capital, which he used to foster needed industries, such as paper milling, iron smelting, and beet sugar production.[18] His wish that spiritual and temporal interests of the Mormons be further combined found a promising model in cooperatives founded in the Utah towns of Lehi and Brigham City in the mid-1860s.

The Brigham City cooperative, under Lorenzo Snow, was particularly successful. Supported by English converts who had been familiar with the Owenite Rochdale cooperative system in Lancashire, the enterprise began in 1864 with the founding of a retail store. To encourage widespread membership, shares were offered in small denominations, and commodities, such as butter and eggs, were accepted in lieu of cash. Profits from the store were put into producers' cooperatives that grew to include a tannery; a shoe shop; a sawmill; a furniture factory; sheep, cattle, and dairy farms; a textile mill, with cotton and flax farms; a millinery factory; a tin shop; a rope factory; and several administrative departments, including an education and a "tramp" department (to provide employment to itinerants who stopped in the town seeking a handout). Most adults among the 800 townspeople were both shareholders and employees of the cooperatives. Through their labors the town became 85 percent self-sufficient and a model of cooperative endeavor praised by many, including radical labor movement pamphleteer Dyer D. Lum.[19] According to the Snow family, Edward Bellamy spent several days in

DEAN L. MAY

Brigham City with Lorenzo Snow prior to writing his famous utopian novel *Looking Backward*.

Brigham Young was also impressed with Snow's accomplishments and no doubt was pleased that they were made in his namesake city. With the transcontinental railroad approaching and an increasingly brisk trade in imported goods being carried on by Gentile merchants, Young decided to reverse his earlier policy of discouraging Mormons from fostering such trade. In 1868 he founded Zion's Cooperative Mercantile Institution (ZCMI), a church-sponsored retail trading system that he hoped would drive out Gentile merchants and be profitable enough to provide the capital needed to foster local cooperative industries. With the Salt Lake City ZCMI as a central wholesaling facility, Young encouraged the establishment of local branches in almost every Mormon town and village. Some 150 cooperative stores were opened the length and breadth of Mormondom, all displaying a logo of clasped hands of brotherhood and the motto Holiness to the Lord. A few, as Young had hoped, followed the Brigham City model by branching out into manufacturing enterprises of various kinds, though most did not move beyond retail merchandising. In time, the five- and ten-dollar shares drifted into the hands of the more wealthy, and though retaining the name, the stores in the system lost their cooperative character. The ZCMI was the only store in many communities until well into the twentieth century. It remains a powerful and important department store chain in Utah and surrounding states.

Despite the apparent short-term success of ZCMI, Young still wrestled with the problem of keeping the Saints apart culturally and economically from the incoming flood of Gentiles attracted by gold and silver strikes in Utah's mountains. The panic of 1873 provided a particularly sharp lesson in the dangers of integration with the national economy. Those areas of Utah tied to mining suffered severely, while Brigham City seemed relatively unaffected. Observing poverty, dispiritedness, and disaffection as he traveled south to his winter home in St. George during the winter of 1873–74, the aging Young considered how best to control the situation.

That winter he drew again from the substructure of Mormonism, the sermon Lorenzo Snow had preached the previous October perhaps still ringing in his ears. "It is more than forty years since the [communal] Order of Enoch was introduced, and rejected. One would naturally think, that it is now about time to begin to honor it." Borrowing the name that had been applied to a cooperative manufacturing effort under Joseph Smith, Young began in February urging each settlement to organize under the United Order of Enoch. Telegraphing his initial successes to his counselors in Salt Lake City he was unabashedly jubilant. "We have organized six companies after the order of Enoch. . . . The brethren and sisters all seem ready to go into this order of oneness heart and hand and all the settlements are pressing us to come and organize them preparatory for the spring work. Thank the Lord the people as so prepared for with the fire of the gospel burning thus brightly, we need not fear the efforts of our enemies."[20]

By the next fall some 200 United Orders had been organized, at least on paper, among both rural and urban congregations. Yet only here and there was attachment to the program sufficient to sustain the effort beyond the 1874 season. Many never got beyond the stage of electing officers. The disappointing result perhaps could have been predicted. Young was attempting at a stroke to transform a frail but functioning economy, serving some 80,000 persons, into a commonwealth of communes. Aware that some would resist, he specifically ordered that no one be coerced. Moreover, he placed on the bishop of each congregation the responsibility of determining how far his flock was willing to go in the direction of cooperation and urged bishops not to push them further than they were willing. The result was a bewildering variety of organizations and a good deal of fighting within congregations as to what form their United Order should take. In no instance was the specific form of Smith's Law of Consecration and Stewardship followed.

Several northern communities, such as Brigham City, already had well-developed community cooperatives. They merely changed the name of their organization and continued business as usual. The Brigham City Mercantile and Manufacturing Association was a stock company making few demands on the private lives of its shareholders. Its leaders changed the name to the Brigham City United Order but did not change its accustomed mode of operation.

Many of the city congregations in Salt Lake, Ogden, and Provo, after some stumbling, attempted to found a manufacturing enterprise, contributing capital and labor to establish a community-owned meat market, hat factory, or soap factory. Yet city bishops were perhaps of all Young's lieutenants most tied to the Gentile economy, profiting as suppliers to the new industries brought in by the railroads and mines. Most were not eager to lead their flock into the United Order. Moreover, they noted that Young was not quick to offer his own considerable resources in support of the community-owned cooperatives. Only two or three of the city wards (congregations) formed viable organizations.[21]

The more common orders were in the congregations of rural towns, such as at St. George, where land and farm equipment were placed under the direction of an elected committee, which supervised production, deciding such matters as crops to be grown. The directors attempted to improve efficiency by dividing labor, assigning able-bodied men, women, and older children to specialize in tasks at which they might be most adept and carefully controlling the extent and nature of any attempts to move or work outside the order. There was, however, no effort to prescribe common dress or uniform housing, to eat at a common table, or to regiment personal lives, beyond seeing that the work due the order was accomplished. Moreover, as the orders began to disband in the fall of 1874, the members seemed to have no difficulty identifying the property they had contributed.

Another form of United Order was urged by those who felt a fully communal life would be the only one consistent with Brigham Young's aims. Their devotion to what was called the gospel plan was such that in at least two instances severe strains developed between the communalists and those desiring something less than an all-encompassing cooperative. In Kanab the bishop suspended the sacrament (communion) for several months because there was such rancor between the two camps. In Mt. Carmel the breach became so great that it could not be healed. Those favoring the gospel plan seceded from the town in 1875 and founded their own two miles away, which they named Orderville. Orderville became the symbol for the most communal United Order and a model for a number of orders, especially in the southern portions of Mormon country.

The Orderville Saints went far beyond what Joseph Smith had envisioned in the Law of Consecration and Stewardship. Initially in Orderville the entire community arose for prayers at the sound of a bugle or bell. All ate together in a common dining hall, wore uniform clothing made by Orderville industries, and lived in uniform apartments. All activity, including entertainment, schooling, cooking, clothing manufacture, and farming, was under the supervision of an elected board. Private property did not exist, though personal possessions were assigned as a Stewardship to each individual.

Yet under this regimen the order prospered both materially and spiritually. Assets of the eighty families tripled from $21,551 to $69,562 in the first four years of operation and reached nearly $80,000 by 1883. One visitor in 1877 "found peace, plenty and harmony prevailing. Like fraternal brothers they were furnishing Bro. Lott Smith's camp [a struggling new Arizona settlement] with a large quantity of bread stuff. A united order indeed with purpose and effect against the day of want and famine." Another visitor that same year noted that "they work in perfect harmony and they have the power 'to do' that cannot be found in any other place among the saints."[22]

Adjustments were made as time went on. In 1877 the earlier loose dependence on willingness to contribute was replaced with an accounting system that placed uniform values on labor and commodities (the wages varying by age and sex, but not type of work). A flood in 1880 destroyed the dining facilities. After the cleanup, communal dining was not resumed. In 1883 Erastus Snow, a regional church official, recommended moving to an unequal wage and partial stewardship system, the latter giving each family a plot of ground to till for its own use. Evolution away from the original communal purity continued as specific enterprises were leased to their operators for a fee retained by the order.

External pressures took their toll as well. The largely polygamous leadership of the community was decimated after the U.S. Congress passed the Edmunds Act of 1882. This act stimulated a vigorous campaign to enforce federal antipolygamy statutes, leading to the imprisonment or forced exile of many local leaders. In 1885 central church leaders, eager to reduce the range of federal complaints against Mormon peculiarities (the government was hostile to Mormon economic as well as marital practices), counseled the members to disband the order, which, as Francis Porter reported, they agreed reluctantly to do. They retained community ownership of the tannery, the woolen mill, and the sheep ranch until 1889 and finally let the corporation lapse in 1904. In time the memory of tensions and problems in the commune faded, and dozens of memoirs affirmed historian Andrew Jenson's conclusion that the people "never felt happier in their lives than they did when the Order was in complete running order and they were devoting their entire time, talent and strength for the common good. Good feelings, brotherly love and unselfish motives characterized most of those who were members until the last."[23]

Although the less communal stock company system of Brigham City was at least as successful financially as was Orderville, it did not capture the imagination and live on in the collective memory of Mormons. Orderville became the symbol of the United Order for subsequent Saints, a daring and near-successful effort to build the City of God on earth. Celebrated in song and legend, Orderville is in the minds of most Mormons today a model of selflessness, devotion, and future obligation. In fact few today seem to realize that the United Order of Enoch was attempted outside Orderville.

Sporadic efforts were made to implement some form of the United Order into the 1880s, especially in the founding of new colonies, and of course some organizations, such as Orderville and Brigham City, continued for a decade or more after founding. Yet it was clear by 1876 that the mass involvement Young had hoped for would not materialize. Asked in the last year of his life if he had launched the effort on his own or through revelation, he replied that he "had been inspired by the gift and power of God to call upon the

Saints to enter into the United Order of Enoch and that now was the time, but he could not get the Saints to live it and his skirts are clear if he never says another word about it."[24]

Faced with unremitting federal pressures toward conformity, Young's successors were content to retreat from advocating an active communal life and to nourish the substance of communalism that remained central to Mormonism. As southern Utah leader Erastus Snow put it, "Murmur as little as possible; complain as little as possible; and if we are not yet advanced enough to all eat at one table, all work in one company, at least feel that we all have one common interest and are all children of one Father; and let us each do what we can to save ourselves and each other."[25]

Perhaps it is no surprise that the United Order experience did not turn the Mormons against the communal values that had so long been important to their identity as a people. On the contrary, the regret in Brigham Young's complaint that he "could not get the Saints to live it" and the promise in Erastus Snow's observation that "we are not yet advanced enough" resonated long in Mormon country. A blueprint for a perfect society could be readily forgotten, but not a failed effort to build it. It would seem that as members discerned the divisive consequences of their attempt to institute economic communalism, they turned away from it in order to protect their social communalism.[26]

Like the thwarted effort to live the Law of Consecration and Stewardship in Missouri, the United Order movement, far from dampening Mormon communitarian impulses, heightened them and made their future implementation a necessity. For generations a common folk catechism among Mormons was "Could you live the United Order if asked to do so?" In the late 1940s Mormon bean farmers in Ramah, New Mexico, were asked by a Harvard team of researchers to describe the perfect society. In contrast to that of other Americans in the area, whose response was expansive, individualistic, and materialistic, the Mormon response, as summarized by the researchers, evoked in powerfully direct words their communal past: "I've often commented to myself that I'd like a newly man-made community. I think we ought to have a big reservoir the first thing to take care of the water supply. I believe I would put it under the United Order. . . . There would be just one people, all of one belief, where they treat everybody equal, no injustice to any of them, each looking out for the other's welfare. I think that used to be done in years back."[27] The plain people of Ramah clearly expressed Joseph Smith's communal values more than a century after his death.

By the early decades of the twentieth century Brigham Young's dream of economic independence for Utah had been lost. The state had become fully integrated into the national economy, with natural resources—both mineral and agricultural—its principal exports. The unusually high demand for such products stimulated by World War I brought prosperity until the war orders ceased. Beginning in 1919 Utah descended into a depression that persisted until the 1930s and then deepened as the Great Depression struck the rest of the nation. Because the Utah economy plummeted from a much lower base than that elsewhere, the depression was unusually devastating in its human consequences.[28]

As in the past, church leaders, feeling a responsibility for the temporal as well as spiritual welfare of the members, cast about for a solution. Again, as in the 1850s and the 1870s, a severe crisis caused them to draw on their reserve of communal values. In 1936 they announced plans for what came to be known as the Church Welfare Plan. In announcing it one high church leader described the program not as something new, "but a return to that which is old." Another avowed that it "goes back to the principles which were given the Church over a hundred years ago, [and] puts us once more on the road leading to the establishment of a Christian rule."[29]

Under the plan each stake (a diocesan level church unit consisting of several wards) was to acquire a farm or factory that would grow or manufacture essential household commodities. The goods were then to be shipped to regional warehousing and distribution centers from which they were redistributed to each stake, so local bishops would have a completely stocked storehouse to draw on in aiding the poor. The farms or factories were owned by the stake members and though there were paid managers, volunteers were recruited to assist in labor-intensive operations, such as weeding, harvesting, or canning. Local bishops and relief society presidents (women's leaders in each ward) were in charge of distribution. Being neighbors of those needing assistance, they could tailor aid to their needs, asking the recipients to work for assistance where possible. The central principles, according to Harold B. Lee, founder of the program, were cooperation and united effort. "Every member . . . gives what he is able to give and receives in return whatever he needs for the sustenance of himself and his family."[30]

The welfare plan remains in operation today. In addition to providing regular assistance to the poor, it has responded to major world disasters, sending blankets, food, and other commodities to assist victims of floods, earthquakes, and wars. Though Mormons grouse at the occasional assignments to make soap, weed fields, and pick fruits or vegetables and can them, they generally respond in sufficient numbers to make the program viable and to provide memorable and often warm experiences in cooperative enterprise. Though not as far reaching as Consecration and Stewardship or the United

DEAN L. MAY

Order, the program for half a century has implemented in a concrete way the communal values that Mormons exhibit in many other aspects of their lives. As Marion G. Romney, late president of the Quorum of Twelve Apostles, said of the program in 1973,

> From the very beginning I felt that the program would eventually move into the Law of Consecration and that this is the trial pattern. Until I can pay my tithing and make liberal contributions of my money and labor to the Welfare Program, . . . I will not be prepared to go into the United Order, which will require me to consecrate everything I have and thereafter give all my surplus for the benefit of the kingdom. I think the United Order will be the last principle of the gospel we will learn to live and that doing so will bring in the millennium.[31]

The historical interaction between the base of Mormon communal values laid down in Joseph Smith's time and recurrent efforts to implement them in communal organizations provides a fascinating study. Joseph Smith, concerned by the centrifugal forces tearing at the old social order in the early republic, sought a means of preserving order, unity, and an older sense of community within that society. Whether by genius or inspiration (his followers would stress the latter), Smith used scriptural precedent, his own teachings, and historical experience to alter for his followers widely held American assumptions about freedom, individualism, the nature of authority, property rights, distinctions between the secular and the religious, the obligations of the individual to society, and the nature and role of the family in society.

In all of these spheres the impetus was toward integration. Men and women are ordained by God to be free, but primarily so that they might freely choose to make covenants to God that will greatly restrict their actions and bind them with sacred obligations. The individual is important but finds his or her greatest fulfillment through learning to control selfish impulses so he or she might act in concert and harmony with others. A regard for clearly designated authority, based on the confidence and trust of the followers, is essential to an orderly and unified society. All property belongs to God, and men and women are only stewards over that which they possess. Stewardship creates obligations to God and to mankind—past, present, and future. There should properly be no distinction between the secular and the religious. All of God's children are under sacred obligation to use both time and possessions in a socially beneficial way. And the family—including past, present, and future members—is a sacred and enduring institution, both nurturing and obligating the individual. A harmonious and loving family is indeed the very model of a perfect society.

The Mormons began to imbibe these values before Smith revealed the communal order that was intended to implement them. At no time were all members required, as a condition of their membership, to live under that communal order. Yet the heroic attempt on the part of some to do so was held up as a model that reinforced the underlying values and placed all under a future obligation to develop the collective character necessary to implement them at some future time. Recurrent crises led leaders in the 1850s, 1870s, and 1930s to call the members to commit these values to the cause of caring for the poor and achieving a more just society. Both failures and successes in these endeavors enhanced the underlying communal value system. But the fact that communal living has been a sign of exceptional devotion rather than a condition of membership has made it relatively easy for the group to accommodate large numbers of converts and still keep its communal values intact.

At the present, Mormon communalism is most evident in the welfare program and in the structure and operations of church government, which are larded with terms and metaphors drawn from the Law of Consecration and Stewardship. Mormon congregations or wards are geographically defined and deliberately limited in size. The preoccupation of members with the ward community often causes non-Mormons to see them, quite accurately, as clannish and inward looking. There may be other negative consequences of that communal impulse. In the arts Mormons seem more accomplished in ensemble than individual expression: bands, choirs, the theater, and dance, over painting, sculpture, or creative writing. Employers complain at times that Mormons are good followers but poor innovators. Visitors to Brigham Young University campus are impressed by its tidiness but wonder if such order and apparent unity are conducive to creative thought. To the degree that these widely held impressions reflect reality, they may indicate trade-offs communal societies make for the mutual support, efficiency, and strength their common endeavor affords. And though many in today's liberal society would not be willing to make that trade, it may be that such communalists possess the means to mitigate the great fear Alexis de Tocqueville, writing in the 1830s, had for America, that "each man is forever thrown back on himself alone, and there is danger that he may be shut up in the solitude of his own heart."[32]

Communal values are essential to the Mormon church as it presently functions, though recent leaders have tried to distance the church from any organized structure of communal living and from its communal past. It is not likely that in normal times the present leaders would move the members again toward such an organized structure. Yet the world is so precarious that one could readily imagine a crisis sufficient to stir the millennial impulse still strong in Mormonism and cause its leaders to reach again into their rich storehouse of communal resources in dealing with that crisis.

The Mormon prophet in 1993 was Ezra Taft Benson, known for his political conservatism. Yet as a young man he was active in helping farmers to organize marketing cooperatives—hardly the action we would expect of a dedicated free-enterprise capitalist. It may be that the tide of Mormon communalism runs more deeply than the professed political ideologies of its present leaders and that anyone wishing to understand the prospects for future communal initiatives on their part should pay more attention to what they do than to what they say.

Chronology

Dec. 1805	Joseph Smith is born in Sharon, Vt.
1816	The Smith family moves to western New York.
Spring 1820	Smith has a vision in which he is told to join no church.
Sept. 1823	Smith learns in vision of the buried plates, later "translated" as the Book of Mormon.
Apr. 1830	The Church of Jesus Christ of Latter-day Saints is organized in Fayette, N.Y.
Oct. 1830	Mormon missionaries in Ohio convert Campbellite minister Sidney Rigdon and his congregation, some of them living communally.
Dec. 1830	The Enoch vision describing the city of Zion is received.
Jan. 1831	Joseph Smith moves to Kirtland, Ohio, area.
Feb. 1831	The "Law of the Church" revelation outlines Consecration and Stewardship.
July 1831	Jackson County, Mo., revealed as the site of the new Zion; Mormons begin to "gather" there; Edward Partridge implements Consecration and Stewardship.
July 1833	Mob destroys Mormon press and warns Saints to leave Jackson County.
Nov. 1833	Mormons forced to flee Jackson County; they settle in Clay County.
Mar./Apr. 1836	Kirtland, Ohio, Temple dedicated.
Summer 1836	Mormons asked to leave Clay County, Mo.; they settle in Caldwell County.
Winter 1838/39	Missouri expels Mormons; refuge found in Quincy, Ill.
May 1839	Former Commerce, Ill., renamed Nauvoo, is new gathering place for Mormons.
July 1838	Consecration and Stewardship amended by a tithing system.
June 1844	Joseph Smith and brother killed in Carthage, Ill.
Aug. 1844	Brigham Young assumes leadership of main body of Mormons.
Feb. 1846	Mormons begin to move west; they camp on Missouri River.
July 1847	Pioneer company arrives in Utah.
1854–58	Consecration movement in Utah; nearly half of family heads deed property to church.
1864	Brigham City cooperative founded.

1869	Zion's Cooperative Mercantile Institution founded; transcontinental rail line completed.
1873	Panic of 1873 affects Utah.
Feb. 1874	United Order of Enoch movement launched in St. George.
July 1875	United Order of Orderville founded.
Sept. 1876	Brigham Young says he was inspired by God to implement the United Order.
Aug. 1877	Death of Brigham Young.
1882	Edmunds Act leads to vigorous prosecution of polygamists.
1885	Communal labors in Orderville abandoned.
1895	Brigham City Coop goes into receivership.
1919	Severe postwar depression lingers through 1920s in Utah.
Oct. 1929	Stock market crash commences Great Depression.
Apr. 1936	Church Welfare Plan announced.
Nov. 1975	Church leader Marion G. Romney affirms that the welfare plan is to lead to the United Order.

Notes

1. Cited in Leonard J. Arrington, Feramorz Y. Fox, and Dean L. May, *Building the City of God: Community and Cooperation among the Mormons* (Salt Lake City: Deseret Book Co., 1976), 468, from Porter to Bleak, August 9, 1904, James G. Bleak Manuscripts, Henry E. Huntington Library, San Marino, Calif. *Building the City of God* details much of the material covered in the present essay and remains the most comprehensive study of Mormon communitarianism. A new edition was published by the University of Illinois Press in 1992.

2. Robert N. Bellah, Richard Madsen, William M. Sullivan, Ann Swidler, and Steven M. Tipton, *Habits of the Heart: Individualism and Commitment in American Life* (Berkeley: University of California Press, 1985), 39.

3. Richard L. Bushman treats the family-centered character of early Mormonism in *Joseph Smith and the Beginnings of Mormonism* (Champaign: University of Illinois Press, 1984).

4. Smith's history is readily available in a Mormon scripture called the Pearl of Great Price, "Writings of Joseph Smith, 2."

5. References are in another Mormon scripture, Doctrine and Covenants 1:14–16, 38:27, and 58:55.

6. Book of Mormon, Fourth Nephi, verse 3; Pearl of Great Price, Moses 7:18.

7. Doctrine and Covenants 42:30–38.

8. Psalms 24:1.

9. Gordon Eric Wagner has analyzed the system in "Consecration and Stewardship: A Socially Efficient System of Justice" (Ph.D. diss., Cornell University, 1977).

10. The early communal efforts of the Mormons, including the significance of the Plat of the City of Zion are treated by Mario S. De Pillis in "The Development of Mormon Communitarianism, 1826–1846" (Ph.D. diss., Yale University, 1960).

11. *Autobiography of Parley Parker Pratt*, ed. Parley P. Pratt Jr., 3d ed. (Salt Lake City: Deseret Book Co., 1938), 72, 93; Brigham Young sermon, April 7, 1873, in the *Journal of Discourses*, 26 vols. (Liverpool: F. D. Richards, 1855–1884), 16:11.

12. The identification with ancient Israel, profoundly important in understanding Mormonism, is discussed in Jan Shipps, *Mormonism: The Story of a New Religious Tradition* (Urbana: University of Illinois Press, 1985).

13. Lyndon W. Cook offers an alternative interpretation of the continuing significance of Consecration and Stewardship in *Joseph Smith and the Law of Consecration* (Provo, Utah: Grandin, 1985). He sees the system as having been reduced to a vague advocacy of "spiritual commitment and love" by the time of Joseph Smith's death. He does not explain why Brigham Young remained so devoted to the communitarianism in Smith's original vision or why subsequent church leaders have maintained the Mormons will live a communal life as their ultimate preparation for the millennium. Dean L. May included a response to Cook in "The Economics of Zion," *Sunstone* 14 (August 1990): 15–22.

14. The hymn was in the first (1835) edition of *Latter-day Saint Hymns* and has been in all subsequent editions. Young's burial instructions are in Leonard J. Arrington's *Brigham Young: American Moses* (New York: Knopf, 1985), 400.

15. Klaus J. Hansen, *Quest for Empire: The Political Kingdom of God and the Council of Fifty in Mormon History* (East Lansing: Michigan State University Press, 1967), and D. Michael Quinn, "The Council of Fifty and Its Members, 1844–1945," *Brigham Young University Studies* 20 (Winter 1980): 163–97.

16. Young was sustained as prophet at Winter Quarters, a Mormon settlement on the Missouri, in December 1847. See D. Michael Quinn, "The Mormon Succession Crisis of 1844," *Brigham Young University Studies* 16 (Winter 1976): 187–233.

17. See Richard E. Bennett, *Mormons at the Missouri, 1846–1852: "And Should We Die . . . ,"* (Norman: University of Oklahoma Press, 1987).

18. Mormon economic development in Utah is the principal theme of Leonard J. Arrington's classic study *Great Basin Kingdom: An Economic History of the Latter-day Saints, 1830–1900* (Cambrige, Mass.: Harvard University Press, 1958).

19. See [Dyer D. Lum], *Social Problems of Today; or, the Mormon Question in Its Economic Aspects* (Port Jervis, N.Y.: Dyer D. Lum, 1886).

20. The above descriptions of cooperative endeavor in Utah draw from relevant chapters in Arrington et al., *Building the City*. The telegram is Brigham Young to D. H. Wells et al., February 28, 1874, Brigham Young Telegrams, MS, LDS Church Archives, Salt Lake City, Utah.

21. Dean L. May, "Brigham Young and the Bishops: The United Order in the City," in *New Views of Mormon History: A Collection of Essays*, ed. Davis Bitton and Maureen Ursenbach Beecher (Salt Lake City: University of Utah Press, 1987), 115–37.

22. John Oakley to Brigham Young, January 16, 1877, MS, Brigham Young Incoming Correspondence, LDS Church Archives; *Deseret News*, January 13, 1877, as cited in Arrington et al., *Building the City*, 263, 276.

23. *Deseret News*, March 4, 28, 1892, as cited in Arrington et al., *Building the City*, 293.

24. Presiding Bishopric, Bishops' Meeting Minutes, 1862–1879, September 21, 1876, LDS Church Archives.

25. St. George Stake Manuscript History, June 9, 1878, LDS Church Archives, as cited in Arrington et al., *Building the City*, 175.

26. Dean L. May makes this point in his *Three Frontiers: Family, Land, and Society in the American West, 1850–1900* (New York: Cambridge University Press, 1994). See esp. chap. 6, "The Place Where We Lived."

27. Evon Z. Vogt and Ethel M. Albert, eds., *People of Rimrock: A Study of Values in Five Cultures* (Cambridge, Mass.: Harvard University Press, 1966), 28.

28. An excellent recent overview of Latter-day Saint efforts at poor relief is Garth L. Mangum and Bruce D. Blumell, *The Mormons' War on Poverty : A History of LDS Welfare, 1830–1990* (Salt Lake City: University of Utah Press, 1993).

29. *LDS Conference Report*, October 3, 4, 1936, 59, 114. The quotes are from Joseph Fielding Smith and J. Reuben Clark Jr.

30. *Improvement Era*, December 1938, 740.

31. Oral interview, January 4, 1973, LDS Church Archives. See also *Ensign*, November 1975, 127. A review of the history philanthropic outreach by the Latter-day Saints is in Dean L. May, "Body and Soul: The Record of Mormon Religious Philanthropy," *Church History* 57 (September 1988): 322–36.

32. Cited in Bellah et al., *Habits of the Heart*, 37.

Selected Bibliography

Allen, Edward J. *The Second United Order among the Mormons*. New York: Columbia University Press, 1936.

Arrington, Leonard J. *Great Basin Kingdom: An Economic History of the Latter-day Saints, 1830–1900*. Cambridge, Mass.: Harvard University Press, 1958.

Arrington, Leonard J., Feramorz Y. Fox, and Dean L. May. *Building the City of God: Community and Cooperation among the Mormons*. Salt Lake City: Deseret Book Co., 1976. 2d ed., Urbana: University of Illinois Press, 1992.

Cook, Lyndon W. *Joseph Smith and the Law of Consecration*. Provo, Utah: Grandin, 1985.

De Pillis, Mario S. "The Development of Mormon Communitarianism, 1826–1846." Ph.D. diss., Yale University, 1960.

Flanders, Robert B. *Nauvoo: Kingdom on the Mississippi*. Urbana: University of Illinois Press, 1965.

Gardner, Hamilton. "Communism among the Mormons." *Quarterly Journal of Economics* 37 (1923): 134–74.

———. "Cooperation among the Mormons." *Quarterly Journal of Economics* 31 (1917): 461–99.

Geddes, Joseph A. *The United Order among the Mormons (Missouri Phase)*. Salt Lake City: Deseret News Press, 1924.

Lucas, James W., and Warner P. Woodworth. *Working toward Zion: Principles of the United Order for the Modern World*. Salt Lake City: Aspen Books, 1996.

[Lum, Dyer D.] *Social Problems of Today; or, the Mormon Question in its Economic Aspects*. Port Jervis, N.Y.: Dyer D. Lum, 1886.

Mangum, Garth L., and Bruce D. Blumell. *The Mormons' War on Poverty : A History of LDS Welfare, 1830–1990*. Salt Lake City: University of Utah Press, 1993.

May, Dean L. "Brigham Young and the Bishops: The United Order in the City." In *New Views of Mormon History: A Collection of Essays*, edited by Davis Bitton and Maureen Ursenbach Beecher, 115–37. Salt Lake City: University of Utah Press, 1987.

Olsen, Arden Beal. "The History of Mormon Mercantile Cooperation in Utah." Ph.D. diss., University of California, Berkeley, 1935.

Stegner, Wallace. *The Gathering of Zion: The Story of the Mormon Trail*. New York: McGraw-Hill, 1971.

Vogt, Evon Z., and Ethel M. Albert, eds. *People of Rimrock: A Study of Values in Five Cultures*. Cambridge, Mass.: Harvard University Press, 1966.

Wagner, Gordon Eric. "Consecration and Stewardship: A Socially Efficient System of Justice." Ph.D. diss., Cornell University, 1977.

CARL J. GUARNERI

Brook Farm and the Fourierist Phalanxes

Immediatism, Gradualism, and American Utopian Socialism

Born in Besançon, France, in 1772 into an age of revolutionary up-heaval, Charles Fourier saw with a clarity that bordered on madness that his mission was to bring order and justice to humanity. During his career as a traveling salesman and commercial employee, Fourier became fed up with the frauds of commerce: adulteration of products, loan sharking, speculation in currency, and the creation of devastating artificial shortages. In Lyons the misery of silk workers fighting with master merchants over declining wages awakened him to the coming Industrial Revolution. To reconcile conflicting social interests, Fourier began to tinker with schemes for model cities and cooperative warehouses. By the time he was thirty, he had come to believe that an entire economic system based on the anarchy of free competition was wrong. A radical change was necessary, but it must be con-structive, orderly, and peaceful. Having lost his inheritance in the French Revolution when Parisian troops destroyed his entire stock of goods, Fourier hated social conflict and hoped instead for a society guaranteeing class har-mony through scientific organization.[1]

About the same time that his fellow utopian visionaries Henri de Saint-Simon in France and Robert Owen in Scotland were developing their ideas of social reform, Fourier decided that the cure for the evils of competitive civilization was the establishment of meticulously planned cooperative com-

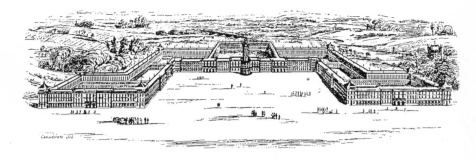

This design for a Phalanstery, Charles Fourier's concept of the communal palace
that was to house the world in exactly 2,985,984 communities, was published
by Victor Considerant in *Description du phalanstère* in Paris in 1848.

munities called "phalanxes," which would gather persons of all classes and
characters and spread throughout the world. In each community there would
be a huge central dwelling or "phalanstery" located on a large countryside
plot and surrounded by the workshops, fields, and cultural institutions that
provided a varied and fulfilling existence for every resident. Beginning in
1808 Fourier described this communal vision with painstaking detail in dis-
organized and difficult writings that went virtually unread until in the wake of
the July revolution of 1830 a circle of young French intellectuals embraced
them as the bible of their movement.[2]

Nothing was known of Fourier's theory in the United States until it was
brought across the Atlantic by a young and energetic American convert. Albert Brisbane, the pampered and somewhat pushy son of an upstate New
York landowner, embarked on a student's tour of Europe in 1828. His search
for a creed took Brisbane to Victor Cousin's lectures at the Sorbonne, to
Hegel's in Berlin, to Saint-Simonian soirees in Paris, and finally in 1832 to
Fourier himself, whose private lessons converted the American into a dedicated phalansterian within two months. The encounter gave Brisbane his life's
work. Henceforth his "only aim," he wrote to a friend, was "to transmit the
thought of Charles Fourier to my countrymen." For a year and a half Brisbane
remained in Paris, working with Fourier's French disciples. Upon his return
to New York he tried to accumulate enough funds through land speculation
to finance personally the first American Fourierist community. But when the
bank panic of 1837 and subsequent depression ruined this scheme, Brisbane
had to rethink his plans. Instead of sponsoring a community himself, he
would translate Fourier's works and initiate a utopian socialist journal in the
hope of building popular support for a phalanx experiment. In *Social Destiny
of Man*, published in 1840, Brisbane provided the clearest and most compre-

hensive exposition of Fourier's theory then available in English. He had no inkling, however, that a few years after its publication over two dozen miniature phalanxes would be established in the United States, or that Fourierism (pronounced here as "Foor-yur-ism") would become America's most popular and dynamic secular community movement of the entire nineteenth century.[3]

Though they are often lumped together as "utopian," American movements that have employed communal living have had varied constituents and purposes. Some were immigrant groups fleeing persecution or seeking to preserve an Old World way of life in a New World setting; others were religious sects that established godly enclaves apart from the world in order to practice their beliefs or await Christ's second coming. There have also been anarchist or single-tax advocates attempting to demonstrate a monetary theory in a controlled setting, secular reformers experimenting with new lifestyles, and even profit-seeking colonization companies tinged with elements of cooperation.

Among America's communal utopias the Fourierist phalanxes hold a special place. They are the classic case of the nineteenth-century ideology that Marx and Engels derisively called "utopian socialism," as opposed to their allegedly "scientific" brand. A more neutral name was supplied by Arthur Bestor, who called these kinds of plans "communitarian socialism." Whatever the label, the idea was to supplant existing society with model communities derived from a rational philosophy and a clear blueprint. In the aftermath of the Enlightenment, communitarianism emerged as a reform program that might leapfrog over the slow, piecemeal changes of politics, yet also avoid the violence of revolution. This "third force," discovered by reason and spread through example, would reconstruct society totally but peacefully.[4] The Fourierists were the most persuasive of those preaching such an all-embracing "social science." Unlike the Shakers, Mormons, or Oneidans, they were not a religious sect, nor did they adopt communalism provisionally or practice it in isolation from the world. Like the Owenites or the Icarians, but with a far larger American contingent and a much clearer program, they embraced communalism as the form by which—and to which—they hoped to convert all of society. The phalanxes were self-consciously part of a movement that aimed to reshape a conflict-ridden and disordered society into a new world of harmony and order. Model communities were both the levers of social change and the ultimate form the renovated society would take.

In fact, for Fourierists, as for no other group, the precise form of the utopian future was clearly marked out.[5] Humanity, according to Fourier, was inexorably progressing through increasingly complex stages of existence beginning with Savagery and Barbarism and continuing through Civilization and would eventually culminate in a Harmonic society of intricately planned phalanxes. But there was a much shorter road to utopia. Ever since the Greeks, the material preconditions of Harmony had been satisfied; only the correct theory was missing. It was Fourier's genius—as he immodestly proclaimed—to have discovered this "divine social code," the precise arrangements that would impel a sudden leap to Harmony. Deducing the details of phalanx existence from a scientific analysis of human "passions," Fourier claimed that they had all the rigor of mathematical calculations. Fourierist communities were thus demonstrations rather than experiments, intended to illustrate scientific truth rather than to proceed by trial and error. To Fourier's mind, a communal way of life did not develop; it was simply set up in full dress from a rational plan.

That plan was grandiose as well as specific. According to Fourier, exactly 1,620 men, women, and children—twice the number of distinctive human personality types that Fourier had found—were to inhabit a sprawling, multistory phalanstery whose wings enclosed landscaped inner courtyards and whose entrance faced a vast parade ground. Inside, a splendid variety of apartments, communal rooms, and circulation galleries would house residents and promote spontaneous association. Across from the main dwelling, workshops and storehouses would frame the public square. This central cluster of buildings would be situated on a beautiful tract of 6,000 acres with abundant gardens, carefully tended orchards, and inviting forests. Members would arrange themselves through the simple force of attraction into hundreds of specialized work groups gratifying every interest, and their contented labor would produce so much that consumption and leisure, not production, would be their main preoccupation.

The grand and all-too-specific vision of Fourier's phalanx dazzled American reformers in search of a concrete community plan, but ultimately it hurt the Fourierist movement. With expectations for palatial living aroused so absurdly high, Fourierists were too easily disappointed with struggling little communities that looked nothing like Fourier's phalanx. And Fourier's "instant" rather than gradual approach to communalism steered movement leaders in the wrong direction when they were faced with scaled-down projects and real-world decisions. In the end, leaders such as Brisbane and the faithful rank and file found it hard to accept that the American phalanxes might never approach Fourier's monumental plan.

Few commentators have recognized, however, that the Fourierist movement involved far more than phalanxes. Hoping to demonstrate cooperative principles and to spread their influence in the larger society, the Fourierists established outside the phalanxes a reform network comprising dozens of local clubs, mutual insurance groups, cooperative stores, and urban communes. Fourier himself had paid only fleeting attention to such transitional projects; they represented an important amendment by his disciples to the "instant community" idea. Ironically, it was in these gradualist institutions, more than in the short-lived phalanxes, that the impact of American Fourierism endured.

Fourier's theory was actually a vast and eccentric universal philosophy that included ideas about the origins and demise of the solar system, the psychological makeup of humanity, and the course of human and animal history, as well as visions—much too explicit for most nineteenth-century tastes—of a free-love utopia where "passional attraction" governed relationships. When Brisbane and his American colleagues imported it, they carefully edited the master's ideas, peeling away what Fourier called "the new amorous world" from "the new industrial world," then paring down the remainder to a practical communitarian program while still preserving enough of the larger theory to show that their blueprint was "scientific." Basically three main ideas were left: a critique of present-day society, a community plan, and an overlay of propaganda harmonizing Fourierism with prevalent American beliefs.[6]

At the start there was the conviction that the competitive system of the present must be replaced. Competition under capitalism reduced society to an "insane war of efforts and interests" whose waste, anxieties, and exploitations victimized all classes.[7] With uncanny foresight the Fourierists predicted that unlimited competition would lead to an "industrial feudalism" where people would either endure enslavement by monopolies and corporations or lead a bloody rebellion against them. European society was mired in poverty and oppression, but in the New World there was still time and space to plant the seed of a different order.

Fourier's phalanx was that seed. In contrast to the chaos of current "Civilization" the world of the phalanx would be both personally fulfilling and socially harmonious. In these model communities individuals would voluntarily form "groups" and then "series" of groups oriented around one task, such as carpentry, education, household work, or gardening. Working in teams and alternating jobs about every two hours, community members would be stimulated to greater productivity and at the same time develop the various aptitudes of their personal makeup. Cooperation would be ensured by guaranteeing everyone a minimum wage and maintenance in sickness or old age; by adopting a complex system of dividing up the community's profits (certain fractions going to labor, capital, and skill); and by having each member own part of the community through joint-stock shares.

Finally, the Fourierists presented their theory as a universal and all-reconciling reform. While declaring that theirs was a nonsectarian venture in which all religions were welcome, Brisbane and the American Fourierists made a special appeal to evangelical and liberal Protestants. To these they asserted that the phalanx was Christian love in practice and its dissemination would bring the millennium so many nineteenth-century Americans thought was at hand. To temperance, peace, and antislavery reformers, the Fourierists extended their sympathies and presented communitarianism as the indispensable precondition for realizing their goals. To conservatives worried about overturning established society, Fourierists demonstrated that their proposal was nonviolent, respected the rights of capital, and created a true "harmony of interests" between social groups and classes. To those wary of pledging allegiance to a single philosopher's doctrine, the Fourierists explained that the principles of "social science" were universal, and they adopted the name "Association" rather than "Fourierism" for their creed.

Fourier himself would settle for nothing less than the full complement of 1,620 Harmonians ensconced in a Versailles-like palace. Legend has it that the Frenchman waited in his apartment every noon for the millionaire who would underwrite the first phalanx. But Brisbane, impatient for success and sensing that the time was ripe, streamlined Fourier's blueprint for the American audience. In his popular pamphlet *Association* (1843), he advocated stripped-down phalanxes of a few hundred persons in the countryside not far from major cities, and he provided a model constitution. Brisbane stressed the compatibility of the phalanx plan with American ideals of self-government, personal freedom, equity, and social progress. Nowhere in French Fourierist literature did such a simple and practical version of the phalanx appear.

Within just three years after addressing the public, Brisbane was rewarded with two major victories. The first was the conversion of Horace Greeley, the colorful and soon-to-be famous editor of the *New York Tribune*. When he read the copy of *Social Destiny of Man* that Brisbane presented to him, Greeley sensed in Fourier's plan the kind of partnership between labor and capital he had been preaching as a Whig publicist. Greeley promptly offered Brisbane a column in his daily paper, and on March 1, 1842, a series of articles, "Association; or, Principles of a True Organization of Society," was inaugurated. Through the *Tribune* and other papers that picked up the column Brisbane was able to introduce Fourier's theory into thousands of reform-minded households across the northern states. Long after the editorial agreement terminated, Greeley gave the Associationist movement valuable publicity, defended it against critics, attended its conventions, and invested thousands of dollars in its phalanxes.[8]

Brisbane's second major triumph came when Brook Farm enlisted in the Fourierist movement. Perhaps the most celebrated of all American communal experiments, Brook Farm was founded in 1841 at West Roxbury, Massachusetts, outside Boston by George Ripley and a circle of Transcendentalist ministers, reformers, and writers. Among them was the young Nathaniel Hawthorne, who drew on his brief Brook Farm experience for the novel *Blithedale Romance* (1852). Ripley's idea, as he wrote Ralph Waldo Emerson, was to share the Transcendentalist version of the good life in a model cooperative society:

> Our objects, as you know, are to insure a more natural union between intellectual labor than now exists; to combine the thinker and the worker, as far as possible, in the same individual; to guarantee the highest mental freedom, by providing all with labor, adapted to their tastes and talents, and securing to them the fruits of their industry; . . . and thus to prepare a society of liberal, intelligent, and cultivated persons, whose relations with each other would permit a more simple and wholesome life, than can be led amidst the pressure of our competitive institutions.[9]

Emerson, like the spirited feminist Margaret Fuller, was too individualistic to join such a community, but Ripley attracted a talented group of young idealists. Throughout its brief life Brook Farm had a campuslike atmosphere, where unmarried men and women in their twenties predominated, social and literary discussion flourished, and room visits and moonlight walks created a casual and free—though quite proper—social life. Its showpiece was the community's school, which attracted students from around the country and gave them excellent practical as well as classical training.

By late 1843 the Brook Farmers wanted to broaden their membership and increase the community's efficiency. Through Brisbane's badgering, Ripley and other Transcendentalists were already familiar with Fourier's theory, and they were encouraged to adopt it by Greeley, a frequent visitor, and by their friend William Henry Channing, nephew of the great Unitarian preacher William Ellery Channing. Early in 1844 the Brook Farm Association announced its intention to become the Brook Farm Phalanx. The transition to Fourierism was actually quite smooth, contrary to the assertions of Lindsay Swift and others.[10] Ripley had always envisioned Brook Farm as a model experiment in class cooperation, and Fourierism linked this mission to a growing national movement, boosting the community's morale and democratizing

Josiah Wolcott's *Large Landscape of Brook Farm* pictures the tranquil rural setting of the Fourierist community in the 1840s. The urban expansion of nearby Boston later swallowed this scene.

its membership through the recruitment of carpenters, shoemakers, and other artisans. Brook Farm, in turn, became the Associationists' propaganda headquarters, whose members took over the Fourierist weekly *Harbinger*, made it into a first-class organ of literary and social criticism, and lectured on Association across New England and upstate New York.[11] Until a disastrous fire destroyed its new phalanstery in March 1846, the community was the lively center of American Fourierism.

With Brisbane and the Brook Farmers promoting Association and Greeley endorsing it, Fourierism was bound to command a hearing in reform circles. But no one was prepared for the enthusiastic, almost frenetic response to communitarian socialism in the early 1840s. The depression of the late 1830s had put clerks and craftsmen out of work; religious revivals left converts anxious to practice a more fervent Christianity; and middle-class Americans were swept up in a wave of reform enthusiasm. Fourier's rejection of partial and gradual measures coincided with the emergence of a new romantic faith in immediate and drastic action among reformers on both sides of the Atlantic.[12] These events converged with long-term trends such as the decline of artisan

CARL J. GUARNERI

self-employment under early industrial capitalism and the rise of journalism and reform as legitimate career choices for middle-class youths. The stage had been set for communal experimentation, and Fourierism's assurance of rapid success, its appeal to American ideals, its prestigious backers, and its seemingly scientific blueprint made it the preferred doctrine among communitarians. The Associationists' propaganda succeeded beyond their wildest dreams: no less than twenty-eight miniature phalanxes sprang up on American soil between 1843 and 1858. At least 15,000 Americans became personally involved at one time or another in the Fourierist movement.

A brief look at three of the most important phalanxes illustrates some of the forces at work in the rise and fall of the communal phase of the Fourierist movement. The Sodus Bay Phalanx was one of several communities founded in the "Burned-over District" of western New York. This region was a notorious seedbed of new religions and reform crusades—Finneyite revivalism, the Millerite movement, and Mormonism among them—and after Brisbane's lecture tour late in 1843, Fourierism swept through it like wildfire.[13] Spurred by local religious revivals and reeling from declining wheat prices and the slowdown of traffic on the Erie Canal—effects of the recent depression—Rochester Fourierists flocked into four different phalanx attempts. The Sodus Bay, the most promising of them, was established in 1844 at a scenic site on Lake Erie formerly inhabited by Shakers. Yet despite the community's strategic location and the substantial buildings and fine orchards it inherited, the experiment was a disastrous failure. A too-generous admission policy and the promise of a year's sustenance before any payment was due brought a rush of unqualified applicants who quickly put the community in debt. Overcrowded accommodations hastened the spread of typhoid fever, which depleted the labor force. To add to the community's problems, a serious dispute broke out between evangelical Protestants and religious liberals over issues such as work on Sunday and control of phalanx education. The two factions became, according to one observer, "opposite and hostile elements, which have no more affinity for each other than water and oil, or fire and gunpowder."[14] As families began leaving in 1845, the community sold its crops to repay them for cash advances and went bankrupt. In April 1846 the handful of remaining members dissolved the experiment.

Although it was a much more efficient and prosperous community, the Wisconsin Phalanx nevertheless fell prey to some of the same difficulties. Founded in 1844, it was representative of the Fourierist communities on the midwestern frontier. Southport (now Kenosha), Wisconsin, had been settled by migrants from upstate New York and Vermont. When business in the Lake Michigan seaport stagnated, this band of artisans gathered to discuss Brisbane's *Tribune* columns, then headed inland with their families to try cooperative farming. (Unlike Brook Farm the western phalanxes recruited members with farming experience and had almost as many children as adults.) As hard workers without the busy social life of the Brook Farmers, they built a solid economic base: the community ran a successful farm and reduced its debt year by year. But there were underlying conflicts and pressures. While the community's leader, Warren Chase, was a militant freethinker, other members were Baptists and Methodists committed to a strict code of personal conduct. And whereas Chase and his followers wanted to adopt Fourier's communal system as quickly as possible, other members were interested in cooperative production but not in "unitary dwellings" and shared meals. Finally in 1850, when key members leaped at the chance to sell their property at a hefty profit, the Wisconsin Phalanx disbanded.[15]

The North American Phalanx was established in 1843 with Brisbane's assistance by a group of Albany storekeepers and artisans. Within a few years it became, according to a contemporary observer, "the test-experiment on which Fourierism practically staked its all in this country."[16] On the sandy soil of New Jersey a diverse band of Associationists recruited from throughout the northern states built the most profitable and carefully organized phalanx. As the Fourierist community closest to New York City, the North American attracted a steady stream of visitors, received ample publicity in the *Tribune*, and benefited from the investment capital of sympathetic New York merchants. And as the last surviving phalanx, it attracted faithful Fourierist veterans from communities that had already dissolved. The surges of both capital and membership were mixed blessings, however. There was constant tension because Brisbane and the New York patrons wanted to build the North American into a full-scale model phalanx immediately, while resident members preferred to evolve slowly. In addition, some influential members, mostly nonresidents, wanted to make the phalanx more religious. In 1852 they split off to form a competing phalanx, the Raritan Bay Union, a few miles away. When in September 1854 the North American Phalanx's mill burned down, the remaining members voted not to rebuild it with outside capital. One year later the community closed.[17]

Each of the twenty-eight antebellum phalanxes had its own history, and important differences existed among them; but from this distance one can see common patterns. In the initial excitement neighbors and strangers organized the little phalanxes far too hastily and with too little capital. Most of them compounded the problem either by failing to secure full title to the property or by buying far too much acreage for their needs. Added to this was the failure to screen new members carefully: in many cases a useful skill or some capital to invest was the only requirement, and the probationary period was allowed to pass without a careful look at the candidate. The result was that, as Horace Greeley lamented, "scores of the conceited, . . . the selfish, . . . the pugnacious, . . . [and] the idle" were permitted to join the new phalanxes.[18]

All the phalanxes faced the problem of how far they should—or could—implement Fourier's formidable plan. Brook Farm was unique in that as a pre-existing communal experiment converted to Association it expected to adopt Fourierist practices gradually. All the other communities were founded under the Fourierist rubric, but they too had to compromise. Because of their limited membership and capital, none could aim to be a model phalanx along Fourier's guidelines. But most communities put into practice, to the degree they felt was possible or desirable, Fourier's system of work in groups and his idea of differential rewards for different kinds of work. Most gathered together persons from diverse religious and occupational backgrounds: far from being havens of dreamy ministers and intellectuals, as many people today still believe, the phalanxes attracted an artisan majority—large numbers of formerly self-employed carpenters, printers, masons, and shoemakers—but unfortunately in most communities not enough farmers.[19] Most community members lived in scaled-down phalansteries that resembled modern two-story apartment buildings and shared their meals in a common dining hall, although a few families inhabited separate cottages. Despite Fourier's dictates to the contrary, all the phalanxes were conservative in sexual and family relations: within a somewhat freer social atmosphere than Victorian households, the traditional nuclear family still predominated, sex roles were governed by nineteenth-century stereotypes, and children were raised by their parents. Thus for reasons ranging from lack of capital to ideological disagreement, Fourier's specifications for a full-blown model phalanx could not be met.

In many ways Fourierism had promised everything to everybody with the idea that "social science" would harmonize any differences that resulted from full freedom. Behind this lay the naive faith that under the proper conditions Baptists would get along with freethinkers and intellectuals would make great farmers. It did not work out that way. Disputes arose at various phalanxes over issues such as compulsory religious services, communal dining, drinking of alcohol, and differential wages.[20] Even when phalanxes were successful, there was always the temptation to sell one's shares at a profit and buy cheap land nearby. Faced with these kinds of pressures and disagreements, most of the antebellum phalanxes died early deaths. Twelve lasted just one year, only eight survived for more than three years, and the longest-lived, the North American Phalanx, held out for a mere dozen years.

Studies of long-lived utopian communities have found that genuine communal feeling is something that takes root among like-minded people rather than being imposed by a structure. Communal entrants have to be willing to sacrifice individual expression for the benefits of group identity and cohesion.[21] The Fourierists' confidence that their "scientific" arrangements could quickly and painlessly reconcile religious, ideological, class, and personality differences was perhaps the greatest illusion of their master's mechanical community blueprint. Fourier's complex organization, his "visible hand," worked no better than the laissez-faire capitalists' invisible one, which supposedly guided self-interested action automatically toward the common good.

Since the founding of phalanxes was meant to be the culmination of the Associationist movement, in theory at least, they should not have been established until the Fourierists organized local clubs, rallied public support through systematic national propaganda, and amassed a huge building fund. In practice, the virtually spontaneous rush into phalanxes made this impossible. Only after the first wave of little phalanxes began to crash did Brisbane, Ripley, Parke Godwin, and other national Fourierist leaders begin to gain control over the movement. Through *The Harbinger* they attempted to standardize doctrine and answer the Fourierists' critics. In 1846 they formed the American Union of Associationists, which organized local "unions" or Fourierist clubs, held annual conventions at which movement policy was voted on, underwrote extensive lecture tours, and opened subscriptions to a fund to build a model phalanx.

Viewed from a developmental perspective, the Fourierist movement really proceeded backward, beginning with the founding of communities and only then moving to organize a support network for them. Yet the situation might have been salvageable had Associationist leaders not compounded the problem by abandoning the existing communities in favor of an ever-elusive model phalanx yet to be established. Faced with fledgling communal experiments they viewed as unacceptable, national leaders decided to start over again, in effect dooming a dozen little self-proclaimed phalanxes still struggling to stay alive. Brisbane and his colleagues had shown admirable flexibility in the early 1840s when they pared down Fourier's blueprint and encouraged modest communal ventures. But when they reversed their course and retreated unimaginatively to Fourierist orthodoxy, they made a major strategic mistake. Despite their protests that the miniature phalanxes were not fair trials of Fourier's theory, public opinion identified them as Fourierist, and the decision to let the communities die fatally discredited the movement. A true model phalanx was so elaborate and expensive it could never be set up. There was absolutely no guarantee that it would succeed, either. On the other hand, there was the real possibility that a few of the existing phalanxes could have progressed through experiment and with outside support into stable cooperative communities—not exactly according to Fourier's blueprint, but worthy nonetheless.

All these points were driven home in a debate between Brisbane and John Humphrey Noyes, the Fourierists' rival and the shrewd, charismatic founding father of the Oneida Community. In response to Brisbane's statement of Fourier's scientific claims, Noyes made a distinction between the "deductive socialism" of the utopian socialists and his own "inductive" brand. "We do not believe," Noyes wrote, "that cogitation without experiment is the right way to a true social theory." Enduring communities evolved gradually from experience rather than from a preconceived blueprint, however imposing and apparently scientific. By patiently building consensus rather than expecting it as "the miraculous result of getting together vast assemblages," the Oneidans claimed to sidestep "the limitations and impossible conditions of Fourierism."[22] Noyes, whose Oneida experiment lasted thirty-three years, had the better of the argument. Clearly Fourier's vision of an immediate, monumental, and conclusive communal demonstration damaged the Associationist movement. Once they had read Fourier's splendid description and seen the palatial phalanstery in the engraving Brisbane brought back from France, Associationist leaders could not let go of the dream of a grand model phalanx established quickly from a "fresh start."

The last such fresh start was attempted in 1855 as the North American Phalanx was breaking up. For years Brisbane had been trying to interest Victor Considerant, the leader of the French Fourierists, in founding a Fourierist colony on the American frontier. When Louis Napoleon's coup d'état put an end to socialist agitation in France, Considerant finally looked to the New World. In 1853 he and Brisbane toured the American West on horseback and chose a site near present-day Dallas for a gathering of the Fourierist remnant from two continents. The result was the ill-fated colony of La Réunion, where a few dozen Americans and 300 Frenchmen struggled with drought, rattlesnakes, and internal divisions before giving up in 1859.[23] Thus as an organized community movement Fourierism was dead in the United States by the Civil War, though an impressive but isolated experiment, Silkville, was established by a wealthy Franco-American patron in Kansas in 1869.[24]

The American phalanxes were not, as it turned out, the germs of a new social world. But they did serve in more subtle ways as agents of change. The experience of living in community, however short lived, was not easily forgotten. As Paul Goodman once observed about small communal experiments, "Per-

haps the very transitoriness of such intensely motivated intentional communities is part of their perfection. Disintegrating, they irradiate society with
people who have been profoundly touched by the excitement of community
life, who do not forget the advantages but try to realize them in new ways. . . .
Perhaps these communities are like those 'little magazines' and 'little theatres'
that do not outlive their first few performances, yet from them comes all the
vitality of the next generation of everybody's literature."[25]

From this point of view communal experiments are educational environments that send out "graduates" to enact many of the group's ideals through
their lives in the larger society. The later careers of the Associationist movement's "alumni" testify to their enduring commitment to innovation and reform. Several phalanx leaders, most notably Charles Sears, Nathan Meeker,
and Alcander Longley, led or joined subsequent communitarian experiments
after the Civil War. Albert Brisbane and other ex-Fourierists helped to organize the reform-oriented American Social Science Association in 1865.
John Orvis of Brook Farm carried cooperative principles to the Gilded Age
labor movement through his leadership of the Sovereigns of Industry and
the Knights of Labor. Building on their apprenticeship with *The Harbinger*,
George Ripley later became the dean of American book reviewers, and his former colleague John Dwight was recognized as America's leading music critic.
Elizabeth Blackwell of the Philadelphia Associationists graduated as the first
woman medical doctor in America, and Fourierist ideals played an important part in her lifelong drive to extend medical care to women and the
poor. Henry James Sr., father of the great novelist, blended Fourierism with
the mystical theology of Swedenborg to emerge as a distinguished philosopher in his own right. Stephen Pearl Andrews became one of the first American anarchists and the man who introduced phonetic shorthand to the United
States. The outspoken, charismatic feminist Marie Howland continued her
Fourierist-inspired campaign for the liberation of women through communal
work and cooperative households into the 1890s. Dozens of Fourierist men
and women, including William Henry Channing and the influential journalist Parke Godwin, played important roles in the Republican Party's crusade
against slavery, seeing it as the culmination of their quest for a just American
society.[26] Even when Fourierist communalism was a brief phase in members'
lives, it made a lasting impact through them on society at large.

It is especially important to recognize that the Fourierist movement encompassed much more than the phalanx experiments. In two dozen cities
Fourierists formed local clubs affiliated with the American Union of Associationists where ordinary people heard utopian-socialist lectures, read and debated Fourier's works, and contributed funds to the national movement. A

"Religious Union of Associationists" was organized, with William Henry Channing as minister, to function as a nondenominational socialist church.[27] The "Woman's Associative Union" made and sold craft work to support the movement. The New England Industrial League promoted workers' producer associations, while the Workingmen's Protective Union organized cooperative stores. These Fourierist-inspired organizations existed simultaneously with the phalanxes, so that at any point in time the movement embodied different forms and degrees of cooperative socialism among which members and sympathizers could choose, ranging from fundraising groups to cooperatives to the phalanxes themselves.

All this represented a substantial innovation in Fourierism. Especially after the sudden leap to Harmony through phalanxes failed to materialize, many Associationists turned to more limited and gradual reforms. These were meant to demonstrate the benefits of Association on a small scale and win new converts. As a series of increasingly encompassing cooperative institutions, they might also serve as stepping stones to full cooperative living in a phalanx. Occasionally in his writings Fourier had mentioned or sketched such transitional institutions as communal kitchens, model farms, and mutual credit institutions, but he never considered them more than an unattractive last resort. As Nicholas Riasnovsky has noted, Fourier's "heart and hope remained in the trial phalanx."[28] His American followers made an important departure from the idea of instant community when the American Union of Associationists embraced such transitional reforms.

In *The Harbinger* local utopian-socialist clubs were urged to create a progressive system of "guarantees" (Fourierist jargon for cooperative institutions) among members. Cooperative stores were established by clubs at Albany, New York, and Lowell and Nantucket, Massachusetts, while Philadelphia and Albany Fourierists also set up disability and life insurance plans.[29] One group of projects, pioneering plans for "unitary dwellings," was especially forward looking. Thirty years before the first large-scale apartment building appeared in America, Fourierists developed elaborate blueprints for hotellike residences with common dining and recreation rooms, to be located in town or in the suburbs near a commuter railroad. Members would live in separate apartments and most would hold jobs in the outside society until enough capital was collected to begin group workshops. Such cooperative households were established in existing housing during the 1840s by two groups from the Boston Union of Associationists, and in the next decade by as many as 100 utopian socialists who joined the "Unitary Household" on Fourteenth Street in New York City. Married and single members moved together into townhouses and ran them as cooperatives, sharing housework, meals, and rental expenses. These "combined households" were America's first urban communes.[30]

Outside the affiliated unions, the Fourierists' publicity and support for gradualist reforms had even greater influence. The Associationists promoted mutual life insurance as a positive reform because the mutual method of democratic control and profit sharing through dividends was a perfect example of Fourierist techniques. One of their warmest supporters, Elizur Wright Jr., became known as the "father of life insurance" for his invention of reliable valuation tables and his crusade to rid the young industry of unethical practices.[31] In addition, such Fourierist authors as Brisbane, Thomas J. Durant, Charles Sears, and Victor Considerant, by promoting interest-free mutual banks and currency reform, contributed to an important debate over "greenbacks" and the credit system among Gilded Age reformers.[32]

The most impressive result of the Associationists' promotion of limited reforms was the cooperative movement. Whereas in England it was Owenite ideas that stimulated working-class cooperatives (through the Rochdale model), in the United States the Fourierists virtually founded the movement. Through their magazines and clubs the Fourierists encouraged and sponsored consumer cooperatives, which they called Protective Unions. By the end of the 1840s more than 230 such Protective Union stores were in operation in New England and New York, and many kept their doors open until the Civil War.[33] When Brisbane and other American Fourierists returned from a visit to France in the late 1840s, they brought with them details of producer associations started among French workers. Thanks to their publicity, by the early 1850s cooperative workshops were organized among ironmolders, tailors, printers, and seamstresses in Cincinnati, Boston, Pittsburgh, Providence, and New York.[34] Through their inspiration and support for cooperatives the Associationists extended genuine practical benefits to tens of thousands of men and women workers—far more than were touched by phalanxes. All these "transitional" organizations expanded the reach of Fourierism, and many of them lived on long after the phalanxes disappeared. The success of such gradualist reforms was a tacit rebuke to the theory of instant community through phalanxes, but it also demonstrated the enduring appeal of Fourierist ideals among nineteenth-century Americans.

Chronology

1772   Charles Fourier is born in Besançon, France.
1808   Fourier publishes *Theory of the Four Movements*, his first substantive work.

1832	First Fourierist journal, *La Réforme industrielle*, published in Paris. Albert Brisbane meets Fourier.
1837	Charles Fourier dies.
1840	Albert Brisbane publishes *Social Destiny of Man*.
1841	Brook Farm founded in West Roxbury (now Boston), Mass.
1842	Brisbane's column in the *New York Tribune* begins. First American phalanx, the Social Reform Unity, established in Pennsylvania.
1843	North American Phalanx begins operations in Monmouth County, N.J.
1844	Brook Farm officially converts to Fourierism. Fourierism peaks with twelve phalanxes founded in 1844, including the Wisconsin Phalanx, near Ripon, Wisc.
1845	First Fourierist-inspired cooperative store set up.
1846	American Union of Associationists formed. Fire at Brook Farm precipitates breakup.
1849	Wave of Fourierist producer cooperatives.
1850	Wisconsin Phalanx disbands.
1855	North American Phalanx dissolves; La Réunion colony of French and American Fourierists settles near present-day Dallas, Tex.
1859	Breakup of La Réunion.
1867	End of the Protective Union (cooperative store) movement.
1869	Kansas Co-operative Farm (Silkville) Phalanx founded near Ottawa, Kans.
1892	Demise of Silkville, the last Fourierist experiment in America.

Notes

1. For an excellent scholarly biography of Fourier, see Jonathan F. Beecher, *Charles Fourier: The Visionary and His World* (Berkeley: University of California Press, 1986).

2. Saint-Simon, Owen, and Fourier were often grouped together by contemporaries, and they even accused one another of plagiarism. See Fourier, *Pièges et charlatanisme des deux sectes Saint-Simon et Owen* (Paris: Bossange, 1831). There is no adequate history of the French Fourierist movement. Hubert Bourgin, *Fourier: Contribution à l'étude du socialisme français* (Paris: Société nouvelle de librairie et d'édition, 1905), 409–536; Henri Desroche, *La Société Festive: Du Fouriérisme écrit aux Fouriérismes practiques* (Paris: Editions du Seuil, 1975), 241–98; and Adolphe Alhaiza, *Historique de l'Ecole Sociétaire Fondée par Charles Fourier* (Paris: La Rénovation, 1894), 19–59, contain important information. See also the sources on Victor Considerant cited in n. 23, below.

3. Brisbane, as quoted in Jean Manesca to Charles Fourier, 30 January 1836, Archives Sociétaires, French National Archives. Brisbane's autobiography, Redelia Brisbane, *Albert Brisbane, a Mental Biography* (Boston: Arena, 1893), details his conversion to Fourierism, but because it was dictated in old age, it contains many inaccuracies. For a more careful reconstruction, see Arthur Bestor Jr., "Albert Brisbane—Propagandist for Socialism in the 1840s," *New York History* 28 (April 1947): 128–40. Bestor's article should be supplemented by Brisbane's correspondence in the French National Archives and his travel diaries of 1830–32 in the Brisbane Papers, George Arents Research Library, Syracuse University, Syracuse, N.Y. The fullest history of the movement Brisbane founded, and the source of much of this chapter's information, is Carl J. Guarneri, *The Utopian Alternative: Fourierism in Nineteenth-Century America* (Ithaca, N.Y.: Cornell University Press, 1991).

4. See Friedrich Engels, *Socialism, Utopian and Scientific* (1892; reprint, New York: International Publishers, 1975), and Arthur Bestor Jr., *Backwoods Utopias: The Sectarian Origins*

and the Owenite Phase of Communitarian Socialism in America, 1663–1829, 2d ed. (Philadelphia: University of Pennsylvania Press, 1970), vii–17, 256.

5. The most complete edition of Fourier's writings is *Oeuvres complètes de Charles Fourier*, 12 vols. (Paris: Editions Anthropos, 1966–68). The heart of Fourier's theory is available in English translation through *The Utopian Vision of Charles Fourier: Selected Texts on Work, Love, and Passionate Attraction*, trans. and ed. Jonathan Beecher and Richard Bienvenu (Columbia: University of Missouri Press, 1983); Mark Poster, ed. and trans., *Harmonian Man* (Garden City, N.Y.: Doubleday, 1971); and Charles Gide, ed., *Design for Utopia*, trans. Julia Franklin (New York: Schocken, 1971). The clearest and most comprehensive survey of Fourier's thought in English is Nicholas V. Riasnovsky, *The Teaching of Charles Fourier* (Berkeley: University of California Press, 1969), but for a penetrating psychological interpretation, see Frank Manuel and Fritzie Manuel, *Utopian Thought in the Western World* (Cambridge, Mass.: Harvard University Press, 1979), 641–75.

6. The following section on the Americanization of Fourierist doctrine is based on Carl J. Guarneri, "Importing Fourierism to America," *Journal of the History of Ideas* 53 (October–December 1982): 581–94.

7. Albert Brisbane and Osborne Macdaniel, "Gradual Abasement of the Producing Classes," *Phalanx* 1 (March 1, 1844): 73.

8. Bestor, "Albert Brisbane," 144–45, 150–53, carefully sorts out conflicting accounts of the Brisbane-Greeley connection. For Greeley's subsequent role in promoting Fourierism, see Cecelia Koretsky, "Horace Greeley and Fourierism in the United States" (M.A. thesis, University of Rochester, 1952).

9. Ripley to Emerson, 9 November 1840, quoted in Octavius Brooks Frothingham, *George Ripley* (Boston: Houghton Mifflin, 1882), 307–8. Histories of Brook Farm include Lindsay Swift, *Brook Farm: Its Members, Scholars, and Visitors* (New York: Macmillan, 1900), and John Thomas Codman, *Brook Farm: Historic and Personal Memoirs* (Boston: Arena, 1894). For other sources, see Joel Myerson, ed., *Brook Farm: An Annotated Bibliography and Resource Guide* (New York: Garland, 1978).

10. Swift, *Brook Farm*, 14, 135, 277–81, stresses the incompatibility of Fourierism with early Brook Farm ideals and practices. But see Charles Crowe, "'This Unnatural Union of Phalansteries and Transcendentalists,'" *Journal of the History of Ideas* 20 (October–December 1959): 495–502; Crowe, "Fourierism and the Founding of Brook Farm," *Boston Public Library Quarterly* 12 (April 1960): 79–88; and Richard Francis, "The Ideology of Brook Farm," *Studies in the American Renaissance* (1977): 1–48, for a useful corrective.

11. A detailed study of *The Harbinger* is Sterling F. Delano, *The Harbinger and New England Transcendentalism: A Portrait of Associationism in America* (Rutherford, N.J.: Fairleigh Dickinson University Press, 1983).

12. See David Brion Davis, "The Emergence of Immediatism in British and American Antislavery Thought," *Mississippi Valley Historical Review* 49 (September 1962): 209–30, and John L. Thomas, "Romantic Reform in America, 1815–1865," *American Quarterly* 17 (Winter 1965): 656–81.

13. The classic study of agitation in the region, Whitney R. Cross, *The Burned-over District: The Social and Intellectual History of Enthusiastic Religion in Western New York, 1800–1850* (Ithaca, N.Y.: Cornell University Press, 1950), should now be supplemented by Paul E. Johnson, *A Shopkeeper's Millennium: Society and Revivals in Rochester, New York, 1815–1837* (New York: Hill and Wang, 1978), and Michael Barkun, *Crucible of the Millennium: The Burned-over District of New York in the 1840s* (Syracuse, N.Y.: Syracuse University Press, 1986). Arthur Bestor's pioneering study, "American Phalanxes: A Study of Fourierist Socialism in the United States (with Special Reference to the Movement in West-

ern New York)" (Ph.D. diss., Yale University, 1938), contains the best account of the Sodus Bay Phalanx.

14. John A. Collins, quoted in John Humphrey Noyes, *History of American Socialisms* (Philadelphia: Lippincott, 1870; reprint, New York: Dover, 1966), 290.

15. For histories of the Wisconsin Phalanx, see S. M. Pedrick, "The Wisconsin Phalanx at Ceresco," *Proceedings of the State Historical Society of Wisconsin* (1902): 190–226, and Joan Elias, "The Wisconsin Phalanx: An Experiment in Association" (M.A. thesis, University of Wisconsin, 1968). The phalanx's records are in the Ceresco Community Papers, State Historical Society of Wisconsin. Noyes, *American Socialisms*, 411–48, reprints valuable contemporary accounts.

16. Noyes, *American Socialisms*, 449.

17. Published histories of the North American Phalanx include Herman J. Belz, "The North American Phalanx: Experiment in Socialism," *Proceedings of the New Jersey Historical Society* 81 (October 1963): 215–46; George Kirchmann, "Unsettled Utopias: The North American Phalanx and the Raritan Bay Union," *New Jersey History* 97 (Spring 1979): 25–36; and Dolores Hayden, *Seven American Utopias: The Architecture of Communitarian Socialism, 1790–1975* (Cambridge, Mass.: MIT Press, 1976), 148–85. The phalanx's records are in the Monmouth County (N.J.) Historical Society. Several contemporary accounts are reprinted in Noyes, *American Socialisms*, 449–511.

18. Horace Greeley, *Recollections of a Busy Life* (New York: J. B. Ford, 1868), 154.

19. For an occupational profile of the phalanxes, see Carl Guarneri, "Who Were the Utopian Socialists?: Patterns of Membership in American Fourierist Communities," *Communal Societies* 5 (1985): 65–81.

20. Noyes, *American Socialisms*, 648–53, gloomily reviews the causes of conflict in the phalanxes.

21. See Benjamin Zablocki, *The Joyful Community: An Account of the Bruderhof, a Communal Movement Now in Its Third Generation* (Baltimore: Penguin, 1972); Rosabeth M. Kanter, *Commitment and Community: Communes and Utopias in Sociological Perspective* (Cambridge, Mass.: Harvard University Press, 1972); and David French and Elena French, *Working Communally: Patterns and Possibilities* (New York: Russell Sage Foundation, 1975). Two contemporary observers of nineteenth-century communitarianism concurred. John Humphrey Noyes stressed that successful community life required "subordination" of self and a prior "bond of agreement." See Noyes, *American Socialisms*, 656, 672. Charles Nordhoff concluded that "patience, submission[, and] self-sacrifice" were the most important determinants of communal success. See Nordhoff, *The Communistic Societies of the United States: From Personal Visit and Observation* (New York: Harper and Bros., 1875; reprint, New York: Schocken, 1965), 409.

22. Noyes, *American Socialisms*, 667, 672.

23. For the history of La Réunion, see Russell M. Jones, "Victor Considerant's American Experience, 1852–1869," *French-American Review* 1 (1976–77): 65–94, 124–50; Rondel V. Davidson, "Victor Considerant and the Failure of La Réunion," *Southwestern Historical Quarterly* 76 (January 1973): 277–96; William J. Hammond and Margaret Hammond, *La Réunion: A French Settlement in Texas* (Dallas: Royal, 1958); and Jonathan Beecher, "Une utopie manquée au Texas: Victor Considerant et Réunion," *Cahiers Charles Fourier* 4 (1993): 40–79.

24. Garrett R. Carpenter, "Silkville: A Kansas Attempt in the History of Fourierist Utopias, 1869–1892," *Emporia State Research Studies* 3 (December 1954): 3–29.

25. Paul Goodman and Percival Goodman, *Communitas: Means of Livelihood and Ways of Life* (New York: Vintage, 1960), 109.

26. On Longley's later ventures, see Hal Sears, "Alcander Longley, Missouri Communist: A History of Reunion Community and a Study of the Constitutions of Reunion and Friendship," *Missouri Historical Society Bulletin* 25 (1969): 123–37. Meeker's role in the Union Colony of Colorado is noted in Hayden, *Seven American Utopias*, 260–87. Sears's continuing involvement in communitarianism is evident in Carpenter, "Silkville," 22–29. For the Fourierist connections of the American Social Science Association, see Luther Bernard and Jessie Bernard, *Origins of American Sociology: The Social Science Movement in the United States* (New York: Crowell, 1943), 527–67. On Orvis, see Swift, *Brook Farm*, 175–81, and David Montgomery, *Beyond Equality: Labor and the Radical Republicans, 1862–1872* (New York: Vintage, 1967), 414. For Ripley's later career, see Frothingham, *Ripley*, 199–305; for Dwight's, see George Willis Cooke, *John Sullivan Dwight, Brook Farmer, Editor, and Critic of Music* (Boston: Small, Maynard, 1898). Fourierist influence on Blackwell is apparent in her memoirs, *Pioneer Work in Opening the Medical Profession to Women*, Everyman's Library Edition (London: J. M. Dent & Sons, 1914), 10–11, 47, but can be traced most clearly in the Blackwell Family Papers, Library of Congress. On James, see Alfred Habegger, *The Father: A Life of Henry James, Sr.* (New York: Farrar, Straus & Giroux, 1994). Andrews's adventures are followed in Madeleine B. Stern, *The Pantarch: A Biography of Stephen Pearl Andrews* (Austin: University of Texas Press, 1968). For Howland's life and ideas, see Dolores Hayden, *The Grand Domestic Revolution: A History of Feminist Designs for American Homes, Neighborhoods, and Cities* (Cambridge, Mass.: MIT Press, 1981), 91–113, and Paul M. Gaston, *Women of Fair Hope* (Athens: University of Georgia Press, 1984), 19–65. Godwin's contribution to the antislavery Republican Party is outlined in John R. Wennersten, "A Reformer's Odyssey: The Public Career of Parke Godwin of the New York *Evening Post*, 1837–1870" (Ph.D. diss., University of Maryland, 1970).

27. *Harbinger* 7 (17 June 1848): 56, reported Affiliated Unions of the American Union of Associationists functioning in Bangor, Maine; Boston, Lowell, Newburyport, Mattapoisett, New Bedford, Amesbury, Nantucket, and Springfield, Mass.; Brandon, Clarendon, Middlebury, and Pittsford, Vt.; Providence, R.I.; Albany, King's Ferry, Utica, Westmoreland, and New York, N.Y.; Philadelphia and Pittsburgh, Pa.; Wheeling, Va.; Cincinnati, Ohio; and Ceresco, Wisc. Two other unions, at Washington, D.C., and Manchester, N.H., were formed later. For the Religious Union of Associationists, see Charles Crowe, "Christian Socialism and the First Church of Humanity," *Church History* 35 (1966): 93–106, and Sterling F. Delano, "A Calendar of the Meetings of the 'Boston Religious Union of Associationists,'" in *Studies in the American Renaissance 1985*, ed. Joel Myerson (Charlottesville: University of Virginia Press, 1985), 187–267.

28. Riasnovsky, *Teaching of Fourier*, 138.

29. "Doings in Albany," *Harbinger* 6 (22 January 1848): 93; "Annual Meeting of the American Union of Associationists," *Harbinger* 7 (13 May 1848): 13; Philadelphia Union of Associationists, *Constitution of the Group of Actuation* (Philadelphia: n.p., n.d.).

30. The most detailed plan for such a "unitary dwelling" was the *Constitution of the Philadelphia Unitary Building Association* (Philadelphia: U.S. Job Printing Office, 1849). For one Boston "combined household," see Helen Dwight Orvis, "A Note on Anna Q. T. Parsons," in Marianne Dwight, *Letters from Brook Farm, 1844–1847*, ed. Amy L. Reed (Poughkeepsie, N.Y.: Vassar College Press, 1928), xv; Cooke, *Dwight*, 129–30; and William Henry Channing to Julia Channing, 29 November 1848, William Allen Family Papers, Houghton Library, Harvard University, Cambridge, Mass. This and the second commune can be found in the Manuscript Population Schedules of the Seventh Census of the United States, Suffolk County, Mass. For the New York "Unitary Household," see Laura Stedman

and George M. Gould, *Life and Letters of Edmund Clarence Stedman* (New York: Moffat, Yard, 1910), 1:151–77, and Luisa Cetti, *Un falansterio a New York: L'Unitary Household (1858–1860) e il riformismo prebellico americano* (Palermo: Sellerio, 1992).

31. Wright attended Associationist meetings and, like Greeley, arranged for a column of his newspaper to carry Fourierist news and ideas. A sparkling summary of Wright's work in insurance reform is in Daniel J. Boorstin, *The Americans: The Democratic Experience* (New York: Random House, 1974), 175–80.

32. See Albert Brisbane, *The Philosophy of Money* (n.p., 1863); Thomas J. Durant, *Free Money, Free Credit and Free Exchange* (Washington, D.C.: Gibson Bros., 1874); Charles Sears, *Representative Money* (Ottawa, Kans.: n.p., 1878); and Victor Considerant, *Three Hundred Millions of Dollars Saved in Specie by the Meaning of a Word* (New York: n.p., 1867).

33. Edwin C. Rozwenc, *Cooperatives Come to America: The History of the Protective Union Store Movement, 1845–1867* (1941; reprint, Philadelphia: Porcupine Press, 1975).

34. Albert Brisbane, "Co-Operation in America," *Christian Socialist* 2 (27 September 1851): 202–4; James Harrison Wilson, *Life of Charles A. Dana* (New York: Harper and Bros., 1907), 92–94; Norman J. Ware, *The Industrial Worker, 1840–1860* (Boston: Houghton Mifflin, 1924), 193–97.

Selected Bibliography

Bassett, T. D. Seymour. "The Secular Utopian Socialists." In *Socialism and American Life*, edited by Donald Drew Egbert and Stow Persons, 1:155–211. Princeton: Princeton University Press, 1952.

Beecher, Jonathan F. *Charles Fourier: The Visionary and His World*. Berkeley: University of California Press, 1986.

Belz, Herman J. "The North American Phalanx: Experiment in Socialism." *Proceedings of the New Jersey Historical Society* 81 (October 1963): 215–46.

Bestor, Arthur, Jr. "Albert Brisbane—Propagandist for Socialism in the 1840s." *New York History* 28 (April 1947): 128–58.

———. "American Phalanxes: A Study of Fourierist Socialism in the United States (with Special Reference to the Movement in Western New York)." Ph.D. diss., Yale University, 1938.

———. "The Communitarian Point of View." In *Backwoods Utopias: The Sectarian Origins and the Owenite Phase of Communitarian Socialism in America, 1663–1829*, by Arthur Bestor Jr., 1–19. 2d ed. Philadelphia: University of Pennsylvania Press, 1970.

Brisbane, Albert. *Social Destiny of Man; or Association and Reorganization of Industry*. 1840. Reprint, New York: Burt Franklin, 1967.

Crowe, Charles. *George Ripley, Transcendentalist and Utopian Socialist*. Athens: University of Georgia Press, 1967.

Delano, Sterling F. *The Harbinger and New England Transcendentalism: A Portrait of Associationism in America*. Rutherford, N.J.: Fairleigh Dickinson University Press, 1983.

Dwight, Marianne. *Letters from Brook Farm, 1844–1847*. Edited by Amy L. Reed. Poughkeepsie, N.Y.: Vassar College Press, 1928.

Fourier, Charles. *The Utopian Vision of Charles Fourier: Selected Texts on Work, Love, and Passionate Attraction*. Translated and edited by Jonathan Beecher and Richard Bienvenu. Columbia: University of Missouri Press, 1983.

Guarneri, Carl J. *The Utopian Alternative: Fourierism in Nineteenth-Century America*. Ithaca, N.Y.: Cornell University Press, 1991.

Hayden, Dolores. *Seven American Utopias: The Architecture of Communitarian Socialism, 1790–1975*. Cambridge, Mass.: MIT Press, 1976, 148–85.

Jones, Russell M. "Victor Considerant's American Experience (1852–1869)." *French-American Review* 1 (1976–77): 65–94, 124–50.

Noyes, John Humphrey. *History of American Socialisms*. Philadelphia: Lippincott, 1870. Reprint, New York: Dover, 1966.

Riasnovsky, Nicholas V. *The Teaching of Charles Fourier*. Berkeley: University of California Press, 1969.

Rose, Anne C. *Transcendentalism as a Social Movement, 1830–1850*. New Haven: Yale University Press, 1981.

Rozwenc, Edwin C. *Cooperatives Come to America: The History of the Protective Union Store Movement, 1845–1867*. 1941. Reprint, Philadelphia: Porcupine Press, 1975.

Spann, Edward K. *Brotherly Tomorrows: Movements for a Cooperative Society in America, 1820–1920*. New York: Columbia University Press, 1989.

Spurlock, John C. *Free Love: Marriage and Middle-Class Radicalism in America, 1825–1860*. New York: New York University Press, 1988.

Swift, Lindsay. *Brook Farm: Its Members, Scholars, and Visitors*. New York, Macmillan, 1900.

Ware, Norman J. *The Industrial Worker, 1840–1860*. Boston: Houghton Mifflin, 1924. Reprint, Chicago: Quadrangle, 1964.

JONATHAN G. ANDELSON

The Community of True Inspiration from Germany to the Amana Colonies

In gently rolling countryside along the Iowa River in east-central Iowa are the seven small villages of the Amana Colonies, home to one of the most successful communal societies in American history. The villages nestle into the flanks of the valley on either side of the river, which meanders southeast toward the Mississippi River seventy-five miles away. Five of the villages lie in a scraggly line one or two miles apart on the north side of the river. The other two are separated by five miles on the south side of the river. The bottomland adjacent to the river and some of the higher hills are forested. The rest of the land has been cleared and is used for cattle grazing and crops; fields of corn, soybeans, and hay thrive in the rich alluvial soil. Good stewardship is evident in every direction.

Six of the villages have a grid-shaped layout, while one consists of a single long street. Virtually all of the buildings on Amana property are located in the villages. Numerous barns and other farm buildings can be found in one or two clusters near the perimeter of each village. Modern houses, with widely varying architecture, are concentrated in several locations. The core of each village consists of houses, outbuildings, and shops dating from the nineteenth century and obviously built according to a general plan. The architecture is reminiscent of Georgian style: orthogonal lines, symmetrical form, and a solid, no-nonsense look. The discerning eye can catch occasional intrusive elements, such as picture windows, shutters, elaborate porches, and half-timbering, all twentieth-century additions.

Amana Inspirationists' homes, kitchen gardens, and barns, as well as the canal
that powered their calico and woolen mills, as seen in a panorama from the
Amana Woolen Mill smokestack around 1910. (Photographic Collection,
Amana Heritage Society. Photograph by Bertha Shambaugh.)

In the center of each village stands the church, larger than the other buildings but otherwise indistinguishable from them. No cross, spire, belfry, or
sign marks its identity. The main sanctuary within is equally plain. The walls
are painted pale blue; the wood floor is unpainted and unvarnished. Unpainted wooden benches are arranged in a dozen rows facing one of the long
walls. In the front of the room, facing the rows of benches, stands a chair and
a small table as well as four benches. There are no icons of any kind, or any
musical instruments. The sanctuary, indeed the entire building, bespeaks a
directness and simplicity in religious attitude uncommon in the modern
world.

The Sunday morning service in the Amana churches has not changed ap-
preciably for 150 years. Men in somber suits enter the church through one
door and sit on one side of the room; women in plain dresses and wearing
traditional black aprons, shawls, and caps enter through another door and sit
on the other side. The church "elders" occupy the benches at the front of the
room that face the congregation. The presiding elder, seated at the table,
reads from Scripture and from a collection of books unique to the Amanas
containing inspired pronouncements delivered by early leaders of the church

JONATHAN G. ANDELSON

over a century ago. Following the readings the congregation joins in the recitation of prayers, hymns, and the Apostle's Creed. The unvarying form and content of the church service gives an impression of timelessness and simple piety.

A short distance from the church in Middle Amana, the village closest to the geographical center of the colonies, across well-manicured lawns and down a grassy slope, stands Amana Refrigeration, Inc., an enormous modern factory where the manufacture of freezers, refrigerators, and microwave ovens is controlled by computer. It employs over 2,000 workers, most of whom commute from neighboring cities and towns. In the main village, simply called Amana, in spring, summer, and fall, and again around Christmas, the streets are filled with thousands of tourists shopping at a myriad of gift shops, wineries, and stores and perhaps sampling the fare at one of several restaurants in the villages.

Many of the tourists who crowd the streets, and many Americans who own Amana appliances, are unaware of the juxtaposition in Amana of modern business and traditional religion. But the residents of Amana, and especially those whose parents and grandparents lived there, know very well that the spirit of an unusual past survives in the midst of their modern, affluent present. Some of their traditions date back to the early eighteenth century, when the spiritual ancestors of today's church members separated from the state church in Germany to form the Community of True Inspiration. Others date from the mid-nineteenth century, when members of the sect came to this country in search of religious freedom and, first in New York and then in Iowa, set up a communal economic order to insure their survival as a religious society. The communal order ended in 1932, but the church and a strong sense of community remain. This essay reviews highlights in the history of the Amana Colonies, focusing on their adoption and then abandonment of communal organization.

European Origins

At the beginning of the eighteenth century, Protestant Germany was attempting to come to terms with a newly promulgated theological teaching known as Pietism. The most famous Pietist of the time, Philip Jakob Spener, pastor of the Lutheran Church in Frankfurt am Main, criticized the church's emphasis on an intellectual interpretation of religious doctrines. Spener believed that the proper way to worship God was not through reasoned debate over theological questions, but through simple, direct, and loving communion, both individually and congregationally, based on the study and contemplation of the Word of God as presented in Scripture. For Spener and his followers the church was necessary but not sufficient to insure salvation. Within a context provided by the church, individual Christians themselves must seek the means to attain true piety.

Other Pietists, more radical than Spener, believed the church (by which they meant the Lutheran, or Evangelical, Church) had become too didactic and hierarchical to admit such reforms. They maintained that a truly Christian life could be found only by those who separated from the church and worshiped together in small congregations or "conventicles." Under the influence of these Radical Pietists, many Germans withdrew from the church and became known as Separatists. Their existence threatened both the church's hegemony and, by implication, the authority of civil government, since the Evangelical Church was the official state-supported religion in most of Germany.

The perceived threat of Separatism was heightened by "inspirationism," a sometimes associated phenomenon referring to any claim that individuals or groups of individuals were divinely inspired, or in other words, possessed by the Holy Spirit. Inspirationism had broken out among French Huguenots in the late seventeenth century. Facing persecution, some of the inspired Huguenots fled early in the eighteenth century to England, where they were known as the "French Prophets" and where they influenced the development of Quakerism. Some of the French Prophets traveled on to Germany, where their views were well received among some Pietists. Inspirationism represented a special threat to the established church because of its claim to direct divine authority.

Separatists experienced severe punishments as a result of their beliefs. They were imprisoned, flogged, denied property rights, relieved of their positions, and expelled from their homelands. But rarely does religious persecution achieve its purpose. The martyr's blood nourishes the faithful, and the prison cell renews their conviction. So it was with the German Separatists. After persecution weeded out the faint of heart, the remaining believers emerged more determined than ever to spread their message and win converts. In the turbulent years of the early eighteenth century, several groups consolidated around the belief that God spoke to them through divinely inspired instruments (*Werkzeuge*), much as in the days of the biblical prophets.

In 1714 several of these inspired instruments came to the town of Himbach, in the principality of Hesse, to visit two eminent Separatists who had sought refuge there some years earlier after being banished from Stuttgart on the charge of attending Pietist conventicles. Eberhard Ludwig Gruber and Johann Friedrich Rock were living quietly under the protection of the count of

JONATHAN G. ANDELSON

Ysenburg, a man of liberal religious views. The visit from the inspired renewed the two men's spiritual enthusiasm, and at a meeting on November 16, 1714, Gruber, Rock, and several others forged an association they called the Community of True Inspiration. It differed from other groups of inspired in emphasizing the importance of distinguishing between true inspiration (from God) and false inspiration (from Satan).

It is significant that the Community of True Inspiration, which throughout its history has remained flexible and adaptive, was founded by two leaders. A single leader may dictate; co-leaders of differing abilities and personalities must compromise. Gruber was the group's theoretician and thinker, its heart and soul. He articulated the doctrines of Inspirationism in a number of early tracts, and he developed many of the practical rules governing daily life. Gruber also held the title of "Overseer of the *Werkzeuge*," for although he himself never became inspired, it was believed that he possessed the crucial ability to discriminate between true and false inspiration.

Rock had been one of several *Werkzeuge* early in the group's history, but he alone retained the "gift" of inspiration for the remainder of his life. In contrast to Gruber, Rock was a man of action, the sect's back and legs. For thirty years he traveled widely in Germany, Switzerland, Alsace, and Austria, speaking out wherever and whenever the Spirit of the Lord moved him, proselytizing and holding together the scattered congregations of the faithful. Gruber died in 1728 at age sixty-three, and Rock became the principal figure in the group. When he died in 1749 at age seventy, he left the Inspirationists with a strong faith and a sound organization, entrusted after his death to the care of the elders.

For fifty more years the elders steered the congregations along the "narrow path" of piety, but by the beginning of the nineteenth century the faith that Rock and Gruber had labored so hard to instill was fading. Many left the fold, and a few of the old congregations disappeared entirely as death claimed the remaining members. It was at this time, providentially, as modern Amanans will say, that the Lord sent new *Werkzeuge* to "reawaken" the sleeping remnant.

The Reawakening

The reawakening was triggered in 1817 by Michael Krausert, a journeyman tailor from Strassburg and a man searching for spiritual meaning in his life. In the course of his wanderings he was directed to the Inspirationist congregation in Bischweiler, Alsace, where, in the words of the community's historian, "Several of Br. Rock's testimony books came into Krausert's hands and in these he found the key to his mysterious inner longings. Through these testimonies, his spiritual inquisitiveness was guided and given direction. More and more, the Lord adapted him to His service. He favored and endowed him to become an inspired instrument."[1] Some members of the "old community" did not accept Krausert as a *Werkzeug*, but as he traveled from congregation to congregation, trying to rekindle the faith of old, many others did accept him, and they became the nucleus of the "new community."

The following year, 1818, a second instrument appeared. Barbara Heinemann, an uneducated and worldly innkeeper's helper in the Alsatian town of Sulz, was twenty-two years old when in the summer of 1817 a crisis of faith and a growing concern for her salvation led her to the True Inspirationist congregation in Sulz, where she heard one of Rock's testimonies read and was greatly moved. Shortly afterward Krausert came to Sulz, met Heinemann there, and had a divine revelation that she would soon receive "the divine gift of inspiration." Following a period of inner struggle in which she doubted Krausert as well as her own purpose, she, too, became inspired. Some of the Inspirationists looked down on her poor social standing and lack of education; but Krausert supported her, and soon she joined him in advancing the renewal of the century-old faith.

In the fall of 1819 Krausert and Heinemann quarreled irreconcilably, putting their followers under enormous strain. The crisis was resolved when Krausert admitted the falseness of at least some of his own inspirations and withdrew from the community. Heinemann was left as the sole *Werkzeug*, and for three years she led the Inspirationists through numerous trials associated with the Reawakening. Then in 1823 she fell in love with a young schoolteacher in the community, George Landmann. Although the elders urged Heinemann to resist the temptation to marry him for the sake of her spiritual condition (most of the earlier *Werkzeuge* had been unmarried, and the feeling prevailed among the Inspirationists that God chose only those without earthly, sensual attachments to serve as His instruments), she yielded to it and immediately lost the gift of inspiration. Unlike Krausert, who left the group after his fall from grace, Barbara Heinemann Landmann remained an Inspirationist. Twenty-six years later, after the Inspirationists had emigrated to America, God again selected her as His servant, and she remained a *Werkzeug* until her death in 1883.

Fortunately for the community, Heinemann's fall coincided with the appearance of a third *Werkzeug*. A divine prophecy transmitted earlier through Heinemann—that Christian Metz, an ardent young supporter of the Reawakening, would one day become inspired—was fulfilled in 1823. Metz had been born into an old Inspirationist family at the Ronneburg Castle, a tradi-

JONATHAN G. ANDELSON

tional center of Inspirationist activity near Buedingen, in Hesse; his grandfather had been an elder in the old community, and young Christian proved to have exceptional leadership abilities and emerged as the central figure of nineteenth-century Inspirationism. Like Rock, Metz proselytized widely in Germany, Switzerland, and Alsace. His success was met with harassment from civic and church authorities, and the Inspirationists were banished from one region after another. Many of them came to the more tolerant principality of Hesse, where beginning in 1833 Metz arranged for the leasing of several estates near the Ronneburg on which these refugees could gather. Most were artisans or merchants, and while some continued to ply their trades on the estates, others worked in agricultural production or in one of the businesses operated by wealthier members. Property was not held in common at this time, but greater cooperation and a fuller sense of shared destiny began to develop.

Even in liberal Hesse, however, the Inspirationists' freedom was not guaranteed indefinitely. When high rents and hostile magistrates began to threaten them early in the 1840s, they resolved to emigrate to America. The decision was not lightly made, even though many Germans were emigrating at that time, for it meant leaving behind non-Inspirationist relatives and friends and the familiar places and culture of their homeland. Yet they left with more hope than despair because they expected to find a place where their collective efforts to lead a life pleasing to God would insure their individual salvation.

As the Inspirationists prepared for their departure, they faced the questions of where and how to settle in the new land. For most of their existence they had lived in small, widely dispersed congregations. Although they had experimented with a more centralized social organization on the Hessian estates, their time there was too short and their population there too much in flux for it to have crystallized. Consequently they might have reverted to a dispersed settlement pattern in America. However, since most of them spoke no English and had little knowledge of their adopted land, it was more practical for them to live together. Besides that, the persecutions and relocations in Europe, coupled with the sense of mission that accompanied the prospect of immigration to America, created in the Inspirationists a high level of religious enthusiasm. More than ever they conceived of themselves as a *Gemeinde*, in the rich sense conveyed by that German word that our translation as "community" does not quite capture. They called one another "brother" and "sister," and like many Pietists they distrusted the profane influences of "the world" and wished to minimize contact with it.

For these reasons the Inspirationists decided to settle in America separate from the world in a community of their own. Upon locating a suitable tract of land near Buffalo, New York, they pooled their money to purchase it and pay ship's passage for those members willing and able to undertake the arduous journey. Nearly 700 came between April 1843 and August 1844. Others followed in the years to come as their circumstances permitted, and by mid-century the Community of True Inspiration effectively ceased to exist in Germany. The Inspirationists called their new home "Ebenezer," after a name in the first book of Samuel that means "Hitherto hath the Lord helped us."

Communalism

Once a start was made at Ebenezer, a second question had to be answered, namely on what basis the community's social and economic organization would be established. Should each family remain economically independent, earning its own way and choosing how to spend its income, or should the families collectivize their labor, their incomes, their consumption, or all of these? The first way would maximize individual freedom of choice, but at the same time it would make the community less cohesive and could lead to inequities. Conversely, to the degree that collectivization existed, a more rapid deployment of resources and a fuller sense of community would be possible, but would require more complex and delicate administrative functions.

Although the construction of Ebenezer clearly required collectivized resources, some members wanted the community to revert to an individualistic economy as quickly as possible. But for others economics was not the only consideration. The biblical description of the original apostolic community appeared to them to favor a community of goods: "And all that believed were together, and had all things common. . . . And the multitude of them that believed were of one heart and of one soul: neither said any of them that aught of the things which he possessed was his own; but they had all things common" (Acts 2:44 and 4:32).

These lines have often been cited by communal and monastic groups as authorization for adopting common property. The True Inspirationists were well aware of the existence of such groups. In fact Christian Metz had visited one—the Zoar Society in Ohio—shortly after arriving in New York, and he returned to Ebenezer convinced that the Inspirationists should adopt communal organization. Some Inspirationists resisted the idea, but Metz's charisma was so strong that when, under the influence of divine inspiration, he sanctified the collective system, the objections were overcome. In January 1846 the Inspirationists adopted a constitution that established a modified form of communalism. Land and the means of production were owned

JONATHAN G. ANDELSON

jointly, and members worked for the community (called the Ebenezer Society) without pay. The society in turn provided food, housing, and health care for members as well as an annual spending allowance with which they purchased items for personal use. Furniture and other household property were privately owned and passed on within families, which retained their traditional form. The constitution made clear that these arrangements existed in the context of a community of faith.

How should the modern student of communal societies view the Inspirationists' adoption of communal property? When Christian Metz said that a divine curse would rest on those who opposed the communal system, was he speaking entirely out of religious conviction, or was he using religion to justify what the community's leaders felt to be a practical necessity? In fact, neither explanation precludes the other, nor is one logically prior to the other. That communalism is part of the Christian tradition is self-evident, as is the Inspirationists' difficult financial situation at the time of their immigration.

By adopting communalism the Inspirationists simply reconciled practical necessity with Christian tradition. Although the apostolic community apparently adopted common property out of spiritual conviction rather than need, it does not follow that because the Inspirationists acted out of need they therefore lacked conviction. Furthermore, the fact that some members required inspired testimonies by Metz to convince them to accept communalism supports the argument that those members (and probably others) maintained a religious, not a secular, orientation to the question. It is impossible to say for certain whether Inspirationists in 1846 thought they were adopting communalism permanently, or if they could foresee a time when they would abandon it. There is no doubt, however, that the community held to the system of common ownership until 1932, enabling us to credit them with being the fourth longest-lived communal society in American history after only the Shakers, the Hutterites, and the Rappites.[2]

Common ownership permitted the Inspirationists to embark on a rapid and impressive program of building and economic development at Ebenezer. Within a few years they had constructed four principal villages (Middle Ebenezer, Lower Ebenezer, Upper Ebenezer, and New Ebenezer), each with a church, residences, communal kitchens, mills, workshops, and farms. Two small satellite villages (Canada Ebenezer and Kenneberg) were established across the Niagara River on land acquired when several families of German immigrants joined the community. By 1855 two woolen mills, a calico print mill, three sawmills, two grist mills, and an oil mill were in operation. Carpenters, masons, blacksmiths, saddlers, locksmiths, soapmakers, watchmakers, shoemakers, tanners, coopers, wagonmakers, butchers, bakers, and basket-makers met nearly all of Ebenezer's material needs. Others worked on the community's farms and with the livestock. The goods and produce of the mills and farms were sold in Buffalo and New York City. With the income, the community purchased things it could not produce on its own, provided members with a credit allowance in the colony stores, and paid taxes and passage for more members from Europe.

Amana

Although the Inspirationists prospered in Ebenezer, problems arose that compelled them to migrate again. The arrival of additional members from Europe swelled their ranks to over a thousand, and more land proved difficult to obtain nearby and at a reasonable price. Metz and the elders also disliked the proximity of Buffalo, a growing and boisterous city that threatened to engulf the community in a "flood of sin." In an effort to locate a more isolated spot where the community could settle, Metz led an exploration party to Kansas in 1854, the year it became a territory. They found nothing there that suited their needs, but on a second expedition, to Iowa, already a state for eight years, a second party discovered a promising location along the Iowa River, twenty miles west of Iowa City, then the state capital. The land was fertile, there was water to generate power for their mills, and timber covered much of the property. Two outcroppings of sandstone could be quarried and used for construction, and there was clay suitable for making brick.

The Inspirationists were able to purchase a sizable contiguous tract of land on either side of the river, ultimately acquiring a total of 26,000 acres. They incorporated under Iowa law as a religious association called the Amana Society, after a name in the Song of Solomon, and gradually established seven villages, five on the north side of the river (Amana, East Amana, Middle Amana, High Amana, and West Amana) and two on the south side (South Amana and Homestead). The relocation from Ebenezer took nine years, and by the time the last member arrived in Amana in 1864, the population there had reached 1,300.

Amana was built up in much the same way that Ebenezer had been. In every village the Inspirationists erected numerous residential units (each typically containing four apartments), a school, a general store, a bakery, a meat market, shops for the various craftsmen, several community kitchenhouses, and barns and other agricultural buildings. They built two woolen mills, a calico print works, a tannery, a soap works, and several flour mills and sawmills. When the small creek they expected to provide water for the mills proved unreliable, they dug a seven-mile-long canal, or mill race, to bring

Communal kitchen workers are shown sorting onions in Homestead, Iowa, about 1913. Most onions were used by the community, although surplus onions were sold to outside markets. The clothing worn by the women is Amana calico. The lap trays and baskets were also produced by the Amana community. (Photographic Collection, Amana Heritage Society)

water to the mills from the Iowa River. They situated the church at the center of each village, and at the edge they set aside land for a cemetery that they surrounded with evergreen trees, symbolizing eternal life. Members were buried in the order of death under plain, uniform headstones. The cemeteries, like the churches, expressed the Inspirationists' ethos of simplicity and equality.

Amana's economy was based on manufacturing and agriculture. The woolen mills produced an extensive line for wholesale, including blankets, skirting flannel, socks, gloves, and yarn. The print works purchased calico cloth and dyed it with indigo in dozens of subdued, patterned prints. Both the woolens and indigo prints were sold nationally. Other items were marketed locally, including soap, lumber, shingles, laths, and laundry bluing. Agricultural production was equally diverse. The society produced and sold onions and onion sets, potatoes, celery, hay, barley, wheat flour, and corn meal and raised cattle, hogs, and poultry for mostly local consumption.

The Amana Colonies

Horses provided traction and transportation, and the society's herds of sheep provided much of the wool used in the mills. Bees were also kept, and the society sold the honey.

Boys and girls began working for the society at age fourteen, when they finished eighth grade. Boys were assigned to farm, factory, or craft work, often (but not necessarily) following their fathers. While it was possible for a man to change jobs, there was no formal system of job rotation. A few young men were sent out of the community to receive training in medicine, dentistry, pharmacy, or education. Girls began working in the community kitchens, where teams of three or four cooked and served meals for as many as forty people. Older women worked in the kitchen gardens, and a few taught sewing and other forms of handwork to schoolchildren. Far fewer work options existed for women than for men, and the only job with real responsibility available to a woman was that of kitchen "boss." Both men and women generally did some kind of work until ill health or old age forced them to retire.

The business affairs of the society were supervised at several levels. A thirteen-member Great Council, elected annually by voting members of the society (men over twenty-one and single women over thirty), rendered decisions about general operations: new businesses, construction projects, wages paid to hired hands, members' spending allowances, admission of new members, intervillage transfers of members, and matters concerning the kitchen houses. Day-to-day decisions about the operation of particular businesses—such as production quotas and product marketing—were made by the managers of the businesses in consultation with local councils in each village, comprised of between three and six elders appointed by the Great Council. The local councils also assigned members their housing. The *Werkzeuge* rarely spoke in inspiration about the community's temporal affairs, but when they did their words were sovereign.

Life in communal Amana was balanced between efforts to achieve spiritual piety and a state of divine grace on one hand, and economic solvency on the other, with a tilt in the early years toward religion. The Inspirationists' pragmatism kept them from adopting extreme postures in matters of religion, and their religiosity restrained their profit seeking. They insisted on marketing only the highest-quality products, on dealing scrupulously with their business partners, on paying a fair wage to their hired hands, and on the priority of worship over work. They attended eleven church services a week where they heard Metz, Barbara Landmann, and the elders exhort them to put aside material concerns and "the vanity of the world"; to turn their backs on selfishness, arrogance, and cleverness; and to repent of their past sins and "wake up" and sin no more. Transgressors against God's law or the community's code of conduct were warned and reprimanded, in public if necessary. Habitual offenders faced expulsion, though this was rarely resorted to, because as Christian Metz once told the members, "A doorway to the world is always open for those who do not wish to obey."

In the early years most Amanans did obey the rules, for life in the colonies was as secure as it was spiritually fulfilling. No one went hungry or unclothed. Members' apartments, though not spacious by today's standards, were solidly built and comfortably appointed. All members of the community received free medical and dental care supplemented by a system of preventive medicine that included maternity leaves (two years), day care, job security, and assistance to the elderly and infirm. The average member had no economic worries and was largely protected from dishonest salesmen, shyster lawyers, and corrupt politicians. Even burial was at the society's expense. In short, colony life was probably as carefree from cradle to grave as one could have found in nineteenth-century America. The elders undoubtedly felt a burden of responsibility for the community's continued well-being, but by sharing the burden with one another they were able to alleviate it.

Strains and Discontent

To observe that every social system is flawed is to utter a truism. Every solution to any problem of social life is likely to generate problems of its own. For that reason, life in a community is never static; it is a process, an unending series of readjustments and hopeful balancing acts aimed at achieving the private and collective ends of a group of individuals.

The True Inspirationists adopted communal organization in 1843 because it allowed them to live together as a *Gemeinde* at a precarious period in their history. In time, however, some Amanans stopped wanting to obey some of the rules associated with communal living. The countless minor regulations governing dress, deportment, leisure activities, dining habits, and even the manner of greeting other community members all created an orderly but, some thought, small-minded atmosphere in the community. They wanted to be free to play card games or baseball, to have birthday parties or to bob their hair, all proscribed by the elders as "dangerous worldly distractions." Perhaps a family wanted to eat its meals together at home rather than in the community dining hall, where men and women ate at separate tables. And one rule, requiring a couple to wait up to two years after their engagement before marrying, was especially frustrating to young people.

Some members chafed at their inability to satisfy their material desires in

Amana's cashless and frugal economy. The communal system provided every family with an annual credit in the colony store against the purchase of shoes, clothing, tobacco, and other items for personal use. A typical family of four in 1900 received an annual spending allowance of seventy or eighty dollars, with all other sources of income proscribed. While many lived within these limits, there were others who acquired a taste for more expensive things. The council not only enforced the credit limit but instructed members not to acquire various "worldly" possessions, including baby carriages, certain types of apparel, most musical instruments, fancy fabrics, and bicycles. Ironically, some of these very items were carried in colony stores for sale to outsiders. Another complaint, voiced occasionally by the parents of larger families, was that the council did not assign to them spending allowances sufficient to meet even basic needs comfortably.

The last point raises an issue that contributed further to the dissatisfaction of some Amanans, namely their impression that privilege and partiality existed in what was ostensibly an egalitarian community. In fact, some members did receive privileges denied to others because of their positions in the community. The doctors had their own automobiles; business managers who dealt with outsiders had larger spending allowances than farmhands in recognition of their "need" to dress more suitably; and church elders "maybe got a little something extra in the community kitchen." When such observations were coupled with the realization that certain families held most of the positions of privilege in the community, momentary jealousies could easily become gnawing frustrations. The complaint from large families mentioned above could have arisen from more subtle, but related, causes. Inspirationist doctrine advocated sexual restraint, favoring celibacy over marriage and, within marriage, small rather than large families. Couples who were about to become parents were even demoted in church rank for one year. If, as one Amana woman said, "large families were just looked down on a little," it was a short step from there to subtly unequal treatment like barely sufficient spending allowances.

Limited opportunities for personal development disconcerted the more ambitious Amanans. The society provided only an eighth-grade education for all but the select few it sent to medical or teachers' college for the community's benefit. One young man, directed by the council to attend pharmacy school, left the society when the elders denied his request to go on for a medical education. Others caviled at the choice of jobs available to them in the community. Women were especially justified in this feeling, since they had few options from which to choose. Some men felt that their alternatives were

JONATHAN G. ANDELSON

restricted because of their family's social standing in the community; the son of a farmworker was unlikely to become a clerk in a colony store.

Those who disliked living under the rules of Amana's communal system had several options. If thoroughly dissatisfied, they were, as Christian Metz had said, free to leave. By the end of the nineteenth century some of the factors that militated against this choice when the Inspirationists first arrived had disappeared. No longer were Amana's young people separated from the outside world by a language barrier, because all of them learned English in the Amana schools. They also had been exposed to more and more elements of the wider society, despite the elders' best efforts. To judge from the available figures, apostasy began to occur with increasing frequency in the mid-1880s. Amana's population reached an all-time peak of 1,813 in 1881. Ten years later the population had fallen to 1,722, a decline of 91 during a decade when births and adult deaths were evenly matched. Although the population recovered somewhat over the next fifteen years, after 1905 (population, 1,770) an almost steady decline occurred until a nadir of 1,365 was reached in 1932. (From 1906 until 1931, adult deaths outnumbered births by only 15, accounting for only 3 percent of the decline.) Most of the apostates were between sixteen and forty years of age and usually went to nearby Cedar Rapids or Davenport, or to St. Louis or Chicago to look for work. Despite new rules from the council restricting their freedom on return trips to the colonies, apostates inevitably fueled nascent discontent simply by their periodic visits home.

Those unwilling to go so far as severing their connection with the society could attempt to make life more tolerable by ignoring or surreptitiously breaking the rules they did not like. Such behavior was quite common after the turn of the century. Young men sneaked off to play baseball or cards; young women bobbed their hair or wore an item of red apparel (a forbidden color). Some sold homemade wine to outsiders to raise pocket money. One enterprising individual arranged for a Cedar Rapids company to send him bulk ice cream, which he then resold to his friends for a modest profit. Others bred rabbits for sale. A man who preferred a day of fishing to a day in the fields might feign illness when the work boss came to his house, then slip out the back door and through the woods to the river. Young couples managed to arrange trysts away from the eyes of their parents or the elders. If detected in transgressions like these, community members received a word of reprimand and warning from the elders and possibly would be banished from church for a week or two. Such a sentence might deter the culprits for a time, but just as often they would find clever ways to circumvent the rules. Once some young men, caught playing baseball and enjoined from repeating the offense, explained when caught again a few days later that, yes, they had understood, but now they were playing softball!

In spite of the discontent felt by some Amanans, many members followed most of the rules most of the time. They worked hard, enjoyed what material possessions they could afford to acquire with their spending allowances, attended church, and avoided contact with outsiders as much as possible. If everyone had done so, if there had been no apostates and no malingering, it is possible that the Amana Society would not have found itself, on the eve of the nation's great economic depression of 1929, in desperate financial straits.

The human factor was only one source of Amana's economic difficulties. Some of the businesses were ailing for reasons beyond the colonists' control. The calico print works was forced to halt production during World War I when dye from Germany could not be imported. After the war, clothing styles changed, the demand for calico fell drastically, and the business never re-opened. The colonies' farms and woolen mills, which experienced good profits during the war years, suffered during the 1920s from irregular but generally unsatisfactory markets. Meanwhile expenses were rising all around, from raw materials to the cost of wages for the hired hands the society employed (and had for over fifty years). Another financial setback came from disastrous fires in the mills in the 1920s. Not believing in insurance of any kind, the society had to absorb the losses. Add to all of this a labor force that, although skilled and productive, was not efficient according to the "world's" measure and that in any case was declining in size and advancing in age, and one can clearly see the society's precarious economic position. The stock market crash on October 29, 1929, merely compounded Amana's economic woes.

Reorganization

To many observers of the day, both in and out of the Amanas, the source of the society's difficulties was obvious: communal ownership. A committee appointed by the Great Council to consider the society's situation drew up a questionnaire which in May 1931 it sent to all 917 adult members of the society. The questionnaire contained only two questions, which members were asked to answer "yes" or "no":

1. Is it, in your opinion, possible to go back to the old lifestyle of denial wholly and completely, as it is prescribed, and are you and your family willing to tread this path without reservation?

JONATHAN G. ANDELSON

2. Is it, in your opinion, possible that by reorganization (which is described as fully as can be at this time in the accompanying letter), the building-up of our community can be effected according to Article V of our present Constitution, and are you and your family willing to present your plans and views before the Committee and then to assist in carrying out the plan approved by the Trustees and the majority of brothers and sisters?[3]

Ballots were counted on June 10, and the committee interpreted the results to indicate a strong preference for reorganization. A year later, after a good deal of study and legal analysis, Amana made its "Great Change" from the communal system to a joint-stock corporation with the power to operate the businesses of the old community and to regulate any new private enterprises that might be established. The popular press picked up the story and announced the "failure of communism" in Amana.

Today, more than fifty years after the reorganization, most Amanans agree with the view expressed to the author that "something at that time had to change; the communal system wasn't working any more." Scholars who have analyzed Amana's economic records concur.[4] There is no doubt that the society's profits were going down before 1932 and that they began to go up after the reorganization. However, this does not by itself establish what some, both in and out of Amana, have claimed: that because common ownership was "not working" in Amana, it was an inherently flawed system that could not work there. It is a mistake to emphasize the economic causes of Amana's reorganization to the neglect of other factors.

Could the old Amana Society have modified its economic operations in ways that would have permitted it to be solvent while retaining communal ownership? Although there is no way to answer this question with certainty, a case can be made that this would have been possible. Some of the unprofitable businesses that were maintained only for the convenience of the members, such as the several shoemaker shops and the watchmaker shop, could have been closed, as many were after 1932. The council could have instituted a system of job rotation for members that would have provided more stimulating work experience and eliminated jealousy over job assignments, and possibly also reduced the need for hired labor. A more careful and accurate accounting system could have provided clearer feedback to the business managers about operating costs and their relationship to profits.[5] It could have also helped reduce pilfering from the community coffers, something that contemporary Amana folklore maintains took place regularly. None of these steps would have been inimical to the essential spirit behind Amana's communal economy, and although they do not address all of the flaws in the system, they would have corrected some of the shortcomings of Amana's communalism.

It is less the case that communalism could not work in Amana than that many members no longer wanted it to and were able to persuade the others (and even themselves) that it could not. Several facts account for this development. First, the last divinely inspired leader of the community, Barbara Landmann, died in 1883 at an advanced age. Without a *Werkzeug* the community's religious leadership grew more diffuse, as eighty-five elders (the number in 1885) attempted to steer the Inspirationists along the difficult path of piety. The elders, however, lacked the authority of the inspired word, and therefore they often failed to establish credible policies or to reprimand transgressors of those policies effectively. Those who misused their position to gain privilege further undermined their legitimacy. Second, a substantial group of new members, about 250, immigrated to the community from Saxony between 1875 and 1881 at the society's invitation. None of them grew up with Inspirationist doctrines, and they lived for at most a few years under the guidance of a *Werkzeug* before Landmann's death. It is likely that this group was less committed to communalism than members of long standing. Finally, the longer the Inspirationists remained in America, the more exposure they had to the worldly ways of a fast-changing society. The outside world was especially difficult for the elders to combat because of the freedoms it offered and the inexhaustible supply of distractions it presented. No sooner had they proscribed one worldly influence than another appeared. This combination of factors lured members away from the path of communal piety, and there was less and less to pull them back to it.

The reorganization vote can also be reexamined in light of these conclusions.[6] The results of the questionnaire appear to be straightforward. Nine hundred members returned questionnaires, and 676 of these answered "yes" to the second question. This was interpreted by the committee to mean that three-quarters of the members of the Amana Society (676 of 917) favored a reorganization away from the communal system. However, the vote varied considerably among residents of the different villages. In East Amana only two-thirds of the members supported reorganization; in High Amana only half did; and in Middle Amana, the second largest village, only one-quarter of the members did. Furthermore, some of those who indicated a willingness to cooperate with the reorganization plan ("yes" on question 2) also voted in favor of returning to the old system ("yes" on question 1). For example, while only 4.5 percent of the East Amanans voted against reorganization, over 22 percent actually voted in favor of returning to the old system. Discrepancies also exist in the other direction. In High Amana nearly a quarter of the members voted not to support the reorganization effort ("no" on question 2), but only 16 percent wanted to go back to the "life of denial."

In short, a measure of ambiguity exists in the results of Amana's reorganization vote. While some of the above figures, by dealing with percentages rather than absolute numbers, represent mere number juggling, on the whole the conclusions emerge that (1) Amanans did not view the two questions as opposites and (2) the total number who either preferred the old system, opposed the tentative reorganization plan, or could envision other (unstated) alternatives could easily have been more than a third of the population, and possibly as much as half.

I do not intend the foregoing speculations as an attempt to rewrite history. A majority of Amanans probably wanted to reorganize in some fashion in 1932, and an even larger majority today believes the change was a good idea. Rather, the speculations may help us to evaluate the reorganization with a greater degree of caution than its interpreters have traditionally exercised. Amana's Great Change did not result from economic factors alone; the abandonment of communalism may not have been the only solution to the very real strains that their communal system was producing; and the degree of support for decollectivization may have been smaller than is generally claimed.

Amana since Reorganization

Reorganization turned the old Amana Society into two autonomous units: the new Amana Society, a for-profit, joint-stock business corporation, and the Amana Church Society, which maintains the spiritual and religious values of the old community. The church retains its simplicity and its emphasis on the equality of the faithful, which is still shown in traditional church garb and the uniform gravestones in Amana cemeteries. The church buildings and the order of worship are essentially unchanged from communal days, and men and women still sit separately. Some significant changes have occurred. The number of church services has been reduced from eleven per week to one; the number of elders has fallen from a high of ninety to about twenty; a group of "English elders" conduct many services in English; and some of the rituals have been modified.

Change is even more noticeable in Amana's economic aspects. The new corporation has operated according to a stricter economic rationalism, eliminating unprofitable businesses and modifying successful ones to keep pace with changing economic conditions. Whereas the old community raised a substantial proportion of the food it consumed, today Amana's farm operation is highly specialized, like that of Iowa generally. Even the manufacture of woolens, a part of the community's economy since the 1830s, was reduced and recently almost completely eliminated as the Amana mill found itself unable to produce woolen goods profitably; during the same period, the retail sale of woolens expanded considerably and today is a thriving corporate business, although most of the woolens are produced elsewhere. Until recently the corporation also regulated (rather liberally) the operation of privately owned businesses in the community.

One of the most significant economic developments was the establishment of a new industry to manufacture freezers and refrigerators. Started by two Amana natives in the 1930s and soon taken over by the corporation, the "refrigeration division" grew so rapidly that it became too large for the corporation to manage successfully. It was sold in 1950 to a group of industrialists from Cedar Rapids, Iowa, who in turn sold it in 1965 to Raytheon Corporation of Massachusetts. Today the factory employs about 2,000 workers in the manufacture of freezers, refrigerators, air conditioners, and microwave ovens that are sold nationally under the Amana name.

The economic change with the most far-reaching implications for the residents of the Amana Colonies has been the rise of tourism. Even before 1932 tourists visited Amana by car and rail from as far away as Chicago to see the distinctive architecture, purchase Amana-made goods, and sample Amana food at the hotel or in a kitchen house. The shift to a profit-seeking economic system opened the door for fuller development of Amana's tourist potential, initially by private entrepreneurs and later by the corporation itself. Shortly after the reorganization the first privately owned restaurant opened for business, followed over the years by half a dozen others. Several members of the community also received licenses to make and sell wine. These and some of the corporation's businesses—the general stores, two meat markets, a furniture factory, and a bakery—attracted a moderate, but gradually increasing, number of tourists through the mid-1960s.

In the last thirty years the flow of tourists to Amana has increased dramatically. In 1965 the United States Department of the Interior designated the Amana Colonies a National Historic Landmark, further legitimizing tourist interest and resulting in substantially more publicity. At about the same time, Interstate 80 was completed across Iowa five miles from the colonies. With new reasons for visiting Amana and easier access to it, tourists came in greater numbers than ever, and both the corporation and private entrepreneurs responded vigorously. In 1980 the Iowa Supreme Court, in a decision growing

JONATHAN G. ANDELSON

out of a suit filed earlier by the Amana Society, denied to the corporation the power to regulate private business operating within the colonies. By 1995 nearly seventy-five privately owned restaurants, wineries, and shops, plus half a dozen corporation-operated shops, catered to tourists. Another seven operate at the Amana exit along Interstate 80. By some estimates, a million visitors were patronizing Amana businesses each year in the late 1970s and 1980s.

Accompanying the tourist boom, and in part even caused by it, was a heightened awareness among Amanans of their own cultural and historical heritage. Once they had distanced themselves from the old communal system, which took about forty years, or a little more than a generation, they began to develop a concern for protecting the surviving reminders of that bygone era. Whereas many Amanans had been quick to modernize their homes and their lifestyles following the reorganization in 1932, by the late 1960s the children of those who engineered the change were becoming aware that modernization was obliterating their heritage. Members of the community formed the Amana Heritage Society and later the Amana Preservation Foundation in an effort to preserve and protect the material culture and the architecture of communal Amana. Through the efforts of these groups, everything from communal-era willow baskets and tinware to old letters and photographs have been preserved and displayed in the Museum of Amana History, and many neglected buildings have been protected and restored to their former appearance. Interest in some of the communal crafts, including quilting, tinsmithing, and basket making, has also been revived through the efforts of the Amana Arts Guild.

Although Amana was a communal society for eighty-nine years, certainly a noteworthy accomplishment, it has surpassed its 150th year of existence as a community and is approaching its 300th year as a religious association. Obviously communalism was only one phase, though an important one, in the long history of this group. Today Amana appears to be a thriving, progressive community that not only retains an appreciation of its past but is able to use that past in order to gain for itself an identity in the present and the prospect of security for the future.

Chronology

1714   Community of True Inspiration founded in Hesse, Germany, by Eberhard Ludwig Gruber, Johann Friedrich Rock, and other Separatists. Central tenet that God communicates through divinely inspired instruments (*Werkzeuge*) established.

1728   Eberhard Ludwig Gruber dies.

1749	Johann Friedrich Rock dies, last inspired instrument of the eighteenth century. Leadership passes to church elders.
1817	"Reawakening" of the Community of True Inspiration through Michael Krausert, Barbara Heinemann, and Christian Metz as inspired instruments.
1819	Michael Krausert falls from grace.
1833	Barbara Heinemann marries; loses gift of inspiration.
1843	Christian Metz leads 700 members of Community of True Inspiration from Germany to United States. Communal living adopted in six villages called the Ebenezer Society (Lower, Middle, Upper, and New Ebenezer near Buffalo in Erie County, N.Y., and Kenneberg and Canada Ebenezer in Ontario, Canada).
1849	Barbara Heinemann Landmann reacquires the gift of inspiration.
1854–61	Community of True Inspiration migrates to Iowa County, Iowa. Establishes seven communal villages known as the Amana Society (Amana, East Amana, High Amana, Middle Amana, South Amana, West Amana, and Homestead).
1867	Christian Metz dies at Amana.
1883	Barbara Heinemann Landmann dies at Amana, last inspired instrument of nineteenth century.
1923	Fire in woolen mill and other economic difficulties weaken the Amana Society.
1931	Plan to reorganize Community of True Inspiration without communal ownership approved by large majority of members.
1932	The "Great Change" occurs. Communal economy replaced by new Amana Society as joint-stock corporation. Religious movement continues as the Amana Church Society without controlling Amana businesses or enforcing traditional restrictions on personal property or behavior.
1936–50	Amana Refrigeration operated as business within the Amana Society, then incorporated separately.
1960	Amana Church Society begins services in English in addition to German. Process of translating inspired testimonies and other historic writings into English begins.
1980	Amana Society loses control over private businesses operating within the society's domain. Tourism becomes major component of Amana Colonies' economy.
1992	Amana Society charter renewal vote.

Notes

1. Gottlieb Scheuner, *Inspirations-Historie*, vol. 2, *1729–1817*, trans. and with an introduction by Janet W. Zuber (1884; reprint, Amana, Iowa: Amana Church Society, 1978), 303.

2. Some current communities, including the Vedanta Ashram of San Francisco, may surpass the Inspirationists' eighty-nine years as a communal society. Many monastic orders already surpass it, although their connection to powerful institutions of the wider society places them in a slightly different category.

3. Lawrence L. Rettig, *Amana Today: A History of the Amana Colonies from 1932 to Present* (Amana, Iowa: Amana Society, 1975), 13–14.

4. See Gary Carman, "The Amana Colonies' Change from Communalism to Capitalism in 1932," *Social Science Journal* 24 (1987): 157–67; Jonathan G. Andelson, "The Double-

Bind and Social Change in Communal Amana," *Human Relations* 34 (1981): 111–25; Diane Barthel, *Amana: From Pietist Sect to American Community* (Lincoln: University of Nebraska Press, 1984); Bertha M. H. Shambaugh, *Amana That Was and Amana That Is* (Iowa City: State Historical Society of Iowa, 1932).

5. Carman, "Amana Colonies' Change," 160–62.

6. This discussion depends entirely on data presented by Rettig, *Amana Today*, 123.

Selected Bibliography

Albers, Marjorie K. *The Amana People and Their Furniture*. Ames: Iowa State University Press, 1990.

Andelson, Jonathan G. *Communalism and Change in the Amana Society, 1855–1932*. Ann Arbor, Mich.: University Microfilms, 1974.

———. "The Double-Bind and Social Change in Communal Amana." *Human Relations* 34 (1981): 111–25.

———. "The Gift to Be Single: Celibacy and Religious Enthusiasm in the Community of True Inspiration." *Communal Societies* 5 (1985): 1–32.

———. "Living the Mean: The Ethos, Practice, and Genius of Amana." *Communities: Journal of Cooperation* 68 (Winter 1985): 32–38.

———. "Postcharismatic Authority in the Amana Society: The Legacy of Christian Metz." In *When Prophets Die: The Postcharismatic Fate of New Religious Movements*, edited by Timothy Miller, 29–45. Albany: SUNY Press, 1991.

———. "Routinization of Behavior in a Charismatic Leader." *American Ethnologist* 7 (1980): 716–33.

———. "Tradition, Innovation, and Assimilation in Iowa's Amana Colonies." *Palimpsest* 69 (Spring 1988): 2–15.

Barthel, Diane L. *Amana: From Pietist Sect to American Community*. Lincoln: University of Nebraska Press, 1984.

Carman, Gary D. "The Amana Colonies' Change from Communalism to Capitalism in 1932." *Social Science Journal* 24 (1987): 157–67.

Dow, James R., and Madeline Roemig. "Amana Folk Art and Craftsmanship." *Palimpsest* 58 (1977): 54–63.

Lankes, Frank J. *The Ebenezer Society*. West Seneca, N.Y.: West Seneca Historical Society, 1963.

Perkins, William Rufus, and Barthinius L. Wick. *History of the Amana Society*. 1891. Reprint, New York: Arno, 1975.

Rettig, Lawrence L. *Amana Today: A History of the Amana Colonies from 1932 to Present*. Amana, Iowa: Amana Society, 1975.

Richling, Barnett. "The Amana Society: A History of Change." *Palimpsest* 58 (1977): 34–47.

Scheuner, Gottlieb. *Inspirations-Historie*. Vol. 1, *1714–1728*; vol. 2, *1729–1817*; vol. 3, *1817–1850*. Translated by Janet W. Zuber. Amana, Iowa: Amana Church Society, 1978. Originally published in 1884 (vols. 1–2) and 1891 (vol. 3).

Shambaugh, Bertha M. H. *Amana That Was and Amana That Is*. Iowa City: State Historical Society of Iowa, 1932.

Webber, Philip E. *Kolonie-Deutsch: Life and Language in Amana*. Ames: Iowa State University Press, 1993.

LAWRENCE J. McCRANK

Religious Orders and Monastic Communalism in America

C ommunal living in America is often motivated by religious faith, corresponding ethics and self-discipline, and reversion to unbridled materialism. It is a compromise between having to live in this world yet separating oneself from it. Membership is based on similar religious persuasions and commitment to a common lifestyle that is shaped by tradition. Its socialism stems from both this antimaterialism and, more positively, a Christian social-service ethic. Its utopianism is a blend of progressivism, Christian humanism, and a continuity-oriented historicism that links improvement in this life with hope for a better afterlife. Its spirituality is the social gospel combined with Christian mysticism, and its withdrawal ethos is individually ascetic and collectively monastic. Motives for religious communal living are often idealistic and nostalgic, imbued with a consciousness of salvation history, tradition, and the relationship of self, society, and environment in the broadest context imaginable.

Because of this reliance on tradition for the formation of religious communities and their maintenance, and this Augustinian or linear historicism, New World communalism seldom divorces itself from its Old World antecedents. But in the same way that communes are deliberately segregated and their traditions are denominational, their history is usually written in equally segregated, individualistic, and vertical rather than horizontal or comparative terms. Members of religious communes live within their own traditions. Their lives are shaped by them, and thus the tradition lives. Whereas Catholicism stresses continuity, and this trait is shared by most religious communities, Protestantism harkens back to the Reformation and then to biblicalism rather than seeing a continual ancestry that would link modern communities with medieval, patristic, and biblical asceticism and monasticism.[1] American scholarship has tended to retain this Protestant outlook and, therefore, to separate communal and monastic history.[2] Monasticism is seen as Catholic and Orthodox only, more mystic in its spirituality, entwined with the notion of a special priesthood rather than a lay ministry, and its practice of celibacy means that the community must be sustained through recruitment and adoption rather than marriage and procreation. These are significant differences, but they do not overcome the more pervasive and overarching similarities between Protestant and Catholic communalism, their separatism and collective personalities of communities formed by religious orders and denominations, their rules and engineered lifestyles, motivations and spiritualism, and patterns of development. They are parallel traditions with a common ancestry. Such historical and religious ecumenism motivates the inclusion of Catholic religious orders and monasticism in these studies of American communalism.[3] It is anachronistic to perceive of religious communalism in nationalist terms, and somewhat perverse to see it as peculiarly American Protestant. A comparative perspective of Protestant and Catholic forms is necessary to discern in Western culture a continuing Christian communal tradition, the persistence of dissent to secularism, and an alternative lifestyle that appeals to an elitist minority and more devout practitioner than the common Christian. Such a communalistic tradition links the Old and New Worlds, and the world to come.

A longer-range, more balanced view of American religious communalism may be understood better (1) when linking Protestant and Catholic forms by stressing commonalities more than differences; (2) in providing a brief historical overview of Western monastic tradition, not only for historical perspective but to understand the seminal role a conscious historicism plays in monastic thought; (3) by showing how monastic communities build group identity through a strong sense of genealogy and relationships between communities here and elsewhere, and between American members and their European forbearers; (4) through contrasts between ideals and reality in monastic history; and (5) by discussing contemporary problems in preserving continuity, community survival, and coping with rapid changes in secular society and reform within modern Roman Catholicism.

The Monastic Way

Not all forms of monasticism have been communal, as indicated by the etymology of the term "monk" from its Anglo-Saxon *munuc* or Latin *monachus*.[4]

They mean oneness or being alone, suggesting therefore a life of solitude and withdrawal from secular society. On the other hand, the Fathers of the Church, including St. Augustine, whose influence was paramount in the West, tended to place individuals among other monks and to stress their unity in commitment and shared lifestyle. Complete loners could be seen as selfish and contradictory to the notion of Church—that is, the Christian community. Therefore collectivism seemed necessary to balance any extremes in asceticism inherited from eremitical movements such as radical antisocial behavior or complete isolationism advocated by some of the Desert Fathers.[5]

Monastic life has come to be interpreted almost paradoxically as solitude through association, a sodality and confraternity bound by common observances, traditions, oaths or vows, and habits.[6] One practitioner describes monasticism as "living together alone."[7] The monastic mentality is explained by the Benedictine David Steindl-Rast:[8]

> The monk in us is very closely related to the child in us, or, if you want, to the mystic in us—and we are all meant to be mystics. . . . I lose myself and I discover that so I have found myself. . . . I'm alone with all, and when I'm really one with all, I'm alone. . . .
>
> . . . the whole idea is to get beyond self-will altogether. . . . Obedience means literally a thorough listening; . . . you cannot attribute deafness to the source of the sound. . . .
>
> . . . to live recollectively . . . means the same thing as mindfulness, wholeheartedness, openness to meaning. . . . Faith is ultimately courageous trust in life. Faith versus fear—that is the key issue of religion. . . . Faith is precisely letting go.

Monastic communities have been described, perhaps unfairly, as religious aristocracies where spiritual rather than material wealth is the goal. The vocation pursued is beyond the expectations of most Christians but is a call to perfection based on the Evangelical Counsels, especially Christ's enjoinder (Matt. 19:16) to perfect one's life through poverty. This is a powerful motif in monastic literature. It underlies the monastic *gnosis* or wisdom, which like Platonism identifies spiritual rather than material things as real and of lasting importance.

The variant traditions within Roman Catholicism when given canonical sanction are considered *ordos* or ordered ways of life—that is, religious orders—in the same sense as the term "Holy Orders" for the priesthood and "ordination" for the initiation rite. But not all "religious" in orders are priests, which in the Roman rite is limited to males, and religious orders usually have counterparts for both genders.[9] In popular parlance, men are "monks" and are called "brothers," while women are "nuns" (who live in a nunnery or convent, a female monastery) and are called "sisters."[10] Not all religious are monastics: friars, for example, are mendicants, not monks, who congregate and foster both fraternities and sororities; Jesuits in military fashion and tactical mentality form companies.[11] Mendicants, moreover, generally are not bound by the vow of stability or permanent residence that characterizes Benedictine monasticism and its reformed versions. Although both mendicants and monks form separate female and male communities that are related through institutional and constitutional associations, like extended families called "congregations," mendicant communalism is more a network of distributed personnel or houses with residents coming and going, without the same kind of stable, centralized, villagelike community associated with cloistered monks and nuns.[12]

The monastery is the home for a monastic community, its legal incorporation, and its physical embodiment. It is a religious commune. The monastic mentality in Europe and America has sought serenity, a natural landscape, and geographic isolation to reinforce its claustration and to mirror the inner sanctuary (often a cloister garden, with a fount symbolic of the water of eternal life) with congenial outer surroundings. More practically, monastic communities like other communes in America have relied on farming and livestock (especially dairy cattle and sheep, as well as bees) for their own sustenance and support themselves by selling agricultural produce and surplus foodstuffs. Both through architecture and landscaping monks often try to create miniature environments, replete with religious fine art, conducive for their religious development.[13] A monastic complex usually consists of a church and sometimes a separate chapel for private devotions and Masses, adjacent cloisters or walkways for outdoor but sheltered meditation, a chapter room for business meetings, a refectory or dining hall, practical group dormitories or modest individual cells, an infirmary, a library, offices, and sometimes guest houses, plus areas and outbuildings typical of a farm (such as pastures and corrals, pens and stalls, barns, tool and equipment sheds, stores and granaries, and coolers and wineries) or monastic businesses (such as schools, print shops, garages, stores, and utilities).[14] The monastery is therefore a self-contained world within the world, yet set apart from it. The individual is thus able to withdraw into a regulated life, while the community as a corporation remains part of the secular time and place. His or her individual necessities, modest by comparison with secular lifestyles, are provided by the community; a rich communal culture can evolve that frees the individual from material concerns. Each member in turn supports the overall welfare of the commune by contributing labor, talent, and prayer. While the individual remains poor and lives on modest means, the community can develop considerable resources and even wealth. Individual personalities become camouflaged by the persona of the community. The corporation goes on, constantly accumulating; time is decisive in understanding religious communalism.

The other keys to understanding monastic movements are tradition linked to families or organizational genealogies, and affiliation within and between groups that is most often international. While the designation of a religious order is mainly a constitutional concern requiring official recognition by the Holy See, there are other forms of affiliation and group identification that affect an individual member's identity with a community. Most monasteries retain allegiances to motherhouses, like children to parents, and these form natural hereditary families or more artificial mergers, both called "congregations" within orders. These loyalties are often enforced by customs or traditional ways of doing things (governance, daily schedule, ritual and liturgy, dress and address, standardized in customals) that identify individuals with the group and characterize daily life; these form habits. Religious garb, called habits, reflect such formed behaviors and methods of social control. Not only does uniform dress affect identification with the community and promote obedience thereby, but less consciously such habits condition behavior by cloaking one's individuality and making all acts simultaneously official and sacrificial. One dresses for the part one acts and then plays the role. Even when alone or when traveling among seculars, the monastic could live thereby within a special habitat. This is the meaning behind the characterization of religious and the ministry as men (or women) "of the cloth." Each member inherits a cultural tradition through the order when he or she joins a community, part of which is a strong sense of belonging and personal well-being. The emotional security thus conveyed and personalized reinforces commitment. The whole experience transforms personality, changes behavior, and induces expected conformity while freeing the individual spiritually.

Monasticism sometimes seems to exist as a church within the Church, as a semiautonomous infrastructure. Indeed, "monk" itself is not an official term used by the Roman Catholic Church in its Tridentine self-image, whereby its tripartite membership was seen as the clergy, the religious, and the laity. There has always been a certain tension between the secular and the regular clergy, mendicants and monastics, and nuns and monks.[15] The conflicts between abbots/abbesses and bishops or religious and clergy often reflect a variety of town-versus-country polarities, including the latter's tendency to want modernization to keep abreast with secular developments and to associate automatically monasticism with conservatism—theological and political. Monasteries are ideally apolitical and otherworldly, and although they perform corporate charity and provide hospitality, they tend to avoid individual ministries except under pressure from bishops who in contemporary society are desperately short of diocesan priests. Typically monastic establishments perform corporate service to the Church, such as in maintaining schools, seminaries, and hospitals. Women religious have tended to be more directly involved in teaching, nursing, and social service outside the community. The degree to which a religious order undertakes social service often is the dividing line between monastic and mendicant. Monastics subordinate social action to their primary calling to worship.

Religious men and women consecrate themselves to God by choosing to follow the evangelical counsels, adhering to public vows of poverty, chastity (hence celibacy), and obedience. They combine individual contemplation and private prayer with communal worship as a harmonious duality, and each community assumes some form of apostolate to perform Christian charity. Their special ministries, modes of interaction and service, means of livelihood, approach to contemplation, and emphases on liturgy distinguish one order from another.[16] Because monastics do not self-procreate, in medieval times (as still is the case in Oriental monasticism) monks and nuns adopted children and reared them as members of the community. In America religious communities have relied on external recruitment that is dependent on contact through their ministries and the patronage of lay families. This form of regeneration is itself a motive to engage the secular world one way or another.

Some orders formed support or patronage groups such as lay confraternities whose families were the source for recruits and financial assistance. They were often affiliated with the community, had special privileges such as burial in hallowed ground around the monastic church, and were commemorated thereafter in the communal prayers for the dead. Others, such as the Cistercians, developed brotherhoods (conversi) who provided labor and support by becoming semimonastic, but they were not formed as a source of recruits into the core community. Such devoted labor is seen as a living endowment, a giving of one's self in kind and spirit. In the Middle Ages and extending through early modern times, devout Catholic families often placed their children in monastic schools; others participated in monastic choirs, and the religious would also take in orphans. Such affiliation of youth from the outside with the community could be a source of recruits, since such proximity and familiarity created the option of monastic life that would be unknown to those unexposed to this alternative lifestyle.

Within monastic communities there are stages of initiation and varying degrees of membership. Sometimes outer rings of associates are affiliated formally with an order or individual monastery: lay patrons, laity who benefit from a community's ministry (schoolchildren and their families, orphans, the elderly, and others in the community's care), and lay brothers and sisters who are often organized as oblates.[17] Within a monastic commune there may be a core community of monks, such as the choir monks who worship in unison (chorus or central union), as distinct from visitors, novices, and unprofessed members. Some reform movements were directed against such distinctions, promoted a more immediate egalitarianism, and flattened hierarchies; others reinforced distinctiveness within the community. Sometimes such distinction is between temporary "simple" vows anticipating permanently binding "solemn" vows for those fully professed. Age sometimes defines social sets within a community, formed by common experiences such as the same novitiates, just as in college, pledge classes in fraternities form abiding friendships. Leaders and officers emerge as in any organization. Some orders stress a functional difference and career path between laymen and those ordained as priests, similar to but not as canonically defined as the differentiation in Eastern Orthodoxy between the Black (regular, often monastic) and White (secular) clergy. Nevertheless, orders of male religious are often characterized by their balance between ordained and lay members. The Benedictines, for example, tend to have more monks ordained as priests than do the Cistercians. The denial of the priesthood for women enforces differences in the chosen ministries between men and women religious.[18]

Whatever the station or office held, the daily regimen is basically the same for everyone living in community according to a set schedule or *horarium*. A strict observance might model itself after a medieval schedule as follows:[19]

Time	Activity	Hours	(Divine Office)[20]
1:45–2:00 A.M.	Rise and breakfast		
2:15–3:15	Prayer	Matins	Lenten Vigils
3:30–4:00	Meditation	Prime	Sunrise
5:00–8:30	Work		
8:30–8:45	Prayer	Terce	Sext
9:00–11:30	Meditation and reading		
12:00 noon	Midday meal	Rest	
2:30–3:00 P.M.	Prayer	None	
3:00–5:15	Work		
5:15–6:00	Prayer	Vespers	
6:00–6:30	Evening meal	Collation	
6:30–7:00	Meditation and reading	Compline	Sunset
7:00–7:30	Retirement	Meditation	

Monastic daily routines vary by usages, seasons, and times within the church year, and the hours of moderate observances push back the hours to begin after sunrise. The ordering of time is a notion intrinsic to living an orderly life.

This notion of a peaceful, regular pace of daily life is in keeping with living by a rule—most commonly the Benedictine rule, which is known for its moderation.[21] There are also accoutrements over time from interpretation, innovation, and reform. These customs are often embodied in customals. Dissent within the parameters of obedience and necessary requirement of community cohesion is tolerated, but radical deviation from community norms has limits. The spectrum of hermitage to social community allows for considerable diversity, thus easing any tendency toward repressive conformity. Sometimes parent houses deliberately found new monasteries because of internal pressures; at others, groups split away to found new houses, and reform movements can lead to new orders. Many communes in the United States were formed because of conflict in Europe, both external, in the case of war, and internal divisions.[22] In individual cases leave can be arranged to reconsider one's vocation, and in some instances of personal disavowal, total secularization is possible by a dispensation from vows. Group dynamics often pull in opposite directions, oddly producing a kind of stability through moderating tensions. No matter the ideal, monastic communities are human societies with admitted imperfections.

Monasticism in America is a transplant from Europe that shares a long tradition. Western monasticism is mainly a medieval development that was almost snuffed out in the Early Modern Age but that was revived, reformed, and expanded. Although the foundations of monastic thought are biblical (both Old and New Testaments) and monastic life was originally imitative of ancient ascetic models (for example, Sts. Anthony, Athanasius, and Pachomius) including Christ's withdrawal during the formative years before his public ministry, its maturation is associated with the Middle Ages.[23] Monastics study their past enthusiastically.[24] Historicism is not an embellishment of monastic life; it is essential. It fosters an intellectualism that the Benedictine Jean Leclercq graciously characterized as "a love of learning and the desire for God," which embodies the notion of the remaking of Man.[25] Such thinking sees civilization (for example, in St. Augustine's *City of God*) as a secular counterpart to gradual salvation, the conversion from the primitive and savage to the domestic and civilized that has so influenced Western concepts of education.[26] It was never accidental that monasticism, monastic *scholia* and schools, *scriptoria* and literacy, libraries, and the formation of Western education were so entwined.[27] A genealogy of Western monasticism known to all monks and nuns would read like a litany of saints. Origins of the Western monastic tradition, based on connections with the Greek East and the homeland of Christianity in the Near East, would include transition figures such as Sts. Martin of Tours, Ambrose of Milan, Augustine of Hippo, and Ceasarius of Arles and the masters Cassiodorus of Vivarium and John Cassian, but the key founder would be St. Benedict of Nursia (480–546).[28] His rule overtook all others, including those variants from St. Columban's missions, the Iberian peninsula, and mysterious survivals such as the famous *Regula Magistri* or Rule of the Master. Benedictine monasticism underwent two major reforms, in its spread to Germany by the missions of St. Boniface (672/5?–754), and from the center of Cluny after 909–11. It was largely Cluniac Benedictinism to which Cistercians reacted in the twelfth century. The two versions were often contrasted by their habits representing different approaches to monastic living, such as the Black and White monks. Other regional reform movements led to the Camaldolese, the Vallambrosans, and the Carthusians who formed villages of hermitages. Friars contrasted themselves to monks by moving into cities; both Franciscans and Dominicans were early thirteenth-century reform movements consciously differentiating themselves from older monastic orders by their social activism. This trend toward leaving the communal refuge, a fortress for renewal, to labor in the secular world was epitomized by Ignatius of Loyola's Jesuits who conditioned themselves through *Spiritual Exercises* and served as the vanguard of the Counter-Reformation. Although Benedictine monasticism in the intervening millennium had spawned such varieties of communal organization, spirituality, and ministerial specialization, the mendicant and Jesuit reforms were seen as something different.

The pattern of monastic history in the West seems to be continuous reformation—reformation characterized by periods of formation, growth and aging, decay and decline, reform and rejuvenation, expansion, and so on. Monastic history is thus a paradigm for the contemporary monastic experience, illustrating the ideal and the futility of its permanent achievement on earth. The continued attempt at perfection, the process of salvation, and continual witness and prophecy in monastic life override any significant accomplishment in any time or place, or the importance of any particular foundation.

Reform and Expansion to America

The Protestant and Catholic reformations demarcate the transition from medieval to early modern worlds according to modernist periodization. Both reformulated religious life, its organization and institutional character, and sense of Christian unity. Monasticism, originally a lay movement that had already blurred the distinctions between clergy and laity, was in some ways co-opted by the Protestant extension of the priesthood to a lay ministry. This confusion of priestly and ministerial roles, and the Protestant position regarding good works as nice but nonessential for salvation, also undermined the distinctiveness of the mendicants. In essence Protestantism was an accelerated laicization in thought and action of certain trends already evident in Western religious life long before Luther, and which still has pertinence for Catholic communalism today.

Whereas medieval monasticism was characteristically confederate, collegial, regional, and Benedictine, its Romanization made it more defined, canonical, legalistic, and institutionalized than ever before. The reform of monasticism contemporary with the Protestant Reformation was characterized by networking of individual houses into regional unions or congregations and a standardization of practices and norms. Monastic reform ideology can be identified with the synod of monks at Peterhausen in 1417, revivals in Bavaria and Austria exemplified by Kastl and Melk, and the union of sixty houses by Bursfield Abbey in northern Germany that outlasted the Reformation and survived until 1802. In France the convent of Montmartre and the abbey of Liessies under Blossius were exemplary; in Spain the reform was spread by the congregation of Valladolid; and in Italy Sta. Giustina in Padua and Monte Cassino led monastic revivals and reorganizations. These monastic reform movements may be seen as part of the larger reformations occurring within Christendom and amidst Catholic versus Protestant rivalries, but they fared less well against the radical secularism that followed the wars of religion (1592–93) with the rise of absolute monarchies, widespread anticlericalism, and the political instability of Europe epitomized by the French Revolution and the reorganization of the continent after Napoleon. The suppression of England's 800 religious houses begun after 1536 by Henry VIII was a ruthless takeover, whereas on the Continent many houses were simply abandoned. But state secularization continued through 1835 when, for example, Joseph Bonaparte finished suppressing fifty-six communities in the Iberian peninsula. Even the famous Monte Cassino succumbed; symbolically it became a repository for Italy's national archives in care of its laicized members. Dom David Knowles, OSB, lamented that by 1810 Europe had fewer monasteries than at the time of St. Augustine. This famous Benedictine historian reckoned that there were more than 1,000 Benedictine and Cistercian monasteries in Europe before 1750, but by the 1820s the Black monks lived in their dozen houses and the White monks were scattered in thirty more.[29]

It seemed that Western monastic communalism should have died after this,

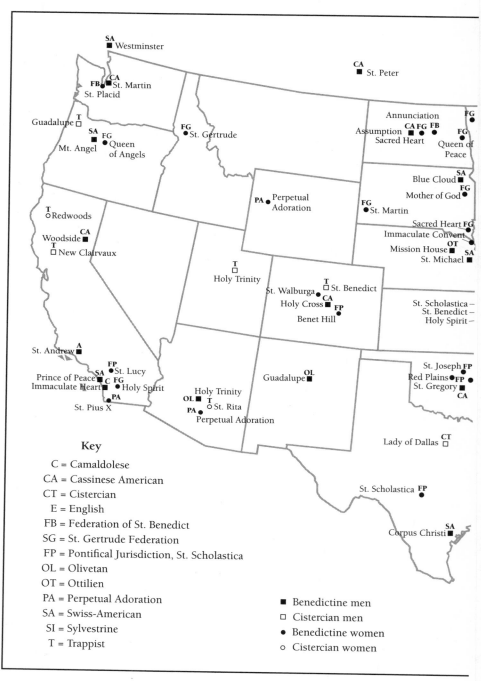

Major Benedictine and Cistercian monastic communities in the United States

LAWRENCE J. McCRANK

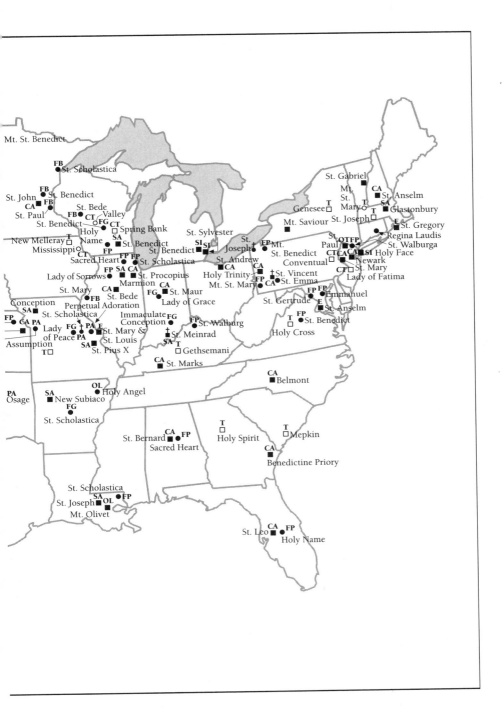

Mt. St. Benedict

FB
●St. Scholastica

FB
St. John ●St. Benedict
CA ■ ●**FB**
St. Paul ■
St. Benedict **FB** ●St. Bede
CT■Valley
New Melleray○ **FG**○ □Spring Bank
□ **CT**
Holy ●**CT** St. Sylvester
T■ Name
Mississippi□ ●**SA** ●■St. Benedict
FP FP ●■St. Benedict **SI**
CT ●■ **SI**
Sacred Heart **FP FP** ■St. Scholastica St.
FP SA CA ●■ Joseph
Lady of Sorrows● ■ ●St. Procopius †■ **FP**Mt.
CA■Marmion **CA**St. Andrew St. Benedict
St. Mary **CA** **FG** ●■St. Maur **CA** Conventual□
Conception● ●**FB** ●St. Bede ●Lady of Grace Holy Trinity
SA■ Perpetual Adoration Mt. St. Mary●
FP■ **CA PA** ■St. Scholastica Immaculate **FG**
CA PA ● Conception● **FP**●St. Walburg
Lady ●**FG** †■**PA**■**E** ●**FG** St. Gertrude
of Peace **PA** ●St. Mary & †■St. Meinrad
Assumption ●●St. Louis **SA T**
T□ **SA**■ St. Pius X □Gethsemani
CA Holy Cross
●St. Marks

PA **OL**
Osage ●Holy Angel
SA
■New Subiaco
FG●
St. Scholastica

St. Gabriel
Mt. **CA**
St. ■St. Anselm
Genesee□ **T** St. Mary○ **T SA**■
T ■Glastonbury
Mt. Saviour■ St. Joseph□ **T**
E■St. Gregory
St. **OT FP** ▼Regina Laudis
Paul●**CT CA CA** **SI**●St. Walburga
CT□ Newark ■Holy Face
St. Vincent **CT**□■St. Mary
†● St. Emma Lady of Fatima
●**CA**●
FP FP
●□Emmanuel
E
■St. Anselm
FP
T□ ●St. Benedict

CA
■Belmont

St. Bernard■ **CA** ●**FP** **T**□ **T**□Mepkin
Sacred Heart Holy Spirit
CA■
Benedictine Priory

St. Scholastica
SA■ **OL**
St. Joseph ●**FP**
Mt. Olivet

St. Leo●**CA** ■**FP**
Holy Name

the great "dissolution," but scattered communities survived in diaspora. In the process of canonical definition so characteristic of Trentine Catholicism, and in reorganizing after the onslaught of Protestantism, the Roman Catholic Church reaffirmed the distinct stature of an ordained priesthood in the church, centralized authority, classified and imposed order from the papacy downward on all orders, and realigned communities with episcopal government or directly under the Holy See. Popes from Pius IX through St. Pius XI, all ascetics, from the papal exile of 1848 until the outbreak of World War I, fostered monasticism to counter nationalism and ultraliberalism. The papacy itself was forced (hence the term "imprisonment" of the Vatican) into a kind of monastic enclosure with the creation of Vatican City as a walled papal state. The monastic tradition thus survived, was rejuvenated from a few centers, and tended to gain papal protection and support. It was this tough-minded, reform-oriented, pro-papal monasticism that spread to the New World. American monasticism thereby inherited a proud heritage, a long intellectual tradition, stronger multicommunity organizations, and a sense of continuity and historical nostalgia. Their precarious political environs, diminished financial resources, and delimitation of such traditional social services as education by the state ministries prompted monks to seek new homelands like other immigrant groups including Protestant communities, who sought in America religious freedom to continue their forms of Christian utopian living. The American experience was to be a new beginning.

The resilient comeback of religious communalism in nineteenth-century Europe was characterized by a resolve and fervor reacting to the previous near-destruction of monasticism. While some rural communities adopted an almost fortress mentality, their suburban counterparts developed a parallel ghetto territoriality. Many houses in the United States, monastic and mendicant, were safeguards against still possible repression in Europe. They were the retreats to which a suppressed community might flee. This defensiveness meant that some New World monks clung tenaciously to old ways and assiduously tried to replicate Old World models. This conservatism isolated them even more from modernist American tendencies. On the other hand, monks who came to the United States as scouts for their communities back home were often the most individualistic, pioneering, and nonconformist among their numbers, and several embarked on self-proclaimed missions. This produced certain anachronisms that came to distinguish many American foundations from their European motherhouses.[30]

The whole Roman Catholic Church in America is an immigrant and mission church, extremely conscious of its minority stature.[31] New foundations found themselves either surrounded by Protestants, or when they moved beyond eastern seaboard settlement to find privacy in open land, they seemed to be engulfed by paganism of either Native Americans or uneducated and unchurched frontiersmen. It is no accident that German monks saw themselves as successors to St. Boniface, the eighth-century monk-bishop apostle to the German barbarians. History was being repeated. The profound awareness monks have of their own monastic history is reflected in the naming of American foundations such as "New" Engelberg (Mt. Angel) or New Melleray in the same way that secular immigrants named their new cities, such as "New York." It is also apparent in their production of centennial histories as a genre of corporate biography.[32]

Most historians of Western monasticism would trace the nineteenth-century revival from which most American Benedictine foundations sprung to one man, Prosper Gueranger (1805–75), a secular priest who founded Solesmes in 1833. It became the center for reconstructing the intellectual heritage of monastic thought and reviving the liturgical arts (especially music), and the parent of a far-flung congregation throughout Europe and North and South America. In France friars and monks, sisters and nuns, were allowed again in 1816 to wear religious garb. Remnants of suppressed communities also regrouped under the Benedictines of Perpetual Adoration. By 1854 such reformed congregations were spreading their revival into Germany. Under the patronage of King Ludwig I of Bavaria, who reopened Metten in 1827, and with papal canonical restoration in 1858 of the old southern German congregation, Benedictinism received new inspiration from two brothers, Maurus and Placidus Wolter. Dom Maurus (1825–90) refounded the abbey of Beuron with financial aid from Princess Katherine of Hohenzollern. It became an archabbey, like old Bursfeld, which borrowed the artistic revival from Solesmes and a strict interpretation of the rule that seemed to resemble Trappist sensibilities. Beuronese monasticism spread with the resuscitation of old houses, but the German unification movement from the north and the *Kulturkampf* (1876–87) interrupted this revival. One of its monks, Hildebrandt de Hemptine, fled to Belgium to found the famous abbey of Maredsous, which in turn founded other daughterhouses. Maria Laach in the Rhineland became a second Beuron when the culture war waned. Both men's and women's communities continued to be organized. Pius IX patronized reorganization of the Italian Benedictines in a reconstituted congregation of Monte Cassino, taking as its model the previous reform of Sta. Giustina. Austrian abbeys regrouped into two congregations; five clustered together in Hungary; and in Switzerland, where civil law forbade additional foundations, the old abbeys of Einsiedeln and Engelberg were revived.

The Cistercians underwent similar vicissitudes. A remnant of a suppressed community of White monks founded the La Trappe as a refuge. One of its leaders, Dom Augustin de Lastrange, returned from exile in America to revive the European order. Adherents to the Common and to the Strict Observance continued to splinter and regroup until finally in 1892 the two formed separate orders. By 1895 the Sacred Order of Cîteaux had over 800 members, and despite two world wars that devastated many of their latifundia-like farms, the monks increased by another third by the mid-twentieth century.[33] The French-based Trappists grew even more, despite their strictness, but a series of suppressions in the 1880s forced many into exile. In 1891 there were 2,900 such Cistercians in fifty-two monasteries; by 1940 there were 3,700 with an additional six houses; and by the outbreak of World War II there were seventy-two communes of White monks.[34]

In contrast, purely monastic life for women declined in favor of more active, laicized roles as sisters of charity, missionaries, and teachers. Whereas Germany once had 100 Benedictine and 200 Cistercian communities of cloistered contemplative nuns, by the close of World War II it had only 10 of the former and 7 of the latter. At the same time more women than ever before joined women's communities with semimonastic enclosure and active social ministries. In contrast, the war trauma drew more men than ever into the most austere monastic communities: by 1976 there were over 700 professed Cistercians of the Strict Observance in the United States. The increased numbers of monks and nuns in American communities compared with the total membership in religious orders is a phenomenon of the last century alone, contemporary with and assuredly related to two World Wars and the Great Depression.

Although monasticism has always been a significant aspect of Western religious life, and in America monastics form a distinctive and important cadre in Roman Catholicism, there are interestingly enough no panoramic views of American monasticism or adequate syntheses of the many histories of individual houses and groupings.[35] American Catholic history has been largely ecclesiastical history wherein the secular "official" clergy predominate.[36] This is perhaps because the latter are all male and so much of religious communalism is female, but today historical revisionism abounds. The impact of women religious in America, still largely unknown, cannot be overemphasized.

The earliest representatives of religious orders in America were missionaries far from their continental communities: Castilian Franciscans in Spanish-claimed territories. The eastern seaboard was served by First and Third Orders, Recollects, and Capuchines, followed by Jesuits and Sulpicians. The Ursulines were the first women religious to support these missions, mainly by running boarding schools after 1727 when they arrived in New Orleans. The Carmelites, Augustinians, Visitandines, Poor Clares, and Dominicans followed in small teams reliant on financial backing from Europe to support a mission church. Educational need was a magnet pulling religious into every diocese during the latter 1800s as the American bishops after the Plenary Council of Baltimore in 1852 launched an unprecedented drive to establish a parochial school system on a national scale. Religious who lived communally in convents and monasteries near hospitals, schools, and parishes in towns as well as on rural farms were targets for American Protestants in their Nativist campaigns,[37] and their supply of faculty for Catholic schools made the parochial versus public school controversies worse.[38] Most Protestants thought of religious in communities, their group settlement, and association with schools as a severe threat, more than the occasional contact with a parish priest or some charitable sisters caring for the poor or nursing the sick. Groups of religious in habit seemed organized, formidable, and like a vanguard for the papacy: the worst American Nativist propaganda and mob attacks were aimed at Catholic communities.[39]

Contrary to its opposition's premise, however, Roman Catholicism in America never provided a united front. It was internally divided along ethnic lines, especially Irish versus German—a division realigned as Irish American prelates looked suspiciously at German-built monastic communities. Added tension to this uneasy alliance within Catholicism came from pressures on the bishops for more diocesan clergy to fill an ever-present manpower shortage, the need for women as teachers and nurses, and the demand for both men and women religious as missionaries. The secular needs of the church mitigated against unqualified support of bishops for monks and nuns, which often came in the form of land and subsidies for the initial foundation, unless the latter found ways institutionally to return such favor. Just as Bishop John Carrol of Baltimore (1735–1815) urged the Carmelites to leave their cloisters for his schoolhouses, an Irish Kentuckian prelate thought that the French Cistercians of the Strict Observance should do the same. Such "brick and mortar" prelates were less supportive of the contemplative ambitions of monastics than might be assumed. Finally, the apostolates of monastic and mendicant orders were never well coordinated. Massive duplication, failure to achieve an economy of scale for efficient administration of some social services and expensive ministries such as hospitals, and even competition for spheres of influence made for a movement more haphazard than was understood by anti-Catholics. What was lacking in corporate marketing of service and multi-organizational coordination was compensated by esprit d'corps and personal

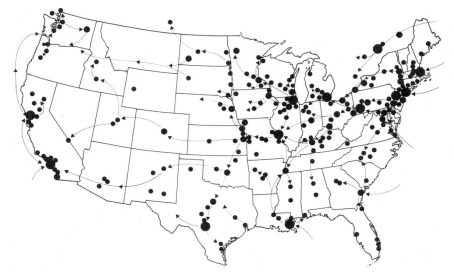

Concentrations of Roman Catholic religious communities in the United States

spirit, devotion, and sacrifice. In this, Catholic religious communalism shares a similar history with Protestant denominationalism.

The numerical growth of Catholic religious communities in the United States paralleled increases in immigration from Catholic areas of Europe—first from Spain and France, then from southern Germany and Austria, and last from Italy and Ireland—before monastic and mendicant houses were able to recruit monks and nuns from American families. Whereas a quarter-million Catholics immigrated in the 1830s, the subsequent decade nearly tripled that number, and despite the slowdown during the Civil War over a million came in the 1860s.[40] The spread of Catholic religious communities therefore reflects a general immigration pattern east to west across the northern United States, with a slow drift into the Protestant-dominated South. Until the second quarter of the twentieth century most religious houses in America retained their dominant language and cultural affinities with the larger immigrant communities they were ministering to and from where they took new members.[41] The world wars, however, broke much of the allegiance of monastics to their European roots and forced clearer distinctions between their motherlands and motherhouses.

Eleven immigrant and indigenous communities were organized in the United States before 1830 in two concentrations: (1) old pockets of French and Spanish settlement, such as New Orleans and St. Louis, with movements along river routes, and (2) the mid-Atlantic base with movement due west. Women often formed the vanguards. The first included Vincentians, who

LAWRENCE J. McCRANK

came from New Orleans to Arkansas and Missouri, and the Sacred Heart Madames, who came to St. Louis, where they were later joined by the Sisters of St. Joseph of Carondolet. The second consisted of Carmelites, Poor Clares, and Sisters of Charity (that is, Mother Elizabeth Seton's foundation at Emmitsburg and then Baltimore) who emigrated from Maryland to Cincinnati as the Sisters of Charity or Our Lady of Mercy. The Sisters of Loretto (founded as the Literary and Benevolent Institution in 1812) traveled down the Ohio River to northern Kentucky, where they were joined by Sisters of Charity. They were followed by Dominicans. Augustinians settled outside Philadelphia, where Villanova is today, while the Sisters of Charity of the Blessed Virgin chose the city. The Visitandines came to Catholic Georgetown before the arrival of Jesuits there and at Woodstock.

The rate of religious immigrations and native foundations of communities increased dramatically after 1840. Baltimore's parochial schools were bolstered by the Brothers of Christian Schools, and the Sisters of Mercy in New York joined their male counterparts, Paulists, and Franciscan Brothers in New York. The second wave of German immigration in the latter half of the century consolidated the so-called "German Belt" with reinforcements from Catholic religious communities. The Black monks first and then Benedictine nuns came to the Pittsburgh region; from the 1850s onward a series of communities were founded farther west from these initial settlements. The greatest change came in the Ohio-Indiana route. Cincinnati was not only a center of religious controversy such as the Cambellite debates, but the city became a stopover and training center for European religious coming to America and then an exporter of Catholicism to the West. There the Sisters of Notre Dame de Namur, Franciscan Friars, and Marianists settled, and the Good Shepherd community formed nearby in Kentucky. The French Trappists found safe haven after 1848 in the Catholic-settled midlands of Kentucky from Bardstown to Louisville. The earliest transplant of Trappists in 1805 failed, but the monks of Melleray Abbey near Nantes were able to colonize Gethsemani Abbey.[42] The Sisters of Providence pushed as far as Terre Haute, literally settling in St. Mary "of the Woods" at the edge of Indian territory and the jumping-off place from old Route 40 for St. Louis and connections with the Oregon Trail. The Holy Cross Fathers came to Notre Dame, which was then equally austere and remote. Franciscan sisters penetrated Wisconsin. Like a pincher's movement across westward overland and along the Ohio River, the southern contingent moved upward on the Mississippi. New Orleans was reinforced by Brothers of the Sacred Heart, Sisters of the Holy Family, and Marianite Fathers of the Holy Cross, and the Sisters of the Precious Blood moved straight onward to St. Louis. While Daughters of the Cross founded schools in Louisiana, Sisters of Charity of the Incarnate Word headed for Texas and the Spanish borderlands.

The movement of Catholic religious communities into the American frontier is remarkable. Far-flung missions were staffed by the Missionary Oblates of Mary Immaculate, who would work among the Plains Indians in the Canadian West and American Pacific Northwest. The crafty French Canadian missionary archbishop of Oregon, Francis N. Blanchet, lured religious men and women by ship and over the Oregon Trail to the West Coast. First the Sisters of Holy Name of Jesus and Mary came from Quebec, and then came reinforcements from Notre Dame de Namur in Belgium, to establish schools in the Willamette valley. The Sisters of Providence were attracted to the boom towns of Portland and Seattle. At the end of his episcopate he finally arranged for Swiss Benedictines, after failing to induce German Benedictines to migrate so far west, to found a monastery in Oregon, Mt. Angel, which in turn attracted a community of Benedictine nuns. They settled in the valley not far from where other utopian communities were to form, such as the Aurora colony. Many of these monastic settlements are scattered in the same geographic areas as Protestant communes because of patterns of immigration and land availability.

Communities formed in such numbers and varieties that Catholics, much less Protestants, could not keep track of their different names, origins, habits, apostolates, or numbers. Sisters seemed to appear in small bands like "angels of mercy" in schools, hospitals, and poorhouses and disappear as nuns into their convents. Brothers worked similarly, while friars ventured out alone or in pairs. Monks and cloistered nuns formed larger but more remote and less visible corporations that seemed to supply a growing stream of American recruits for an American-born clergy but never enough to meet an insatiable demand with western expansionism and the influx of Catholic laity in the nineteenth century.

The consolidation of the so-called German Belt across the American Midwest included the implant of reform-oriented Benedictinism related to the *Missionsverein*, which was a union of lay and church organizations for the propagation of the faith "among the heathens and unbelievers, principally in Asia and North America."[43] The archetype of the "pioneer" Benedictine was Boniface Sebastian Wimmer, a monk of Metten whose activity in the German Mission Society led in 1846 to his founding St. Vincent's Archabbey on a less-than-hospitable hilltop in Pennsylvania. The history of this fledgling community reads like one misadventure after another, with hardship interspersed with adversity, and conflict between German and Irish and between secular and regular clerical interests. The community's detractors criticized the monastery's "merry atmosphere" and more vehemently attacked the abbot's entrepreneurialism. Four adherents to a more strict lifestyle, led by Peter Lechner, formerly prior at Scheyern, were temporarily disaffected, and some returned to Europe. The community remained severely split through Wimmer's contested leadership, especially over such controversies as the abbey's operation of a brewery. The community grew, however, and its teaching ministry prospered with the assistance of a cadre from Eichstatt of Benedictine nuns nearby, under the much more stable administration of Mother Benedicta Riepp. By 1855, with support of the Cassinese Congregation and papal backing overriding opposition of the bishop of Pittsburgh, the priory became an abbey with enough manpower to send out its first colonies in 1856 to St. John's in Minnesota and St. Benedict's in Kansas.[44] Subsequently colonies founded daughterhouses in New Jersey, Texas, Virginia, North Carolina, Georgia, Illinois, Colorado, and Alabama. By Abbot Wimmer's death in 1877 five of these foundations had become independent abbeys. Under Abbot Alexius Edelbrock (1843–1908) St. John's monks, who eventually comprised the largest monastery in America (over 400 monks under Abbot Alcuin Deutsch, d. 1952), spread Benedictinism westward into Saskatchewan (1882) and Washington (1895).

The missionary work of the German men and women Benedictines was augmented by Swiss foundations. Monks from Einsiedeln, disillusioned by the Sonesbund war in the homeland, were invited by the bishop of Vincennes into southern Indiana. Abbot Martin Marty (1870–80) introduced the Beuronese reform at St. Meinrad's that founded a Swiss American congregation separate from the Cassinese Benedictines. Both congregations served the swell of German-speaking immigrants and missions to Native Americans from the Dakotas to Texas, the Pacific Northwest, and by the twentieth century, Alaska as well. The Swiss migrated into Missouri, where they founded Conception Abbey, which in turn established Mt. Angel in 1882 in far-off Oregon.[45] Swiss monks settled in Arkansas (Subiaco, 1878) and Louisiana (St. Joseph, 1889) and in a revival after World War II spread to South Dakota (Blue Cloud Abbey, 1952) and California (1958). Subsequently American monks founded a priory in Peru (1962), although an earlier effort in Uruguay failed. English Benedictines also established themselves in Washington, D.C. (St. Anselm's, 1919), and later in Missouri (1955). Both communities ran college preparatory boys' schools.

The history of Cistercian and Benedictine communities of women in the United States is closely connected to apostolates begun by monks in missions, parish work, schools, and relief agencies. Cistercian nuns, never plentiful, remained cloistered and drawn to a more contemplative life. The Trappistines, however, built relatively large communities of sixty nuns at Wrentham, Massachusetts, and in Dubuque, Iowa. The Benedictine sisters were far more numerous and active, with their Cluniac organizational model and reform inspiration from Beuron. Mother Benedicta's convent at St. Joseph, Pennsylvania, eventually founded nine daughterhouses, and these in turn became thirty-one in number. Periodic influx of contingents from St. Walburga in Eichstatt and from Tutzing added to these communities. Swiss Benedictine sisters from Maria Rickenback, Sarnen, and Melchthal Abbeys founded six houses in Missouri, the Dakotas, Arkansas, Idaho, and Oregon. They eventually formed a congregation named after St. Gertrude (1937), which by the mid-1960s had 1,700 sisters in eleven motherhouses. Another female congregation had formed from St. Scholastica in Kansas, but this was not sanctioned officially until 1930. These houses allied with the St. Benedict group, and both aligned themselves with the American Cassinese Congregation of monks. Together they had 2,600 sisters in sixteen motherhouses and another 2,175 sisters in seven convents. While the sisters of St. Scholastica tended to teach kindergarten through women's college levels, others diversified their apostolates to hospitals, nursing homes, and orphanages. A fourth congregation formed in 1925, the Sisters of Perpetual Adoration founded in 1875 from Maria Rickenback, remained contemplatives and became known for their liturgical arts. The Olivetan Benedictines and other independent houses remained outside congregations and fell under the jurisdiction of local bishops.

By the Vatican Council II, 57 percent of the world's 22,600 Benedictine sisters lived in the United States.[46] They operated over 600 schools, ten colleges, fifty-seven hospitals, and countless parish centers. While the sisterhood declined in Europe, it flourished in America. The organized and institutionalized character of monasticism, for both men and women, contributed immeasurably to American socioeconomic and cultural development.

Monasticism Today: Crisis and Change

American religious communities, having survived the initial trial of precarious foundations and a dramatic geographic redistribution during the late nineteenth century, entered a period of sustained numerical and fiscal growth throughout the mid-twentieth century, which they began to regard as normal. After the mid-1960s, however, vocations in the church began to decline, first for secular priests, then for male religious and especially the lay brotherhood, and finally for women religious as well. In what could have been a period of retrenchment, activist reform attitudes generated in and around Vatican Council II and subsequently by an episcopate and papacy that regarded reli-

The modern architecture of the cloister in the monastery of Saint Meinrad Archabbey at St. Meinrad, Indiana, embodies the centuries-old tradition of a religious communal sanctuary. (Courtesy of Saint Meinrad Archabbey Archives)

gious orders as a wellspring of spirituality have made religious life anything but insulated and withdrawn. Vatican Council II (October 11, 1962–December 8, 1965) was a major turning point in the history of Catholicism—a landmark as momentous as the Council of Trent—which has had a profound influence on religious communities everywhere.[47] It demarks the initial terminus for a period of transition characterized by tremendous institutional changes and intellectual ferment, ending in 1984 with the codification by the Vatican Congregation for Religious and for Secular Institutes of *The Essential Elements in Church Teaching on Religious Life*.[48]

American Catholicism's institutional and numerical expansion has always outdistanced the church's supply of secular clergy, so the bishops have continually pulled religious communities into overexpansion and broad geographic distribution. It is no accident that so many monastic communities placed themselves under papal protection to preserve autonomy and freedom from diocesan service so they could cultivate contemplative, communal lifestyles. Even so, the tendency in American monasticism to engage in active ministries outside the community, and even place large portions of their memberships at mission and parish sites without the continual reinforcement of communal life, has introduced a polarization between eremitical, private living and totally social, secular lifestyles in the personal lives of these men and women. It is not uncommon today for a third of the priests in some dioceses to be members of religious orders. They must be brought back into community periodically to resuscitate their common identification and spirituality. In these tendencies lay dangers to traditional monastic values that, to some, have been compromised by both "modernism" and "Americanism."[49] Active ministries and contemplative lives can be pursued by both laity and religious, monastics and nonmonastics; it is the blend that distinguishes them, or that blurs their distinctiveness as in the case of the Paulists and model established by Fr. Issac Hecker.

The tendency to dismantle the religious community for social ministries is sometimes called "laicization." All laypeople are being drawn to social action as part of post–Vatican II renewal (for example, in the revival of the deaconate for parish work), which means that the ministries of the religious are not unique to communal or celibate life. Additionally, more paid laymen have entered church service, and even communal members working with their vows of poverty donate their salaries to assist community finances. One can serve today without envisioning a special vocation. The declines in vocations for religious life and numerical recession in communities reflect a larger problem in the recruitment of priests for the Catholic Church, and perhaps also the problem of organized religion in general in maintaining an active membership. The largest decline in religious vocations in the 1970s was coincidental with the most significant rise in the number of Catholics leaving the church or who longer attended Mass regularly.[50] The reasons for this overall disengagement are unclear: a demythologizing of religion with accompanying materialism, a crisis in leadership and strong dissent to papal views (especially against *Humanae Vitae*), and the transition from immigrant to indigenous Catholicism. All of these contribute to the crisis of Catholic religious communalism in America.

The crisis is usually stated in numerical terms.[51] At the close of the last decade 2,416 Benedictine monks lived in fifty communities in the United States and another half-dozen in Canada. Of these 1,404 were in the American Cassinese congregation, and a third of these lived in three monasteries: St. John's, St. Vincent's, and St. Benedict's Abbeys. Another 791 monks live in fourteen houses comprising the Swiss American congregation, the largest being St. Meinrad and Mt. Angel Abbeys. Another 300 live in English, Camaldolese, Olivetan, Sylvestrine, and Ottilien houses. These communities are still vigorous and vital, operating a half-dozen priories, 15 institutions of higher education, 16 secondary schools, and providing manpower to 230 parishes, 64 chaplaincies, and 30 missions, plus numerous retreat centers; but the largest houses have 20 percent fewer members now than at their numerical peak three decades ago. The numerical decline of American Cistercian monks, 30 percent over the last two decades, likewise reflects a parallel decrease in membership worldwide.[52] Trappists number 573, with the largest communities at Gethsemani, St. Joseph's, New Melleray, and Holy Spirit Abbeys. All other orders are comparatively small. These numbers are also more meaningful when contrasted with mendicants in the United States: 2,677 Franciscan friars live in and out of 146 friaries organized into ten provinces; 1,134 Dominicans are organized into five provinces; and 5,579 Jesuits form nine provinces. Despite overall decline, there is still a higher ratio of monks to mendicants and Jesuits in the United States than worldwide.[53]

Women in religious communities in the United States outnumber men four to one, but they are more splintered: 366 separate orders. Benedictines are most numerous, with 5,274 members or twice the number of their confreres. About 1,730 sisters living in twenty-one abbeys and priories form the Federation of St. Scholastica (1922–; 1930–) under pontifical jurisdiction; the largest communities are St. Scholastica Abbeys in Kansas and Chicago, St. Walburga in Kentucky, and Mt. St. Benedict and Mt. St. Mary's in Pennsylvania. They administer a college, over eighty-six schools, five hospitals, seven nursing homes, and numerous parish centers. Fourteen houses with 1,541 members comprise the second Federation of St. Gertrude (1937–), the largest being Sacred Heart convent in South Dakota, Mt. St. Benedict in Minnesota, Immaculate Conception in Indiana and St. Scholastica in Arkansas. They run nine colleges, sixty-nine schools, eighteen hospitals, nine homes, and over fifty-seven parish centers. The third Federation of St. Benedict (1947–) included 1,480 nuns in seven communities, with the largest center in St. Cloud, Minnesota. They are concentrated in a single ecclesiastical province and provide seven colleges, seventy-eight schools, fifteen hospitals, eight homes, and over twenty mission and parish ministries. Together the Congregation of Perpetual Adoration (1874–; 1936–; 1966–), Olivetans, and Missionary Benedictines have another nine houses in the United States. Other orders distribute their personnel in more houses, fewer in each one, such as the totally contemplative Discalced Carmelites, whose 1,790 members live in sixty-four convents.

In contrast to totally cloistered, contemplative orders such as the Discalced Carmelites, Poor Clares, or the Dominican Nuns of Perpetual Adoration (1880–; 222 members in eight convents) and the Franciscan Third Order of Perpetual Adoration (1849–; 739 nuns in five convents, which do run hospitals and schools at home bases), which ordinarily live in small communities of ten to thirty members, some orders are split between contemplative and activist counterparts (for example, Sisters of Charity of the Cross and Sisters of Our Lady of Charity of the Good Shepherd, respectively). The Dominican Sisters (Congregation of the Third Order, 1822–) are both. Their 10,169 members live in thirty-two houses, some of which are huge (Holy Cross in Amityville, New York, and Most Holy Rosary in Sinsinawa, Wisconsin, number more than 1,000 each). Other large communities are located in Columbus, Ohio; Newburgh, New York; Racine, Wisconsin; Sparkhill, New York; San Jose, California; Grand Rapids, Michigan; and Caldwell, New Jersey. They operate 15 colleges, over 600 schools, 14 hospitals, and a dozen homes as well as mission and retreat centers. The Maryknolls (1912–), who are also under the patronage of St. Dominic, have nearly 1,000 sisters devoted to foreign missions like their male counterparts.

The Franciscans are divided like the Dominicans into smaller organizations, often with special territorial foci for mission work. The Franciscan sisters per se have 3,321 women affiliated with fifteen houses, of which the largest are in Manitowoc, Wisconsin; Little Falls, Minnesota; Hamburg, New York; St. Louis and Springfield, Missouri; and around Chicago. There are an additional 1,293 Sisters of St. Francis (1900–) in four communities, and an older group by the same name (1881–) that includes 2,278 members. The proliferation of orders, the affiliation of communities within them, their evocation of various saints for patronage, and their regional communal differentiation make their nomenclature confusing. They have common heritages, entwined histories, and patterns of settlement along major immigration routes, however, and their ministries tend to concentrate on certain foci.

It is not uncommon for the large orders of socially active women religious to have one-third to one-half of their membership outside their communities at any one time. This is especially true of the Daughters of Charity, who form sixteen main groups. Those of St. Vincent de Paul (1809–) number approximately 1,650 in five houses; the Sacred Heart and Daughters of Divine Charity add 300 more; nearly 1,000 Sisters of Charity call Cincinnati home (Mt. St. Joseph's, 1908–) in addition to the 578 who have settled in Kansas; and over 650 Sisters of Charity of Nazareth are concentrated in Tennessee and Kentucky. Eastern seaboard communities include more than 1,000 Sisters of St. Elizabeth who put their place-name on the New Jersey map; 797 sisters remain associated with the Emmitsburg, Maryland (1809–) community, and another 524 belong to the Seton Hill group (1870–); and 1,178 sisters reside around Boston. In addition to those who immigrated to the Great Plains, 1,370 Sisters of Charity of the Blessed Virgin focused their attention on Iowa.

An extensive array of buildings for worship, education, production, and hospitality suggest the many facets of Mount Angel Abbey in St. Benedict, Oregon. (Courtesy of Mount Angel Abbey Library Archives)

All are devoted to charitable work in schools, hospitals, nursing homes, diocesan relief agencies, and other welfare and social services. Even while working outside their communities in small groups, they remain affiliated with thirty-one motherhouses ranging in size from 30 to over 500 residents. The largest are in Boston; Greensburg, Pennsylvania; Emmitsburg, Maryland; Cincinnati, Ohio; St. Louis, Missouri; and Leavenworth, Kansas. Their related Sisters of Providence (408 members, 1843–) ventured farther west to found three houses in the Pacific Northwest.

Other large orders of women in the United States include the Felicians (1874–), who have 2,467 sisters in seven motherhouses; Holy Cross Sisters (1843–; 950 members) associated with St. Mary's in Indiana; and the Sisters of the Holy Name (1859–; 1,194 professed sisters).[54] The Sisters of Providence (separate from the aforementioned communities in the Northwest) and of Divine Providence (organized into five main groups: 1840–, 1856–, 1876–, 1889–, etc.) have over 1,600 members. Their main house is St. Mary's of the Woods near Terre Haute, Indiana. Seven groups of 3,971

Religious Orders and Monastic Communalism   229

women form the Immaculate Heart sisters (1871–, 1889–, etc.), with large motherhouses in Pennsylvania and Michigan. But the most numerous are the Sisters of Mercy (1863–), who have two unions, numbering 4,454 and 4,264 for a total of 8,718 women religious in twenty-four provincial motherhouses and dependent convents scattered all over the United States. Those invoking the patronage of St. Joseph (1873–) are even more numerous: 9,026 sisters in nineteen independent motherhouses loosely affiliated, with large concentrations in Boston (1,176 professed sisters), Philadelphia (2,056), and New York (1,329). The Sisters of St. Joseph of Carondolet (1836–) are comprised of another 2,456 members in four provinces.[55] The Ursulines, who first came to America in 1727, now number 1,607 in seven communities.

Despite these seemingly impressive numbers and the array of organizational creativity reflected in the proliferation of these orders, the women in these communities are aging, and the total number of women religious continues to decline as vocations dwindle. At their peak in 1965 Catholic sisterhoods embraced 181,421 women religious, but within fifteen years their numerical strength of 126,517 had weakened by 30 percent. The result is a decline in productivity and service; increased financial strain on communities by their aging and increased dependence on fewer young members; a contraction of charitable and educational institutions run by monastic, mendicant, and other religious communities; and the drying up of the reserve of priests for Catholic bishops.[56] Ironically Vatican II's focus on active ministries and the critical reexamination of Christian values the reform induced may have contributed to the problem. It reflects a mentality pervasive in modern Catholicism that has produced massive laicization. Although the total number of Catholics in the United States is rising, this overall increase sometimes hides the movement out of the church in record numbers. The combination of the decline in religious vocations with this dropout symptom constitutes a serious problem for Roman Catholicism. During the 1950s it was estimated that 7 percent of Catholics in the United States were nominal (nonpracticing) or were consciously leaving the church.[57] The estimate today is variously 14 to 16 percent, which is coincidental with the increased numbers of religious leaving orders.[58] This suggests that the problems now faced by religious communities seeking vocations to fill their ranks is less related to communalism itself than to the overall health of American Catholicism.[59]

A long-range perspective, however, suggests that the dramatic growth periods of religious communalism resulting from nineteenth-century immigration and hard times and world war from the late 1920s through the 1950s may be seen as waves in the continuous ebb and flow in monastic history. First, contemporary immigration is increasingly from non-Christian countries or areas with inherent anticlericalism. Second, global conflict has been reduced to regional turmoil, which does not produce the same impulse to flee from secular life. A third explanation lies in the nature of monasticism as a transplant from European to American soil, rather than an indigenous movement. Sisterhoods have been more innovative than brotherhoods in adapting to their American environs, although sometimes at the expense of their monastic values and lifestyles. Issac Hecker, a convert to Catholicism who in 1858 founded the Paulists, would be an exception, but he advocated a social activist ministry and community action centered around revitalized parishes more related to many of the women's movements than older cloistered monasticism. Monastics have held tenaciously to old ways, despite starting anew in America. This has placed them in opposition to Americanists in the secular clergy who argue for the uniqueness of American Catholicism, has often aligned monastic leadership with conservative elements in the hierarchy, and has continued the alliance with Rome.

Monastic recruits came largely from German and Irish immigrant communities and the working class in America, whereas the mendicants have drawn more from Hispanic and Italian American families.[60] Such sources for the novitiate have changed considerably since 1950; they are more diffuse, more mobile economically and socially, and less dependent on the church for avenues of advancement. These populations also have less-stable families with increased divorces, and family size has shrunk. Put another way, the church has ever more competition even for ministerial careers and charitable work. One can engage in these activities without joining the clergy or entering a religious community. Such changes have little to do with the intrinsic merits of monastic life, but they do influence all religious communities profoundly.

A major theme in the literature analyzing modern Catholicism is its Americanization, which may also be interpreted as secularization, and in terms of vocations, a laicization. Whether or not there is a distinctive "American monasticism" is much debated.[61] The conversion of German immigrants' Old World loyalties to American nationalism in response to Germany's role in two world wars, for example, could also weaken any sense of continuity in religious tradition with European foundations. Catholic laity have been wrenched from traditions in a variety of ways, including the reform's renewal stressing the vernacular and the end of the Latin Mass, to which monastic communities clung. The transition in musical and liturgical arts, language and modern translations, and other changes caused no little anxiety and even paranoia within Catholicism. The polarization wrought by the Vatican Council, coupled with demographic shifts and dramatic changes in social values and allegiances, has made recruiting into religious communities a difficult and even perilous venture.[62] Old policies have been reexamined, such as traditional forms of recruitment of novices from Catholic schools and parish ministries directly into formal novitiates and from there to an early proclamation of permanent vows. This has been replaced by an emphasis on formal education, lasting commitment, and postponement of vows until all uncertainly is past. There is also increased openness to monastic life as a second career; widows and widowers are finding second homes and fulfillment in religious life, and the church benefits from a hitherto wasted pool of talent.

Finally, there seems to be greater understanding and even empathy toward those who leave a community, without the former exclaustration and heart-wrenching denial of friendships and common ground. Whereas once all ties were broken, now many ex-religious often retain close ties with their former companions and continue in service to the community informally and formally as oblates, almost like a lay brotherhood or sisterhood or the old notion of confraternities. Nonpracticing priests, former monks and nuns, and married clergy canonically removed from their ministries find communion with the core communities.[63] The problem is the degree to which their personal decision to renounce their vows and leave monastic or religious life challenges those who remain.[64] Does their influence from outside the community dilute or add to its religious life? Does an extension of friendship form a healthy symbiotic relationship in keeping with Christian charity, or does it constitute a threat to the membership by the reversal of recruitment into the community?[65]

Such questioning is typical of the inspection to which modern monasticism has been subjected by its own practitioners. Among the more discernible themes in monastic and religious literature is the idea that a monastic vocation is a blessing from God and a gift of opportunity to be devoted entirely to God. This is related to the notion that monastic life is itself a witness to Christ.[66] The idea of a calling falls within a long-standing tradition, as does testimonial ideology,[67] but current literature uses almost militaristic terms, as in the writings of St. Benedict, who spoke of monastic discipline as soldiering. This is carried further in Ignatian spirituality of Jesuit authors who couple vocation with combat—for example, good versus evil.[68] These old themes are receiving new twists, however, as American secularism qua materialism is identified as *the* enemy. This is reminiscent of old controversies and papal condemnations, but the issues are put in different terms to avoid the polarization between a modern secular clergy versus an antiquarian regular clergy and monastic laity. Religious orders want to avoid the stigma of being behind the times, but instead try to engage the contemporary and offer an alternative. This critical confrontation with modern culture and popular values

The communal quality of life is clearly reflected in the enclosed nature of the central complex of Saint Joseph's Abbey, Order of Cistercians of the Strict Observance (Trappists), in Spencer, Massachusetts. (Courtesy of Saint Joseph's Abbey)

in North America (more so in the United States than Canada) continues a historical dialectic, but it is colored by a pervasive socialism (if not a communism) associated with communalism. It is not overtly Marxist or aligned with any nationalist ideology, but it nevertheless challenges American materialism and relativism. Paradoxically, the so-called Americanization of monasticism is producing a counterethic and an intellectual posturing that appears on the offensive, which may be ascribed to a defensiveness and need for self-justification. This modern proactive rhetoric appears to be progressive within Western monastic tradition. Such debate is increasing recognition of monasticism as a counterculture, now as when it spread in the late Roman Empire. Its very survival is important as a witness to Christ's gospel.

These themes of alternative lifestyle and counterculture are related to the traditional monastic vow of poverty, and hence monastic renewal reidentifies with the poor.[69] Purposeful poverty is itself a form of witnessing.[70] This ideology deemphasizes the physical building of a monastic institution and accumulation for fiscal stability of the community, parallel to the "brick and mortar" episcopal concerns for the early twentieth-century church in America. It allows new group formation, somewhat similar to local cults, without the structure of religious orders, and which appear to be another form of laiciza-tion. Concern with the apostolate is often evident even when its support is a financial risk to the community. Consequently, religious communities appear more individually and collectively activist than ever before, and they display intervention-oriented attitudes in offering assistance to the needy, which seem contrapuntal to contemplative monasticism.[71]

Although most American houses were founded for specific missions, his-torically the approach to their ministries has been collective. Increasingly small groups now leave their communities like fifth-column movements, in-filtrating areas of poverty to offer assistance and then returning to the com-munity periodically. Many sisters work with laymen and -women, imitating the example of Mother Theresa and other exemplary nuns; monastic priests go individually to assigned stations as chaplains and parish rectors. This means that monastics tend to confront secular culture today more directly than before, and their lives become more emotionally entwined with those whom they serve.[72] They risk emotional involvement in ways previously re-garded as dangerous because the ideal of service is displacing the self-preser-vation instinct of the community. Such daily contact not only challenges their dedication to celibacy, but it affects attitudes toward other cherished monas-tic traditions such as stability, obedience, and contemplative withdrawal or striving toward peace that is often seen as pacifism. In any case, such activism and individual response to charitable causes diffuse the community and spread a membership over wide areas, instead of the previous pattern of com-munities splintering and sending off new missions to found new houses. The older model based on Cluny, with large, centralized motherhouses and cen-tralized governance structures, from which authority radiates from a single hub to a circle of dependent houses, is being changed into a distributed net-work linking monasteries and their retreat centers with parishes, missions, chaplaincies, hospitals, and other agencies. This has produced greater flexi-bility in responding to the challenges of Vatican II and overcoming some of the limitations of declining numbers, but at risk is the survival of monastic communalism in America.[73]

Such issues amid the overall intellectual ferment and organizational change promoted by Vatican II became very evident in discussions during Pope John Paul II's visit to the United States in September 1987. Two subsequent papal visits, one directed specifically at American Catholic youth, have kept the pa-pacy in the center of Catholic debate. Especially controversial are the rele-vancy of celibacy and human sexuality, the permanence of vows and commitments, the role of women in the church, and changing attitudes toward ecclesiastical authority and governance. Perhaps most difficult to discuss objectively is the question of sex in the religious sphere, especially in America, with its ingrained puritanism that pervades Catholic as well as Protestant mentalities, juxtaposed with increased sexual permissiveness in secular society. Deviation from church social teaching in the common practice of birth control among American Catholics indicates the constant difference between ideal and reality. Such a difference pertains to religious life as well. The priestly vocation, Holy Orders, in the Roman Catholic tradition back to the early church and especially enforced since the Gregorian Reform, calls for celibacy as a special consecration to God. Celibacy is the self-denial of all sex, duo or solo, regardless of one's hetero- or homosexual orientation, which should make little difference in the context of total celibacy. The ideology of sexual abstinence is partially related to the notion of original sin and to general venality as the human condition, although the disavowal of sex as impure counters the sanctification of marriage, the idealization of motherhood, and several basic tenets of natural theology. Monastic circles especially extolled virginity, confused it with the concept of purity, glorified the virtue of chastity, and interpreted celibacy as penance and absolute denial. It has been interpreted so strictly as even to deny acknowledgment of any basic urge, to say nothing of thought or act. Now, however, celibacy is being viewed more as sexual abstinence while in a state of vowed chastity; it is a commitment with parameters, and there is less guilt associated with sexual encounters outside this state or with awareness of one's continued sexuality into religious life. An obvious awareness exists of celibacy as a gift, a special vocation, and an opportunity to dedicate oneself fully to God. Instead of denial, the focus is a positive concentration on the spiritual that necessarily downplays physical sex without purging all sexuality.[74] Consequently, this controversial issue is recognized as a legitimate concern of religious life. It is being discussed more openly than ever before.

Although the very notion of celibacy has been challenged, especially as something required by the church rather than volunteered by the individual, the ideal of chaste living is very much alive. Certainly casual and recreational sex is held in disdain, and the official teaching of the church about legitimate sex within monogamous marriage for procreation and including censures of birth control are held onto more rigorously in monastic and religious circles than in the Catholic laity as a whole. Sexual behavior by Catholics in general, such as common premarital sex and the widespread use of birth control, while remaining conservative about abortion, must influence religious thought about sexuality and morality. Catholics are outraged by instances of pedophilia and child abuse by clerics and related cover-ups by their superiors that have been publicized during the past decade, often with the taint of revived American Nativism, but the laity seems less scandalized by traces of homosexuality among the religious and more open to the idea of married clergy. Nevertheless, the resulting critical temperament of American Catholics and modern sexual permissiveness reflecting changing moral and social values among the laity form the context around religious debate about sexual abstinence in religious life. Must such denial be permanent? The monastic argument is often one of temporary versus lifelong vows.[75] The questions are numerous: Is imposed sexual abstinence meaningful, spiritually beneficial? Or psychologically harmful, and detrimental to human affection and Christian love? If interpreted too legalistically, is celibacy properly related to chastity as an attribute? Is chastity virtuous when enforced by social norms and fear of scandal more than by inner character?

The issue of sex is no longer taboo to discuss, but it remains highly controversial not only because this high standard of conduct in human affairs is so juxtaposed with normal behavior, but because of the intensity of religious zeal added to the debate within Catholicism and Orthodoxy. The American public lives with a double standard, allowing permissive behavior but reacting with censure when adherents fail the test. The scandal within the church is even more pronounced by the uncelibate in the public media. As Fr. Andrew Greeley has disclosed, the church is not immune from sexual transgressions of societal norms by its clergy.[76] It should not be surprising, therefore, that there are homo- and heterosexual encounters between community members, and between religious and laymen and -women.[77] Homosexuality, however, has been especially taboo for communalism more than for secular clergy, ironically because of fear that it may thrive in communities segregated by sex to guard against heterosexual activity. As in a case of military enclosure, monastic communalism could incubate homosexuality. Whereas unwanted pregnancy may once have been the worst outcome of illicit union, now AIDS makes such encounters potentially even more tragic. Moreover, the AIDS epidemic has made such behavior public. Cases among the clergy and religious at first embarrassed the church's hierarchy. Apprehension about a rekindled American Nativism from the Religious Right in the United States, legitimate concern about scandal and defamation that hurts the church's fundraising and charitable efforts, or an initial reaction of betrayal of community standards all must be overcome by Christian compassion and charity. This is not easy. Consequently, human sexuality is being reassessed as never before with reinvestigation of church history, tradition, theological foundations, biblical exegesis, ecclesiology, and explorations into the very heart of human psychology.[78] Such probes strike into the depths of Christian consciousness.

Although some Catholic women may aspire to the priesthood, and in some female religious circles eucharistic sacramental rites are being performed by unordained women, an overwhelming movement in Roman Catholicism to ordain women as priests is not discernible. Indeed, the opposition in the hierarchy and from monastic and religious orders seems overpowering, and the laity generally seems less open to this than to priests marrying. Greater support is given to expanded roles of women in various ministries, the liturgy, preaching, and even governance.[79] To some, women religious by virtue of their vocations and self-direction unwittingly have been feminist leaders.[80] Within their communities women enjoy full and rewarding careers, including senior administration, short of access to the episcopacy. The centuries-old contention over subordination of female communities to a male hierarchy remains, but without confusion between equity and sameness that pervades the secular debate or a movement to double houses and procreative communal life.[81] Apart from the prohibition against ordination of women, and the obstacle this creates to entrance into their hierarchy, few oppose women playing important roles in the social ministry of the church, and close partnerships between male and female communities continue. The quest for greater flexibility and self-direction in these roles seems less related to any liberation movement than to a move toward participative management and a refinement of the ideology of obedience with notions of shared, mutual responsibilities.[82]

Epilogue

After a period of disillusionment and factionalism in monastic and other religious circles during the implementation of Vatican II reforms in the 1970s, when variants of "death of God" theology spread along with questioning of old values and experimentation in liturgy, a "back to basics" movement can be discerned and a reinterpretation rather than a denial of tradition. Moreover, the great disaffection with vocations seems to be subsiding, although a critical shortage of clergy and religious remains. Celibacy is not being discarded, but it is being framed by a post–Vatican II mentality that is less judgmental than a Tridentine perspective. The older view of monastic life as witnessing is being reinterpreted in charismatic fashion almost as a form of prophecy because it constitutes daily reaffirmation of Christian expectations of an afterlife that has continuity with this life.[83] The older divisions between human and divine are less pronounced, strains of Christian humanism are healthy, the uncritical embrace of death-of-God theology seems reversed, Catholic literature is less cynical, and situational ethics, sensitivity training, and business management principles without moral foundations are falling into disrepute. The already rich tradition of spirituality, counseling, communal ethics, and freedom of thought in the Augustinian rather than the libertarian sense is alive and well. Likewise, monastics are reconsidering being pulled into such active lives that their ministry is at the expense of their meditative spirituality, periodic retreat to solitude, communal prayer and devotion, and camaraderie of the community. Old monastic values are being revindicated even in nonmonastic circles: this balance of the *vita activa* and *vita contemplativa* reflects St. Benedict's sense of moderation.

Such rethinking of the monastic tradition amounts to a reconciliation of polarized attitudes toward the human and divine in Christian thought and a potential reformation of monasticism.[84] The refocus on community formation in monasticism, turning from a reactionary withdrawal and rejection response to secular life that were sometimes at the expense of caring for the larger Christian community and mankind in general, is a choice to live life at the fullest, to disentangle oneself from encumbrances, and to maximize one's personal talents by channeling them through communal action. There is an openness by monastic and religious communities to new forms of affiliation with those outside the community; cloistered walls are coming down, and earlier boundaries are becoming extended zones of degrees of association measured by religious intent, proximity, and time of life.

Any assessment of the current milieu must remain preliminary, but the resilience of monasticism in the past would lead to the prediction that religious men and women will transcend the current crisis and anxieties, and they will come together to share their religious convictions and life for mutual reinforcement. Certainly dire predictions about the destruction of Western monasticism are premature. If one can appreciate the current ferment as a sign of vitality rather than death and decay, optimism should prevail. If no one cared about the problems religious communities discuss so passionately, that would more clearly signal such a demise. This is not the case. Instead, if historical cycles hold true, one should expect a renewal in monastic spirituality and religious communalism in America. Moreover, foundations from America will flourish elsewhere.

LAWRENCE J. McCRANK

Chronology

1500s	Earliest Spanish and French missions to North America.
1600s	Jesuits establish missions in North America.
1727	Ursuline nuns arrive in New Orleans. American Catholic Church organized by Bishop John Carrol of Baltimore.
1789	French Revolution begins and later produces suppression of monasteries and convents.
1790	Discalced Carmelite nuns enter Maryland.
1796	Augustinian monks come to Philadelphia.
1799	Visitation nuns at Georgetown, Del.
1805	French Trappists attempt unsuccessfully to found American monastery.
1808	Daughters of Charity founded by Mother Elizabeth Seton in Maryland.
1809	Sisters of Charity of St. Vincent and Sisters of Charity of Cincinnati formed.
1812	Sisters of Charity of Nazareth and Sisters of Loretto Institute begun.
1833	First Jesuits in Maryland. St. Louis mission church started. Sisters of Charity B.M.V. formed.
1834	Charlestown Ursuline convent burned by Nativists.
1836	Oregon Catholic mission begun. St. Joseph of Carondolet sisters founded. Maria Monk publishes *Awful Disclosures* as anti-Catholic writings increase.
1840	Notre Dame de Namur sisters from Belgium pioneer schools. Sisters of Providence formed in Indiana.
1841	Holy Cross fathers and brothers founded.
1843	Holy Cross sisters organized in Indiana. Marianites enter United States. Sisters of Mercy immigrate from Ireland.
1844	Franciscan friars organized. Precious Blood sisters started in Ohio. German monastic revival under patronage of King Ludwig I.
1845	Christian Brothers schools opened.
1846	Boniface Wimmer, as one leader of German Missionary movements, helps Benedictines in Pennsylvania found St. Vincent's priory; becomes abbey in 1855.
1847	Issac Hecker: Paulists founded. Notre Dame school sisters begun.
1848	Trappists at Gethsemani in Kentucky.
1849	Trappists in Iowa. Perpetual Adoration Franciscans founded.
1850	Redemptorists in Baltimore.
1852	Benedictine nuns arrive in America, found St. Mary's motherhouse in Pennsylvania. Sisters of Charity formed in Cincinnati. Plenary Council of Baltimore held. Conventual Franciscans come to United States.
1854	Swiss Benedictines establish St. Meinrad's priory in Indiana; becomes abbey in 1870, now archabbey. Presentation sisters from Ireland come to California.
1855	Grey Nuns come to United States from Canada (formed there in 1737). Eudist sisters arrive from France. Franciscan sisters in Philadelphia.
1856	Benedictines begin St. John's in Minnesota.
1857	Benedictine monks start St. Benedict's in Kansas and nuns found St. Joseph's in Minnesota. Capuchin Friars enter United States. Benedictines in New Jersey.
1859	Holy Name sisters immigrate from Canada. American Cassinese Federation founded.
1860	Sisters of Charity (Incarnate Word) formed in Texas.

1861	Benedictine nuns in Chicago.
1863	Benedictine nuns enter Kansas. Marists in Louisiana.
1865	Franciscan missionary sisters begun.
1866	Sisters of Providence in Texas.
1867	Vincentians in Pennsylvania. Benedictine nuns start Convent of the Immaculate Conception in Indiana.
1870	Adoration sisters immigrate from Italy. Benedictine nuns in Pittsburgh.
1871	Immaculate Heart sisters formed.
1873	Benedictines enter Nebraska. Sisters of Charity immigrate from Germany.
1874	Benedictine nuns at Clyde, Mo. Perpetual Adoration Congregation founded. Felician sisters come from Poland, and Notre Dame sisters from Germany.
1875	Poor Clares come to the United States, and Hospitaler Franciscans are formed.
1876	Sacred Heart Franciscans founded.
1878	Benedictines enter Arkansas. Jesuit New York province begun.
1880	Benedictine nuns in the Dakotas. Cloistered Dominican nuns formed.
1881	American Swiss Federation started.
1882	Congregations of Dominican sisters formed in the United States, and Benedictine nuns enter Oregon. Good Shepherd sisters come from Canada.
1883	Oblates organized in United States. Second wave of German immigration. Irish and Italian immigration.
1885	Holy Family sisters arrive from Italy.
1887	Olivetan Benedictine sisters formed.
1891	Franciscan sisters in Minnesota.
1892	St. Scholastica established in Minnesota.
1894	Bernardine Franciscans formed.
1900	Sisters of St. Francis started. Papal reaction to "Modernism."
1909	Pallatines come to America.
1910	Tertiary Franciscans organized; American foreign mission movement begins. Olivetan Benedictines in United States.
1911	Maryknoll missionaries in United States.
1918	Canon Law codification.
1919	English Benedictines come to New England, then Washington, D.C.
1922	St. Scholastica Federation organized.
1931	Carmelite fathers started.
1934	Missionary Benedictine sisters organized.
1935	Discalced Carmelite fathers established.
1936	Perpetual Adoration Congregation reconstituted.
1937	Federation of St. Gertrude established.
1939–45	Hungarian Cistercian refugees come to United States as monastic exiles.
1944	Benedictine nuns in Mexico.
1947	Federation of St. Benedict organized.
1949	Trappistines enter New England. Cistercian nuns come to Midwest.
1951	Carthusians enter New England.
1962–65	Vatican Council II (1962–65). Liturgical reform. Religious orders reach numerical peaks in America. Apostolate reconsidered. International Congregation of Benedictines (1964).
1966	Pope Paul VI's *Ecclesia sanctae*.
1969	Conferences of Major Superiors of Religious men and women.

1970s	Laicization. Numerical decline of monastic membership, and reconsideration of religious life.
1980s	Reformation of monastic communal life. John Paul II's *Essential Elements in the Church's Teaching on Religious Life. . . .* New Code of Canon Law.
1990s	Monastic renewal, stabilization and strategic planning of apostolates holds potential for the emergence of a vital, distinct "American monasticism."

Notes

1. This is actually a post-Reformation phenomenon, since monastic theology and Protestant thought remained entwined, especially in approaches to communalism: see Gerard Valle, "Luther and Monastic Theology: Notes on *Anfectung* and *Compunctio*," *Archiv fur Reformationsgeschichte* 75 (1984): 290–97.

2. Martin E. Marty, "The American Religious History Canon," *Social Research* 53, no. 3 (1986): 513–28.

3. Still, the conceptualization of this book reveals this underlying bias and separatism that pervades communal history. Essays on individual communities allow great detail, while Catholic religious and monastic orders, which have fostered more communities in the United States than all Protestant denominations combined, must be compressed into a single essay. Likewise, this book pays more attention to defunct communities than to those that survive and to those that, over time, have had far fewer numbers, smaller geographic spread, and less socioeconomic impact on regional development than those ignored by collapsing the treatment of over 125 living Catholic monasteries in the United States into one essay. The result is a lack of congruence or balance, not by design, but by an unconscious perseverance of a traditional white Anglo-Saxon Protestant conceptualization of American history.

4. From the Greek μοναχός: *Oxford English Dictionary* (Oxford: Clarendon Press, 1933; reprint, 1961), 6:610 (hereafter referred to as *OED*).

5. Hermits, solitaries devoted to austere asceticism, were identified as practicing a conscious way of life when they refused to join monastic communities, especially after the Council of Chalcedon in A.D. 451, which attempted to subject them to ecclesiastical controls. While hermits resisted regularization, anchorites (a Greek-derived term for retirement and withdrawal) were able to blend living alone within a community. Cf. Helen Waddell, trans., *The Desert Fathers* (New York, 1936; reprint, Ann Arbor: University of Michigan Press, 1957), and Benedicta Ward, trans., *The Sayings of the Desert Fathers* (London: Mowbrays, 1975). The canonical difference that evolved in the Middle Ages between anchorites and cenobites was one of distance and integration into community; hermits lived truly alone and isolated, but anchorites sometimes resided near a commune, sometimes as dependents. Cenobites were those whose withdrawal from secular society was into a religious community. For such distinctions, which last to this day, see *The New Catholic Encyclopedia* (New York: McGraw-Hill, 1967), 1:486, 6:1077 (hereafter referred to as *NCE*).

6. Monastic communities are not as uniform as tightly organized regimes, but organization and teamwork do differentiate them from spontaneous movements, purely charismatic leadership, or absolute distinctions between anchoritic and cenobitic forms. Sometimes hermitages grew into monasteries, some of which remained clusters of hermitages, and sometimes monasteries shrank to mere hermitages. The difference is like comparing a microcosm with a macrocosm, or it is a constitutional distinction. The term

"monastery" (*NCE*, 6:601) refers to a group of individual cells within an enclosure or protective wall.

7. Charles A. Fracchia, *Living Together Alone: The New American Monasticism* (New York: Harper and Row, 1979).

8. David Steindl-Rast, "The Monk in Us," *Epiphany* 1, no. 3 (1981): 14–25 (quoted pp. 14, 18–19, 21–22, 25).

9. Unlike communes of married couples and families, Catholic religious communes have always been segregated by sex. In the Middle Ages there were "double houses," one community with separate sections for female and male members (such as medieval Fontevrault, a matriarchy where monks served the nuns), but gradually communities divided into two, moved apart but nearby, and remained parallel (often participating in the same ministries), such as the Benedictine nuns of St. Benedict and monks of St. Johns in Minnesota.

10. Women have used "nun," from *nuncus*, meaning negation of secular values including denial of sex in favor of virginity, rather than the feminine of "monks" (*monachae*) or the Romance *moniales* (*OED*, 6:610). The patristic distinctions between nuns and virgins versus laywomen were based on sexual abstinence, but while the former withdrew into communities of women, the latter could continue in secular life, often in social ministries. Consider the idea of virginity and celibate living as sacrifices being a form of continuous prayer: Paul Hinnebusch, "The Consecrated Virgin: Efficacious Sign of the Church," in *Religious Life: A Living Liturgy* (New York: Sheed and Ward, 1965), 3–9. Canonists have tried without much success to distinguish clearly between convents of nuns and communities of sisters on the basis of the former having solemn vows, enclosure, and a full monastic office, while the latter observe simple vows and serve the diocesan ordinary.

11. The terminology is confusing for most people. "Mendicant" comes from the Latin *mendicare*, i.e., "to beg," and hence to live on alms (*OED*, 6:355), so their labor is their ministry. Monks labor for their own sustenance, and their ministry is less social service and more concentrated on the *Opus Dei*, or worship. In the same way that monastics are called "monks," mendicants are called "friars," from the Romance *fraile* and Latin *frater*, meaning "brother" (*OED*, 6:542–43), primarily for the four principal orders of friars: Franciscans or Friars Minor, Dominicans or Friars Preachers, Augustine or Austin Friars (distinct from Augustinian Canons), and Carmelites or White Friars. Friars live in friaries, monks reside in monasteries, and nuns who are either mendicants or monastics live in monasteries often called convents (from *conventus*, a juridical unit). Monasteries are also often called "cloisters" from the "closed" lifestyle of closetlike cellular enclosure. A friary is a brotherhood or fraternity, and hence also a fraternity house for mendicants. But these terms have double meanings, like "church" and "Church" referring to either the physical or sociopolitical edifice. "Brother" is used to address unordained monks and friars, as "sister" is used for women in religious orders; ordained monks and friars ("regular" clergy living by rules, from the Latin *regula*) are addressed as "father" like secular priests (living in this time and world, from the Latin *saecula*). Unordained men and women in religious orders are technically laity rather than clergy. It is no longer proper to confuse the nomenclature of monk and friar—hence the bifurcated title of this essay, which emphasizes monastic communities because they most closely resemble Protestant communes except in their segregation by sex.

12. Mendicants have historically been drawn to cities where they minister to the urban poor, while monastics have remained rural and pastoral, retaining their affinity for nature and disdaining the urbanity that seems the epitome of materialism. This "back to nature" calling translated to America is not dissimilar from Thoreau's *Walden* or other modern ex-

istentialism and utopian ideas. Such naturalism is not typically Protestant but belongs to a larger spiritual tradition; see Claude Peifer, *Monastic Spirituality* (New York: Sheed and Ward, 1955; reprint, 1966).

13. For religious fine arts and architecture, consult journals such as *L'Art de l'Eglise* (1930–), *Liturgical Arts* (1931–), *L'Art Sacre* (1947–), and the journals produced by the various orders, e.g., *Revue Benedictine* and *Analecta Cistercienses*. Cf. P. M. Busquets, "Monastic Art and Architecture," in *NCE*, 9:1023–31; Kevin Seasoltz, "Contemporary Monastic Architecture and Life in America," in *Monasticism and the Arts*, ed. Timothy Verdon (Syracuse, N.Y.: Syracuse University Press, 1984), 313–44; and, for monastic church architecture, Seasoltz, "Living Stones Built on Christ," *Worship* 57 (1983): 98–122, updating A. Christ-Janer and M. M. Foley, *Modern Church Architecture* (New York: McGraw-Hill, 1962), 29–328.

14. For older sites, cf. David Knowles and S. K. St. Joseph, *Monastic Sites from the Air* (Cambridge: Cambridge University Press, 1952); J. Evans, *Monastic Architecture in France from Renaissance to Revolution* (Cambridge: Cambridge University Press, 1964); and Anselm Dimier and J. Porcher, *L'Art Cistercien* (Paris: Zodiaque, 1962), with parallel English translations and excellent photographs.

15. The secular ecclesiastic hierarchy goes from minor orders to the deaconate; priests as pastors, deans, and monsignors; urban-based bishops and archbishops; cardinals and the curia; and the pope, or bishop of Rome. Religious communities are flatter organizations, with various members assigned spheres of influence and specific responsibilities in accord with their talents (e.g., singers as cantors, or scholars as librarians); the prior or prioress, who is the chief business officer; and the abbot or abbess, who is a spiritual and often charismatic leader. Monastic government by canon law is subordinated to the episcopal system, except when exempted through papal intervention, but the exact relations between prelates often appear confusing. This is especially so when monastics transfer to secular service, as when an abbot becomes a bishop. Historically the medieval idea of a monk-bishop was to preserve the charisma of the episcopate and guard against oversecularization of the Church. This has been institutionalized in Orthodox Christianity by its distinction between the White (secular) and the Black (regular) clergy, whereby careerists must be monastics.

16. The contemplative mode distinguishes monastic communities from one another, as does liturgy, as in the case of Benedictine, Cistercian, and Trappist, which may be seen liturgically as a continued digression from high-church or more to less elaborate worship and simplicity in taste, coupled with a different emphasis in a continuum from intellectual to manual work. Likewise, Jesuits are known as reformers and political protagonists; Dominicans are known for their education and preaching; Franciscans are revered for spiritual counseling and service to the poor; and the Paulists excel in pastoral work. All religious embrace some form of contemplative life and spiritualism. Some mendicants, such as the cloistered Carmelite sisters who fall into the Franciscan spiritual tradition, live as monastics under the strictest regulation and total claustration. It is indeed very hard to generalize about the character of any religious body because of this mixing of variant traditions. Little is orderly in the evolution of religious orders!

17. Several terms denote affiliation of laborers and patrons with a monastery: *conversi* (from *convertere* or "to turn about," but who may not go all the way, as meant in "conversion") are associated with Cistercians (*OED*, 2:942–43). Others are *devoti, donati,* or *commissi,* taking their meaning from devoting, giving, or commissioning oneself to God in a solemn commitment. Oblates are secular men and women who ally with a monastery to look after its material interests (from the pluperfect of *offerre* in the sense of sacrificial of-

fering: *OED*, 7:18). See St. John's Abbey, *Manual for Oblates of St. Benedict* (Collegeville, Minn.: St. John's Abbey Press, 1953–), or Leonard Boyle's introduction, "Oblates," in *NCE*, 10:610–11. From the thirteenth century onward secular oblates were organized as support groups for bishops, abbots, and abbesses; seven major congregations were formed. The Oblates of Mary Immaculate have been especially influential in the mission fields of the American and Canadian West. They formed communities resembling religious orders, including imitation of monastic life. Their statutes, approved in 1888 by the Holy See, incorporate many ideas from the Rule of St. Benedict.

18. Although monasticism was originally a lay movement, and priesthood was considered to be a separate vocation, the elaboration of ritual and emphasis on the Eucharistic service as a concelebrated Mass in Benedictine monasteries since the Cluniac reform has promoted the merger of the two into a monk-priest tradition. Some monastic reforms (e.g., the Cistercians) attempted to return to a lay emphasis. For the modern debate, see Ivan Havener, "Monastic Priesthood: Some Thoughts on Its Future in America," *Worship* 56 (1982): 431–41.

19. This schedule is a hybrid of the three traditional seasons (winter, lent, and summer) from a reconstruction of a daily schedule for the eighth through the tenth centuries, diagramed by V. Gellhaus, "Monasticism, 600–1500," in *NCE*, 10:1037–38. The hours gradually shifted back so that modern French communities, for example, tend to rise at 5:00 A.M.; spend the morning in readings, prayer, and Mass; eat dinner at 1:00 P.M.; participate in recreation and work, and vespers and study until a late supper at 7:30 P.M., followed by retirement after 8:30 P.M. The strict observance of the Trappists still calls for early-hour vigils. The *horarium* introduced at St. Vincent's Abbey for American Benedictines started the day at 3:45 A.M. for Matins and Lauds, then meditation; Primate at 6:00 A.M. and a conventual Mass thereafter, followed by a speedy breakfast and, at 7:00 A.M., classes and work time; 9:00 A.M. Terce and Sext, and examination of consciences. Dinner at 11:00 A.M. was followed by devotions, Nones, and recreation past noon; 1:00 P.M. study and labor again; 3:00 P.M. Vespers and study; 5:00 P.M. review of the Rule and its application (not common, but important for new communities lacking practice); 6:00 P.M. supper, social hour and recreation, and reading; 7:30 P.M., Compline, Rosary recitation, and retirement by 9:30 P.M.

20. These are the canonical hours of Roman liturgy, consisting of psalmody, antiphons, responsories, hymns, and lessons, arranged according to the seasons and the church year in repetitive three-year cycles. Monks usually celebrate these communally, in antiphonal choirs that respond to one another and enter into unison prayer and song (plain chant), or the liturgical hours. For an introduction to monastic liturgy, see W. Lipphardt, "Divine Office," in *NCE*, 4:920–22.

21. Timothy Fry and I. Baker, eds., *The Rule of St. Benedict* (Collegeville, Minn.: St. John's Liturgical Press, 1981). The notes and commentary of Justin McCann are still cogent: *The Rule of St. Benedict* (Westminster, Md.: Newman Press, 1952).

22. Robert H. Winthrop, "Leadership and Tradition in the Regulation of Catholic Monasticism," *Anthropological Quarterly* 58 (1985): 30–38, relates enculturation or authority or leadership in the monastic tradition. He claims that the interruption of continuity after the Napoleonic Wars and the creation of "reform-oriented" monasteries in the United States resulted in major shifts in the understanding of the monastic tradition.

23. For a historical overview, see David Knowles, *Christian Monasticism* (New York: Mc-Graw-Hill, 1969; reprint, 1977).

24. The theme of medievalism in contemporary monastic culture is treated by Lee Braude, "The Medieval Strain in Contemporary Culture: A Debate with Weber's Ghost," *Phylon* 32, no. 3 (1971): 244–36.

25. Jean Leclercq, *The Love of Learning and the Desire for God*, trans. C. Misrahi (New York: Fordham University Press, 1961).

26. Cf. Robert Redfield, *The Primitive World and Its Transformations* (Ithaca, N.Y.: Cornell University Press, 1953; reprint, 1968), 22–25; Jack Goody, *The Domestication of the Savage Mind* (Cambridge: Cambridge University Press, 1977), 1–18.

27. The relevant literature is vast; see the select guide by Giles Constable, *Medieval Monasticism: A Select Bibliography* (Toronto: University of Toronto Press, 1976), updated by standard indexing and abstract services, i.e., *Index of Medieval Bibliography*, *Historical Abstracts*, etc.

28. The Benedictine Order's history is surveyed by Philip Schmitz, *Histoire de l'ordre de St. Benedict*, 7 vols. (Maredsous: Benedictine Press, 1942–56); it was translated into German (Zurich, 1946–50), but only the early volumes are available in English.

29. Knowles, *Christian Monasticism*, 158, 175–76.

30. See Joel Rippinger, "The Origins and Development of Benedictine Monasticism in the United States," in *The Continuing Quest for God: Monastic Spirituality in Tradition and Transition*, ed. William Skudlarek (Collegeville, Minn: St. John's Liturgical Press, 1982), 160–69; cf. Thomas M. Gannon, "The Religious Order in American Catholicism," *American Review of Social Science and Religion* 3 (1979): 17–57.

31. James Hennesey, "Immigrants Become the Church," in *American Catholics: A History of the Roman Catholic Community in the United States* (New York: Oxford University Press, 1981), 116–27.

32. The literature about American monastic and religious communities is immense: cf. Oliver Kapsner, *A Benedictine Bibliography*, 2d ed. plus supplement (Collegeville, Minn.: St. John's Abbey, 1967); John Tracy Ellis and Robert Trisco, *A Guide to American Catholic History*, 2d ed. (Santa Barbara, Calif.: ABC-Clio Press, 1982); James Hennesey, *American Catholic Bibliography, 1970–1982* (Notre Dame, Ind.: Cushwa Center for the Study of American Catholicism, 1982). For syntheses, see Claude Peifer, "Monastic Studies in the United States," in *Regulae Benedicti Studia I: Annuarium Internationale*, ed. B. Jaspert (Heldesheim, W. Germany: Verlag Gerstenberg, 1972).

33. Louis J. Lekai, *The Cistercians: Ideals and Reality* (Kent, Ohio: Kent State University Press, 1977), esp. pp. 480–86 for tabulated statistics.

34. Knowles, *Christian Monasticism*, 196–97.

35. See Karen Kennelly, "Historical Perspectives on the Experience of Religious Life in the American Church," in *Religious Life in the U.S. Church: The New Dialogue*, ed. Robert J. Daly (New York: Paulist Press, 1984), 79–97, with a comparative chart or timetable for the introduction of major religious orders to America.

36. See, for example, the standard surveys of John Tracy Ellis, *American Catholicism* (Chicago: University of Chicago Press, 1969), which indexes no references to major monastic orders; Thomas T. McAvoy, *A History of the Catholic Church in the United States* (South Bend, Ind.: University of Notre Dame Press, 1969), where the Benedictines and Cistercians together earn no more than one mention; and Hennesey, *American Catholics*, 81–88, 218–24, for brief mentions of the Benedictines interwoven with comments about the immigrant church.

37. For the connection between immigrant Catholicism, settlement patterns, Protestant reaction, and American Nativism, see John Higham, *Strangers in the Land: Patterns of American Nativism, 1860–1925*, rev. ed. (New York: Atheneum, 1965), 35–96, and his interpretative "Another Look at Nativism," *Catholic Historical Review* 44 (1958): 147–58. However, these studies do not focus clearly on the extraordinary problems of Catholic monastic communities and Nativist reactions to their corporate economies, large-scale farming, and fortresslike institutionalism.

38. For the great American school controversy, cf. Hennesey, *American Catholics*, pp. 108–9, and Lawrence A. Cremin, *American Education: The National Experience, 1873–1876* (New York: Harper and Row, 1980), pp. 148–85, for summation, and in more detail, Vincent P. Lannie, *Public Money and Parochial Education: Bishop Hughes, Governor Seward, and the New York School Controversy* (Cleveland, Ohio: Case-Western Reserve University Press, 1968); Diane Ravitch, *The Great School Wars: New York City, 1805–1973* (New York: Basic Books, 1974), for longer-range perspective; and for the Catholic side, Harold A. Buetow, *Of Singular Benefit: The Story of Catholic Education in the United States* (New York: Macmillan, 1970).

39. Cf. the seminal study of Ray Allen Billington, *The Protestant Crusade, 1800–1860: A Case Study in the Origins of American Nativism* (New York: Rinehart, 1939). Consider the "best seller" of the antimonastic genre in American Nativist literature, e.g., Maria Monk [pseud.], *Disclosures of Maria Monk, as exhibited in a narrative of her sufferings during a residence of five years as a novice and two years as a black nun, in the Hotel Dieu nunnery in Montreal* . . . (Paisely, N.Y.: A Gardner, 1836). One of the most controversial of all incidents was in Philadelphia: cf. James Kennelly, "The Burning of the Ursuline Convent: A Different View," *Records of the American Catholic Historical Society of Philadelphia* 90 (1979): 15–21, set into a larger context of widespread disorder by Theodore M. Hammett, "Two Mobs of Jacksonian Boston: Ideology and Interest," *Journal of American History* 62, no. 4 (1976): 845–68, which compares such anti-Catholic riots with violence against antislavery headquarters.

40. Thomas T. McAvoy, "The Growth of the Catholic Minority in the Later Nineteenth Century," *Review of Politics* 15 (1953): 275–302.

41. For the cohesion and endurance of religious orders because of ethnic identification, cf. Mary Ewens, "The Leadership of Nuns in Immigrant Catholicism," in *Women and Religion in America: The Nineteenth Century* (San Francisco: Harper and Row, 1981), ed. Rosemary Radford Ruether and Rosemary Skinner Keller, 101–49, and William V. Calabro, "Recruitment and Socialization in a Normative Organization: A Case Study" (paper before the Association for Sociology of Religion, 1980), which from a sample of 1,200 women religious indicated that they are still recruited from a rather narrow segment of U.S. Catholics.

42. The community grew to about 44 monks and by 1851 had achieved abbatial status under Eutropius Proust, but it almost became extinct by 1900 and had to be revived under Abbot Edmond Obrecht (1889–1935), who led it into a virtual renaissance during the late 1930s. It gained worldwide notoriety through its foremost author, Thomas Merton, but is also famous for its acclaimed fruitcakes and cheeses. Its growth to 279 members by the 1950s seems almost an anomaly for Strict Observance Trappists in the modern world. For their spirituality, read Merton's *The Waters of Silo* (New York: Harcourt, Brace, 1949); cf. M. Raymond Flanagan, *Burnt Out Incense* (New York: P. J. Kennedy, 1949). Gethsemani's colonies founded monasteries in 1944 at Conyers, Ga.; in 1947 at Huntsville, Utah; at Mepkin Abbey in South Carolina in 1949; at Piffard, N.Y., in 1951; and at Vina ranch in the Sacramento Valley in 1955 before attrition set in that eventually reduced the motherhouse's membership to fewer than 100.

43. Jerome Oetgen, *An American Abbot: Boniface Wimmer, OSB (1809–1887)* (Latrobe, Pa.: St. Vincent Archabbey, 1976), initially published in parts in the *American Benedictine Review* 22 (1971): 147–76 (quote p. 148); 23 (1972): 282–313; 24 (1973): 1–28; cf. Coleman J. Barry, "Boniface Wimmer, Pioneer of the American Benedictines," *Catholic Historical Review* 41 (1955): 272–96.

44. Cf. Peter Beckman, *Kansas Monks: A History of St. Benedict Abbey* (Atchison, Kans.:

Abbey Student Press, 1957); Colman J. Barry, *Worship and Work: Saint John's Abbey and University, 1856–1980*, 2d ed. (Collegeville, Minn.: St. John's Liturgical Press, 1980).

45. Cf. Albert Kelber, *History of St. Meinrad Archabbey, 1854–1954* (St. Meinrad, Ind.: Grail, 1954); Charles Gedert, "The Swiss-American Congregation of Benedictines and Its Contributions to the American Catholic Church" (B.A. thesis, Atheneum College of Liberal Arts, Cincinnati, Ohio, 1956); and Joel Rippinger, "The Swiss American Congregation: A Centennial Survey," *American Benedictine Review* 32 (1981): 87–99. For key daughter-houses, see Edward Malone, *Conception: A History of the First Century, 1858–* (Elkhorn, Neb.: Michaeleen Press, 1971), and Lawrence J. McCrank, *Mt. Angel Abbey: A Centennial History of a Benedictine Community and Its Library, 1882–1982* (Wilmington, Del.: Scholarly Resources, 1983).

46. Stephan Hilpisch, *History of Benedictine Nuns*, ed. Leonard Boyle, trans. M. Joanne Muggli (Collegeville, Minn.: St. John's Abbey Press, 1958), lists for 1955 9,493 nuns in 247 houses and 11,105 sisters in 120 monasteries of the Benedictine Order throughout the world.

47. Consider, for example, Michael Whitley, "Determining Organizational Changes Reflecting the Impact of Vatican II and the Decline of the Immigrant Church Paradigm of American Catholicism" (paper before the Midwest Sociological Society, 1979 [ms. Sterling collection, KS; cf. *Sociological Abstracts*, no. 383000]), who calls attention to the coincidence between the renewal of Vatican II and the decline of the "immigrant model" of the American Catholic Church. For the legal reconfirmation of monastic life and its reinterpretation according to revised canon law (1983), see Elio Gambari, *Religious Life According to Vatican II and the New Code of Canon Law*, trans. Daughters of St. Paul (Boston: Paulist Press, 1985), 6:1–192.

48. Cf. David Flemming, ed., *Religious Life at the Crossroads: Papers form the Conferences of Major Superiors of Men Religious, Selected from Meetings, 1975–1985* (New York: Paulist Press, 1985), and Daly, *Religious Life in the U.S. Church*, 311–42, for discussion of the *Essential Elements*. For the impact of the council of monastic spirituality, see Skudlarek, *Continuing Quest for God*.

49. Modernism is not to be confused with secularism in the general sense but applies specifically to views condemned by Pius X's encyclical *Pascendi* in 1907, especially agnosticism, immanent thought, and an evolutionary/naturalist approach to doctrine. The church took a conservative stand against the notion that canon law, dogmatic theology, etc., should automatically accommodate the modern world. Instead the immutable, universal, and transcendent have been emphasized. On the other hand, Americanism refers to ideas censored by Leo XIII's apostolic brief in 1899, *Testem benevolentiae*, which rejected the notion of the universal church having to accommodate any particular geographic region or culture for the sake of acceptance. Among the ideas rejected was the notion of the incompatibility of religious vows and religious freedom. Cf. the summaries by J. J. Heaney, "Modernism," in *NCE*, 9:991–98, and Thomas T. McAvoy, "Americanism" in *NCE*, 1:443, whose *The Great Crisis in American Catholic History, 1895–1900* (Chicago: University of Chicago Press, 1957) explored these issues.

50. Hennesey, *American Catholics*, 329, following Andrew M. Greeley, *The American Catholic: A Social Portrait* (New York: Basic Books, 1977), 143, summarizing the National Opinion Research Center studies, 1976–.

51. Compare the annual counts in *The Official Catholic Directory* (Wilmette, Ill.: P. J. Kennedy & Sons, 1984–), e.g., 1035–94, with counts used in the *NCE* articles on each congregation (2:300–303) for the 1960s, and Knowles, *Christian Monasticism*, 248, for 1955 (3,013 monks in three congregations).

52. Cf. *NCE*, 3:888, with Lekai, *Cistercians*, 482–83 (1972 data), with *Catholic Directory* annual counts and Knowles, *Christian Monasticism*, 247, based on the *Annuario Pontifico* (Rome: Vatican, 1955–).

53. Knowles, *Christian Monasticism*, 248, surveys memberships in 1955: 49,500 Franciscans (26,500 OFM; 15,600 OFM Capuchin), 34,700 Dominicans, and 9,500 Jesuits. Compare these numbers with cloistered monks: 688 Carthusians in seventeen houses, 3,770 Trappists in eight monasteries, 1,665 Cistercians in fifty-one abbeys, and 12,070 Benedictines. In 1967 the worldwide population of Catholic monks was 18,667 at their peak. By 1980 that number had dropped to 8,563.

54. Consider the Sisters of Loretto (1812–; 660 members); Presentation Sisters (two groups, 1854– and 1873–, with 595 sisters in one and 861 in the other); Servants of the Immaculate Heart (1870–; 736 sisters); Visitation Nuns (1799–; 323 members); etc.

55. Another 1,182 sisters live in nine unaffiliated communities that are dedicated to St. Joseph, the patron of manual labor.

56. In 1980 there were 59,892 priests and 4,093 deacons serving the Catholic Church in the United States; about 800 men were ordained annually (Hennesey, *American Catholics*, 329). However, the number of seminarians, indicating the future supply of clergy, has declined sharply to an all-time low by 1980 of 13,226 (including an increased number of women in seminaries), or only a third of the enrollment from the 1960s. A quarter of American priests are in religious orders, but less than 5 percent are in monastic orders. Nevertheless, monk-priests constitute a significant portion of the church's priestly manpower. Pope Paul VI in 1966 argued for the harmony of the monastic and priestly vocations as "a special union between two consecrations," and the Catholic Church officially regards the declericalization of religious institutes as an "impoverishment." See Elio Gambari, "Religious Life and the Priesthood," in *Religious Life According to Vatican II and the New Code of Canon Law* (New York: St. Paul Press, 1983), 201–5.

57. See Margaret M. Modde, "Departures from Religious Institutes," in *NCE*, 17:570–71, for a summary, and note the prediction of crisis for religious communities in the 1980s foretold by earlier massive survey questionnaires—for example, Jacques Legare, "Les Religieuses du Canada: Leur Evolution numerique entre 1965 et 1980," *Recherches Sociologiques* 10, no. 1 (1969): 7–21.

58. Hennesey, *American Catholics*, 329.

59. W. Downey, ed., "Why the Sharp and Sudden Decline?," in *Religious Life: What the Church Teaches* (New York: Institute on Religious Life, 1985), 48–56, outlines the major problems: (1) secularization of contemporary society; (2) breakdown of Catholic family life; (3) widespread agnosticism and skepticism; (4) poor public image presented by the American public media reflecting traditional Protestant attitudes; (5) chemical dependency among youth; (6) pervasive relativism; (7) declining enrollments in parochial schools and a dilution of content in religious education; (8) failure of religious themselves to promote religious vocations; (9) secularization of the lifestyles of religious in public, resulting in a failure to inspire by example; and (10) decreased visibility of religious in the public eye (e.g., lay dress, "another sign of transcendence that has disappeared").

60. Note the findings in such case studies as presented by Calabro, "Recruitment and Socialization in a Normative Organization," concerning religious orders of women in northeastern America.

61. Joel Rippinger, "Is There an American Benedictine Spirituality?," in Skudlarek, *Continuing Quest for God*, 279–85.

62. Among the recommendations for encouraging vocations in religious life, as in Downey, *Religious Life*, 57, are (1) improving Catholic education; (2) advocating consider-

ation of the idea of giving oneself, that is, a religious dedication; (3) increasing intensity and zeal of those already in religious life for example; (4) wearing religious garb for identification and higher visibility; (5) building a theology around the evangelical counsels; (6) inculcating an identification with Christ in a more personal manner—i.e, revived mysticism; (7) honestly engaging the effects of sin or creating a clearer opposition of good and evil; and (8) praying for vocations.

63. For the canonical ideal of communion as the aggregation, grouping, linking, and bonding into religious communities, see Gambari, "Communion among Religious," in Gambari, *Religious Life*, 452–64. Compare this ideology with the canonical and procedural issues of exclaustration, dispensation, and dismissal, etc.: Gambari, "Separation from the Institute," in ibid., 579–97.

64. This is the reverse of several notorious cases of husbands and wives voluntarily separating and entering religious orders but not renouncing marriage vows. In one celebrated nineteenth-century case the husband changed his mind and sued for conjugal rights when his wife chose to remain a nun and had vowed celibacy after their separation. The husband never won his case, but the affair so scandalized the bishops and was used by anti-Catholics to defame all religious institutes as the enemies of marriage and family life, that such practices were discouraged.

65. The idea of community flows from the notion of a consecration to and communion with God and with one's communal association. Consider "Communion in Community," in *Essential Elements*, II.2, articles 18–22.

66. Consider Hinnebusch's idea of religious life as a liturgical sign and the whole ideology of signification, signing, and imagery that outwardly signals the spirit of inner Life, as in his "The Religious: As Liturgical Sign," and "Christian Witness: Completion of the Liturgy," in Gambari, *Religious Life*, 71–87, 147–52, 203–10; cf. Downey, "Religious Identity," in Downey, *Religious Life*, 35–56, and "Call and Consecration," in *Essential Elements*, III.1, nos. 1–7, defining a vocation, dedication, and religious profession.

67. The ideas of witnessing, consecration, and vocation are entwined: cf. "Fundamental norms," in *Essential Elements*, III.9, nos. 1–7, 13–17, 35–41.

68. Consider the words of Pope John Paul II in 1984, referring to religious vocations as having "character and spiritual power from the same depth of the mystery of the Redemption," cited by Downey et al., *Religious Life*, 37.

69. Cf. Walter Vogels, ed., *Attentive to the Cry of the Needy*, Conference of the Major Superiors of Canada in 1973 (Ottawa: Canadian Religious Conference, 1973), and Carlos Palmes, ed., *Witnessing to the Kingdom in a Dehumanizing World*, 2d Inter-American Conference of Religious, Bogota, 1974 (Ottawa: Canadian Religious Conference, 1975).

70. Gambari, "Religious Poverty," in Gambari, *Religious Life*, 284–311.

71. The apostolate is often seen as an extension of the evangelical mission of religious life, as defined in *Essential Elements*, II.3, articles 23–27. Thus there is a duality in modern religious communal living, juxtaposing active ministries outside the community with retreat back into the community for spiritual regeneration.

72. Consider the popular literature in which there are numerous attempts to update the common, traditional image of the Catholic nun, which often confuses all women religious as monastics; for example, Collete Dowling, "The Nun's Story," *New York Times Magazine*, November 28, 1976, 34–35, 78–82, 92–96, 100: "Many of the sisters' orders in America are taking on new ways. The change is disturbing to some Catholics—and wrenching for the nuns."

73. Cf. "Government" as a "fundamental norm" in *Essential Elements*, III.9, nos. 42–49, stressing constitutional government and the relation of institutes to the authority of the

church, especially local ordinaries and the Holy See. The "fundamental norm" of community life is outlined in *Essential Elements*, III.2, nos. 8–12: "Religious should live in their own religious house, observing a common life. They should not live alone without serious reason."

74. Gambari, "Religious Chastity," in Gambari, *Religious Life*, 265–83.

75. For the explicit nature of vows, see "Consecration by Public Vows," in *Essential Elements*, II.1, articles 13–17.

76. Greeley, *American Catholic*, 142.

77. Margaret Halstead and Lauro Halstead, "A Sexual Intimacy Survey of Former Nuns and Priests," *Journal of Sex and Marital Therapy* 4, no. 2 (1978): 83–90.

78. Anthony Kosnik, ed., *Human Sexuality: New Directions in American Catholic Thought* (New York: Paulist Press, 1977).

79. Cf. Alice I. Liftin, "Catholic Women's Orders after 1967: Placing Religious Innovation in Sociological Context" (Ph.D. diss., Columbia University, 1986) (see *Dissertation Abstracts International* A [1986], 46, no. 11), available from University Microfilms DA8523196; Diana Trebbi, "Daughters in the Church Becoming Mothers of the Church: A Study of the Roman Catholic Women's Movement" Ph.D. diss., CUNY, 1986) (*Disseration Abstracts International* A [1986], 47, no. 3), available as University Microfilms DA8611387; John Deedy, "Beyond the Convent Wall: Sisters in the Modern World," *Theology Today* 40 (1984): 421–25.

80. Helen Rose Ebaugh, "Catholic Nuns: Unwitting Feminists" (paper before the Southwestern Sociological Association, 1978), suggested that women religious can be viewed as feminists because of their deliberate choice of alternative life roles, professionalism, legitimate status as single females, and opposition to the male-dominated church hierarchy. Some arguments in secular feminism are muted by the ideas of obedience and service in choosing a religious life.

81. To place women religious in the context of female leadership in formal religious movements, cf. Ruether and Keller, *Women and Religion in America*, updated with a contemporary perspective by Lora A. Quiñonez, ed., *Starting Point: Six Essays Based on the Experience of U.S. Women Religious*, vol. 3., *Women Religious* (Washington, D.C.: Leadership Conference of Women Religious, 1980).

82. See Gambari, "Religious Obedience," in Gambari, *Religious Life*, 312–30.

83. "Of its nature, religious life is a witness that should clearly manifest the primacy of love of God and to do so with a strength coming from the Holy Spirit (*Evangelica Testificato*, 1)" from "Public Witness," in *Essential Elements*, II.6, articles 32–37. For the related prophetic nature of religious life, see P. Land and J. Puls, "Pilgrims and Prophets: Some Perspectives on Religious Life in the United States," and J. Provost, "The Church in the United States as Prophet," in Flemming, *Religious Life at the Crossroads*.

84. "Formation," in *Essential Elements*, II.8, articles 44–52.

Selected Bibliography

Ahles, Mary A. *In the Shadow of His Wings: A History of the Franciscan Sisters*. St. Paul, Minn.: North Central, 1977.

Angelus, Gabriel. *The Christian Brothers in the United States, 1848–1948: A Century of Catholic Education*. New York: Declan X. McMullen, 1948.

Barry, Coleman J. *Worship and Work: Saint John's Abbey and University, 1856–1956*. Collegeville, Minn.: St. John's Abbey, 1956. 2d ed., *1856–1980*. Collegeville, Minn.: Liturgical Press, 1980.

Baska, Mary Regina. *The Benedictine Congregation of Saint Scholastica: Its Foundations and Development, 1852–1930*. Washington, D.C.: Catholic University of America, 1935. Published thesis.

Battlesby, William John. *The Christian Brothers in the United States, 1900–1950*. 2 vols. Winona, Minn.: St. Mary's College Press, 1967, 1976.

Beckman, Peter. *Kansas Monks: A History of St. Benedict Abbey*. Atchison, Kans.: Abbey Student Press, 1957.

Benedict of Nursia, St. *The Rule of Saint Benedict*. Translated by Justin McCann. Westminster, Md.: Newman Press, 1952. Cf. *The Rule of St. Benedict in Latin and English with Notes*. Edited by Timothy Fry and I. Baker. Collegeville, Minn.: St. John's Liturgical Press, 1981.

Bittle, Celestine N. *A Romance of Lady Poverty: The History of the Province of St. Joseph of the Capuchin Order in the United States*. Milwaukee, Wisc.: Bruce, 1933.

Butler, E. Cuthbert. *Benedictine Monasticism: Studies in Benedictine Life and Rule*. London, 1916, 1927. Reprint, Cambridge: University Press, 1961.

The Cistercian Heritage. Translation of *La spiritualite de Citeaux*. London, 1958.

Coogan, M. Jane. *The Price of Our Heritage: History of the Sisters of Charity of the Blessed Virgin Mary, 1821–1920*. 2 vols. Dubuque, Iowa: Mt. Carmel, 1978.

Daly, Robert J., ed. *Religious Life in the U.S. Church: The New Dialogue*. New York: Paulist Press, 1984.

Dirvin, Joseph I. *Mrs. Seton: Foundress of the American Sisters of Charity*. New York: Farrar, Straus, and Cudahy, 1962.

Dondero, J. P., and Frary, T. D. *New Pressures, New Responses in Religious Life*. New York: Alba, 1979.

Dudine, M. Federica. *The Castle on the Hill: Centennial History of the Convent of the Immaculate Conception, Ferdinand, Indiana, 1867–1967*. Yankton, S.D.: Sacred Heart Convent, 1971.

Fracchia, Charles A. *Living Together Alone: The New American Monasticism*. New York: Harper and Row, 1979.

Garraghan, Gilbert J. *The Jesuits of the Middle United States*. 3 vols. New York: America Press, 1938. Reprint, New York: Arno, 1978.

Gedert, Charles. "The Swiss-American Congregation of Benedictines and Its Contributions to the American Catholic Church." B.A. thesis, Atheneum College of Liberal Arts, Cincinnati, Ohio, 1956.

Habig, Marion. *Heralds of the King: The Franciscans of the St. Louis-Chicago Province, 1858–1958*. Chicago: Franciscan Herald, 1940.

Hanousek, Mary Eunice. *A New Assisi: The First Hundred Years of the Sisters of St. Francis of Assisi, Milwaukee, Wisconsin, 1849–1949*. Milwaukee, Wisc.: Bruce, 1949.

Hennesey, James. *American Catholics: A History of the Roman Catholic Community in the United States*. New York: Oxford University Press, 1981.

Herbermann, Charles G. *The Sulpicians in the United States*. New York: Encyclopedia Press, 1916.

Herron, Mary Eufalia. *The Sisters of Mercy in the United States, 1843–1928*. New York: Macmillan, 1929.

Hilpisch, Stephan. *Benedictinism through the Centuries*. Translated by F. Doyle. Collegeville, Minn.: St. John's Abbey Press, 1958.

Hoffmann, Mathias. *Arms and the Monk!: The Trappist Saga in Mid-America*. Dubuque, Iowa: William Brown, 1952. A history of New Melleray Abbey.

Isetti, Ronald E. *Called to the Pacific: A History of the Christian Brothers of the San Franciscan District, 1868–1944*. Moraga, Calif.: St. Mary's College, 1979.

Kleber, Albert. *History of St. Meinrad Archabbey, 1854–1954*. St. Meinrad, Ind.: Grail, 1954.

Knowles, David. *Christian Monasticism*. New York: McGraw-Hill, 1969. Reprint, 1977.

Kohler, Mary Hortense. *Rooted in Hope: The Story of the Dominican Sisters of Racine, Wisconsin*. Milwaukee, Wisc.: Bruce, 1962.

Lapomarda, Vincent A. *The Jesuit Heritage in New England*. Worcester, Mass.: Holy Cross, 1977.

McCrank, Lawrence J. *Mt. Angel Abbey: A Centennial History of a Benedictine Community and its Library, 1882–1982*. Vol. 2, *Catalog on Fiche*. Wilmington, Del.: Scholarly Resources, 1983.

McDonald, M. Grace. *With Lamps Burning*. St. Joseph, Minn.: St. Benedict's Press, 1957. Bavarian Benedictine nuns in Minnesota.

Merton, Thomas. *The Waters of Silo*. New York: Harcourt, Brace, 1949. Cistercians in the United States.

Murphy, Joseph. *Tenacious Monks: The Oklahoma Benedictines, 1875–1975: Indian Missionaries, Catholic Founders, Educators, Agriculturalists*. Shawnee, Okla.: St. Gregory's Abbey, 1975.

Neal, Marie Agusta. *Catholic Sisters in Transition from the 1960's to the 1980's*. Wilmington, Del.: Michael Glazier, 1984.

Orsy, Ladisias. *Open to the Spirit: Religious Life after Vatican II*. London: Geoffrey Chapman, 1970.

Rees, Daniel, ed. *Consider Your Call: A Theology of Monastic Life Today*. London: SPCK, 1978. Kalamazoo, Mich.: Cistercian Publications, 1980.

Roemer, Theodore. *The Ludwig-Missionsverein and the Catholic Church in the United States, 1838–1918*. Washington, D.C.: Catholic University of America, 1933. Reprint, New York: AMS, 1974.

Documentary Film

American Broadcasting Company (ABC). *The Monastery*, directed by Helen Whitney. August 20, 1981.

LAWRENCE FOSTER

Free Love and Community

John Humphrey Noyes and the
Oneida Perfectionists

Few communal experiments in America have attracted more attention or generated more controversy than the Oneida Community, founded in nineteenth-century New York state by the eccentric Vermont-born genius John Humphrey Noyes. Historians, sociologists, psychologists, literary scholars, and popular writers alike have continued to be intrigued by the "complex marriage" system at Oneida, which both Noyes and his critics rather misleadingly referred to as "free love."[1] The journalist Charles Nordhoff characterized the system, perhaps most flamboyantly, as an apparently unprecedented "combination of polygamy and polyandry with certain religious and social restraints."[2] Virtually all writers have seen in Oneida a mirror that reflects their own hopes and fears. John Humphrey Noyes has been variously described as a "Yankee Saint," whose sexual attitudes and practices can serve as a model for "liberated" present-day lifestyles; as a "Vermont Cassanova," with sick and exploitative attitudes toward women; and even as a prototype for Hitler, because Noyes's "stirpiculture" or eugenics experiment could be seen as prefiguring some of the most repressive and threatening human engineering experiments of the twentieth century.[3] Seldom have writers tried to understand the strengths and weaknesses of Noyes and his experiments in communal living in terms of the larger goals that he and his followers set for themselves.

To achieve such an understanding of the Oneida Community, both its theoretical underpinnings and its practice, one must first understand its founder, John Humphrey Noyes. To a large extent Oneida is best understood as the lengthened shadow of this one extraordinary man, reflecting his complex personality and concerns. Noyes struggled with unusual intensity to overcome his own religious and sexual problems. Unlike most individuals, who simply seek to reach an accommodation with the larger world, Noyes adopted a prophetic stance, arguing that his insights provided a universally valid model for setting the world straight. Possessed by this extraordinary and compelling idea, unable or unwilling to work within what he considered to be an unstable or inconsistent value framework, Noyes sought "to initiate, both in himself as well as in others, a process of moral regeneration."[4] He projected his ego strengths and weaknesses onto the world. He was one of those individuals about whom William James wrote in whom a "superior intellect" and a "psychopathic temperament" coalesce, thereby creating "the best possible condition for the kind of effective genius that gets into biographical dictionaries. Such figures do not remain merely isolated critics. Their ideas possess them, they inflict them, for better or worse, upon their companions or their age."[5]

The world into which John Humphrey Noyes was born in southern Vermont in 1811 was undergoing disquieting social, political, and religious changes as the young American republic gradually left behind elements of its more cohesive colonial past and moved into the rough-and-tumble world of nineteenth-century capitalist individualism. Like many of the people who would later join his communities, Noyes grew up in a family of higher than average intellectual and social attainments. His father, John, was a successful businessman who served in the United States House of Representatives, while his strong-willed and deeply religious mother, Polly Hayes, was an aunt of Rutherford B. Hayes, who later became the nineteenth president of the United States.

The close-knit family environment in which young John grew up on the family holdings in Putney, Vermont, would later be reflected in many of the features of the organizational life of the Putney and Oneida Communities. The family was emotionally ingrown yet strongly aware of its distinctive talents and capabilities. All four of Noyes's father's brothers had, apparently because of shyness, married close cousins. The elder John Noyes himself had only married Polly Hayes after a long and desultory courtship when he was forty. Young John throughout his life shared his father's intense shyness around women, as well as the related tendency to intellectualize relations with the opposite sex. The complex-marriage system that John Humphrey Noyes eventually instituted among his followers at Putney and Oneida reflected the curious combination of intimacy and distance he had first experienced in his own family.[6]

Oneida community founder John Humphrey Noyes, pictured here about 1851, appears as conventional as his ideas were unconventional. (Courtesy of Oneida Community Historical Committee)

Young John Noyes first began to move out into the world on his own as a result of his conversion in a religious revival in 1831. That conversion sent him off to Andover and then to Yale theological seminaries to study to become a minister. Noyes was an intense and driven young man who seemed to expect absolute perfection of himself. He compulsively read his Bible as much as twelve to sixteen hours a day, trying to discover God's will for his life. Finally, after an intellectual breakthrough in 1834, he realized that God could not expect the impossible of him. The total perfection that God demanded of all true Christians was achieved through a right attitude and an inner sense of salvation from sin, not through any outward acts per se. When Noyes publicly announced that he was "perfect" in this sense, he was viewed as crazy and lost his license to preach. For three emotionally tumultuous years until 1837, he wandered quixotically throughout New England and New York state trying to convert the whole world to his highly idiosyncratic perfectionist religious beliefs. He was determined to establish "right relations with God," a common value framework for the world, but instead he found his message either ignored or ridiculed. On several occasions he experienced such intense psychic turmoil that his family and close associates feared he was temporarily deranged.[7]

During this difficult period when all religious and social truth seemed uncertain, Noyes also began to question and rethink the basis for relations between the sexes. He struggled to understand his own sexual impulses and to determine why so many of the perfectionists with whom he was associated were engaged in such erratic and often self-destructive sexual experimentation. Eventually Noyes applied the same principles to sexual relations that he had to understanding religious truth. He concluded that if one had the right attitude, sexual relations, like other activities in life, would be expressed in an outward manner that would be pleasing to God. The sexual impulse was basically a good one, but it needed to be expressed through proper channels. Noyes declared that neither the act of sexual union nor abstinence from it had any importance in itself. The goal, rather, was "a healthy development and faithful subordination of the sexual susceptibility."[8] As early as 1837 he argued that eventually in the holy community of Christians, love, including sexual love, would be expressed freely among all God's saints.[9]

Public announcement of the latter views temporarily lost Noyes virtually all his remaining supporters. In attempting to justify himself and rehabilitate his reputation, he began during the late 1830s to settle down and establish the organizational forms that would eventually allow him to realize his principles in functioning communal life. After returning home to Putney, Noyes started a Bible School in 1836. Two years later he married Harriet Holton, a socially and financially well connected woman whom he hardly knew personally. Noyes's Bible School evolved into a Society of Inquiry and then into the Putney Community, which, after its relocation to Oneida, New York, in 1848, became the Oneida Community and lasted for more than thirty additional years. The process of development was a gradual one, part of an attempt to find the best way of expressing the group's religious convictions in practice.[10]

LAWRENCE FOSTER

At the core of Noyes's religious beliefs was a millenarian expectation that the ideal patterns of the kingdom of heaven could literally be realized on earth in his communal experiments. Noyes argued that he and his followers were returning to the ideals of early Christianity, the "primitive Christian church." Following his hero St. Paul, Noyes argued that the spirit not the letter of the law was what really mattered. Noyes and his followers did not slavishly seek to follow the *forms* of early Christianity but instead attempted to realize the *spirit* of early Christianity in their particular nineteenth-century setting. "Perfection," not in externals but in internal attitude and a sense of salvation from sin, was required by God of all true Christians on earth.

The complex and highly unorthodox religious beliefs around which Noyes's perfectionists eventually organized their communities at Oneida and its smaller branches were most fully presented and elaborated in Noyes's articles in the community newspapers and in the compendium of those articles published in 1847 as *The Berean: A Manual for the Help of Those Who Seek the Faith of the Primitive Church.* Theologically, the core of Noyes's heresies was his belief that the second coming of Christ had occurred in A.D. 70 when the temple in Jerusalem was destroyed and the great diaspora began. Noyes argued that at that time there was a primary resurrection and judgment in the spiritual world that marked the beginning of the kingdom of God in the heavens. A second and final resurrection judgment was now approaching: "The church on earth is now rising to meet the approaching kingdom in the heavens, and to become its duplicate and representative on earth."[11]

Associated with Noyes's millenarian conviction that the kingdom of heaven could be literally realized on earth was his intense desire to overcome the disruptive individualism of nineteenth-century America by instituting among his followers a new set of religious and social values. Those values stressed the subordination of individuals and their private, selfish interests to the good of the larger community, as interpreted by Noyes. The goal, most briefly stated, was to move beyond the "egotism for two" implicit in monogamous family life to create an "enlarged family" in which all loyalties, including sexual loyalties, would eventually be raised to the level of the entire community.[12] These new values were introduced and internalized during the decade at Putney through the practice of male continence, mutual criticism, and complex marriage.

Male continence, the extraordinary method of birth control used at Putney and Oneida, was developed initially in response to the problems of Noyes's wife, Harriet. During the first six years of their married life, Harriet was traumatized by five difficult childbirths, four of which resulted in the death of the child. Noyes's attempt to spare Harriet such agony in the future led him to explore the distinction between sexual intercourse for "amative" and "propagative" purposes. The primary concern of sexual intercourse was social or amative—to allow the sexes to communicate and express affection for each other. Noyes argued that such intercourse could be separated from propagative intercourse in practice, without artificial aids, by "male continence," a practice that is technically known as *coitus reservatus*. Under male continence, a couple would engage in sexual congress without the man ever ejaculating, either during intercourse or after withdrawal.[13] Noyes saw this practice, which required substantial male self-control, as a logical outgrowth of his principles. In his view, regular intercourse is wasteful, sowing the seed where one does not want or expect it to grow. "Yet it is equally manifest that the natural instinct of our nature demands frequent congress of the sexes, not for propagative, but for social and spiritual purposes. It follows from this that simple congress of the sexes, without the propagative crisis, is the order of nature for the gratification of ordinary amative instincts."[14]

To describe the process of male continence, Noyes used this striking analogy:

> The situation may be compared to a stream in three conditions, viz., 1, a fall, 2, a course of rapids above the fall, and 3, still water above the rapids. The skillful boatman may choose whether he will remain in the still water, or venture more or less down the rapids, or run his boat over the fall. But there is a point on the verge of the fall where he has no control over his course; and just above that there is a point where he will have to struggle with the current in a way which will give his nerves a severe trial, even though he may escape the fall. If he is willing to learn, experience will teach him the wisdom of confining his excursions to the region of easy rowing, unless he has an object in view that is worth the cost of going over the falls.[15]

How well did such an unusual system work? Initial experimentation by Noyes and his followers at Putney in the early 1840s suggested that the procedure was effective in curtailing pregnancies. And during the twenty years between 1848 and 1868 when male continence was almost the sole sanctioned method of sexual relations at Oneida, community records show only twelve unplanned births in a group numbering approximately 200 adults, equally balanced between the sexes and having frequent sexual congress with a variety of partners.[16] Undoubtedly that low birthrate can be traced in part to the practice of having women past menopause induct young men into male continence and having older, more experienced men induct young women. But the effectiveness of male continence as a means of birth control in a regulated community setting is incontestable.

The psychological effects of male continence are more ambiguous. Despite the unfortunate destruction of many community diaries and journals in the late 1940s, much can be gleaned about the workings of the practice from printed sources, including the community newspapers, as well as from other surviving manuscript sources held by the Syracuse University Library that have recently been opened to scholarly research. These sources suggest that although men undoubtedly found male continence more demanding than ordinary intercourse, they experienced no significant adverse physical or emotional effects, even after many years of engaging in the practice. Women evidently found male continence an improvement that allowed them fuller sexual enjoyment, including orgasm.[17]

Male continence can be viewed as an accentuation and synthesis of certain characteristic Victorian sexual attitudes that sought internalized control of sexual expression.[18] The primary importance of the technique was practical, however. Noyes declared that the "Oneida Community in an important sense owed its existence to the discovery of Male Continence" and that "the principle underlying its practice has been the very soul of its working constitution."[19] Male continence undercut the emotional and physical exclusiveness of couples. It prevented the complications that having children would have posed to establishing the primary loyalty to the community in all things. It allowed a degree of sexual pleasure, coupled with stringent self-control and self-denial, not found in artificial methods of birth control. Few would be tempted simply to make a "hobby" of the practice and withdraw from the normal round of community life into exclusive emotional and sexual attachments.

The second form of social control that helped to prepare the way for complex marriage and the close community life associated with it was the practice of "mutual criticism."[20] Under this special form of group feedback and control, which has parallels with a variety of modern techniques from Gestalt therapy to Chinese thought control, the person to receive criticism would be openly and honestly evaluated by other members of the group in order to encourage that individual's character development. Although group criticism sessions were sometimes conducted by the entire adult portion of the community acting as a body, usually they were conducted by groups of between ten and fifteen members, with an approximately equal balance between the sexes. The person to receive criticism would remain silent while other members of the group would, in turn, discuss his or her strengths and weaknesses. The process brought faults and irritating personality characteristics into the open, rather than letting the problems fester in secret. Topics brought up in the sessions could range from ideological issues to the most private personal and sexual matters. In the absence of a formal governmental structure at Oneida, mutual criticism sessions served as the chief means of informally establishing and sustaining community cohesion and norms.

Institutionalization of male continence and mutual criticism among Noyes's followers preceded his further action at Putney in 1846 to move out of traditional monogamous marriage into a new group form called "complex marriage." The details of this difficult transition, which was not completed until the early 1850s at Oneida, have been discussed at length elsewhere and are not important to this analysis.[21] Suffice it to note that the essence of the complex-marriage system Noyes eventually introduced among his followers was the elimination of "selfishness"—the subordination of individual self-interest to the interests of the community, which in turn was dedicated to achieving God's will. Even individual sexual loyalties had to be given up, raised instead to the level of the community, to the enlarged family.

Noyes argued that the resulting ties were at least as binding and demanding as those of ordinary marriage. In the words of the community handbook: "The honor and faithfulness that constitutes an ideal marriage may exist between two hundred as well as two; while the guarantees for women and children are much greater in the Community than they can be in any private family."[22] To sustain such larger ties, any tendencies toward "special love" (exclusive romantic attachments) were rigorously discouraged. Special individual attachments to offspring or close friendships between members of the same sex were similarly broken up. The enlarged family at Oneida eventually lived under one roof in a large Mansion House, ate together, worked together, gathered daily for the religious-and-business meetings of the whole group, and shared all but the most basic personal property in common.[23]

It is interesting to speculate about the psychological motives that could have led Noyes to set up a community in which intense loyalty to the group was required but all exclusive social and sexual attachments were discouraged. The sociologist Maren Lockwood Carden makes the acute, if only partially correct, observation that Noyes was never able "to commit himself completely to any idea, action, or person."[24] A more accurate statement might be, instead, that Noyes always was firmly committed to his own sense of mission and core ideas, but he was never willing to open himself up to close personal relationships, either with men or with women. Until Noyes was able to find followers willing to acknowledge his unique, God-given leadership, he remained intensely shy and insecure. Once his supreme authority was accepted, however, he was able to relax somewhat and benevolently delegate authority to his loyal subordinates, who, in turn, showed great flexibility in putting his ideas into practice.[25] As Robert David Thomas has suggested in

The Man Who Would Be Perfect, Noyes was an individual whose great ego strengths and weaknesses were reflected in a sharp ambivalence about his competing drives for autonomy and dependence.[26] In effect, Noyes skillfully used his communities, with their institutionalized combination of emotional distance and closeness, to overcome his inner divisions and establish a sense of worth and power.

John Humphrey Noyes was far more than an isolated individual propounding idiosyncratic, if very interesting, religious, social, and sexual theories. He also was the founder of a community that at its peak numbered some 300 members at Oneida and its branch communities[27] and that successfully put his theories into practice for more than thirty years. One wonders, therefore, what kinds of people were attracted to Oneida and why. What was the social theory that underlay the Oneida perfectionists' attempt to reorganize relations between men and women? And what was the "practice of perfection" like during the heyday of Oneida's development?

The most striking features of Oneida Community membership were the careful process of selection and the extraordinarily high rate of membership retention. Although a few accessions to the group and a few defections from it would continue to occur throughout the community's existence, 84 of the 109 adults who joined during the first two years at Oneida either died in the community or lived there until the breakup.[28] This impressive degree of membership stability was connected with the carefully selected character of the group. Members were deliberately chosen on the basis of complete loyalty to Noyes's leadership and his perfectionist ideals. Members represented a wide range of occupational backgrounds, personality types, and special interests that could contribute to the good of the community. They came from most of the areas of New York and New England where sizable pockets of Noyes's perfectionist followers lived, and many of them were relatively affluent.[29] By 1857, for example, members had invested almost $108,000 in the Oneida Community and its branches. Only the aid of such a large capital backing allowed the community to continue to function despite a loss of more than $40,000 during the initial decade before Oneida finally began to achieve financial stability.[30]

The psychological attraction of Oneida to new members can be briefly summarized. Most individuals for whom we have data were in an emotionally unsettled state when they joined the community. Frequently they had been religious "seekers," distressed at repeatedly experiencing the emotional ups and downs of revivalistic religion. They yearned for release from this emotional roller coaster and thus were attracted by Noyes's promise to provide "salvation from sin" within a stable, supportive, and authoritative communal structure.[31] Despite the emotionally unsettled state of individuals when they entered Oneida, they do not appear to have had any special "character structure" that could differentiate them from the generality of Americans of their day. The detailed psychological critiques of Oneida members given in mutual criticism sessions and reported in the community newspapers from 1850 onward show the full range of human types, with almost every conceivable character strength and weakness.[32] Oneidans, like converts to any religious or secular ideology that attempts a radical restructuring of the lives of its adherents, found Noyes's system appealing because it helped them to overcome the disorder they experienced and to become resocialized to a more secure and satisfying way of life.[33]

If Noyes's perfectionism stressed the possibility of achieving an ideal society on earth under divine leadership, what was the nature of that society to be? Noyes argued that after restoring right religious principles, the second step in achieving the kingdom of heaven on earth was to restore right relations between the sexes. Existing marriage practices and relations between the sexes were unnatural and harmful. Following Jesus' statement reported in Matthew, Mark, and Luke that there would be no marriage or giving in marriage in the resurrected state, Noyes argued that in the heavenly society he was attempting to realize on earth there would be no monogamous marriage, no exclusive sexual and emotional ties between the sexes, and no ownership of women by men. Instead there would be a complex marriage in which all loved each other and placed the concerns of the community above their private selfish interests.[34] As part of the complex-marriage system at Oneida, women were formally freed to participate in almost all aspects of community religious, economic, and social life, in contrast to the far greater restrictions that they faced in the outside world. Women wore a functional, bloomer-type outfit; cut their hair short; and engaged in virtually any type of community work they wished. Children were reared communally by both male and female caretakers from the group. Within the limits necessary to maintain the primary loyalty to the larger communal order, all individuals were encouraged to develop their highest capacities. Few societies in human history have done more to break down arbitrary distinctions between the sexes than did Oneida.[35]

It might initially seem paradoxical that this significant revision of sex roles and rise in women's status at Oneida should have been accomplished in the face of John Humphrey Noyes's formal belief in the superiority of men over women. The chief reason this could occur was that Noyes's primary concern was not with male and female authority patterns as such, but rather with establishing his own personal authority over all his followers, both men and

Perfectionist women of Oneida shown wearing their bloomer-style outfits and short hair while engaged in a bag-making bee. (Courtesy of Oneida Community Historical Committee)

women. So long as Noyes's male and female followers unquestioningly acknowledged his paternalistic, Godlike authority, he was prepared to be flexible in delegating that authority and making major changes in the interests of both sexes.[36] No one way of organizing relations between the sexes was sacrosanct; the underlying spirit rather than any specific external forms was always Noyes's concern.[37]

In effect, therefore, both men and women at Oneida shared a common personal and religious commitment that radically undercut normal social restrictions. Woman's primary responsibility was not to her husband or to her children, but to God—and all souls were ultimately equal before God.[38] While it was true that St. Paul had said that wives should be subject to their husbands in this life, he had also said that there is "neither male nor female in the Lord."[39] Since the Oneida Community was attempting to realize the heavenly pattern on earth, the conventional juxtaposition of male superiority and female inferiority no longer had much significance for them. If some women were, in fact, spiritually superior to some men—as they recognizably were—they then should exercise more authority at Oneida than *those* men.

Thus, instead of stressing gender as the basis for authority at Oneida, life in the community gradually came to be governed by a philosophy of "ascending and descending fellowship," in which those deemed as being more "spiritual"

The Oneida Perfectionists

Oneida men, women, and children shell peas communally, sometime before 1860, under the watchful eyes of John Humphrey Noyes, seated at left behind the woman with glasses. (Courtesy of Oneida Community Historical Committee)

exercised more authority than those of lesser attainments.[40] Noyes was at the top, along with a handful of the most "spiritual" men, who oversaw most major decisions. Those men cooperated closely with the most spiritual women, who were above the less spiritual men, who were above the less spiritual women, and so forth. Since those who were seen as more spiritual generally were older than the less spiritual, there was an implicit age factor operating in determining community status. Because it was considered desirable to associate with those higher in the ascending fellowship, higher-status individuals had access to a larger range of sexual contacts than did lower-status members. Children appear to have entered this hierarchy of ascending and descending fellowship at puberty and sexual initiation, and at least during their teens and twenties they were expected to associate sexually with older, more spiritually mature men and women. In these and in other ways, authority relations between men and women were restructured at Oneida.

In addition to establishing right relations with God and right relations between the sexes, a third goal of Noyes's ideal society was to establish right economic relations. Noyes was deeply disturbed by the unrestrained individualism, the selfish dog-eat-dog capitalism that characterized Jacksonian America. He argued that the ideal society would follow the pattern of voluntary "Christian communism" described in Acts 2:44–45 in which the early Christians "held all things in common; and they sold their possessions and goods and distributed them to all, as any had need." Movement toward this

LAWRENCE FOSTER

The "enlarged family" of the Oneida community, with John Humphrey Noyes standing in the right foreground. (From C. N. Robertson, *Oneida Community: Autobiography* [1970].)

goal was a gradual process at Putney and Oneida, made on an ad hoc basis as part of an ongoing attempt to find the best way of expressing their religious convictions in practice.[41]

Eventually at Oneida all members lived together in an enlarged family in which everyone had a variety of different roles and shared in "the common roof, the common table, and daily meetings of all [adult] members."[42] The focal point of the community was an imposing Mansion House within which almost all community life took place. As a result of additions over the years, this Victorian Gothic structure eventually sprawled around the quadrangle, surrounded by lawns landscaped with an impressive variety of trees. In keeping with the emphasis on the greater importance of communal over individual concerns, the inside of the house contained a number of small private and semiprivate rooms for sleeping and other purposes, supplemented by a large and attractive library, several communal sitting rooms that provided comfortable furnished centers for group life, and a large hall, which despite its size had an appealing intimacy.

To support itself the Oneida Community engaged in a wide variety of economic pursuits. Initially, like many other communal groups, the perfectionists at Oneida tried to make a living through farming. They soon branched out as well into a number of more lucrative areas of production: sawmilling lumber for neighboring farmers; blacksmithing; canning fruit; producing furniture, baskets, and other items for sale; silk production; and manufacturing the steel traps used by the Hudson's Bay Company and fur trappers throughout the United States. The animal traps, developed by Sewell Newhouse who had joined the community in 1848, eventually became one of the mainstays of the economic success of Oneida. By the time of the breakup of the community in 1881, the combined properties at Oneida and Wallingford were valued at more than $600,000. The community showed ingenuity in developing labor-saving devices and in managing its many activities. An effective system of bookkeeping, for example, allowed the community to know its profit and loss in each enterprise. Twenty-one standing committees managed finances, roads and lawns, education, clothing, painting, water and steam power, patent rights, and arbitration. Duties of administration were divided among forty-eight departments including publication, fruit preservation, printing, carpentry, shoe shop, library, agriculture, travel, children, heating, bedding, and so forth. Despite the number of committees and departments, Oneidans showed remarkable flexibility in dealing with community needs and concerns.[43]

One key to the success of Oneida was the religious-and-business meetings held each evening in the large hall of the Mansion House and attended by all adult members of the community. The community had no formal religious services on Sunday or on other days, and the religious and moral concerns of the group were often raised in the evening meetings, particularly in the extemporaneous "Home Talks" by John Humphrey Noyes. In addition, other activities were planned, ranging from spirited dancing to community-produced plays, musical events, skits, and special productions that helped to vary the normal routine and keep the group lively. New talent was encouraged to develop and perform. Community life, especially in later years, could hardly be characterized as a dour, gloomy pursuit of ascetic perfection. Noyes's son Pierrepont remembered, "The grown folks seemed almost as bent on being happy as they did on being good. Everyone worked; almost everyone had time for play, or perhaps I should say recreation."[44] By the latter years of the community's existence, it also became a popular stop for tourists, and even Sunday School groups enjoyed visiting Oneida. For more than two decades, life at Oneida continued to follow a basically tranquil course.

Despite the many strengths of the Oneida Community, the group eventually experienced sufficient internal and external tension that it gave up complex marriage in 1879 and discontinued its communal form of economic life as well in 1881. What were the chief factors contributing to the end of complex marriage and to the breakup? This complex and fascinating issue has been explored in greatest depth in Constance Noyes Robertson's study *Oneida*

Community: The Breakup, 1876–1881, as well as in a number of other studies.[45] Here only a few points can be highlighted.

The primary factor that brought individuals to Oneida and kept them there was loyalty to John Humphrey Noyes and his ideals. That loyalty—and the implementation of Oneida's ideals in communal life—was strong enough for more than two decades to convince members to override personal desires in favor of larger group goals. By the 1870s, however, a series of subtle but significant changes were occurring that undercut communal cohesiveness. The declining ability of the aging and increasingly deaf John Humphrey Noyes to lead the community set the stage for the breakup. No other leaders emerged who were able to fill Noyes's place successfully. Associated with this leadership vacuum and underlying it was the decline in the commitment of the group to its original religious ideals. A younger generation lacking direct experience of the early struggles of the group on behalf of its ideals showed an ever more skeptical and secular bent. Without a strong commitment to common values, it became more and more difficult to justify the intense self-sacrifice necessary to make the community's distinctive organization work. Actions by the governing central committee members came to be viewed as arbitrary and lacking any rationale other than self-interest.

As common values broke down, specific sexual tensions that had always been present began to be more divisive. Young people and community members of lower status began to chafe under the system of ascending and descending fellowship that limited the sexual contacts of those of lower status. One issue that created special controversy among key leaders had to do with who should have the responsibility for initiating young women into the community's sexual system. A related concern, especially among young women, was the increasing desire to form an exclusive, committed sexual relationship. Further complications were introduced by the stirpiculture or eugenics experiment that Noyes had inaugurated in 1869.[46] As part of Noyes's effort to overcome "involuntary or random procreation," certain men and women volunteered or were chosen, with their consent, to have children as part of an effort to develop the best human beings, both spiritually and physically. Not surprisingly, resentments festered when only certain individuals were deemed good enough to have children. Once children were born, tendencies toward "special affection" began to emerge, even when children were reared communally. With a high degree of commitment to basic ideals, these and other tensions could perhaps have been minimized. In the absence of such commitment, however, factionalization resulted. When an external campaign against the community was launched in the mid-1870s by the Reverend John W.

Mears of Hamilton College, the weakened community was no longer confident of its mission and the loyalty of its members.

In the face of an increasingly uncertain internal and external situation, the community leaders in August 1879 acted gracefully to terminate their distinctive sexual arrangements while their venture could still be counted a success. In discontinuing more than thirty years of unorthodox marital practice, the community announced that it was placing itself "not on the platform of the Shakers, on the one hand, nor of the world, on the other, but on Paul's platform which allows marriage but prefers celibacy." The community also stated, in what may well prove a fitting epitaph,

> The past history of the Oneida Community is at least secure. Its present social position and its future course, whatever they may be, have no power to change the facts of the past; and the more these things are studied, the more remarkable they will appear. These things prove, as does also their present course in giving up that phase of their communal life which has caused offense, that the Communists have not been the reckless bacchanalians a few have represented them. The truth is, as the world will one day see and acknowledge, that they have not been pleasure-seeking sensualists but social architects, with high religious and moral aims, whose experiments and discoveries they have sincerely believed would prove of value to mankind.[47]

As part of the process of ending complex marriage, a major effort was made to disentangle the complex web of relationships that had developed and to formalize new relationships between men and women of the community. Provision was also made for the care of children, even though some were unable to remain with both of their natural parents due to the marriage of their parents to different spouses. Although many Oneidans still hoped to continue communal living following the termination of complex marriage, the community had lost its focus. Increasingly, individuals desired to return to private property and the institutions of the world. Leaders of the group realized that a reorganization of the entire system would be necessary. After careful planning in consultation with the full membership, on January 1, 1881, the Oneida Community was legally transformed into the Oneida Community, Limited, a joint-stock company in which each of the former community members was granted shares. Those who wished could continue to live in the Mansion House, paying for their room and board at cost. Those who wanted to leave could go. Former members who continued to work in Oneida industries would for the first time be paid for their services. The aged and invalids had the option of life support instead of shares of the new company's stock.

The immediate aftermath of the reorganization was difficult for all concerned. In the leadership vacuum that emerged, factionalism and disputes multiplied for more than a decade. The economic health of the company also worsened under the old-fashioned business leadership of a conservative, elderly management accustomed to outmoded mid-nineteenth-century practices. In the wake of the national depression of 1893, Pierrepont Burt Noyes, one of Noyes's sons, was elected to the leadership of the company. He led a successful proxy fight to gain control of the company and modernize its operations. Pierrepont Noyes saw the potential for manufacturing high-quality silverware as a replacement for the declining trap business. He made plans to market the silverware throughout the country. New production and distribution methods, in conjunction with innovative and aggressive promotional efforts that Pierrepont pioneered, allowed the Oneida Community, Limited, to begin making a healthy profit by the turn of the century. Within the company and the community itself, Noyes displayed a paternalistic approach committed to improving the quality of life. By 1935, however, when the company changed its name to Oneida, Limited, much of even that secular idealism was waning, and the company was less and less easy to distinguish from other successful small business enterprises in the United States.[48] Although memories of the earlier communal experiments of John Humphrey Noyes inevitably have dimmed with time, the imposing Mansion House still stands today as a focal point for Oneida, Limited, business meetings and for local community life embodying in new and creative ways the ideals of cooperation that were so central to the original Oneida Community.

What was the larger significance of John Humphrey Noyes and the distinctive communal ventures that he helped establish? Underlying all Noyes's experiments was a concern to overcome the social and religious disorder that he perceived around him. Noyes could see clearly that all existing social patterns were inadequate and subject to change, but he did not make the common mistake of lesser minds and hearts and simply conclude that "anything goes." Instead, he almost compulsively sought a new set of common assumptions and basis for unity to restore the possibility of healthy human relationships. With his strong sense of personal destiny and his unwillingness to try to conform to the shifting and unreliable patterns of society around him (one does not try to stay on board a sinking ship), Noyes sought to create a form of unified community life that would demonstrate the validity of his views. As he put it in 1837, "God has set me to cast up a highway across this chaos, and I am gathering out the stones and grading the track as fast as possible."[49]

Unlike many lesser reformers and religious leaders, Noyes insisted that the intellectual or creative person must accept responsibility for the social consequences of his or her beliefs. Noyes would not break down existing social patterns until he felt he had something better to offer and was convinced that he stood a reasonable chance of introducing the new ways successfully. Between 1834 and 1846 he worked to establish the basis for new ideals and practices within himself and among his followers. Only after he and his followers had internalized this new basis for morality did Noyes lead the way out of the marriage customs of the "apostasy" and into those of the "resurrected state." Throughout this effort, Noyes always sought to maintain a harmonious balance between "the two great principles of human existence," "solidarity" and "liberty," which, though they appeared antithetical, "like the centripetal and centrifugal forces of nature," were in fact "designed to act upon human life in equilibrium."[50]

Although the idiosyncratic sexual life at Oneida has principally attracted the attention of popular and scholarly writers, Noyes's primary importance is as a brilliantly original social thinker and theorizer. For more than forty years at Putney and Oneida, Noyes and his followers struggled with problems of social order and disorder, both in theory and in practice. While they did not achieve a permanent "utopia,"[51] they grappled with fundamental human problems that all thoughtful individuals face during times of rapid change. They made a transition to a radically new way of living, and they made that way of life work for more than twenty years, surely no small achievement given their ambitious goals.

Noyes's observations from his own experience on the problems and prospects of transitional periods of human life rank with the analyses of the best modern theorists. His statement regarding his underlying "conservative" objectives provides a fitting summary of his career and communal efforts:

> The truth is, all present institutions are growths from an imperfect society and are adapted only to a transition state. This is true of religious as well as political institutions, marriage as well as slavery. The spirit of heaven in order to fulfill its development in this world requires that we be willing to forsake all institutions adapted to the selfish state of society, and to expect something new and better. A truly conservative man will be ready for change. He will not violently or unwisely attack any present institutions, but he will be ready and on the lookout for change.[52]

John Humphrey Noyes and his communal experiments deserve the kind of serious scholarly attention that they have only recently begun to receive.

Chronology

1811	John Humphrey Noyes is born in Brattleboro, Vt.
1830	Noyes graduates from Dartmouth College and chooses legal career.
1831	Noyes is converted in revival in Putney, Vt., and enters Andover Theological Seminary to become minister.
1832	Noyes transfers to Yale Divinity School.
1834	Noyes experiences a "second conversion" to Perfectionism (belief that perfect holiness is possible in this life), loses his ministerial license, and begins publishing *The Perfectionist*, the first of his many newspapers.
1834–36	Noyes's three years of emotional turmoil and travel.
1836	Noyes starts Bible School in Putney, Vt.
1837	Most of Noyes's followers desert him after publication of his private letter on marriage in newspaper *The Battle-Axe and Weapons of War*.
1838	Noyes marries Harriet Holton, member of prominent Vermont family.
1841	Formation of Society of Inquiry after death of Noyes's father.
1844	Noyes's Putney Community signs Contract of Partnership; he introduces birth control by "male continence" (*coitus reservatus*) among his Putney followers.
1846	John Humphrey and Harriet Holton Noyes begin practicing complex marriage with George and Mary Cragin at Putney.
1847	Noyes begins complex marriage with his larger Putney Community, is indicted for adultery, and leaves state, forfeiting $2,000 bond.
1848	Noyes and closest disciples start new community at Oneida, N.Y.; Noyes writes "Bible Argument Defining the Relations of the Sexes in the Kingdom of Heaven."
1851	Branch community formed in Wallingford, Conn.
1852	From March through August, Oneida Community temporarily discontinues complex marriage.
1854	Noyes resumes direct leadership of Oneida and consolidates small branch groups after death of his faithful manager, John Miller.
1869	Eugenics experiment at Oneida begins.
1877	Noyes relinquishes leadership of the Oneida Community in favor of son Theodore.
1879	Oneida Community permanently stops complex marriage. *The American Socialist*, Noyes's last newspaper, discontinues publication.
1881	Oneida Community is legally dissolved and transformed into Oneida Community, Limited, a joint-stock company.
1886	John Humphrey Noyes dies near Niagara Falls in Canada.

Notes

1. For John Humphrey Noyes's discussion of the shifting meaning of the term "free love," see his *History of American Socialisms* (Philadelphia: Lippincott, 1870), 638–40. This essay draws heavily on the analysis presented in Lawrence Foster, *Religion and Sexuality: Three American Communal Experiments of the Nineteenth Century* (New York: Oxford University Press, 1981), 72–122, reprinted with identical pagination as *Religion and Sexuality: The Shakers, the Mormons, and the Oneida Community* (Urbana: University of Illinois Press, 1984). Portions of that work are used here with the permission of the copyright holder,

Oxford University Press. The essay also draws from the articles "The Psychology of Free Love: Sexuality in the Oneida Community" and "Free Love and Feminism: John Humphrey Noyes and the Oneida Community," which were reprinted in revised form in Lawrence Foster, *Women, Family, and Utopia: Communal Experiments of the Shakers, the Oneida Community, and the Mormons* (Syracuse, N.Y.: Syracuse University Press, 1991), 75–102.

2. Charles Nordhoff, *The Communistic Societies of the United States: From Personal Visit and Observation* (New York: Harper and Bros., 1875), 271.

3. The characterization of Noyes as a "Yankee Saint" is found in Robert Allerton Parker, *A Yankee Saint: John Humphrey Noyes and the Oneida Community* (New York: G. P. Putnam's Sons, 1935). Mention that Noyes has been treated as a "Vermont Cassanova" appears in Robert David Thomas, *The Man Who Would Be Perfect: John Humphrey Noyes and the Utopian Impulse* (Philadelphia: University of Pennsylvania Press, 1977). For the comparison of Noyes to Hitler, see Eric Achorn, "Mary Cragin: Perfectionist Saint," *New England Quarterly* 28 (1955): 490–518. An interpretation of Noyes that stresses the psychopathological aspects of his efforts is found in Louis J. Kern, *An Ordered Love: Sex Roles and Sexuality in Victorian Utopias—the Shakers, the Mormons, and the Oneida Community* (Chapel Hill: University of North Carolina Press, 1981), 271–79. For more sympathetic interpretations of Noyes's psychology, see Thomas, *Man Who Would Be Perfect*, and Michael Barkun's articles "The Visionary Experiences of John Humphrey Noyes," *Psychohistory Review* 16 (Spring 1988): 313–34, and "'The Wind Sweeping over the Country': John Humphrey Noyes and the Rise of Millerism," in *The Disappointed: Millerism and Millenarianism in the Nineteenth Century*, ed. Ronald L. Numbers and Jonathan M. Butler (Bloomington: Indiana University Press, 1987), 153–72. Lawrence Foster, "The Psychology of Religious Genius: Joseph Smith and the Origins of New Religious Movements," *Dialogue: A Journal of Mormon Thought* 26 (Winter 1993): 1–23, suggests that much of the dynamic creativity of many great religious leaders, including Joseph Smith and John Humphrey Noyes, may have been associated with manic-depressive tendencies.

4. Kenelm Burridge, *New Heaven, New Earth: A Study of Millenarian Activities* (New York: Schocken, 1969), 162.

5. William James, *The Varieties of Religious Experience: A Study in Human Nature* (New York: New American Library, 1958), 36–37.

6. On Noyes's early life, the best treatments are Parker, *Yankee Saint*; Thomas, *Man Who Would Be Perfect*; and George Wallingford Noyes, ed., *Religious Experience of John Humphrey Noyes, Founder of the Oneida Community* (New York: Macmillan, 1923).

7. The perfectionist goals of eventually overcoming sin and achieving human perfection on earth had roots in the earliest development of Christianity, with its millennial expectations of Christ's imminent second coming. As Christianity developed into an established religion, such millennial concerns were largely relegated to an indefinite future. Similar concerns resurfaced, however, at the time of the Protestant Reformation as well as in nineteenth-century America among groups that rejected Calvinist beliefs that human beings were totally depraved and could only be saved by the intervention of a mysterious, utterly transcendent God. Methodists, for example, argued that individuals could play an active role in achieving their salvation and saw salvation as an ongoing process, not absolute or Adamic or angelic perfection in this life, but rather perfect love as called for by Christ.

Some people influenced by perfectionist ideas carried them one step further, however, arguing for all-or-nothing perfection in this life. Such individuals argued that they were already free from sin—or "perfect"—and that inasmuch as they were perfect, they were free to act as they chose, since God's will and their own were identical. While Noyes's views approached such antinomian extremes at times, he was aware of the dangers of the socially anarchic tendencies inherent in such beliefs, and he developed an elaborate theological edifice to guard against the potential excesses of perfectionist individualism. For a detailed introduction to the various schools of Christian perfectionist thought, see Frederick Platt, "Perfection," in *Encyclopedia of Religion and Ethics*, ed. James Hastings (New York: Scribner's, 1917), 9 : 728–37. For Noyes's perfectionism, see John Humphrey Noyes, *Confessions of John H. Noyes*, part 1, *Confession of Religious Experience, Including a History of Modern Perfectionism* (Oneida Reserve, N.Y.: Leonard, 1849); George Wallingford Noyes, *Religious Experience of John Humphrey Noyes*; and Foster, *Religion and Sexuality*, 75–79.

8. "A Word of Warning," *Perfectionist and Theocratic Watchman* 5 (July 12, 1845): 34.

9. This argument was expressed in a private letter to a friend that was published, without Noyes's prior knowledge or approval, in *The Battle-Axe and Weapons of War*, an extravagantly antiestablishment newspaper edited by Theophilous Gates. Among other things, Noyes declared in his letter, "In the holy community, there is no more reason why sexual intercourse should be restricted by law, than why eating and drinking should be—and there is as little occasion for shame in the one case as in the other." The letter was reprinted in *The Witness* 1 (January 23, 1839): 49.

10. For an analysis of the complex motivation underlying Noyes's marriage to Harriet Holton, see Foster, *Religion and Sexuality*, 82–84. Noyes himself ingenuously observed in print, "By this marriage, besides herself, and a good social position, which she held as belonging to the first families of Vermont, I obtained money enough to buy a house and printing-office, and to buy a press and type" ("Financial Romance: How the O.C. Got Its Capital," *Circular* 2, n.s. [January 8, 1866]: 366).

11. *First Annual Report of the Oneida Association* (Oneida Reserve, N.Y.: Leonard, 1849), 11–12. Also see John Humphrey Noyes's *Confessions*; his *The Berean: A Manual for the Help of Those Who Seek the Faith of the Primitive Church* (Putney, Vt.: Office of the *Spiritual Magazine*, 1847); and George Wallingford Noyes, *Religious Experience of John Humphrey Noyes*. Strange though Noyes's specific beliefs might sound, they always represented an attempt to stake out a middle ground between the theological extremes of his day.

12. Foster, *Religion and Sexuality*, 90–93.

13. John Humphrey Noyes, *Male Continence* (Oneida, N.Y.: Office of the *Oneida Circular*, 1872). Robert Dale Owen had earlier drawn a distinction in his pamphlet *Moral Physiology* between sexual intercourse for amative and propagative purposes. Whereas Owen favored *coitus interruptus* as the method for avoiding procreation, however, Noyes, with his characteristically Victorian concerns about wasting the male seed, came to favor *coitus reservatus*. For a lively analysis of Victorian concerns about the loss of male semen, see G. J. Barker-Benfield, "The Spermatic Economy: A Nineteenth-Century View of Sexuality," *Feminist Studies* 1 (Summer 1972): 45–74.

14. John Humphrey Noyes, "Bible Argument Defining the Relations of the Sexes in the Kingdom of Heaven," in *First Annual Report of the Oneida Association*, 32. Noyes appears to have developed his theory and practice of male continence without reference to similar practices in Tantric and other non-Western religious movements. On the latter subject, see Benjamin Walker, *Tantrism: Its Secret Principles and Practices* (Wellingborough, Northamptonshire, England: Aquarian Press, 1982), 49–76.

15. John Humphrey Noyes, *Male Continence*, 7, 9.

16. Maren Lockwood Carden, *Oneida: Utopian Community to Modern Corporation* (Baltimore: Johns Hopkins University Press, 1969), 51, finds evidence that thirty-one births occurred at Oneida between 1848 and 1868, but some of these births were planned. The R. L. Dickinson Papers at the Kinsey Institute indicate that only twelve unplanned births occurred during that period. Whatever the number, the figure for unplanned births was remarkably low.

17. See Theodore E. Noyes, M.D., "Report on Nervous Diseases in the Oneida Community," as printed in John Humphrey Noyes, *Scientific Propagation* (Oneida, N.Y.: Oneida Community, 1872?), 25–32; Ely van de Warker, "Gynecological Study of the Oneida Community," *American Journal of Obstetrics and Diseases of Women and Children* 17 (August 1884): 755–810; and Havelock Ellis, *Sex in Relation to Society*, vol. 6, *Studies in the Psychology of Sex* (Philadelphia: F. A. Davis, 1911), 553.

The recently opened Oneida Community manuscripts held in the Syracuse University Library make possible much more subtle assessment of the nature of Oneida Community sexuality. For a listing of the documents, see Mark F. Weimer, comp., *The Oneida Community Collection in the Syracuse University Libraries: Inventory* ([Syracuse, N.Y.]: Syracuse University, George Arents Research Library for Special Collections, 1986). By far the most valuable of these manuscripts, fully opened to scholars in April 1993, is the George Wallingford Noyes Papers, a 2,200-page typed transcription from original documents, letters, and other manuscripts relating to the Noyes family and the Oneida Community from 1811 to 1880. Also exceptionally revealing on Oneida sexual practices is the Tirza Miller diary. Another important source is the Victor Hawley diary, edited by Robert Fogarty as *Special Love/Special Sex: An Oneida Community Diary* (Syracuse, N.Y.: Syracuse University Press, 1994). The first comprehensive recent history of the Oneida Community to make use of the surviving manuscript records now held by the Syracuse University Library is Spencer Klaw, *Without Sin: The Life and Death of the Oneida Community* (New York: Allen Lane, Penguin, 1993).

It is interesting to note that the classic contemporary analysis of male sexual behavior by Alfred Kinsey and his associates argues that men practicing *coitus reservatus* can achieve orgasm without ejaculation. The study describes the physiological mechanisms by which this can occur. If this work is supported by other research, it suggests that the common understandings of the possible range of male sexuality are extraordinarily limited. See Alfred C. Kinsey, Wardell Pomeroy, and Clyde Martin, *Sexual Behavior in the Human Male* (Philadelphia: W. B. Saunders, 1948), 158–61.

18. See Ben Barker-Benfield, "Spermatic Economy," as well as other essays collected in Thomas Altherr, ed., *Procreation or Pleasure: Sexual Attitudes in American History* (Malabar, Fla.: Robert E. Krieger, 1983).

19. John Humphrey Noyes, *Male Continence*, 21.

20. Primary information on the practice is found in *Mutual Criticism* (Oneida, N.Y.: Office of the *American Socialist*, 1876) and in columns in the community newspapers.

21. Foster, *Religion and Sexuality*, 100–116. During one six-month period between March and August 1852, internal and external pressures were so great that the group appears to have temporarily given up the practice of complex marriage. For a discussion of the significance of this period, see Lawrence Foster, "The Rise and Fall of Utopia: The Oneida Community Crises of 1852 and 1879," in Foster, *Women, Family, and Utopia*, 103–20. Important insights from the recently opened G. W. Noyes Papers are discussed in Lawrence Foster, "The Turbulence of Free Love: New Perspectives on the Early Development of the Oneida Community, 1848–1854" (paper presented at the 1994 Communal Studies Association conference at Oneida, N.Y.).

22. *Handbook of the Oneida Community, No. 2* (Oneida, N.Y.: Oneida Community, 1871), 56.

23. Foster, *Religion and Sexuality*, 116–18.

24. Carden, *Oneida*, 30.

25. Foster, *Religion and Sexuality*, 85–86, 105–6.

26. Thomas's use of modern ego psychology provides one of the most compelling contemporary analyses of Noyes's motivation.

27. In addition to the main community at Oneida, Noyes established small branch "communes" at Wallingford, Conn.; Cambridge, Vt.; Newark, N.J.; and Brooklyn, N.Y., in the early 1850s. He also reestablished a small communal association at Putney, Vt., in 1851. Of these groups, only the Wallingford Community survived for many years. Noyes's perfectionists moved freely between the Oneida and Wallingford Communities during the years prior to the breakup. See Carden, *Oneida*, 40–41.

28. Ibid., 107. Extensive primary and secondary records allow the reconstruction of Oneida membership characteristics. A valuable starting point for such an analysis is Robert Fogarty, "The Oneida Community, 1848–1880: A Study in Conservative Christian Utopiansim" (Ph.D. diss., University of Denver, 1968). Fogarty used the Oneida Family Register, a manuscript giving names and personal data on the first 111 people who joined the community, as well as U.S. census data from 1850 to 1880 and annual reports and newspapers printed at Oneida to reconstruct membership backgrounds and histories. From his work and from other sources such as the even more detailed compendium of information by John B. Teeple, *The Oneida Family: Genealogy of a Nineteenth-Century Perfectionist Commune* (Oneida, N.Y.: Oneida Community Historical Committee, 1985), it becomes apparent that individuals were not attracted to the group because of any narrow social or psychological factors.

29. It is difficult to see how geographical, occupational, or economic characteristics of community members could fully account for their attraction to the group. *Bible Communism: A Compilation from the Annual Reports and Other Publications of the Oneida Association and its Branches* (Brooklyn: Office of the *Circular*, 1853), 22, accurately states that "the main body of those who have joined the Association at Oneida are sober, substantial men and women of good previous character and position in society." Problems with the status anxiety and frustration-aggression models in explaining reform in general and Noyes's efforts in particular are discussed in Robert David Thomas Jr., "The Development of a Utopian Mind: A Psychoanalytic Study of John Humphrey Noyes, 1828–1869" (Ph.D. diss., State University of New York at Stoney Brook, 1973), 1–10.

30. *Handbook of the Oneida Community* (Oneida, N.Y.; Office of the *Oneida Circular*, 1875), 15.

31. Fogarty, "Oneida Community," and Stow Persons, "Christian Communitarianism in America," in *Socialism and American Life*, ed. Donald Drew Egbert and Stow Persons (Princeton: Princeton University Press, 1952), 1:127–51.

32. Foster, *Religion and Sexuality*, 110.

33. Carden's common sense assumption in *Oneida*, 107, that Oneida Community members had an unusual "psychological makeup" that led them to want to participate in complex marriage is not supported by the evidence.

34. Matthew 22:15–22, Mark 12:18–27, and Luke 20:27–40. Noyes's "Bible Argument Defining the Relations of the Sexes in the Kingdom of Heaven," his social and sexual manifesto, was first published in 1849 in *First Annual Report of the Oneida Association*, 18–42. The statement was also reprinted in 1853 in *Bible Communism*, 24–64, and, in condensed form, in Noyes's *History of American Socialisms*, 623–37.

35. See Foster, "Free Love and Feminism," for a fuller discussion of Noyes's attitudes toward equality for women.

36. The overriding concern that Noyes had with his own personal authority and control is stressed in *Spiritual Magazine* 2 (July 1, 1847): 57–59, and by George Wallingford Noyes, ed., *John Humphrey Noyes: The Putney Community* (Oneida, N.Y.: The author, 1931), 25–33. I am grateful to Robert David Thomas for pointing out to me the way in which Noyes logically extended this approach to relations between the sexes. Also see Thomas's observations in *Man Who Would Be Perfect*, and Richard DeMaria, *Communal Love at*

Oneida: A Perfectionist Vision of Authority, Property, and Sexual Order (New York: Edwin Mellen Press, 1978).

37. A concern for the spirit not the letter of the law, faith not works, underlay Noyes's conversion to perfectionism in 1834 and his entire subsequent career. This approach was most eloquently affirmed in 1852 when the community temporarily discontinued complex marriage, declaring, "WE ARE NOT ATTACHED TO FORMS; and in no way could we express this victory so well as by our present movement. To substitute for the fashions of the world, cast-iron fashions of our own, would be no gain. To be able to conform to *any* circumstances, and *any* form of institutions and still preserve spiritual freedom is Paul's standard and what we now claim" (*Circular* 1 [March 7, 1852]: 66).

38. "Woman's Slavery to Children," *Spiritual Magazine* 1 (September 15, 1846): 109–11.

39. Noyes's chief hero was St. Paul, but Noyes always followed the *spirit* of Paul's concerns rather than narrowly adopting the particular *practices* Paul had advocated in response to a particular time and place. In general, Noyes tended to interpret away Paul's more restrictive statements about women and emphasize instead his underlying flexibility of approach—that in Christ there was neither Jew nor Gentile, slave nor free, man nor woman. For instance, see "Marriage Nailed to the Cross," *Witness* 2 (December 10, 1841): 76–77. DeMaria notes that confusion arises in understanding male-female power relationships because Noyes used the terms "male" and "female" in two different senses. On the one hand, humanity is divided into two sexes, male and female. On the other hand, every individual human being reflects the active "male" principle and the receptive "female" principle. To be healthy, Noyes argued, was to achieve a balance within each individual between these two polarities. For an analysis of Noyes's argument for androgyny as the ultimate ideal, see DeMaria, *Communal Love at Oneida*, 96–103.

40. The best secondary accounts of the system of ascending and descending fellowship are found in Parker, *Yankee Saint*; Carden, *Oneida*; DeMaria, *Communal Love at Oneida*; and Klaw, *Without Sin*. Noyes himself usually discussed this informal system obliquely, even while recognizing that it underlay the entire structure of community government. For instance, see *Mutual Criticism*; "Socialism in Two Directions," *Circular* 3 (April 29, 1854): 250; "Home Talk #24," *Circular* 3 (September 19, 1854): 496; and Alfred Barron and George Noyes Miller, eds., *Home Talks by John Humphrey Noyes* (Oneida, N.Y.: Oneida Community, 1875).

41. Foster, *Religion and Sexuality*, 82–87.

42. John Humphrey Noyes, *American Socialisms*, 642.

43. See the Oneida Community *Annual Reports*; Nordhoff, *Communistic Societies*, 277–87; and Constance Noyes Robertson, *Oneida Community: An Autobiography, 1851–1876* (Syracuse, N.Y.: Syracuse University Press, 1970).

44. Pierrepont B. Noyes, *My Father's House: An Oneida Boyhood* (New York: Farrar & Reinhart, 1937), 138.

45. Most of the studies that deal with the breakup of the Oneida Community tend toward a monocausal approach. Fogarty, "Oneida Community," stresses the disruptive role of the stirpiculture or eugenics experiment; Carden, *Oneida*, highlights sexual conflicts over the question of which men should initiate virgins into sexual experience; Parker, *Yankee Saint*, places greater emphasis on external factors; while Spencer C. Olin Jr., "The Oneida Community and the Instability of Charismatic Authority," *Journal of American History* 67 (1980): 285–300, utilizes Weberian theories of leadership. Each of these studies provides useful perspectives, but the only comprehensive, multicausal study of the breakup with full documentation is Constance Noyes Robertson, *Oneida Community: The Breakup, 1876–1881* (Syracuse, N.Y.; Syracuse University Press, 1972). Klaw, *Without Sin*, 299–300, notes that the one flaw of this otherwise important study based on the G. W.

Noyes Papers was its deletion of passages from letters and documents (without any indication of the deletions) dealing with the sexual politics at Oneida and the charges of improper sexual behavior brought against John Humphrey Noyes.

46. On the stirpiculture experiment, see Fogarty, "Oneida Community."

47. Robertson, *The Breakup*, 160.

48. For treatments of Oneida business and community developments since the breakup, see Pierrepont B. Noyes, *A Goodly Heritage* (New York: Rinehart, 1958), and Carden, *Oneida*, 113–212.

49. George Wallingford Noyes, *Religious Experience of John Humphrey Noyes*, 306. This is part of the larger portion of Noyes's letter to George Harrison that was not printed by Theophilous Gates as part of the Battle-Axe Letter.

50. "The Liberty of Union," *Circular* 1 (January 4, 1852): 86.

51. Noyes emphatically denied that his goals were "utopian." Far from seeking an unchanging ideal society, he stressed the importance of continuous change and flexibility. Thus, when his community at Oneida no longer appeared to be working well under its complex-marriage system, Noyes did not hesitate to propose discontinuance of the practice.

52. "Liberty to Change," *Circular* 3 (August 8, 1854): 422.

Selected Bibliography

Bible Communism: A Compilation from the Annual Reports and Other Publications of the Oneida Association and its Branches. Brooklyn: Office of the *Circular*, 1853.

Carden, Maren Lockwood. *Oneida: Utopian Community to Modern Corporation.* Baltimore: Johns Hopkins University Press, 1969.

Fogarty, Robert S., ed. *Special Love/Special Sex: An Oneida Community Diary.* Syracuse, N.Y.: Syracuse University Press, 1994.

Foster, Lawrence. *Religion and Sexuality: Three American Communal Experiments of the Nineteenth Century.* New York: Oxford University Press, 1981. Reprinted as *Religion and Sexuality: The Shakers, the Mormons, and the Oneida Community.* Urbana: University of Illinois Press, 1984.

———. *Women, Family, and Utopia: Communal Experiments of the Shakers, the Oneida Community, and the Mormons.* Syracuse, N.Y.: Syracuse University Press, 1991.

Kern, Louis J. *An Ordered Love: Sex Roles and Sexuality in Victorian Utopias—the Shakers, the Mormons, and the Oneida Community.* Chapel Hill: University of North Carolina Press, 1981.

Klaw, Spencer. *Without Sin: The Life and Death of the Oneida Community.* New York: Allen Lane, Penguin, 1993.

Nordhoff, Charles. *The Communistic Societies of the United States: From Personal Visit and Observation.* New York: Harper and Bros., 1875.

Noyes, George Wallingford, ed. *John Humphrey Noyes: The Putney Community.* Oneida, N.Y.: The author, 1931.

———. *Religious Experience of John Humphrey Noyes, Founder of the Oneida Community.* New York: Macmillan, 1923.

Noyes, John Humphrey. *The Berean: A Manual for the Help of Those Who Seek the Faith of the Primitive Church.* Putney, Vt.: Office of the *Spiritual Magazine*, 1847.

———. *Confessions of John H. Noyes.* Part 1, *Confession of Religious Experience, Including a History of Modern Perfectionism.* Oneida Reserve, N.Y.: Leonard, 1849. Part 2 was never published.

————. *History of American Socialisms*. Philadelphia: Lippincott, 1870.

Noyes, Pierrepont B. *My Father's House: An Oneida Boyhood*. New York: Farrar & Reinhart, 1937.

Parker, Robert Allerton. *A Yankee Saint: John Humphrey Noyes and the Oneida Community*. New York: G. P. Putnam's Sons, 1935.

Robertson, Constance Noyes, ed. *Oneida Community: An Autobiography, 1851–1876*. Syracuse, N.Y.: Syracuse University Press, 1970.

————. *Oneida Community: The Breakup, 1876–1881*. Syracuse, N.Y.: Syracuse University Press, 1972.

Thomas, Robert David. *The Man Who Would Be Perfect: John Humphrey Noyes and the Utopian Impulse*. Philadelphia: University of Pennsylvania Press, 1977.

Weimer, Mark F., comp. *The Oneida Community Collection in the Syracuse University Libraries: Inventory*. [Syracuse, N.Y.]: Syracuse University, George Arents Research Library for Special Collections, 1986. This lists the manuscript holdings.

Wells, Lester G. *The Oneida Community Collection in the Syracuse University Library*. Syracuse, N.Y.: Syracuse University Library, 1961. These monographs and serial publications can be purchased on microfilm through University Microfilms, Ann Arbor, Mich.

ROBERT P. SUTTON

An American Elysium

The Icarian Communities

Throughout most of the last half of the nineteenth century the Icarians tried to build a utopian society in the United States modeled on the ideal community envisioned by their founder, the French political radical Etienne Cabet. They called themselves Icarians after the title of Cabet's *Voyage en Icarie* (Travels in Icaria), a book published in Paris in 1839 that delineated a perfect community without money and private property. Five separate times they attempted to create Icaria. First in Texas; then at Nauvoo, Illinois; St. Louis, Missouri; Corning, Iowa; and finally near Cloverdale, California, they tried to establish what Cabet described as a "new terrestrial paradise," where each member worked "according to his abilities" and received from the community "according to his needs."[1]

The Icarian movement, therefore, began in the fertile imagination of Etienne Cabet. Born of middle-class parents in Dijon on January 1, 1788, he earned a doctorate of jurisprudence at the University of Dijon in May 1812 but three years later was suspended from practicing law because of his outspoken opposition to the monarchy. For the next twenty years he acted as a leading propagandist and demanded, among other changes, the restoration of the French republic. Temporarily appeased by the revolution of 1830, which placed Louis Philippe, Duc d'Orléans, in power, he nevertheless soon became disillusioned with Louis's conservatism and what Cabet called the "perversions of kingcraft." His tirades against the government in his Paris newspaper *Le Populaire* increased. The police retaliated. He was arrested, convicted of treason, and sentenced to either two years in prison or five years in exile. He

Etienne Cabet led his French utopians to America to implement the Icarian
way of life described in his 1839 novel *Voyage en Icarie* (*Travels in Icaria*).
(Courtesy of Center for Icarian Studies, Western Illinois University)

crossed the English Channel in October 1834 and while in London wrote
Voyage en Icarie.[2]

Voyage en Icarie, a novel of over 800 pages, in many ways imitates Thomas
More's *Utopia*, a work Cabet read for the first time in the British Museum
and to which he attributed an enormous influence. Yet Cabet's utopia also
reflected French romanticism, particularly Jean Jacques Rousseau's. He, like
Rousseau, envisioned a return to a simpler, primitive economy where private
property and the selfishness inherent in it never existed. In addition, Cabet's
ideas mirrored the concepts of contemporary French socialists. For example,
Cabet embraced a plan of social progress through the leadership of a natural

ROBERT P. SUTTON

elite identified by equal education for both sexes. He believed that the natural instincts of mankind were sound; only the institutional husks were rotten, and this condition thwarted our innate urges to live together in harmony for mutual benefit. The final influence on the formation of Cabet's Icaria was Robert Owen. During his sojourn in London, Cabet became acquainted with Owen, and from the reformer of New Lanark, Scotland, he borrowed an emphasis on the importance of a healthy physical environment in the creation of a faultless community. To these influences—More's utopianism, Rousseau's romanticism, French socialism, and Owen's environmentalism—Cabet brought his own mystical Christianity. His Icaria emphasized the Golden Rule: "Love your neighbor as yourself. Do not unto others the harm that you would not have others do to you. Do to others the good that you wish for yourself."[3]

After his return from London, Cabet toyed with the idea of putting his Icaria into practice in France. But the rising influence of Marxism among some Icarians, with its push for class conflict instead of Christian brotherhood, discouraged him. Cabet's continued criticisms of the government got him into trouble once more, and in 1847 he was arrested and interrogated. Because of these developments, and probably following the advice of Owen, Cabet looked to the United States, specifically to Texas. There he saw opportunities and conditions that France lacked: abundant land, freedom from police surveillance, and separation of church and state.[4] On November 14, 1847, he proclaimed on the front page of Le Populaire, "C'EST AU TEXAS!" (on to Texas), and on February 3, 1848, the First Advance Guard slipped out of Le Havre for America. Their destination was the Red River valley, where Cabet had purchased—through Owen—some 1 million acres of land. Four months later the Second Advance Guard departed, and over the course of the summer and fall seven other groups left for the New World Icaria, one of them including Cabet himself. By the time he landed in New Orleans in December, he was sixty years old.

At New Orleans Cabet found chaos. Of the 500 or so Icarians who had emigrated, half were packing to go home. The others, waiting for direction from their leader, whom they affectionately called "Papa," told him of a disastrous previous summer in Texas. They had suffered broiling heat and devastating disease. Moreover, the land was sold to Cabet in alternate sections, in a checkerboard fashion that made integrated communal life impossible.[5] By the spring of 1849 only 281 loyal Icarians had decided to stay with Cabet to rebuild Icaria. This time they looked to a northern and more congenial climate up the Mississippi River in Illinois.

The site Cabet chose for his second effort, the previously Mormon town of

After purchasing a section of Nauvoo, Illinois, from the Mormons in 1849, the French Icarians occupied these apartment buildings on the southeast corner of the former Temple Square and adjacent to their own library, office, and print shop. (Courtesy of Center for Icarian Studies, Western Illinois University)

Nauvoo, became the first permanent Icarian community. Created in 1839 as a Zion for the final gathering of the Latter-day Saints, Nauvoo had grown rapidly into the largest city in the state, housing over 12,000 persons by 1845. But when the Mormon prophet Joseph Smith was murdered in 1844 and violence broke out against the Mormons in western Illinois, they abandoned the city and under Brigham Young left for a new Zion farther west. In March 1849 the Mormons sold the Temple Square to the Icarians. Then Cabet and his band boarded the steamship *Rome* with baggage and supplies and paddled upriver to their Icaria. They immediately adopted a formal charter that prescribed a political structure seen in *Voyage en Icarie*. There was a president, elected annually, and four other officers in charge of finance, farming, industry, and education. A prospective member gained admission to the community by approval of a majority vote of adult males after the prospect had lived in the society for four months, pledged $80 (or 600 francs), and forfeited all property.[6]

As in the book, equality was the rule in theory and practice. Men and women participated with equal voice in the weekly community assembly held every Saturday. Each family used the same amount of physical space—two rooms in an apartment building—and was allowed the same amount and kind of furniture. Children over four, as wards of the society, lived apart from

ROBERT P. SUTTON

their parents at a boarding school; only on Sundays could they visit their families. Throughout the week teachers raised them to love the community without developing special affection for parents or family. All Icarians took meals in family groups, however, three times a day, in the large refectory. Cabet assigned every adult a job in one of the workshops or on one of the two farms he had purchased near the city. The Icarians practiced no religion but met on Sundays, voluntarily, in a fellowship called "Cours icarien" to discuss Christian morality, ethics, or any of Cabet's writings and teachings. Moral rectitude was assumed. Marriage was almost insisted upon, and celibacy was condemned as an offense against the community. Divorce was allowed, but it was accompanied by an expectation that individuals would remarry as soon as possible.

Cultural life at Nauvoo was superior to that of any utopian community in that part of the United States. Icarians held regular band concerts and theatrical productions. Their library numbered over 4,000 volumes in English and French—reference works, popular novels, applied science, and biographies—used in the refectory or lent out, making it the largest such collection in Illinois. They published a biweekly newspaper in French called *Colonie Icarienne*. They welcomed visitors to stay as long as they wished in their hotel, located near the refectory, and to participate in their picnics along the banks of the Mississippi.[7]

Troubles came to this bucolic setting, however. The first problem was Cabet's forced return to France in May 1851 to answer charges of fraud in connection with the Texas debacle. He was found innocent, but his absence for fifteen months led to bickering and work slowdowns. By the time he returned in July 1852, other difficulties had surfaced.[8] The community could not produce enough to balance its finances and had been only able to pay their bills with money turned over by new members and with funds sent from Paris, mainly royalties from *Voyage en Icarie* and Cabet's other writings. Moreover, Cabet, by the fall of 1852, detected signs of moral decay: smoking and drinking. In a series of strict edicts he tried to save Icaria from disaster. He forbade tobacco, hard liquor, complaints about the food, and hunting and fishing "for pleasure." He demanded absolute silence in the workshops and "absolute submission to the discipline of the community."[9] Apparently, "discipline of the community" in Cabet's mind meant obedience to him, for early in 1855 he proposed to have himself elected president not just annually but for a four-year term. The new president would also have the right to appoint "inspectors" who would insure that everyone followed his orders. To most Icarians, these steps seemed little different from the repressive and authoritarian monarchy they hated in France.

The Nauvoo Icaria divided into two separate factions. On one side were the Dissidents, led by Alexis Armel Marchand and Jean Baptist Gérard. On the other side were the Cabetists. Both camps showed their dissatisfaction through repeated episodes of food boycotts, work stoppages, and street parades where they shouted obscenities. In the fall of 1856 the Dissidents, consisting of a majority of the adult males, expelled the Cabetists. Cabet and 180 followers steamed downriver to St. Louis, where just a week after arriving there, Cabet died of apoplexy. He was almost seventy years old.[10]

The next year the Cabetists used Cabet's money to put $500 down on a $25,000 mortgage for three buildings and thirty-nine acres at a spot just southwest of the city called Cheltenham.[11] Their new leader, a thirty-two-year-old lawyer named Benjamin Mercadier, later recalled the group's predicament at that time. They were without tools or personal property and ladened with old people, a number of sick and infirm adults, and numerous children with wet nurses. Besides, he said, they were suddenly "exposed to the dangers of a new climate and to the many inconveniences of a large city which we knew very poorly of its language and customs."[12] The Cheltenham Icarians persevered. They adopted a constitution, a facsimile of the Nauvoo document, enrolled their children in public schools, and found well-paying employment in the city as skilled craftsmen. They replicated a miniature version of daily life at Nauvoo with the creation of an orchestra, a theater group, and a library (with about 1,000 books carted from Illinois). They began a newspaper, *Nouvelle Revue Icarienne*. With political acrimony behind them, a sense of harmony prevailed.

By the 1860s, though, circumstances had changed. The Cheltenham property was too small to support a self-sufficient community, and the men had to spend their workdays outside Icaria in the city. Health became a main concern. The Rivière des Pères, which bisected the colony, was in fact an open sewer. In the warm months, with the pollution, heat, and mosquitoes, Icaria was pestilential. Epidemics of dysentery and cholera occurred. After 1862 many young men left to join the nearby Union army. Differences of opinion over leadership festered. The final, unconquerable problem, however, was a financial one. They could not meet the mortgage payments, and in 1864 the property reverted to St. Louis banker Thomas Allen. That same year, in March, most of the members simply left the community; the Cheltenham Icaria ceased to exist.[13]

The 200 or so Icarians left at Nauvoo also experienced difficulties in the late 1850s. Crops failed, and because of the panic of 1857, prices for Icarian products sold at Keokuk, Iowa, plummeted. With Cabet gone, all financial assistance from Paris ended. There were no new members to speak of. Debts mounted. Creditors pressed their claims. Under such conditions the Nauvoo Icarians decided to do what they had planned since 1853: move to southwest Iowa, where new federal lands had just opened for sale at $1.25 an acre, about half the going price of $2.25 an acre for nearby Illinois land. In 1860 they sold their Nauvoo property for more than $21,000 and moved across southern Iowa on the Mormon Trail to Adams County. When they arrived at the site where they had purchased 3,100 acres of farm- and timberland on the Nodaway River, they saw nothing but miles of uninhabited prairie. The nearest supply town was St. Joseph, over 100 miles directly south over roadless hillcountry.

The Corning Icaria, modeled on the Nauvoo layout, was initially a stand of primitive log structures with dirt floors. The largest building, the refectory, functioned as a dining hall, school, laundry, taylor shop, supply store, and library. On the river they built a sawmill and a flour mill. Later they put up log cabins for a blacksmith and shoemaker. Barns for livestock were built on the northeast part of the colony farthest from the living quarters, just as Cabet suggested in his book. Unlike Nauvoo, however, there were no apartments. Now all Icarians lived in private dwellings with their families.

The Civil War brought prosperity, largely because the Icarians sold their products to federal purchasing agents at greatly inflated prices. By 1870 they had redeemed all their debts. By then the Icarians had replaced the crude log cabins with sturdy frame buildings. A new and larger refectory housed a kitchen and storage area in the basement and a sewing room, a tailor shop, and a library (containing over 2,000 volumes) on the top floor. Separate buildings existed for a pharmacy, a bakery, and a laundry. Craft shops crowded together in the southwest quarter of the community. To the northeast sat the barns and slaughterhouses. By 1870, then, a self-sufficient and prosperous communal society had taken shape.

Soon afterward, though, ideological turmoil struck, reminiscent of the Nauvoo crisis. The disruption came from a group of newly arrived and younger converts from France who called themselves the Progressives. Under Emile Péron, they demanded better business management and full voting rights for women. The Conservatives, mostly Nauvoo Icarians led by Alexis Armel Marchand, condemned such changes.[14] A showdown came in the fall of 1877 when the Progressives charged that the Conservatives violated the charter of the colony by maintaining private gardens. They brought the matter to the Circuit Court of Adams County in August 1878, and the judge agreed. He ordered the charter forfeit. Once again, the community divided into separate factions.

Between 1878 and 1884 there were two Icarias at Corning. One, the older group, called itself New Icaria and moved, dragging their homes on logs, about a mile east of the original site. The other group, the Progressives, renamed themselves Young Icaria and remained on the Nodaway River. The Progressives could not survive; within two years they accumulated a $7,000 debt, and membership dwindled to six families. Thus in 1881 one of the Progressives, Armand Dehay, went by train to San Francisco, where he inspected a tract of 885 acres along the Russian River some fifty miles north of the Bay City. Feeling that a better economic opportunity awaited the Icarians in the hilly, grape-growing Sonoma Valley, he bought the land for $15,000 and moved his family from Iowa in the spring of that year. They were soon joined by the Leroux family and by two San Francisco Socialists, Emile Bée and Gustave Provost. They called the colony Icaria Speranza (Icaria of Hope) after the newspaper *L'Espérance*, which Jules Leroux had edited in Kansas in 1858. Two years later the rest of the Progressives moved to California, and in 1884 the community of fifty people, including children, was legally organized in a certificate of co-partnership filed in the Sonoma County courthouse in Santa Rosa.

In some ways Icaria Speranza departed from Cabet's *Voyage en Icarie* more than any other community, largely because of the implementation of some ideas of Saint-Simonian socialism. For example, in contrast to the earlier colonies, this one devised an annual profit-sharing scheme and allowed some private property. Yet most of Icaria Speranza was a duplication of Cabet's plan. They had officers elected by and accountable to a general assembly of all adults in which both men and women voted. They built a refectory where all ate and gathered for social and political occasions. As at Corning, children were taught in a one-room school built on colony land and organized as the Icarian School District within the county system. They increased the French language requirement, though; these Icarians were Francophiles indeed. Now an initiate had to speak and read fluent French, serve a year of probation, and win the approval of nine-tenths of the general assembly.

Economically Icaria Speranza prospered, for a while. They put in zinfandel vines and pressed wine, as they had started to do in Corning. They planted wheat and started a peach tree orchard, but the community never became self-sufficient because there were too few Icarians. For a brief time the money they received from the sale of 800 acres of their Iowa property, about $9,000, helped pay their debts. But this sum trickled in and was never fully collected, and the California Icarians still owed $6,000. They sold a half-section (160 acres) of their best land. They then sold their cattle, horses, and pigs. Early in 1886 some San Francisco men who had invested money as a business enterprise pulled out. In June of that year Icaria Speranza dissolved, and its

The last members of the Corning Icaria in Corning, Iowa, pose in front of one of their community structures about 1880. (Courtesy of Center for Icarian Studies, Western Illinois University)

property was equally distributed among the eleven adult members who remained. As in Iowa, St. Louis, and Nauvoo, some families stayed near the community; most moved away.[15]

The older Icarians at Corning subsisted for another decade or so. They maintained the same way of life that, by then, most of them had known all of their adult lives. However, membership dwindled as children, such as Marie Marchand, the daughter of Alexis Armel Marchand, married outsiders and left Icaria permanently. Elderly Icarians, some of whom had known Cabet, passed away. In 1898 the handful of Icarians still there asked, without acrimony or debate, for the county court to dissolve their community. And so, quietly, a half-century after the First Advance Guard set out from Le Havre to build the new and perfect society in America, the last Icarian utopia died of old age.

Given the differences among the five communities and their dispersal in geography and time, three generations of Icarians showed a striking degree of continuity in their way of life. The explanation of the phenomenon is a simple one: they all referred to, and applied, the ideas of Cabet's *Voyage en Icarie*. It was the sole authority from beginning to end. And the Icarians left behind a voluminous record to prove how conscientiously they tried to approximate the pages of the book in their communities: letters, diaries, newspapers, reminiscences, and visitors' accounts. Every Icarian knew about, embraced, and continually discussed, in French, Cabet's ideas. Such knowledge was a prerequisite for admission to the society. The Icarians shared a common eschatology. They believed that personal salvation lay in a community of brotherly love. They saw two steps to achieving salvation: renouncing the sins of capitalism, and participation in a spiritual regeneration of selflessness in a democratic utopia where each gave according to ability and need. "All for each and each for all!" was their motto.

More than common ideology and vision bound them together. They practiced a tangible communal existence. They ate together, worked together, socialized together, and slept within hearing distance of one another. In the French sense of the word *connaître* (to understand; to experience) they "knew" each other. All Icarians gathered three times a day and ate the same food prepared in their refectory. Breakfast was café au lait, sometimes with eggs. At noon they had their main meal of meat, vegetables, milk, and dessert. Supper consisted of a soup made from leftovers. *La Revue Icarienne* in the spring of 1885, put out by Marchand, had this account of a routine day at the refectory: "At breakfast we have . . . coffee with milk, butter or cheese and often eggs . . . at dinner a dish of meat and one or two vegetables . . . at supper, soup, a dish of vegetables, stewed apples or jam. For beverage, at dinner and supper, milk for those who want and an unlimited supply of very wholesome water. On holidays, we have been indulging ourselves with wine."[16]

Most of the men worked at similar assignments either in agriculture or in workshops, the gristmill, the sawmill, the laundry, the blacksmith's shop, and the tailor's shop. Women's occupations were rotated every week, and they always worked in pairs. There were three tasks for the women: cooking, laundry, and weaving or sewing. The cooking was done by three sets of women. One set prepared the food in large kettles in the basement of the refectory. Upstairs, another set prepared the tables and, after the meals, cleared the dishes, transporting them on a dumbwaiter back to the basement, where they washed them. The third set gathered food supplies from the gardens or cut the meat for the menu. Men washed the clothes, as washing required strength in those days. Young women over age sixteen ironed the clothes, then sorted the clean garments into family baskets for delivery each night to the apartments or homes. Weaving and sewing were the work of young girls under supervision. They made all the community clothing, knitted the socks, and wove the straw hats.[17]

ROBERT P. SUTTON

Sexual equality proved the rule in Icaria, particularly in political and educational matters. Women and men had the same voice in the weekly general assembly, voting on admissions, constitutional changes, and the election of the officer in charge of clothing and lodging. Later the Corning Progressives and those at Icaria Speranza gave women the full franchise. Nowhere, perhaps, was sexual equality reflected more than in the Icarian system of education. Cabet demanded the same education for boys and girls from age five to adulthood. Indeed, he wrote more on education in *Voyage en Icarie* than on any other topic—two extensive chapters. Cabet argued that this education must be more than an accumulation of knowledge. It must produce a better member of society, both academically and morally. Accordingly, the curriculum was rigorous and heavily ladened with an emphasis on moral and civic responsibility. Two of the six categories of instruction at Nauvoo, for instance, described exactly what Cabet wanted. Article 87 of the charter stated, "The moral training has [as] an end the forming of excellent citizens who practice the principle of Brotherhood and who accomplish it in all the duties of social life." Article 91 declared, "Civic training aims to make known the laws, and the political social duties." Emile Vallet, who, as a teenager, lived at the Nauvoo community, remembered that the moral side of his education was handled by Cabet personally, and Papa instructed him regularly on "doing unto others as we wish to be done by." Cabet told them, in Vallet's words, to "protect, love, and work for the feeble, the sick; to forgive; to hold the other cheek when smitten; to be kind, one to another; to love and respect their parents and everybody in general."[18]

Second only to education as a priority in Icaria was the emphasis on cultural and intellectual life. Just as in founding their schools, the Icarians turned to the chapters of *Voyage en Icarie* for guidance. To start with, all the communities had huge libraries. All produced a regular schedule of artistic events on a weekly basis. Following Cabet's specific instructions they stressed music, theater, and festivals or outings. The Nauvoo orchestra was a marvel to all who heard it. Its repertory consisted of popular contemporary music rather than classic concert pieces. Extant Nauvoo scores bear such favorite titles as "Song of the Transporters," "I Conserve It for My Wife," or "No More Cries." At Corning they switched from concerts to operettas, and every other Saturday during the 1860s and 1870s, before the schism, they put on productions in the refectory. On other occasions violins accompanied the community chorus performing Icarian hymns such as "Song of the Departure" or "Hymn of Harmony."[19]

Icarian theater, like the orchestra, was a surprise to outsiders who were invited to its plays. An Austrian visitor to Nauvoo described one such event in the summer of 1855. He noted afterward that such productions were staged at least once a month while he was there. "The stage is at the end of the dining hall. . . . Benches used for the meals are placed in such a way that everyone can see very well. There are some complimentary passes given to a few American families. I attended the performance of *The Salamander, The Hundred Piques, The Miser's Daughter* and I myself was a member of the cast in *The Fisherman's Daughter.*"[20] At Cheltenham the Icarians had their "band of students and fraternal festivals," where they continued to enjoy, in the opinion of one recent French scholar, a high level of theatrical achievement.[21]

Then there were the outings, or promenades, as Cabet labeled them in *Voyage en Icarie*, that combined music, dancing, and fellowship. Again, visitors to Nauvoo left vivid accounts of these excursions. Pierre Bourg, a visitor there in 1849, described in his journal this delightful occasion:

> We were nearly two hundred. . . . Our venerable and venerated Patriarch walked with a joyous air in the middle of us, our whole ensemble formed an appearance of a large and happy family. A magnificent sky, an air pure and fresh, the trees, the flowers, the fruits unknown to us, the prairie, the valleys, the forests, all of this luxury of light, of vegetation, of the vigorous American greenery doubled our feeling of holiday. Our promenade had, besides, a very attractive objective, especially for the women and children, to concentrate on the gathering of walnuts, an inexhaustible crop in this country. After having picked a grove of trees in the woods situated along the river, we went to have our dinner set out on the grass, in a glen, next to a brook, under a tent of foliage; and then, the repast finished, defying a prescription of Raspail, to rest, our orchestra played some quadrilles and waltzes in order to make us sing and pirouette like the mythological hosts of the ancient forest. Finally, at sundown, very tired but happy, we returned to the communal building where at supper, promptly served, we were given a few chilly glances for having kept it waiting.[22]

Jean Lacour, another visitor, depicted in pastoral simplicity another such event held at Nauvoo on June 17, 1855. He called it "Promenade in Icaria."

> The sky this morning promised us a beautiful day. Almost half of the members of the colony are part of this promenade. The band, composed of young men of the school, played several military marches. We descended along the river, arriving in a pretty little wooded area called the Woods of the Young Ladies, each one seated himself on the grass by sections of ten. A wagon contains the dinner which is made up of ham,

radishes, and kneips. The more obliging go to fetch the drinks, which is composed of soft water and muddy water of the Mississippi or of a small brook a little distance away. The musicians organize themselves into a dance orchestra. Some of us take part in the dance.[23]

At the Corning Icaria the festival tradition enjoyed the same popularity. Marie Marchand Ross remembered it from her childhood days in the colony as a regular occasion. One of them, in the fall after the harvest, was called the Fête du Maïs (Corn Festival), and it involved the following events: "Many friends and neighbors came to help with the last day of corn picking. Early in the afternoon, when the harvest was finished all cleaned up and dressed and repaired to the Dining room where a real feast was served. There were speeches and toasts made. Old songs were sung, and after the tables cleared and pushed out of the way the first drama was held on the new floor."[24]

Such memories recall Icaria at its quintessence, as a bucolic mixture of work and play, of reason and fellowship, and the ambiance of community brotherhood. These reminiscences, and others like them, are, as are most such recollections of times past, as selectively distorted as Proust's, for the Icarian experience in America was never quite as perfect as its adherents and descendants portrayed it. Nor was Icaria merely the story of periodic frustration and rancor. Yet historians must attempt to find the essentials of their experience beyond the usual criteria of success or failure.

Viewed from the perspective of developmental communalism, the Icarian experience resembles other movements predicated on a desire to implement an original, fixed, utopian model.[25] The task of exactly duplicating the ideal society through a preconceived communal arrangement often became an unbearable burden. Beyond economic, governmental, and social difficulties, this rigid quest can produce legalism, factionalism, and schism resulting in the undoing of the communities and, sometimes, the movements themselves. Those who ventured to build prototypes of the utopian visions of Robert Owen, Charles Fourier, Laurence Gronlund, Edward Bellamy, and others experienced these negative results in greater or lesser degrees, just as those who pursued Icaria.

No communitarian utopians were ever more committed to the faithful implementation of a model than were the disciples of Etienne Cabet. The Icarians maintained communalism as their permanent and paramount way of life, not as a halfway house or temporary stage in community building. The plan laid down in *Voyage en Icarie* was not a transitional model to another phase of communalism or reform. The Icarians existed only as Icaria, as a homogeneous communal society, or they did not exist; Icarian communal living was preeminent, never secondary. Without a developmental process, their movement lived and died by Cabet's static, utopian model.

A reinterpretation of the Icarian communities emerges with the application of the developmental approach to internal analysis. By thinking developmentally, we become more attentive to arrangements within the communities that promoted or disrupted the society, especially the attitudes of the members. We pay more attention to the critical times and visions that resulted in disruption, schism, and the abandonment of communal ways. We gain new insights into the entire history of the American Icarians.

The internal arrangements of each Icarian community were dramatically unchanging. They all had the same written, rigid, society-adopted rules of organization, admission, conduct, and governance. The rules, likewise, proved for each Icaria largely unrealistic. For example, the Nauvoo constitution required rigorous work discipline in order to create an economy strong enough to support a self-sufficient community. But the work rules were never followed, and Cabet had to resort to coercion to get the jobs done. His later draconian measures to impose discipline were counterproductive and were ignored by most Icarians. Their admission requirements—fluency in French and a thorough knowledge of Cabet's works—likewise were too demanding and, moreover, reflected a peculiar xenophobia or at best an anti-Americanism. What they wanted was a French Icaria, and they built severe barriers for potential American members. This tendency worsened with successive communities so that the admission test for French culture was more stringent at the last Icaria in California than at the first one at Nauvoo.

Their attitudes toward themselves add a dimension, other than xenophobia, to the understanding of their growth, or the lack of it. The élan vital of the Icarians was the emphasis on the importance of the individual and his or her contribution to and participation in the community. Consequently, they opened the door to political participation for women. They believed, and practiced, a system of education that developed the talent and virtue of both sexes. They asserted that every member was intellectually and spiritually equal. Yet this emphasis on individual worth ran against the grain of their need for group cooperation, discipline (as in the workshops), and self-denial for the benefit of the community. So their fundamental attitudes as expressed in their motto "One for all and all for one" were, in practice, an invitation to dissension. A communal society committed at once to individualism and to communism was a society divided emotionally and ideologically against itself.

Another contradiction plagued the Icarians. They were proudly exclusively French. Yet they were incapable of remaining French, of staying away from

ROBERT P. SUTTON

the attractions, or distractions, of American life. They wanted to be separated from American culture but were surrounded by it. As a consequence they were not able to test their Icarian ideas sufficiently removed from and unhampered by the pressures and influences of American society and values. The Nauvoo community, for instance, was never the isolated frontier settlement on the Mississippi River that it is usually pictured to have been after the Mormons left. The Icarians did not come from New Orleans and take over a deserted city. The census manuscripts of 1850 and 1855 reveal that the Icarians were always a small minority in an average-sized river town, not more than 25 percent of the total population. At Nauvoo, just as at Cheltenham (where the Icarians had to work in St. Louis and not in the community), they had to associate continually with Americans who, in contrast to Icarian ideals and way of life, behaved as they wished to behave and worked at a job for the benefit of themselves or their families. The American children, in contrast to the Icarians at Nauvoo, lived with their parents in their homes and not just on weekends in communal apartments. Americans ate meals of their choice when they wished and spent their own money on things they liked, all without the slightest thought about the effect of these personal choices on the brotherhood of mankind. Many Icarians, beset with other problems in their utopia and constantly seeing the alternatives that America had to offer, decided that Cabet had demanded too much. From about 1855 on, they left their communities in steadily increasing numbers.

The Icarians, were, indeed, beset with grave, critical times and with serious divisions that affected them in such a way that, afterward, as developmental communalism suggests, the community divided or decayed or died. There were two such critical times in the history of the American Icarias: the expulsion of Cabet from Nauvoo in 1856, and, twenty years later, the schism at Corning between the Progressives and the Conservatives. In the Nauvoo crisis the community split into two groups, both of which claimed to be the true Icarians. Neither group survived in a condition they had achieved before the fight. The St. Louis Icaria failed to congeal behind a leader to replace Cabet, and they were unable to surmount the subsequent combination of disease, economic failure, and the impact of the Civil War on membership. The Nauvoo majority, likewise, was hit by economic problems and declining membership: by 1863 their total number (men, women, and children) had fallen from just over 200 to only 35 Icarians.[26] The Nauvoo Icarians survived at Corning as an agricultural commune, however. But in 1876, because of the demands of the younger members for changes in the constitution and the resistance of the older Icarians to these changes, the society again split in half. The Progressives soon left for California and a short-lived effort to re-create the community at Cloverdale. The Conservatives lingered at Corning, depleted by age and by the exodus of their children until in 1898 they, too, dissolved the community.

The most remarkable aspect of the American Icarias is the degree to which each community clung to its original blueprint of communal life as put down in Cabet's book, to the dream of a community that would be, as he wrote, a "truly second Promised Land, an Eden, an Elysium, a new Earthy paradise."[27] In the face of severe environmental contrasts between the ideal urban Icaria of the *Voyage* and the realities of life in Texas, Illinois, Missouri, and Iowa, they tried to mimic the scheme of political organization, education, workshops, and culture described in detail by Cabet's pen. In the face of the immediate setback of the Texas fiasco, after a permanent schism of the society in the Nauvoo showdown, after the frustrations at Cheltenham, after the fatal division of the Corning Icaria, and despite continual erosion of followers, they refused to be discouraged in their commitment to build Icaria. Undaunted, they continued, in their letters and newspapers, to write of their hope of realizing, perhaps next time, a community of unselfish practitioners of the Golden Rule. Despite the fact that every Icaria steadily lost members to the unstructured opportunities of American life, the remaining stalwarts were convinced that they had kept the faith. They might have suspected that, because of their persistent French clannishness, they would leave only footprints in the sand of nineteenth-century American social history. Nevertheless, their stubborn, Gallic refusal to surrender their original vision of Cabet's "community of goods," as he called Icaria, still draws the attention of historians to a fascinating epoch in the story of American communal utopias.

Chronology

1788   Etienne Cabet is born in Dijon, France.
1834   Cabet is exiled to England for treason and is influenced by Robert Owen there.
1840   Cabet publishes his utopian novel, *Voyage on Icarie* (Travels in Icaria), in France.
1848   First Advance Guard of Icarians departs France for America and makes an abortive attempt to establish the first Icarian settlement in Texas. Cabet arrives at New Orleans to assume leadership in December.
1849   Nauvoo Icaria founded at Nauvoo, Ill., on the Mississippi River after Icarians purchase the Temple Square from the Mormons.
1852   Cabet leaves Nauvoo for France to stand trial on fraud charges.
1854   Cabet returns to the Nauvoo community in July.
1856   Cabet and his faction of Icarians are expelled from Nauvoo; Cabet dies at St. Louis, Mo.
1857   Cheltenham Icaria founded at Cheltenham, Mo., now part of St. Louis; Benjamin Mercadier is president.

1860   Nauvoo Icaria is moved to Corning, Adams County, Iowa, and called Corning Icaria; Armel Alexis Marchand is president.
1864   Cheltenham Icaria dissolves.
1876   Progressives arrive at the Corning Icaria.
1878   Young Icaria and New Icaria created as the original Corning Icaria community divides because of internal disputes.
1881   Icaria Speranza founded near Cloverdale, Sonoma County, Calif., led by Armand Dehay, Jules Leroux, and his sons Paul and Pierre.
1883   Young Icaria at Corning, Iowa, dissolves.
1886   Icaria Speranza dissolves.
1898   New Icaria dissolves at Corning, Iowa, ending the Icarian movement.

Notes

1. Etienne Cabet, *Travels in Icaria*, trans. Robert P. Sutton (Macomb: Western Illinois University Press, 1985), 3.

2. The standard treatment of Cabet and the early Icarian movement in Europe is Christopher H. Johnson, *Utopian Communism in France: Cabet and the Icarians, 1839–1851* (Ithaca, N.Y.: Cornell University Press, 1974). The most recent full account of the Icarians is Robert P. Sutton, *Les Icariens: The Utopian Dream in Europe and America* (Urbana: University of Illinois Press, 1994). See also the first chapter of Albert Shaw, *Icaria: A Chapter in the History of Communism* (New York: G. P. Putnam's Sons, 1884). For those fluent in French, the best authority is Jules Jean Prudhommeaux, *Icaria et son Fondateur Etienne Cabet* (Paris: Édouard Cornély et Cie, 1907; reprint, Philadelphia: Porcupine Press, 1972).

3. Cabet, *Travels*, 233; Prudhommeaux, *Icarie*, 159–64.

4. Johnson, *Communism in France*, 260–88; H. Roger Grant, "Icarianism and American Utopianism," *Illinois Quarterly* 34 (1972): 5–6.

5. Prudhommeaux, *Icarie*, 219–35.

6. Ibid., 291; Kenneth O. Luke, "Nauvoo since the Exodus of the Mormons, 1846–1973" (Ph.D. diss., St. Louis University, 1973); Thomas Rees, "Nauvoo, Illinois, under Mormon and Icarian Occupation," *Journal of the Illinois Historical Society* 21 (1929): 516.

7. Fernand Rude, *Voyage en Icarie Deux Ouvriers Viennois aux Etats-unis en 1855* (Paris: Presses Universitaires de France, 1952); Prudhommeaux, *Icarie*, 336–37.

8. Prudhommeaux, *Icarie*, 280–83, chaps. 5–6.

9. Ibid., chap. 7; Emile Vallet, *Communism: History of the Experiment at Nauvoo of the Icarian Settlement* (Nauvoo, Ill.: Nauvoo Rustler, 1917), 31–33.

10. Jacques C. Chicoineau, "Etienne Cabet and the Icarians," *Western Illinois Regional Studies* 2 (1979): 5–10. This issue of *Western Illinois Regional Studies* contains three articles on the Icarian communities at Nauvoo and St. Louis. Cabet was first buried with the rites of the Free Masons in Old Riddle Cemetery on Arsenal Street. His followers also placed in the coffin twenty-eight volumes of his published works and a list of the names of his last close friends. In 1972 Cabet's casket was reinterred in the city's New St. Marcus Evangelical Cemetery.

11. Robert P. Sutton, "'Earthly Paradise': The Icarian Experiment in St. Louis," *Gateway Heritage: Quarterly Magazine of the Missouri Historical Society—St. Louis* 12, no. 4 (Spring 1992): 48–59. See also the recent study of Cheltenham by Jeanette C. Lauer and Robert H. Lauer, "Cheltenham: The Search for Bliss in Missouri," *Missouri Historical Review* 81 (Jan-

uary 1987): 173–83. The deed for the property is printed in the Center for Icarian Studies *Newsletter* 9 (Spring 1987): 6.

12. *Comte-rendu de la Gérance à la Communauté* (St. Louis; n.p., 1857).

13. Shaw, *Icaria*, 72, and Lauer and Lauer, "Cheltenham," 172–83.

14. The Progressives began publishing their objections in a newspaper, *Le Jeune Icarie*, edited by Leroux, who, before joining the Icarians in 1876, had printed a socialist newspaper in Kansas called *L'Etoile du Kansas*. See Nadine Dormoy Savage, "Jules Leroux en Icarie," *French Revue* 49 (1976): 1025–40.

15. The only treatment of Icaria Speranza by a historian is Robert V. Hine's "The Icaria Speranza Commune," in his *California's Utopian Colonies*, rev. ed. (Berkeley: University of California Press, 1983).

16. *Revue Icarienne*, April 4, 1885.

17. See Marie Marchand Ross, *Child of Icaria* (New York: City Printing Co., 1938), for details of daily life in Corning Icaria.

18. Vallet, *Communism*, 30–31.

19. See the Center for Icarian Studies *Newsletter* 4 (Spring 1982): 2, for these and other musical scores. See also Elizabeth Ann Rogers, "The Housing and Family Life of the Icarian Colonies" (M.A. thesis, University of Iowa, 1973), 82.

20. Rude, *Deux Ouvriers*, 155.

21. Jacques Rancière, *La nuit des prolétaries* (Paris: Librairie Arthém Fayard, 1981), 411–19.

22. *Le Populaire*, December 15, 1849.

23. Rude, *Deux Ouvriers*, 154.

24. Ross, *Child of Icaria*, 108.

25. Donald E. Pitzer, "Developmental Communalism: An Alternative Approach to Communal Studies," in *Utopian Thought and Communal Experience*, ed. Dennis Hardy and Lorna Davidson (Enfield, England: Middlesex Polytechnic, 1989), 68–76.

26. Prudhommeaux, *Icarie*, 486.

27. Cabet, *Travels*, 3.

Selected Bibliography

Cabet, Etienne. *Travels in Icaria*. Translated by Robert P. Sutton. Macomb: Western Illinois University Press, 1985.

Hine, Robert V. *California's Utopian Colonies*. Rev. ed. Berkeley: University of California Press, 1983.

Johnson, Christopher H. *Utopian Communism in France: Cabet and the Icarians, 1839–1851*. Ithaca, N.Y.: Cornell University Press, 1974.

Prudhommeaux, Jules Jean. *Icarie et son Fondateur Etienne Cabet*. Paris: Édouard Cornély et Cie, 1907.

Ross, Marie Marchand. *Child of Icaria*. New York: City Printing Co., 1938.

Sutton, Robert P. *Les Icariens: The Utopian Dream in Europe and America*. Urbana: University of Illinois Press, 1994.

Vallet, Emile. *Communism: History of the Experiment at Nauvoo of the Icarian Settlement*. Nauvoo, Ill.: Nauvoo Rustler, 1917.

JON WAGNER

Eric Jansson and the Bishop Hill Colony

O ne can only imagine the shock and disbelief the devout Lutherans of Sweden's Hälsingland province experienced as they gathered in the spring of 1844 to watch their neighbors, followers
of the prophet Eric Jansson, burn religious books. Onto the
pyre went hymnbooks, devotional literature, church tracts—even some of
the works of Martin Luther. Later that year the Janssonists burned the Lutheran catechism itself, and with it the last bridge of reconciliation with the
Swedish church. Only the Bible, the sole authority in religious matters besides the prophet, was spared. The Janssonists had set an irreversible course
toward separatism with all the persecution and intransigence that entailed.[1]
Within two short years the Janssonists were to find refuge on the prairies of
Illinois, where they built a community similar in many respects to those of
other European Pietists in America. Not only did they hold a significant place
in the history of American communalism, but they also left far-reaching effects on Swedish society and helped trigger the great Swedish emigration of
the following decades.[2]

Janssonism in Sweden

Had it not been for Eric Jansson, social and religious unrest in Sweden might
have taken a different course. The flames of religious dissent, which had
swept Germany for centuries, had barely touched Sweden by the early nineteenth century. True, there had been an outbreak of German-inspired Pietism
a century earlier, against which the Swedish government had enacted the

Conventicle Edict forbidding Bible reading or other religious meetings without a clergyman present. But those laws were not at first invoked when some conscientious Lutherans in Sweden's northern agricultural province of Hälsingland began to organize Bible study groups and prayer meetings. Like the Pietists of Germany and other parts of Europe, these "readers" (läsare) hoped to reverse the worldly trends they saw in the established church, with its socially privileged clergy, its ties to government, its emphasis on ritual and doctrine, and its indifference to the needs of common people. Hoping to return religion to the simple spiritual purity of the apostolic faith, the Pietists emphasized personal religious devotion over doctrine and ritual, and they challenged the need for clergymen to act as intercessors with God. In addition to these religious concerns, they felt a deep uneasiness about the state of public morality and social well-being, a matter to which we shall return presently. Yet despite this potentially volatile combination of social and religious criticism, some clergy welcomed the readers movement as a means of purifying the church from within, and there was little reason at first to view it as a separatist movement.[3]

Eric Jansson,[4] who was to alter the course of Swedish religious history, was born in Biskopskulla parish in the province of Uppland in 1808, the child of religiously lukewarm parents. Sensitive to spiritual matters as a boy, Jansson experienced a vision at age twenty-six in which the Lord reportedly spoke to him, saying, "It is writ that whatsoever ye shall ask in prayer, believing, ye shall receive; all things are possible to him that believeth. 'If ye shall ask anything in my name, I will do it, saith the Lord.'"[5] Jansson's thirst for spiritual knowledge led him to a close study of the Pietistic devotional literature. Ultimately, he developed his own radical theology that departed from both Lutheranism and mainstream Pietism in rejecting the doctrine of man's inherent sinfulness. In this Jansson may have been influenced by the Hernnhutist doctrine of the spiritual value of man, which had recently spread to Sweden from the Continent, or by Methodism, which had an influential missionary presence in Sweden during the 1830s.[6] But Jansson, like some other religious utopians, embraced the more extreme position of "perfectionism," preaching that those who were truly saved could lead sinless lives and, in fact, were incapable of sinning: "He who is born of God cannot sin, and he who sins is of the devil."[7] Jansson further repudiated the state church of Sweden by proclaiming, contrary to accepted doctrine, that the Bible is a call to social action and a blueprint for Christian society.[8] Eventually Jansson considered himself the second incarnation of Christ, sent to save Christianity from the fallen church; he thought himself and his heirs destined to rule during the millennium in the kingdom of God on earth.[9] These radical teachings, however,

JON WAGNER

reached their full expression only after Jansson's charismatic preaching had already won the support of many of Hälsingland's readers and converted the prominent *läsare* leader Jonas Olsson.

As Jansson's more radical ideas emerged, Janssonist extremism aggravated official persecution and brought followers to his defense. One Janssonist woman, asked if Eric Jansson were her God, defiantly proclaimed that "Eric Jansson is as good as God."[10] Barred from Holy Communion, the Janssonists responded by linking the Lutheran Church with Satan. The book burnings of 1844 were part of this cycle of fanaticism and persecution that culminated in arrests, legal harassment, and mob violence against the Janssonists. Jansson himself, who seemed fated either for martyrdom or imprisonment, was boldly rescued from custody and spirited into Norway during the early months of 1846.

Although one may view Janssonism in strictly religious terms, the religious issues form part of a larger webwork of changes and stresses in Swedish society. Some of these stresses stemmed from demographic pressures: during the preceding century, falling death rates had contributed to substantial population increase and pressure on the land. Expansion of agricultural lands was unable to keep pace, and much of the benefit from this expansion went to those whose holdings were already large, while the landless population grew at several times the rate of the whole population.[11] Thus in a time of economic growth the hopes of a rising number of citizens were frustrated. Not only did Swedish culture tend to define success in terms of membership in the rural landowning class, but the burgeoning urban-industrial economy was not yet able to absorb the landless population, whatever their aspirations.[12]

Not surprisingly, laypeople associated social problems with a vague anxiety about moral decline and looked to religion for a solution. But the state church of Sweden could do little to assuage popular distress, and it was in any case a conservative force allied with, and often indistinguishable from, the privileged classes and the local governmental bureaucracy. Clergymen showed little interest in applying religion to these broad problems or to more specific manifestations, such as alcoholism; rather, they wielded religion as a weapon against change and a shield for their own transparently self-interested behavior (the parish priest, for example, might also own the local distillery). For people who saw God as their deliverer and the Bible as a guide for living, it did not seem contradictory or hypocritical to give religious form to social and political protest. That the *läsare* and Janssonist movements flourished in the northern provinces, which were especially hard hit by such problems, was probably no accident.[13] Nor was it sheer coincidence, perhaps, that the several years preceding the rise of Janssonism had seen severe crop failures, a disastrous drop in the price of linen, and a general recession due to a decline in iron exports.[14] If this were not enough, the Janssonists could also count legal persecution and mob harassment among their woes. Their future in Sweden seemed to offer only more suffering.

This crucial phase of the Janssonist movement fatefully coincided with the first stirrings in Sweden of "America fever." Although there were few Swedish immigrants in America at the time, their reports of religious freedom and economic opportunity presented the Janssonists with what seemed the perfect solution to their troubles. In 1845 they sent an emissary to find a suitable location for a Janssonist colony in America. The Janssonist scout, Olof Olsson, found his way to the town of Victoria in west central Illinois, where a small Swedish Methodist congregation had already been established. His report was more than encouraging: "This land is like the Kingdom of Heaven. It contains all that is good and free . . . a land where the laborer, as well as the regent, may eat his loaf of white bread."[15] Olsson selected lands a few miles to the north while the Janssonists readied themselves for the emigration. Since not everyone in the sect had the means to pay for his or her own passage, the Janssonists decided to pool their wealth. A colony descendant who conducted extensive interviews with the original colonists at the turn of the century writes,

> Their thoughts were directed constantly to the early Christians in apostolic times, so when they decided to emigrate they followed the example of the first Christians at Jerusalem by selling their possessions and forming a common treasury. . . . A common fund was necessary if all should obtain sustenance and transportation across the Atlantic to America and Illinois and support during the first period in their new home. Thus from scriptural example and circumstance the principles of communism were adopted by the Jansonists to be continued during the entire existence of the colony.[16]

The Building of Bishop Hill, 1846–1850

The Janssonists faced extraordinary hardships even by pioneer standards. It had been a bitter parting in Sweden, with Janssonists and anti-Janssonists each prophesying God's wrath upon the other. The ships that carried them were hastily equipped for passengers, and the emigrants knew little of what lay before them or how to prepare for it. Yet despite the uncertainties, nearly all of the Janssonists emigrated to America between 1846 and 1854. Research on the passport and passenger arrival data indicates a total of between 1,300

JON WAGNER

and 1,400, over a thousand of whom embarked for America during the first year of the colony's existence.[17] Not all, however, arrived at the New Jerusalem. Disease and shipwreck claimed scores of lives, especially among children and the aged. Others became disillusioned to find that they could not miraculously speak English upon arrival as the prophet had foreseen, and many left the company at New York or along the arduous three-week journey inland.

In July 1846 ~~Eric Jansson~~ arrived with his small party at the site of the new colony, which was named Bishop's Hill after Jansson's birthplace (the "s" was soon dropped). With little time to prepare for the 400 followers who were to arrive before the onset of winter, they prepared about thirty semiunderground log cabins or "dugouts" in a ravine running through the center of the village site. Food was another matter—they arrived too late to put in a crop and found virtually no place to buy food on the Illinois frontier. "Certainly we had money," a colonist later recalled, "but you couldn't eat money."[18] Weakened from the journey and facing the winter with inadequate food and housing, the Janssonists suffered dreadfully that first winter. "Nearly every morning," writes a historian of the colony, "a fresh corpse was pulled out from the reeking death-traps."[19] They had no time for proper burials, much less keeping mortality statistics, but in Red Oak grove, where some sixty-five or seventy colonists were stationed, there stands a marker for fifty who died in that winter. In all, more than one-third of the 400 perished before spring.[20] Not surprisingly, a stream of deserters left to try their luck elsewhere. The author's impression, drawn from incomplete and somewhat conflicting data, is that the total attrition from death or desertion during the journey or within a few months of arrival must have approached 50 percent.[21]

In light of all this, the spirit and achievements of the faithful proved astounding. On February 9—still in the throes of that first morbid winter—one wrote to a friend in Sweden: "For the land which we have taken is large and wide, and is such a land that nothing on earth is lacking us, for it flows with milk and honey." He goes on to quote Scripture: "We are already a light unto the Gentiles and the glory of the Lord even unto the end of the world, and the word is made flesh among us," to which another colonist adds the postscript, "I and my companions are getting along so well that you cannot believe it."[22]

Anders Larsson, who had left the Janssonists because of doctrinal differences before reaching Bishop Hill, visited the community from June 4 to 10, 1847. His report in a letter to Sweden, as fair-minded and coherent an account of early conditions as any available, bore witness to the colony's stupendous achievements during the few warm months since its founding.[23]

The restored sanctuary of the Bishop Hill Colony Church built in 1848 in Bishop Hill, Illinois, reveals its elegant simplicity. (Photograph by Jon Wagner)

"They've put in quite unbelievable amounts of work there during this short time," he wrote. The Janssonists had built a flour mill (the only one for thirty miles) and were planning another; they had two sawmills, "several brick-works . . . , a tannery, roofing shake facility, and shops of all types." Although planting was still in progress, they had already sown "over 400 acres in wheat, 700 acres in corn, 3- to 400 in barley and oats, many hundreds of acres in potatoes," and had constructed four and a half miles of earthen wall to protect the fields from their abundant livestock. "While I was there," he wrote, "a surveyor measured and adjusted the site of the city itself, which will be built in the shape of a square, with 18 houses on each side externally, and internally [there will be] orchards and planting land, and a large church. All these houses will be exactly alike in all possible dimensions."

Jansson had appointed twelve "apostles" to disseminate the faith, and Larsson reported that "all of these have now gone to an English school since last fall, and haven't concerned themselves with other tasks; . . . they'll soon be fully educated in the English Language." Jansson himself had preached in English for the first time during Larsson's visit, on June 7. Education in the English language was not restricted to the apostles: "All the children go to school and study English, in which a large number are already well-advanced, and are under the care of remarkably capable men and women teachers."

Of Bishop Hill's economic organization, Larsson wrote, "Everything is said

302   JON WAGNER

to be communal, and no one has any more than the other. If someone needs clothes, it's only [necessary] to go to the management, then to the stores, and take what is needed. Cooking and eating takes place in three kitchens. No one works more than he wants, but all live in the belief that the more industrious they are, the more each will get at [the time of division]." Larsson, however, expressed his skepticism about this last point in a footnote: "But when this division will take place, I'll leave unsaid." He went on to say of those who leave the colony, "None of them will get a single shilling back." The preceding fall, he explained, court settlements had obliged the colony to compensate those leaving the community, but since then the Janssonists had appointed district judges who ruled in favor of the colony.

Although clearly impressed by the Janssonists' industry, Larsson did not conceal his distaste for Jansson, whom the colonists called "the prophet" and whom they believed to be "endowed with all the perfections of God." Larsson complained that even failed prophecies, such as the promised "gift of tongues" and a prediction that all the sect would arrive in America by New Year's Day, failed to shake the absolute belief and obedience of the Janssonists. The prophet, however, maintained no monopoly on revelation. Members' dreams and visions were consulted, and various persons preached during the two-hour morning and evening church services, "since all (as they say) are taught by God and thus cannot speak any other word than that which God places in their mouths."

According to Larsson and other sources, Jansson frequently was inspired to order fasting during the early period. One such fast lasted for four days during Larsson's visit. According to Larsson, the fasting served as a test of faith for the "newly arrived guests," the remainder of some 300 or 400 who had left Sweden from December to March and who would have arrived about the same time as Larsson.[24] In practical terms the fast was, Larsson notes, "a masterful improvisation," since it dealt with a shortage of flour and allowed time to install two new baking ovens. Nevertheless, Jansson's fast may have been the last straw for twenty new arrivals who departed during Larsson's visit, leaving about 600 in the colony.

Those who left had no dearth of places to go. Chicago and the nearby town of Galesburg were among the first to have communities of Swedes who had left the Janssonists; these and other Swedish "seed communities" of former Janssonists helped channel the next wave of Swedish emigration into Illinois and Iowa.[25] During the early days of the colony, however, it was Jonas Hedström's Swedish Methodist congregation at Victoria, to which the Janssonist scout Olof Olsson had initially been drawn (and almost converted), that presented the most immediate threat. Hedström's tireless efforts to convert

Janssonists made him, as Larsson observed, "the great means of freeing all who had wished to leave."[26]

The austerity that Larsson witnessed at Bishop Hill proved temporary. Fasting ceased, and the quantity and quality of food improved greatly, although the Janssonists retained a preference for simple foods such as hardtack, corn meal mush, and a nonalcoholic "small beer" from the colony brewery.[27] Housing and other building construction also developed apace, as Janssonists replaced the early dugouts, tents, and sod buildings with adobe structures, then frame buildings, and finally the brick construction that later dominated the colony's architecture. By 1849 one of the colony's notable landmarks, the frame colony church, stood completed, and another, the huge apartment building called "Big Brick," was well under way.[28]

The circumstances of the early years, perhaps combined with the vague distrust of sexuality that was common to many religious groups of the time, led the Janssonists to adopt a policy of celibacy during the pioneering period of the colony. The rule, which is variously described as a total ban on sexual relations or as a mere discouragement of new marriages, seems to have had the desired effect: census records show only three male children born from 1846 to 1849.[29] In 1848, when the economy and housing in the colony had improved, Jansson reversed the earlier policy and paired off many couples "regardless of personal likes or dislikes."[30] Colony records show that Jansson married over fifty couples in weekly ceremonies during the summer of 1848, with as many as twenty-four couples wed in a single day.[31]

Nevertheless the Janssonists, unlike many communal groups, made little effort to interfere with the traditional family. Indeed, contrary to myths about Janssonism tearing families asunder, kinship (even more than regionalism) was the main structuring principle of the Janssonist emigration.[32] One family grouping, for example, contained sixty-four members, almost all from the same parish. Nuclear families occupied single rooms in several communal dwellings, the largest of which was Big Brick, with its seventy-two family rooms and communal dining halls. Although the colonists performed domestic tasks communally, the division of work generally followed traditional lines. Sex roles in Sweden, however, were not especially rigid by Old World standards; in fact, Anders Larsson's letter, cited above, expressed surprise that American women performed such a narrow range of tasks. In Bishop Hill, women made and carried bricks; built bridges, mills, and ponds; and planted crops in addition to their cooking, sewing, spinning, dairying, and other traditional women's jobs.[33]

Colony life was not without its tragedies and setbacks. A cholera epidemic that ravaged the community from July until September 1849 killed about 150

JON WAGNER

Olof Krans came to Bishop Hill, Illinois, from Sweden with his parents at age twelve in 1850. From memory, he later painted many portraits of Eric Jansson's disciples and scenes of their communal activities. This painting of the colonists planting corn is perhaps the most famous. (Courtesy of the Bishop Hill State Museum)

persons, including Jansson's wife and two of their children and many of the colony's best artisans, thus reducing the population to an all-time low of just over 400.[34] The membership was further drained by a steady trickle of colonists who left for other settlements. Figures show that although roughly equal numbers of men and women left Sweden for Bishop Hill,[35] the 1850 sex ratio in the colony favored women by approximately two to one.[36] This suggests a substantial and selective attrition on the part of the men, who would have been in a better position to strike off on their own.

Despite its struggles, Bishop Hill was among the most important settlements in the region from the day of its founding. Quite aside from the considerable labor value of the immigrants themselves, the colony brought $10,000 to $15,000 in gold into circulation between 1846 and 1850, at a time when paper money was almost worthless and much business was transacted by barter.[37]

The colony benefited from an economy of large scale, a high esprit de corps, and a willingness to try new things. In their architecture they readily adopted brick construction, which was virtually unknown in their native provinces, and in 1848–50 they built the massive Big Brick, 200 feet long and four stories tall, said to have been the largest building in America west of Chicago.[38] In farming they took immediately to American crops and often surpassed their neighbors in adopting innovations such as the grain cradle, a hand harvesting tool unknown in Sweden. In 1848 they acquired a threshing machine, which they hauled from farm to farm, taking one-eighth of the grain they processed. A mechanical reaper was used experimentally in 1849, but it proved less satisfactory than the grain cradles, with which some individuals in the colony could harvest as much as fourteen acres in a day.[39] Working together in groups of up to 200, the harvesters made their eighteen-hour workdays occasions for fellowship and communion:

> The young men wielded the cradles—and wonderful feats were performed with the cradle in those days—while the middle-aged men and the women bound the sheaves; boys and girls gathered the sheaves together, while the old men placed them in shocks. In the evening, when the day's work was done and the harvesters were retiring from the field, an interesting spectacle presented itself to the observer. Two by two, in a long procession a couple of hundred strong, the harvesters wended their homeward way, first the men carrying their cradle-scythes over their shoulders, then the women with their hand-rakes, and, finally, the children, all singing some merry harvest-song of their native country, while keeping step to the music. On arriving at the village they repaired to the common dining hall [in Big Brick], where a bountiful repast awaited them on long wooden tables, some of which were set aside for the men, others for the women, and still others for the children.[40]

Thus in 1850, at the end of what has been called the "great decade" of nineteenth-century commune building, Bishop Hill had taken its place alongside such thriving communal groups as Amana, the Shakers, Oneida, Zoar, and the Harmony Society, and it might have seemed that it, too, was destined for many decades of communal prosperity. This bright prospect, however, was not fulfilled.

Administrative Communalism, 1850–1858

The events of 1850 were soon to change the direction of Bishop Hill's development. In 1848 John Root, a Swedish American soldier of fortune, joined the colony and asked for the hand of Jansson's cousin, Charlotta Lovisa. The marriage agreement stipulated that Charlotta would not be removed from the community against her will, which is precisely what Root soon attempted to do. After Charlotta was rescued from Root's possession by a group of Bishop Hill men, Root raised a mob and prepared to attack the colony, only to be turned away by a posse of Bishop Hill's sympathetic neighbors. On May 13,

1850, the frustrated John Root shot and killed Eric Jansson at the county courthouse in Cambridge, where they had each come on other business.

Although colony lore holds that the prophet foresaw his death, he had not named a successor. Notwithstanding an attempt by Jansson's second wife to designate a proxy for his twelve-year old son, public opinion favored a cadre of Jansson's deputies, most notably the former *läsare* leader Jonas Olsson. With the assistance of several others, Olsson led the community in moral and religious matters while Olof Johnson managed secular and external affairs.[41] The arrangement was formalized with the legal incorporation of the colony in 1853, which designated seven "trustees," including Olsson and Johnson, to handle colony business and report to the membership. The 1853 charter also enshrined communalist principles, giving them explicit religious justification and spelling out the communal life already being practiced—with one important change: the 1854 revision of the bylaws allowed persons who left to be compensated for their labor.[42] The charter also allowed land and property to be held in the name of the community, rather than by individual leaders. Jonas Olsson, whom critics have called a religious tyrant, seems to have steered a middle course theologically, retaining the fundamentals of perfectionism while quietly revising or putting aside Jansson's more extreme writings.[43] Olof Johnson's economic management, too, seemed at first to be conservative and quietly competent.

Under the trustees the colony prospered as never before.[44] The workforce was efficiently organized, with each person assigned to a department according to talent and preference, and each department under the leadership of a manager.[45] John Swainson, who visited the colony in 1853, described "fifty young men . . . cultivating a cornfield where every furrow was two miles in length" and fifty milkmaids emptying the milk from 200 cows into huge tubs. "We had never before seen so large a farm, nor one so well cultivated," he wrote. The colony had its own dairy, tannery, gristmill, sawmill, brick factory, brewery, and many specialists including tailors, shoemakers, blacksmiths, carpenters, wheelwrights, and a silversmith. In addition to the many items it produced for its own use, the colony manufactured wagons and carriages for sale outside the community, and in 1851 the women wove more than 30,000 yards of linen cloth and carpeting from colony flax.[46] Broomcorn was also an important cash crop, bringing $36,000 into the community in 1854.[47] By the end of the decade Bishop Hill's landholdings had grown to about 11,500 acres valued at over $400,000,[48] and the population had climbed to about 700.[49] A flurry of building construction, mostly in the early part of the decade, left Bishop Hill looking much as it does today, with its dozen or so large brick and frame buildings, in an eclectic Greek revival style

The Bjorklund Hotel, erected in 1852, stands majestically among other remaining communal structures in Swedish Bishop Hill, Illinois. (Photograph by Donald Janzen)

(with whimsical suggestions of Swedish folk art), rising unexpectedly from the prairie.[50]

But the achievements of the colonists were not only material; what is far more important, from the utopian point of view, is that they led what was by most accounts a satisfying life. Swainson commented on the kindness, hospitality, and good cheer that prevailed in the colony. Anders Wiberg, who also visited in 1853, found himself unexpectedly charmed by that "notorious" place. "Eric Jansson has now gone to his just reward," writes Wiberg, "but praise be the Providence which permits even gross delusions to bring blessed results." Wiberg then quotes at some length from a newspaper account that overflows with praise for the community. "Theirs is an industrial socialism," writes the anonymous journalist after a visit to the colony, "founded on virtue and morality; which lightens their labor, and sanctifies their toil." He tells of his euphoria as he reclines on Alpine-white sheets, falling asleep to the "sweet lullaby" of "industry"—the spinning wheel in a nearby room. At breakfast he is greeted by a delightful scene: "Three to four hundred of both sexes seated on either side of snowy-white-arched columns, no noise, nor confusion. Hark again! slowly, and lowly at first, presently as with one voice, upwards and heaven-wards swells that hymn of praise, and your soul with it, if you have one that is ever capable of rising above this groveling world."[51]

Like most other communal societies of the day, the Bishop Hill colony once established was able to provide well for its members. "No one was obliged to overtax his strength," one account notes, and "on the whole, the members of the community enjoyed a greater amount of comfort and security against want than the struggling pioneer settlers by whom they were surrounded."[52] Philip Stoneberg, whose work on the colony was based on interviews with aging colonists, writes that "each and every one knew that he worked for the welfare of the society. If the work was trying, sometimes it also had its sweet sides. It was a large family who lived together; the daily intercourse within it was not without its pleasure."[53]

Letters from the 1850s confirm the satisfactions of communal life. One, for example, assures relatives in Sweden that the colonists "live in splendidness without any worldly cares." The father of painter Olof Krans writes, "I work with many dear brothers, and one encourages the other with God's words." Another colonist, arriving in 1855, reports that "all people are friendly and religious. They like to carry our burdens for us."[54] Even after the divisive end of the colony, which was soon to come, a departing colonist could still say, "Thanks for good company."[55]

The Dissolution, 1859–1861

Although the charter of 1853 stated that the trustees should be accountable to the membership and report regularly to them, it seems to have entrusted this duty largely to the trustees' good faith. Far from providing practical checks, it gave the trustees sweeping powers to expel persons for "wicked conduct" or "disturbing the peace and harmony." To make matters worse, Olof Johnson gained control over the votes of four other trustees, giving him almost unlimited power to manage the business of the colony while Olsson attended to spiritual matters.[56] None of this seemed important as long as consensus prevailed, but divisive issues had a way of snowballing under such an arrangement.

The first major issue, it seems, was that of celibacy. As the story goes, one or two of the Janssonist "apostles" had returned from the Shaker colony at Pleasant Hill, Kentucky, with the proposal that the Janssonists abolish marriage. What happened after that depends on whom one believes: some suggest that the policy was never more than talk, or at the most, urging, by Olsson and some other trustees; others tell of marriages destroyed and colonists driven from the community by the rule of celibacy.[57] Colony records do show that ten men were expelled in 1855 for spreading antitrustee propaganda but do not specify the cause of their dissent.[58] The claim that celibacy was a rigid doctrine or rule seems to have been popular among hostile outsiders and disgruntled exiles, while official colony records and the letters of loyal members are curiously silent on the subject. Judging from evidence too complex to recount fully here, this author suspects that celibacy was strongly endorsed (but not formally required) by Olsson and some other leaders, and that this provided a focal issue—and a nice bit of scandal—for dissenters, who were inclined to exaggerate its importance. The celibacy ideal seems to have been put aside by 1859, when official records trace a debate over whether young people planning marriage should seek parental consent.[59]

The cracks in communal solidarity became open rifts when Olof Johnson's undisclosed economic speculations began to go amiss. Johnson had made a series of risky investments in the hopes of letting the colony's capital, rather than the people, do the work. All went well until the financial slump of 1858, following the Crimean War, when Illinois lost 250 banks at once.[60] The colony was plunged into irreparable debt, and the situation worsened with the trustees' steadfast refusal to answer pleas for a full disclosure. Amid escalating accusations and reprisals, some members began to agitate for a dissolution of the communal economy. Two factions developed: one, comprising two-thirds of the colonists, wanted to keep a record of individual property and make other reforms, but continue daily communal life as before; the other wanted an end to the communal system.[61] For reasons that are by no means clear, the minority faction prevailed.

The formal dissolution in 1861 did not end the bitterness, for the full extent of debt was not disclosed until the Bishop Hill case had dragged through the courts for more than another decade, and so extensive was the debt that many ex-colonists were forced to sell their shares of land and property in order to pay it.[62] The trustees, who had a large role in the distribution of shares, were accused of favoring themselves. Bishop Hill's industries closed, and its thriving communal economy collapsed, forcing many of the people to move away.

The Role of Communalism

There is general agreement that the practice of communalism was adopted by the Janssonists initially in order to facilitate the emigration, and it was evidently the understanding of at least some colonists that the property was later to be divided and the communal system dismantled. Anna Maria Stråle, one of Jansson's closest followers, wrote in an 1872 letter to Sweden, "for each one of us individually to construct a home with the few assets we had brought over after paying for the trip was an impossibility. We decided thus to build and farm in common. . . . This communality would continue according to what Erik Jansson often said, until we had recovered to the point that we could, without damage to each other, divide up into our own homes."[63] Similarly, Jansson's son, Captain Eric Johnson, stated in 1880 that his father had intended communalism only as a "temporary arrangement," and that "there was no intention of founding the colony on a socialistic basis."[64]

Important as these testimonies are, the place of communalism in Janssonist history is more complex than they suggest. These and many other statements about the communal system date from after the breakup and reflect in some degree the acrimonious debate between pro- and anticommunal factions in the last years of the colony. Resentment of the communal system as advocated and administered by the trustees may have led to an after-the-fact rejection of communal principles by many former colonists; certainly Johnson's claim about his father's intentions is difficult to dissociate from his strong anti-trustee sentiments (and since he was only ten when his father died, he may be a less reliable source on this question than others closer to the colony leadership). Furthermore, those who, like Johnson, wished to protect Jansson's good name in a world unsympathetic to communalism may have felt obliged to play down its significance to his teachings, just as those hostile to Jansson seem to have been more inclined to treat it as a central tenet.[65]

To claim that communalism was never intended as more than a temporary expedient would be to oversimplify a complex aspect of colony history. Indeed, some lines of evidence suggest a growing commitment to communal living. The 1853 articles of incorporation and the revised 1854 bylaws, signed by most of the adult members, unequivocally endorsed communal organization with no mention of its being temporary. A collection of twenty-one letters from colonists in the early to middle 1850s contains testimonials to the moral virtue of communal living and no references to an impending division of property.[66] The 1860 newspaper account by the anonymous but well-informed "settler" (who, despite his sympathy, was no utopian sentimentalist) admitted that two-thirds of the colonists still favored communal life.[67]

Still more significant is the fact that, even during Jansson's lifetime, the colony made a major investment in communal organization by way of its architecture. The town plan of 1847 mentioned by Larsson (who, as we have noted, was already skeptical about the abandonment of communalism) was never implemented. Instead of the seventy-two identical houses, which might have been adapted to either communal or private living, the colony built much larger structures, most notably the megalithic Big Brick with its seventy-two family rooms, communal dining halls, and associated service buildings (bakery, brewery, meat house, etc.). Perhaps the largest building in any American communal settlement, Big Brick was utterly unsuited for private living (as were most colony buildings, to the great inconvenience of later residents) and points instead to a highly ordered and centralized life of communal sharing. Such a form of social organization would have fit nicely with Jansson's apparent taste for personal control of colony affairs.

If communalism was at first employed as a practical plan for the emigration, it nevertheless had its ideological side. The earliest history of Bishop Hill, which appeared in serial form in a local newspaper in 1860, claims that Jansson adopted the notion of Christian communalism at the beginning of his preaching career in 1843.[68] An observer in Sweden confirms that Jansson favored communalism from the start, and Isaksson reports that on the eve of the emigration, Jansson advocated "complete communism" in his essay "A Few Words to God's Congregation."[69] Jansson took his inspiration from Acts 4:34–35: "Neither was there any among them that lacked: for as many as were possessors of lands or houses sold them, and brought the prices of the things that were sold. And laid them down at the apostles' feet: and distribution was made unto every man according as he had need."

The Janssonists present an interesting parallel with the German Pietist groups, including the founders of Ephrata, Zoar, Harmony, and Amana, whose idealization of the apostolic community prompted them to adopt communalism as an expedient for emigration, and who later made communal living a central tenet of faith. Like them, the Janssonists took an interest in other communal groups. For years the colonists carried on a lively economic and cultural intercourse with the Shakers at Pleasant Hill, Kentucky, whose outlook on life they evidently found congenial (a number of them went there after the dissolution).[70] Aside from its religious implications, communalism may have also harkened back to important cooperative aspects of rural life in Sweden; one researcher argues, in fact, that the Janssonists "came from Sweden to return to communal village life."[71]

Why did the communalism of Bishop Hill, whose development paralleled that of groups such as the Inspirationists of nearby Amana, Iowa, come to a relatively abrupt end? Jansson's death proved a setback, but many other groups prospered as communes long after the death of the original leader, and Bishop Hill seemed to do the same in the early 1850s. Perhaps the growing alienation between leaders and members, the dissent over celibacy, and the disagreements concerning economic management can be seen as symptoms of a deeper problem, a loss of common purpose. Two related trends seem to distinguish Bishop Hill from the German settlements. First, the colo-

JON WAGNER

nists increasingly immersed themselves in material pursuits to the apparent detriment of religious concerns. Many colonists and observers seem to agree with Elmen's assessment that "the character of the community began slowly to change from that of poor and pious settlers to reasonably well-off burghers." Even during Jansson's lifetime, a visitor reported that "they now pay less attention to religion and more to industry."[72]

The second, and closely related, trend in the colony was toward a rapid adoption of American ways. Unlike the German communalists who preserved their language as a barrier against the outside, the Bishop Hill colonists began learning English even as they shivered in the dugouts. The Swedish element in colony architecture barely glimmers through the prevailing Greek revival style of mid-nineteenth-century America, and household furnishings had lost their Swedish flavor by the 1860s. The colony maintained a hotel that offered visitors the amenities of a thriving frontier town, and in 1859 they were reportedly considering building a railroad branch to the colony.[73] At the beginning of the Civil War, the colonists must have shocked their German counterparts by mustering a company for the Union army.

Why was Bishop Hill so easily wooed by American culture, as compared with other immigrant communalists who kept it at arm's length, or American communalists who deliberately broke with it? Possibly the answer lies in the fact that the Janssonist movement had formed under very special conditions that were short lived; even Jansson's earliest followers had been together in Sweden only three years, which was not long enough to forge the bonds of identity and commitment that existed among the other immigrant communal sects. If the Janssonists had started earlier, or emigrated later, their ideological commitment might have been more deeply rooted and more resilient. As it was, they had scarcely formed themselves as a society before they found themselves in new circumstances to which the Janssonist religious protest was far less relevant.

The Post-Colony Period

The end of the Bishop Hill commune left a harsh aftermath. Without industry or cash, and unable to pay even the taxes on their shares of the property, many residents moved away, and the population fell to about 200. In neighboring towns the stigma of the colony's nonconformist religious and social doctrines outlived the glory of its material achievements. When Charles Nordhoff came to Bishop Hill to gather material for his book on American communes, he found the community "slowly falling into decay" and the people unwilling to talk about their past.[74] In 1880 Jansson's son claimed that disillusionment with organized religion had placed the majority of Bishop Hill's residents "outside of all congregations."[75] In fact, most of the colonists who remained had not turned away from organized religion, nor had they rejoined the Lutheran Church, as Elmen suggests.[76] Recent studies show that an independent congregation of Adventists continued to meet in the church sanctuary under the leadership of Jonas Olsson, attracting at least sixty-four known former Janssonists. The diehard Janssonists of the procommunal faction seem to have favored this group. Methodism, whose perfectionist teachings are mildly reminiscent of Janssonism, attracted a similar-sized following, while a Swedish Mission Covenant congregation, about which little is known, did about equally well for a time. There was evidently little rivalry between the Adventist and Methodist congregations. The former simply gave way to the latter, as the old hard-core Janssonists sent their children to the Methodist church while they attended the Adventist "Church on the Hill."[77]

Interest in preserving Bishop Hill's unique heritage began as early as 1875, when 3,000 people attended a reunion organized by the newly formed Old Settlers Association.[78] The association was revived in a semicentennial fest in which Jansson's son Eric Johnson shared the podium with John Root, the son of his father's assassin (and the first surviving male child born in Bishop Hill); also in attendance was the aged Jonas Olsson. It was not, however, until the time of the 1946 centennial, when the state of Illinois began to acquire property in the community, that preservation began in earnest. In 1962, after the colony bakery-brewery building was destroyed to enlarge the town softball diamond, the Bishop Hill Heritage Association joined the ranks of the preservationists.

Today the combined efforts of the state of Illinois, the Heritage Association, the Old Settlers Association, and other groups, aided by public and private funding, have made Bishop Hill again a center of cultural life. Seventy-five thousand visitors annually tour restored colony buildings, view the celebrated paintings of colony life by colonist Olof Krans, and enjoy arts and entertainment at seasonal celebrations such as *Jordbruksdagarna*, or Agricultural Days. In 1984 Bishop Hill became officially recognized as a National Historic Landmark. Because of its role in the Swedish emigration and in stimulating debate over social and religious reform, Bishop Hill is perhaps more widely known in Sweden than in America. Many Swedes, including King Carl XVI Gustaf, have visited the site. The government of Sweden, which has contributed to the restoration effort, recently issued a postage stamp commemorating the community. All this might have come as a solace to Jonas Olsson, who wrote in his later years, "It would be a great comfort if we in our old age could be spared witnessing the destruction that has recently threatened us, and if our descendants, after we have gone to our fathers, have nobler things to view when looking back on bygone days than a ruined place intended as a dwelling for the people of God."[79]

Chronology

1808	Eric Jansson is born in Uppland province, Sweden.
1842	Jansson begins preaching to "readers" in Hälsingland, Sweden.
1844	Book burnings; Janssonists become a separatist sect.
1846–55	Janssonists emigrate to Bishop Hill, Ill.
1850	Eric Jansson is assassinated.
1853	Legal incorporation of Bishop Hill under trustees.
1855	Internal dispute over celibacy.
1857	Financial difficulties and accusations of mismanagement.
1861	Formal dissolution of the communal system.
1896	Colony pioneers honored in semicentennial celebration.
1946	Centennial celebration; Bishop Hill becomes a state memorial and restoration begins.
1976	Sweden's King Karl XVI Gustaf visits Bishop Hill.
1984	Bishop Hill recognized as a National Historic Landmark.
1996	Bishop Hill sesquicentennial, in conjunction with Sweden's "Great Migration Sesquicentennial" commemoration.

Notes

1. Silvert Erdahl, *Eric Janson and the Bishop Hill Colony* (Philadelphia: Porcupine Press, 1972; facsimile reprint from *Journal of the Illinois State Historical Society* 28, no. 3 [October 1925]).

2. George M. Stephenson, *The Religious Aspects of the Swedish Immigration* (Minneapolis: University of Minnesota Press, 1932); John E. Norton, "The Causes, Structure and Impact of the Janssonist Emigration from Sweden, 1846–1850," manuscript, Bishop Hill Archives and Research Collection, n.d., Bishop Hill, Ill.

3. Erdahl, *Eric Janson*, pt. 2.

4. Alternative spellings include "Erik Jansson" and "Eric Janson"; the spelling adopted here, except in some titles and quotes, is used by Jansson's American biographer Paul Elmen (see n. 6, below).

5. Michael A. Mikkelsen, *The Bishop Hill Colony: A Religious Communistic Settlement in Henry County, Illinois* (Philadelphia: Porcupine Press; facsimile reprint of series 10, no. 1, of Johns Hopkins Studies in Historical and Political Science, 1892).

6. Paul Elmen, *Wheat Flour Messiah: Eric Jansson of Bishop Hill* (Carbondale: Southern Illinois University Press, 1976), chap. 4; John E. Norton, "The Janssonist Faith," manuscript, Bishop Hill Archives and Research Collection, n.d.

7. Olov Isaksson, *Bishop Hill: A Utopia on the Prairie* (Stockholm: LT Publishing House, 1969), 40.

8. Norton, "Janssonist Faith."

9. Erdahl, *Eric Janson*, pt. 2.

10. Elmen, *Wheat Flour Messiah*, 41.

11. John S. Lindberg, *The Background of the Swedish Immigration* (Chicago: University of

Chicago Press, 1930), and Carolyn Anderson Wilson, "Revitalization, Emigration, and Social Organization: An Ethnohistorical Study of the Bishop Hill Colony, 1846–1861" (honors thesis, Knox College, 1973).

12. Charles H. Nelson, "The Erik Janssonist Movement of Pre-Industrial Sweden," *Sociological Analysis* 38, no. 3 (1977): 209–25. This work is useful for its general discussion of the interplay between social and religious factors in Janssonism.

13. Lindberg, *Background*, 103, 128.

14. Norton, "Causes of Janssonist Emigration" and "This Land Flows with Milk and Honey," manuscript, Bishop Hill Archives and Research Collection, n.d.

15. Wesley Westerberg, trans., "A Letter from Olof Olsson, Follower of Erik Jansson, to his Mother and Loved Ones, December 1845," *Swedish Pioneer Historical Quarterly* 23 (April 1972).

16. Philip J. Stoneberg, "The Bishop Hill Colony," in *History of Henry County, Illinois*, ed. Henry L. Kiner (Chicago: Pioneer, 1910), 630.

17. Carolyn Anderson Wilson, "Revitalization, Emigration, and Social Organization," estimates the total at 1,399; Norton, "Causes of Janssonist Emigration," puts the figure tentatively at 1,311, not counting mortality at sea.

18. John E. Norton, "This Land Flows of Milk and Honey: A Documentary Survey of Pioneering Agriculture at the Swedish Colony of Bishop Hill, Illinois, 1846–1854," manuscript, Bishop Hill Archives and Research Collection, 1972, 4.

19. Mikkelsen, *Bishop Hill Colony*, 30.

20. Ronald E. Nelson, "The Role of Colonies in the Pioneer Settlement of Henry County, Illinois" (Ph.D. diss., University of Nebraska, 1969), 137.

21. See, for example, Larsson's figures in John E. Norton, "'For It Flows with Milk and Honey': Two Immigrant Letters about Bishop Hill," *Swedish Pioneer Historical Quarterly* 24 (July 1973), and Carolyn Anderson Wilson's estimates in "Revitalization, Emigration, and Social Organization," 72.

22. Norton, "'For It Flows with Milk and Honey,'" 166.

23. All references to Larsson's letter are from Norton's translation, ibid.

24. Norton, "Causes of Janssonist Emigration," 35; cf. Carolyn Anderson Wilson, "Revitalization, Emigration, and Social Organization," 72.

25. Norton, "Causes of Janssonist Emigration."

26. Erdahl (*Eric Janson*, 543) claims that Hedström converted between 200 and 300 Janssonists to his Methodist congregation in the fall of 1848, but Carolyn Anderson Wilson ("Revitalization, Emigration, and Social Organization," 72) notes that population figures for Victoria in 1850 make this unlikely.

27. Norton, "This Land Flows of Milk and Honey," 12–13.

28. John E. Norton, "Bishop Hill: The Building of Utopia," manuscript, Bishop Hill Archives and Research Collection, 1972.

29. Carolyn Anderson Wilson, "Revitalization, Emigration, and Social Organization," 72.

30. Stoneberg, "Bishop Hill Colony," 637.

31. Colony Record Book, Bishop Hill Archives and Research Collection.

32. Charles H. Nelson, "Erik Janssonist Movement," 72–76, contrasts this with later Swedish emigration patterns.

33. Carolyn Anderson Wilson, "Revitalization, Emigration, and Social Organization," 66, 86–88.

34. Mikkelsen, *Bishop Hill Colony*, 35, gives a figure of 143, but other cholera mortality estimates range up to 200; see, for example, Elmen, *Wheat Flour Messiah*, 148.

35. Carolyn Anderson Wilson, "Revitalization, Emigration, and Social Organization," 67 and appendix, and Norton, "Causes of Janssonist Emigration," 26.

36. Letter from Britton A. Hill, quoted in Elmen, *Wheat Flour Messiah*, 148; Carolyn Anderson Wilson, "Revitalization, Emigration, and Social Organization," 72.

37. Mikkelsen, *Bishop Hill Colony*, 37.

38. Isaksson, *Bishop Hill*, 85.

39. Norton, "This Land Flows of Milk and Honey," 15, 25.

40. Mikkelsen, *Bishop Hill Colony*, 34.

41. Anonymous "Settler," *Henry County Chronicle*, March 20, 1860.

42. "Colony Charter and By-Laws," as quoted in Mikkelsen, *Bishop Hill Colony*, appendix; "Records and Papers in Custody of E. Hedstrom," preamble to the charter, microfilm, Bishop Hill Archives and Research Collection.

43. Mikkelsen, *Bishop Hill Colony*, 58.

44. Ronald E. Nelson, "Role of Colonies," 154–83, documents in detail the prosperity of this period.

45. Philip J. Stoneberg, translated in J. Hiram Wilson, "Property as a Social Institution in the Bishop Hill Colony: An Ethnohistorical Study" (honors thesis, Knox College, 1973), 35.

46. Mikkelsen, *Bishop Hill Colony*, 35.

47. Norton, "This Land Flows of Milk and Honey," 14.

48. J. Hiram Wilson, "Property as a Social Institution," 64.

49. Population estimates for the late 1850s range from 655 (Stoneberg, "Bishop Hill Colony," 645) to 800 ("The Bishop Hill Colony, Henry County, Illinois," *Revue Icarienne*, February 1, 1859).

50. Although most colony buildings have been restored, Big Brick was destroyed by fire in 1928.

51. "Anders Wiberg's Account of a Trip to the United States in 1852–1853," *Swedish Pioneer Historical Quarterly* 29 (April 1978).

52. Mikkelsen, *Bishop Hill Colony*, 58.

53. Translated in J. Hiram Wilson, "Property as a Social Institution," 35.

54. Lilly Setterdahl, "Emigrant Letters by Bishop Hill Colonists from Nora Parish," *Western Illinois Regional Studies* 1 (1978): 121–75.

55. Philip Stoneberg's interview with J. P. Chaiser (September 28, 1908), Knox College Archives, Galesburg, Ill.

56. Mikkelsen, *Bishop Hill Colony*, 62.

57. For example, Erdahl, *Eric Janson*, 62, and Elmen, *Wheat Flour Messiah*, 200.

58. "Records and Papers in the Custody of E. Hedstrom," microfilm, Bishop Hill Heritage Association Archives and Research Collection.

59. Ibid.

60. Mikkelsen, *Bishop Hill Colony*, 630.

61. "Settler," *Henry County Chronicle*, April 16, 1860.

62. Hiram Bigelow's *The Bishop Hill Colony*, Transactions of the Illinois State Historical Society, no. 7 (1902), contains a detailed account of the Bishop Hill court case.

63. Norton, "Causes of Janssonist Emigration," addendum.

64. Isaksson, *Bishop Hill*, 123–26.

65. For example, Ernst Olson, an anti-Janssonist, examines and rejects evidence such as that cited above, in his *History of the Swedes of Illinois* (Chicago: Engberg-Holmberg, 1908), 221–22.

66. Setterdahl, "Emigrant Letters."

67. "Settler," *Henry County Chronicle*, April 16, 1860.

68. Ibid., January 24, 1960. The anonymous writer (a county resident but not a Janssonist) was seemingly well acquainted with many details of colony history but does not discuss the sources of his information. His evident sympathy with the Janssonists, together

with his dislike of communalism, may lend a degree of credibility to this statement.

69. Isaksson, *Bishop Hill*, 55.

70. Elmen, *Wheat Flour Messiah*, 163.

71. Carolyn Anderson Wilson, "Revitalization, Emigration, and Social Organization," 91.

72. Elmen, *Wheat Flour Messiah*, 126–27.

73. *Revue Icarienne*.

74. Charles Nordhoff, *The Communistic Societies of the United States: From Personal Visit and Observation* (New York: Harper and Bros., 1875; reprint, New York: Dover, 1966), 348–49.

75. Erdahl, *Eric Janson*, 571.

76. Elmen, *Wheat Flour Messiah*, 178.

77. Eric Miller, "Janssonism and Post-Janssonist Religion in Bishop Hill" (honors thesis, Knox College, 1986), gives a detailed analysis and offers membership statistics that support the similar conclusions reached independently by Lilly Setterdahl, "The End of Eric Jansonism: Religious Life in Bishop Hill in the Post-Colony Period," *Western Illinois Regional Studies* 11 (1988).

78. University of Illinois, Department of Urban and Regional Planning, "Historic Bishop Hill: Preservation and Planning" (UP 320 Class Report, summer 1976).

79. Isaksson, *Bishop Hill*, 154.

Selected Bibliography

Elmen, Paul. *Wheat Flour Messiah: Eric Jansson of Bishop Hill*. Carbondale: Southern Illinois University Press, 1976.

Isaksson, Olov. *Bishop Hill: A Utopia on the Prairie*. Photographs by Soren Hallgren. Stockholm: LT Publishing House, 1969.

Mikkelsen, Michael A. *The Bishop Hill Colony: A Religious Communistic Settlement in Henry County, Illinois*. Philadelphia: Porcupine Press, 1972. Reprint of series 10, no. 1, of Johns Hopkins Studies in Historical and Political Science, 1892.

Swank, George. *Bishop Hill, Swedish-American Showcase: History of the Bishop Hill Colony*. Galva, Ill.: Galvaland Press, 1987.

———. *Painter Krans: OK of Bishop Hill*. Galva, Ill.: Galvaland Press, 1976. Both works by Swank are distributed by Bishop Hill Heritage Association, P.O. Box 1853, Bishop Hill, IL 61419.

Wagner, Jon, "Living in Community: Daily Life in the Bishop Hill Colony." *Western Illinois Regional Studies* 12 (Fall 1989): 2.

Film and Video

Bishop Hill. 1979. Film distributed by Bishop Hill Heritage Association, P.O. Box 1853, Bishop Hill, IL 61419.

The Building of Utopia: Work and the Workplace in Bishop Hill. 1988. Video distributed by Bishop Hill Heritage Association, P.O. Box 1853, Bishop Hill, IL 61419.

JON WAGNER

GERTRUDE E. HUNTINGTON

Living in the Ark

Four Centuries of Hutterite
Faith and Community

The low rays of the late afternoon sun emphasize the contrast between the deep snow and the black suit and long dark dress of the minister and his wife as he leads the way along a straight, neatly shoveled concrete walk between the uniform living houses to the building in which evening service (*Gebet*) is held. Doors open from each apartment, and the family clusters follow the minister. As they enter the large, orderly, unadorned room, the family members separate—each to occupy his or her God-given place, determined by the age-sex hierarchy of colony life. No bell calls the Hutterites to worship. Centuries of tradition, a lifetime of colony living, and a consciousness of submitting to the collective will all contribute to the seemingly spontaneous assembling for evening prayer that takes place each day in almost 400 Hutterite colonies scattered across the plains states and prairie provinces.

A vigorous, growing population of communards, the Hutterites combine unchanging religious beliefs and changeless social structure with flexible utilization of modern technology and economic adaptability.[1] Within the marketplace each Hutterite colony is a corporation, well adapted to our modern capitalistic economy. In contrast, within the corporation everything is owned communally, "no one shall have any private possessions," and each one "gives and surrenders himself . . . with all that he has and is able to do."[2] "No one . . . seeks his own advantage or wants to live a selfish life. Instead, each one lives for the others."[3] In contemporary terminology, "Each and

319

Concrete walks often connect single-family dwellings and community buildings in Hutterite colonies called *bruderhofs*. Barrels at the corner of each house collect rain water. The large silo suggests the massive agricultural and livestock endeavors that sustain the economies of nearly 400 Hutterite colonies.

every member of said corporation shall give and devote all his or her time, labor, services, earnings and energies to the said corporation, and the purposes for which it is formed, freely, voluntarily and without compensation or reward of any kind whatsoever, other than herein expressed."[4] Fringe benefits have been worked out long ago, and no energy is wasted discussing wages.

The Hutterites, with a history of more than four and a half centuries, are the oldest family communal group in the Western world. Given the difficulty of living "in Community," this is a remarkable achievement.[5] Equally unusual, and of particular interest to the student of developmental communalism, is the Hutterite ability, virtually unique, to reestablish a total community of goods after communalism had been lost. Contemporary Hutterites are in their third period of communalism, having abandoned community in favor of individual ownership for about seventy years in the eighteenth century (1693–1763) and for forty years in the nineteenth century (1818–59).[6] Their population has fluctuated from over 20,000 while living in Moravia, down to 19 individuals in Transylvania, to perhaps 1,000 in Russia, to 443 when they first settled in colonies in North America. By 1995 the Hutterites had a population of approximately 36,000[7] living in about 390 colonies. With the exception of the Roman Catholic religious orders, the Hutterites exceed in numbers

GERTRUDE E. HUNTINGTON

and wealth all other communally organized movements in the history of North America.

To what can the endurance of the Hutterite movement be ascribed? Of course no single, simple answer suffices. The various explanations reflect the background and worldview of the individual making the interpretation. A Hutterite could perceive God's purpose in a period of growth, peace, and plenty in the following way: "God granted his people quiet times and rich blessings. . . . This he did to see how they would prove themselves in such times and to make sure that his work and plans would be publicly carried out and become known to all people far and wide."[8] A secular historian could try to give the "reasons" for this prosperity without understanding the event as "revealed truth" showing the Lord's work and plans.[9] The spiritual Hutterite would *know* how God was working in history; the contemporary academic would *examine* the economic, geographic, and sociological forces at work to explain the growth. It is difficult for intellectually trained, scientifically oriented, highly individualist people of the twentieth century to understand the thought processes that led to the founding of the Hutterites and which, to a remarkable degree the Hutterites have been able to maintain to this day. Yet in order to explain their longevity and their economic strength one must comprehend what motivates them to aspire to a way of life most contemporary westerners consider austere and severely circumscribed.

Institutionalization of Community of Goods and the Written Word

The Hutterites or Hutterian Brethren arose during a period of great social, political, and economic upheaval. During the turn of the sixteenth century, Sir Thomas More published his *Utopia* (1516), Martin Luther pounded his ninety-five theses on the Wittenberg church door (1517), Erasmus settled in Basel (1521), Zwingli became the Great Minister in Zurich (1519), and in 1536 John Calvin published his *Institutes of the Christian Religion*. The Peasant War erupted (1524–26), and the Turks captured Belgrade in 1521 and defeated Hungary in 1529. Peasants were deserting the land, cities were growing, and capitalism was on the rise.

At a meeting in Zurich, Switzerland, in 1525 George Blaurock, a former priest, asked Conrad Grebel "to baptize him with true Christian baptism." This Anabaptist act repudiated infant baptism and allegiance to a state church. It made faith a matter of personal, voluntary commitment. Hutterites believe this baptism on the confession of faith "was the beginning of separation from the world and its evil ways."[10] As participants in the radical left wing of the

Reformation, the Hutterites hold theological positions making them the most radical of the Anabaptists.[11] They not only renounce infant baptism and all warfare but also believe Christians should neither judge those outside the Christian community nor physically resist evil, because judgment and punishment are God's prerogatives. Voluntary adult baptism symbolizes, for the Hutterites, the individual's separation from the world, which they believe is a precondition for holding all goods in common and therefore a precondition for living in community, which is required of all true Christians.

Community of goods is so central to Hutterite faith that they date their beginning to 1528, when they instituted communal sharing. At that time about 200 adults attempting to flee persecution crossed Moravia, a region of central Czechoslovakia. This rootless band of wanderers "took counsel together in the Lord because of their immediate need and distress and appointed servants for temporal affairs. . . . These [servants] then spread out a cloak in front of the people, and each one laid his possessions on it with a willing heart— without being forced—so that the needy might be supported in accordance with the teaching of the prophets and apostles."[12] Thus, occasioned by necessity and the first-century Christian communal precedent, these earliest Hutterites made community of goods a vital part of their way of life and a sacred tenet of their faith.[13]

Community of goods for its own sake is not a Hutterite goal. Living communally is an outcome of a belief in brotherly love and of submitting oneself completely and obediently to the will of God. "Our community way of life is not an invention or a social system devised by the Hutterians, nor is it always to our liking to live this life," wrote Montana Hutterites in 1963. "But herein we have no choice. If Christ is our Savior, then we must obey his teachings and follow in his footsteps as He taught."[14] The earliest Hutterite *Ordnung* or church discipline (1529) emphasized the absolute yieldingness required of each convert: all material goods, all gifts from God, one's life and limb, must be surrendered to God and the church. Each member must submit to discipline by the group and by God, accepting all discipline with joy, thanks, and patience.[15] Complete submission is still taught. A recent reprint of a 1906 tract, "How Admission is Made to the Hutterite Church and Congregation of the Godly," states in the first article, "Into this Community [the Church of Christ] we are brought into true submission: that is, into the spiritual Ark of Noah, in which we can be preserved."[16] In 1966 a Hutterite minister wrote, "In this ark of Noah's you surrender everything."[17] Total submission is necessary because the group is considered to be more important than the individual.[18] The group must be preserved because one cannot be truly Christian or honor God properly unless one lives in community.[19] Only within such a community can the individual achieve everlasting life.[20] However, unlike many Christian groups personal salvation is not stressed; rather, salvation is the natural climax of a lifetime shared with one's brethren in obedience and submission to God and the community.

The basic religious beliefs, ceremonial observances, and social organization of the Hutterites were thoroughly developed, implemented, and put into print within thirteen years of the founding of the church.[21] Jakob Hutter, after whom the movement is named, inspired and oversaw the early development before his martyrdom in 1536. Hutter is particularly remembered for his missionary labors and his skillful leadership in enforcing the practice of community of goods among new converts.[22] Letters to various colonies still survive.[23] The sixteenth-century *Confession of Faith* clearly and simply explained the Hutterites' worldview, their daily activities, and the biblical faith that still underlies their communal life in the United States and Canada.[24] Everyone could easily understand Hutterite teachings regardless of whether they were recent converts, resident founders of new Hutterite colonies, authorities who imprisoned Hutterians, clergy who attempted to dissuade them from their radicalism, or the landed gentry who might either hire them or banish them. Hutterite flexibility in what they considered nonessential areas of belief and practice, such as keeping Sunday rather than some other holy day, aided in their being tolerated by the outside society.[25]

Though the Hutterite social system and way of life were institutionalized in the sixteenth century, religious expression remained spontaneous, vigorous, and widespread among members. Anyone in prison might write hymns, send letters back to the colony, and create confessions of faith with their answers to interrogation.[26] Sermons were biblical, varied, and inspired. An able servant of the Word "preached the Gospel with power . . . [even] though he did not know the alphabet."[27] In contrast, a century later, after religious expression had become ritualized and sermons were generally read, a servant of the Gospel was "relieved of the service at his request because of his weak eyesight."[28]

During the golden years of the Hutterite movement from 1565–91, a generation of believers grew up in the relative safety of the large Moravian communities. Some of the economically diversified Hutterite colonies in Moravia and Hungary were said to have more than 1,000 inhabitants, though 450 may be a realistic average.[29] The accommodation of large numbers in the communal Hutterite *bruderhofs* became possible because they included converts from nearly every profession and trade practiced in the sixteenth century. Although professionals and a few petty nobles joined the Hutterites, the majority joining were farmers and artisans.[30] According to a 1569 description of the church, "All sorts of honest, useful trades were represented: those of mason, scythesmith, blacksmith, coppersmith, locksmith, clock maker, cutler, plumber, tanner, furrier, cobbler, saddler, harness maker, bag maker, wagon maker, blanket maker, weaver, rope maker, sieve maker, glazier, potter, beer brewer, barber-surgeon, and physician."[31] The Hutterites were skilled metalworkers, created high-quality pottery that is now found in many European museums, and produced excellent linen.

The variety of adherents and the apprentice system within the *bruderhof* or communal colony contributed to the Hutterites' economic strength. Communal sharing involving both community of production and community of consumption encouraged the development of a meritocracy. For unlike much of European feudal society and the sixteenth-century guild system, social status did not dictate one's contribution. One's natural ability or God-given grace determined one's role in the community. The well-run, highly rational enterprises supported the Hutterite population and served as solid economic assets for their protectors among the landed nobility.

The second generation of Hutterites coming to maturity in these prosperous communal surroundings had not experienced the stress and excitement of the founding years and needed the strengthened commitment that could be stimulated by an intimate knowledge of the original cost of forming the Hutterite church separate from the world. Partly to serve this need, the Hutterites began documenting their own history in the 1560s.[32] A century later, massive amounts of primary material had been collected in a manuscript known as *Das grosse Geschichtsbuch* in German and as the Great Chronicle in English. Personal correspondence and accounts of torture and prison confessions as well as community records, disciplines, appointments, and excommunications compose this invaluable record of Hutterite history.[33] In documents as late as 1665, this chronicle graphically illustrated to young Hutterites, by simple, eyewitness accounts, how God worked in history through the dedication of his chosen people and how the Hutterite communities strove to live as obedient Christians separate from, but physically within, a sinful world. The personal detail recorded simply and without sentimentality or embellishment enabled the readers to identify with the struggling, yet spiritually joyful brethren. The "private side of history" is preserved by accurate historians who can be master storytellers.

The Great Chronicle reveals a world distinctly divided between good and evil, God and Satan, eternal and temporal, spiritual and carnal, the church and the world, and Hutterites and non-Hutterites. One is either in the ark or not in the ark. Over the centuries this dualistic approach has enabled the Hutterites to think differently about affairs inside the community of believers

GERTRUDE E. HUNTINGTON

from matters involving the outside world of unbelievers. Thus, throughout their long history, they continue socially and religiously traditional, submissive to the authority of their own group, which they see as the eternal kingdom of God. Simultaneously, they are assertive and progressive in economic matters and in their dealings with the transitory, secular world. Herein lies one of the secrets of the vitality and longevity of their movement. From their perspective it is not inconsistent for present-day Hutterite colonies to raise pigs in automated, air-conditioned barns while colonists use outhouses.[34]

In the sixteenth century the controversy between the Hutterites and the world centered around five articles of faith: (1) adult baptism, which undermined the state church; (2) celebrating the Lord's Supper only with fellow members of Christ's body in remembrance of his death, thereby ritually negating a state church; (3) community of goods, which altered the individual's relationship to his family, the feudal lords, the guilds, and the city-state; (4) governing authority, rejection of oaths, rejection of war, and rejection of participating in government but including a willingness to pay all tithes and taxes that did not support war; and (5) the separation of believing and nonbelieving marriage partners, which was seen as undermining the family.[35] The five ideological tenets were religious in nature but had political implications that threatened those holding secular power. During the 1570s these five articles of faith were formulated into a book that affirmed the brotherhood and their criticism of the world. The mood of the *Great Article Book* is reflected in its full title: *A Beautiful, Joyful Book Containing a Number of the Main Articles of Our Christian Faith, Made by Compiling Much Godly Evidence; Also How the World has Perverted [The Christian Faith] and Lives and Strives Against It.*[36] The *Great Article Book*, the Great Chronicle, Riedemann's *Confession of Faith*, early baptismal sermons, and the school discipline of 1568 were important elements in the institutionalization of the Hutterites and continue to be influential today.[37] This early literature dealt with the theme of a church of communards, purified, obedient, and loving, who separated themselves from a sinful, antagonistic, violent world.

Although the major institutionalization took place during the sixteenth century, the intellectual development of the Hutterites continued to be influenced by the surrounding culture.[38] There was constant intellectual interaction with the dominant society, and missionaries recruited a steady stream of converts for the growing church.[39] After the Hutterites were expelled from Moravia in 1622, missionary activity declined sharply.

During the leadership of Andreas Ehrenpreis (*Vorsteher* [elder], 1639–62), in addition to many church disciplines and exhorting letters, between 200 and 300 sermons were written and preserved.[40] These sermons, which minis-

Hutterite society is strongly patriarchal. Couples, like this husband and wife, marry for life and usually raise large families.

ters read in church services today, are the basis of the ritualization of religious expression and the institutionalization of a way of thinking. Several teachings on child rearing, for example, reflect prevalent seventeenth-century European attitudes.[41] In other ways, too, the Hutterites still think as seventeenth-century Europeans; the Enlightenment barely touched them, and Descartes and Freud did not inform their outlook. Part of the impetus behind the formation of a center, almost a seminary for preachers, and the production of church disciplines and sermons was a desire to stem the decline the church experienced during and after the banishment from Moravia.[42] These sermons have played a crucial role in the survival of the Hutterite movement.[43]

In Russia, Johannes Waldner (*Vorsteher*, 1794–1824) also tried to fight spiritual decline with the written word. He compiled the *Klein-Geschichtsbuch der Hutterischen Brüder* (*The Small Chronicle of the Hutterian Brethren*), in which he summarized their early history, bringing the record to 1802.[44] He included various sermons (mostly from the Ehrenpreis period), church disciplines, and contemporary descriptions of Hutterite life in Russia. Johannes Waldner revived the time-honored custom of reading sermons. He carefully collected old sermons. Hutterites consider these sermons equivalent to Scripture and therefore part of God.[45] Although Waldner's efforts did not prevent the loss of community of goods, his work did contribute to the reestablishment of communalism among the Hutterites.

GERTRUDE E. HUNTINGTON

Since migrating to North America in 1874, the Hutterites have printed and photocopied some of their old handwritten sermons, confessions of faith, epistles, church disciplines, hymnals, and histories.[46] They have reproduced some of their German School pedagogical material used by the children to copy and memorize. Even though there is easy access to photocopying on the colony, the children are taught the old Gothic script and spend hours making beautifully written copies of hymns, sermons, and stories from their history. The Hutterites have also written a few books describing and sometimes defending their beliefs and culture.[47]

As with many religious movements the written word is a major uniting factor. Memorized prayers, hymns, and oft-repeated stories and sermons are an integral part of the socialization process that continues throughout each Hutterite's entire life. Beginning in infancy they memorize their literature. Although referred to as the written word, Hutterite writing is in the oral tradition. The words are to be spoken aloud, listened to, and shared. On Saturday evening, which functionally is the beginning of the Hutterian Sunday, colony residents gather and tell stories from the Great or Small Chronicles or from old sermons or hymns. Hutterite literature is social, written not for scholars—not to impress—but to explain, to inform, and to be enjoyed communally. The shared word is available to everyone and contributes to their collective sense of identity, an identity that includes the past, the period of the martyrs, and the present colony. Words, like spirit, can belong to eternity. Hutterites believe material objects decay, but the word of truth is incorruptible.[48]

From the Edge of Society to the Loss of Community

The Hutterites' belief in living separate from the world, and the persecution this often precipitated, led them to niches on the "edge" of society. Centuries ago in Moravia a symbiotic relationship evolved between the Hutterites and the Moravian landed nobles. Both strove to maintain themselves politically and economically independent of larger governing units. When the Hutterites migrated to the Ukraine in 1770, they settled on recently acquired lands that were underdeveloped and on the edge of Russian territory. In North America the Hutterites formed their first colony (Bon Homme) in 1874 in the remote Dakota Territory, now southeastern South Dakota. Even in modern times their colonies in the United States and Canada occupy the sparsely populated fringes of agriculturally productive regions. Some of the newest colonies are being established farther and farther north, or on pockets of good soil in poorer agricultural regions.[49] Religiously, politically, and economically the Hutterites are most successful when interaction with the larger society exists on a limited basis.[50]

Historically a variety of circumstances caused Hutterites to temporarily abandon community of goods. During the first decade of their existence in the early 1500s, roving groups of banished Hutterites were sometimes refused all provisions, even water, by the local population. To survive they had to break up into groups of eight or ten.[51] Even when physically separated from their communal coreligionists, however, they had no desire to establish individual ownership, and their sense of community and interdependence was maintained by a network of traveling servants (ministers). Thus, their loss of community was temporary and superficial. In spite of the severe persecution throughout the early years, missionary zeal and spiritual commitment rapidly brought in new converts. Imprisonment and public executions advertised Hutterite beliefs. During the years in Moravia, missionary activity continued, and persecution, though limited, remained a threat. However, as persecution declined during the good years (1554–64) and the golden years (1565–91), the Hutterites experienced a concomitant decline in the intense, personal dedication that had characterized the earliest years.

Converts swelled Hutterite ranks, but not always for purely religious reasons or with a strong desire to live communally and to work hard for the common good. The Great Chronicle records that "several hundred people from Switzerland joined the community. Many had been forced to move because of the famine, but they wanted to accept the faith and change their lives. We took them in with this same hope and agreed to try it with them."[52] Later, "There was a steady increase in the number of the indolent who apparently had united with the Church from a desire to live off the fruit of the hard work of others, rather than from religious conviction."[53] One seventeenth-century Hutterite minister complained, "This excellent practice of community of goods has brought forth many lazy people. . . . There is no diligence nor conscientiousness such as there was formerly."[54] As individual commitment waned, *Ordnungen*, written church disciplines, became even more necessary. Members were assigned certain amounts of work but began asking if they could use extra time beyond their community obligation to work for personal interest. Those who labored away from the community for wages were tempted by supplementary jobs and individual pay. Some who worked as personal servants for the petty nobles violated Hutterite practice by dressing in worldly fashion. The faithful concluded that "since the descendants of the Hutterian Brotherhood had . . . fallen away and not walked faithfully in the light of the Gospel, God finally withdrew from them his light and grace."[55]

GERTRUDE E. HUNTINGTON

In addition to a loss of spiritual zeal, the Hutterite colonies were subjected to devastation, and their residents to torture at the hands of marauding armies and bandits during the Thirty Years' War. Men, women, and children were carried off into slavery. Hutterite sisters were forced to travel with the armies as camp prostitutes.[56] The Great Chronicle vividly states, "So we lost our community at Farkeschin. Everything was gone—people and goods and chattels."[57] Famine gripped the lands, and the large colony storehouses and barns of the nonresistant Hutterites were plundered and torched.[58] The Hutterites were utterly ruined, having lost members, buildings, and resources. Finally, "Compelled by the greatest poverty it was ordered that everyone should pay for himself."[59]

Thus all Hutterites abandoned community of goods in the late seventeenth century, the first colony in Hungary in 1684, the last in Transylvania in 1695.[60] Though unable to practice their belief in the principle of communal living, their movement continued. In spite of severe pressure to convert to Catholicism, they clung to the essentials of their radical Christian faith and functioned as congregations for half a century.[61] However, by 1762 all but nineteen of the Hutterites had converted, at least nominally, to Catholicism.[62] Community of goods was reestablished in 1763 when the movement was revitalized by a small influx of converts. Seven years later, in 1770, sixty communal Hutterites immigrated to the Russian Ukraine.

The situation in Russia that led the Hutterites to abandon community of goods a half-century later (by 1818) was quite different from that of Central Europe. The Hutterites in Russia were not persecuted. In fact, "the government was friendly to them because of their honesty and was happy for the work of the congregation."[63] During the first generation the community developed many trades and established itself on a firm economic basis. The members were thankful for peace and worked diligently. There was some internal disagreement over religious matters, but using the Great Chronicle as an authoritative source, innovation was rejected. Two dissenting members wanted to modify some of the religious practices, advocating a return to missionary activity and the establishment of new communities. Both suggestions were rejected, and eventually the men left the colony.[64]

Isolation characterized the Hutterite community in the Ukraine. Except for the fifty-six former Hutterites who joined them by 1784 and contact with their Mennonite neighbors after moving to the southern section of the Ukraine in 1842, the Hutterites experienced complete isolation from the German-speaking world. They carried on no missionary activity.[65] They had little social or intellectual interaction with their Russian neighbors, and no Hutterite literature was translated into Russian.[66] Consequently, no Russians were converted. To insure spiritual purity and separation from the world, workshop supervisors saw that the young brethren read the Bible on Sundays and holidays; they were forbidden to read newspapers and worldly books.[67] A few individuals who joined in the mid-nineteenth century were neighboring Mennonites.[68]

Peace and prosperity in the Ukraine brought the Hutterites problems similar to those plaguing some other communal religious movements that also prospered economically while weakening spiritually.[69] As the second generation of Hutterites in Russia assumed leadership positions, "selfishness, self-interest and dishonesty grew in the congregation, chiefly among the foremen in the handicrafts."[70] "The fields and meadows were in prosperous condition, however, the work was preferably done by hired servants from among the neighboring Russians."[71] The lack of all but routine economic interaction led to social and intellectual stagnation. Colonists were fearful of establishing new communities, and as their population increased, they did not have enough land. They rented a tract of land from the government that yielded a nice income for the congregation as long "as it was supervised by true and faithful brethren." But foremen did not turn in money, only accounts. They were careless in their supervision; outside help was hired, a practice that often proves destructive of communal enterprise. The Hutterite congregation deteriorated into poverty and "fell into disrepute and was even disregarded by many of its own members." A move to new lands in 1802 did not improve the situation. The two leading ministers continued to disagree, the older wanting to strengthen community of goods, the younger wanting to abolish community. After a very difficult period community of goods was dissolved, although a fairly strong community structure remained.[72] The emotion accompanying this development can be sensed from a short sentence in a list of baptisms: "Dec. 26, 1820—Jacob Walter baptized the following [four women]. These were the first so baptized after community living ceased and through him destroyed."[73]

The Hutterite experiences in Central Europe and Russia from the seventeenth to the nineteenth centuries raise questions concerning the relation of community of goods to spiritual commitment, economic prosperity, and external resistance and persecution. In Europe the Hutterites suffered physical loss of members (through murder, capture, and imprisonment), loss of buildings, and loss of produce. They were assaulted by efforts to convert them to the state religion. In Russia the Hutterites were free from external attack, both physical and intellectual, but they were so inward-looking and isolated from stimulation that they stagnated, lost enthusiasm for their unique way of life, became fearful of anything new, and finally declined into poverty. Because it

GERTRUDE E. HUNTINGTON

is so difficult for most individuals to live in a sharing community, breakdown of community of goods is generally attributed to spiritual decline. However, it is not clear whether the loss of community results from spiritual decline or if the decline in dedication and morale is only one aspect of general decline. Religious commitment can enable a community to flourish under seemingly impossible conditions. Low morale can lead to degeneration no matter how comfortably community members live. Internal and external factors interact to induce abandonment of community. In the Hutterite movement, external circumstances were probably more important in Europe; internal decline in vigor was more significant in Russia.

Community of Goods Regained

During periods of individual ownership the Hutterites never abandoned their belief that community of goods was a tenet of their religion. The Hutterite movement possessed sufficient content, strength, and flexibility to keep its teachings alive. Even after the Hutterites abandoned Christian communalism for individual ownership in Europe and Russia, their church congregations continued, and many of the cooperative aspects of community were maintained. In both Central Europe and Russia the Hutterites were living in foreign lands.[74] Therefore, there existed a natural ethnic and cultural barrier that reinforced their group identity and protected their requirement that members marry within the church. In Central Europe when they gave up community of goods the Hutterites did not move from their communal colonies. In Russia they moved as a congregation, not as individual families. In both instances much of their social structure remained intact.

Furthermore, as mentioned earlier, the written word has been of unusual significance in maintaining group identity. Unlike the theological expositions of many religious groups, Hutterite literature is primarily communication with the beloved brotherhood: it is for the edification of all members. The hymns, letters, confessions of faith, sermons, and *Ordnungen* are clear, concrete, logical, and personal. A great many of their beliefs and history have been recorded in hymns, some with over 100 verses.[75] These hymns are memorized in their entirety by the children from kindergarten through Sunday School, and adults (especially women) continue to memorize hymns and sing them as they work. Hymns are much easier to commit to memory than any other religious material, so they form an excellent vehicle for internalizing Hutterite history and religious doctrine.[76] During the periods of individual ownership, members continued to sing the old hymns in the church services and listen to the traditional sermons being read. Thus the importance of community of goods continued to be preached even though it was not being practiced.

After sixty years of private ownership the reestablishment of communal living among the Hutterites of Transylvania came about in 1763 for three discernible reasons. First, the members still maintained a tightly knit congregation that read the old sermons and books and sang the traditional hymns. Second, a group of Lutheran exiles from Carinthia converted to Hutterite teachings. With the zeal of new converts, these Carinthians awakened the congregation to the imperative in the old Hutterite writings that demanded that true Christians must hold all things in common.[77] In 1763 the congregation responded by ordaining ministers, starting a school, and establishing a communal kitchen. Members stopped working for outsiders and began earning a good income from spinning and weaving linens. The third factor pushing them back to communalism was the great pressure upon the Hutterites to embrace Catholicism. In their attempt to eradicate the brotherhood, authorities sent Hutterites to prison and to different parts of Transylvania. When these attempts failed, the Jesuits planned to put all the children in an orphanage and banish their parents. Before this could be done, the community, consisting of sixteen "old" Hutterites and fifty-one Carinthian Hutterites, fled over the mountains into Wallachia, in present-day Romania. The "rite of passage" of the migration and the need for cooperation in establishing a new community in a new region fused the small group together and made obvious the advantages, practical as well as spiritual, of community of goods.

The situation was quite different in Russia, where there was never any external persecution. Individual ownership had not kept the congregation from further deterioration. Members were poverty stricken both temporally and spiritually. They gave up their school for the only time in Hutterite history, and a generation reached adulthood who were illiterate. With insufficient acreage to support their growing population, they petitioned the government for permission to move to new lands. This was denied, but a compassionate and able Mennonite who was a government official agreed to sponsor them. Moving the Hutterites in 1842 to land in the southern Ukraine near the Mennonite settlements, Cornies demanded total Hutterite compliance. He required the ninety-one Hutterite children to attend village school. An equal number of adults requested a teacher for evening classes.[78] Adolescents and young adults were placed on Mennonite farms to learn modern farming practices. Other Hutterite young people were required to go to various Mennonite villages to learn trades. In contrast to the isolation they had experienced for seventy years, they were now in contact with a thriving, German-speaking community of about 6,000. The Hutterites maintained their own church congregation, dress style, and dialect, and although they lived in individual family dwelling units, they had their own village. In ten years the Hutterites had made sufficient economic progress to found a second village, though not without considerable internal disunity over the matter. During the next fourteen years they formed three more villages. The fear of branching and other innovations that had characterized their first seventy years in Russia had been somewhat overcome.

Hutterite experiences since 1818 had made clear to them that individual ownership also has its limitations and tribulations. Some individual Hutterites began to be concerned that they were not living in common ownership as their forefathers did. The strict community teachings of their forefathers were being preached, and they possessed many books on community life, in which it was pointed out that the only way of salvation and the only way to combat the weakness or faults of their congregations was through community ownership.[79]

Many problems remained to be solved, however, and various attempts at community of goods failed. "The women especially showed very little interest in common living." One member, Michael Waldner, had a vision of heaven and hell. During his trance he was asked "Can you tell me whether any person was saved from the Great Flood besides those in the ark? . . . The ark is the *Gemeinschaft* of the Holy Spirit to which you no longer belong."[80] Religious experiences like this are unusual among the pragmatic Hutterites but are related occasionally in the Great Chronicle and undoubtedly strengthened Waldner in the difficult task of reestablishing communal living. Confidence in his vision is evidenced by his being chosen servant of the Word, or minister. He and his fellow preacher, Jakob Hofer, prayed "from their innermost heart to God that he might help them by his grace to carry out the intended enterprise in the right fashion and with the right spirit."[81] The two ministers accepted each other into a *Gemeinschaft* and also accepted their wives. Then they invited the brethren to join the community of goods they had reinstituted. In this way in 1853 the Schmiedeleut, one of the three endogamous Hutterite groups in the United States and Canada today, came into being.[82] By 1870 when the Russian government decided to withdraw special privileges from the German minority, there were two congregations of about sixteen families each practicing community of goods. Faced with the prospect of loss of their own schools and mandatory military service, the Hutterites decided, once again, to migrate.

Religious freedom and the availability of land recommended North America as a place for relocation for German dissidents living in Russia. In 1873 two Hutterite leaders traveled to North America to look at land and evaluate

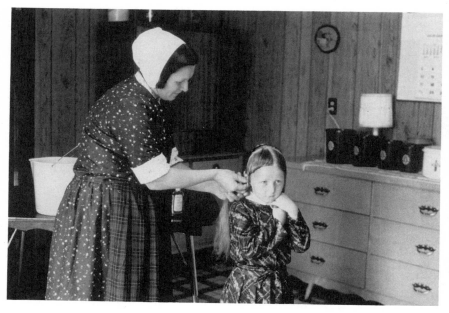

A Hutterite mother carefully arranges her daughter's hair in the traditional way.

the political climate. They met personally with President Ulysses Grant and petitioned him for fifty years of freedom from military obligation and inquired about living in colonies, having their own schools and their own local government, and whether or not they could be free from oath taking, office-holding, jury service, and the requirement to vote. They received the reply that most of these matters were under the control of the specific states, and the president could not exempt them from state laws or from military obligations. However, the president replied, "for the next fifty years we will not be entangled in another war in which military service will be necessary." [83]

In 1874 the first of 1,267 Hutterites emigrated from Russia to the United States. Land was available for both private and communal ownership. All but 443 decided to accept the terms of the Homestead Act of 1862 and become individual family farmers. Three congregations decided to remain true to the communal tenet of their faith and established colonies in the region that became South Dakota. The Schmiedeleut founded the first: Bon Homme Colony, in Bon Homme County on the Missouri River in 1874. The Darius-leut settled at Wolf Creek in 1875. The Lehrerleut, who did not become communal until reaching America, began its first *bruderhof* at Elmspring in 1877. Thus amicably freed from both Russian coercion and influence from fellow Hutterites who did not want to live communally, communalism was firmly

GERTRUDE E. HUNTINGTON

reestablished. The three colonies started by the original 443 Russian immigrants have grown, 120 years later, into almost 400 colonies in the United States and Canada, with an estimated 36,000 inhabitants.[84]

The importance of migration to the reestablishment of community cannot be overemphasized. In both the eighteenth and nineteenth centuries, community of goods was consolidated in the process of community building in a new environment where there was little incentive and little opportunity to return to individual ownership. In a sense, the process developed by the Hutterites in America of constantly branching to found daughter colonies as their rapidly expanding populations reach 110 or so constitutes "minor migrations" from the point of view of the individuals involved. Each generation has at least one experience of being a part of a small, intimate group that goes forth, that migrates to a new location and builds, together, a new community.[85] The experience of beginning a new community reinforces the innate sense of personal control that is a significant aspect of the Hutterite ability to maintain and to reestablish community. The renewal of communal and religious zeal stimulated by this procedure and the slight changes that may occur in practices in the new colony are undoubtedly reasons why Hutterites in the last century have found it possible to sustain the vigor of their movement within a communal framework.

It might appear paradoxical that a belief in the superiority of the community over the individual should result in strong individuals. However, Hutterites, although they believe in an all-powerful God who has a plan for everything, are not fatalistic. They are fiercely individualistic in that they strongly believe that each person has the freedom to decide whether or not to belong to or stay in community. Individual responsibility rates very high both in deciding one's own destiny and also in protecting and maintaining the group. Even under torture Hutterites protected their fellow believers. They believe also that the way they live influences what God allows to happen. If they follow his will and his order, they will thrive, but if they turn away from God, "what formerly served for his (man's) profit, good and well-being, now on the contrary serveth for his injury."[86] Therefore individual Hutterites have a sense of control.

Hutterites participate vigorously in group decisions. Leaders, both religious and secular, are chosen by the baptized men and can be removed by them. The leaders are servants; the minister is called the "servant of the word." The group, the church of God, which includes all baptized adults, both male and female, is of more importance than any specific leader. Leaders are expected to be farsighted and caring and to reflect the beliefs of those who chose them. An essential part of the Hutterite concept of self is the individual's identification with the colony, which makes this type of individuality highly functional for the maintenance of community.

Two twentieth-century religious movements, one in Japan and one in Germany, have been attracted to the communalism and Anabaptist theology of the Hutterian Brethren. Japanese Christians started the Owa Community in the mid-1950s. They became familiar with the Hutterites in the early 1970s and have exchanged visits with the Alberta Hutterites. The Japanese Hutterites also have taken advantage of translations into Japanese of Anabaptist literature by Gan Sakakibara.[87]

Reading early Hutterian writings led founders of the Society of Brothers in Germany to seek affiliation with the contemporary Hutterites.[88] Before he visited the Hutterites and was ordained a servant of the Word in 1931, Eberhard Arnold of the Society of Brothers wrote, "Decisive for us is the *Confession* of our religion, doctrine, and faith by Peter Ridemann with all the books, writings, songs, and Orders of the Church of God as it was established anew by Jakob Hutter."[89] Eberhard's wife, Emmy, later explained, "We were particularly happy when Eberhard brought home books and manuscripts about the Hutterian Brothers from libraries and archives. We felt deeply that the same Spirit had called these Brother, who had experienced so much martyrdom, and had independently called us to this life."[90] In spite of their twentieth-century origin and outlook, the Society of Brothers has consistently and aggressively sought to be identified with the traditional Hutterites. However, deep-seated differences in areas such as economic behavior, child rearing, and attitudes toward nature, drama, music, art, and the external society lead to conflicts and misunderstandings. In 1955, about a year after the Society of Brothers established their first *bruderhof* in North America, the traditional Hutterites severed formal relations with them. In 1974 the two groups reaffiliated. However, in 1990 the Dariusleut and the Lehrerleut informed the Society of Brothers that they no longer recognized them as Brothers in Faith and asked them to refrain from using the Hutterite name.[91] By 1996 the Schmiedeleut had also severed their relations with the Society of Brothers, although there remained some internal divisions within the Schmiedeleut.

Hutterites and Society

In common with all Anabaptists the Hutterites have a pessimistic view of society and an optimistic view of the church. Society is hopeless, the kingdom of satan, totally of the temporal world. The Christian must withdraw from this world into the kingdom of God, into a church that is "without spot or blemish," a collection of saints. Although the Hutterites believe that humans are basically sinful, with the grace of God and complete submission and obedience each individual can choose sainthood and eventually reach the point where he or she is not tempted to sin. Until that time his (or her) brothers (and sisters) will watch over him (or her), correct him (or her), and protect him (or her) from wrongdoing. These beliefs demand the separation of church and state. The Hutterites were among the first to insist on and to try to live in such a separation. Sixteenth-century Hutterites advocated religious freedom, civil liberties, a better status for women, and education for every child. Because society was not their responsibility, other than to lead people out of society, the Hutterites advocated these liberties only for their own members. However, the Hutterites' demand for freedom to practice their own religion contributed to the separation of church and state and helped to protect religious freedom for all of society. In North America the Hutterite preference for separation even from neighbors has sometimes brought suspicion, gossip, pranks, destruction of property, and repressive legislation from the outside society.[92]

Hutterites are not typical citizens who participate fully in government. However, short of compromising their religious beliefs, they are law-abiding citizens.[93] As pacifists they refuse to give military service in the conviction that bloodshed is not the will of God. Throughout the four and one-half centuries of their church not one Hutterite has been known to commit murder. When the United States entered World War I in 1917, the Hutterites faced the issue of conscription as forthrightly as before in other lands; they would rather migrate or be martyred than be part of any army. No laws provided for alternative service for conscientious objectors in 1917. Although the leaders appealed to Washington, young Hutterite men were drafted, court-martialed, and kept in separate army barracks and guardhouses.[94] The patriotic pressures during World War I were the closest Hutterites had come to persecution since their immigration to North America. Attempts were made to force colonists to buy war bonds and to stop using their native German language. They refused to change their language or to support the war financially. The ridicule and calculated mistreatment of four drafted Hutterites resulted in the deaths of two of them and precipitated the mass migration of Hutterites to Canada beginning in 1918. By the outbreak of World War II, during which time both the United States and Canadian governments had made arrangements for pacifists to serve in nonmilitary ways, there were fifty-two Hutterite colonies in North America, of which only six were in the United states—five in South Dakota and one in Montana.[95]

Hutterite Faith and Community

337

The Hutterite practices of child care described by Peter Riedemann in 1545 are still followed in North American Hutterite colonies.[96] Babies and young children under three years of age are cared for and fed in the living houses by their parents, babysitters, or relatives. At the age of about three years children enter the colony kindergarten, where they learn prayers, hymns, and how to function as a part of their colony-determined age group. On his or her sixth birthday the child leaves kindergarten to join the German School. These children eat, work, and study together under the care of the German School teacher, who teaches them Hutterite history, traditions, and regulations and how to read and write the old German script. They sleep at home with their family, but most of their waking hours are directed by the German School teacher. At age fifteen the child leaves German School, enters the adult dining room, and participates in the adult work of the colony. When the young adult is baptized, he or she becomes socially an adult.

During most of their history the Hutterites have made, relative to their size, a significant economic contribution to society and have provided for the needs of their members through communal enterprise. No government today spends money for Hutterites who are unemployed, disabled, aged, or retired. No Hutterites are homeless street people or permanent residents of mental institutions. None are malnourished, battered, or born with drug addiction or fetal alcohol syndrome. Hutterites are keenly aware that in order to maintain their desired independence from the surrounding culture their colonies must rest on a sound economic basis. In Moravia the Hutterites exchanged economic productivity for protection. In Manitoba the contribution of the Hutterite colonies to the agricultural economy "is of a magnitude far greater than the proportion of land owned by these people."[97]

Until very recently the economic basis of all Hutterite colonies was large-scale diversified agriculture involving the growing of wheat, oats, barley, and truck gardens and the raising of hogs, beef cattle, dairy cattle, laying hens, broilers, turkeys, geese, ducks, and bees. Today individual colonies also may raise rape, sunflower, and flax. In 1990 a specific Hutterite colony in North Dakota with a population of thirty-four adults and thirty-seven children had a hog barn that held 1,200 hogs, two chicken barns that together housed 44,000 chickens, a pullet barn for 20,000 pullets, and a cow barn with 50 dairy cows and an addition for calves. The colony raised grain for their livestock and had their own storage elevators and feed mill. They worked three truck garden plots and raised potatoes on two quarters of irrigated land. The potatoes were stored in a building they owned in a nearby town. The colony had its own electric shop, carpenter shop, blacksmith shop, and garage.

GERTRUDE E. HUNTINGTON

Hutterite women enjoy a mid-morning lunch outside the butcher house where they are dressing turkeys for market.

High-quality equipment was purchased in the United States, Canada, and Germany. All equipment is serviced on the colony. For seven years the colony ran a grain salvage business that took them throughout the upper Midwest. They continue to take demolition jobs in their immediate area.[98]

Hutterites constantly exchange information among colonies and have been pioneers in introducing new farming practices. The two-litter-a-year hog cycle was introduced into Manitoba by a Hutterite colony. Colonies keep computerized records, striving to produce twenty-five weanling pigs per sow per year. Specialty potato production in Alberta was pioneered by a Hutterite colony. Hutterites continually experiment with different seed varieties, sometimes beginning with as little as an envelope of gift seed. They have used the most modern milking machines for many years. In their processing, milk never comes in contact with the air. It goes directly from the cow to refrigerated bulk tanks from which the milk company picks it up. Hutterite dairy parlors may be completely computerized, with the total milk production and amount of feed given each cow recorded and adjusted daily. Cow barn floors may be flushed mechanically several times a day by automated machines. The effluent is held in a large lagoon until used to fertilize the fields. The Hutterites construct their own buildings, make their own furniture, manufacture some of the farm and kitchen equipment, and maintain and repair everything they use.

Colony lands range in size from 20 to 24,000 acres, depending on availability and fertility of the land and the economic enterprises of the specific colony. As land becomes more difficult to obtain and as agriculture becomes more specialized and subject to greater governmental regulation, Hutterite farming is tending toward specialization. However, each colony attempts to maintain sufficient diversification to supply most of its own needs, to keep all its members busy, and to insure enough economic flexibility to cushion itself against weather and market fluctuations. A further response to land pressure and government regulation is the growing economic importance of small-scale manufacturing. Thus a colony with small landholdings may specialize in raising feeder pigs and also in manufacturing plastic counters, sinks, and tubs for kitchens and bathrooms.

Fear of Hutterite economic success and expansion have occasioned opposition from neighbors in adverse regulation by local, state, and provincial governments. A 1942 wartime law in Alberta went so far as to forbid the sale of land to Hutterites. This was changed in 1947 to permit the purchase of 6,400 acres for any new colony if it was forty miles from the nearest existing one. In 1960 the forty-mile restriction was lifted, and in 1973 a more informal agreement was reached in which land acquisitions were channeled through a liaison office. Legal discrimination in Alberta induced Hutterites to found new colonies in Montana after 1948, Saskatchewan after 1952, and Washington state after 1960. Restrictive legislation is periodically introduced in various provinces. South Dakota, where legal and extralegal coercion induced Hutterite emigration to Canada during World War I, invited the colonies back during the dark days of the Great Depression when the state needed tax revenue and people to farm the deserted lands. Colonies returned only to be threatened with restrictive legislation introduced into, but rarely passed by, various state legislatures.[99] As long as Hutterite communal solidarity, business enterprise, and numerical growth persist, Hutterites will contribute to the general development of the regions they occupy. In spite of their contribution they will likely continue to be perceived as real or imagined threats by some who feel Hutterian colonies must be regulated.

Although superficially unchanging, the Hutterite culture is far from stagnant. Colony size, family size, and relations among the various *Leut* and with the outside society are changing. Lack of homogeneity is apparent as differences between *Leut* and among colonies increase. Details of daily life— dress, food, recreation, and housing—remain fairly traditional in some colonies and are modernizing in others. Viewed from the perspective of historic Hutterianism, individualism appears to be increasing, but viewed from the perspective of the contemporary American, the Hutterites are still staunchly dedicated communards, maintaining their traditional social structure and adhering to the teachings of the Bible, Riedemann's *Confession of Faith*, and the Great Chronicle.

For the scholar the Hutterites constitute a unique experiment, a natural laboratory. Their extensive records offer specialized, accurate information for historians. Their descriptions of their colonies, their confessions of faith, and their *Ordnungen* give a historic perspective to sociologists and anthropologists as well as to communitarians. Their contemporary life offers information for sociologists, anthropologists, and psychologists as well as economists and agronomists. Their accurate genealogical records are invaluable for geneticists and demographers. Even representatives of the large agricultural equipment companies visit the colonies to see what mechanical improvements the Hutterites have devised.[100]

Ultimately, the Hutterite movement carries a utopian mission for its own members and the people of the outside society. The Hutterites believe that they are a saving remnant, a people who justify the continuance of the human race. People were created solely for God's honor and praise.[101] Only true Christians can honor God properly.[102] And one can be a true Christian only by submitting one's will and by living obediently in community.[103] Seen in this light, the Hutterites make a contribution to society similar to that made, say, by sequestered nuns or Eastern hermits, reminding secular society that there are those who elect another way. For its own believers the Hutterian Church provides assurances of security not only in this life but into eternity. All Hutterites who choose obedience become heirs to the promise of life everlasting. Within the boundaries and regulations of a healthy colony lie a sense of satisfaction and freedom. One knows exactly what is expected, and these expectations can usually be met. Human frailty is accepted. With the help of the brethren (including sisters), one grows more saintly as one grows older and becomes more responsible. Though happiness in this life is believed to be meaningless, a quiet contentment surrounds the dedicated Hutterites as they strive for their own salvation and for the salvation of their loved ones. Each Hutterite has a temporal goal, that the colony may be successful and flourish. Each has a social goal, that through his or her efforts the ark may be preserved, enabling all the brethren to reach heaven. And, finally, each Hutterite has a personal goal, that death will bring life eternal in the perfect colony.

Chronology

Beginnings
1525   Founding of Swiss Anabaptist movement in Zurick by Conrad Grebel, George Blaurock, Felix Mantz, and others. Adult baptism.

First period of community of goods, 1528–1695
1528   Founding of the Hutterites. While fleeing, group of about 200 adults began practicing community of goods.
1529   Community discipline adopted by some Anabaptists. Article 4 specifies community of goods.
1530–1622, Moravia (central Czechoslovakia)
1533   Jakob Hutter, chief organizer of *bruderhofs*, becomes first *Vorsteher* (elder), 1533–36.
1536   Jakob Hutter executed in Innsbruck. Church inherits the name "Hutterian."
1542   Peter Reidemann, *Vorsteher*, 1542–56.
1545   Peter Reidemann writes *Account of Our Religion, Doctrine and Faith . . .* known to the Hutterites as the *Confession of Faith*. Only book printed by Hutterites during the sixteenth century.
1545–1762, Slovakia (Hungary)
1554–64   The Good Years.
1565–91   The Golden Years. Approximately ninety *bruderhofs* flourish under the protection of the nobility. Population exceeds 20,000. Peter Walpot, *Vorsteher*, 1565–78. Compilation of the Great Chronicle (*Das grosse Geschichtsbuch*) begun. The Great Article Book written.
1592–1618 Renewed persecution: war between Hapsburgs and Turkey.
1618–48   Sharp decline in Hutterite membership during Thirty Years' War.
1621–22   All Hutterites expelled from Moravia.
1621–1767, Transylvania (Romania)
1639–62   Andreas Ehrenpreis collects and preserves Hutterite sermons and documents.
1665   Writing of the Great Chronicle completed.
1695–1763 Hutterites abandon communal living.
1756   Carinthian Lutheran refugees revitalize remnant of declining Hutterites.
1761–63   *Vorsteher* of the Hutterites, Zacharias Walter, imprisoned by Jesuits, converted to Catholicism. Hutterites forcibly converted to Catholicism, maintained some traditional communal social structure. Only nineteen Hutterites did not convert.

Second period of community of goods, 1763–1818
1763   Community reestablished with *bruderhof* of forty-six people, in Transylvania.
1767–70, Wallachia (Romania)
1767   Sixty-seven Hutterites emigrate from Transylvania to Wallachia—sixteen old Hutterites and fifty-one Carinthian Hutterites.
1770–1874, Ukraine, Russia
1770   Hutterites migrate to Russia, sixty in original party during next fourteen years joined by fifty-six former Hutterites.
1802   Moved from private estate to government land.
1818–59   Communal living abandoned.

| 1824 | Death of Johannes Waldner, *Vorsteher*, 1794–1824, author of *Das Klein-Geschichtsbuch* (1793–1802). Born in Carinthia in 1749, transmigrated to Transylvania, to the Ukraine. |
| 1842 | Hutterites moved to southern Ukraine near Mennonite settlements. |

Third period of community of goods, 1859–present
| 1859 | Community of goods restored by Schmiedeleut congregation. |
| 1873 | Hutterite delegates visit the United States and Canada to investigate colonization prospects. |

1874–present, United States
1874	1,265 Hutterites migrate from Russia to Dakota Territory. All but 443 chose to homestead as individual families, later called Prairieleut. Schmiedeleut established first *bruderhof* in America, Bon Homme colony in present-day South Dakota.
1875	Dariusleut colony founded at Wolf Creek, now South Dakota.
1877	Lehrerleut reestablish communal living in Elmspring, colony founded near present day Parkston, S.D.
1880	443 Hutterites living in community in the United States. No communal Hutterites left in Europe.
1905	Hutterites in South Dakota form corporation.

1918–present, Canada
1918	Seventeen new colonies formed in Alberta and Manitoba by South Dakota Hutterites following the deaths of two Hutterite conscientious objectors from mistreatment in military barracks.
1930–31	Eberhard Arnold (1883–1935) founder of the Society of Brothers in Germany visits North American colonies; ordained servant of the Word at Standoff Colony.
1942	Land Sales Prohibition Act in Alberta prohibits the sale of land to enemy aliens and Hutterites. Later modified and then replaced by more informal agreement in 1974.
1950	Constitution of the Hutterian Brethren Church subscribed to by all Canadian colonies to facilitate legal relations with the government.
1955	Formal relations with the Society of Brothers severed.
1974	Formal relations restored between Hutterites and Society of Brothers.
1977	Izomi Izeki, founder of the Owa Christian Community of New Hutterite Brethren in Japan, appointed servant of the Word.
1990	The Leherleut and Dariusleut revoke the 1974 unification with the Society of Brothers.
1992	Schmiedeleut divide into faction that identifies with the Hutterites and faction that goes with Jake Kleinsasser and the Society of Brothers.
1995	Second faction of Schmiedeleut sever relation with Society of Brothers. Nigerian church supported by second faction of Schmiedeleut but not by Society of Brothers.
1996	The Society of Brothers is now officially known as the Bruderhof Communities and has a population of about 1,200 living in eight communities: three in New York, two in Pennsylvania, one in Connecticut, and two in England. Somewhat over 100 of those living in Society of Brothers *bruderhofs* are ethnic Hutterites. Hutterites themselves have a population of approximately 36,000 living in about 390 colonies. Ninety-five percent live in Alberta, Manitoba, South Dakota, Saskatchewan, and Montana.

Notes

1. Although the religious beliefs and, specifically, the religious teachings of Hutterites are unchanging, their religious practices, especially in relation to the external world, change with circumstances. Missionary zeal was a primary activity during the first century of the movement's development. Today, missionizing is done by being an example to the world and, to a very limited extent, by circulating literature. No effort is made to bring in new converts other than their own children. When a Hutterite minister permitted me to photocopy his sermon collection, he said, "We don't go out and missionize, but our sermons can."

2. *The Hutterian Brethren of Montana* (Augusta, Mont.: [1963]), 17; also "What the Church of Christ Is and How One May Join It," in *The Hutterian Brethren of America* (n.p., n.d.), 11.

3. Jakob Hutter, *Brotherly Faithfulness: Epistles from a Time of Persecution (1535)* (Rifton, N.Y.: Plough, 1979), 172.

4. "Articles of Incorporation of the Hutterische Brudergemeinde" in *Das Klein-Geschichtsbuch der Hutterischen Brüder* (*The Small Chronicle of the Hutterian Brethren*), ed. and comp. A. I. F. Zieglschmid (Philadelphia: Carl Schurz Memorial Foundation, 1947), 615.

5. See John A. Hostetler's excellent discussion "The Problems and Techniques of Survival," pt. 3 of *Hutterite Society* (Baltimore: Johns Hopkins University Press, 1974), 255–83. Also Karl A. Peter, "The Survival and Institutional Evolution of Hutterite Society," in *The Dynamics of Hutterite Society: An Analytical Approach* (Edmonton: University of Alberta Press, 1987), 3–23.

6. The exact year of abandonment of community of goods is difficult to determine. Various members and communities moved into individual ownership at different times, therefore different accounts will give different dates. Often 1690 and 1685 are given as the year community was first abandoned. See John Hofer, David Wiebe, and Gerhard Ens, *The History of the Hutterites*, rev. ed. (Elie, Manitoba: Hutterian Educational Committee, 1988), 43, 46, 69; Hostetler, *Society*, 291; Victor Peters, *All Things Common: The Hutterian Way of Life* (Minneapolis: University Minnesota Press, 1965), 26; and Zieglschmid, *Klein-Geschichtsbuch*, 223. Most colonies had abandoned communalism by 1685. By 1695 there were no communal colonies left.

7. In addition to the mainstream Hutterites, the Society of Brothers (Bruderhof Communities) chose to identify themselves as Hutterites. They listed themselves as Hutterian Brethren in most of their publications, and therefore they are so listed in the selected bibliography. The traditional, ethnic Hutterites strongly object to the Society of Brothers using the name Hutterite or Hutterian. In 1996 the Society of Brothers changed their legal name from Hutterian Brethren of New York to Bruderhof Communities of New York.

The Society of Brothers began in Germany in 1920 and affiliated with the Hutterites in 1931 and again in 1974. In 1990 the Dariusleut and the Lehrerleut severed connections with the Society of Brothers, and in 1995 the Schmiedeleut severed relations. In 1996 the Society of Brothers had six colonies in North America and two in England, was closing the only colony in Germany, and had withdrawn a lawsuit against the colony they started in Nigeria. The Nigerian church is being supported by some of the Schmiedeleut.

There is one small Christian colony in Japan that is affiliated with the Dariusleut.

8. Hutterian Brethren, eds. and trans., *The [Great] Chronicle of the Hutterian Brethren*, vol. 1, *Das grosse Geschichtsbuch der Hutterischen Brüder* (Rifton, N.Y.: Plough, 1987), 402. This work is commonly referred to in English as the "Great Chronicle" and appears as such throughout this essay. The compilation and writing of this chronicle of Hutterite history

GERTRUDE E. HUNTINGTON

was begun in the 1560s and continued until 1665. It circulated in manuscript form until it was first printed in 1923 as Rudolf Wolkan, ed. *Geschichts-Buch der Hutterischen Brüder, Herausgegeben von den Hutterischen Brudern in Amerika*, Canada (Macleod, Alberta: Stand-off-Colony, 1923; reprint, Cayley, Alberta, 1974). Another edition, largely ignored by the Hutterites, was brought out by A. J. F. Zieglschmid, ed., *Die alteste Chronik der Hutterischen Brüder* (Philadelphia: Carl Schurz Memorial Foundation, 1943).

9. "A Hutterite tract of the 16th century is entitled: 'Why are there no University graduates (Hochgelehrte) in our midst?' Answer: Intellectual sophistication kills simplicity, and with it faith. . . . Anabaptists had chosen the type of faith, which embraces the revealed truth, . . . the significant distinction between reason and understanding, . . . that is between logical (Greek) rationality and Biblical spirituality" (Peter S. Tschetter, *The Hutterian Brethren of Yesterday and Today: A True History of Christians and Non-Christians, a Guide for Those Who Want to Be Guided* [Minburn, Alberta, Canada: Mixburn Colony, 1966], 16).

10. Hutterian Brethren, *Chronicle*, 44–45.

11. Franklin H. Littel, *The Anabaptist View of the Church: An Introduction to Sectarian Protestantism* (n.p.: American Society of Church History, 1952), 52–57.

12. Hutterian Brethren, *Chronicle*, 81.

13. This belief in the community of property is as sacred to the Hutterites as the seven sacraments are to the Greek and Roman Catholics. See *Hutterian Brethren of America*, 14.

14. *Hutterian Brethren of Montana*, 6–17.

15. Hutterian Brethren, *Chronicle*, 77–79; Wolkan, *Geschichts-Buch*, 60–61; Robert Friedmann, "The Oldest Church Discipline of the Anabaptists," *Mennonite Quarterly Review* 29 (1955): 162–66.

16. Paul S. Gross, *Hutterian Brethren: Life and Religion* (Pincher Creek, Alberta: n.p., n.d.) 23–30.

17. Tschetter, *Hutterian Brethren*, 10.

18. John Hofer, David Wiebe, and Gerhard Ens, *The History of the Hutterites* (Elie, Manitoba: Hutterian Educational Committee, 1982), 70. The foreword states, "The Hutterian Educational Committee has examined all chapters of this text and we found the content according to historical facts and to our interpretation of our history" (iii). For a discussion of the Hutterite concept of self, see Gertrude Enders Huntington, "Freedom and the Hutterite Communal Family Pattern," in Proceedings of the Fifteenth Conference on Mennonite Educational and Cultural Problems, Bluffton College, Bluffton, Ohio, 1965, 88–111. Also Bert Kaplan and Thomas F. A. Plaut, *Personality in a Communal Society: An Analysis of the Mental Health of the Hutterites* (Lawrence: University of Kansas Publications, 1956); Joseph W. Eaton and Hobert J. Weil, *Culture and Mental Disorders: A Comparative Study of Hutterites and Other Populations* (Glencoe, Ill.: The Press, 1955); and P. Stephenson, *The Hutterian People: Ritual and Rebirth in the Evolution of Communal Life* (Lantham, Md.: University Press of America, 1991).

19. Peter Riedemann, *Account of Our Religion, Doctrine and Faith Given by Peter Rideman [Riedemann] of the Brothers Whom Men Call Hutterians*, 2d ed. (*Rechenschaft unserer Religion, Lehr und Glaubens, von den Brudern, so man die Hutterischen nennt, ausgangen durch Peter Rideman, 1545*) (Rifton, N.Y.: Plough, 1970), 93, 94, 108; subsequent references cite this work as *Confession of Faith*. Tschetter, *Hutterian Brethren*, 16, 17; Emil J. Waltner, *Banished for Faith* (Freeman, S.D.: Pine Hill Press, 1968), 26, 132.

20. Waltner, *Banished*, 132.

21. Riedemann, *Confession of Faith*, was first printed in 1545.

22. Jakob Hutter, Vorsteher, 1533–36; Hutterian Brethren, *Chronicle*, 146, 65–110.

23. Hutter, *Brotherly Faithfulness*.

24. Paul S. Gross, a present-day Hutterite minister, writes of the *Confession of Faith*, "This

book expresses the fundamentals of faith that have governed the life of the Hutterians over the course of four centuries. . . . It expresses the faith underlying the communal life of the older Hutterian communities as well as that of the later times in the United States and Canada" (*Who Are the Hutterites* [n.p.: Mennonite Publishing House, n.d], 15).

25. Riedemann, *Confession of Faith*, 19, 126.

26. Robert Friedmann, *Hutterite Studies* (Goshen, Ind.: Mennonite Historical Society, 1961), 163, notes that "almost all the theological tracts of the Hutterites originated with lay members."

27. 1537, Hutterian Brethren, *Chronicle*, 161.

28. 1641, Ibid., 736.

29. Paul S. Gross, personal correspondence, September 28, 1988. In Hungry some thirty households arose, the largest of which consisted of about 500 families. See Eberhard Arnold in Riedemann, *Confession of Faith*, 284.

30. Hostetler, *Society*, 11; Peter Brock, *Pacifism in Europe to 1914* (Princeton: Princeton University Press, 1972), 135. Professionals who joined included priests, physicians, barber-surgeons, and apothecaries (Hutterian Brethren, *Chronicle*, 46, 48, 52, 54, 57, 174, 383, 494, 496, 764). Nobles are mentioned in the Hutterian Brethren, *Chronicle*, 160, 349.

31. Hutterian Brethren, *Chronicle*, 406. Sources disagree on the actual composition of the early Hutterite colonies. John W. Bennett, *Hutterian Brethren; The Agricultural Economy and Social Organization of a Communal People* (Stanford, Calif.: Stanford University Press, 1967), 49, 50, suggests about three-fourths of the converts were peasants. Peter, *Dynamics of Hutterite Society*, 14, comments that "Hutterites were predominately craftsmen although they tended to maintain an agricultural base." Paul S. Gross, in a letter to the author, September 28, 1988, wrote that "they were craftsmen; their base was handicraft, manual labor."

32. Leonard Gross, *The Golden Years of the Hutterites: The Witness and Thought of the Communal Moravian Anabaptists during the Walpot Era, 1565–1578* (Scottdale, Pa.: Herald, 1980), 200–204. Robert Friedmann, "Second Generation Anabaptism as Illustrated by the Walpot Era of the Hutterites," *Mennonite Quarterly Review* 44 (1970): 390–93.

33. See n. 8 above.

34. During the last decade almost all Hutterite colonies have installed indoor plumbing in family houses. In some colonies apartments have thermostats in each room and microwave ovens in the apartment kitchenette; telephones connect all apartments and shops, but not the outside world. Portable phones or a radio system may be used to communicate with operators of the large agricultural equipment or with members doing business outside the colony.

35. Hutterian Brethren, *Chronicle*, 251–93.

36. Leonard Gross, *Golden Years*, 202; see also Harold S. Bender, Cornelius Krahn, C. Henry Smith, and Melvin Gingerich, eds., *The Mennonite Encyclopedia: A Comprehensive Reference Work on the Anabaptist-Mennonite Movement*, 5 vols. (Hillsboro, Kans: Mennonite Brethren, 1955–1990), 1:173–74.

37. Hostetler, *Society*, 321–28, and Harold S. Bender, ed. and trans., "A Hutterite School Discipline of 1578 [1568] and Peter Scherer's Address of 1568 to the School Masters," *Mennonite Quarterly Review* 5 (1931): 231–41.

38. For a different but compelling analysis of Hutterite institutionalization, see Peter, *Dynamics of Hutterite Society*, 3–45.

39. An outstanding example of intellectual interaction is a document written by the Hutterites around 1561, "Handbook Countering the 'Proceedings,' Issued in 1557 at Worms on the Rhine Against the Brethren who are Called Hutterites, and Signed by Philipp Melanchthon and Johannes Brenz, Among Others from Their Midst," in Leonard Gross, *Golden Years*, 90–93. Paul S. Gross translated, edited, and printed the document

privately under the title *Hand Book Against the (process) procedure or action that took place at Worms on the Rhine against an Anabaptist Group-folk known as the Hutterian in the year 1557.*

40. Friedmann, *Hutterite Studies*, 107–10; Friedmann, "Anabaptist Ordinance of 1663 on Nonresistance," *Mennonite Quarterly Review* 25 (1951): 116–27, 161; Friedmann, "Hutterite Worship and Preaching," *Mennonite Quarterly Review* 40 (1966): 9.

41. Andreas Ehrenpreis, "On Rearing Children, 1652," and "An Exhortation to Parents and Children and Their Mutual Responsibilities," in John A. Hostetler, ed., "Sources on Child Rearing and Socialization: The Hutterian Brethren," photocopy, 1967, 17–24; Philippe Aries, *Centuries of Childhood: A Social History of Family Life* (New York: Knopf, 1962), 42–43, 46–49. For a discussion of contemporary Hutterite child rearing, see Gertrude Enders Huntington, "Children of the Hutterites," *Natural History* 90 (February 1981): 34–47; Huntington, "Order Rules the World: Our Children among the Communal Society of the Hutterites," in *Children and Anthropological Research*, ed. Barbara Butler and Diane Michalski Turner (New York: Plenum, 1987), 53–71; Hostetler, "Total Socialization: Modern Hutterite Educational Practices," *Mennonite Quarterly Review* 44 (1970): 72–84; Hostetler and Huntington, "Communal Socialization Patterns in Hutterite Society," *Ethnology* 8 (October 1969): 331–55; Paul S. Gross, *The Hutterite Way: The Inside Story of the Life, Customs, Religion, and Traditions of the Hutterites* (Saskatoon, Canada: Freeman, 1965), 47–71; Eduard Schluderman and Shirin Schluderman, "Developmental Aspects of Social Role Perception in Hutterite Communal Society," in *Child Development: Selected Readings*, ed. L. Brockman, J. Whiteley, and J. Zubcek (Toronto: McClelland and Stewart, 1973); Elisabeth Peters, *Hutterian Education*, Monographs in Education XI, ed. Alexander Gregor and Keith Wilson (Winnipeg, Manitoba: University of Manitoba, 1984); Claudia Sue Konker, "Child Abuse in America: Cultural Variation in Definition and Behavior" (Ph.D. diss., University of Washington, 1992); Peter, *Dynamics of Hutterite Society*, 61–132.

42. Friedmann, *Hutterite Studies*, 184.

43. In 1990 the Dariusleut and Lehrerleut wrote to the Society of Brothers, "The main downfall of your people is, that you do not preach the Hutterian Sermons or Lehren, which to us are so sacred, and indeed biblical, and were written by men of suffering and inspiration of the Holy Ghost, and were sealed with blood and tears. These sermons are the solid foundation that keeps our church alive and in order, and Jesus is the head of this true church."

44. Zieglschmid, *Klein-Geschichtsbuch*. The heart of this book is the work of Johannes Waldner, who wrote it in Russia between 1793 and 1802. Zieglschmid assembled documents from 1802 to 1947 in an effort to bring the chronicle up to date. Emil J. Waltner, *Banished for Faith* (Freeman, S.D.: Pine Hill Press, 1968), 10–134, translates sections of the *Klein-Geschichtsbuch*, as did John Horsch in *The Hutterian Brethren, 1528–1931: A Story of Martyrdom and Loyalty* (Goshen, Ind.: Mennonite Historical Society, 1931).

45. "In the beginning was the word." God's words are believed to be forever part of him and cannot break away from him (Riedemann, *Confession of Faith*, 24). It is not the old sermon books that are valuable but the contents. Just as the human body is temporal and the spirit is eternal, Hutterites feel that old sermon books may be discarded in a coffin to decay with the body while the spirit continues. In baptism it is the word, not the water, that is holy (ibid., 186). Memorized words rather than objects, relics, or rosaries are the basis of Hutterian ritual and sense of security. The belief is that recited or read words, rather than spontaneous utterances, strengthen the community and do not call attention to the individual. Personal charisma is not esteemed. Hutterites hold that no one should delete anything from the gospel or add anything to the gospel (ibid., 173).

46. Handwritten sermons may be carefully photocopied and then bound. This is done by individual Hutterites or by hired commercial printers. The Reverend Paul S. Gross also

has transcribed many sermons on the typewriter, translated some himself, and made some available for translation (Paul S. Gross and Elizabeth Bender, trans., "A Hutterite Sermon of the Seventeenth Century," *Mennonite Quarterly Review* 44 [1970]: 85–91).

47. These books and booklets are published privately or by local presses. During the years the Society of Brothers was affiliated with the ethnic Hutterites the Plough Publishing House produced some material in German and published translations of original Hutterite manuscripts. These translations are accurate and capture the tone of the original in idiomatic English. In addition, scholarly footnotes help contemporary readers. The Society of Brothers publishes a periodical, in-group literature, books describing aspects of their history and their community life, and works for the edification of the outside society.

48. Riedemann, *Confession of Faith*, 24.

49. John Ryan, *The Agricultural Economy of Manitoba Hutterite Colonies* (Ottawa: Institute of Canadian Studies, Carleton University, 1977), 264.

50. For a description of aspects of contemporary Hutterite colony life, see John A. Hostetler and Gertrude Enders Huntington, *The Hutterites in North America*, 3d ed. (Fort Worth, Tex.: Harcourt Brace College Publishers, 1996). Also Michael Holzach, *The Forgotten People: A Year among the Hutterites*, trans. Stephan Lhotzky (Sioux Falls, S.D.: Ex Machina, 1993).

51. Hutterian Brethren, *Chronicle*, 142.

52. Ibid., 507.

53. Horsch, *Hutterian Brethren*, 70.

54. Ibid., 77.

55. Quoted in ibid., 78.

56. Hutterian Brethren, *Chronicle*, 651, 652, 700, 749, 780–81, 784, 786,

57. Ibid., 779.

58. Ibid., 779, 781, 783.

59. As quoted in Horsch, *Hutterian Brethren*, 75.

60. Zieglschmid, *Klein-Geschichtsbuch*, 223.

61. Victor Peters, *All Things Common*, 26.

62. Hostetler, *Society*, 85–90; Hofer et al., *History of the Hutterites*, 47. Those who converted were known as *Habaner*. Although no longer subscribing to the Hutterite religion, they retained a semicommunal organization with various cooperative activities that persisted until after World War I (*Mennonite Encyclopedia*, 2:619).

63. Waltner, *Banished*, 100.

64. Hostetler, *Society*, 96–99.

65. In Zieglschmid, *Klein-Geschichtsbuch*, 553, is a comment made in 1793 that for a long time no new people had been joining.

66. Paul S. Gross, *Hutterite Way*, 192–93.

67. Waltner, *Banished*, 100.

68. Hutterite Centennial Steering Committee, *Hutterite Roots* (Freeman, S.D.: Pine Hill Press, 1985), 83.

69. Paul S. Gross, *Hutterite Way*, 195.

70. Waltner, *Banished*, 110.

71. From an official report of a Russian government inspector. Waltner, *Banished*, 102; Zieglschmid, *Klein-Geschichtsbuch*, 412.

72. Waltner, *Banished*, 100, 113–15.

73. Hutterite Centennial Steering Committee, *Hutterite Roots*, 83.

74. Attempts at establishing *bruderhofs* in Germany in 1603 and 1654 failed. After initial success, social and economic integration into the surrounding German culture led to the dissolution of the Hutterite community (Victor Peters, *All Things Common*, 28).

GERTRUDE E. HUNTINGTON

75. For an example, see a hymn about Christian belief and baptism in *Die Lieder der Hutterischen Brüder* (Winnipeg, Canada: Christian Press, 1953), 351–62.

76. For a discussion of Hutterite hymns, see *Mennonite Encyclopedia*, 3:339–40.

77. Waltner, *Banished*, 18; Hostetler, *Society*, 76; Zieglschmid, *Klein-Geschichtsbuch*, 268–70.

78. Waltner, *Banished*, 119; Zieglschmid, *Klein-Geschichtsbuch*, 439.

79. Waltner, *Banished*, 120, 132; Zieglschmid, *Klein-Geschichtsbuch*, 442.

80. Robert Friedmann, "The Re-Establishment of Communal Life among the Hutterites in Russia (1858)," *Mennonite Quarterly Review* 39 (1965), 150.

81. Ibid., 151.

82. Hostetler, *Society*, 105–12.

83. "The Diary of Paul Tschetter, 1873," ed. and trans. J. M. Hofer, in *The History of the Hutterite Mennonites* (Freeman, S.D.: Hutterite Mennonite Centennial, 1974), 29–47. Also published in the *Mennonite Quarterly Review* 5 (1931): 112–26, 198–220.

84. Joseph K. Wipf, *1995 Hutterite Telephone and Address Book* (Cranford, Alberta, Canada: Joseph K. Wipf, Lakeside Hutterian Brethren, 1995). One hundred eleven Lehrerleut colonies, 130 Dariusleut colonies, and 154 Schmiedeleut colonies (not including Society of Brothers) give a total of 395 colonies in Alberta (138), Manitoba (91), Saskatchewan (54), South Dakota (52), Montana (42), North Dakota (6), Washington (6), Minnesota (5), and British Columbia (1).

85. Even those individuals who do not move from the mother colony participate in building the daughter colony. Classically, though not always in practice, when it is time to actually move to the new location, the family heads align with one of the two ministers in such a way that the age structure of each group is similar and nuclear families are not broken up. Everyone packs, then on the day the move is to take place, lots are drawn. Depending on how the lot falls, each family either moves or unpacks.

86. Riedemann, *Confession of Faith*, 199.

87. Joshua Hofer, *Japanese Hutterites: Visit to Owa Community* (Altona, Manitoba: Friesen and Sons, 1985), 11–13, 64–70A.

88. Hutterian Brethren, eds., *Brothers Unite: An Account of the Uniting of Eberhard Arnold and the Rhon Bruderhof with the Hutterian Church* (Rifton, N.Y.: Plough, 1988). For descriptions of the Society of Brothers, see Emmy Arnold, *Torches Together: The Beginning and Early Years of the Bruderhof Communities* (Rifton, N.Y.: Plough, 1971); Benjamin Zablocki, *The Joyful Community: An Account of the Bruderhof, a Communal Movement Now in Its Third Generation* (Chicago: University of Chicago Press, 1971, 1980); Ulrich Eggers, *Community for Life* (Scottdale, Pa.: Herald, 1988); and Donald Durnbaugh, "Relocation of the German Bruderhof to England, South America, and North America," *Communal Societies* 11 (1991): 62–67. For a view of the Society of Brothers from former members, see *KIT* (Keep in Touch) *Newsletter*, a project of the Peregrine Foundation, P.O. Box 460146, San Francisco, CA 94146; Roger Allain, *The Community That Failed: An Account of Twenty-Two Years in Bruderhof Communes in Europe and South America* (San Francisco: Carrier Pigeon Press, 1992); Elizabeth Bohlken-Zumpe, *Torches Extinguished: Memories of a Communal Bruderhof Childhood in Paraguay, Europe, and the USA* (San Francisco: Carrier Pigeon Press), 1993; and Nadine Moonje Pleil, *Free from Bondage: After Forty Years in Bruderhof Communities on Three Continents* (San Francisco: Carrier Pigeon Press, 1994).

89. Eberhard Arnold, *Foundations and Orders, 1920–29* (Rifton, N.Y.: Plough, 1976), 2. In the same source (51, 52) he states, "In August 1924 we met . . . to read important old Hutterian confessions of faith and orders; we declared our complete agreement with Hutterian life and faith. . . . But it was not until 1927 that we came into personal contact with the present-day Hutterians."

90. Emmy Arnold, *Torches Together*, 125.

91. "From The Hutterian Brethren Church of the Darius and Lehrerleut Conference, To Society of Brothers who call themselves Hutterian Brethren," December 11, 1990, typed letter.

92. Hostetler and Huntington, *Hutterites in North America*, 102–4 (3d ed., 100–107); David Flint, *The Hutterites: A Study in Prejudice* (Toronto: Oxford University Press, 1975).

93. For a Hutterite interpretation, "Concerning Voting and Citizenship," see *Hutterian Brethren of Montana*, 28–29.

94. "An Account, by Jakob Waldner, Diary of a Conscientious Objector in World War I," ed. Theron Schlabach, trans. Ilse Reist and Elizabeth Bender, *Mennonite Quarterly Review* 48 (1974): 73–111.

95. Hostetler and Huntington, *Hutterites in North America*, 9–10, 100–101 (2d ed., 92–94).

96. Riedemann, *Confession of Faith*, 130–31.

97. Ryan, *Agricultural Economy*, 245.

98. Tony Waldner, *History of Forest River Community* (Fordville, N.D.: Forest River Community, 1990).

99. Hostetler and Huntington, *Hutterites in North America*, 104–7.

100. For example, Hutterites enclosed cabs and added strong headlights to combines long before these were generally available.

101. Riedemann, *Confession of Faith*, 15, 19.

102. Ibid., 93–94; Tschetter, *Hutterian Brethren*, 17.

103. Riedemann, *Confession of Faith*, 108; Tschetter, *Hutterian Brethren*, 16; Waltner, *Banished*, 26, 132.

Selected Bibliography

Allain, Roger. *The Community That Failed: An Account of Twenty-Two Years in Bruderhof Communes in Europe and South America.* San Francisco: Carrier Pigeon Press, 1992.

Arnold, Emmy. *Torches Together: The Beginning and Early Years of the Bruderhof Communities.* Rifton, N.Y.: Plough, 1964.

Bohlken-Zumpe, Elizabeth. *Torches Extinguished: Memories of a Communal Bruderhof Childhood in Paraguay, Europe, and the USA.* Women from Utopia Series, edited by Gertrude Enders Huntington. San Francisco: Carrier Pigeon Press, 1993.

Colin, Paul K. *Two Paths to Utopia: The Hutterites and the Llano Colony.* Lincoln: University of Nebraska Press, 1964.

Eggers, Ulrich. *Community for Life.* Foreword by John A. Hostetler. Scottdale, Pa.: Herald, 1988.

Gross, Leonard. *The Golden Years of the Hutterites: The Witness and Thought of the Communal Moravian Anabaptists during the Walpot Era, 1565–1578.* Scottdale, Pa.: Herald, 1980.

Gross, Paul S. *The Hutterite Way: The Inside Story of the Life, Customs, Religion, and Traditions of the Hutterites.* Saskatoon, Canada: Freeman, 1965.

Hofer, John, David Wiebe, and Gerhard Ens. *The History of the Hutterites.* Elie, Manitoba: Hutterian Educational Committee, 1982. Rev. ed., 1988.

Hofer, Joshua. *Japanese Hutterites: Visit to Owa Community.* Altona, Manitoba: Friesen and Sons, 1985.

Holzach, Michael. *The Forgotten People: A Year among the Hutterites.* Translated from the German by Stephan Lhotzky. Souix Falls, S.D.: Ex Machina, 1993.

Horsch, John. *The Hutterian Brethren, 1528–1931: A Story of Martyrdom and Loyalty.* Goshen, Ind.: Mennonite Historical Society, 1931.

Hostetler, John A. *Hutterite Life.* Scottdale, Pa.: Herald, 1983.

———. *Hutterite Society.* Baltimore: Johns Hopkins University Press, 1974.

Hostetler, John A., and Gertrude Enders Huntington. "Communal Socialization Patterns in Hutterite Society." *Ethnology* 8 (October 1968): 331–55.

———. *The Hutterites in North America.* 3d ed. Case Studies in Cultural Anthropology, edited by George and Louise Spindler. Fort Worth, Tex.: Harcourt Brace College Publishers, 1996.

Huntington, Gertrude Enders. "Children of the Hutterites." *Natural History* 90 (February 1981): 34–47.

———. "Order Rules the World: Our Children among the Communal Society of the Hutterites." In *Children and Anthropology Research*, edited by Barbara Butler and Diane Turner, 53–71. New York: Plenum, 1987.

Hutterian Brethren, eds. *Brothers Unite: An Account of the Uniting of Eberhard Arnold and the Rhon Bruderhof with the Hutterian Church.* Rifton, N.Y.: Plough, 1988.

———, eds. and trans. *The [Great] Chronicle of the Hutterian Brethren.* Rifton, N.Y.: Plough, 1987.

Janzen, Rod. "The Prairieleut: A Forgotten Hutterite People." *Communal Societies* 14 (1994): 67–89.

Kaplan, Bert, and Thomas F. A. Plaut. *Personality in a Communal Society: An Analysis of the Mental Health of the Hutterites.* Lawrence: University of Kansas Publications, 1956.

Peter, Karl A. *The Dynamics of Hutterite Society: An Analytical Approach.* Edmonton: University of Alberta Press, 1987.

Peters, Victor, *All Things Common: The Hutterian Way of Life.* Minneapolis: University of Minnesota Press, 1965.

Pleil, Nadine Moonje. *Free from Bondage: After Forty Years in Bruderhof Communities on Three Continents.* Women from Utopia Series, edited by Gertrude Enders Huntington. San Francisco: Carrier Pigeon Press, 1994.

Zablocki, Benjamin. *The Joyful Community: An Account of the Bruderhof, a Communal Movement Now in Its Third Generation.* Chicago: University of Chicago Press, 1971, 1980.

Films and Video

The Hutterites: To Care and Not to Care. 1984. Produced by Buller Films, Inc., Herderson, Neb., for R. H. B. Productions. John L. Ruth, writer and director. 58 minutes and 25 minutes, color, 16mm and video.

The Hutterites. Educational film produced by the National Film Board of Canada, Montreal, Quebec. 28 minutes, black and white. 16mm.

Life Together: The Hutterian Bruderhof. 1988. 22-minute video about the Society of Brothers. Produced by Hutterian Brethren (now known as the Bruderhof Communities), Ulster Park, N.Y.

PEARL W. BARTELT

American Jewish Agricultural Colonies

Introduction

Among the large numbers of communal societies that emerged in nineteenth- and early twentieth-century America, none exhibited as wide a variety of types of settlement and were as widely dispersed or as disparate in their communal identity as those of the Jewish agricultural colony movement. Fueled by the same European social and political forces that gave rise to Zionism and the kibbutz movement, the most significant time for these societies corresponds with the substantial growth of the Russian Jewish emigration in the last two decades of the nineteenth century and the first decade of the twentieth century. Indeed, it is most striking that this movement to establish rural agricultural communities reached its zenith during the peak of American urbanization.

The Jewish agricultural colony movement broadens our understanding of the dynamics of community formation and survival as well as our sense of the variety of communal societies. While all shared in a commitment to establish communities in which collective efforts dominated, patterns of property ownership, leadership, sponsorship, and size varied tremendously from settlement to settlement.

Three purposes drive this essay. First, these groups left a rich legacy of descriptive materials that provide a wealth of insight into the difficulties in establishing communities that cut against the tide of American urbanization. Second, the variety of experiences reflected in this history provides a useful added perspective to the discussions of communal and utopian societies.

Third, the distinctive contributions of many of these communities can be seen by applying a developmental perspective to them. While most communities were short lived, many helped shape the cultural geography of their surroundings. In other cases, the origins of many contemporary aspects of the Jewish American community can be seen.

Background

The history of Jewish agricultural colonies in the United States is closely linked to the social forces that affected Russia and America in the late nineteenth and early twentieth centuries. Most of the nearly 100 Jewish communal settlements in North America emerged from the great wave of Russian Jewish immigration after 1881. History in general has emphasized the urban context of that migration, as most Jews arrived on the East Coast and stayed in the cities of the East and the industrial Midwest. Many others, however, dispersed across the continent, founding more communities than any immigrant groups except Roman Catholics and the Hutterites. These Russian Jews were driven by the religious hostility of the pogroms, officially sanctioned violence against Jews and their property, and attracted by American agricultural opportunities. The further attraction of landownership for a population forbidden to hold property in their homeland contributed as well.

Many found a supportive ideology in the Am Olam movement (discussed more fully below), which began in Odessa in 1881. But no central leader or philosophy integrated all the Jewish colonies. With few resources available within Russia, Am Olam eventually developed strategic alliances with both European and American sources of support for their movement. Their reliance on external funding agencies set them apart from other American communal utopians and proved both beneficial and detrimental to the development of their immigrant communities.

Although German Jews formed the earliest Jewish agricultural colonies in America in the 1820s, the Russian immigration beginning in the 1880s far exceeded the German initiative. This shift reflected the clear change in emigration patterns from North Central to Eastern Europe as well as the effects of the pogroms in accelerating such emigration. The first part of the twentieth century marked the end of the major wave of agricultural colonization, although a colony was founded as late as the 1930s.

These colonies were dispersed over much of the United States. Although New Jersey and North Dakota were the states with the largest numbers of Jewish agricultural colonies, many communities developed across the continental United States. The concentration of settlements in these two states is relatively easy to understand. While New Jersey was close to both the New York and Philadelphia ports of entry, success in growing and selling wheat as well as in acquiring available land under the homestead laws in North Dakota made it easier to acquire property there than many other locations.[1]

While these colonies are no longer in existence, they played an important role in United States Jewish immigration history. They were instrumental in moving Jews out of the Northeast and involving them in agricultural pursuits that continued long after the colonies had ceased to exist, developing a network of Jewish charitable organizations. The communities are also linked to the establishment of rural credit bureaus in the United States.[2]

At least four Jewish agricultural colonies in America predated the Russian immigration in the 1880s: Ararat and Shalom in New York, Alachua County in Florida, and Atwood in Colorado. Ararat, started in 1820, is generally recognized as the first Jewish agricultural colony in the United States. This colony, referred to as "a City of Refuge for the Jews," was started by Major Mordecai Manuel North on Grand Island in the Niagara River in New York state.[3] Shalom was begun seventeen years later in 1837 in Warwarsing, Ulster County, New York, by Moses Cohen. This community evidenced the first indications of the basic problems that plagued the Jewish colonies: lack of farming expertise, poor soil, and insufficient funds. The settlers at Shalom persisted for five years.[4]

The proliferation of Jewish agricultural colonies in America began in the 1880s. In 1881 the Russian Czar Alexander III succeeded the assassinated Alexander II and, possibly reacting to the false accusation of Jewish involvement in Alexander II's assassination, began a series of pogroms. One feature of Alexander's pogroms officially barred Jews from farming—an activity in which they had, in any event, long been underrepresented. (In 1870 90 percent of the Russians were living on farms, but only 5 percent of the Jews were farmers.[5]) The May Laws of 1882 directly banned Jews from owning land and engaging in agricultural pursuits.[6]

Two groups were formed in Russia to promote Jewish opportunities in agriculture as well as to help Jews escape from the pogroms. One, Am Olam ("Eternal People"), was organized by young Jewish intellectuals in 1881 as a defense group in Odessa to protect Jews from the increasing violence against them.[7] Its goal was to found, support, and populate Jewish agricultural colonies in the United States; its emblem was a plow with the Ten Commandments. The plow represented the agricultural goal, while the Ten Commandments illustrated the identification with Judaism.[8]

The second group was called BILU, for the beginning letters of the Hebrew words that mean "House of Jacob, Let Us Go."[9] Its goal was emigration to

·PEARL W. BARTELT

Palestine, which was under Turkish rule at that time; there the emigrants would work as farmers or laborers.

The Am Olam group's interest in farming had important implications for the settlement of the Jewish agricultural colonies in America. Many felt that Russian anti-Semitism was caused by the types of economic activities in which the Jews of Russia engaged. Even though the Jews were banned from owning land, their work as peddlers, middlemen, and merchants led them to be stereotyped as parasites. Emigration to the United States, Am Olam leaders felt, would change that.[10] The larger world of nineteenth-century reform literature influenced the movement as well. As historian Abraham Menes has written, "The plan was to found cooperative colonies in America in the spirit of Robert Owen, Charles Fourier, and Tolstoy."[11]

A crucial factor in the establishment of the American Jewish agricultural colonies was the emergence of charitable assistance organizations. Many Russian refugees were aided in their travels to the United States by the Alliance Israelite Universelle, a French group founded in Paris in 1860 that helped Russian Jews settle in the United States.[12] The Mansion House Committee of London was similarly active during this period.[13] The Jewish Colonization Society, founded by Baron de Hirsch, had as its goal the movement of Russian Jews to agricultural colonies in countries that would be "favorable" to them.[14] In the United States the Hebrew Emigrant Aid Society was formed to deal with the large influx of Russian Jews.[15] These groups, along with other charitable and funding organizations, played an important role in the formation of the Jewish agricultural colonies in the United States.[16]

It would be erroneous to conclude, however, that the support of various charitable organizations signified an acceptance of the Russian Jews by the German Jews who had emigrated to the United States decades earlier. In fact, Russian Jews and German Jews were culturally quite different. The Russian Jews were generally Orthodox; required strict adherence to the religious laws; spoke Yiddish, a German dialect combining parts of Hebrew, Russian, and Polish; and often emigrated in large, multifamily groups from their Russian communities of origin. German Jews, on the other hand, were usually Reform Jews, with a less restrictive set of religious laws. They spoke German and usually emigrated on a family-by-family basis.[17] The language distinction was especially important. The German Jews tended to consider themselves Germans first, Jewish second. The vast majority of emigrating Russian Jews spoke a language that set them apart from the rest of the Russian population and were considered by the Russian government, and often by themselves, as Jewish rather than Russian.[18]

An important component of the settlement process was the great change in

Baron Maurice de Hirsch founded the Jewish Colonization Society, which assisted many Russian Jews in finding homes in agricultural colonies in the United States and elsewhere. (Archives of the YIVO Institute for Jewish Research)

American society that occurred contemporaneously with the wave of Russian Jewish immigration. The Jewish agricultural colonies developed during a period of rapid urbanization in the United States. In 1880 28 percent of the population lived in urban areas; by 1920 this had increased to 51 percent, with more than 88 percent of the Russian immigrants living in cities.[19] Thus, the agricultural colonies developed in opposition to the demographics of the times. Still, other utopian/communal groups were forming as well. Rugby

PEARL W. BARTELT

was formed in Tennessee; the Titioute Colony of the Hutterites, in South Dakota; Kaweah Cooperative Commonwealth, in the Sierra Nevadas; Shalam, in New Mexico; the Mormon United Order Community, at Orderville; and the Woman's Commonwealth, in Texas.[20] Regardless of different geographical locations or religious origins, the founders of these communities shared a commitment to small, agriculturally rooted societies.

After their arrival in the United States, Russian Jews were encouraged by Jewish immigration agencies to move out of the eastern urban areas. This was done to ease the strain on the tenements but also to increase the assimilation process of these Russian Jews.[21] The German Jews, dominant in the assistance agencies, wanted the Russian Jews to be Americanized and dispersed from the urban areas that they, the German Jews, inhabited. Thus German Jews oversaw the development of many of the agricultural colonies—a fact that directly influenced the fate of these communities.

Travel to the outlying rural areas of the United States was not easy in the 1880s, as one description of the journey to New Odessa in Oregon indicated. "In July, 1882, twenty-five members of Am Olam left New York by steamer for Colon, Panama, crossed the Isthmus by foot and wagon, boarded another steamer for San Francisco and yet another coastal ship for Portland, Oregon."[22] Before embarking on this venture, these migrants had already traveled from Russia to the United States. While only a small proportion of Russian Jewish immigrants joined colonies, those who did moved to diverse parts of the United States very early in the colonization movement.

The story of the Jewish agricultural colony movement is thus a complex one. The original goal of Am Olam—to gain ownership of land in the United States through collective agricultural development—attracted the financial support of European Jewish organizations (French and English, for the most part). The settlement process in the United States was mainly handled through charitable organizations or congregations dominated by more-established German Jewish communities located in urban areas. Given these factors, it is not surprising that the survival of many of these communities depended on their proximity to established, urban settlements and the continued support of their patrons. Not to be taken lightly was still a third factor—the availability of agriculturally viable land. As we examine the histories of many of the communities, these points recur time and again.

Early Russian Immigrant Colonies

The decade of the 1880s marked the initial phase of the Jewish agricultural colony movement in the United States. While it would be tempting to typify geographically or ideologically the colonies at this or the other time periods, a review of the available descriptions of these communities leaves the reader with a sense of their tremendous variation across a wide expanse of the country. In this and each of the succeeding two sections of this essay, the experiences of some of these colonies are summarized. Because of the uneven nature of the documentation for the widespread colonization effort, some descriptions contain more detail than others. I have chosen to include many of the more detailed descriptions in order to provide a richer flavor of the hardships and difficulties, as well as achievements, experienced by these colonies.

Russian Jews created their first American colony, Sicily Island, in Catahoula Parish, Louisiana, in 1881. The colonists had assistance from three funding organizations: the Alliance Israelite Universelle, the New York Emigration Committee, and the New Orleans Agricultural Society. A local Louisiana coroner named Eillinger located and obtained the land for the colony, but it was quite unsuited for agriculture.[23] Sicily Island lay in a deserted swamp. The hot climate and continued flooding of the Mississippi River contributed to high rates of malaria and yellow fever.[24] While the colonists had varied occupational backgrounds (including bookkeeper, cigar/cigarette maker, clerk, lawyer, merchant, professor, saddler, student, tinsmith, tobacco cutter, and tobacco manufacturer), only a few were farmers.[25] The adult men preceded the women and children at the site; they undertook the chores of building cottages, fencing the grounds, and planting corn, vegetables, and trees. Then they built more substantial houses and opened a general store. When the children were brought up from New Orleans, a school was started. Two of the colonists who knew English served as the teachers.[26]

Sicily Island had a detailed constitution that specified that "all lands, farming utensils, implements, stock and furniture shall remain the property of the association or colony."[27] The well-defined system of governance included a seven-member governing board that arbitrated disputes and handled the business of the colony.[28] The colony, however, was far from New Orleans, and therefore far from any Jewish community. Despite the high hopes and careful planning, it lasted less than a year.

After the dissolution of Sicily Island, many of the participants moved with Herman Rosenthal, their leader, to the Cremieux colony in South Dakota. This colony was named after Adolphe Cremieux, president of the Alliance Israelite Universelle. In the colonists' first year at Cremieux, the crops of oats, wheat, rye, and barley produced a solid yield. In the second year a wheat bug destroyed many of the crops and severe drought killed the cattle, while in the third year, thunderstorms ruined the crops. The colonists were forced to mortgage their farms but were unable to remain solvent while paying the high interest rates. The colony then disbanded.[29]

Colony formation in the United States reached a peak in 1882. In that year alone, twenty Jewish agricultural colonies were founded in ten different states ranging from North Dakota in the north, Arkansas in the south, New Jersey in the east, and Oregon in the west.[30]

The New Odessa colony was founded in Douglas County, Oregon, by members of the Am Olam group with participants who had lived in Odessa. Before they moved to Oregon, the group had spent time in New York raising funds. Realizing their need for agricultural training, they worked for a time outside Hartford, Connecticut, learning farming techniques.[31] After checking different potential locations, they selected Oregon because contacts with western railroad developers enabled them to purchase land where an extension of the Oregon and California Railroad was being built. This meant that the colony, which owned the land collectively and had a detailed constitution, was able to raise immediate income from selling timber to the railroad to serve as fuel and railroad ties.[32]

The New Odessa colony was soon torn by internal conflict between two factions, one led by Paul Kaplan, a radical communist, and the other by William Frey, a non-Jew promoting a highly structured lifestyle, multiple marriage partners, and a "religion of humanity." Both men had joined the group in 1883. The conflict culminated in 1885 when Frey and fifteen other members left.[33] The isolation of the colony, the small amount of land available for cultivation, the destruction of common buildings in a fire, lack of privacy, and the unavailability of wives for the single men led to the dispersion of the members out of the Pacific Northwest.

Some of the longest-lasting colonies begun in this period were in New Jersey. Located in the southern part of the state, Alliance, Carmel, Estelleville, and Rosenhayn had the advantage of being close to New York City and Philadelphia, with railroad access enabling them to get their produce to market. Further, these groups combined industry with agriculture; thus they could survive with low crop yields. Shirt, cigar, and clothing factories were established in the Alliance colony.[34] Carmel had clothing factories, and Rosenhayn boasted both a clothing and a brick factory.[35]

Possibly because of their proximity to the large Jewish communities of New York and Philadelphia, the New Jersey colonies were funded at a higher level and from a greater variety of sources. Alliance received support from the Alliance Israelite Universelle (for which the colony was named), the Hebrew Emigrant Aid Society, the Alliance Land Trust, and the Mansion House

Founded in 1882 and pictured here on August 12, 1889, Carmel Colony
in southern New Jersey combined agriculture and industry. (Archives of
the YIVO Institute for Jewish Research)

Committee of London, which established the Alliance Trust Fund.[36] This
more sound financial base doubtless contributed to the greater longevity of
Alliance.

The colonists first arrived at Alliance by train. They disembarked at the
Bradway train station (which later became Norma, another Jewish colony)
and were taken to the site of their colony, which was mainly scrub oak and
pine woods. Three large framed barracks were already on the land. These
they named "Castle Garden" after the New York port of entry. The colonists
lived in them communally for approximately six months until the small frame
houses that were to dominate the settlement were built. Two of the Castle
Garden barracks were then torn down, while the third was converted into a
cigar factory. Two years later it was again used as housing for new arrivals.

Family farms were twelve to fifteen acres in size and were assigned by lot.
The individual houses were made up of two rooms (one upstairs, one down-
stairs) and a cellar.[37] These houses sold for $150 each and, being cheaply
built, were cold in the winter and hot in the summer.[38] In the center of the
compound flew an American flag. The streets were named in honor of the
trustees of the Alliance Land Trust. On October 22, 1889, eighty members of
the Alliance colony received their naturalization papers in Salem and became
citizens of the United States.[39]

Education of the children was a priority. Very early in the existence of the
settlement temporary schools were established to teach the children English,

preparing them to enter the public schools in nearby Vineland. Religion was also well integrated into life at Alliance; there was no work on Saturday, the Sabbath, and initially kosher meat was imported from Philadelphia. Eventually the colony built four synagogues. There was also an active cultural life at Alliance. At the Sabbath school Yiddish poems were read and Jewish events discussed. In addition, the colony boasted a public library, a night school for adults, lectures, concerts, and music lessons. A benevolent society sponsored political meetings followed by refreshments of herring, crackers, and beer.[40] For recreation the unmarried members of the colony would socialize on a walk to the post office in the evenings.[41]

Along with the cigar and shirt factories at Alliance, tailoring became a home industry providing additional income. In 1884 Leonard Lewisohn of New York City donated a sewing machine to each family.[42] In 1897 Maurice and Joseph Fels of the Fels-Naphtha Soap Company of Philadelphia became involved with the colony, establishing the Allivine Cannery. This facilitated the marketing of Alliance's produce. This varied economic base further contributed to the longevity of the colony.

The Kansas colony of Beersheba, founded in 1884 with the sponsorship of the Hebrew Union Agricultural Society in Cincinnati, had quite a different experience. The colonists in Beersheba viewed their interlude there as a beginning, a chance to become Americanized, and an opportunity to acquire financial assets.[43] Beersheba was a transitional phase in their lives; when it was dissolved, some of the members continued to be a part of the farming community in that area.

In 1884, two years after its formation, the settlers of Beersheba leased part of their land to a syndicate seeking to enlarge cattle trails. The Hebrew Union Agricultural Society, "rose in righteous wrath at such action" even though the colonists had not sold the lands, but only leased them.[44] Angered by the community's decision, the sponsoring organization felt it had the legitimate right not just to countermand the settlers but to punish the community. The Hebrew Union Agricultural Society proceeded to take the animals, farm implements, and even some personal belongings of the settlers and sell them to a neighbor. This illustrates the significant power that the funding organizations often had over the colonies. Rarely in the history of communal groups did a sponsoring agency exert such direct control over the group. Yet as evidence of a general pattern of continued close oversight, this was not an isolated incident in the American Jewish agricultural colonies.[45]

The recurring themes of external funding and the harsh economic physical realities of nineteenth-century farming emerged in the histories of several other societies as well. The Painted Woods colony, founded near what is now

Bismarck, North Dakota, in 1882, was funded in part by the Jews of St. Paul, Minnesota. It was also underwritten by the Baron de Hirsch Fund as well as the Montefiore Agricultural Aid Society. At the time of the colony's beginning, the area was still the Dakota Territory. Given the harsh climate, it is remarkable that the colony existed for as long as it did: six years. Winter was long, and summer saw drought and winds, bringing, not surprisingly, major crop failure. Insufficient funds and prairie fires further destroyed Painted Woods' viability, eventually causing the colony to disband, with some members relocating at Devil's Lake.[46] Cotopaxi, near Canon City in Colorado, was located in an arid region of the state. In addition to problems created by internal conflicts, difficult winters, and the lack of regular rainfall, spring floods from the mountains disrupted farming in that community.[47]

Before the 1880s ended, nine more colonies were begun. Five of these were in Kansas, two were in North Dakota, and one was in New Jersey. As in the case of Sicily Island, some of whose members had traveled from Louisiana to Cremieux in South Dakota; the disbanding of one colony led to the settlement of another. The Devil's Lake colony was founded in Ramsey County, North Dakota, by members of the Painted Woods colony that had disbanded in 1887.[48] The soil and drainage were somewhat better at Devil's Lake, and the farmers were more successful than they had been at Painted Woods; but this too disbanded.[49]

The Continued Development of the Jewish Agricultural Colonies: The 1890s

The early 1890s were an important time in the continued development of Jewish agricultural colonies in the United States. In 1889, persecution of Jews in Russia began afresh. Immigration to the United States increased, as did the need for funds. The Baron de Hirsch Fund was incorporated in 1891 in New York with over $2 million in assets to assist the colonists.[50] By 1899 600 Jewish farmers had been assisted by the fund.[51] This organization provided funding support for colonies and was instrumental in the development of other groups such as the Jewish Agricultural Society.

During this time the Michigan colonies of Twelve Corners and Palestine were founded. Twelve Corners, in Berrien County on Lake Michigan, was funded by the Jewish Agriculturists' Aid Society of Chicago.[52] The colony of Palestine, often called Bad Axe, after the town where it was located, is distinctive relative to most of the other Jewish agricultural colonies in that settlers purchased their own land. Nevertheless the colony was still involved with a larger funding organizational structure, since it was under the "protection" of the Detroit Reform Jewish Community and also received support from the Baron de Hirsch Fund. The land was owned by Langdon Hubbard and his son Frank, bankers and landowners, who sold it to the colonists when Hyman Lewenberg, the founder, brought together a large group of Jewish purchasers.[53]

At first the Palestine colonists lived in tents or in the open air. When the weather turned cold, the families went back to Bay City, and the men had to resort to peddling to survive the first winter.[54] They built five or six small shacks comprised of one unplastered room each. Religious services were originally held in one of the shacks until a small synagogue was built. Meat was delivered from Detroit since there was no kosher butcher in the colony. When a peddler told Marin Butzel, the president of Temple Beth El Hebrew Relief Society, about the difficult life in Palestine, he sent his good friend, a retired and experienced farmer, Emanuel Woodic, to investigate. Woodic's report indicated that Palestine consisted of twenty-three adults and thirty-four children living in ten shacks, with only seven horses and two cows among them.[55] Returning to Detroit, Woodic raised funds for the colony and returned a few months later. As a result, each farmer got a cow and a small amount of groceries. Woodic stayed to assist in training the farmers in growing oats, peas, and potatoes, which became the major crops of the colony.[56]

The settlers at Palestine did not have experience as farmers, the land was poor, their winters were bitter, they were far from markets, and they had great difficulty making the necessary payments on their land.[57] Not surprisingly, in 1899 colonists began leaving.[58] It would be easy to label Palestine as a failure, yet the Bad Axe experience helped inspire the founding, in 1900, of the Jewish Agricultural Society.[59]

Woodbine, one of the best-known colonies of the early 1890s, was founded in New Jersey. Like Alliance, it was a combined agricultural/industrial venture. Besides its agricultural endeavors, Woodbine housed a machine shop, two clothing factories, a knitting mill, and both hat and box factories.[60] One of the most significant features of Woodbine was the establishment of the Baron de Hirsch Agricultural School. This tuition-free, coeducational school, founded in 1891, held its first regular class in 1894 and was open to students fourteen years old and over.[61] Although the first class consisted of only fifteen students—all boys—by 1900 the school listed eighty boys and fifteen girls in attendance.[62] The aim of the Baron de Hirsch Agricultural School, according to the school catalog, was to offer "Jewish young men a course in agriculture, which is to teach young men practical agricultural work, and make them true tillers of the soil, intelligent farm help and managers, enabling them to earn a living as such and eventually to take up farming for themselves."[63] Fulfilling this promise until 1917, the school offered a fully developed curriculum with a wide array of subjects in what may have been the first school in the United States to provide a secondary-level education in agriculture.[64]

In April 1903 Woodbine was incorporated as a separate borough in the New Jersey county of Cape May.[65] In 1941, after allowing individual settlers to purchase land, the Baron de Hirsch Fund turned over the remaining land to the borough of Woodbine.[66] The town still exists, as well as many of the buildings and the cemeteries of the original colony, although its population is no longer predominantly Jewish.

The Baron de Hirsch Agricultural School was not the only educational institution started in the 1890s by someone supportive of the Jewish agricultural colonies.[67] In 1896 Rabbi Joseph Krauskopf founded the National Farm School in Doylestown, Pennsylvania. This was a tuition-free, four-year school established to provide agricultural training for young men not prepared to enter the state agricultural colleges.[68] Rabbi Krauskopf, while visiting Russia, had been told by Count Tolstoy to return to the United States and start a school in which Jewish boys could learn a trade.[69] The school was never exclusively for Jews, however, and had no religious services associated with it. In 1948 the National Farm School was approved as a senior college, and its name was changed to the National Agriculture College. In 1960 it became the Delaware Valley College of Science and Agriculture.

Jewish Agricultural Colonies from the Turn of the Century

Although the Jewish colonies formed in the early 1900s are generally not as well known as those that arose in the 1880s, colonies were founded in sixteen states during the first ten years of the century.[70] The Arpin colony was started in Wisconsin in 1904. The Milwaukee Jewish Agricultural Association, under the leadership of Adolph W. Rich, assisted in the settlement in Wood County, Wisconsin, 150 miles northwest of Milwaukee. As with many other groups, the work was heavy and the winters cold. But, according to historian Louis J. Swichkow, "the primary reasons for the ultimate dissolution of the colony were the lack of secondary educational facilities, social contacts with fellow Jews, and, above all, the fear of intermarriage."[71] The concern for education and potential marriage partners was part of the developmental process in the dissolution of this and other colonies. This was one reason later colonizers attempted to situate their communities near large Jewish population centers.

Happyville in South Carolina (founded 1905) had a funding base much different from that of the other colonies. Ebbie Julian Watson, the South Carolina commissioner of agriculture, wanted European immigrants to come to the South, where he felt they would help bring prosperity. To that end South Carolina established an office on Wall Street in New York City to recruit Russian Jews. Happyville was funded by the South Carolina State Immigration Bureau rather than by the traditional Jewish charities. Watson selected Charles Weintraub and Morris Latterman to assist in the selection of land. Twenty-five Russian immigrants formed the Incorporative Farming Association to finance the colony. Membership entitled the colonists to a portion of the crops they raised as well as wages.[72] Following a familiar trajectory, Happyville lasted under three years. Poor soil, internal disagreements, and the settlers' lack of farming experience all contributed to its end.

Clarion colony in Utah, another twentieth-century colony, received funding from both a traditional Jewish funding agency, the Jewish Agricultural and Colonial Association, and an unexpected source, the Mormon Church. Like South Carolina, the state of Utah actively recruited settlers to the area, often participating in expositions for this purpose. Clarion colony actually had its origins in a meeting in Philadelphia in January 1910. A year and a half later, in August 1911, the settlers arrived. "In September 1911, on a barren hill in south central Utah," writes Robert Alan Goldberg, "twelve Jewish farmers hoisted an American flag to signal the transformation of a dream into reality. A Jewish agricultural colony had arisen from the desert."[73] Initially they lived communally in large white tents, and all produce went into a common storehouse.[74] Even when the living arrangements centered on nuclear families, the farmwork was done communally and the colony boasted a cooperative store and a common granary. By 1913 thirty-three homes and a school had been constructed, although some families still resided in tents.[75] The houses were twenty-five-foot-square, one-room shacks set on concrete that had been covered with boards. There was no running water. A wood-fueled stove was used for cooking and heat, while kerosene lamps were used for light.[76] The school had two rooms for grades one through five. The local Mormon school board agreed to supply the teacher if the colonists built the school, and to allow the colonists to hire a second teacher to provide religious instruction in Judaism.[77]

Clarion's leader, Benjamin Brown, was born Benjamin Lipshitz in Russia. He took his last name from the American farmer for whom he worked when he was a student in the National Farm School. Rabbi Joseph Krauskopf of the National Farm School had contacts in Utah and felt that the Mormons would be more receptive than most Americans to a Jewish colony.[78] The Mormons, who understood communal living from their own experiences in Ohio, Missouri, Illinois, and Utah, sympathized with the Jews as biblical brethren.[79]

American Jewish Agricultural Colonies 365

The needs of the Jewish colonists and those of state officials blended nicely. Lack of water posed a major problem, however.[80] While the Board of Land Commissioners foreclosed the colony and offered it for public sale on November 5, 1915, this did not end the colonists' agricultural influence in the area.[81] Benjamin Brown and more than ten families remained on the land, paying rent to the state. In 1923 they formed the Utah Poultry Producers Cooperative Association. The association later expanded into the Intermountain Farmers Association, which in 1967 did over $9 million worth of business.[82]

The early years of the twentieth century, a time of organizational ferment and "progressive" reform in American agriculture generally, also saw a flurry of activism in the Jewish agricultural movement. In 1908 the Jewish Agricultural and Industrial Aid Society started the *Jewish Farmer*, a Yiddish farming publication that eventually was published in English as well.[83] A year later thirteen different associations organized the Federation of Jewish Farmers of America and held the first annual convention of Jewish farmers.[84] But the great era of Jewish agricultural communities had passed. Only one more venture in Jewish rural communal living would be founded in America. The Sunrise colony started in Michigan in 1933 and moved to Virginia after six years. It was quite different from the other Jewish agricultural colonies discussed in this essay, in that the members were not immigrants but native-born Jews. It lasted for six years in Michigan and another two years in Virginia.[85] Thereafter, Jewish farming continued in the United States but on an individual, not a collective, basis.

Conclusions

What conclusions about communal or utopian societies can be drawn from the experiences of Jewish agricultural colonies in the United States? Their relative lack of longevity, their variety, and the distinctive nature of these colonies make such an effort difficult, unless a developmental perspective is applied to both the colonies and their patrons. For the study of Jewish agricultural colonies is also a study of charitable and social service organizations. These include the Alliance Israelite Universelle, the Baron de Hirsch Fund, the Hebrew Colonization Society, the Hebrew Emigrant Aid Society, the Montefiore Agricultural Aid Society, and the Russian Emigrant Relief Committee.[86] In addition, local philanthropic societies in many areas, such as the Jewish Agriculturists' Aid Society of Chicago, Milwaukee's Jewish Agricultural Association, and the Hebrew Union Agricultural Society in Cincinnati, also helped underwrite these agricultural ventures.

PEARL W. BARTELT

This exhibit of the Sanitation Department of the Jewish Agricultural Society
was one of many of its efforts to improve the living standards of rural settlers.
(Archives of the YIVO Institute for Jewish Research)

Despite the brief duration of individual Jewish agricultural colonies, taken together they contributed importantly to the dispersion of immigrant Jews throughout the United States and to the Americanization of Russian Jewish immigrants. Considering the problems they faced—including poor land selection, inadequate funding, agricultural inexperience, and the changes in post–Civil War American agriculture associated with industrialization and the revolution in transportation—they did a remarkable job of adapting to economic, organizational, and physical conditions that in the main were disruptive of small-scale rural communities of any kind, and especially of communal ones.

What, then, is the significance and legacy of these communities? As we have seen, the Jewish agricultural colonies contributed to the nationwide dispersion of Jewish immigrants, played an important role in the Americanization of the pre–World War II Jewish immigrants, and figured prominently in the emergence of a large network of mutual assistance organizations. In addition, Russian Jews were in the vanguard of the rural-credit movement in America. They organized cooperatives such as the Cooperative Poultrymen's Association in Woodbine, New Jersey, the Cooperative Fire Insurance Companies of New York State, and the Intermountain Farmers Association in Utah.[87] The experience in Bad Axe inspired the founding of the Jewish Agricultural Society, which performed inspections for the government to ensure sanitary conditions on farms and operated an extension department, a purchasing bureau, and a farm labor bureau.[88]

The colony at Woodbine resulted in an incorporated borough in New Jersey. Other settlements throughout the Vineland-Millville area of New Jersey, such as Alliance, helped develop the agricultural and light industrial character of the area. The National Farm School in Doylestown, Pennsylvania, still exists as the Delaware Valley College of Science and Agriculture.

A World War II press release from the Jewish Agricultural Society suggested the impact of the early Jewish agricultural colonies. After noting the growth in the number of Jewish farmers in America from fewer than 1,000 in 1900 to over 100,000 by 1937, it went on: "The history of early Jewish attempts to found farm colonies are as interesting as any chapter of American pioneer days. While most of the early settlement attempts failed, yet the seeds of the desire remained, culminating in a rising community of Jewish farmers and agriculturists who are today contributing to the science and economy of American farming, and who are producing precious food for an America at war."[89]

The Jewish agricultural colony movement spanned a full century in the history of American society. Shaped by the patterns of immigration to the United States, the movement reached its height during the heaviest period of Eastern European/Russian emigration from 1880 to 1920. The histories of these communities clearly reflect the demands of survival and the widely varying levels and conditions of their sponsors' funding and support. Unlike many other types of communal societies, the Jewish agricultural colonies were dominated more by the practicalities of survival than by ideological considerations.

The developmental paradigm suggests that communal societies do not simply disappear from a society but interact with and live on in their impact on the society. The Jewish agricultural colonies spawned towns and communities that emerged from their cigar factories and canning operations; they developed an agricultural education program that included the founding of an agricultural college; and they began at least one continuing major agricultural cooperative, the Intermountain Farmers Association.

But perhaps more important than such specific results of the movement are the more institutionalized forms of activity. This essay has emphasized two major features of American life linked to this movement. The first of these is the integration of Jewish immigrants into rural settings, and across a much wider geographic area, than would have otherwise been expected. This is especially noteworthy given the discrimination, ghettoization, and spatial concentration experienced by large segments of the American Jewish community.

The second is the relationship of the ventures to the establishment of a system of Jewish philanthropy. This system persists to the present day, at times replete with the politics and sponsorship issues of the past. In this sense, the influence of the Jewish agricultural colonies' experience in American society is both identifiable and significant.

Chronology

1820	Ararat, first of nearly 100 immigrant agricultural colonies, is founded on Grand Island in the Niagara River in Erie County, N.Y., by German Jews led by Mordecai Manuel Noah. (See Appendix for complete list.)
1825	Alachua colony of German Jews established in Alachua County, Fla., led by Moses Elias Levy.
1837–42	Shalom colony of German Jews in Ulster County, N.Y.
1860	Alliance Israelite Universelle is established in Paris to aid Russian refugees traveling to America. Many other immigrant aid societies appear in the nineteenth century, including the Mansion House Committee of London and, in the United States, the Hebrew Emigrant Aid Society, the Jewish Agricultural Society, the Hebrew Colonial Society of Baltimore, and the Jewish Agricultural and Industrial Aid Society.
1865	Last German Jewish colony is formed in Atwood County, Colo.
1881	Pogroms in Russia; the Am Olam movement is begun in Odessa by young Jewish intellectuals to found agricultural colonies in America. First Russian Jewish colony is established at Sicily Island in Catahoula Parish, La.; led by Herman Rosenthal and dissolved in 1882.
1882	Peak of Jewish colonization; no fewer than twenty Russian Jewish colonies set up in Arkansas, Colorado, Kansas, Maryland, Michigan, North Dakota, New Jersey, Oregon, South Dakota, and Virginia (see Appendix).
1891	Baron de Hirsch Fund is incorporated.
1894	Baron de Hirsch Agricultural School is begun in Woodbine, N.J.
1900	Jewish Agricultural Society is started.
1908	*The Jewish Farmer* begins publication.
1909	Federation of Jewish Farmers of America is started.
1938	Last Jewish colony is begun by Joseph Cohen at Sunrise, Va.; dissolves in 1940.
1959	*The Jewish Farmer* ends publication.

Notes

1. Richard E. Singer, "The American Jew in Agriculture: Past History and Present Condition" (unpublished prize-winning essay, Hebrew Union College, Cincinnati, Ohio, 1941), 395.

2. Each colony discussed is listed in the Appendix under Jewish Agricultural Colonies. Where discrepancies of dates occur in the literature, decisions were made based on the primary sources.

3. Leonard G. Robinson, *Agricultural Activities of the Jews in America*, reprint from the *American Jewish Year Book 5673* (New York: American Jewish Committee, 1912), 28.

4. George M. Price, "The Russian Jews in America," trans. Leo Shpall, *American Jewish Historical Quarterly* 48 (1958): 100–101. Although New York state did not have agricultural colonies per se, the region became an important geographical area for individually owned Jewish farms and summer boardinghouses that eventually developed into an area noted for the large hotel establishments of the Catskills. By 1909 there were at least ten noncommunal Jewish farming communities in New York state: Liberty, Hurleyville, Ferndale, Fallsburg, Monticello, Centerville, Mountaindale, Summitville, Ellenville, and Nassau. See also David M. Gold, "Jewish Agriculture in the Catskills, 1900–1920," *Agricultural History* 55 (1981): 40. The use of Jewish farms for summer boarding to augment income occurred in Connecticut, Massachusetts, and New Jersey as well.

5. Ruth Marcus Patt, ed., *The Jewish Scene in the Central Jersey Rural Areas*, supplement no. 2 (New Brunswick: Jewish Historical Society of Central Jersey, 1982), 4.

6. Ibid.

7. Helen E. Blumenthal, "The New Odessa Colony of Oregon, 1882–1886," *Western States Jewish Historical Quarterly* 14 (1982): 321.

8. Ibid.

9. Ibid.

10. Joseph Brandes, *Immigrants to Freedom: Jewish Communities in Rural New Jersey since 1882* (Philadelphia: University of Pennsylvania Press, 1971), 21; Abraham Menes, "The Am Oylom Movement," in *Studies in Modern Jewish Social History*, ed. Joshua A. Fishman (New York: Ktav, 1977), 157.

11. Menes, "Am Oylom Movement," 159. Many assume that modern Jewish agricultural communitarianism began in Israel with the formation of the kibbutz movement. Actually, Jewish agricultural colonies in America employed communal methods decades before the first Zionists in Palestine did so at the initial kibbutz, Degania, in 1909. See Robert Alan Goldberg, *Back to the Soil: The Jewish Farmers of Clarion, Utah, and Their World* (Salt Lake City: University of Utah Press, 1986), 142. By 1909 more than seventy Jewish colonies existed in America. There is no explicit evidence, incidentally, that cross-fertilization of utopian perspectives occurred across organizations, although it would be surprising if this did not occur to some extent, given the emergence of external support for both efforts.

12. Robinson, *Agricultural Activities*, 39.

13. Ibid.

14. Lois Fields Schwarz, "Early Jewish Agricultural Colonies in North Dakota," *North Dakota History* 34 (1965): 221.

15. Robinson, *Agricultural Activities*, 40.

16. Funding organizations are included in the Appendix.

17. A. James Rudin, "Beersheba, Kansas: 'God's Pure Air on Government Land,'" *Kansas Historical Quarterly* 34 (1968): 282.

18. Although this was not the case for the Am Olam members, who spoke Russian, the earlier arriving German Jews did not separate different groups of the new arrivals for preferential treatment.

19. David Ward, *Cities and Immigrants* (New York: Oxford University Press, 1981), 6, 56.

20. Timothy Miller, ed., *American Communes, 1860–1960: A Bibliography* (New York: Garland, 1990).

21. Joel S. Geffen, "Jewish Agricultural Colonies as Reported in the Pages of the Russian Hebrew Press," *American Jewish Historical Quarterly* 60 (1971): 356.

22. Blumenthal, "New Odessa Colony," 323.

23. M. Peissackwotch, "The Jewish Agriculture Colonies in America" (unpublished paper, YIVO Institute for Jewish Research, New York, n.d.), 3.

24. Leo Shpall, "Jewish Agricultural Colonies in the United States," *Agricultural History* 34 (1950): 130; Price, "Russian Jews in America," 85.

25. Singer, "American Jew In Agriculture," 326.

26. Menes, "Am Oylom Movement," 24; Singer, "American Jew in Agriculture," 35.

27. Leo Shpall, "A Jewish Agricultural Colony in Louisiana," *Louisiana Historical Quarterly* 20 (1937): 830.

28. Uri D. Herscher, *Jewish Agricultural Utopias in America, 1880–1910* (Detroit: Wayne State University Press, 1981), 35.

29. Milton Reizenstein, "Agricultural Colonies in the United States," in *Jewish Encyclopedia*, 12 vols., ed. Isadore Singer (New York: Funk and Wagnalls, 1906), 1:257–58.

30. Newport and the Arkansas Colony in Arkansas; Cotopaxi in Colorado; Beersheba and Hebron in Kansas; Baltimore in Maryland; Carp Lake in Michigan; Alliance, Carmel, Estelleville, and Rosenhayn in New Jersey; Devil's Lake and Painted Woods in what became North Dakota; New Odessa in Oregon; Adler, Bethlehem Yehudah, Cremieux, and Mendelsohn in the present state of South Dakota; and Middlesex County and Waterview in Virginia.

31. Shpall, "Jewish Agricultural Colonies," 134.

32. Blumenthal, "New Odessa Colony," 323.

33. Ibid., 326, 329.

34. Shpall, "Jewish Agricultural Colonies," 141.

35. Philip Reuben Goldstein, *Social Aspects of the Jewish Colonies of South Jersey* (New York: League Printing Co., 1921), 41. This work began as a Ph.D. dissertation at the University of Pennsylvania.

36. Shpall, "Jewish Agricultural Colonies," 141–42.

37. Brandes, *Immigrants to Freedom*, 57.

38. Sidney Bailey, "The First Fifty Years," in "Yoral: A Symposium upon the First Fifty Years of the Jewish Farming Colonies of Alliance, Norma and Brotmanville, New Jersey," ed. Herman Eisenberg et al. (unpublished booklet, New Jersey State Library, Trenton, 1932), 13.

39. Moses Klein, "The Alliance Colony in 1889," in Eisenberg et al., "Yoral," 40.

40. Bailey, "First Fifty Years," 19.

41. Elizabeth Reidnick Levin, "Pioneer Women of the Colonies," in Eisenberg et al., "Yoral," 32.

42. Singer, "American Jew in Agriculture," 266.

43. Lipman Goldman Feld, "New Light on the Lost Jewish Colony of Beersheba, Kansas, 1882–1886," *American Jewish Historical Quarterly* 60 (1970): 168.

44. Ibid., 165.

45. In the early 1900s the Jewish Agricultural and Industrial Aid Society took back plows and other equipment it had given the colonists in Laramie, Wyoming. The colonists had used monies for other than their intended use and would not give real estate mortgages as security on the loaned monies. See Singer, "American Jew in Agriculture," 524–25.

46. Price, "Russian Jews in America," 87; Robinson, *Agricultural Activities*, 43.

47. Robinson, *Agricultural Activities*, 43.

48. Ibid.

49. Singer, "American Jew in Agriculture," 423.

50. Robinson, *Agricultural Activities*, 49–50.

51. Singer, "American Jew in Agriculture," 199.

52. Robinson, *Agricultural Activities*, 74.

53. Gabriel Davidson, "The Palestine Colony in Michigan: An Adventure in Colonization," *American Jewish Historical Society* 34 (1925): 62. Names of the initial settlers were Baerman, Beckman, Eckstein, Goldman, Kahn, Lipowsky, Malinoff, Rosenberg, and Steinborn.

54. Singer, "American Jew in Agriculture," 362.

55. Davidson, "Palestine Colony," 65.

56. A. James Rudin, "Bad Axe, Michigan: An Experiment in Jewish Agricultural Settlement," *Michigan History* 56 (1972): 123.

57. Ibid., 127–30.

58. Davidson, "Palestine Colony," 73.

59. Ibid., 130. The Jewish Agricultural Society responded to the problems of the agricultural colonies and provided financial and technical assistance to later generations of Jewish farmers, both in colonies and on individual farms.

60. Robinson, *Agricultural Activities*, 69.

61. *Catalogue of the Baron de Hirsch Agricultural and Industrial School at Woodbine, N.J.* (New York: DeLeeuw and Oppenheimer, 1898), 9–10.

62. "Souvenir Programme: Dedication of the Baron de Hirsch Agricultural and Industrial School, Woodbine, New Jersey, 1900" (YIVO Institute for Jewish Research), 14.

63. "The Baron de Hirsch Agricultural School—Woodbine, New Jersey" (YIVO Institute for Jewish Research, n.d.), 5.

64. *Baron de Hirsch Fund 75th Anniversary Exhibit* (Washington, D.C.: B'nai B'rith Jewish Historical Committee, 1966), 10; *Catalogue of the Baron de Hirsch Agricultural and Industrial School*, 11–13. The first-year curriculum, which was almost the same for boys and girls, consisted of English, arithmetic, drawing, history, geography, chemistry, physics, bookkeeping and correspondence, and botany. In the second and third years the curriculum differed somewhat by gender, although all students were expected to do "practical work" every term. Also see Robinson, *Agricultural Activities*, 86.

65. Goldstein, *Social Aspects*, 55.

66. *Baron de Hirsch Fund*, 10.

67. Benjamin Brown, "The Story of the Jewish Colony, Clarion in Utah" (unpublished translation of Benjamin Brown's Yiddish manuscript, translator unknown, YIVO Institute for Jewish Research, n.d.), 3.

68. Robinson, *Agricultural Activities*, 87.

69. Mrs. Gourley, Secretary to the Corporation, Delaware Valley College of Science and Agriculture, telephone interview, March 1989.

70. Ellington and Hartford in Connecticut; Flora in Illinois; Sulzberger in Kansas; Ellicott and Yaazor in Maryland; Bolystown, Rutland, and Sandisfield in Massachusetts; Cherry County in Nebraska; Flemington, Six Points, and Toms River in New Jersey; Rensselaer and Syracuse in New York; Bowman and Burleigh County in North Dakota; Happyville in South Carolina; Perkins County in South Dakota; Tyler in Texas; Clarion County in Utah; Arpin in Wisconsin; and Laramie in Wyoming.

71. Louis J. Swichkow, "The Jewish Agricultural Colony of Arpin, Wisconsin," *American Jewish Historical Quarterly* 54 (1964): 91.

72. Arnold Shankman, "Happyville, the Forgotten Colony," *American Jewish Archives* 30 (1978): 8.

73. Goldberg, *Back to the Soil*, 3.

74. Ibid., 64. Evertt L. Cooley, "Clarion, Utah: Jewish Colony in 'Zion,'" *Utah Historical Quarterly* 36 (1968): 121.

75. Cooley, "Clarion Utah," 122.

76. Goldberg, *Back to the Soil*, 103.

77. Ibid., 101.

78. Ibid., 43.

79. Ibid., 57.

80. Cooley, "Clarion, Utah," 130.

81. Goldberg, *Back to the Soil*, 124.

82. Cooley, "Clarion, Utah," 131.

83. *Baron de Hirsch Fund*, 12.

84. Robinson, *Agricultural Activities*, 83.

85. For further information, see Joseph J. Cohen, *In Quest of Heaven: The Story of the Sunrise Co-operative Farm Community* (New York: Sunrise History Publishing Committee, 1957), and Christina M. Lemieux, "Michigan Utopia: The Sunrise Cooperative Farm Community," *Chronicle* 23 (1988): 4–8.

86. Cooley, "Clarion, Utah," 137.

87. Singer, "American Jew in Agriculture," 569.

88. Ibid., 565.

89. Jewish Agricultural Society, "Our Jewish Farmers" (YIVO Institute for Jewish Research, n.d.), 1.

Selected Bibliography

Brandes, Joseph. *Immigrants to Freedom: Jewish Communities in Rural New Jersey since 1882.* Philadelphia: University of Pennsylvania Press, 1971.

Eisenberg, Ellen. *Jewish Agricultural Societies in New Jersey, 1882–1920.* Syracuse, N.Y.: Syracuse University Press, 1995.

Goering, Violet, and Orlando Goering. "The Agricultural Communes of the Am Olam." *Communal Societies* 4 (1984): 74–86.

Gold, David M. "Jewish Agriculture in the Catskills, 1900–1920." *Agricultural History* 55 (1981): 31–49.

Goldstein, Philip Reuben. *Social Aspects of the Jewish Colonies of South Jersey.* New York: League Printing Co., 1921.

Herscher, Uri D. *Jewish Agricultural Utopias in America, 1880–1910.* Detroit: Wayne State University Press, 1981.

Menes, Abraham. "The Am Oylom Movement." In *Studies in Modern Jewish Social History*, edited by Joshua A. Fishman, 155–79. New York: Ktav, 1977.

Peissackwotch, M. "The Jewish Agriculture Colonies in America." Unpublished paper at YIVO Institute for Jewish Research, New York, n.d.

Price, George M. "The Russian Jews in America." Translated by Leo Shpall. *American Jewish Historical Quarterly* 48 (1958): 26–62, 78–133.

Reizenstein, Milton. "Agricultural Colonies in the United States." In *Jewish Encyclopedia*, 12 vols., ed. Isadore Singer. New York: Funk and Wagnalls, 1906), 1:256–62.

Shpall, Leo. "Jewish Agricultural Colonies in the United States." *Agricultural History* 24 (1950): 120–46.

Singer, Richard E. "The American Jew in Agriculture: Past History and Present Condition." Unpublished prize-winning essay. Hebrew Union College, Cincinnati, Ohio, 1941.

"Souvenir Programme: Dedication of the Baron de Hirsch Agricultural and Industrial School, Woodbine, New Jersey, 1900." YIVO Institute for Jewish Research, New York.
"Yoral: A Symposium upon the First Fifty Years of the Jewish Farming Colonies of Alliance, Norma and Brotmanville, New Jersey." Edited by Herman Eisenberg et al. Unpublished booklet, New Jersey State Library, Trenton, 1932.

PEARL W. BARTELT

JAMES E. LANDING

Cyrus Reed Teed and the Koreshan Unity

The emergence of communal life in twentieth-century America brought increasing attention to earlier attempts to found utopian communities. Although all such groups have individual histories, a few, at least, seem to have been founded by leaders increasingly confounded by religious, technological, and social developments of the nineteenth century. The emergence at that time of newer forms of biblical criticism and theological expression, the rise of the scientific method of analysis as exemplified in Darwinian biology, and the scale of social change emanating from industrial capitalism, among other developments, had upset what was, to many, the established order. Disturbed by the conceptualization of an infinite universe, of an organic evolution stretching backward into a vast unknown, and of social rearrangement only yet dimly understood, there was, to some, comfort to be found in finiteness, boundedness, order, and less complex arrangements.

Emanating from the unique circumstances of the late nineteenth century, a host of individual perspectives arose, making an effort to reconcile such discomforts: a flat earth or a hollow earth, with the safety of known limits; a definite time and place in which creation became manifest; a social structure and social life that, at one and the same time, could take advantage of the new but remain rooted in the old. In short, a simple universe that by mental analogy was one with beauty, symmetry, ordered arrangement, and not the least important, godliness. Perhaps this is a frame of reference for beginning an understanding of Koreshanity and its founder, Cyrus R. Teed. For it was not

375

so much in the uniqueness of any single belief as it was in the integration of science, religion, and social economics that the movement of Teed became known.

Cyrus Reed Teed

In 1839 Cyrus Reed Teed was born near Trout Creek in Delaware County, New York, the second son in a family of eight.[1] Soon after his birth, the family moved to Utica, and, at eleven, Cyrus left school for a job on the Erie Canal. His parents were, apparently, devout Baptists, and Teed was urged to study for the ministry because of his powers of oratory. Instead, in 1859 he began the study of medicine in the office of Samuel Teed, his uncle, in Utica. He married Delia M. Row, fathered a son Douglas (who later gained renown as an artist in the Binghamton area[2]), and joined the Union army medical service during the Civil War, where he was attached to a field hospital.[3] After the war Teed continued his medical studies at the New York Eclectic College, graduated, and in 1868 established his own practice in Utica, just one year before the remarkable experience that was to transform not only his life but also that of countless followers to come.

Teed was a learned man full of curiosity; but his training in medical science began to lean more toward the occult, and he was preoccupied with alchemy. According to his own account these pursuits were not without reward, because he immodestly claimed to have discovered that which had eluded the sages of countless centuries prior to his own work. "I had succeeded in transforming matter of one kind to its equivalent energy, and in reducing this energy, through polaric influence, to matter of another kind. . . . The 'philosopher's stone' had been discovered, and I was the humble instrument for the exploiter of so magnitudinous a result."[4]

According to Teed, it was near midnight on an autumn eve in 1869 as he sat in his "electro-alchemical" laboratory pondering his successes and hoping to perfect further the laws of transmutation, when an even more singular incident occurred. In Teed's words one can feel the creative force of his prose, recognize the scientist at work, and come close to his very self.

I bent myself to the task of projecting into tangibility the creative principle. Suddenly, I experienced a relaxation at the occiput or back part of the brain, and a peculiar buzzing tension at the forehead or sinciput; succeeding this was a sensation as of a Faradic battery of the softest tension, about the organs of the brain called the lyra, crura pinealis, and conarium. There gradually spread from the center of my brain to the ex-

　　　　　　　　　JAMES E. LANDING

Dr. Cyrus Reed Teed, who took the name "Koresh" (Hebrew for Cyrus) and founded the Koreshan Unity. (Frontispiece from Koresh and U. G. Morrow, *The Cellular Cosmogony . . . Or . . . The Earth a Concave Sphere* [1889].)

tremities of my body, and, apparently to me, into the auric sphere of my being, miles outside of my body, a vibration so gentle, soft, and dulciferous that I was impressed to lay myself upon the bosom of this gently oscillating ocean of magnetic and spiritual ecstasy. I realized myself gently yielding to the impulse of reclining upon the vibratory sea of this, my newly-found delight. My every thought but one had departed from the contemplation of earthly and material things. I had but a lingering, vague remembrance of natural consciousness and desire.[5]

As Teed luxuriated in his plane of astral projection, he suddenly saw a "light of dazzling brilliancy"[6] that slowly materialized into the form of a beautiful woman who addressed him: "Fear not, my son, thou satisfactory offspring of my profoundest yearnings! I have nurtured thee through countless embodiments."[7] A lengthy dialogue followed, but two statements of the celestial vision that had visited Teed's laboratory stand out as being of special significance: (1) "Offspring of my most potential desire, thou art chosen to redeem the race,"[8] and (2) "I have brought thee to this birth to sacrifice thee upon the altar of all human hopes, that through thy quickening of me, thy Mother and Bride, the Sons of God shall spring into visible creation."[9] There was no doubt that Teed was to be the new Messiah.

As a result of this illumination Teed began practicing medicine in conjunction with preaching. Finding some succor from his immediate family, he soon began to preach to his patients. But Utica was, at that time, not the scene for a doctor to begin espousing strange doctrines, for "it lay in that psychically fertile earth of a broad mystic highway running across New York State."[10] New Yorkers, already acquainted with the Rappites, Joseph Smith and his Mormons, the Oneida Community of John Humphrey Noyes, Ann Lee's Shakers, the Society of True Inspiration, and the strange beginnings of American Spiritualism at the Fox home in Hydesville, New York, held little tolerance for what they believed was another expression of deviance. Teed's medical practice languished, and he drifted from one New York town to another, discovering that his patients preferred doctoring to his strange preachings.[11] In 1880, discouraged and disillusioned, he moved to Moravia, where he took over the operation of his parents' small mop-making business and established his first group following. Known to many as "Cyrus the Messenger,"[12] Teed himself Hebraized his given name into the pseudonym "Koresh" and went by this name until his death, forsaking it only once when he authored a work of visionistic fiction under the pseudonym Lord Chester.[13]

It is difficult to reconstruct exactly what Teed taught in the early days. Although many writers[14] and Teed's later followers[15] claim that his teachings had been revealed to him that strange night in his laboratory, one searches Teed's account of his "illumination" in vain for any specific doctrine, religious or secular, other than vague references to reincarnation, ascendancy to the astral plane, immortality, and the annunciation of Teed's messiahship. Teed himself mentioned the fact that his discovery of the laws of transmutation and his illumination were separate events. By 1880, however, several basic doctrines crystallized that would later be refined and better articulated. Among these were the communalization of the social order, the abolition of private property, the sanctity of celibacy, and a vague awareness of the coming of the millennium. Teed's communal ideas may have developed as a result of his contacts with the Shakers, the Perfectionists at Oneida, and especially the Rappites or Harmonists who had returned from Indiana and established their new communal order at Economy, Pennsylvania.[16] At one time the Harmonists and the followers of Teed contemplated some sort of merger, but the demise of the society at Economy prevented this from taking place.[17] Celibacy was a major tenet of the Shakers, but Teed especially emphasized chastity as a means of preserving sexual energy, a doctrine that may have owed much to the Oneida colonists. The millennial doctrine, of course, was a common religious topic of the nineteenth century.

These were not, however, the doctrines that made Teed's movement distinctly different. He integrated them into a unique universal structure held together by the concept for which he has become most noted, that of the hollow earth. Teed, pondering the significance of Isaiah 40:12—"Who has measured the waters in the hollow of his hand and marked off the heavens with a span, enclosed the dust of the earth in a measure and weighed the mountains in scales and the hills in a balance?"—became convinced that man lived "in" the earth rather than "on" it and was impressed by the key scriptural words "hollow" and "enclosed." It was, apparently, this attack on the Copernican view of astronomy that earned Teed the appellation in central New York of "that crazy doctor."[18]

Teed revealed this idea, which he termed the "Cellular Cosmogony," in conjunction with his ideas on the nature of the social order and referred to his beliefs as Koreshanity, or the Koreshan Universology. One can only speculate on the origins of the hollow earth concept in Teed's mind, but the basic idea had illustrious proponents before his time. One was the Scottish physicist Sir John Leslie, known for his works on the properties of heat. Even earlier, Dr. Edmund Halley, of comet fame, had theorized such a possibility, as did the Swiss inventor of binary logarithms, Leonhard Euler.[19] Such an idea had also been espoused by Cotton Mather, but the most devoted apostle, prior to Teed, was a veteran of the War of 1812, Captain John Cleves Symmes, who spent a fruitless life trying to convince the world that the interior of the earth was habitable and could be reached through two large entry holes located at the poles.[20] A copy of Symmes's work appeared in 1868 under the name of Professor W. F. Lyons, entitled *A Hollow Globe* and published just a year before Teed's illumination. Jules Verne's fictionalized version of the hollow earth first appeared in 1864. Doubtless, Teed was influenced by some of these writings.

Whatever the background of his thinking, Teed's later years appear to fall into three distinct periods, although overlapping chronologically: an early or

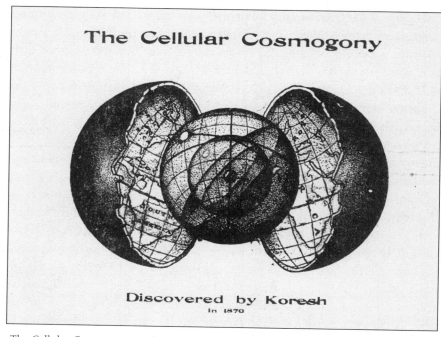

The Cellular Cosmogony

Discovered by Koresh
In 1870

The Cellular Cosmogony, as discovered by Koresh in 1870 and pictured here, suggested a "hollow globe" with the oceans and continents on the inside and the heavenly bodies with all the universe within the earth. (From back cover of *The Flaming Sword* [1948].)

formative period, centered largely around cosmological ideas and contemporary science; a middle or investigative period, during which Teed and his adherents made prodigious attempts to validate his beliefs empirically; and a late or social period, during which he synthesized his ideas and translated them into a new form of religious movement and social order.

Teed in the Formative Period

Within two years the mop-making business at Moravia had failed, and Teed, with several followers, went to Syracuse for a short time. Failing to receive converts, they moved to New York City in a third floor flat near 135th Street and Eighth Avenue.[21] Here Teed established a Koreshan colony consisting of himself and four women, including his sister and a cousin. They were about to abandon New York when Teed was asked to address the National Association for Mental Health in Chicago in September 1886. His oratorical powers must have been at their best, for he was elected president of the association and was invited to present more lectures. Immediately Teed and his devoted little band moved to south Chicago.

JAMES E. LANDING

The next seventeen years were extremely productive ones for Teed. Organization was rapid. A communal, celibate colony was established in a large mansion, called Beth-Ophra, in the suburb of Washington Heights (now part of Chicago). In the Englewood district of south Chicago he also established a central office, the Guiding Star Publishing House, and the College of Life, soon renamed the Koreshan University. Teed was also able to purchase several small businesses on the west side of Chicago through which he hoped to demonstrate the fallacies of the capitalistic system.

The rationale for this system of organization was beautifully articulated in Teed's typical neat and tidy manner in a schematic diagram in which the universal and earthly physical and social systems were woven together to form the Koreshan Unity, and in which the tripartite integrative organizational systems are obvious. Teed described this arrangement as follows:

The Koreshan Unity is an organic system of religious, social, economic reform, projected and executed from the basis of the form and function of the physical cosmos. The interpretation of universal nature, the anatomy, so to speak, of the great cosmos, is the guide to the construction of human society into one grand climax of integralism, having all the correlate activities, laws, motions, and function of the only natural and scientific pattern. Man sustains a specific relation to the physical world; aggregate humanity constitutes a universe which is analogous to the physical cosmos. The form and functions of the human body are analogous to the form and functions of the universe, consequently, the human world must be governed in accordance with the laws which govern the great physical world and the analogous form of the human body; the righteous structure of human society and government must therefore be in the form of the physical universe.[22]

This statement was clearly indicative of Teed's view of the world as one of integrative "systems" of interlocking parts, but the effort to translate this schema of the "cellular" structure (clearly, Teed's euphemism for "atom") of the physical universe to the social order led to results that appear to be ill defined. All Koreshan Unity falls into three major classes: a Secular System, a Commercial System, and an Educational System. These three cells are supposed to be mutually exclusive, but it is never made clear why the educational and commercial systems are not also "secular."

The inner circle of the Koreshan Unity consisted of three groups: the Society Arch-Triumphant, which consisted of the celibate, communal members (representing the Secular System); the Koreshan University (representing the Educational System); and the Church Triumphant, which was the income-

The Koreshan Unity.

The Cellular Universe is the Natural Basis and Pattern for the Construction of Human Government and Society.

Koreshanity is the Imperial System of Theocracy of the Golden Age.

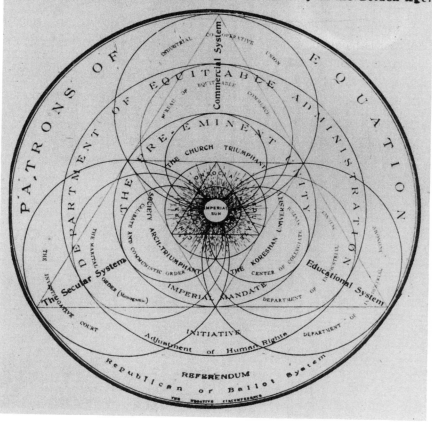

Schematic diagram of the "Koreshan Unity." (From Koresh and U. G. Morrow, *The Cellular Cosmogony . . . Or . . . The Earth a Concave Sphere* [1889], 191.)

producing sector of the group. These three, called by Teed the "Pre-Eminent Unity," had an "Imperial Mandate" to conduct their affairs and were likened to the "Imperial Sun" of the physical universe as the "Central Consociate Groupate."

The next and more outer layer of the Koreshan Unity consisted of the Department of Equitable Administration, again divided into three groups. The

JAMES E. LANDING

Marital Order (monogamous) represented the Secular System and consisted of the married members who chose not to live in a communal fashion. The Bureau of Equitable Commerce was the extension of the Commercial System to serve them, but it was never clear just how this functioned. The Department of Industrial Science was the Educational System for those in this outer circle, but its function was never clear. Those belonging to the Department of Equitable Administration were to govern their affairs through the use of the initiative process.

The third social layer, those most distantly removed from the Pre-Eminent Unity, were designated the Patrons of Equation and, once again, consisted of three groups. The Secular group was the Investigative Court, composed of those who believed in Koreshanity but chose not to live in the colony and those who were demonstrating interest in the group and seeking information. The Educational function was fulfilled by the Department of Industrial Cooperative Union. Teed described the latter as follows: "The I.C.U. is the result of practical applications of the principles of industry and commercial exchange; it is a genuine crusade against the competitive system. It owns and controls a number of industries, and desires the cooperation of all who wish to escape the bondage of the competitive world and to move in the direction of human and economic liberation."[23]

In the Chicago period some emphasis was placed on the outer two layers of this universal social scheme, but once the group left Chicago and moved to Florida, only the Pre-Eminent Unity maintained any recognizable identity and function.

With the establishment of the Guiding Star Publishing House, the Koreshans began sending forth a steady stream of literature, practically all consisting of Teed's writings. The first issue of their weekly journal, *The Guiding Star*, was published in 1887, but the name was changed in November 1889 to *The Flaming Sword* ("and he placed at the east of the garden of Eden Cherubims, and flaming sword which turned every way, to keep the way of the tree of life" [Genesis 3:24]). One list of Teed's publications included thirty-one titles, and it was not complete.[24]

Teed's oratory, powers of persuasion, and doctrines apparently had appeal for south Chicagoans, and the number of his adherents grew. Within a few years he had 126 members at Beth-Ophra and at other locations in Englewood.[25] Before the turn of the century, the Koreshans claimed to have 10,000 followers, of whom 505 were members of the Society Arch-Triumphant (celibate, communal). They had a communal branch in San Francisco and organized groups in Baltimore, Boston, Pittsburgh, Denver, Ogden, Tacoma, Portland, Lynn, and Springfield.[26]

In 1891 Teed gave a talk in Pittsburgh in which he captivated his audience with some of the practical applications of the power that would be unleashed when the governments of the world had fallen under his leadership. He proposed to employ a million men to build a six-track railroad from the Atlantic to the Pacific coasts, planned to construct a pneumatic tunnel that would carry persons on nonwheeled vehicles from New York to San Francisco in twelve hours, and claimed to have applied for a patent for a device by which he could sit in his office in Chicago and set type by wire for every newspaper in the country.[27] Although some see in Teed's words the delusions of grandeur, it is just as easy to see a sort of technological prophecy akin to that of Jules Verne.

In 1893 the World Parliament of Religions was held in Chicago. The impact of presentations on Eastern religions, metaphysical philosophies, and occult topics and the personal appearance of teachers from throughout the world was enormous. Some writers claim that Teed borrowed most of his basic ideas from various doctrines discussed at the parliament,[28] but this would imply that he came to Chicago in 1886 without having some well-developed system of his own. His activities in south Chicago between 1886 and 1893 seem to belie this, although his interest in mediumship seems to have emerged from contact with Swedenborgianism at the parliament.[29]

In 1894 the Koreshan group in Chicago had become, in a small way, a success. It was at this time Teed entered the second, or investigative, period of his movement.

Teed the Cosmological Investigator

Although Koreshanity appeared to be in the ascendancy, Teed was not without his critics, and he readily admitted that many did not believe. "In this effort we have been held up to insolent ridicule and most bitter persecution, consonant with which the public sentiment is subject. . . . We have pushed our claims to a knowledge of cosmology until the advocates of the spurious 'sciences' begin to feel their insecurity." [30]

It is small wonder that scientists of the day were not responsive to Teed's teachings. In addition to his denial of Copernican astronomy, he rewrote Huttonian geology. To Teed the earth's surface was concave and contained the entire universe. Outside the earth was nothing. The crust of the earth was composed of seventeen layers and was but 100 miles thick. The "inner" five layers were geological strata that were underlain by five mineral layers. The "outer" seven were layers of the noble metals, the outermost one being pure gold. Beyond gold, the most noble of the noble metals, there could be nothing.

JAMES E. LANDING

Within the earth's surface was found the central sun, always half lit and half dark, thus explaining day and night, and this was the power battery of the entire universe. Our sun, however, was only a projection of the central sun and followed the path of the ecliptic. The planets were reflections of mercurial "disci" floating in space between the various layers of the crust, and the moon was a sphere of crystallic energy forming an x-ray picture of the earth's surface, which was radiated to us on the surface through the moon's own energy radiation. Stars were focal points of light and mere reflections of the mercurial disci.[31] Energy was matter and matter was energy, energy flowing into and out of the central sun, materializing into matter in the crust, and reenergizing and reradiating back to the central sun.

It had long been Teed's opinion that persons assumed the earth's surface was convex only because they did not understand the principles of perspective and the laws of optics. Social and scientific pressure soon convinced Teed that explanations of the laws of optics were not enough to convince a cynical public of the truths of Koreshanity, and he began a diligent search for empirical proof of his beliefs. The search had two major dimensions. The first was to find an area suitable for his construction of a New Jerusalem where he could gather the Society Arch-Triumphant in a single body under his leadership and vindicate his views through living example. The second was to scientifically validate his theory that the earth's surface was actually concave, thus vindicating the principles of Koreshan Universology. The two searches were inextricably intertwined.

Whether by coincidence, revelation, or messianic destiny, Teed received in 1893 a letter from Gustav Damkohler, a German immigrant who had settled along the Estero Bay area of Florida south of Fort Myers on the Gulf Coast. Damkohler had accidentally come across some of the writings of Koresh, and this strange German, who had also claimed to have received celestial vibrations of some sort,[32] invited Teed to come and investigate the area. Accordingly, on January 1, 1894, Teed and three Koreshan women from Chicago reached Damkohler and were greatly impressed by Estero. Teed concluded this section of Florida was "the vitellus of the cosmogenic egg, the vital beginning of the new order."[33] Estero was to be the site of the New Jerusalem. The first search had ended.

In the meantime, plans were made to conduct experiments on the nature of the shape of the earth's surface. Teed's major assistant in this work was Professor U. G. Morrow, about whom little is known except that he was an "astronomer and geodesist."[34] The first experiments were conducted in July 1896 along the Illinois and Michigan Canal and along beaches in south Chicago and Roby (now part of Hammond), Indiana.[35] Encouraged by this work, Teed and his group decided to complete the experiments along the flat, sandy beaches near Naples, Florida, close to the site of the Estero settlement, which had attracted a score of residents.

The Koreshan geodetic staff arrived in Florida on January 2, 1897, established headquarters at Naples on the property of Col. W. N. Haldeman, owner and publisher of the *Courier Journal* of Louisville, Kentucky, and under the direction of Morrow began their work. Morrow had developed a surveying device known as a "rectilineator" and extended an "air line" (a horizontal line rather than a line following the curvature of the earth's surface) for four miles along the Naples beach. Near Gordon's Pass they discovered that the surface of the ocean, when viewed through a telescope with a hairline, had actually curved upward above the air line rather than downward as would be believed by most surveyors and engineers. Teed explained:

> The scientific cause for this discrepancy resides in the optical illusion referred to above, namely, that on one side of the visual line there are two factors entering into the formation of a picture on the retina, as follows: The perpendicular post producing the effect of retinal impression, is shortened or elongated proportionally to the distance of the object in perspective; and in addition to this, the geolinear foreshortening (the line along the earth's surface) induces a corresponding effect upon the retinal membrane. We confront, then, two kinds of foreshortening—the one geolinear, the other perpendicular—in all geodetic observations, and an optical phenomenon which should be attributed to the principle of perspective foreshortening is ignorantly attributed to curvature.[36]

With the work of Morrow providing satisfaction for Teed's basic contentions, the two published the accounts of their experiments in 1899.[37] Needless to say, the activities along the beach at Naples did not fail to attract the attention of the contemporary press.[38]

The work of Koresh and Morrow, *The Cellular Cosmogony . . . Or . . . The Earth A Concave Sphere*, remains the basic text for all Koreshan belief. It is divided into two parts: the first, by Koresh, explaining the principles of Koreshan Unity, and the second, by Morrow, describing all the survey experiments. The dedication of the volume well describes Teed's philosophy. "This little work is part of the skirmish line of the Army of Revolution; it shall never cease its influence until every vestige of the fallacies and evils of a perverted science and religion shall have been relegated to oblivion. To the first fruits of the Resurrection, offspring of the Lord, I supremely dedicate it; thence to all men in all grades of progress in their liberation from thraldom to ignorance and the hells of the competitive system."[39]

But it is an inconspicuous paragraph in the book's introduction that provides the synthesis between concavity and Teed's view of the social order resulting in the Koreshan Unity or Universology. It asserted that "to know the Lord Christ absolutely, is to be in the consciousness of the Deity; and to become like Him is to sit upon the throne of his glory. This knowledge is so related to the structured alchemico-organic macrocosm, that to know of the earth's concavity and its relation to universal form, is to know God; while to believe in the earth's convexity is to deny him and all his works. All that is opposed to Koreshanity is Antichrist."[40]

The fabric was completely woven. The geography of the earth became the religion of Koreshanity, and the religion of Koreshanity became the geography of the earth. There could be no separation. "The secret is claimed to have been found, the 'philosopher's stone' is being applied, the circle has been squared, baser metals have been transmuted into gold, the Bible is now understood, and its laws clearly analyzed by the founder of Koreshanity."[41] Teed now moved into his life's final period, structuring the social order at the New Jerusalem site along the Estero River.

Teed the Social Reformer

Within a month following the arrival of Teed on the Estero River, and after receiving a gift of land from Damkohler, twenty-four eager Koreshans journeyed to the site of the New Jerusalem. They built a log shelter to house themselves as they began their work. Teed envisioned a star-shaped city with streets 400 feet in width. It was to be the greatest city "in" the earth.[42] Teed's own description is undeniably ecstatic.

> Like a thousand world's fair cities, Estero will manifest one great panorama of architectural beauty, one great system of orderly activity, where every obstruction to the free motion of every human orb in its circle of progress will be removed. Here is to exist the climax, the crowning glory, of civilization's greatest cosmopolitan center and capital. We may stand upon the site of ancient Babylon—in the present wilderness of Assyria—and wonder at the existence of one of the world's greatest cities of the past. We may stand upon the site of the Greater Estero-to-be, and think not of the past with its ruins and its dead, but of the future when, through the influence of scientific truth in its application to life and

human relations, there springs into the world a new element of human progress, which shall loudly call to all the world for millions of progressive minds and hearts to leave the turmoil of the great time of trouble, and make their homes in the Guiding Star City.[43]

For a decade, from 1894 to 1903, the Koreshans diligently worked to develop their colony sixteen miles south of Fort Myers. When construction reached a point to accommodate Teed's followers, he liquidated his Chicago holdings, and the Society Arch-Triumphant moved as a body to its new home.

The work had not been easy. Lacking any experience in such a venture, the Koreshans literally hacked the New Jerusalem out of the palmetto wilderness of western Florida. They dredged the Estero River, dug drainage ditches, straightened ravines, landscaped, and constructed more than thirty-five buildings. By 1906 the Koreshan Unity had acquired nearly 7,000 acres of land and figured their capital assets at nearly a quarter-million dollars.[44]

Unlike many communal societies, the Koreshans were a gay lot. Although there were never more than about 200 resident Koreshans in the colony at a time, Teed's intellectual bent placed great emphasis on activities such as music, art, and dancing, and the colony had a renowned band and orchestra. Teed ruled this theocratic state jointly with one of his most devoted followers from Chicago, Anne G. Ordway, whom he designated as Victoria Gratia, Pre-Eminent. She was, Teed claimed, the embodiment of the celestial vision that had provided him with his illumination. The governmental structure was cosmic, with Koresh and Victoria Gratia being the central duality presiding over a Planetary Chamber of six women, a Stellar Chamber of four men, and a Signet Chamber of six men and six women. This represented a synthesis, through what was termed a process of "correspondential analogy," of the cosmogony and social order as Teed preached it. A friendly Shaker visited Estero about this time and left the following account:

The buildings are mostly set in a park along the right bank of the Estero River for about a mile. This park contains sunken gardens filled with flowers, banana trees loaded with fruit, paw-paw trees in fruit, palm trees of many varieties, the tall and stately eucalyptus, the bamboo waving its beautiful foliage, and many flowering trees and shrubs. Mounds are cast up, and crowned with large urns or vases for flowering plants. Steps lead down into the sunken gardens and to the water's edge at the river. This land, where the park and the buildings are located, was at times overflowed with water before the Koreshans came. They expended $3,000 or more in dredging the river, besides making a deep ravine to

Leaders of the Koreshan Unity at Estero, Florida, in the early 1900s. Koresh and Anne Ordway ("Victoria Gratia, Pre-Eminent") are shown in the front row center. Among this group were those Teed called the Central Duality (himself and Victoria Gratia), the Planetary Chamber (six women), the Stellar Chamber (four men), and the Signet Chamber (six men and six women). (From William A. Hinds, *American Communities and Cooperative Colonies* [1908], following 474.)

carry off the surplus water into the river. This ravine is now beautified with Para and Guinea grasses, both natives of Cuba, and is crossed by several artistic foot-bridges made of bamboo and other woods. Almost every kind of tropical fruit possible to grow in Florida can be found in this delightful garden, flowering vines cover the verandas of the houses and the foot-bridges in the park. Steps leading down to the boat landing, made of concrete colored with red clay, are quite grand, and were made and designed by the brethren. In fact, all the work in this magnificent garden is the product of home brains and industry. Koresh says he intends parking the river on both sides down to the bay, a distance of five miles.[45]

A conservatory, a library, and a new Koreshan University were also being planned.

The nature of Koreshan communitarianism seems to have been strongly influenced by the early family support provided Teed by his wife and other relatives. The New York experience was largely centered around close friends and his wife, his sister, his cousin, and other relatives. Even while Teed espoused celibacy and chastity, his wife, Delia Teed, remained a faithful member of the society.

Cyrus Reed Teed and the Koreshan Unity

How much Teed was influenced by views of socialists is unknown. He seems to have been unfamiliar with Marx or Engels or the works of the European anarchists. Yet he espoused the abolition of private property and the communalization of the social order. These ideas undoubtedly came from intensive contacts with the Oneida colonists, the Harmonists, and the Shakers. The uniqueness of the Koreshan Unity seems to have been in Teed's integration of the nature of the social order with his concept of the universe being contained entirely within the earth's outer circumference.

The sudden influx of several hundred Chicagoans who voted as a bloc was a great disturbance to the politicians of Fort Myers and Lee County. Soon efforts were made to disenfranchise the Koreshan group, and the customary rumors that surround all communal orders—immorality, drunkenness, occult and bizarre doings—began to circulate. In defiance of the Democratic machine, Teed inaugurated his own political party, the progressive Liberty Party, and began publishing a secular newspaper, the *American Eagle*, which had no small influence on nearby Florida voters. It was 1906, an election year, and the county politicians were unhappy with Teed since his influence had made the election outcome uncertain. On October 13, as the Koreshans tell the story, Teed was attacked and struck down by the town marshal of Fort Myers and suffered grievous injuries from which he never recovered. A painful nervous disorder developed, and Cyrus Reed Teed of Trout Creek, Cyrus the Messenger, Koresh, the Messiah, and the founder of the City of the Guiding Star died at Estero three days before Christmas in 1908.

The immediate aftermath provided no less drama. Despite his own prediction, made in 1892, that he would suffer martyrdom at the hands of a "people who professed the religion of Jesus Christ the God," Teed was also a believer in his own immortality and reembodiment. The Koreshans were divided. There were those reconciled to his death, but the majority took Teed at his word and mandated that no burial be allowed for three days so that the body of Koresh could materialize. Christmas came and Christmas went, but Koresh made no move. Finally the county health authorities ordered burial, and the Koreshans placed the remains of their departed leader in a concrete mausoleum on Estero Island, engraving on the front simply, "Cyrus, Shepherd Stone of Israel."[46]

The death of their leader resulted in disunity among the Koreshan Unity. One man, Gustav Faber, claimed that on his deathbed Teed had requested that Faber assume leadership. Victoria Gratia claimed supreme authority. Others rejected both, quietly awaiting the return of their prophet. These demanded to be allowed to investigate the status of Teed's remains. Denied, they attempted to raid the tomb, and a watchman had to be assigned. Just how long the watch was kept is unknown, but it became unnecessary after a still October day in 1921. A terrific windstorm blew across the landscape of Estero Island and swept the tomb of Koresh into the Gulf of Mexico. For the true Koreshans, the messianic destiny had been fulfilled. Koresh was freed from his mortal prison and would soon return.

Estero after Teed

Disunity was no stranger at Estero. The early days of development had been hard, and many became disillusioned and left the group. Since their possessions belonged to the colony, some residents just left to get away, but a number sued in the Lee County courts. Even Gustav Damkohler, the benefactor of the site of New Jerusalem, sued the Koreshans for return of his land, but the courts granted him only half.[47]

The mainstays of the colony were the celibates. Without Teed's leadership, converts to the Society Arch-Triumphant declined, and even the families of the marital order began to drift away. When historian Carl Carmer visited the Koreshans shortly after World War II, he found only six men and six women left, supported by a trust established around the Koreshan business activities and landholdings. They ran a general store on the Tamiami Trail, a main north-south artery through Florida; a gasoline station; a curio shop; and a trailer court leasing much of their land.

In 1947 a dispute broke out among the surviving Koreshans that threatened the continued existence of Estero. As a result of lawsuits, land had to be sold, and the aged management was forced to consider new alternatives for perpetuation.[48] They recognized that young people were not interested in Estero, and some wished only a place to live, so leadership passed into the hands of Laurence W. Bubbett, whose parents had been early Teed converts in Chicago. Bubbett spent most of his life in New York City as a copyreader but returned to the scene of his boyhood to take over the affairs of the colony. He was determined that Estero would not become an infirmary for the aged.

Bubbett was authorized to approach Florida state officials about the possibilities of perpetuating the remnant of the Koreshan landscape as a historical monument. Discussions commenced in 1952, but not until 1961 did the state of Florida accept from the Koreshans, "in the name of humanity," 305 acres of property to be designated as the Florida Koreshan State Park. Most of the colony buildings are now within the park, and the large Art Hall, one of the earliest structures erected at the New Jerusalem site, is now a combination art and Koreshan museum, containing many paintings by Teed's son, Morrow's rectilineator, Teed's Koreshanic charts, and his globe showing the continents on the inside.

The Koreshan Unity, Incorporated, is still a functional entity at Estero. Following World War II, Hedwig Michel became president, and her presence was evidence of the impact of Teed's teachings. While working as a headmistress in a Jewish school in Germany in the 1930s, she hired Peter Bender, a wounded aviator of World War I days, to teach mathematics. Bender had read Teed's cosmogony and was successful in converting Michel. Bender himself became so infatuated with the cellular cosmogony that he soon came to believe that he was the reincarnation of Koresh. Just before the war Michel headed to Estero, and Peter Bender's messianic destiny ended in a Nazi concentration camp.[49] Hedwig Michel passed away in 1982 and was succeeded by Mrs. Jo Bigelow as the seventh president of the Koreshan Unity, the third woman to hold that position.

The Koreshans still publish their monthly journal, *The American Eagle*, now largely devoted to historical and conservation articles related to the local area. The *Flaming Sword* was last issued in October 1948; a fire shortly thereafter destroyed the Guiding Star Publishing House. But the magazine did not die with a whimper. On page 11 of that issue is a copy of the letter that Bubbett sent to the editor of *Life* magazine pointing out his error in interpreting a high altitude photo of the Bonneville salt flats as revealing the earth's convexity. To the Koreshans, we still live "inside."[50]

Chronology

1839	Cyrus Reed Teed born in Delaware County, N.Y.
1859	Teed begins study of medicine.
1862–64	Teed serves in hospitals in the Union army during the Civil War.
1868	Teed graduates from the New York Eclectic College in medicine and establishes his own medical practice in Utica, N.Y.
1869	Teed experiences what he called his illumination, during which he was proclaimed the new Messiah.
1869–80	Teed formulates his ideas that he called the Koreshan Universology or the Koreshan Unity.
1880	Teed abandons medical practice and establishes a small communal group in Moravia, N.Y., where he Hebraized his name Cyrus to "Koresh."
1880–86	Teed moves his communal group to Syracuse, N.Y., then to New York City.
1886	Teed speaks before the National Association for Mental Health in Chicago.
1886–1903	Teed establishes his communal group in Chicago, founds a publishing house, several cooperative businesses, and his university. Begins empirical studies to prove that the earth is hollow.

ca. 1890–91	Teed maintains a branch of the Koreshan Unity in San Francisco.
1894–1903	Teed and other Chicago Koreshans travel to Estero, Fla., and begin the development of the "New Jerusalem."
1897–99	Teed and his Koreshan geodetic staff finish empirical studies at Estero to prove the earth hollow; publication of *The Cellular Cosmogony* by Teed and Morrow in 1899.
1903	Teed liquidates his Chicago holdings, and the Koreshans move to Estero, just south of Ft. Myers, Fla.
1908	Teed dies at Estero on December 22.
1947	Laurence Bubbett becomes leader of Koreshans at Estero.
1961	Koreshan Unity conveys 305 acres to state of Florida for Koreshan State Park.
ca. 1946–82	Hedwig Michel is president of Koreshan Unity, Inc.
1982–present	Jo Bigelow is president of Koreshan Unity, Inc.

Notes

This essay is a revised version of "Cyrus R. Teed, Koreshanity and Cellular Cosmogony," *Communal Societies* 1 (Autumn 1981): 1–17.

1. Hedwig Michel, *A Gift to the People* (Estero, Fla.: Koreshan Unity, n.d.), 2; an extensive account of Teed is Carl Carmer, *Dark Trees to the Wind: A Cycle of New York State Years* (New York: McKay, 1949; reprint, 1956), 260–89, 368; see also Robert S. Fogarty, introduction in the reprint of Cyrus Reed Teed, *The Cellular Cosmogony . . . Or . . . The Earth a Concave Sphere* (Philadelphia: Porcupine Press, 1975); an excellent interpretation of Koreshan religious belief is found in Elmer Talmadge Clark, *The Small Sects in America* (New York: Abingdon, 1949), 147–50.

2. Carmer, *Dark Trees*, 262. It should also be mentioned that Teed may have been a distant cousin of Mormon Joseph Smith.

3. Martin Gardner, *Fads and Fallacies in the Name of Science* (New York: Dover, 1957), 22–23.

4. Koresh, *The Illumination of Koresh: Marvelous Experiences of the Great Alchemist Thirty Years Ago, at Utica, N.Y.* (Chicago: Guiding Star, n.d. [ca. 1899]), 5–6.

5. Ibid., 7–8.

6. Ibid., 11.

7. Ibid., 10.

8. Ibid., 17.

9. Ibid., 12.

10. Carmer, *Dark Trees*, 260. For a development of the mystic belt of New York, see Whitney R. Cross, *The Burned-over District: The Social and Intellectual History of Enthusiastic Religion in Western New York, 1800–1850* (New York: Harper Torchbooks, 1965), and Michael Barkun, *Crucible of the Millennium: The Burned-over District in the 1840s* (Syracuse, N.Y.: Syracuse University Press, 1986).

11. Carmer, *Dark Trees*, 258–69; Fogarty, introduction to Teed, *Cellular Cosmogony*.

12. Everett Webber, *Escape to Utopia: The Communal Movement in America* (New York: Hastings House, 1959), 355, a rather shallow and cynical piece of work.

13. Lord Chester, *The Great Red Dragon; Or, the Flaming Devil of the Orient* (Estero, Fla.: Guiding Star, 1909). Since Teed died in 1908, this was published posthumously.

14. Examples are Clark, *Small Sects*, 147, and Gardner, *Fads*, 23.

15. Michel, *A Gift*, 2: "This illumination was the revelation of the mysteries of life and death, of the form and character of the universe, of the relation of man to God and man's

ultimate destiny in God. It was the revelation of universal knowledge." See the excellent account of William A. Hinds, *American Communities and Co-operative Colonies*, 2d ed. (Chicago: C. H. Kerr, 1908), 480. Since Teed's published writings began to appear only in the late 1880s, much of his account of the earlier days was probably apocryphal.

16. Michel, *A Gift*, 3; Fogarty, introduction to Teed, *Cellular Cosmogony*. The possible fact that Teed and Anne Ordway were novitiates in the Shaker colony at Mount Lebanon, N.Y., is puzzling without more detail (information in a letter from T. W. Beasley, December 19, 1979).

17. Michel, *A Gift*, 3; Karl J. R. Arndt, "Koreshanity, Topolobampo, Olombia, and the Harmonist Millions," *Western Pennsylvania Historical Magazine* 56 (1973): 71–86; Arndt, *George Rapp's Successors and Material Heirs, 1847–1916* (Rutherford, N.J.: Fairleigh Dickinson University Press, 1975), 230–32.

18. Carmer, *Dark Trees*, 268.

19. W. Ley, "The Hollow Earth," *Galaxy*, March 1956, 71–81; Gardner, *Fads*, 21; Warren Smith, *The Hidden Secrets of the Hollow Earth* (New York: Zebra Books, 1976).

20. Ley, "Hollow Earth"; Gardner, *Fads*.

21. Carmer, *Dark Trees*, 269.

22. Koresh and U. G. Morrow, *The Cellular Cosmogony . . . Or . . . The Earth a Concave Sphere* (Chicago: Guiding Star, 1899 [anno Koresh 60]), 192. Republished with addenda by Guiding Star Publishing House at Estero, Fla., in 1905, 1922, and 1927. Reprinted in 1975 by Porcupine Press (see n. 1, above).

23. Koresh and Morrow, *Cellular Cosmogony*, 194.

24. Mary Burnham, ed., *The United States Catalog: Books in Print, January 1, 1928*, 4th ed. (New York: H. W. Wilson, 1928), 2814.

25. Unfortunately for the historical and geographical urbanist, all tangible evidence of Koreshan existence in south Chicago is gone. All the Englewood buildings were removed for the development of the Dan Ryan Expressway, and Beth-Ophra has been replaced by a rail line.

26. Carmer, *Dark Trees*, 270. Hinds, *American Communities*, 473–74.

27. Carmer, *Dark Trees*, 270–71.

28. Clark, *Small Sects*, 147; R. R. Mathison, *Faith, Cults, and Sects of America from Atheism to Zen* (Indianapolis: Bobbs-Merrill, 1960), 87; see also n. 15, above.

29. Koresh, *Emanual Swedenborg: His Mission, and What Constitutes Mediumship and Materialization* (Chicago: Guiding Star, n.d.).

30. Gardner, *Fads*, 25.

31. Teed's ideas are fully explained in *Cellular Cosmogony*.

32. Carmer, *Dark Trees*, esp. 271; Michel, *A Gift*.

33. Hinds, *American Communities*, 472.

34. Koresh and Morrow, *Cellular Cosmogony*, title page, 192.

35. Ibid., 76.

36. Ibid., 35.

37. Ibid., 36.

38. Feature stories appeared in the *Chicago Times-Herald*, December 4, 1896, July 24, 25, 1897; the *Louisville Courier-Journal*, May 2, July 25, 1897; the *Chicago Journal*, October 17, 1896; and the *Pittsburgh Post*, May 2, 1897. Other newspapers throughout the nation carried stories on the work of the Koreshan geodetic staff.

39. Koresh and Morrow, *Cellular Cosmogony*, 1.

40. Ibid., 9.

41. Ibid., 161.

42. Webber, *Escape to Utopia*, 256.

JAMES E. LANDING

43. Hinds, *American Communities*, 472–73.

44. Ibid., 472.

45. Ibid., 477. Early landholding figures must be interpreted with care. Although it is frequently cited that Estero was incorporated as the fourth or fifth largest city in area in the United States, the Koreshans never filed a plat for a village, nor did they incorporate (personal letter, D. T. Farabee, Clerk of the Circuit Court, Lee County, Fla., July 23, 1971).

46. Carmer, *Dark Trees*, 280. Most accounts contain no version of Teed's beating.

47. Webber, *Escape to Utopia*, 357.

48. Carmer, *Dark Trees*, 283–85; *Newsweek*, December 6, 1948, 26.

49. Carmer, *Dark Trees*, 284–85.

50. The hollow earth concept did not die with Teed. In 1914 and 1920 Gardner published works espousing the idea in great detail (Ley, "Hollow Earth," 81; Gardner, *Fads*, 1957). A German, Karl Neuper, revived Morrow's work under his own name in 1925, and high officials in Nazi Germany had been influenced by the teachings of Peter Bender (Gardner, *Fads*, 1957; G. S. Kuiper, *Popular Astronomy*, 1946; L. Pauwels and J. Bergier, *The Morning of the Magicians* [New York: Avon, 1968], 266). During World War II, radar experiments based on the hollow earth concept were conducted on the island of Rugen by German scientists (Pauwels and Bergier, *Morning*, 265–67). Two other accounts of the hollow earth were put forward as recently as 1947 (*Time*, July 14, 1947, 59). For a wide variety of views on the hollow earth, see Smith, *Hidden Secrets*, 1976.

Selected Bibliography

Arndt, Karl J. R. "Koreshanity, Topolobampo, Olombia, and the Harmonist Millions." *Western Pennsylvania Historical Magazine* 56 (January 1973): 71–86. Documents Teed's contact with members of the Harmony Society and indicates that some Harmonists accepted Teed's teachings.

Carmer, Carl. "The Great Alchemist at Utica." Chap. 14 in *Dark Trees to the Wind: A Cycle of York State Years*. New York: McKay, 1949. Reprint, 1956.

Clark, Elmer Talmadge. *The Small Sects in America*. New York: Abingdon, 1944, 147–50.

Hinds, William A. *American Communities and Co-operative Colonies*. 2d ed. Chicago: C. H. Kerr, 1908, 470–85.

Kitch, Sally L. *Chaste Liberation: Celibacy and Female Cultural Status*. Urbana: University of Illinois Press, 1989. This work contains Florida references not available to this writer (see pp. 20–21 of the work).

Koresh. *The Illumination of Koresh: Marvelous Experiences of the Great Alchemist Thirty Years Ago, at Utica, N.Y.* Chicago: Guiding Star, n.d. [ca. 1899]. The most extensive personal account of Teed's "illumination."

———. *Fundamentals of Koreshan Universology*. Estero, Fla.: Guiding Star, 1927.

Koresh and U. G. Morrow. *The Cellular Cosmogony . . . Or . . . The Earth a Concave Sphere*. Chicago: Guiding Star, 1899. Reprint, with addenda, Estero, Fla.: Guiding Star, 1905, 1922, 1927. The classic account of Koreshan beliefs and the studies done by Morrow to prove the earth is hollow.

Landing, J. E. "Cyrus R. Teed, Koreshanity, and Cellular Cosmogony." *Communal Societies*, Autumn 1981, 1–17.

Teed, Cyrus Reed. *The Cellular Cosmogony . . . Or . . . The Earth a Concave Sphere*. Philadelphia: Porcupine Press, 1975. Reprint of the classic work of 1899 by Koresh and Morrow. Contains an excellent introduction by Robert S. Fogarty titled "We Live on the Inside." Also reprinted by Koreshan Unity, Inc., Estero, Fla., 1983.

The Theosophical Communities and Their Ideal of Universal Brotherhood

I n 1889 Madame Helena Petrovna Blavatsky, one of the founders of the recently formed Theosophical Society, informed the members internationally of the organization of an even newer movement: "The organization of Society, depicted by Edward Bellamy, in his magnificent work *Looking Backward*, admirably represents the Theosophical ideal of what should be the first great step towards the full realization of universal brotherhood. . . . Have you not heard of the Nationalist clubs and party which have sprung up in America since the publication of Bellamy's book?"[1]

This quote, by which Blavatsky offered her blessing to the Nationalist clubs as a true expression of Theosophy, has frequently been depicted as the origin of a brief episode during which the Theosophists heartily supported the Nationalist movement and just as quickly withdrew their support to pursue other interests, their association being of little importance to either movement. End of story. Viewed developmentally, however, especially from the perspective of Theosophy, the encounter with the Nationalist movement is an important initiatory phase in what became a continuing attempt to bring to "visible expression" the society's own utopian goal of universal brotherhood. Once the break with the Nationalists occurred, Theosophy would continue to draw inspiration from Bellamy and would seek other means to the ends that drew it to the Nationalist cause in the first place. The hopes that had emerged so prominently in the Bellamyite enthusiasm would be redirected in the early twentieth century into the establishment of a number of model communities, several of which survive to this day. These communities are of interest in themselves, but placed in the larger context of Theosophy and utopian ideals, their story also provides an additional illustration of the continuing ripples still visible from Edward Bellamy's original casting of *Looking Backward* into the pond of American culture.

The Origin of the
Bellamy-Theosophical Connection

As is well known to students of Bellamy's utopianism, *Looking Backward*[2] sold very slowly during the first months after its release in January 1888. It was not until the following year that it became a bestseller. However, among the early readers was a Theosophist, Cyrus Field Willard, a newspaperman for the *Boston Globe*. Willard had been among the first to affiliate with the Theosophical Society, which had formed two lodges in Massachusetts (Boston and Malden) soon after its formal chartering in 1883. Following his reading of *Looking Backward*, Willard initiated correspondence with Bellamy. In one of these letters he first raised the possibility of the formation of an association to propagate the ideal of the book.

Unbeknownst to Willard, a second Theosophist, another newspaperman, Sylvester Baxter, an editorial writer on the *Boston Herald*, had written with a similar suggestion. Baxter had penned the first book review of any length of *Looking Backward*. In spite of their offices being across the street from each other, their mutual membership in the Theosophical Society, and their shared enthusiasm for Bellamy, the two were unknown to each other until introduced through their correspondence with Bellamy. However, the two were soon busy planning the new organization. Its first meeting was on December 1, 1888. At a subsequent meeting on December 15, four officers were elected, Willard and Baxter among them. Willard also organized a committee to write a statement of purposes. The committee consisted entirely of Theosophists, including, besides himself and Baxter, Henry W. Austin, Arthur B. Griggs (president of the Boston Theosophical Society), and George D. Ayres (president of the Malden Theosophical Society).

The Nationalist principles took their keynote from the first stated objective of the society: "To form a nucleus of a Universal Brotherhood of Humanity, without distinction of race, creed, sex, caste, or color." It began, "The principle of the Brotherhood of Humanity is one of the eternal truths that govern the world's progress on lines which distinguish human nature from brute nature."[3] As the statement was circulated, clubs began to spring up in urban centers around the United States and in Canada.

There is every reason to believe that Willard and/or Baxter alerted both William Q. Judge, head of the American branch of the society, and Madame Blavatsky (then residing in England) to *Looking Backward*. Shortly after the publication of the principles, in February 1889, Judge wrote Bellamy, "Theosophy . . . is, as you know, founded on the principle of Universal Brotherhood. I thus conceive of it as closely linked to Theosophy, and desirable means whereby Theosophists may assist in the ethical advancement of the race, substituting brotherhood and co-operation for competition, and do good work on the practical plane. Hence I desire to popularize Nationalism, showing it in the above fraternal light."[4] Judge also placed a review of the book in the March 1889 issue of *The Path*, the magazine he edited. At about this same time, Blavatsky prepared a review for *Lucifer*, the British Theosophical magazine, and was penning her famous comments for *The Key to Theosophy*, still an extremely popular book within the Theosophical Society. In her statement she quoted the principles approvingly, thus adding her blessings to the mixing of Bellamyites and Theosophists. During 1889–90 the Nationalist movement attracted many non-Theosophists to its program, but wherever a Theosophical group formed, a Nationalist club also soon opened its doors.

While the seeming convergence of Bellamy's plan for the Army of Industry with the Theosophical ideal of a universal brotherhood was the most prominent point of agreement between Bellamy and the Theosophists, other shared ideas should not go unnoticed. For example, Blavatsky, her successor Annie Besant, and Judge's successor Katherine Tingley, could each appreciate Bellamy's liberation of women in Boston in A.D. 2000. Blavatsky could agree on a non-Darwinian form of evolution that she shared with the liberal Protestant Dr. Barton (*Looking Backward*'s slightly disguised Unitarian pastor), not to mention the parson's emphasis on the "divinity within" each person.

But as Nationalism ran rampant through Theosophy, warnings were sounded. Blavatsky was the first to voice her concern, within months of giving her initial support. In her message to the American Theosophical Society convention of April 1890 she cautioned the members, "The Nationalist Movement is an application of Theosophy. But remember, all of you, that if Nationalism is an application of Theosophy, it is the latter which must ever stand first in your sight. Theosophy is indeed the life, the indwelling spirit which makes every true reform a vital reality, for Theosophy is Universal Brotherhood, the very foundation as well as the keystone of all movement toward the amelioration of our condition."[5]

However, as both the Theosophists and the Nationalists began to work out the practical aspects of moving society toward that pictured by Bellamy, they were forced to grapple with the issue Bellamy avoided in his novel—how society could move from its present state to the ideal condition. Theosophists assumed that the movement was nonpartisan and gentlemanly and placed their faith in the power of truth to woo even the rich and established leaders into a change of heart. Bellamy and the non-Theosophical Nationalist clubs began to espouse a more radical approach that emphasized the need to engage society itself and work for more systemic change. The divergence of approach surfaced most decidedly when Henry R. Legate, president of the Second Nationalist Club of Boston, aligned that club with what Willard and the Theosophists in the First Nationalist Club perceived to be corrupt politicians. With the Nationalist clubs positioning themselves for battles in the political arena, and set to align themselves with the socialist-oriented Peoples Party, the Theosophists were forced to choose between them and the society, which had strict policies against associating the Theosophical Society with partisan political efforts and legislative solutions. Willard, Baxter, Ayres, all the leading Theosophists in Boston, and then around the country began to drop away from Bellamy. In a short time, many of the Nationalist clubs disappeared, and the thrust of the movement was absorbed by the Peoples Party and the Socialists.

The substance of the concern that divided Theosophists and Nationalists can be fruitfully seen in terms of the shared contradictory notions held by both Bellamy and Blavatsky. On the one hand, both had affirmed the divinity within, a concept with extremely individualistic connotations. While Bellamy did little to develop the idea, Blavatsky elevated it to particular prominence. Both also looked for a collective social ideal, but Theosophists subordinated their search for universal brotherhood to the development of the divinity of the individual. Brotherhood would come as the divinity was brought forth. Bellamy did little to develop the concept of divinity within as a working principle and opted for a program of direct social action to realize the more important utopian goals.

For many the story ends at this point. To be sure, there is little in the Theosophical side for the next few years but the expression of bitterness over their experience with the Nationalists. In 1893 Judge personally repented of his earlier endorsement of Bellamy in an article in *The Path*. "We have been asked about this labor struggle? We have been asked why we do not join the Bellamyites and other cooperative societies? Do you want to go in, go in. The Theosophical Society, as such, has nothing to do with it. I am personally satisfied to live where I am and do my duty where I stand, without any new law on property, or with it, whichever you please. . . . The Theosophist know [sic] that legislation changes nothing whatever"[6]

But while that was the end of any active participation by Theosophists in the Bellamyite cause, it was the end of neither their relation to Bellamy nor their search for some means to realize more fully and visibly their stated goal of universal brotherhood. Given the permanent place of *The Key to Theosophy* in the movement, Theosophists would continually return to Bellamy for some inspiration and guidance. In later years, unable to relate to a congenial Nationalist movement, they would seek other means to give visible expression to their goal. But to understand the altered direction taken by Theosophists, one must know a little bit about the society.

The Development of Theosophy
through the 1890s

The Theosophical Society was formed in New York City in 1875 by Blavatsky, Judge, and Henry S. Olcott to collect and diffuse knowledge of the laws that govern the universe. As formally outlined in the 1880s, it accepted three objectives:

> 1. To form a nucleus of a Universal Brotherhood of Humanity, without distinction of race, creed, sex, caste, or color;
> 2. The study of ancient and modern religions, philosophies and sciences, and the demonstration of the importance of such study; and
> 3. The investigation of the unexplained laws of nature and the psychic powers latent in man.[7]

As noted above, the society's first objective lent itself readily to utopian speculations. But in spite of the enthusiasms of Willard and the Bellamyites, most Theosophists tended to subordinate this interest in Brotherhood to the more intriguing task of exploring the occult.

In 1878 Blavatsky and Olcott had moved to India, eventually establishing headquarters at Adyar, near Madras. They left the development of the American section to Judge. Blavatsky devoted much of her time to writing, while Olcott administered the day-to-day affairs of the growing society. Blavatsky began to develop a set of occult teachings around the concept of the Masters. The Masters, according to Blavatsky, formed a cosmic spiritual hierarchy guiding the destiny and evolution of the race. While Olcott personally believed in the Masters, he saw the society as more of an open philosophical discussion group. He recognized Blavatsky's teachings but opposed limiting the concept of Theosophy to her ideas and of identifying the society exclusively with the Masters. In the mid-1880s Blavatsky moved to Europe, and Olcott reorganized the society following his more open perspective. Blavatsky responded by drawing around her a group of students dedicated to the Masters and their esoteric teachings, and among them she disseminated a set of secret occult instructions.

Initially opposed to her actions, Olcott changed his mind after reading a letter purportedly from one of the Masters, whose opinions he personally valued. In 1888 he announced the formation of the Esoteric Section of the Theosophical Society (ES), though he wanted it to be understood that the ES was to be an entirely separate organization and to have only an informal relationship to the society. This separate but intimate relationship between the ES and the Theosophical Society was to have crucial importance for the history of the movement. It should also be remembered that it was during these formative months of the ES that Blavatsky became aware of Bellamy and wrote *The Key to Theosophy*, and that those who accepted the somewhat ascetic disciplines imposed on the members of the ES were most enthusiastic for its utopian visions. During the remaining three years of Blavatsky's life, the ES spread through the membership of the society around the world. Judge assumed leadership of the American section of the ES just as he became aware of Bellamy's work.

Among the students drawn into the ES was Annie Besant, who had left atheism and efforts with the Fabian Society in England to work with Blavatsky. In her earlier years she had lectured on Bellamy and was thus already acquainted with his ideas. Though appearing only at the end of Blavatsky's life, Besant quickly moved to the fore as her most promising student, and Blavatsky designated her as her successor. Offended, Judge suggested that at least the responsibilities should be divided, with him continuing to head the ES in America, and Besant to lead in Europe and India. Two years later, accusations that Judge had been circulating spurious messages from the Masters initiated a series of events that led him in 1894 to declare himself the sole head of the ES. The following year, when Judge broke completely with Olcott and Besant, the American membership declared itself to be the Theosophical Society in America. The fourteen lodges that remained loyal to Besant and the Adyar headquarters in India reorganized as the American Section of the Theosophical Society (Adyar).

As these events that first split the Theosophical Society progressed, Judge had made the acquaintance of a former social worker and Spiritualist, Katherine A. Tingley. Like Besant, Tingley brought a commitment to the larger human community to Theosophy. Impressed with her abilities, much as Blavatsky had been impressed with Besant's, Judge appointed Tingley head of the ES. When Judge died the year after the break with Adyar, E. T. Hargrove declared himself Judge's successor; but he resigned in 1897, and Tingley stepped into the top office. She did not, however, command the allegiance of all. In swift succession the Syracuse and New York City lodges withdrew and became independent organizations: the Temple of the People and the Theosophical Society of New York. Within a decade Robert Crosbie bolted with a group of Los Angeles members to form the United Lodge of Theosophy, the first of a host to follow during the twentieth century.[8]

Thus, just as Theosophy was disconnecting from the Nationalist cause, it was entering a period of inner turmoil. Blavatsky died in 1891. Judge's and Besant's struggle for control then split the society. Judge died in 1896, and the American work was further splintered by people who rejected his successor. By the end of the century both the American and Adyar branches of the movement and, as we shall see, at least one of the prominent splinters was headed by individuals committed to the ideals of universal brotherhood and creating a visible expression of the same. Besant would do this in a variety of ways and is most remembered for the many social programs she initiated in India. However, those who had read *The Key to Theosophy* led the several branches of the movement in the initiation and support of experimental communities where the universal brotherhood ideals could be modeled before the world. The impulse to community began just as the century ended and continued for over a generation. Katherine Tingley was the first to initiate a new community in 1897, quickly followed by the Temple of the People and the American branch of the Adyar Theosophists. The attempt to found new communities continued into the 1920s, climaxing in the formation of the Aquarian Foundation and its establishing a colony on Vancouver Island in British Columbia.

Point Loma: Theosophical Society in America

The first and by far the most famous of the Theosophical communities began as the vision of Katherine Tingley.[9] Following Judge's death, she began a round-the-world tour, partly to raise money for her newly inherited organization. Tingley brought to her new job years of effort as a social worker, and she combined her social perspective with her more recently acquired occult insights. She saw the opportunity to put Theosophy, heretofore largely limited to spreading its message by lectures and print, into manifestation on a practical working level.

Over the years Tingley had developed a social critique. A typical statement of her views appears in one of her more autobiographical books, *The Gods Await* (1926):

J. GORDON MELTON

The Point Loma Theosophical community near San Diego, California, as it appeared about 1907. Visible are the curved seating area for America's first open-air Greek Theater (built in 1901) and founder Katherine Tingley's residence and office building (right center), with the Raja Yoga Academy behind on the right and the Temple behind on the left. (Courtesy of The Theosophical Society Archives, Pasadena, California)

The curse of our nations is separateness. We are not agreed upon any scheme of life or thought or action. We are separated one from another by the imaginary interests of daily life; and competition carried too far is ringing the death-knell of our civilization. Money has become such a power as to make men lose sight of their souls and conscience, and forget that they are a part of Universal Life. . . . The greed of the world is the death of the world. The man whose mind is occupied with trying to get control of others that he may stand before the public as powerful and prosperous—that man is, from his soul's standpoint, in his death-throes.[10]

Tingley had also developed a program for correcting the ills of society. Possessing little hope for changing her own generation, she conceived of a "school of prevention" in which the conditions and causes of crime and poverty could be removed from the children, the next generation. The idea of a school closely followed the Theosophical worldview, which tended to see life as a school in which the developing soul through successive reincarnations grew into godlikeness. According to Tingley's version of Theosophy, truth began in understanding humankind's twofold nature. Through discipline, training, and perfection the soul could realize its divine nature. This perfecting process was best accomplished through service to others.

Tingley softened her severe critique of society by locating the problem in the heart of individual humans (who gave too much attention to their animal nature) rather than in the distorted social structure. She, for example, largely ignored the tensions of family life, the relations of capital and labor, and the divisions among social classes. Hence her solutions were essentially pietistic, seeking change in the inner self rather than the basic structures of society. In like measure, the role of the community at Point Loma was not to promote social change directly but to provide a congenial, if intense, atmosphere for the development of the changed individuals.[11]

Tingley placed the school of Raja Yoga at the heart of the new community. To Tingley, the ideal of Raja Yoga stood for an integrated education that emphasized personal scholarship and culture while giving prime attention to each student's spiritual evolvement. Raja Yoga represented a radical expansion of Theosophy originally articulated by the society's founders.

During her initial world tour Tingley purchased 330 acres on Point Loma, a peninsula on the Pacific coast at San Diego, where she proposed to create her "School for the Revival of the Lost Mysteries of Antiquity." To climax her world tour in January 1897, she laid a cornerstone for the first building. Then to bring her vision into manifestation, she created a new organization, the Universal Brotherhood. At the annual meeting of the Theosophical Society in February, she forced the merger of the society into the brotherhood as its literary branch. She invited the members of the new organization to join her in her experiment in brotherly living at the Point.

Members began to gather in 1899, the first completed building being that of a sanitarium erected by a member who was also a physician. Most of the early residents used tents until more permanent houses were constructed. In 1900 Tingley moved both the headquarters of the brotherhood and her home from New York to Point Loma. With Tingley in residence, the community flowered. Members around the country sent their children to be educated at the Raja Yoga School. They were soon joined by a number of Cuban children who arrived at Point Loma as a result of a relief project that Tingley had developed to give humanitarian aid in the wake of the Spanish-American War. The sanitarium, renamed the Academy, became the school's headquarters. In 1901 an outdoor Greek-style theater (the first in America) was constructed and was made the site of lavish classical plays performed by community residents. The following year the old Fisher Theater in downtown San Diego was

The Raja Yoga children of Katherine Tingley's Point Loma about 1902, many brought from Cuba after the Spanish-American War. The photograph was taken in the 1901 Temple before Reginald Machell carved the large front doors and painted the murals and pillars. (Courtesy of The Theosophical Society Archives, Pasadena, California)

purchased. Renamed the Isis Theater, it became the scene of regular Sunday evening dramatic productions staged by the community for the town's residents. A community press published the society's magazine, *The Theosophical Path*, and a number of books.

Rather than adhering to classical utopian communal ideas, Tingley transformed the Theosophical ideal of universal brotherhood into a utopian vision of the Theosophical Society of America spearheading a worldwide cultural and ethical renovation of the next generation through education. Thus, in considering the community's organization, it is not surprising to discover many of the more definitive aspects of traditional communes weak or missing. For example, members of the community did not have to abandon private property, though many of them did. In general, a $500 entrance fee was required as well as monthly payments for room and board. The scale was adjusted upward for wealthier members and downward for the poor. In return, the community supplied all of a resident's basic needs—food, clothes, shelter, education, and medical care. Money was dispensed on a basis of individual need, though few seemed to need it. Communal housing was available, but community members could and a few did construct their own homes on the community's land. Dress tended to be uniform, as most clothes were manufactured by the community following very simple patterns.

The community strove for self-sufficiency. A prosperous fruit and vegetable garden supplied much of its food. Financial support came from the society

The Theosophical Permanent Peace Committee poses in the Point Loma
Temple of Peace in 1923. Katherine Tingley is seated in the center.
(Courtesy of The Theosophical Society Archives, Pasadena, California)

scattered across the United States and Europe and the sale of literature from
the Point Loma press. Most of the children came from the homes of nonresident society members who accepted Tingley's education philosophy and who
paid up to several thousand dollars annually for their education. At its height
Point Loma had approximately 500 residents, of whom 300 were children
and 65 were instructors. Only a few residents, such as wealthy sports-equip-
ment manufacturer A. P. Spalding, continued to be employed outside.

The community was controlled by Tingley, who had been elected head
of the society for life. She appointed a thirteen-person cabinet to handle
the financial and administrative duties. Tingley's emergence as a charismatic
leader, quite as powerful as Blavatsky had been a generation before, allowed
Point Loma to survive as a vigorous enterprise, though it never attained the
financial stability for which it strove. The beginning of its demise can be
dated with Tingley's accidental death on July 11, 1929, while on a fundraising
tour in Europe. Her death occurred only a few months before the stock market crash. Geoffrey de Purucker, who succeeded Tingley as head of both the
society and the community, found Point Loma heavily in debt. He attempted
to solve the problems by cutting back on community activities, finally closing
the school in 1940. He tried to sell small tracts of land to pay some of the

J. GORDON MELTON

more pressing debts, intensified by an increasing tax burden—as only the school was tax exempt.

For another thirteen years de Purucker was able to keep the community together. However, with the beginning of World War II and the added fears of possible violent activity centered on the naval station adjacent to the community, de Purucker gave up and sold the property. In this way Tingley's vision ended, and the society reverted to its noncommunal, pre-Tingley structure. Without a charismatic leader like Tingley, it was never able to return to its former glory, the national and international work having suffered severely from a generation of neglect in favor of the almost total dedication to the now abandoned Point Loma experiment. Headquarters was moved first to Covina, California, and eventually to Pasadena, where it remains today.

Temple of the People

Among the first to reject Katherine Tingley's leadership were members of the Syracuse, New York, Lodge, under the leadership of Frances LaDue and William H. Dower, a physician. Both Dower and LaDue, but principally the latter, as messengers or "channels" for the Masters, founded the Temple of the People.[12] Following the Masters' instruction given through LaDue, the small group moved to Halcyon, a community they created several miles south of Pismo Beach, California, where the temple is still headquartered. The first members to arrive in Halcyon settled in 1903 and assisted Dower in opening a clinic, which in time became noted for its treatment of alcoholics. The new community saw itself as the center of a larger movement of people sympathetic to Theosophical ideals across North America and the world. Local groups that subscribed to the temple teachings were termed squares, and by 1905 no less than twenty-two such squares existed across the United States.

In 1905, following a directive received from the Masters, community residents organized a separate corporation designed along largely utopian lines: the Temple Home Association. Interestingly, while the overall critique of society by the temple was much less severe than that of Katherine Tingley at Point Loma, it included what the association founders considered a major structural flaw in society, the distorted relationship between capital and labor. As an ultimate goal, they envisioned a time in which all of the land would "be owned all of the time by all of the people; where all the means of production and distribution, tools, machinery and natural resources will be owned by the people—the Community; and Capital and Labor may meet on equal terms with no special privileges to either." Each resident member was to receive living expenses, a small monthly allowance, and a half-acre upon which she or he could live. The land could not be sold, though any improvements to the property could be considered one's personal possession. As the experiment proceeded, members studied the cooperative ventures and sought further guidance from the Masters through the messengers who led the temple. They published their findings in the monthly *Temple Artisan*.

Membership in the association was granted upon payment of a $100 fee. Additional financial investments, while not granting increased voting power, entitled members to a greater share of projected profits. Nonresident members around the country were encouraged to join and invest, and they could vote (by proxy if necessary) in the annual association business meeting. Ideally a resident member initiated each new association business (department). The association then provided the necessary land, permanent improvements, and some cash capital. The head of the department and his/her assistants (employees) provided all labor and ongoing expenses. At the end of the year the association (capital) and those engaged in the business (labor) shared equally in the profits. Thus the workers would gain first from their labor and second, as association members, from their capital investment in all departments. Early departments centered on poultry raising, construction, and farming the available land.

The Masters' plan sought to avoid both the selfish competition of the world and the extremes of other socialist endeavors, but problems with it appeared as early as August 1907, when the *Temple Artisan* took notice of some internal dissension. In response to criticism, the governing board of the association organized a monthly meeting of members to advise the board on the management of the association's life and businesses. These meetings brought to light a crucial flaw in the Masters' plan. Since the businesses were as yet showing no profit, the association was receiving no money to retire the heavy mortgages. Capital was drying up. After due consideration, on January 1, 1909, the board revised the plan and realigned the departments and the association. The departments began to pay the association a regular monthly amount, in place of sharing profit (or loss). This plan shifted the major financial responsibility for business failure to laborers, rather than to the association. It also amounted to the abandonment of the most significant element in the temple's social critique. But even this makeshift solution could survive only a few years. Continued problems, especially the draining of funds to meet mortgage payments, plagued the colony. Thus in 1912 the association abandoned the cooperative economic arrangements, cut its ties to the members' businesses, and sold some of the land to pay off all the outstanding mortgages.

While leaving behind its cooperative arrangement, the community itself prospered. Residents developed some successful businesses, including a locally famous pottery shop. A temple building was erected in the 1920s, by which time the community had grown to include approximately fifty residents. Today both the Temple of the People, a spiritual/religious fellowship, and the Temple Home Association, a holding company for the land in Halcyon, remain active. *The Temple Artisan* continues to be published quarterly. The community, minus its utopian elements, still serves as a center for temple activities, primarily publishing and the annual international membership gatherings every August. The temple has members across the United States and in several foreign lands, with an especially strong following that emerged in Germany after World War II. The temple is headed by the guardian-in-chief, the inner guard, the treasurer, and the scribe, all residents of Halcyon. The Temple Home Association holds the trust and manages the Halcyon property. Most, but not all, of the approximately thirty current residents are temple members.

Krotona: American Section of the Theosophical Society (Adyar)

At the beginning of the century, A. P. Warrington, an active member of the remnant Adyar faction of American Theosophists, attempted to found a Theosophical colony in Virginia but met with little success. Eventually his hope converged with Annie Besant's vision of a Theosophical community somewhere in the Southwest, and by 1906 Warrington was advocating the establishment of a community in southern California. Meanwhile, Besant appointed Warrington head of the Esoteric Section for America, and early in the second decade of the century sanctioned his purchase of a site in Hollywood (located approximately halfway between Point Loma and the Temple of the People) for the new Esoteric Section headquarters. A separate nonprofit corporation, the Krotona Institute of Theosophy, was created.[13] Besant was named president, and administration was placed in the hands of Warrington as vice-president and a fifteen-member board of trustees, all of whom had to be members of the Esoteric Section. The site originally consisted of ten acres at the end of Vista del Mar Avenue, upon which a Spanish-style headquarters building was erected. The initial down payment was made with a $10,000 gift from one of the board members. Soon thirteen more acres had been acquired, and individual members had purchased adjoining lots.

No sooner had Krotona been purchased, however, than leadership of the American Section of the Theosophical Society (Adyar) and the still-independent ES were united by Warrington's becoming the society's general secretary. Warrington then moved the headquarters of the society from Chicago to Krotona and on June 2, 1912 (a day chosen because of its freedom from all astrological afflictions) laid the cornerstone for a new headquarters-administration building. Before the end of the month the out-of-doors Greek theater opened. Warrington was justly optimistic about the future. Within a year there were forty-five community residents, and in April 1913 he enthusiastically reported to the society's membership: "Coming out of the small beginning, which has now only in latency the communal elements, I long to see, some day, a community fully exemplifying the life of the future under a truly scientific system of growth on all planes." [14]

The promising new community now housed the headquarters of both the ES and the section, a press, a vegetarian cafeteria, a temple (in which a variety of Theosophical organizations met), and a library. Among the most important structures at Krotona was the School of Theosophy, which annually offered a variety of programs, classes, and seminars on Theosophical philosophy and its application to contemporary life and world needs. The Liberal Catholic Church, a liturgical worship community that interpreted traditional Western Christianity in light of Theosophy, erected a cathedral adjacent to Krotona.

Astrological considerations aside, the first decade of Krotona was largely determined by financial afflictions. By 1917 the balance of debt on the original purchase stood at $25,000. That same year a member donated an adjoining estate, complete with an additional $16,000 mortgage. Warrington's initial attempts to eliminate the debt raised questions concerning the nature of any equity that the society might have in Krotona, questions regularly tabled during his administration. But controversy never died, and in 1920 Warrington resigned his office. The new section head, L. W. Rogers, faced the task of settling the issues surrounding Krotona.

Rogers was quite aware of Warrington's conflict of interest created by the joint leadership of the section and the ES. For a fee, Krotona happily gave headquarters space to the section, with all of its departments, but granted no equity in the property. As head of the section, Warrington had raised significant sums of money for Krotona but had failed to communicate satisfactorily to the donors that the gifts were destined for the institute rather than the section. Rogers clearly saw that the financially sound section was Krotona's only hope of retiring its debts. But an initial proposal that the property (and the debts) be transferred to the section merely ignited increased controversy. Rogers could, however, take some action unilaterally, and he immediately abandoned Krotona and returned the section's headquarters to Chicago. The financially strapped board sold a portion of the property to reduce the mortgage burden and to pay back members who had understood the recipient of their gift to be the section, not the ES. Finally, after two years of rancor, the issue was submitted to Annie Besant, the official head of the ES.

Besant divided the assets. The majority of the land was sold, and the money was dispersed according to perceived needs. The section received the larger part for its expanding program. The ES retained the remaining land and money deemed sufficient for its program. In 1924 the board sold the land in Hollywood and purchased an 118-acre estate in Ojai, California (a favorite location of Besant's), onto which the institute moved. The new hillside site housed the headquarters of the ES, a library, a bookshop, resident housing, a guest house, and the School of Theosophy. All mention of Krotona dropped out of the society's periodical, which otherwise featured the work of the local Theosophical centers.[15]

For many years Krotona remained a small, marginal activity hardly noticed by most Theosophists. It did not revive until the 1960s, when it took on new life as an educational center for the society. The main activity of Krotona today is the School of Theosophy, which annually, from September to May, supports three quarters of seminars, workshops, and classes. It sees itself as a support center for Theosophy, where "students could be trained to become more useful and effective workers for the Theosophical Society." The establishment of the Taomina Theosophical Retirement Community on nearby property in 1967 expanded the community's outreach substantially. Also, when the Liberal Catholic Church was forced to abandon its Hollywood property, it rebuilt in Ojai, several miles from Krotona. Its presiding bishop lives on the Krotona property.

The intensity of the controversy over Krotona and the abandonment of the Hollywood property were soon forgotten by the majority of Adyar Theosophists. The mid-1920s were the heyday of Besant's promotion of Jiddu Krishnamurti as the vehicle for the coming world teacher to initiate a new age. By becoming the new focus of controversy within the society, Krishnamurti inadvertently assumed an important role in the formation of the fourth and last of the major community experiments within the Theosophical movement, the Aquarian Foundation.

The Aquarian Foundation

The fourth prominent community related to theosophy was founded in 1927 by Edward Arthur Wilson, better known under his foundation name, Brother XII.[16] The Aquarian Foundation can be traced to early 1926, when Wilson had been "translated in spirit to the higher realms in order to meet the eleven

Masters of Wisdom." That summer a series of articles and announcements by him appeared in *The Occult Review*, a prominent metaphysical journal published in London, England. The major item was printed in the August issue, "A Message from the Masters of Wisdom." Later reprinted as a leaflet, it announced a "Further Work" to be done by the Theosophical Masters. It denied the imminent appearance of a world teacher, at that time being promoted by Annie Besant in the persona of Jiddu Krishnamurti, suggesting instead that the Masters wished to again raise the standard of universal brotherhood. This new work would prepare the way for a world teacher who would appear around 1975. At the beginning of 1927 Wilson announced the formation of a community in British Columbia, and in January he left England for his native Canada. Over 100 Theosophists followed him.

Along the way he made contact with another independent Theosophical group, the Sun Group of Akron, Ohio, which ran the small Sun Publishing Company. Sun Publishing printed a booklet, *The Three Truths*,[17] in which Wilson as Brother XII outlined his most important ideas to his American audience. *The Three Truths* was quickly followed by a more substantial volume, *Foundation Letters and Teachings*,[18] which contained a membership application and a request for financial support, the foundation having neither membership fees nor monthly dues. The contact address was given as Cedar, British Columbia, Canada.

Wilson returned to British Columbia, where earlier in his life he had had a visionary experience, and established his colony near Nanaimo, at Cedar-by-the-Sea, on Vancouver Island. Initially attracting several prominent American Theosophists as well as a few well-to-do disciples, the colony flourished. Unlike the other Theosophical communities, the Aquarian Foundation never lacked money. Members turned over their assets to Wilson, and other donors gave monetary gifts in the tens of thousands. Property holdings even included some nearby islands. These gifts, along with the produce of their fame, supported the colony until the disasters of 1934. American Theosophists joined their British counterparts in the growing enterprise.

Once the colony was established, Brother XII introduced some new sexual teachings derived from his conviction that foundation members were to give birth to a new advanced generation, which were to be, in Theosophical terminology, the coming sixth rootrace. Designated colony females, married or single, were to mate with Brother XII up to nine times. Present members would then train the resultant children to receive the coming world teacher due to arrive in the 1970s. A keystone to the new teaching was the special work of Myrtle Baumgartner, whom Wilson had recruited during one of his early fundraising trips. He convinced Baumgartner that in a previous incarnation they were Osiris and Isis and that in this incarnation, through him, she was destined to bear Horus, the expected world teacher. When she moved to the community, he ordered the building of a house for their "work." He also set aside a section of Valdes Island as a protective refuge for the soon-to-arrive children of the new sixth rootrace.

About 1930 Mabel Skottowe moved to the colony from Canada. Known among colonists as Madame Zee, she soon replaced Baumgartner, who had some problems in producing a male child and later experienced a mental collapse, as Wilson's favorite. She assumed the position as coleader with Wilson. The colony had a quiet existence for several years, but the fabric of the foundation began to unravel in 1933. Two lawsuits were filed by former members claiming harsh treatment and misuse of foundation funds by Wilson.

The lawsuits were both heard in 1934. They detailed horrors similar to those that have come out of the "cult wars" of the 1970s. Members told of personal abuse from Wilson and Madame Zee. One told of being ordered to kill a Canadian government official through "black magic." Both trials were decided in favor of the plaintiffs, and the court gave large sums of money and most of the property to the plaintiffs. During the trial, one of Wilson's yachts was dynamited, and a cache of gold disappeared. The unfavorable court decisions, the violence, and the loss of the gold that had been the community's financial reserve doomed the colony. Brother XII and Madame Zee disappeared to never be heard from again, their eventual fate still a matter of speculation.

Conclusion

Theosophy is alive and well. It is a worldwide movement narrowly defined in the several competing organizations that bear the name seeded by the several branches of the Theosophical Society.[19] The communal impulse emerged early in the society's history and flourished in its second generation. But then as the movement grew, expanded, and splintered through the first decades of the twentieth century, communal speculation seemed to disappear, though both the Temple of the People and Krotona continue as alternative communities. The communal impulse initially arose among those Theosophists who saw community building as the natural means for creating universal brotherhood. From almost the beginning of the movement, spurred by Edward Bellamy's work, society members united occult speculations with various communal ideals. But even with the backing of Blavatsky, the united Theosophical communal ideal was favored by only a minority of members, though they were among the most dedicated and committed.

To survive, the communal life must be supported by both a critique of society's structures and a communal organization that embodies the commune's solutions to society's problems. In contrast, Theosophists have seen their communities primarily as places of gatherings for like-minded individuals who wish a congenial atmosphere in which to cultivate the Theosophical life. If otherwise financially viable, such communities could easily continue after the communal aspect disintegrated.

Further, the communal impulse, however logical it seemed to some Theosophists, was doomed from the beginning. In the long run, it was simply at odds with the occult essence of the teachings, which are intensely individualistic. They emphasize the personal journey of the soul through time via reincarnations and the individual search for the divine within. Thus, while communalism is one logical interpretation of the society's first objective, communalism could just as logically be seen as the invasion of a foreign ideal into Theosophy by way of Bellamy's philanthropy. When these early secondary enthusiasms failed to inspire a new generation, Theosophists abandoned the search for community for its more primary occult concerns. The once flourishing communal impulse survives as shared social and religious life of Krotona and Halcyon.

Finally, the Theosophical communities were hindered in their prospects by their inability to gain an independent standing. Their fortunes were always tied to a larger supporting organization. The several Theosophical organizations, while committed to the Theosophical worldview, possessed little or no interest in communal experimentation or the immediate concerns of the various communities. At the same time, the communities always depended on the nonresident organization membership for ongoing financial support. When the larger group withdrew or weakened its support, the communities immediately suffered, often fatally. Thus while the movement continued on its natural course, the communities died, no longer able to convince the larger movement of their viability or worth.

The communal impulse is but a fading memory of the several contemporary Theosophical societies that have for many decades shown no interest in initiating new communal experiments. However, in the 1970s the New Age movement, a recent innovation within the larger occult-metaphysical community dominated by Theosophical ideology, provided the context for a revived communal impulse. Young New Age occultists formed a host of communities combining planetary ideals, critiques of contemporary society, insights from Eastern religions, and communications with the Masters of Wisdom.[20] Several of these communities, such as Findhorn in northern Scotland and

The Farm in Tennessee, continue in spite of some near-fatal problems and subsequent reorganizations. It is, however, still too early to know if some of these new communes will establish themselves as anything more than one extreme and ephemeral element of the New Age world.

Chronology

1875	Theosophical Society is founded in New York City by Helena P. Blavatsky, Henry Steel Olcott, and William Q. Judge.
1878	Blavatsky and Olcott move to India, leaving the American work to Judge.
1888	Blavatsky founds the Esoteric Section of Theosophy.
1891	Blavatsky dies; Annie Besant becomes joint leader of the Esoteric Section with Judge.
1895	After a year of controversy, Judge breaks with Besant and reorganizes the Theosophical Society in America independently of the Indian and European work.
1896	Judge dies; the leadership of the society falls to Katherine A. Tingley; schisms follow.
1897	Temple of the People is formed in Syracuse, N.Y.; Tingley lays cornerstone for the new community on Point Loma near San Diego.
1900	Headquarters of the Theosophical Society in America is moved to Point Loma.
1903	Following a directive of the Masters, members of the Temple of the People colonize Halcyon, Calif.
1905	Temple Home Association is organized communally.
1912	Krotona Institute of Theosophy is founded and property is purchased in Hollywood, Calif., for the development of a community. Temple Home Association abandons cooperative economic arrangements but continues holding property to present in Halcyon, where most residents are still temple members.
1924	Krotona Institute is relocated to Ojai, Calif., with communal arrangements largely abandoned.
1925	Short-lived theosophical colony is founded in Western North Carolina.
1927	Aquarian Foundation is founded in British Columbia, Canada.
1929	Tingley dies following an accident while on tour in Europe.
1934	Aquarian Foundation dissolves in wake of lawsuits and violence; leaders disappear.
1942	Property on Point Loma is sold by Theosophical Society in America and colony is dispersed.
1942	Present Theosophical Society continues with headquarters now at Pasadena, Calif.

Notes

1. H. P. Blavatsky, *The Key to Theosophy* (London: Theosophical Pub. Co., 1889), 44–45.

2. For information on Bellamy and the Nationalist movement, see Arthur E. Morgan, *Edward Bellamy* (New York: Columbia University Press, 1944); Morgan, *The Philosophy of Edward Bellamy* (New York: King's Crown Press, 1945); Sylvia E. Bowman, *Edward Bellamy*

Abroad (New York: Twayne, 1962); and Bowman, *The Year 2000* (New York: Bookman Associates, 1958). While Morgan has been most quoted as a source for information on Bellamy and Theosophy, Bowman has important corrective insights about the continuing use of Bellamy within the Theosophical movement.

3. Quoted in Morgan, *Edward Bellamy*, 262.

4. Ibid., 262–63.

5. *H. P. Blavatsky to the American Conventions* (Pasadena: Theosophical University Press, 1979), 29.

6. William Q. Judge, *Echoes of the Orient* (San Diego: Point Loma Publications, 1980), 143.

7. The text of the objectives of the society were revised on several occasions through the first decade of its existence. The present text, finally adopted in 1886, appeared essentially as at present in Blavatsky's *The Key to Theosophy* (1889). The story of the development of the text is told in Josephine Ransom, *A Short History of the Theosophical Society* (Adyar, Madras, India: Theosophical Publishing House, 1938).

8. This essay builds on the earlier treatment of theosophical communities in Robert V. Hine, *California's Utopian Colonies* (New Haven: Yale University Press, 1953), and Paul Kagan, *New World Utopias: A Photographic History of the Search for Community* (Baltimore: Penguin, 1975). For general background on Theosophy, see Bruce F. Campbell, *Ancient Wisdom Revised* (Berkeley: University of California Press, 1980); Alvin B. Kuhn, *Theosophy: A Modern Revival of Ancient Wisdom* (New York: Henry Holt, 1930); Josephine Ransom, *Short History of the Theosophical Society*, and James A. Santucci, *The Theosophical Movement* (Los Angeles: Cunningham, 1951). On Blavatsky, the best single source is Marion Meade, *Madame Blavatsky* (New York: G. P. Putnam's Sons, 1980), though a more sympathetic treatment is Charles J. Ryan, *H. P. Blavatsky and the Theosophical Movement* (Pasadena: Theosophical University Press, 1975).

9. This treatment of the Point Loma experiment is based on the substantial work of Emmett A. Greenwalt, *California Utopia: Point Loma, 1897–1942* (San Diego: Point Loma Publications, 1978), with important supplemental data drawn from Iverson Harris, "Reminiscences of Lomaland," *Journal of San Diego History* 20, no. 3 (Summer 1974): 1–32.

10. Katherine Tingley, *The Gods Await* (Point Loma, Calif.: Woman's International Theosophical League, 1926), 42–43.

11. In an oft-quoted statement for public consumption, though not entirely conforming to the reality of what she created, Tingley stated her understanding of the Point Loma experiment in explicit terms: "The headquarters of the Organization at Point Loma, and the buildings and the grounds pertaining thereto, are no 'Community,' 'Settlement,' or 'Colony.' They form no experiment in Socialism, Communism, nor anything of similar nature, but are what they stand for: the Central Executive Office of a worldwide organization where the business of the same is carried on, and where the teachings of theosophy are being demonstrated" (quoted in Greenwalt, *California Utopia*, 146).

12. Apart from the brief treatments by Hine and Kagan, the Temple of the People has been rarely mentioned in the secondary literature on theosophy. This account has been largely taken from early volumes of *The Temple Artisan* found in the collection of the Institute for the Study of American Religions, now the American Religions Collection located at the Davidson Library at the University of California, Santa Barbara.

13. The history of Krotona has yet to be compiled, though a start has been made by Joseph E. Ross in *Krotona of Old Hollywood, 1866–1913* (Montecito, Calif.: El Montecito Oaks Press, 1989). For the history of the Ojai phase, material was assembled from the recent history of the American Section of the Theosophical Society by Joy Mills, *100 Years of Theosophy* (Wheaton, Ill.: Theosophical Publishing House, 1987); descriptive brochures is-

J. GORDON MELTON

sued by the Krotona Institute; the early issues of *The Messenger* (the official periodical of the American sections); and scattered issues of *The Krotonian* (the biannual periodical of the institute).

14. *The Messenger*, April 1913, 614–15.

15. Following its move to Ojai, all mention of the Krotona Institute dropped out of the publications of the section, most noticeably of *The Messenger*, which otherwise covered the activity of all the Theosophical centers across the United States. In like measure, Joy Mills deleted any mention of the institute after the events of 1924 in her recent history of the American Section. Though formerly president of the American Section, Mills is currently the director of the Krotona Institute School of Theosophy.

16. For the account of the Aquarian Foundation, I am indebted to the initial labors of James Santucci of California State University, Fullerton. His paper, "Brother XII and the Aquarian Foundation," delivered at the 1987 meeting of the Western Section of the American Academy of Religion and published in revised form as "The Aquarian Foundation" in *Communal Societies* 9 (1989): 39–61, alerted me to the foundation and its role in Theosophical history. His paper has been supplemented by the foundation's publications, including its periodical, *The Chalice*, and the writings of a prominent member, Will Levington Comfort, all found in the collection of the Institute for the Study of American Religion. In 1991 a helpful study of the foundation by John Oliphant appeared as *Brother Twelve: The Incredible Story of Canada's False Prophet* (Toronto: McClelland & Stewart, 1991).

17. Akron: Sun Publishing Co., 1927.

18. Akron: Sun Publishing Co., 1927.

19. Out of Theosophy have come such diverse organizations as the Liberal Catholic Church, the Agni Yoga Society (Nicolas and Helena Roerich), the Arcane School (Alice Bailey), the Anthroposophical Society (Rudolf Steiner), the Rosicrucian Fellowship (Max Heindel), the "I AM" Religious Activity, the Word Foundation (Harold W. Percival), and the Universariun Foundation (a flying saucer contactee group). Most of these have in turn given birth to even more new groups. In the 1970s a number of individuals who psychically "channel" from the Masters have emerged to found a whole new generation of Theosophically inspired organizations. For brief descriptions of these groups, see J. Gordon Melton, *Encyclopedia of American Religions* (Detroit: Gale Research, 1996).

20. On the New Age communes, see Cris Popenoe and Oliver Popenoe, *Seeds of Tomorrow* (San Francisco: Harper and Row, 1984), and Corinne McLaughlin and Gordon Davidson, *Builders of the Dawn: Community Lifestyles in a Changing World* (Shutesbury, Mass.: Sirius, 1986).

Selected Bibliography

Blavatsky, H. P. *The Key to Theosophy*. London: Theosophical Pub. Co., 1889.

Campbell, Bruce F. *Ancient Wisdom Revised*. Berkeley: University of California Press, 1980.

Greenwalt, Emmett A. *California Utopia: Point Loma, 1897–1942*. San Diego: Point Loma Publications, 1978.

Kuhn, Alvin B. *Theosophy: A Modern Revival of Ancient Wisdom*. New York: Henry Holt, 1930.

Meade, Marion. *Madame Blavatsky*. New York: G. P. Putnam's Sons, 1980.

Mills, Joy. *100 Years of Theosophy*. Wheaton, Ill.: Theosophical Publishing House, 1987.

Oliphant, John. *Brother Twelve: The Incredible Story of Canada's False Prophet*. Toronto: McClelland & Stewart, 1991.

Ransom, Josephine. *A Short History of the Theosophical Society*. Adyar, Madras, India: Theosophical Publishing House, 1938.

Ross, Joseph E. *Krotona of Old Hollywood, 1866–1913*. Montecito, Calif.: El Montecito Oaks Press, 1989.

Ryan, Charles J. *H. P. Blavatsky and the Theosophical Movement*. Pasadena: Theosophical University Press, 1975.

Santucci, James A. "The Aquarian Foundation." *Communal Societies* 9 (1989): 39–61.

The Theosophical Movement. Los Angeles: Cunningham, 1951.

Tingley, Katherine A. *The Gods Await*. Point Loma, Calif.: Woman's International Theosophical League, 1926.

California's Socialist Utopias

S truggling with the impacts of industrialism, Europe after the French Revolution produced a series of socialist thinkers and rebels who believed that private property and the exploitation of workers were at the root of social evil. Karl Marx, the most significant, saw a solution in terms of class struggle, but many of his socialist predecessors, the so-called utopian socialists, such as Henri Saint-Simon, Charles Fourier, and Robert Owen, were less concerned with class revolution and more interested in the cooperation of all classes in communal experiments that would demonstrate the evils of the capitalist system while extolling the advantages of cooperation. These socialists understood that communities based on religion invariably work better, or at least last longer, than those structured on secular ideology. In a sense, the motivation of socialist utopias since the mid-nineteenth century has been to transfer the successes of religious community into a more secular context. In their efforts the economy becomes the religion, and the creed becomes ownership by the community of the means of production.[1]

California, along with Washington state, early became a western center for such experimentation. Some religious colonies, like those of the Mormons in San Bernardino (1852) and the followers of Thomas Lake Harris near Santa Rosa (1875), often included secular assumptions and so organized their economies with the community controlling all production, but these economies existed only as part of an overriding theocracy in which all the parts were subservient to the whole.

Compared with their religious counterparts, secular socialist colonies have been generally more democratic, even more individualistic, and far less dominated by single leaders. As Benjamin Zablocki would say, they were the products of alienation, not charisma—reactions against the prevailing society rather than attractions to a magnetic personality.[2] They may have reflected minor brushes with Marxism, but they were more often the offspring of that utopian socialism that Marx had so derided. Fourier and Saint-Simon, for example, were according to Marx hopelessly naive about the necessity of violent action to dislodge the capitalist class from its privileges. California socialists tended to be of that naive type and often followed American thinkers such as Edward Bellamy or William Dean Howells. Their colonial lives were relatively short; still they enjoyed exciting, colorful, and humane histories.

One of the earliest California expressions did indeed stand in a direct line from a European utopian socialist, Etienne Cabet.[3] His enthusiastic French followers struggled with an abortive effort at colonization in Texas and then followed their leader up the Mississippi River to Nauvoo, Illinois. There they moved into the recently abandoned Mormon settlement and enjoyed moderate success with nearly 500 members during the early 1850s. After some unfortunate schisms, they moved, like their Mormon predecessors, farther west and by 1857 had set up a fresh start on the Iowa frontier near Corning. Seceding groups formed other colonies, and one of those splinters in 1883 arrived near Cloverdale in the Napa Valley on the banks of the Russian River to form Icaria Speranza.

The California members included a few who had fought on the barricades for the Paris Commune in 1871; Jules Leroux brought the ideas of Henri Saint-Simon; Emile Bée represented the Socialist Labor Party; but most were simple farmers. Whatever their backgrounds, they all decried competition as sick with "dollaromania." For the new cooperative society they set to work constructing a sawmill, raising vineyards and a winery, and planting plum orchards. Because they remained an island of French culture, even avoiding the use of the English language, their pool of potential membership was never large. Debts mounted. Some unfortunate schemes backfired, like one to import blooded Percheron horses from France. A more detailed story of their decline is related elsewhere in this volume, but here suffice it to say that their fraternal life gradually faded before the decade ended.

A most impressive nineteenth-century socialist colony, the Kaweah Cooperative Commonwealth, was far more American in its roots. Burnette G. Haskell, its instigator, was an enthusiastic, imaginative, powerful, but erratic labor organizer in San Francisco. He was a reader of Laurence Gronlund and the recently popular Edward Bellamy.[4] Out of these authors Haskell and his seamen and intellectual friends conceived a socialist, communitarian experiment. They sought and found a site, and for half a decade in the 1880s their efforts dominated San Francisco Bay socialist thinking like a colossus. Eventually over 300 of them boarded the new railroad cars and traveled south to Visalia in the San Joaquin Valley. From there they hauled their belongings on buckboards to Kaweah in the Sierra foothills beneath the future Sequoia National Park.

For five years they wrestled with the meaning and organization of a new society based on cooperation and socialist brotherhood. The life they built had its measure of success. Believing a staple product was essential for communitarian health, they constructed a road into the higher altitudes in order to tap the lumber resources of the giant redwoods. They dreamed realistically of providing wood products for the burgeoning San Joaquin Valley and less realistically of exporting redwood veneers on their own steamers to Australia, India, and Europe. The road became a symbol of their future glory, but it was built at heavy cost, economically and physically. For four years the colony picked and shoveled eighteen miles of granite ledges to an altitude of 8,000 feet. For many years after the colony disbanded, its road was the only access from the valley to the higher Sequoia forests.

After days of work, there were all manner of recreational activities. Their newspaper, the *Commonwealth*, carried thoughtful articles, especially on the problems of workingpeople. Adult literary classes met. The local Nationalist Club held heated discussions. There were Saturday dances. A band and an orchestra rehearsed and performed under summer stars.

Nonresident members of Kaweah sent dues from as far away as Boston and New York. The residents, however, included a share of "assorted cranks of many creeds and none,"[5] and in time factionalism and political backbiting grew rampant. Even matters such as a publication of the list of members called up interminable debate and even schisms. Haskell's personality caused many ruptures. And the debt mounted.

Hopes for overcoming these obstacles internally were not unfounded. External hostilities, on the other hand, were virtually insurmountable. Railroads, lumber interests, and newspapers viciously attacked Kaweah, a measure, perhaps, of the potential threat the colony posed. But in 1890 the federal government dashed any possibilities of communal success when it withdrew all the colony's land claims (in spite of their legality) in order to form Sequoia National Park. Though it vigorously sought justice, the colony was never reimbursed for its labor, its improvements (including its road), and the fact that in good faith for five years it had believed the land its own to work, to wrestle with, and to dream over.

Between 1890 and 1915, the period of Progressive reformism and also the high tide of national political socialism under Eugene V. Debs, the socialist movement spawned at least four colonies: Winters Island, Altruria, the Army of Industry, and Llano del Rio.

Winters Island in the San Joaquin delta behind San Francisco Bay in 1893 was inspired by Erastus Kelsey, an Oakland Nationalist and follower of Haskell's Kaweah. He was joined by Kate Lockwood Nevins, who had been an organizer for both the Farmers' Alliance and the Populist Party. They brought together some 100 paying members, generally Populist and labor unionist in ideology. By 1896 a quarter of these were living and working on the Winters Island cooperative farm in the delta. They built impressive dikes to keep out the high tides and were especially successful in growing onions for market. The depression of the 1890s hit them decisively, however, and through that period of seriously declining prices they could not sustain their commitment to the cooperative life.

Altruria was the product of high-minded Unitarians who had read William Dean Howells' *A Traveler from Altruria*.[6] They were led by Unitarian social gospel minister Edward Biron Payne, a zealous tubercular anxious to serve the working class through Christian socialism. He had undoubtedly heard George D. Herron, the social gospelist, and Laurence Gronlund, the socialist who inspired Kaweah, lecture in San Francisco in the early 1890s. During 1894–95 his followers expected to translate Howells's socialist principles into reality along Mark West Creek near Santa Rosa in the Sonoma Valley. The colony published a newspaper, raised an impressive, though uncompleted, three-story hotel, and built cabins and cottages scattered through the woods. They lived a year of high hope and joy, including sociable Sundays with lectures under the trees, picnics, hiking, and songfests. They wove cottons and woolens and rugs, manned a smithy and woodworking shops, fashioned rustic chairs and screens and easels, and raised their own vegetables, fruit, honey, poultry, and meat.

But finances dogged them, especially consequences from the hotel construction, the fundamental lack of initial capital, and the widespread depression of the early 1890s. The deaths of two children in rapid succession curbed a part of the spirit. They tried for a time to break up into three smaller units on firmer financial footings, but the enthusiasm by then was largely gone. Still, they parted happily, and even after they dispersed, some of the members lived cooperatively in Santa Rosa and others started a cooperative farm near Cloverdale.

A group of radicals and IWW (Industrial Workers of the World) unionists gathered in 1915 in a colony near Auburn and called themselves the Army of Industry. They followed Gerald Geraldson, a humanitarian fruit rancher and

Job Harriman, founder of the Llano del Rio Cooperative Colony near Los Angeles in 1914, was a prominent figure in Socialist and Labor movements for thirty years.

member of a local San Joaquin Valley Socialist club. As a good socialist, he believed that without the incubus of private property, people could learn to live cooperatively. He inherited his ideas from Edward Bellamy and from contacts with Kaweah. In 1914 he began remodeling his ranch and brought in workers to prove his theories. They eventually lived and worked in ten buildings, which included a communal dining hall. The colony, never numbering more than thirty, encouraged those who had suffered from private ownership and welcomed society's derelicts as well as its idealists. It could not survive the disruptions of World War I, however, and at any rate Geraldson always felt that America was too prosperous to provide the best soil for communitarianism.

Many of the Army of Industry's members were lured away by the most interesting and important of California's socialist experiments, Llano del Rio, which was being organized about the same time in southern California. Llano was born in 1914 in the rocky desert foothills of the Antelope Valley on the Mojave Desert about sixty miles east of Los Angeles. Its creation was the dream of a prominent national socialist, Job Harriman.

Harriman was an Indianan who switched from the ministry to the law before coming to California in 1886.[7] In San Francisco he became a socialist, joined the Bellamy Nationalists, and was made a state organizer for the Socialist Labor Party. He rose in socialist circles until in 1899 he ran as vice-president of the United States on the Socialist Labor Party ticket headed by Eugene V. Debs.

Suffering from tuberculosis, he moved to Los Angeles, and there for the election of 1911, socialists and labor unions united behind his candidacy for mayor. This period was the high tide of American socialism; his campaign was enthusiastically supported, and it was widely assumed that Harriman would win the election. Such success would have come in spite of the fumings of the arch-conservative Harrison Gray Otis and his *Los Angeles Times*. Otis saw Harriman as a threat to all he stood for—a Los Angeles free of labor unions and a general business orientation in the city's political life.

In 1910 the *Times* was crippled by a typographers' strike, and in the turmoil a bomb ripped open its building and killed twenty men. Unionists and radicals sincerely believed that the explosives had been planted by the virulently antiunion Otis faction in an effort to discredit the union movement. In 1911 three union men were placed on trial.[8]

Labor supporters flocked to the side of the leading defendants, James and John McNamara. Harriman, one of the lawyers for the defense, staked his prestige and political future on the innocence of the brothers. But four days before the election in a dramatic reversal the defendants confessed their guilt. The consequences for Los Angeles were historic, and for Harriman, cataclysmic. His chances for election were scuttled, and the episode left him not just politically defeated but deeply disillusioned with the state as a means of social change. He turned from politics and theory to economics and practice and set out to create a model community as a visible demonstration of how socialism might in fact work. Thus the Llano colony was born.

Llano del Rio was planned as a stock-issuing corporation. Depending on time of entrance, colonists paid from $500 to $1,500 for their individual limit of one share per member. Stock conferred voting rights, residence, and work in the colony at an alluring wage of $4 per day. A part of these earnings could be applied to up to three-quarters of the cost of the shares.

In 1914 a strip of desert land in the Antelope Valley near Palmdale was purchased from the Mescal Land and Water Company on the site of a former temperance colony. In May five families built the first houses of wood and canvas. Within a few months the residents numbered 100. Three years later their numbers approached 900.[9]

Life was demanding. Some adobe dwellings rose, but for many years tents stood everywhere, inadequate for some winter nights and many summer

A roofing crew and other workers construct Job Harriman's socialistic Llano del Rio community outside Los Angeles about 1915.

days. The adobe houses gradually spread, an impressive dormitory of stone rose where bachelors and temporary residents slept, and the scene was early dominated by a sturdy hotel with four heavy porch pillars and two enormous fireplaces of native stone from the nearby washes. Meetings there provided relief from labor in the fields, which was hard. Creosote and Joshua trees were cleared; wagonloads of stones were removed; alfalfa, pear orchards, corn, and grain were planted.

Yet the colony grew and prospered, promoted energetically by the *Western Comrade*, a regional socialist monthly (which later actually moved from Los Angeles to the colony).[10] Operations came to include a ranch, a dairy, an apiary, and a rabbitry, plus an industries department that supervised canning, leather work, shoemaking, laundry, and woodworking.[11] The print shop published both the monthly *Western Comrade* and the weekly *Llano Colonist*.

Llano in California lasted four years, and the majority of its members claimed they were exciting years, to say the least.[12] Most enjoyed the refuge from capitalist competition. They seemed to relish the mass participation in its democracy. The flip side of such participation lay in the general assembly's interminable discussions and debates on every detail of colony life, its sessions often lasting far into the night. Reversals of decisions were commonplace. The "brush gang" (named for an early dissident welfare league that met behind the creosote bushes and wore sprigs of brush) accused Harriman and the board of dictatorial practices. Shirkers were yelled at as Gibbonites, after

Two workers at Llano del Rio, Joseph Lewitsky (left) and friend,
pause for a picture about 1916. (Courtesy of Sarah Shuldiner)

a lazy Wobbly who once lived there.[13] The result was a subversive discontent that grew alongside the happiness. The unwanted economic competition of the outside world was often replaced by political discord within.

In 1915 the California commissioner of corporations investigated allegations of mismanagement, but though his report was harsh, he found no grounds for revocation of the colony's charter. This investigation was only the tip of an iceberg of outside hostility. Throughout Llano's California existence, the established business community led by Otis's *Los Angeles Times* never ceased to rail against the socialist experiment.

Nevertheless, the Llano experience provided real advantages to its members. Education was always a primary emphasis. Regular state grammar and high schools were established. In addition one of California's first Montessori schools was opened. Also, the Sierra Madre School, generally referred to as the Kid Kolony, taught trades and practical skills to teenagers. Adults met for Esperanto classes and reading circles. The colony library was well used. Lecturers came from the University of California Agricultural Extension and from the socialist circuit.

Every week adults and youngsters held separate dances. Two orchestras performed and even traveled to neighboring towns and the county fair. Children and adults both presented plays, and the *Western Comrade* enthusiastically reviewed them. After hours, workers frequently hiked into the nearby mountains or played football, baseball, basketball, or billiards. One of the biggest celebrations was the annual anniversary party held on May 1, coincidental with the international socialist holiday. The day was marked with a parade, speeches, plays, musicals, and a community dinner. Life at Llano was varied and exciting, far richer than the former lives of most of its members.

The nature of the people drawn to the community is revealed in the 1916 Great Register of Voters for the Llano precinct. Within the colony the Socialists held a majority of 83 percent, followed in order by Republicans, Prohibitionists, and Democrats. The gender breakdown of those registered showed 65 percent male and 35 percent female. About half were married. Thirty percent identified themselves as housewives, 25 percent as laborers (including 10 percent construction workers), 22 percent as ranchers, 12 percent as farmers, 5 percent as professionals (doctors and lawyers), 2 percent as clericals, and 1 percent as teachers.[14]

Whatever their origins or occupations, Llano members, realizing there must be growing pains, nevertheless claimed to be held together by a new ethical understanding, based on "equal ownership, equal wages, and equal social opportunities." It was an elusive spirit, a shared belief among the members that they were part of a grand experiment, partners in the triumph of socialism across America and throughout the world. The colony, as one visitor observed, "possessed a charm which held its members when the hardships of subjugating the desert nearly overwhelmed them." [15]

Such a driving spirit filled the life of one of the colony's key members, Walter Millsap. In the little town of Woodland in the Sierra Nevada foothills, Millsap had been a bicycle repairman, motion picture projectionist, and active member of the local socialist party. In Woodland's political meetings, seriously seeking an escape from the competitive world, he learned of Job Harriman's plans for a socialist experiment in the southern California desert, and while recovering from a bout of "sexual neurasthenia," he decided to join the colony. He arrived at Llano in July 1915 and entered enthusiastically into its life. He played in the orchestra, worked to raise the level of musical talent, and generally became an ardent community promoter. One of his closest Llano friends came to be Alice Constance Austin, the socialist architect who was developing the master plan for "the future socialist city." [16] Millsap's voluminous correspondence expounded on the glories of Llano. He constantly urged his friends to join. In frequent letters to his parents and his aunts he continuously referred to his joy at finding Eden.

The unforeseen snake in Llano's garden proved to be the problem of inadequate water. The unexpectedly large population and the varied activities, especially the farming, demanded major engineering efforts to provide irrigation in the desert. Original plans called for ditches from Big Rock Creek, and at great labor these were constructed. However, they ran through extremely porous soil and needed concrete lining, but even so protected, they could not avert the water shortages that began to affect hopes for expansion.

In 1918 the colony implemented a wrenching decision, and 100 of its members moved to a new site, 40,000 acres with an abandoned lumber town near Leesville in Louisiana. The entire experiment was thus transplanted halfway across the country and to an area where social radicalism was not held in high esteem. On official forms racially liberated colonists often filled the blanks for color with the word "red." During the Great Depression its numbers swelled, but most of the newcomers were unemployed down-and-outers seeking asylum. Newllano lasted in Louisiana from 1918 until 1937, when it surrendered to internal disputes and the financial disasters of the depression years.

Walter Millsap joined the colony in its long move east. But the humid gulf climate forced him to return to southern California. Thereafter he maintained an organization of former Llano colonists. As late as 1969 Millsap was still acting as treasurer of that group, which issued a newsletter and gathered at annual picnics. He worked for the Upton Sinclair EPIC program and, as a logical outgrowth of his ideas, established the United Cooperative Industries, a self-help cooperative. Clearly the rest of his life was an effort to recapture the enthusiasm of those early days in the Antelope Valley, to develop its ideas in other settings, and to further the basic socialist dream of a reformed economy and a happier humankind.

Thus though Llano ended, its spirit remained. Until he died, Millsap viewed Llano as the high point of his life. In the 1940s the historian Carey McWilliams met with former Llano members and concluded, "The enthusiasm of most of them has not abated. They still speak of those early days at Llano-on-the-desert with an elation which has survived through the years."[17]

Socialist utopias, relatively small and short lived, each fed into a broader story. They tended to be discussed in socialist circles; each inspired others to try. Their final community stood above place and time. Llano and Kaweah, like most socialist utopias, each in its day added to the collective memory and formed another binding tie for their generation of labor unionists and anti-establishment idealists.

As utopianism moved, however, through the twentieth century and into the flush of communes of the 1960s, it became clear that early in the century socialism and communitarianism had parted company. Socialism on the whole returned to Marx's contention that such experiments were dated, naive, and useless. Organized labor felt no need to experiment with the cooperative life, for in the New Deal it achieved its establishment status. Yet in the development of the ideal society socialist communitarianism has always played an important role. Historical networks are labyrinthine, and the paths to social change may yet again double back on themselves and lead to serious communitarian experiments.

Chronology

1883	Icarians arrive at Cloverdale to form Icaria Speranza.
1884	Laurence Gronlund's *Cooperative Commonwealth* published.
1885	Colonists arrive on land of Kaweah Cooperative Commonwealth.
1888	Edward Bellamy's *Looking Backward* published.
1890–92	Legal actions leading to final demise of Kaweah.
1893–98	Winters Island in San Joaquin delta founded.
1894	William Dean Howells's *Traveler from Altruria* published.
1894–95	The Altrurian colony in Napa Valley formed.
1915–18	Army of Industry near Auburn established.
1911	Job Harriman defends McNamara brothers in *Los Angeles Times* bombing trial.
1914	First colonists move to Llano colony in Antelope Valley.

1918   Llano colony moves to Louisiana as Newllano.
1923   Walter Millsap founds United Cooperative Industries in Los Angeles.
1937   Newllano goes bankrupt.

Notes

1. Some of the material in this essay is taken from Michael E. Dermody and Robert V. Hine, "The Llano Colony and California's Socialist Utopias," *Communities* 68 (Winter 1985): 55–58.

2. Benjamin Zablocki, *Alienation and Charisma: A Study of Contemporary American Communes* (New York: Free Press, 1980).

3. *Voyage en Icarie: Roman Philosophique et Social*, 2 vols. (Paris, 1840).

4. Laurence Gronlund's *Co-operative Commonwealth* appeared in 1884 and Edward Bellamy's *Looking Backward* in 1888.

5. Edgar Philip Winser, "Memories," manuscript, Huntington Library, San Marino, Calif., 1931, 120.

6. New York: Harper and Bros., 1894.

7. Knox Mellon, "Job Harriman: The Early and Middle Years, 1861–1925" (Ph.D. diss., Claremont Graduate School, Claremont, Calif., 1972).

8. For one treatment, see Robert Gottlieb and Irene Wolt, *Thinking Big: The Story of the Los Angeles Times, Its Publishers, and Their Influence on Southern California* (New York: Putnam's, 1977), 82–100.

9. Archie Roy Clifton, "History of the Communistic Colony Llano del Rio," *Historical Society of Southern California Annual Publications* 9 (1918): 82.

10. Ibid.

11. Ernest Wooster, *Communities of the Past and Present* (Newllano, La.: Llano Colonist, 1924), 122–23.

12. For one good example, see correspondence between Walter Millsap and A. J. Hooper, Millsap Papers, Special Collections, Tomás Rivera Library, University of California, Riverside.

13. Ernest Wooster, "Bread and Hyacinths," *Sunset*, August 1924, 21.

14. Index to Register of Voters, Los Angeles County, Llano Precinct, 1916, California State Library. In contrast with these statistics, a survey in 1917 found former occupations to have been 41 percent farmers, 29 percent businessmen, 7 percent manufacturers, 6 percent professionals, 4 percent clericals, 3 percent miners, 2 percent transportation workers, 2 percent printers, and 5 percent in various construction trades (Clifton, "History," 90).

15. Carey McWilliams, *Southern California Country* (New York: Duell, Sloan, Pearce, 1946), 286.

16. For Austin, see Dolores Hayden, *Seven American Utopias: The Architecture of Communitarian Socialism, 1790–1975* (Cambridge, Mass.: MIT Press, 1976), 300–310; for Millsap's relations with her, see Millsap Papers.

17. McWilliams, *Southern California Country*, 287.

Selected Bibliography

Conkin, Paul K. *Two Paths to Utopia: The Hutterites and the Llano Colony*. Lincoln: University of Nebraska Press, 1964.

Fellman, Michael. *The Unbounded Frame: Freedom and Community in Nineteenth-Century American Utopianism*. Westport, Conn.: Greenwood, 1973.

Fogarty, Robert. *Dictionary of American Communal and Utopian History*. Westport, Conn.: Greenwood, 1980.

Hayden, Dolores. *Seven American Utopias: The Architecture of Communitarian Socialism, 1790–1975*. Cambridge, Mass.: MIT Press, 1976.

Hine, Robert V. *California's Utopian Colonies*. Berkeley: University of California Press, 1983.

———. *California Utopianism: Contemplations of Eden*. San Francisco: Boyd and Fraser, 1981.

———. *Community on the American Frontier: Separate but Not Alone*. Norman: University of Oklahoma Press, 1980.

Kagan, Paul. *New World Utopias: A Photographic History of the Search for Community*. New York: Penguin, 1975.

Kanter, Rosabeth M. *Commitment and Community: Communes and Utopias in Sociological Perspective*. Cambridge, Mass.: Harvard University Press, 1972.

Kraft, James P. "The Fall of Job Harriman's Socialist Party." *Southern California Quarterly* 60 (Spring 1988): 43–68.

Mason, George. *The Kaweah Colony and Indigenous American Socialism*. M.A. thesis, University of California, Irvine, 1984.

Mellon, Knox. "Job Harriman: The Early and Middle Years, 1861–1925." Ph.D. diss., Claremont Graduate School, Claremont, Calif., 1972.

———. "Job Harriman and Llano del Rio: The Chimerical Quest for a Secular Utopia." *Communal Societies* 5 (Fall 1985): 194–206.

Olin, Spencer C., and Nathaniel Bliss. "In Praise of Utopian Socialism in America." *Alternative Futures* 3 (Winter 1980): 51–70.

———. "Utopianism." In *Encyclopedia of American and Political History*, edited by Jack P. Greene, 1321–31. New York: Scribner's, 1984.

Shaw, Albert. *Icaria: A Chapter in the History of Communism*. New York: G. P. Putnam's Sons, 1884.

Swift, Morrison I. "Altruria in California." *Overland Monthly* 29 (June 1897): 643–45.

Veysey, Laurence. *The Communal Experience: Anarchist and Mystical Counter-Cultures in America*. New York: Harper and Row, 1973.

Wooster, Ernest S. *Communities of the Past and Present*. Newllano, La.: Llano Colonist, 1924.

Father Divine and the Peace Mission

The Peace Mission movement, led by a black minister known as Father Divine, flourished during the 1930s in Harlem and other ghettos especially hard hit by poverty and unemployment. Although it was but one among hundreds of ghetto-based, emotionally expressive religious groups, the Peace Mission stood out for its thriving cooperative enterprises and its social activism. Amid the hardships of the depression era, this movement offered its members spiritual comfort, economic security, and self-esteem as crusaders for racial justice.

The record of the Peace Mission is to a great extent the story of one man's charismatic leadership. Father Divine was born into a southern black farm laborer's family in Rockville, Maryland, in 1879 and became an itinerant preacher of messianic tidings to eager audiences of poor blacks.[1] Citing a line from I Corinthians (3:16), "The spirit of God dwelleth in you," he assured his listeners that all people had the same divine spirit and thus merited the same rights and dignified treatment. But opposition by local black ministers and several arrests stemming from his claims to represent God on earth—in Valdosta, Georgia, in 1914 a trial writ listed him as "John Doe, alias God"[2]—eventually led this short, balding exhorter to leave the South. In 1915 he settled with a small but devoted following in New York City, then well toward becoming the center of African American culture and religious life.

The spiritual and social world that Father Divine entered was rapidly changing amid a vast migration by blacks from the rural South. In New York City there had been only thirteen black churches in 1865; that number increased slowly until the early twentieth century, when it skyrocketed to some

Peace Mission founder, Father Divine, along with three of his secretaries and Brother Lamb, an aide, answer a mound of correspondence at his headquarters in Harlem. (UPI/Corbis-Bettmann)

200 by the 1920s.[3] Many of the new churches were simple renovations of vacated storefronts, created by recent urban arrivals who found the ghetto's established churches too formal and socially aloof. Typically these churches featured highly emotional worship and close social ties similar to those the congregants had left behind in the rural South. Frequently, too, the worship of storefront congregations centered on charismatic ministers who presented themselves as unique surrogates for God. Their extraordinary authority provided a sense of order, confidence, and guidance amid the harsh and impersonal world of the urban slums.

These alternative religious movements encompassed a range of faiths and forms, from Islam to Judaism, but most embraced evangelical Christianity as vital to the African American heritage. They sought to restore to black worship the emotional power that marked religion in the rural South but had become attenuated in the ghetto's conventional churches. Typically such religious groups minimized overt racial considerations in their quest for religious ecstasy. Several of the largest included some white members, a situation not unknown among black Pentecostal and Holiness movements that influenced black religion in the rural South.

Father Divine and the Peace Mission

433

Divine spent four years as a religious leader in black New York. There he observed the styles of leading evangelists but avoided their competition for followers and appeared intent on a respite from the turbulence that marked his past. In 1919 he relocated to the small town of Sayville, Long Island. As the sole black resident of Sayville, Divine calmed initial racial tensions with infinite courtesy, impeccable care of his property, and efforts to secure for neighbors reliable domestic help from among his disciples. For ten years, under the name Major J. Divine, he quietly instructed a handful of disciples in a religion that blended Christianity, Eastern mysticism, and communal ideals. Then in late 1929 the widespread economic collapse stimulated wider interest in Divine's communalism as a shield against both emotional and economic distress. As his modest commune continued to prosper during the depression, the minister gained renown for presenting free Sunday banquets to all visitors and for helping needy guests find jobs. Crowds came regularly from Harlem and Newark, venerating this mysterious provider as a heaven-sent deliverer.

Father Divine might have remained in relative anonymity had he been among numerous other pastors energetically aiding lower-class ghetto residents at the outset of the depression. Instead his ministry coincided with a crisis of social leadership in the black church. The crisis was triggered by the persistent otherworldly orientation of many ministers even as growing numbers of destitute people looked to their churches—the central community institutions—to provide economic relief. A survey of 600 black churches in both North and South, conducted during the first years of the depression, showed that while nearly all gave some relief to the poor, only eighteen (3 percent) provided food for the unemployed, and only two (0.3 percent) helped the unemployed find work.[4] In time a growing number of clerical activists, such as Adam Clayton Powell Sr. of Harlem's prestigious Abyssinian Baptist Church, led the clergy to become more involved in programs of social and economic uplift. But in the early 1930s the philanthropy that marked Divine's ministry still appeared to many black preachers as peripheral to their main, spiritual mission.

The social malaise in church leadership even seeped into the conduct of religious services, which increasingly divided the mass of blacks from a self-conscious elite. While the depression accented lower-class desires for an emotionally expressive religion, numerous urban churches preferred a more formal, decorous service, in imitation of their white counterparts and as a display of bourgeois "refinement." Poor blacks increasingly flocked to movements led by charismatic evangelists who encouraged uninhibited emotional display. Yet, like the conventional churches, most of these movements did

ROBERT S. WEISBROT

little to promote economic uplift. Conspicuous among their leaders for both his popularity and his greed was Charles "Daddy Grace" Emmanuel. Tall, with flowing locks and a piercing gaze, the self-anointed "Bishop" Grace conducted mass baptisms along the East Coast while pitting branches of his United House of Prayer for All People into competitions to raise money for his private use.[5] Like many other self-proclaimed prophets of the day, Bishop Grace essentially democratized the opportunities for spiritual ecstasy without redressing the limitations of the black churches in providing material aid to their congregants.

Father Divine emerged during the early 1930s amid this fragmentation of northern black religious life. Pastors in the most progressive middle-class black churches sought to aid the poorest ghetto dwellers but drew relatively few into their congregations. The evangelical preachers meanwhile commanded loyalty and even cultlike veneration from the poor and the outcast, but with few exceptions their philanthropic and reform interests remained inchoate. Bridging these two worlds with a blend of communal idealism and charismatic evangelism, Father Divine bolted into prominence among the residents of Harlem and other ghettos.

The minister's burgeoning fame brought adversity as well. Many of Sayville's white residents feared that his movement was creating a "Negro colony" in their neighborhood, and in November 1931 they had the minister and some eighty disciples arrested for disturbing the peace. Among the bill of particulars was the revealing claim that at his "so-called religious services . . . colored and white people did congregate and mingle together in large numbers."[6] Although unable to discover evidence of specific crimes, the conservative white magistrate nevertheless sentenced Divine to a year in prison and a $500 fine on the grounds that he was "a menace to society."[7] The defendant was taken away to jail amid loud objections by his followers that the court decision had offended the Almighty. Three days later the judge suddenly died, and journalists flocked to tell the imprisoned minister. Divine reportedly said, "I hated to do it."[8] This episode, culminating in a reversal of Divine's conviction, amplified the minister's aura of supernatural power and gave his fledgling movement new stature in the ghettos and beyond.

As word spread of Divine's brush with martyrdom and his judge's abrupt demise, groups of converts formed in widely scattered locales. They dedicated themselves to his will and adopted his cooperative economic system, which had helped insure a modicum of well-being in an era of 25 percent unemployment nationwide. The new centers, known collectively as the Peace Mission, reflected Father Divine's advocacy of racial harmony, nonviolence, and inner serenity.

Membership and Organization

The Peace Mission became a melting pot of the discontented. A majority of followers were poor black women, often widowed or divorced, and generally from the lowest strata of ghetto society. But others, men and women, held well-paying jobs and were highly educated, including a substantial minority of affluent whites who were drawn to Divine out of idealism or spiritual emptiness. In New York and New Jersey, states which contained the heart of Divine's support, the following was 85 to 90 percent black. In states farther west the proportion of blacks in the movement often dropped sharply but almost never fell below a third of the disciples in any Peace Mission center.

Estimates of the total Peace Mission membership during the 1930s varied sharply. At its peak in the mid-1930s, the movement had perhaps 10,000 hard-core followers who believed fervently in Father Divine's deity, devoted all their possessions to the Peace Mission, and lived in one of the more than 150 movement centers.[9] This conservative count excludes many ghetto residents who disdained notions of Father Divine's godhood yet admired his leadership as a philanthropist and champion of racial equality.

Divine's followers adhered to a rigorous code of discipline, living chastely; abstaining from alcohol, tobacco, and drugs; and repaying debts that sometimes went back years. Disciples also left behind all inherited social and cultural barriers. Whites and blacks, West Indians and Native Americans, rural southern migrants and long-settled Harlem residents, and Baptists and Christian Scientists all coexisted easily in the Peace Mission. Whether they came for sustenance, spiritual truth, or shelter from personal troubles, they shared the unifying belief that only Father Divine could fill some vital lack in each of their lives.

The banquet table was the center of communal activity in every Peace Mission branch. There hundreds gathered to praise Father Divine as an all-providing benefactor, while enjoying repasts to awe many a doubting Thomas outside the movement. The sharing of elaborate and well-prepared meals had, of course, a special meaning in an age of widespread deprivation. The banquets also represented a timeless aspect of religious life: the search for God through human fellowship and devotion to a common spiritual leader.

Banquets served as occasions for free-spirited movement (though no close mingling of the sexes was allowed), hearty songs of praise, and above all, testimony. Individuals took turns recounting in emotional tones their transformation, through Father Divine's inspiration, from a dissolute existence to a scrupulously ascetic and pure-minded life. No banquet service proved complete without a message from Father Divine. At most gatherings, of necessity,

On a cold Easter in 1937, members of the New York congregation of the Peace Mission parade in praise of the leader they revered as God. Although most members were black and female, Father Divine strongly advocated racial and sexual equality, and his movement attracted many whites and males. (Corbis-Bettmann)

a secretary read aloud from a reprinted sermon that the minister had given at some other function. But when Divine himself attended a banquet, enthusiastic cheers verging on pandemonium greeted his addresses. Although his sermons varied widely in their specific themes, each one exhorted his listeners to cultivate their characters, while his words assured the poor, the powerless, and the uprooted of their closeness to God.

Peace Mission disciples were not formally required to live in the movement's communal centers, but most chose to do so. In the large cities of the East and West, many of these "kingdom extensions" included separate dormitories for men and women, assembly halls, kitchens, and dining rooms. A special "studio" was almost always set apart for Father Divine, no matter how remote the chance that he would avail himself of this architectural tithe. The majority of the kingdom extensions functioned in the humbler portions of a city. San Francisco disciples renovated a modest brick building in the notorious Barbary Coast district. Seattle's Peace Mission conducted its evangelical affairs in the equally discouraging haunt known as Skid Road. Peace Missions in the Northeast operated chiefly among the poorest streets of ghetto neighborhoods.

As the Peace Mission spread and diversified, operating hundreds of varied businesses, specialization among the membership became imperative. During the early 1930s the movement developed an informal class of administrators to supervise the kingdom extensions, disseminate information, provide legal counsel, and attend to Father Divine's personal needs. This rapidly expanding bureaucracy oversaw a successful transition from a modest commune to a far-flung network that reportedly handled over $15 million in business annually by the latter part of the decade.

The Peace Mission as a
Force for Social Reform

In a time when legal segregation permeated the South and informal segregation shaped northern race relations, the Peace Mission reflected Father Divine's driving desire to see a country free of racial prejudice. The interracial character of the movement was rare in American religious organizations. The movement further reflected Divine's views—common to a growing number of black ministers and secular leaders—that religious movements had to respond to the racial and economic crises of the day. Of the ghetto churches that persisted in devoting themselves exclusively to the hope of otherworldly salvation, Divine declared, "I would not give five cents for a god who could not help me here on the earth."[10]

The Peace Mission's reform activity during the depression decade represented, to an extraordinary degree, the range of ideas and strategies among contemporary organizations that sought to promote racial equality. More than most groups the Peace Mission had the necessary mass membership, financial resources, and executive leadership to implement widely plans for individual betterment, desegregation, economic cooperation, and political action against discrimination.

The Peace Mission became particularly well known for its aggressive efforts to expand into exclusively white neighborhoods. In one community after another, Divine used white disciples as intermediaries to circumvent restrictive housing clauses, then moved in his interracial following. New Rochelle's luxurious Sutton Manor, the beach resort of Brigantine Island near Atlantic City, a 500-acre estate called "Krum Elbow" across the river from President Franklin D. Roosevelt's mansion in Hyde Park, and other areas all became Peace Mission sites. Divine also elicited statements by Eleanor Roosevelt and, through a personal secretary, the president, affirming that every American should have the right to purchase any home he or she could afford.[11]

Economic uplift was another crucial Peace Mission concern. The cooperative ideal that the movement exemplified was already widely popular among activists for black rights. The Peace Mission's distinctive contribution lay in giving practical large-scale expression to this objective. Peace Mission centers were by far the most successful black cooperative ventures in both scope and profitability. Disciples opened inexpensive restaurants, clothing stores, and numerous other businesses, volunteering their labor and sharing all income. By the mid-1930s the Peace Mission had become a major economic force in Harlem: it was the largest realty holder in the ghetto, with three apartment houses, nine private houses, fifteen to twenty flats, and several meeting halls with dormitories on the upper floors. In addition, followers in Harlem operated two restaurants, six groceries, ten barber shops, ten cleaning stores, two dozen huckster wagons with clams and oysters or fresh vegetables, and a coal business with three trucks driving from Harlem to the mines in Pennsylvania. A variety of Peace Mission businesses also operated in other areas from New England to California.[12]

Father Divine encouraged his disciples to enter business as a constructive act and a sign of their independence. Hundreds with minimal business experience responded by becoming merchants. Followers enjoyed wide latitude in selecting and operating businesses, yet seemed less interested in financial gain than in actively serving their movement. Most apparently returned their net profits to the common funds of the Peace Mission, relying on Father Divine's bounty to provide for their needs. Similarly, some voluntarily worked for others who had established businesses and received no wages except to cover transportation and other job-related expenses.

How did the Peace Mission businesses flourish amid the wreckage of so many other ghetto-based trades in the depression? The nature of the religious movement itself aided greatly, for it promoted the accumulation of capital. Communal living arrangements afforded important economies of scale in purchasing food and in housing the faithful snugly—often several to a room—in "Peace Mission evangelical hotels." Communal expenditures were pared further by the injunctions, on moral grounds, against tobacco, liquor, cosmetics, and other common but costly pleasures. Strictures against insurance plans truncated still another possible siphon of funds from the common pool. It was therefore a relatively easy task for Peace Mission enterprises, in conjunction with wages from outside work, to meet the basic needs of the members and still provide a large supply of liquid capital. This in turn facilitated investment in new properties and enterprises, always in cash payments to avoid debt and the burden of interest on loans.

Under Divine's guidance, Peace Mission members sold quality goods at bargain prices, taking advantage of the movement's low cost of living and relying on sheer volume of trade to sustain revenues. Peace Mission coal vendors charged for their wares $7.50 a ton in 1935, a full dollar below the prevailing market price. Peace Mission restaurants gained national renown for selling complete and nourishing meals for fifteen cents, a price substantially lower than could be found almost anywhere else in Harlem. Lodgings, too, were inexpensive at $1 to $2 a week. If quarters were often crowded, a comparison with most other dwellings in the same neighborhoods left virtually no cause for complaint. Divine's followers consequently did a thriving trade with customers whose sole connection with the movement was an appreciation for low-priced goods. Given the high cost of living in the ghettos, these stores provided a vital service by helping marginally independent workers survive the depression.[13]

The Peace Mission's interest in social rehabilitation extended to rural as well as urban enterprises. The idea of resettling poor urban dwellers in rural areas was highly popular during the depression, but federal efforts tended to slight poor blacks most in need of such programs. To help this overlooked element, Father Divine created in 1935 a "Promised Land" of rural cooperatives in Ulster County, New York. In sharp and deliberate contrast to the world of the sharecroppers, these cooperatives were interracial, debt free, and located on excellent farmland.[14] Within a few years the centers were thriving and even supplying Father Divine's urban cooperatives with agricultural products. It was indicative of Divine's organizing talent that his rural experiments, perhaps the most productive ever devised primarily for disadvantaged ghetto residents, were merely a sidelight among many other "utopian" programs that Divine successfully nurtured during this period.

The Peace Mission became increasingly involved in politics during the mid-1930s and early 1940s, reflecting the black community's growing optimism about the prospects for reform during the Roosevelt presidency. Campaigns against lynching, which engaged the vigorous efforts of many civil rights groups in this period, found Divine drafting model bills to send to congressmen, while his followers gathered 250,000 signatures on a petition in 1940 to pass federal antilynching legislation.[15]

Peace Mission members displayed a reform zeal typical of many social movements in the depression decade when they staged a convention in January 1936 to set forth guidelines for a just society. The key plank in their Righteous Government Platform proposed sweeping civil rights legislation

ROBERT S. WEISBROT

"making it a crime to discriminate in any public place against any individual on account of race, creed, or color, abolishing all segregated neighborhoods in cities and towns, making it a crime for landlords or hotels to refuse tenants on such grounds; abolishing all segregated schools and colleges, and all segregated areas in churches, theaters, public conveyances, and other public areas."[16] In this and all of its political actions the Peace Mission combined a faith in American democratic principles with a warning that the government strictly honor these principles or face massive protest.

The Changing Movement

The Peace Mission evolved after 1940 from a mass movement wholly dependent on its founding father to a formal organization featuring an elaborate bureaucracy. While such trends frequently overtake charismatic movements sometime after the passing of the original leader, the Peace Mission was transformed while Father Divine still lived and firmly controlled its affairs. Under the pressures of advancing age and growing legal problems related to local and federal efforts to ascertain and tax his movement's full revenues, Divine increasingly focused on building institutional guarantees for the movement he had once sustained through sheer vitality and seemingly endless ingenuity. As a result of these changes the Peace Mission proved able to survive even the great trauma of Father Divine's death in 1965, but at the cost—exacted well in advance—of virtually all the movement's original social energy and impact.

The final, conservative phase of Father Divine's leadership was inaugurated by a bitter court fight, spanning more than five years and exposing the fragility of the movement's financial and legal state. A former follower, Verinda Brown, sued Father Divine in 1937 for money allegedly given to him in trust while a disciple. Although Brown lacked any direct evidence and had obviously enjoyed numerous material benefits while a Peace Mission member for five years, a New York court ruled against Divine, placing the burden of proof on him and implicitly viewing his leadership as outside the full protection of the law. Fearing that this decision would tempt other disgruntled or greedy disciples to launch similar suits, Divine acted decisively to ensure his personal freedom and the security of his kingdom.

Beginning in the spring of 1940 followers of Father Divine incorporated several key Peace Mission centers in the Northeast. This marked a decisive break with Divine's earlier stress on an "invisible" church. Yet for a movement plagued by damaging defections and litigation, incorporation offered major advantages. It afforded the Peace Mission legal status on a par with other churches, providing at least a partial antidote to the tendency of trial judges to treat the Peace Mission as a barely legitimate "racket." Incorporation also entitled each official church to deed property in its own name, so that no disciple could claim any of the movement's assets upon leaving the Peace Mission.[17]

Unlike the Righteous Government Platform of 1936, which consisted of several dozen prescriptions for improving the world, the Peace Mission's corporate bylaws modestly confined themselves to problems of institutional continuity. The document created individual church trusteeships, presidencies, and other offices to simplify questions of delegated leadership.[18] For the first time, then, Father Divine formally recognized a special bureaucratic class in the Peace Mission, despite his earlier denunciations of elitist divisions among his disciples. The necessities of the movement in "middle age" simply took precedence over Divine's egalitarian instincts.

The corporate charter's bylaws also formally enshrined the absolute leadership role of Father Divine. In earlier years Divine had nominally renounced any special privilege or rank. He was, in the polite fiction of his own rhetoric, simply serving as "a sample and an example" for those who wished to lead the life he advocated. The bylaws now explicitly listed him as "supreme spiritual authority" while stipulating that he be called by various terms used to describe images of the Supreme Being.[19] Divine thus sought to embalm for all time the charisma that had marked his personal rule, just as the Peace Mission entered a new, more impersonal stage of its existence.

In July 1942, threatened with arrest for failure to pay a $7,000 judgment from Verinda Brown's lawsuit, Father Divine permanently relocated with several hundred followers to Philadelphia, safely beyond the jurisdiction of New York authorities. Divine's sudden self-exile from Harlem, coming just when renewed national prosperity and high employment were fast eroding the Peace Mission's communal economic appeal, contributed to a sharp decline in his following. Yet this appeared not to affect the minister greatly, for he was by then becoming absorbed with consolidating his corporate creation, to the increasing neglect of mass-based social activity.

The Peace Mission's growing conservatism was perhaps a typical response by a socially militant cult when other organizations emerge to assume its activist role.[20] The fact that the Peace Mission's sharp turn from radical politics came just when civil rights groups were forging a strong national coalition appears, in this light, more than coincidence or sad irony alone. Finally, Father Divine may well have seen that the progressive and communal aspects of his ministry no longer held a special attraction for ghetto dwellers and could be jettisoned without significant disruption of the movement. Such a perception

ROBERT S. WEISBROT

would have done much to ease his transition from active social reformer to secluded corporate planner.

The Peace Mission's search for accommodation with the wider society coincided with a pronounced rightward shift in its political rhetoric. During the depression, Father Divine's emphasis had been on making the United States a more democratic nation. In the years after World War II, while still strongly advocating racial equality, he increasingly denounced communists and labor unions, often in combination, as his social vision took on some of the most conservative features of American politics during the Cold War era.

The fading of the Peace Mission occurred in the economic as well as the political realm. Its businesses sharply contracted during the 1940s, and most of them outside Philadelphia, Newark, and Harlem eventually closed, including those in the vaunted Promised Land. The main problem, which worsened with the years, lay not with the businesses themselves; rather, in a time of growing prosperity, the continued economic advantages of cooperation no longer seemed a widely compelling reason to forsake all for Father Divine. In short, as converts diminished in number and old disciples left the movement or shifted from rural branches back to the cities, a flourishing, multimillion-dollar cooperative network languished for lack of personnel.[21]

As the Peace Mission lost its former scope and influence, it strived to enhance its status as a legitimate religious institution. There arose new orders of the devoted, each with its own elaborate code of conduct and special liturgical functions. "Rosebuds" were young women disciples; "Lily-Buds," somewhat older women; and "Crusaders," men of all ages. If one already lived a chaste life, as Father Divine advocated, it was not very difficult to attain membership in one of these orders: about half the active disciples belonged. Nor were these privileged orders, except insofar as they were entitled to lead hymns of praise to Father Divine. Initiates did, however, wear special uniforms, brightly colored to distinguish them from their brethren in the organization. The institution of specific religious orders underscored the advent of the Peace Mission as an established church rather than simply a spontaneous evangelical assembly.[22]

One final act of institutional continuity was Father Divine's marriage, in 1946, to a twenty-one-year-old white follower from Canada, Edna Rose Ritchings, called "Sweet Angel." Divine assured disciples that his was a purely spiritual union and exalted his "spotless virgin bride," now known as Mother Divine. Over the years, in conjunction with an able secretarial staff, she was groomed to act as her husband's vicar in administering and representing the Peace Mission. Although not an innovator or social crusader as Father Divine had been in his prime, Mother Divine proved well suited to lead the Peace

Nine years after his first wife died, Father Divine married twenty-one-year-old Edna Rose Ritchings of Canada. Here the couple trades smiles shortly after their wedding in 1946. The Second Mother Divine later succeeded Father Divine as head of the Peace Mission, which she still leads. (Urban Archives, Temple University)

Mission in its search for spiritual purity and organizational stability. It was clear that Divine's earlier social radicalism was to be merely revered, not revived, but within the Peace Mission's own centers, the Father's vision of a chaste, integrated communal society would go on as before.

Legacy of the Peace Mission Movement

Father Divine died in September 1965 after a decade of severe illness during which he had seldom appeared in public. Among civil rights leaders, his passing did not go unmourned. Roy Wilkins, director of the National Association for the Advancement of Colored People, recalled Divine as having done "a lot of good" as a social leader who "held up an example to the Negro community of cooperative endeavor."[23] One of the younger generation of activists who acknowledged a debt to Divine and his Peace Mission was Leon Sullivan, a black pastor who gained national fame for assisting poor youths and for demands that American businesses in South Africa implement principles of racial equality in their plants. Sullivan described Divine as "the forerunner . . . of much that we see in the practical aspects of religion today. While many people were yet talking about what religion could do about integration and self determination and human dignity, he was practicing it."[24]

The Peace Mission's social legacy has only belatedly gained recognition. The fact that the era of its greatest activity, the 1930s, witnessed neither the sustained protest nor the sweeping civil rights legislation of later decades only partly explains this neglect. More damaging to the Peace Mission's image was Father Divine's status as a cult leader, which tended to absorb the attention of numerous scholars and journalists to the exclusion of interest in his social policies. Divine surely enjoyed—and encouraged—the cultlike reverence that disciples accorded him. Yet rather than bask, immobile, in this adulation of his followers, Divine redirected their devotion outward, in support of the reform causes he valued: integration, equal rights, and economic cooperation. The Peace Mission "cult" thus became the highly effective vehicle of Father Divine's crusade for justice.

In Harlem and other ghettos the Peace Mission set a formidable standard of social activism that numerous ministers, keenly aware of Father Divine's fast-spreading popularity, increasingly sought to match, whether to emulate or to compete with him. At the same time, by aiding and uniting thousands of the most disadvantaged elements of ghetto society, the Peace Mission reminded middle-class blacks as well as whites that racial justice rested as much on alleviating poverty and unemployment as on eliminating Jim Crow practices. Utilizing the benefits of communal living, Father Divine's Peace Mission movement formed a distinctive part of the process by which black religious leaders moved from an era of absorbing spirituality to one of vital commitment to the struggle for equality. This was a trend whose influence on American race relations became ever more visible—and decisive—in succeeding decades.

Chronology

1879 Father Divine (George Baker) is born in Rockville, Md.
1919 Divine moves to Sayville, Long Island, N.Y.
1931 Divine is arrested in Sayville.
1932 Divine is tried, imprisoned, and released. Divine relocates to Harlem in New York City.
1935 Rural "Promised Land" venture begins in Ulster County, N.Y.
1936 Righteous Government Convention takes place in New York City.
1937 Divine is sued by Verinda Brown.

Notes

1. Accounts of Father Divine's early years have variously located his birthplace in Maryland, Virginia, the Carolinas, Georgia, and islands of the southeastern United States, and his birthdate between the end of the Civil War in 1865 and the late 1870s. Jill Watts, *God, Harlem U.S.A.: The Father Divine Story* (Berkeley: University of California Press, 1992), 5, 184, offers the most persuasive case to date, tracing from census and other records Divine's likely birth in 1879 in Rockville, Maryland, near Washington, D.C.

2. St. Clair McKelway and A. J. Liebling, "Who Is This King of Glory?," pt. 1, *New Yorker*, June 13, 1936, 24–25. On Divine's trial and subsequent departure from the South, see 25–26.

3. Seth M. Scheiner, "The Negro Church and the Northern City, 1890–1930," in *Seven on Black: Reflections on the Negro Experience in America*, ed. William G. Shade and Roy C. Herrenkohl (Philadelphia: Lippincott, 1969), 99.

4. Benjamin E. Mays and Joseph W. Nicholson, *The Negro's Church* (New York: Institute of Social and Religious Research, 1933), 122–23.

5. See the brief but penetrating analysis of Daddy Grace's movement in Arthur Huff Fausett, *Black Gods of the Metropolis: Negro Religious Cults of the Urban North* (1944; reprint, Philadelphia: University of Pennsylvania Press, 1971), esp. 22–30.

6. Sara Harris, with the assistance of Harriet Crittendon, *Father Divine*, enl. ed. (New York: Collier, 1971), 34.

7. *New York Amsterdam News*, June 8, 1932, 8.

8. John Hoshor, *God in a Rolls-Royce: The Rise of Father Divine, Madman, Menace, or Messiah* . . . (New York: Hillman-Curl, 1936), 85; but Robert A. Parker, *Incredible Messiah: The Deification of Father Divine* (Boston: Little, Brown, 1937), 28, maintains that Divine remained silent.

9. A more detailed examination of the scope of Peace Mission membership may be found in Robert Weisbrot, *Father Divine and the Struggle for Racial Equality* (Urbana: University of Illinois Press, 1983), 68–71. Varying calculations of Father Divine's following are found in Parker, *Incredible Messiah*, 134; Hoshor, *God in a Rolls Royce*, 139; "Messiah's Troubles," *Time*, May 3, 1937, 61; and St. Clair McKelway and A. J. Liebling, "Who Is This King of Glory?," pt. 3, *New Yorker*, June 27, 1936, 28.

10. Sermon of February 20, 1938, in *New Day*, March 3, 1938, 20.

11. Stephen Early to Father Divine, August 14, 1939, in *New Day*, August 17, 1939, 99–100; Eleanor Roosevelt to Father Divine, August 12, 1939, in ibid., August 17, 1939, 97.

12. McKelway and Liebling, "Who Is This King of Glory?," 22, 23, 25, 26; *Spoken Word*, February 9, 1935, 15.

13. Father Divine went so far as to brand the government's imposition of minimum

price laws "an unjust ruling" and suggested some barely legal means to circumvent them. See his sermon of September 5, 1936, in *New Day*, January 22, 1977, 7.

14. The scope and profitability of the "Promised Land" is treated in Jack Alexander, "All God's Chillun Got Heavens," *Saturday Evening Post*, November 18, 1939, 64.

15. "Is It Wonderful?," editorial in *Baltimore Afro-American*, July 20, 1940.

16. Righteous Government Platform, Introductory Plank 2. The platform is reprinted in its entirety in the *Spoken Word*, January 14, 1936, 7–16.

17. Stephen Zwick, "The Father Divine Peace Mission Movement" (senior history thesis, Princeton University, 1971), 120.

18. Kenneth Burnham, *God Comes to America: Father Divine and the Peace Mission Movement* (Boston: Lambeth Press, 1979), 74.

19. Ibid., 107.

20. See the penetrating analysis of this phenomenon in Peter Worsley, *The Trumpet Shall Sound: A Study of "Cargo" Cults in Melanesia*, 2d ed. (New York: Schocken, 1967), 232.

21. Zwick, "Father Divine Peace Mission Movement," 129–30, insightfully examines why the Promised Land declined.

22. See Burnham, *God Comes to America*, 84–96, for a description of the various religious orders, and Zwick, "Father Divine Peace Mission Movement," 108–9, for a provocative discussion of why they were created.

23. *New York Amsterdam News*, September 18, 1965.

24. William L. Banks, *The Black Church in the U.S.* (Chicago: Moody Bible Institute, 1972), 61.

Selected Bibliography

The indispensable sources for examining Father Divine's Peace Mission are the two major journals of the movement, the *Spoken Word* (October 20, 1934–July 31, 1937) and the *New Day* (May 21, 1936–December 26, 1992). These journals contain stenographic records of Divine's statements in over 10,000 sermons, letters, interview, and office talks, as well as testimony by disciples. The journals also offer a running commentary on the events in which Peace Mission members participated and the programs Father Divine created or aided.

Books on Father Divine and the Peace Mission movement include the following:

Burnham, Kenneth. *God Comes to America: Father Divine and the Peace Mission Movement.* Boston: Lambeth Press, 1979.

Harris, Sara, with the assistance of Harriet Crittendon. *Father Divine.* New York: Doubleday, 1953. Enl. ed., New York: Collier, 1971.

Hoshor, John. *God in a Rolls-Royce: The Rise of Father Divine, Madman, Menace, or Messiah . . . .* New York: Hillman-Curl, 1936.

Parker, Robert A. *Incredible Messiah: The Deification of Father Divine.* Boston: Little, Brown, 1937.

Watts, Jill. *God, Harlem U.S.A.: The Father Divine Story.* Berkeley: University of California Press, 1992.

Weisbrot, Robert. *Father Divine and the Struggle for Racial Equality.* Urbana: University of Illinois Press, 1983. Reprint, Boston: Beacon, 1984. This volume contains an annotated listing of primary and secondary sources for further study, pp. 224–32.

Appendix:
America's Communal Utopias
Founded by 1965

This compilation of American communal utopias established by 1965 is structured to illustrate clearly that many movements have chosen to found communal units as part of a process known as developmental communalism. Individual communities are listed alphabetically for easy reference and, where applicable, cross-listed with the movements that created and sometimes outlived them. Because of their large numbers, most Hutterite colonies, Jewish agricultural settlements, Roman Catholic monasteries and convents, and the settlements and towns of the New Deal Community Program are listed only with their founding movements. Within movements, communities are shown alphabetically by state in the United States, province in Canada, and country. Alternate names of communities and movements are given and, if important, cross-listed. Each community included here practiced or continues to practice communal, collective, or cooperative economies and lifestyles.

The information for this comprehensive listing has been gathered from all available previously printed lists, works on individual communities, and histories of the larger religious and secular movements that organized communally. A selected number of these principal sources appears at the end of this appendix. The bibliographical essay in this volume describes the broad spectrum of works on communal utopias. Primary sources are available in the archival collection of the Center for Communal Studies of the University of Southern Indiana, Evansville, Indiana, and elsewhere.

Where sources differ, those facts determined most reliable are presented. Founding dates for communities often vary among sources, depending on whether they represent the time of organization, incorporation, or actual settlement. The most inclusive dates are presented here, for both movements and communities. Since entire information has not been found for all communities and movements, some entries are not complete.

Key to sequence of information format for listings:
community or movement name/alternate name(s); founding and ending dates; founders and/or leaders; location(s); type of community.

Adonai Shomo Corporation/Community of Fullerites. *See* Millerite Adventist Movement

Alfred. *See* Shaker Movement

Alliance Colony. *See* Jewish Agricultural Colonies

Alphadelphia Phalanx. *See* Fourierist Movement

Altruist Community. *See* Longley Communities

Altruria (1894–1895); Edward Biron Payne; Sonoma County, California; Christian Socialist.

Amana Colonies. *See* Inspirationist Movement

Amenia Community. *See* Spiritualist Movement of Thomas Lake Harris

American Colony (1870s); Chicago, Illinois.

American Settlers Association (1898–1899); Duke (now Ruskin), Ware County, Georgia; settlement.

Amity/Fort Amity. *See* Salvation Army Movement

Am Olam Group Settlement. *See* Jewish Agricultural Colonies

Anarchist Movement

New Jersey: Ferrer Colony (1915–1956); Harry Kelly, Joseph Cohen, Leonard Abbot; Stelton (now Edison), Middlesex County.

Washington: Home Colony/Mutual Home Association (1896–1921); Oliver A. Verity, George H. Allen, B. F. Odell; Von Geldern Cove (now Home), Pierce County.

Anthroposophy Movement. *See* Camphill Movement

Antietam. *See* Seventh Day Baptist Movement

Antislavery Movement (1700s–1865). Private individuals and organizations, including the Canadian Anti-Slavery and the British and Foreign Anti-Slavery Societies, formed or aided communal efforts involving 3,500 to 5,000 blacks from 1819 to the 1860s in Ohio, Indiana, Illinois, Michigan, Tennessee, Pennsylvania, and South Carolina, and in British Columbia and Ontario, Canada. The United States government conducted a communal effort to manage the 10,000 or so slaves taken in the invasion of the South Carolina Sea Islands (1862–1863). Emancipation/Training of Slaves and Freedmen.

Canada

British Columbia: Vancouver Island (1850); Vancouver Island. Attempted only.

Ontario: **1.** Dawn (1842–1868); Josiah Henson, Hiram Wilson, John Scoble; near Dresden. **2.** Elgin (1849–1873); William King; near Chatham. **3.** Refugee Home Society (1852–1865); E. P. Benham, Horace Hallock, Josiah Henson, David Hotchkiss, Henry and Mary Bibb; near Windsor. **4.** Wilberforce Settlement (1829–ca. 1836); Israel Lewis, Thomas Cresap; near Lucan.

United States

Illinois: Edwards Coles's Settlement (1819–?); near Edwardsville, Madison County.

Indiana: Names and locations unknown.

Michigan: Saunders's Colony (1847–ca. 1860s); Mr. Saunders; Cass County.

Ohio: **1.** Attempted settlement of slaves freed in will of John Randolph of Roanoke rejected by Ohio residents (1846–1847); Mr. Caldwell; Mercer County. **2.** Carthagena Settlement (1836–ca. 1855); Augustus Wattles; near present Carthagena, Mercer County. **3.** Nathaniel Beaufort's Colony (?–?); Nathaniel Beaufort; Smithfield, Jefferson County. **4.** Samuel Gist's Settlement/Upper Camp and Lower Camp for Virginia slaves freed in will of Englishman Samuel Gist (1819–ca. 1835); William Wickham/Carter Page; on White Oakland Straight Creeks in Brown County. **5.** Settlement of freed slaves of Mrs. Ware of Kentucky (?–?). **6.** Settlement of freed slaves of the Conway family of Virginia (?–?). **7.** Settlement of freed slaves of William M. Colgin of Kentucky (?–?).

Pennsylvania: **1.** Colony of freed slaves (1827–?); York, York County. **2.** Silver Lake Community (1836–1838); Robert H. Rose; Silver Lake, Susquehanna County.

South Carolina: **1.** Port Royal Experiment of Edward Philbrick (1863–1866); Edward Philbrick; South Carolina Sea Islands. **2.** Port Royal Experiment of the United States Government (1862–1863); Edward Pierce appointed by the U.S. Treasury Department; South Carolina Sea Islands.

Tennessee: Nashoba (1826–1830); Frances Wright; near Memphis, Shelby County. *See also* Owenite Movement

Apalachicella (1900–1904); Florida.

Aquarian Foundation. *See* Theosophical Movement

Arden. *See* Single Tax Movement

Ardencroft. *See* Single Tax Movement

Ardentown. *See* Single Tax Movement

Army of Industry (1914–1918); Gerald Geraldson; Auburn, Placer County, California; Socialist.

Artesia. *See* Hugh MacRae's Immigrant Colonies

Arthurdale (1933–1947); near Reedsville, West Virginia. First New Deal Community Project; became town of Arthurdale. *See* New Deal Community Program for listing of all ninety-nine Federal unemployment relief communities

Association of Beneficents. *See* Domain Community

Aurora. *See* Keilite Movement

Bass Lake Farm (1941–?); Minneapolis, Minnesota.

Bayard Lane. *See* School of Living Movement

Bayside Communistic Colony (?–?); Bayside, Long Island, New York.

Benedictine Monastic Movement (early 6th century–present); St. Benedict of Nursia; Subiaco and Monte Cassino, Italy (A.D. 529), and worldwide; Roman Catholic Religious Order.

Benedictine Monasteries in America

American Cassinese Federation (1855–present)

Alabama: St. Bernard Abbey (1891–present); Cullman.

California: Woodside Priory (?–?); Portola Valley.

Colorado: Holy Cross Abbey (1886; 1925–present); Canon City.

Florida: St. Leo Abbey (1889; 1902–present); Pasco County.

Georgia: Benedictine Priory (?–?); Savannah.

Illinois: **1.** St. Bede Abbey (1910–present); Per. **2.** St. Procopius Abbey (1885; 1894–present); Lisle.

Indiana: St. Maur Priory (?–?); Indianapolis.

Kansas: St. Benedict's Abbey (1857; 1876); Atchison.

Kentucky: St. Mark's Priory (?–?); South Union.

Minnesota: St. John's Abbey (1856; 1866–present); Collegeville.

New Hampshire: St. Anselm's Abbey (1889; 1927–present); Manchester.

New Jersey: **1.** Newark Abbey (1857; 1884–1956; 1968–present); Newark. **2.** St. Mary's Abbey (1858; 1884–present); Morristown.

North Carolina: Belmont Abbey (1876; 1884–present); Belmont.

North Dakota: Assumption Abbey (1893; 1903–present); Richardson.

Ohio: St. Andrew Abbey (1922; 1934–present); Cleveland.

Oklahoma: St. Gregory's Abbey (1875; 1896–present); Shawnee.
Pennsylvania: **1.** Holy Trinity Priory (?–?); Butler. **2.** St. Vincent Archabbey (1846; 1855–present); Latrobe.
Washington: St. Martin's Abbey (1895; 1914–present); Lacey.

Camaldolese Congregation

California: Immaculate Heart Hermitage (1958–present); Big Sur.

Congregation of St. Ottilien

Nebraska: Mission House (?–?); Schuyler.
New Jersey: St. Paul's Abbey (1924; 1947–present); Newton.

Congregation of the Annunciation

California: St. Andrews Priory (?–?); Valyermo.

English Congregation

District of Columbia: St. Anselm's Abbey (1924–present).
Missouri: Priory of St. Mary and St. Louis (1955; 1973); St. Louis.
Rhode Island: St. Gregory's Abbey (1919–present); Portsmouth.

Olivetan Congregation

Arizona: Holy Trinity Monastery (?–?); St. David.
Louisiana: Our Lady of Mt. Olivet Monastery (1932–present); St. Charles.
New Mexico: Our Lady of Guadalupe Abbey (?–?); Pecos.

Swiss-American Federation (1870; 1881–present)

Canada
Westminster Abbey (1939; 1953–present); British Columbia.
United States
Alaska: New Subiaco Abbey (1878; 1891–present); Subiaco.
California: Prince of Peace Abbey (196?–present); Oceanside.
Illinois: Marmion Abbey (1882; 1947–present); Aurora.
Indiana: St. Meinrad Archabbey (1854; 1870–present); St. Meinrad.
Louisiana: St. Joseph Abbey (1890–present); St. Benedict.
Massachusetts: Glastonbury Abbey (1954; 1973–present); Hingham.
Missouri: **1.** Conception Abbey (1873; 1881–present); Conception. **2.** St. Pius X Abbey (1951–present); Pevely.
Nebraska: St. Michael Abbey (1956–present); Elkhorn.
Oregon: Mt. Angel Abbey (1882; 1904–present); St. Benedict.
South Dakota: Blue Cloud Abbey (1950; 1952; 1954–present); Marion.
Texas: Corpus Christi Abbey (1927–present); Sandia.
Wisconsin: St. Benedict's Abbey (1945; 1952–present); Benet Lake.

Sylvestrine Congregation

Michigan: **1.** St. Benedict's Monastery (1910–present); Oxford. **2.** St. Sylvester Monastery (1910–present); Detroit.
New Jersey: Holy Face Monastery (?–?); Clifton.

Unaffiliated

New York: Mt. Saviour Monastery (1950; 1957–present); Pine City.
Vermont: Conventual Abbey of St. Gabriel the Archangel (?–?); Weston.

Benedictine Convents in America

Benedictine Sisters

Colorado: St. Walburga Convent (1934–present); Boulder.
Pennsylvania: St. Vincent Archabbey and St. Emma's Convent (1852–present); Latrobe and Greensburg.

Congregation of Perpetual Adoration-Pontifical Jurisdiction

Arizona: Priory (?–?); Tucson.
California: St. Pius X Priory (1954–present); San Diego.
Missouri: **1.** Convent of Perpetual Adoration (1966–present); St. Louis. **2.** Holy Spirit Priory (1943–present); Kansas City. **3.** St. Scholastica's Priory (1874–present); Clyde.
Oklahoma: Osage Monastery (1950s–present); Sand Springs.
Wyoming: Priory (?–?); Casper.

Federation of Pontifical Jurisdiction, Scholastica (1922; 1930–present)

Alabama: Sacred Heart Convent (1902–present); Cullman.
California: St. Lucy's Priory (1956–present); Glendora.
Colorado: Benet Hill Priory (1963–present); Colorado Springs.
Florida: Holy Name Priory (1889–present); St. Leo.
Illinois: **1.** Our Lady of Sorrows (1951–present); Oak Forest. **2.** Sacred Heart Convent (1895–present); Lisle. **3.** St. Scholastica's Priory (1861–present); Chicago.
Kansas: Mount St. Scholastica (1863–present); Atchison.
Kentucky: St. Walburg's Monastery (1859–present); Covington.
Louisiana: St. Scholastica's Priory (1870–present); Covington.
Maryland: **1.** Emmanuel Priory (?–?); Baltimore. **2.** St. Gertrude's Priory (1857–present); Ridgely.
New Jersey: St. Walburga's Priory (1868–present); Elizabeth.
Oklahoma: **1.** Red Plains Priory (1968–present); Oklahoma City. **2.** St. Joseph's Priory (1879–present); Tulsa.
Pennsylvania: **1.** Mt. St. Benedict Priory (1856–present); Erie. **2.** Mt. St. Mary Priory (1870–present); Pittsburgh. **3.** St. Joseph's Convent (1852–present); Erie.
Texas: St. Scholastica's Convent (1911–present); Boerne.
Virginia: St. Benedict's Convent (1868–present); Bristow.
Wisconsin: Holy Name Priory (1849–present); Benet Lake.

Missionary Benedictine Sisters (1934–present)

Nebraska: Immaculata Convent (1923–present); Norfolk.

Olivetan Benedictine Sisters

Arkansas: Holy Angel Convent (1887–present); Jonesboro.

Primitive Observance (1948–present)

Connecticut: Abbey of Regina Laudis (1948–present); Bethlehem.

Second Federation of St. Gertrude (1937–present)

Arkansas: St. Scholastica's Convent (1878–present); Little Rock.

California: Holy Spirit Convent (1972–present); Sunnymead.

Idaho: Priory of St. Gertrude (1882–present); Cottonwood.

Indiana: **1.** Immaculate Conception (1867–present); Ferdinand. **2.** Our Lady of Grace Convent (1956–present); Indianapolis.

Minnesota: Mt. St. Benedict (1919–present); Crookston.

Missouri: Our Lady of Peace Convent (?–?); Columbia.

North Dakota: **1.** Queen of Peace Priory (1963–present); Fargo. **2.** Sacred Heart Priory (1916–present); Richardton.

Oregon: Queen of Angels Convent (1882–present); Mt. Angel.

South Dakota: **1.** Mother of God Priory (1961–present); Watertown. **2.** Sacred Heart Convent (1880–present); Yankton. **3.** St. Martin's Convent (1889–present); Rapid City.

Wisconsin: St. Benedict's Priory (1897–present); Madison.

Third Federation of St. Benedict

Illinois: St. Mary's Priory (1874–present); Nauvoo.

Minnesota: **1.** St. Benedict's Convent (1857–present); St. Joseph. **2.** St. Paul's Priory (1948–present); St. Paul. **3.** St. Scholastica's Priory (1892–present); Duluth.

North Dakota: Annunciation Priory (1947–present); Bismarck.

Washington: St. Placid's Priory (1952–present); Olympia.

Wisconsin: St. Bede's Priory (1948–present); Eau Claire.

Bennett Co-operative Colony (1837–1877); Long Lane, Dallas County, Missouri.

Berea (1836–1837); Cuyahoga County, Ohio.

Berlin Community (1865–1881); Berlin Heights, Erie County, Ohio; free love.

Berlin Heights (1854–1858); Berlin Heights, Erie County, Ohio.

Bermudian Creek. *See* Seventh Day Baptist Movement

Bethabara. *See* Moravian Movement

Bethany Fellowship (1945–present?); Minneapolis, Minnesota; Evangelical Christian.

Bethel Community in Bethel, Missouri. *See* Keilite Movement

Bethel Community in Philadelphia. *See* Jehovah's Witnesses Movement

Bethlehem. *See* Moravian Movement

Bethlehem Jehudah. *See* Jewish Agricultural Colonies

Bettina (1847–1848); West of Fredricksburg, Gillespie County, Texas.

Bible Community (ca. 1879–?); John C. Priegal; Plattsburg, Clinton County, Missouri.

Birthright Leasehold. *See* School of Living Movement

Bishop Hill. *See* Janssonist Movement

Black Emancipation Communities. *See* Antislavery Movement

Black Oak Ranch (1965–present); Laytonville, California; counterculture, extended family unit of the Hog Farm. *See* Hog Farm

Bloomfield Union Association. *See* Fourierist Movement

Blooming Grove Colony (1804–?); Dr. P. F. C. Haller; Lycoming County, Pennsylvania; German community under Haller, who came to America with advance party of Harmonist leader George Rapp in 1803; Radical Pietist. *See* Harmonist Movement

Blue Spring Community. *See* Owenite Movement

Bohemia Manor. *See* Labadist Movement

Bohemian Colonies

 Tennessee: Bohemian Co-operative Farming Company (1913–1916); near Mayland, Cumberland County; Bohemian Immigrant.

 Virginia: Rys (1897–?).

Bohemian Co-operative Farming Company. *See* Bohemian Colonies

Bon Homme (1874–present); Michael Waldner; Bon Homme County, Dakota Territory (now South Dakota); First American Hutterite Colony. *See* Hutterite Movement for listing of all Hutterite Colonies; *see also* Society of Brothers Movement for affiliated *bruderhofs*

Bookwalter (1879–?); Pawnee County, Nebraska.

Branch Davidian Movement/Branch Seventh-Day Adventists/Davidian Seventh-Day Adventists Association (1930s–present); Victor Houteff; Mount Carmel Center near Waco, Texas, and nationwide; Adventist Christian. Houteff, a member of the Seventh-Day Adventist Church, founded the Mount Carmel Center in 1935. It lasted until its destruction by fire in 1993 during a siege by U.S. government agents. Houteff began the Davidian Seventh-Day Adventists Association as he split with the Seventh-Day Adventist Church in 1942. His own movement splintered when he died in 1959 and many Davidians refused the leadership of his wife, Florence. Mount Carmel continued to function as a Davidian community, however, under the leadership of Florence Houteff, Ben and Lois Roden, George Roden, and, finally, Vernon Howell, who took the name David Koresh. The Branch Davidian movement continues among the faithful not consumed in the fire at Mount Carmel and those Davidians belonging to other Davidian factions that emerged in 1959; one is headquartered at Exeter, Missouri.

Briggs and his Devouts (1920–?); Coconino County, Arizona.

Brocton. *See* Spiritualist Movement of Thomas Lake Harris

Brook Farm (1841–1847); George Ripley; West Roxbury, Suffolk County, near Boston, Massachusetts; Transcendentalist/Fourierist. *See* Fourierist Movement

(The) Brotherhood (1847–?); John O. Wattles; Franklin Township, Clermont County, Ohio.

Brotherhood of Light Movement (1880s–ca. 1910s); John B. Newburgh; nationwide; care and training of children, spiritualism, vegetarianism. *See also* New Era Union Movement

 Colorado: **1.** Brotherhood of Light Community—Arboles (1902–1906); Charles W. Caryl; Arboles, Archuleta County. **2.** Brotherhood of Light Community—University Park (1901–1902); Charles W. Caryl; University Park, near Denver.

Brotherhood of the Co-operative Commonwealth Movement (1895–1907); Norman Wallace Lemond; Warren, Maine, and nationwide; Socialist.

 Washington: **1.** Equality (1897–1907); Norman W. Lemond, Ed Pelton; near Bellingham, Skagit County, Washington; Socialist/Bellamy/Nationalist. **2.** Freeland. *See* Freeland Association

Brotherhood of the New Life. *See* Spiritualist Movement of Thomas Lake Harris

Bruderhof. *See* Hutterite Movement and Society of Brothers Movement

Bryn Gweled Homesteads (1940–present); Southampton, Pennsylvania; planned neighborhood.

Buckley (1890s); E. L. Robinson; thirty miles inland from Puget Sound, Washington; Socialist.

Buddhist Communities
California: Santa Barbara (1934–?).
Vermont: Thetford (1934–?).

Buena Vista Colony/Great Western Co-operative Home-Building Association
(1901?–1919); Buena Vista, Colorado; settlement.

Bureau County Phalanx. *See* Fourierist Movement

Burley. *See* Social Democracy of America Movement

Burning Bush (1912–1919); Bullard, Smith, and Cherokee Counties, Texas; Evangelical Protestant.

Busro. *See* West Union under Shaker Movement

Byrdcliffe (1902–?); Woodstock, New York.

California State Colonization Program (1916–?); land settlement. State legislature appointed a commission on land colonization and rural credits. Experiments in controlled colonization at Delhi in Merced County and Durham in Butte County proved unworkable.

Camphill Movement/Anthroposophy (late nineteenth century–present); founded by Austrian-born Dr. Rudolf Steiner (1861–1925); no fewer than seventy "Camphill communities" worldwide, seven in North America; Anthroposophy ("the wisdom of man"), care for mentally retarded and handicapped.
Minnesota: Camphill Village Minnesota, Inc. (1980–present); Sauk Centre.
New Hampshire: Tobias Community (1988–present); Charles W. Frank; Wilton.
New York: **1.** Camphill Village U.S.A., Inc. (1961–present); Dr. Karl Koenig; Copake. **2.** Fellowship Community (1967–present); Spring Valley. **3.** Triform (1977–present); Hudson.
Pennsylvania: **1.** Camphill Special Schools (1963–present); Beaver Run, Glenmoore. **2.** Camphill Village Kimberton Hills, Inc. (1972–present); Kimberton.

Camphill Special Schools. *See* Camphill Movement

Camphill Village Kimberton Hills, Inc. *See* Camphill Movement

Camphill Village Minnesota, Inc. *See* Camphill Movement

Camphill Village U.S.A., Inc. *See* Camphill Movement

Canterbury. *See* Shaker Movement

Canton Phalanx. *See* Fourierist Movement

Carthagena Settlement. *See* Antislavery Movement

Caryl Co-operative Industrial System. *See* New Era Union Movement

Castle Haynes. *See* Hugh MacRae's Immigrant Colonies

Cedar-by-the-Sea. *See* Theosophical Movement

Cedarvale (1875–1877); Cedarvale, Chautauqua County, Kansas.

Celestia (1852–1864); Peter Armstrong; Sullivan County, Pennsylvania; Adventist.

Celo (1937–present); Burnsville, North Carolina. Claims to be oldest land trust community in America.

Charleston. *See* Moravian Movement

Cheltenham. *See* Icarian Movement

Chicago-Colorado Colony (1871–1972); Andrew C. Todd; Evans, Weld County, Colorado.

Chicago-Colorado Colony (1871–1873); Longmont, Boulder County, Colorado.

Children of the Light (1949–present); Dateland, Arizona.

Christian Commonwealth Colony (1896–1900); Ralph Albertson, George Howard Gibson; Columbus, Muskogee County, Georgia; Christian Socialist. *See* Right Relationship League

Christian Cooperative Association (1898–1902?); Clay Center, Clay County, Kansas.

Christian Co-operative Association (1898–ca. 1902); Muskogee County, Georgia.

Christian Cooperative Colony (1898–?); Sunnyside, Washington; Progressive Brethren Church members, land development.

Christian Corporation (1896–1897); George Howard Gibson; Lincoln, Lancaster County, Nebraska; Christian Socialist.

Christian Republic (1865–1866); Berlin, Ohio.

Christian Social Association (1899–1904); Sarona, Wisconsin.

Church of God and Saints of Christ (1900–?); William Crowely; Belleville, Virginia.

Church of Jesus Christ of Latter-day Saints. *See* Mormon Movement

Church of the Living God. *See* Shiloh Movement

Church of the Redeemer (noncommunal before 1965; communal 1965–present); Houston, Texas; Evangelical Christian, Charismatic.

Church of the Savior (1946–?); Washington, D.C.

Church Triumphant (1870–?); Rockford, Illinois.

Circle Pines Center (1938–present?); Delton, Michigan.

Cistercian Monastic Movement (1098–present); founded by St. Robert in France as reaction to laxity in Cluniac order; to various countries, and United States after 1825; Roman Catholic.

Cistercian Monasteries in America

Congregation of Casamari

New Jersey: Our Lady of Fatima (?–?); Mt. Laurel.

Congregation of Zirc (in dispersion)

Mississippi: Our Lady of Gerowvall (?–?); Paulding.
Texas: Our Lady of Dallas (1955–present); Irving.
Wisconsin: Our Lady of Spring Bank (1928–present); Oconomowoc (Okauchee).

Order of Cistercians of the Strict Observance (Trappists)

California: New Clairvaux Abbey (1955–present); Vina.
Colorado: St. Benedict's Monastery (1956–present); Snowmass.
Georgia: Holy Spirit Monastery (1944–present); Conyers.
Iowa: Our Lady of New Melleray (1849–present); Dubuque.
Kentucky: Gethsemani Abbey (1848–present); Trappist.
Massachusetts: St. Joseph's Abbey (1825–present); Spencer.
Missouri: Our Lady of the Assumption (195?–present); Ava.
New York: Genesee Abbey (1951–present); Piffard.
Oregon: Our Lady of Guadalupe (1847–present); Lafayette.
South Carolina: Mepkin Abbey (1949–present); Moncks Corner.
Utah: Our Lady of the Holy Trinity (1947–present); Huntsville.
Virginia: Our Lady of the Holy Cross (1950–present); Berryville.

Unaffiliated

Pennsylvania: Cistercian Conventual Priory (?–?); New Ringgold.

Cistercian Convents in America

Arizona: St. Rita Abbey (?–?); Sonoita.
California: Redwoods Abbey (?–?); Whitehorn.
Iowa: Abbey of Our Lady of the Mississippi (?–?); Dubuque.
Massachusetts: Mt. St. Mary's Abbey (1949–present); Wrentham.
Wisconsin: Valley of Our Lady Monastery (?–?); Prairie au Sac.

City of David/Israelite City of David (1930–present); Mary Purnell; Benton Harbor, Berrien County, Michigan; Millennialist. *See* House of David Movement

Clarion. *See* Jewish Agricultural Colonies

Clarkson Association. *See* Fourierist Movement

Clear Water. *See* Emissaries of Divine Light Movement

Clermont Phalanx. *See* Fourierist Movement

Coal Creek Community and Church of God. *See* Owenite Movement

Colony of Equality. *See* Owenite Movement

Colorado Cooperative Community. *See* Single Tax Movement

Columbia Co-operative Colony/Nehalem Valley Co-operative (1886–1892); Julia E. William; Mist, Columbia County, Oregon.

Columbian Phalanx/Columbian Association. *See* Fourierist Movement

Common Ground. *See* School of Living Movement

Commonwealth College (1923–1940); Mena, Arkansas.

Commonwealth of Israel (1899–1902); Mason County, Texas.

Communia (1847–1856); Wilhelm Weitling; Communia, Clayton County, Iowa; Socialist.

Community Farm (ca. 1930s–present?); Bright, Ontario, Canada; Protestant Christian, Hutterite influenced.

Community of United Christians (1836–1837); Berea, Cuyahoga County, Ohio.

Congregation of Saints (1843); Lexington, La Grange County, Indiana.

Co-operative Association of America (1900–ca. 1906); Lewiston, Androscoggin County, Maine.

Co-operative Brotherhood/Burley. *See* Social Democracy of America Movement

Co-operative Brotherhood of Winters Island (1893–1898); Erastus Kelsey, Kate Lockwood Nevins; Winters Island in Suisun Bay, Contra Costa County, California; Socialist.

Co-operative Christian Federation (1902–1902); Christadelphia, Benton County, Oregon.

Co-operative Commonwealth Company/Burley. *See* Social Democracy of America Movement

Co-operative Commonwealth of Idaho (ca. 1898–?).

Co-operative Farm (1951–?); Eugene, Oregon.

Co-operative Industrial Colony (ca. 1899–ca. 1901); Milner's Store, Camp Creek, Georgia.

Co-operative Union (1901–1901); Ocala, Florida.

Cosme Colony (1901–1902?); Paraguay, South America.

Count de Leon Movement. *See* Muellerite Movement

Cremieux. *See* Jewish Agricultural Colonies

Danish Colony (1877–?); Hays, Kansas.

Danish Colony (?); Solvang, California.

Dansville Sanitarium. *See* Our Home on the Hillside

Davidian Seventh-Day Adventists. *See* Branch Davidian Movement

Davidian Movement. *See* Branch Davidian Movement

Davisite Kingdom of Heaven (1867–1881); William W. Davis; near Walla Walla County, Washington; Mystic.

Dawn. *See* Antislavery Movement

Dawn Valcour Movement (1874–1875); Oren Shipman, John Wilcox; Vermont and New York; Spiritualist.

New York: Valcour Island (1874–1875); Valcour Island.

Vermont: Colchester (1874–1875); Colchester.

Deep Run Farm. *See* School of Living Movement

Deer Spring/Evergreen. *See* Society of Brothers Movement

Delhi. *See* California State Colonization Program

Delta Cooperative Farm (1936–?); Hillhouse, Mississippi.

Domain, Harmonia, Kiantone Community/Association of Beneficents (1853–1863); John Murray Spear; Kiantone Creek, Chautauqua County, New York; Spiritualist.

Dorrilites (1798–1799); Mr. Dorril; adjoining properties in Leyden, Franklin County, Massachusetts, and Guilford, Widham County, Vermont; vegetarian.

Doukhobor Movement (1899–present); Transcaucasus, Russia, and Manitoba, Canada; numerous congregations with varied degrees of cooperative activities; Christian.

Dr. Abram Brooke's Experiment (1843–1845); Abram Brooke; Oakland, Clinton County, Ohio.

Drop City (1965–1973); Clark Richert and other artists and college students; near Trinidad, Colorado; counterculture.

Durham. *See* California State Colonization Program

Ebenezer Community. *See* Inspirationist Movement

Eclectic Phalanx. *See* Fourierist Movement, Virginia Phalanx

Economy/Oeconomie. *See* Harmonist Movement

Ecumenical Institute (1957–present); Chicago, Illinois.

Ecumenical Institute. *See* Global Order Movement

Eden Society (1907–1908); Baxter Springs, Cherokee County, Kansas.

Edenvale. *See* Emissaries of Divine Light Movement

Eglinton (1882–?); Taney City, Missouri.

Elgin. *See* Antislavery Movement

Elim. *See* Keilite Movement

Emissaries of Divine Light Movement/Emissary Foundation International (1932–present); Lloyd Meeker to 1954, Martin (Cecil) Exeter to 1988, Michael and Nancy (Meeker) Exeter 1988–present; 200 noncommunal Emissary Centers in major cities worldwide with about 4,000 adherents; fewer than 1,000 now living in current Emissary Communities, nine in the United States and Canada, one each in Australia, England, France, and South Africa; Spiritual/Harmony.

Australia

Hillier Park (1979–present); near Adelaide.

Canada

British Columbia: **1.** 100 Mile Lodge (1948–present); Martin (Cecil) Exeter; 100 Mile House. **2.** Edenvale (1973–present); near Vancouver.

Ontario: **1.** King View (1972–present); near Toronto. **2.** Twin Valleys Community (1971–1983); George J. Bullied, David and Dianne Pasikov; near Wardsville.

England

Mickleton (1980–present); near Stratford-upon-Avon.

South Africa
Hohenort Hotel (1978–present); Capetown.
United States
California: Glen Ivy (1977–present); near Corona.
Colorado: Sunrise Ranch (1945–present); Lloyd Meeker; Loveland.
Indiana: Oakwood Farm (1973–present); near Selma.
New Hampshire: Green Pastures Estate (1963–present); near Epping.
New York: **1.** Clear Water (1975–1983); near Livingston. **2.** Lake Rest (1971–1983); near Livingston.
Oregon: Still Meadow (1976–present); near Portland.

Enfield Shaker Village, Enfield, Connecticut. *See* Shaker Movement
Enfield Shaker Village, Enfield, New Hampshire. *See* Shaker Movement
English Colony (?); in the Burns Valley near Clear Lake, California.
English Colony (?); Rosedale near Bakersfield, California.
Enterprise Community (1872–?); Long Lane, Missouri.
Ephraim (1849–1853). *See* Moravian Movement
Ephraim (1853–1864). *See* Moravian Movement
Ephrata. *See* Seventh Day Baptist Movement
Equality. *See* Brotherhood of the Co-operative Commonwealth Movement
Equality/Colony of Equality. *See* Owenite Movement
Equality Industrial Association (1899?–1901?); Pottawatomie County, Oklahoma.
Equity Community. *See* Time Store Cooperative Movement and Owenite Movement
Esoteric Fraternity (1893?–1907); Applegate, California.
Esperanza (1877–1878); N. T. Romaine; Urbana, Neosho County, Kansas.
Estero. *See* Koreshan Unity Movement
Evergreen/Deer Spring. *See* Society of Brothers Movement
Fairhope. *See* Single Tax Movement
Farist Community (1870?); Monticello, Minnesota.
The Farm (1909–?); West Newbury, Massachusetts.
Farmers and Mechanics Co-operative Association (1870?); Missouri.
Farmers' Incorporated Co-operative Society (1889–1902?); Rockwell, Iowa.
Farm Security Administration Homesteads. *See* New Deal Community Program
Father Divine Kingdoms. *See* Peace Mission Movement
Fellowship Community. *See* Camphill Movement
Fellowship Farm Association (1908–1918); George E. Littlefield; Westwood, Norfolk County, Massachusetts; land settlement.
Fellowship Farms (1912–1926); Kate D. Bucks; Puenta, California; land settlement.
Ferrer Colony. *See* Anarchist Movement
First Community of Man's Free Brotherhood (1833–1835); Isaac Romine; Covington, Fountain County, Indiana.
Forestville Community. *See* Owenite Movement
Fort Amity. *See* Salvation Army Movement
Fort Herrick. *See* Salvation Army Movement
Fort Romie. *See* Salvation Army Movement
Fountain Grove. *See* Spiritualist Movement of Thomas Lake Harris
Fourierist Movement (1808–1890s); Charles Fourier, Albert Brisbane; France and United States; Utopian Socialist.
Illinois: **1.** Bureau County Phalanx (1843–1844); La Moille, Bureau County. **2.** Canton Phalanx (1845–1845); John F. Randolph; Fulton County. **3.** Integral Phalanx (1845–1847); John S. Williams; Loami Township, Sangamon County.

Indiana: **1.** Fourier Phalanx (1858–1858); Sparta Township, Dearborn County. **2.** Grand Prairie Harmonial Institute (1853–1854); John O. Wattles; Warren County; Fourierist influence. **3.** La Grange Phalanx (1843–1847); Mongo, Springfield Township, La Grange County. **4.** Philadelphia Industrial Association (1845–1847); South Bend, German Township, St. Joseph County.

Iowa: Iowa Pioneer Phalanx (1844–1845); Scott Township, Mahaska County.

Kansas: Kansas Co-operative Farm/Prairie Home Colony/Silkville Colony (1869–1892); Ernest Valeton de Boissiere; Silkville, Williamsburg Township, Franklin County.

Massachusetts: Brook Farm (1841–1847); George Ripley; West Roxbury (now in Boston), Suffolk County; initially Transcendentalist.

Michigan: Alphadelphia Phalanx (1844–1847); near Galesburg, Comstock Township, Kalamazoo.

New Jersey: **1.** North American Phalanx (1843–1855); Albert Brisbane/Horace Greeley; Atlantic Township, Manmouth County. **2.** Raritan Bay Union/Eagleswood (1853–1857); Marcus Spring/Perth Amboy, Middlesex County.

New York: **1.** Bloomfield Union Association (1844–1846); Edwin A. Stillman; North Bloomfield, at juncture of Livingston and Ontario Counties. **2.** Clarkson Association (1844–1845); Hamlin Township, Monroe County. **3.** Jefferson County Industrial Association (1843–1844); Alonzo M. Watson; Cold Creek, Jefferson County. **4.** Mixville Association (1844–1845); Wiscoy, Hume Township, Allegany County. **5.** Morehouse Union (1843–1844); Piseco, Arietta Township, Hamilton County. **6.** Ontario Union/Manchester Union (1844–1845); Theron C. Leland; Littleville, Manchester, and Hopewell Townships, Ontarion County. **7.** Sodus Bay Phalanx (1844–1846); Benjamin Fish; Sodus and Huron Townships, Wayne County.

Ohio: **1.** Clermont Phalanx (1844–1846); Franklin Township, Clermont County. **2.** Columbian Phalanx/Columbian Association (1845–1845); Zanesville, Muskingum County. **3.** Ohio Phalanx (1844–1845); Bellaire, Pultny Township, Belmont County. **4.** Trumbull Phalanx (1844–1848 and 1849–1852); Post Office, Phalanx Station, Braceville Township, Trumbull County.

Pennsylvania: **1.** Leraysville Phalanx (1844–1845); Lemuel C. Belding; Leraysville, Pike Township, Bradford County. **2.** Social Reform Unity (1842–1843); Barrett Township Monroe County. **3.** Sylvania Association/Sylvania Phalanx (1843–1844); Horace Greeley; Lackawaxen Township, Pike County.

Texas: La Reunion (1855–1859); Victor Considerant; Cement City, Dallas County.

Virginia: Virginia Phalanx/Eclectic Phalanx (1845–1850); Gilmer County.

Wisconsin: **1.** Pigeon River Fourier Colony (1846–1847); Sheboygan County. **2.** Spring Farm Phalanx (1846–1849); Dr. P. Cady; Sheboygan County. **3.** Wisconsin Phalanx (1844–1850); Warren B. Chase; Ripon Township, Kenosha, Fond du Lac County.

Fourier Phalanx. *See* Fourierist Movement

Franklin Community. *See* Owenite Movement

Free Acres Association (1910–1950)

New Jersey: Berkeley Heights (?–?); Berkeley Heights, Union County.

Tennessee: New Providence (?–?); New Providence.

The Free Community. *See* Union Home

Freedom Colony (1897–1905); Fulton, Bourbon County, Kansas.

Freeland Association (1901–1907); James P. Gleason and dissidents from Equality; Whidbey Island, Island County, Washington; Socialist, Rochdale, land development. *See* Brotherhood of the Co-operative Commonwealth Movement

The Free Lovers at Davis House (1854–1858); Francis Barry; Berlin Heights, Erie County, Ohio; Spiritualist, free love.

Friedheim (1899–1900); Virginia.

Friendly Association for Mutual Interests, Stark County, Ohio. *See* Owenite Movement

Friendly Association for Mutual Interests, Valley Forge, Pennsylvania. *See* Owenite Movement

Friendship Community. *See* Longley Communities

Friendship House. *See* Koinonia Farm

Fruit Crest (1911–1912); C. B. Hoffman, George Littlefield; Independence, Missouri; Socialist.

Fruithills (1845–1852); Orson S. Murray; Warren County, Ohio.

Fruitlands (1843–1844); A. Bronson Alcott, Charles Lane, Henry Wright; Harvard, Massachusetts; Transcendentalist, anarchist.

Garden Grove Community (1848–?); Garden Grove, Decatur County, Iowa.

German Colonization Company (1869–1871); Carl Wulsten; near Canon City, Custer County, Colorado.

Germania Company. *See* Millerite Adventist Movement

Germantown. *See* Muellerite Movement

Gibbs Co-operative Colony (1901–1905?); Gibbs, Santa Cruz County, California.

Glen Gardner Cooperative Colony/St. Francis Acres (1950s–?); Glen Gardner, New Jersey.

Glen Ivy. *See* Emissaries of Divine Light Movement

Glenmore (late 1880s–?); New York.

Glennis Cooperative Colony (1894–1896); Oliver A. Verity; Eatonville/Tacoma, Pierce County, Washington; Bellamy Nationalist.

Global Order Movement (1954–present); operates the Ecumenical Institute and the Institute of Cultural Affairs in thirty-five countries worldwide with twenty-five communal residential communities, four in the United States; intercultural communities planning.
    Arizona: Order Ecumenical/Institute of Cultural Affairs—Phoenix Headquarters (1954–present); Phoenix.
    Colorado: Institute of Cultural Affairs—Oklahoma City (?–present); Oklahoma City.
    Washington: Institute of Cultural Affairs—Seattle (?–present); Seattle.

Golden Life Community (1904?); Independence, Minnesota.

Goose Pond Community. *See* Owenite Movement and/or Society of One-Mentians

Gorda Mountain (1962–1968); Amelia Newell; near Gorda, California; counterculture.

Gorham. *See* Shaker Movement

Goshen Community (1825–1826); Goshen Field, Posey County, Indiana.

Gould Farm (1913–present); Monterey, Berkshire County, Massachusetts; psychological treatment/rehabilitation.

Grand Ecore. *See* Muellerite Movement

Grand Prairie Community (1845–1847); Rainsville, Warren County, Indiana; Fourierist influence.

Grand Prairie Harmonial Institute. *See* Fourierist Movement

Great Western Co-operative Home-Building Association. *See* Buena Vista Colony

Green Bay (1850–1853); Nils Otto Tank; Green Bay, Brown County, Wisconsin.

Green Pastures. *See* Emissaries of Divine Light Movement

Groveland. *See* Shaker Movement

Guru Ram Das Ashram. *See* Healthy, Happy, Holy Organization Movement

Halidon. *See* Single Tax Movement

Hancock. *See* Shaker Movement

Harmonia. *See* Domain Community

Harmonial Vegetarian Society (1860–1864); Harmony Springs near Maysville, Benton County, Arkansas.

Harmonist Movement/Harmony Society (1785–1914); George (Johann Georg) Rapp; Württemberg, Germany, and United States; Radical Pietist.

　Indiana: Harmony/Harmonie/New Harmony (1814–1824); George Rapp; New Harmony, Posey County.

　Louisiana: *See* Grand Ecore and Germantown under Muellerite Movement as communities of Harmonist secessionists

　Missouri: *See* Bethel under Keilite Movement as community of Harmonist secessionists

　Ohio: Followers of George Rapp, who did not join his community at Harmony, Pennsylvania, settled at Bull Creek in Columbiana County, Ohio, in 1803. In 1827, under the leadership of Peter Kaufman and other Harmonist secessionists from Economy, they formed the Society of the United Germans, also known as Teutonia. *See* Society of the United Germans

　Oregon: *See* Aurora and Willapa under Keilite Movement as communities of Harmonist secessionists

　Pennsylvania: **1.** Economy/Oeconomie (1824–1905); George Rapp; Beaver County, Economy (now Ambridge). **2.** Harmony/Harmonie (1805–1814); George Rapp; Harmony, Beaver County. **3.** Lycoming County Rappites (1804–?); Dr. P. F. C. Haller led many of George Rapp's followers who arrived on the ship *Margaretha* at Philadelphia in 1804 to settle in Lycoming County. **4.** *See* Blooming Grove Colony **5.** *See* New Philadelphia Society under Muellerite Movement as community of Harmonist secessionists **6.** Tidioute Colony (1884–1886); Harmony Society sponsored this group of Hutterites from the Tripp Colony in South Dakota to settle on Harmonist land near Titusville, Warren County; Hutterite.

Harmony (1899–?); Washington.

Harmony/Harmonie. *See* Harmonist Movement

Harmony/New Harmony/Harmonie. *See* Harmonist Movement and/or Owenite Movement

Harmony Colony/Harmony (1899); S. M. Dunn; Lewis County, Washington; Populist, Socialist.

Harmony Co-operative Industrial Association (1906?); East Assiniboia, Canada.

Harmony Island (1901–1905); British Columbia, Canada; Finnish Utopian.

Harmony Society. *See* Harmonist Movement

Harvard. *See* Shaker Movement

Hays City Danish Colony (1877–?); Louis Albert François Pio; Ellis County, Kansas; Socialist.

Healthy, Happy, Holy Organization Movement/3HO (ca. 1965–present); Yogi Bhaian (Siri Singh Sahib); North America and worldwide; numerous communal centers in North America; Sikh Dharma religion dating to fifteenth century India/Kundalini Yoga.

Canada

Ontario: 3HO (?–present); Toronto.

United States

California: 3HO International Headquarters/Guru Ram Das Ashram (ca. 1965–present); Los Angeles.

Massachusetts: 3HO Guru Ram Das Ashram (?–present); Leverett.

New Mexico: 3HO New Mexico/Hacienda De Guru Ram Das (?–present); Espanola.
Virginia: 3HO Center (?–present); Herndon.
Washington, D.C.: 3HO Foundation (ca. 1965–?).

Heathcote. *See* School of Living Movement

Heaven City (1923–1927); Albert J. Moore; Harvard, Illinois.

Heaven Colony (1867–?); Walla Walla, Washington.

Hebron. *See* Keilite Movement

Helicon Hall Colony (1906–1907); Upton Sinclair; near Englewood, Bergen County,
New Jersey.

Hiawatha Village Association (1893–1896); Walter Thomas Mills, Abraham Byers;
Hiawatha, Schoolcraft County, Michigan; Socialist/Time Credit for Labor.

Hidden Springs (1953–?); Neshanic Station, New Jersey.

Highland Home (1844–1844); Zanesfield, Logan County, Ohio.

Himalaya Academy (1962–present?); Master Subramuniya; Virginia City, Nevada;
Hindu-Christian monastic life and training.

Hog Farm (1965–present); Berkeley, California; counterculture. *See also* Black Oak
Ranch

Holy Band (1903?–?); Maysville, Mason County (or Brown and Adams Counties),
Kentucky.

Holy City (1918–1958); William E. Ricker; near Santa Cruz, Santa Clara County, California; Religious.

Home Colony. *See* Anarchist Movement

Home Employment Co-operative Colony (1894–1906); William H. Bennett; Long
Lane, Dallas County, Missouri.

Home Industrial College (1901–?); Liberty County, Texas.

Hopedale Community (1842–1867); Adin Ballou; Milford, Worcester County, Massachusetts; Christian Socialist, Fourierist influence.

House of David/Israelite House of David (1903–1928); Benjamin and Mary Purnell;
Benton Harbor, Berrien County, Michigan; Millennialist. *See* City of David

Hugh MacRae's Immigrant Colonies/Model Farm Communities Movement
(1905–1930s); Hugh MacRae and the Carolina Trucking and Development Company
formed colonies for immigrants in Pender, Columbus, and New Hanover Counties,
North Carolina; immigrant settlement.
North Carolina: **1.** Artesia (1905–?); Hugh MacRae; near Wilmington; English and
Polish settlement. **2.** Castle Haynes (1905–?); Hugh MacRae; near Wilmington, New
Hanover County; American, Dutch, Hungarian, Polish, and Norwegian settlement.
3. Marathon Colony (1905); Hugh MacRae; near Wilmington; Greek settlement.
4. New Berlin Colony (1906–?); Hugh MacRae; Columbus County; German and
Hungarian settlement. **5.** New Hanover Colony (1906–?); Hugh MacRae; New
Hanover County; Northern Italian and Polish settlement. **6.** St. Helena (1905–?);
Hugh MacRae. **7.** VanEeden (ca. 1908–ca. 1938); Hugh MacRae, Frederik Van-
Eeden; thirty miles north of Wilmington; Dutch settlement.

Hutterian Brethren. *See* Hutterite Movement and Society of Brothers Movement

Hutterite Movement/Bruderhof (1528–present). Founded by Jakob Hutter in Moravia,
spread to Hungary, Transylvania, Wallachia, and the Russian Ukraine. Immigration to
the United States in 1874 resulted in establishment of Bon Homme Colony (*bruderhof*)
led by Michael Waldner, near Tabor in the Dakota Territory (now South Dakota).
Three Hutterite "people," or "leut" (Schmiedeleut, Dariusleut, and Lehrerleut), named
after their earliest leaders in America, began the first three colonies of Bon Homme,
Silver Lake, and Elmspring that have branched into about 390 with a population of

over 36,000, including some 15,000 members. *Prairieleut (or "Prairie People")* (1874–present) are "non-colony" Hutterites who immigrated from Russia in 1874 and chose to acquire private lands under the Homestead Act instead of joining communal colonies. Most Prairieleut became associated with nearby Mennonites. The Society of Brothers (see Society of Brothers Movement) that arose in Germany in 1920 under the leadership of Eberhard and Emmy Arnold has been somewhat affiliated with certain Hutterites at times since the 1950s. Anabaptist Christian, Pacifist.

Schmiedeleut (or "Schmiede People") (1874–present); led by Michael Waldner at Bon Homme Colony (1874–present); Bon Homme, near Tabor, Dakota Territory (now South Dakota).

Canada

Manitoba: **1.** Airport (1972–present); MacDonald. **2.** Alsask (?–1932). **3.** Aspenheim (1988–?); Bagot. **4.** Baker (1973–present); Macgregor. **5.** Barickman (1920––present); Headingly. **6.** Beaver Creek (1971–present); Bagot. **7.** Bloomfield (1957–present); Westbourne. **8.** Blumengard (1922–present); PlumCoulee. **9.** Bon Homme (1918–present); Elie. **10.** Brightstone (1959–present); Lac Du Bonnet. **11.** Broad Valley (1974–present); Arborg. **12.** Cascade (?); Katrime. **13.** Clearview (1982–present); Elm Creek. **14.** Clearwater (1960–present); Balmoral. **15.** Cool Springs (1988–present); Mennedosa. **16.** Concord (1985–present); Winnipeg. **17.** Crystal Spring (1954–present); Ste. Agathe. **18.** Cypress (1975–present); Cypress River. **19.** Decker (1981–present); Decker. **20.** Deerboine (1959–present); Alexander. **21.** Delta (1981–present); Austin. **22.** Elm River (1982–present); Newton Siding. **23.** Espbenheim (?); Macgregor. **24.** Evergreen (1975–present); Somerset. **25.** Fairholm (1959–present); Portage La Prairie. **26.** Glenway (1965–present); Dominion City. **27.** Good Hope (1988–present); Portage La Prairie. **28.** Grand (1958–present); Oakville. **29.** Grass River (1972–present); Glenella. **30.** Green Acres (?); Glen Souris. **31.** Greenwald (1955–present); Beuasejour. **32.** Hidden Valley (1968–present); Austin. **33.** Hillside (1958–present); Justice. **34.** Holmfield (1975–present); Killarney. **35.** Homewood (1960–present); Starbuck. **36.** Huron (1918–present); Elie. **37.** Iberville (1919–present); Headingly. **38.** Interlake (1961–present); Teulon. **39.** James Valley (1918–present); Elie. **40.** Lakeside (1946–present); Headingly. **41.** Maple Grove (1987–present); Lauder. **42.** Marble Ridge (1972–present); Hodgeson. **43.** Maxwell (1918–present); Headingly. **44.** Mayfair (1972–present); Killarney. **45.** Miami (1966–present); Morden. **46.** Miami Farm (?); Morden. **47.** Milltown (1918–present); Elie. **48.** New Dale (1972–present); Brandon. **49.** Newdale Farm (1974–present); Minnedosa. **50.** New Haven (1977–present); Argyle. **51.** New Rosedale (1944–present); Portage La Prairie. **52.** Oak Bluff (1952–present); Morris. **53.** Oak Ridge (1967–present); Holland. **54.** Parkview (1964–present); Riding Mountain. **55.** Pembina (1961–present); Darlingford. **56.** Pine Creek (1973–?). **57.** Plainview (1973–present); Elkhorn. **58.** Poplar Point (1936–present); Poplar Point. **59.** Rainbow (1964–present); Lorette. **60.** Ridgeland (1965–present); Dugald. **61.** Riverbend (1969–present); Carberry. **62.** Riverdale (1946–present); Gladstone. **63.** Riverside (1934–present); Arden. **64.** Rocklake (1947–present); Gross Isle. **65.** Rose Bank (?); Miami. **66.** Rosedale (1918–present); Elie. **67.** Roseisle (1929–?). **68.** Rose Valley (1957–present); Graysville. **69.** Shady Lane (?); Treherne. **70.** Shamrock (1982–present); Baldur. **71.** Sommerfield (1981–present); Highbluff. **72.** Souris River (1977–?); Elgin. **73.** Springfield (1950–present); Anola. **74.** Springhill (1964–present); Nee Pawa. **75.** Spring Valley (1956–present); Brandon. **76.** Spruce Wood (1977––present); Brookdale. **77.** Starlite (1981–present); Starbuck. **78.** Sturgeon Creek

(1938–present); Headingly. **79.** Suncrest (1969–present); Touround. **80.** Sunnyside (1942–present); Newton Siding. **81.** Teulon (1934–?). **82.** Treesbank (1982–present); Wawanesa. **83.** Trileaf (1987–present); Buldur. **84.** Valley View (1986–present); Swan Lake. **85.** Vermillion (1990–present); Sanford. **86.** Waldheim (1934–present); Elie. **87.** Wellwood (1970–present); Dunrea. **88.** West Plan (?–present); Sturgeon Creek Headingly. **89.** West Rock (?–present); Westbourne. **90.** Whiteshell (1961–present); Riverhills. **91.** Willow Creek (1978–present); Cartwright. **92.** Windy Bay (1978–present); Swan Lake. **93.** Wingham; Elm Creek. **94.** Woodland (1971–present); Poplar Point.

United States

Minnesota: **1.** Big Stone (1958–present); Graceville. **2.** Oakwood (?); Dexter. **3.** Spring Prairie (1980–present); Hawley. **4.** Starland (?–present); Gibbon.

North Dakota: **1.** Fairview (1971–present); Lamoure. **2.** Forest River (1950–present); Fordville. **3.** Maple River (1969–present); Fullerton. **4.** Spring Creek (1961–present); Forbes. **5.** Sundale (1985–present); Milnor. **6.** Willow Bank (1984–present); Edgeley.

Pennsylvania: Tidioute (1884–1886); Warren County (Hutterite group from the Tripp Colony of South Dakota sponsored by the Harmony Society on its own land near the Titusville oil fields).

South Dakota: **1.** Beadle (1905–1918); Beadle County, moved to West Raley, Alberta. **2.** Blumengard (1952–present); Wacota. **3.** Bon Homme (1874–present); founded by Michael Waldner as first communal settlement of Hutterites in North America, near Tabor. **4.** Brentwood (1987–present); Faulkton. **5.** Buffalo (1907–1913); Beadle County. **6.** Cedar Grove (1972–present); Platte. **7.** Claremont (?–present); Castle Wood. **8.** Clark (1955–present); Raymond. **9.** Clearfield (?–present). **10.** Cloverleaf (1962–present); Howard. **11.** Deerfield (1962–present); Ipswich. **12.** Elmspring (later called Old Elmspring) (1877–1929); near Parkston, Hutchinson County, moved to Warner, Alberta; first Lehrerleut colony founded by Hutterites just arrived from Russia in 1877. **13.** Fordham (1977–present); Carpenter. **14.** Glendale (1949–present); Frankfort. **15.** Gracevale (1948–present); Winfred. **16.** Grass Land (1990–present); Westport. **17.** Grass Ranch (1990–present); Kimball. **18.** Greenwood (1979–present); Delmont. **19.** Hillcrest (1979–present); Graden City. **20.** Hillside (1961–present); Doland. **21.** Huron (1906–1918); Huron. **22.** Huron (1944–present); Huron. **23.** Hutterville (1982–present); Stratford. **24.** James Valley (1913–1918); James Valley Junction, moved to Elie, Manitoba. **25.** Jamesville (1886–1918; 1937–present); near Utica, moved to Rockyford, Alberta, during World War I. **26.** Kutter (1892–1918); near Mitchell, moved to Redlands, Alberta. **27.** Lakeview (1963–present); Lake Andes. **28.** Long Lake (1990–present); Wetonka. **29.** Mayfield (1987–present); Vienna. **30.** Maxwell (1900–?). **31.** Maxwell (1949–present); Scotland. **32.** Millford (1910–1918); Beadle County, moved to Raymond, Alberta. **33.** Millbrook (1983–present); Mitchell. **34.** Millerdale (1949–present); Miller. **35.** Milltown (1886–1907); Milltown, Hutchinson County. **36.** Newdale (1979–present); Elkton. **37.** New Elmspring (1900–1918; 1936–present); Ethan, moved to Magrath, Alberta, during World War I. **38.** Newport (1987–present); Claremont. **39.** Oaklane (1986–present); Alexandria. **40.** Old Elmspring (?); Parkston. **41.** Orland (?–present); Montrose. **42.** Pearl Creek (1949–present); Iroquois. **43.** Pembrook (1977–present); Ipswich. **44.** Plainview (1958–present); Leola. **45.** Platte (1949–present); Academy. **46.** Pleasant Valley (1973–present); Flandreau. **47.** Pointsett (1967–present); Estelline. **48.** Richards (1906–1918); Sanborn County, moved to Lethbridge, Alberta. **49.** Riverside

(1949–present); Huron. **50.** Rockport (1888–present); Alexandria, moved to Magrath, Alberta, at one time. **51.** Roland (1978–present); White. **52.** Rosedale (1901–1918); Hanson County, moved to Elie, Manitoba. **53.** Rosedale (1945–present); Mitchell. **54.** Silver Lake (1874–1875); led by Darius Walter as first Dariusleut colony. **55.** Spink (1904–1918); Spink County, moved to Fort Macleod, Alberta. **56.** Spink (1945–present); Frankfort. **57.** Spring Lake (1978–present); Arlington. **58.** Spring Valley (1964–present); Wessington Springs. **59.** Sunset (1977–present); Britton. **60.** Thunderbird (1963–present); Wecota. **61.** Trippe (1878–1884); Trippe, Hutchinson County; first "daughter colony" of Bon Homme Colony; Moved to lands donated by the Harmony Society in Pennsylvania in 1884. **62.** Tschetter (1942–present); Olivet. **63.** Upland (1982–present); Mitchell. **64.** White Rock (1968–present); Rosholt. **65.** Wolf Creek (1875–1936); near Freeman; led by Darius Walter from Silver Lake Colony; during World War I moved to Stirling, Alberta, then returned near Olivet in 1964. **66.** Wolf Creek (1964–present); Olivet.

Dariusleut (or "Darius People") (1874–present); founded by Darius Walter first at Silver Lake (1874–1875) and then Wolf Creek (1875–1936), near Freeman, Dakota Territory (now South Dakota).

Canada

Alberta: **1.** Alix (?); Alix. **2.** Athabaska (1961–present); Athabaska. **3.** Beiseker (1926–present); Beiseker. **4.** Berry Creek (1981–present); Hanna. **5.** Blue Sky (1981–present); Drumheller. **6.** Brocket (?); Pincher Creek. **7.** Byemoore (?–present); Box 66, Byemoore. **8.** Cameron (1972–present); Turin. **9.** Camrose (1948–present); Camrose. **10.** Carmangay (1974–present); Carmangay. **11.** Cayley (1937–present); Cayley. **12.** Clear Lake (1982–present); High River. **13.** Cluny (1961–present); Cluny. **14.** Craigmyle (1982–present); Craigmyle. **15.** Donalda (1978–present); Donalda. **16.** East Cardston (1918–present); Cardston. **17.** East Raymond (?); Raymond. **18.** Elk Water (1979–present); Irvine. **19.** Enchant (1979–present); Enchant. **20.** Erskine (1976–present); Erskine. **21.** Ewelme (1925–present); Fort Macleod. **22.** Fairview (1944–present); Crossfield. **23.** Felger (1926–present). **24.** Ferrybank (1949–present); Ponoka. **25.** Gadsby (?–?); Gadsby. **26.** Goldbridge (?–present); Box 207, Turin. **27.** Grandview (1977–present); Grand Prairie. **28.** Granum (1930–present); Granum. **29.** Hardisty (1930); Hardisty. **30.** High River (1982–present); High River. **31.** Hillview (1982–present); Rosebud. **32.** Holden (1971–present); Holden. **33.** Holt (1949–present); Irma. **34.** Hughenden (1973–present); Hughenden. **35.** Huxley (1958–present); Huxley. **36.** Iron Creek (1979–present); Bruce. **37.** Kehoe Lake (1981–present); Barons. **38.** Lakeside (1935–present); Cranford. **39.** Lavoy (1970–present); Vegreville. **40.** Leedale (1977–present); Rimbey. **41.** Little Bow (1982–present); Champion. **42.** Lomond (?–present); Lamond. **43.** Mannville (?); Mannville. **44.** Mayfield (1981–present); Etzikom. **45.** Mixburn (1960–present); Minburn. **46.** Mountain View (?–present); Strathmore. **47.** Morinville (1971–present); Morinville. **48.** New York (1924–present); Lethbridge. **49.** O.B. (1957–present); Marwayne. **50.** Pibroch (1953–present); Pibroch. **51.** Pincher Creek (1926–present); Pincher Creek. **52.** Pine Hill (1948–present); Red Deer. **53.** Plain Lake (1969–present); Two Hills. **54.** Pleasant Valley (1969–present); Clive. **55.** Prairie View (?–present); Sibbald. **56.** Red Willow (1949–present); Stettler. **57.** Ribstone (1969–present); Edgerton. **58.** Ridge Valley (1979–present); Crooked Creek. **59.** Riverside (1933–present); Fort Macleod. **60.** Rosebud (1918–present); Rockyford. **61.** Sandhills (1936–present); Beiseker. **62.** Scotford (1954–present); Fort Saskatch. **63.** Smoky Lake (1969–present);

Smoky Lake. **64.** South Lake (?–present); Gadsby. **65.** Spring Creek (1912–1920); Lewiston, moved to Rockford, Alberta. **66.** Spring Creek (1956–present); Walsh. **67.** Spring Point (1960–present); Pincher Creek. **68.** Springvale (1918–present); Rockyford. **69.** Stahlville (1919–present); Rockyford. **70.** Standoff (1918–present); Fort Macleod. **71.** Starland (1972–present); Drumheller. **72.** Sunnie Bend (?); Westlock. **73.** Sunshine (1956–present); Hussar. **74.** Thompson (1939–present); Glenwood. **75.** Tschetter (1948–present); Irricana. **76.** Turin (1971–present); Turin. **77.** Valley View (1971–present); Tarrington. **78.** Valley View (1973–present); Valleyview. **79.** Vegreville (1970–present); Vegreville. **80.** Veteran (1956–present); Veteran. **81.** Viking (?–present); Viking. **82.** Warburg (1964–present); Warburg. **83.** Waterton (1961–present); Hillspring. **84.** West Raley (1918–present); Cardston. **85.** White Lake (1973–present); Barons. **86.** Wildwood (1964–?). **87.** Willow Creek (1949–present); Red Willow. **88.** Wilson Siding (1918–present); Lethbridge. **89.** Wolf Creek (1930–present); Stirling.

British Columbia: South Peace (1977–present); Dawson Creek.

Manitoba: Dominion City (1893–?).

Saskatchewan: **1.** Arm River (1964–present); Lumsden. **2.** Belle Plain (?–present); Box 61, Belle Plain. **3.** Big Rose (?–present); Box 160, Biggar. **4.** Box Elder (1960–present); Walsh. **5.** Downie Lake (1958–present); Maple Creek. **6.** Eagle Creek (?–present); Asquith. **7.** Estuary (1958–present); Leader. **8.** Fort Pitt (1969–present); Lloydminster. **9.** Hillcrest (1964–present); Dundurn. **10.** Hillsvale (1961–present); Balwinton. **11.** Hodgeville (1971–present); Hodgeville. **12.** LaJorde (1979–present); White City. **13.** Lakeview (1970–present); Unity. **14.** Leask (1953–present); Leask. **15.** Ponteix (1970–present); Ponteix. **16.** Quill Lake (1975–present); Quill Lake. **17.** River View (1955–present); Sutherland. **18.** Simmie (1961–present); Admiral. **19.** Spring Lake (?); Swift Current. **20.** Springwater (?); Ruthilda. **21.** Star City (1977–present); Star City. **22.** Sunny Dale (1990–present); Hillsvale. **23.** Swift Current (1978–present); Swift Current. **24.** Webb (?–present); Webb. **25.** West Bench (1960–present); Eastend. **26.** Willow Park (1979–present); Tessier.

United States

Montana: **1.** Ayers (1945–present); Grass Range. **2.** Deerfield (1947–present); Lewiston. **3.** East Malta (1981–present); Malta. **4.** Flat Willow (1980–present); Colony Road. **5.** Fords Creek (1980–present); Grass Ranch. **6.** Forty Mile (?–?); Lodge Grass. **7.** Gilford (1982–present); Gilford. **8.** Kings Ranch (1925–present); Lewiston. **9.** Loring (1981–present); Loring. **10.** North Harlem (1960–present); Harlem. **11.** Spring Creek (1912–1918; 1945–present); Lewiston, moved to Rockford, Alberta, during World War I. **12.** Surprise Creek (1963–present); Stanford. **13.** Turner (1959–present); Turner. **14.** Warren Range (1913–1918); Fergus County, moved to Cardston, Alberta.

South Dakota: **1.** Beadle (1905–1918); Beadle County. **2.** Jamesville (1886–?). **3.** Kutter (1892–?). **4.** Richards (1906–?). **5.** Silver Lake (1874–1875); led by Darius Walter as first "Dariusleut" colony. **6.** Spink (1904–?). **7.** Wold Creek (1874–1936); led by Darius Walter from Silver Lake Colony, near Freeman, Hutchinson County (during World War I moved to Stirling, Alberta, Canada); resettled upon return from Canada, and continues presently.

Washington: **1.** Asponola (1960–present); Riordan. **2.** Marlin (1974–present); Marlin. **3.** Schoonover (?–?); Odessa. **4.** Spokane (1959–present); Reardan. **5.** Stahlville (1980–present); Odessa. **6.** Warden (1973–present); Walter.

Lehrerleut (or *"Lehrer People"*) (1877–present); emigrated from Russia in 1877 and began communal living at Elmspring Colony (later called Old Elmspring) (1877–1929), near Parkston, Hutchinson County, South Dakota.

Canada

Alberta: **1.** Acadia (1952–present); Oyen. **2.** Big Bend (1920–present); Eardston. **3.** Bow City (1964–present); Site 2 Brook. **4.** Brant (1968–present); Brant. **5.** Castor (1965–present); Castor. **6.** Clear Lake (1982–present); Claresholm. **7.** Clearview (1975–present); Bassano. **8.** Crystal Spring (1931–?). **9.** Crystal Spring (1937–present); Magrath. **10.** Deerfield (?); Magrath. **11.** Elm Spring (1929–present); Warner. **12.** Fairlane (1986–present); Skiff. **13.** Fairville (1986–present); Bassano. **14.** Handhill (1956–present); Hanna. **15.** Hutterville (1932–present); Magrath. **16.** Jenner (1983–present); Jenner. **17.** Kings Lake (1976–present); Foremost. **18.** MacMillan (1937–present); Caley. **19.** Mialta (?); Vulcan. **20.** Miami (1924–present); New Dayton. **21.** Midland (1982–present); Taber. **22.** Milford (1918–present); Raymond. **23.** Miltow (?); Warner. **24.** New Dale (1949–present); Milo. **25.** New Dorf (?); Crossfield. **26.** Newell (1962–present); Bassano. **27.** New Elmspring (1918–present); Magrath. **28.** New Rockport (1932–present); New Dayton. **29.** O.K. (1934–present); Raymond. **30.** Old Elmspring (1918–present); Magrath. **31.** Parkland (1972–present); Parkland. **32.** Plainview (1975–present); Warner. **33.** Ponderosa (1974–present); Grassy Lake. **34.** Ridgeland (?); Bassano. **35.** River Bend (1976–present); Mossleigh. **36.** River Road (1985–present); Milk River. **37.** Rocklake (1935–present); Coaldale. **38.** Rockport (1918–present); Magrath. **39.** Rosedale (1953–present); Etzikom. **40.** Roseglen (1970–present); Hilda. **41.** South Bend (1965–present); Alliance. **42.** Spring Side (1955–present); Duchess. **43.** Springview (1979–present); Gem. **44.** Standard (1987–present); Standard. **45.** Starbrite (1989–present); Foremost. **46.** Suncrest (1983–present); Castor. **47.** Sunnyside (1935–present); Warner. **48.** Sunrise (1978–present); Etzikom. **49.** Twilight (1986–present); Falher. **50.** Verdant Valley (1974–present); Drumheller. **51.** Wild Rose (1990–present); Vulcan. **52.** Willow Creek (?); Nanton. **53.** Winifred (1953–present); Medicine Hat.

Saskatchewan: **1.** Abbey (1971–present); Abbey. **2.** Baildon (1968–present); Moose Jaw. **3.** Beechy (1981–present); Beechy. **4.** Bench (1953–present); Shaunavon. **5.** Bone Creek (?); Tompkins. **6.** Butte (?); Val Marie. **7.** Carmichel (1984–present); Gull Lake. **8.** Clear Spring (1971–present); Kenniston. **9.** Cypress (1953–present); Maple Creek. **10.** Dinsmore (1978–present); Dinsmore. **11.** Eatonia (1987); Etonia. **12.** Glidden (1963–present); Kindersly. **13.** Golden View (1981–present); Biggar. **14.** Haven (1967–present); Fox Valley. **15.** Huron (1969–present); Brownlee. **16.** Kyle (1970–present); Kyle. **17.** Main Center (1963–present); Rush Lake. **18.** Rose Valley (1986–present); Assiniboia. **19.** Rosetown (1970–present); Rosetown. **20.** Sand Lake (1966–present); Val Marie. **21.** Slate (1952–present); Tompkins. **22.** Smiley (1968–present); Smiley. **23.** Springfield (?); Kindersly. **24.** Tompkins (1954–present); Tompkins. **25.** Vanguard (1980–present); Aneroid. **26.** Waldeck (1963–present); Swift Current. **27.** Wheatland (1987–present); Box 110, Carbi.

United States

Montana: **1.** Big Sky (1978–present); Cut Bank. **2.** Big Stone (1985–present); Sand Coulee. **3.** Birch Creek (1948–present); Valier. **4.** Cascade (1969–present); Fort Shaw. **5.** Duncan Ranch (1963–present); Harlowton. **6.** Eagle Creek (1982–present); Galata. **7.** East End (1977–present); Havre. **8.** Fair Haven (1980–present);

Ulm. **9.** Glacier (1951–present); Cut Bank. **10.** Glendale (1969–present) Cut Bank. **11.** Golden Valley (1978–present); Ryegate. **12.** Hilldale (1963–present); Havre. **13.** Hillside (1951–present); Sweet Grass. **14.** Kingsbury (1981–present); Valier. **15.** Martinsdale (1959–present); Martinsdale. **16.** Miami (1948–present); Conrad. **17.** Milford (1947–present); Wolf Creek. **18.** Miller (1949–present); Choteau. **19.** New Rockport (1948–present); Choteau. **20.** Pleasant Valley (1989–present); Belt McCoy Rd. **21.** Rimrock (1963–present); Sunburst. **22.** Riverview (1980–present); Chester. **23.** Rockport (1948–present); Pendroy. **24.** Sage Creek (1960–present); Chester. **25.** Seville (1982–present); Cut Bank. **26.** Springdale (1959–present) White Sulphur Spring. **27.** Springwater (1981–present); Harlowton.

South Dakota: **1.** Elmspring/Old Elmspring (1877–1929); founded as first communal settlement of the Lehrerleut who immigrated in 1877 from Russia and located near Parkston, Hutchinson County. **2.** Milford (1910–?). **3.** New Elmspring (1900–present). **4.** Rockport (1892–present).

Hygeiana (ca. 1850s–ca. 1850s); Dr. Trall; Chillicothe, Ohio.

Icarian Movement (1840–1898); Etienne Cabet; France and United States; Utopian Socialist.

California: Icaria Speranza (1881–1886); Armand Dehay, Jules Leroux; near Cloverdale, Sonoma County.

Illinois: Nauvoo Icaria (1849–1859); Etienne Cabet; Hancock County.

Iowa: **1.** Corning Icaria (1860–1878); Alexis Armel Marchand; Corning, Adams County. **2.** New Icaria (1878–1898); Corning, Adams County. **3.** Young Icaria (1878–1883); Corning, Adams County.

Missouri: Cheltenham Icaria (1857–1864); Benjamin Mercedier; Cheltenham (now part of St. Louis), St. Louis County.

Texas: Texas Icarian Community attempted (1848); Oliver Creek, Denton County.

Industrial Brotherhood (1898?–?); Maine.

Inspirationist Movement/Society of True Inspiration/Ebenezer Society/Amana Society (1714–present). Founded by Eberhard Ludwig Gruber and Johann Friedrich Rock, Hesse, Germany. Christian Metz led Inspirationists to United States and founded communes near Buffalo, New York; Ontario, Canada; and Iowa City, Iowa, after 1843. Radical Pietist.

Canada

Ontario: Ebenezer Society (1843–1855); Christian Metz, Barbara Heinemann Landmann; near Niagara Falls. Two colonies: **1.** Canada Ebenezer **2.** Kenneberg.

United States

Iowa: Amana Society (1854–1832; non-communal to present); Christian Metz, Barbara Heinemann Landmann; near Iowa City in Johnson County, Iowa. Seven colonies: **1.** Amana **2.** East Amana **3.** High Amana **4.** Homestead **5.** Middle Amana **6.** South Amana **7.** West Amana.

New York: Ebenezer Society (1843–1861); Christian Metz, Barbara Heinemann Landmann; near Buffalo, Erie County. Four colonies: **1.** Lower Ebenezer **2.** Middle Ebenezer **3.** New Ebenezer **4.** Upper Ebenezer.

Institute of Cultural Affairs. *See* Global Order Movement

Integral Phalanx. *See* Fourierist Movement

Investigating Community (1875–1876); Kansas.

Investigation Community (1857–?); William Frey; Chautauqua County, Pennsylvania.

Iowa Pioneer Phalanx. *See* Fourierist Movement

Irenia True Church of Brotherly Love (1697–?); Bernard Köster; Plymouth, Pennsylvania.

Israelites (1895–1920); Polk County, Texas; Canadian; vegetarian.

Italian-Swiss Colony (1881–?); Asti, California; immigrant settlement.

Jamestown Colony (1609–1616; not communal thereafter); Virginia. In an effort to insure the survival of the colony it had founded at Jamestown in 1607, the Virginia Company secured a second charter in 1609 that permitted the company to reorganize its settlers under a collective arrangement by which they agreed to give seven years of service. During that period they received food, clothing, and shelter from the company, and 100 acres of free land at the end of the collective period. The "indentured servant" arrangement under which thousands later came to America has roots in such adoption of communal means for colonial survival. Settlement, colony development.

Janssonist Movement (1843–ca. 1860s); Eric Jansson; Sweden and Illinois; Swedish Christian Separatist.

   Illinois: Bishop Hill (1846–1861); Bishop Hill, Henry County.

Jasper Colony (1851–1853); Lenox Township, Iowa County, Iowa.

Jefferson County Industrial Association. *See* Fourierist Movement

Jehovah's Witnesses Movement/Watch Tower Bible and Tract Society (ca. 1868–present); Charles Taze Russell, Joseph Franklin Rutherford; nationwide and worldwide; Millennialism. Communal living practiced in various locations, including the organizational headquarters in Brooklyn, New York, and the Bethel Community in Philadelphia.

Jerusalem/Society of Universal Friends (1788–1820); Jemima Wilkinson; Yates County, New York.

Jewish Agricultural Colonies (1820–1940s); various emigrant aid associations and individuals; nationwide; Jewish immigrant settlement.

   Arkansas: **1.** Am Olam Group Settlement/Arkansas Colony (1882–1883). **2.** Newport (1882–1884); Jackson County.

   California: **1.** Orangevale (1890s–?); David Lubin, Harry Weinstock; Sacramento County. **2.** Porterville (1891–1897); Philip Nettre Lilienthal (funded by Russian Jewish Alliance); Tulare County.

   Colorado: **1.** Atwood Colony (1865–?); Logan County. **2.** Cotopaxi (1882–1884); Julius Schwarz (funded by Hebrew Emigrant Aid Society); Fremont County. **3.** Wellington Smith's Valley (1897–?); Larimer County.

   Connecticut: **1.** Chesterfield (1890–1893); (funded by Baron de Hirsch Fund); New London County. **2.** Colchester (1891–?); New London County. **3.** Ellington (1904–?) (funded by Jewish Agricultural and Industrial Aid Society); Tolland County. **4.** Hartford (1905–?); Hartford County.

   Florida: Alachua County (1825–?); Moses Elias Levy.

   Illinois: Flora (1910–?) (funded by Jewish Agricultural and Industrial Aid Society); Clay County.

   Kansas: **1.** Beersheba (1882–1885); Joseph Baum (funded by Hebrew Union Agricultural Society in Cincinnati); Hodgeman County. **2.** Gilead (1886–?); Commanche County. **3.** Hebron (1882–1887) (funded by Montefiore Agricultural Aid Society); Barber County. **4.** Lasker (1884–1886) (funded by Montefiore Agricultural Aid Society); Commanche County. **5.** Leeser (1886–?); Finney County. **6.** Montefiore (1884–1885); named for Moses Montefiore (funded by Hebrew Emigrant Aid Society and Montefiore Agricultural Aid Society); Ford County. **7.** Touro (1886–1887); Finney County. **8.** Wyandotte (1882–?); Kansas City.

   Louisiana: Sicily Island (1881–1882); Herman Rosenthal (funded by Alliance Israelite Universelle, New York Emigration Committee, and New Orleans Agricultural Society); Catahoula Parish.

Maryland: **1.** Baltimore (1882–?) (funded by Hebrew Russian Relief Committee of Baltimore); Baltimore County. **2.** Ellicott City (1902–?) (funded by Jewish Agricultural and Industrial Aid Society); Howard County. **3.** Yaazor (1902–?) (funded by Hebrew Colonial Society of Baltimore).

Massachusetts: **1.** Bolystown (1908–?); Worcester County. **2.** Holliston (1890–?); Max Mitchell (funded by Baron de Hirsch Fund); Middlesex County. **3.** Medway (?–?). **4.** Millis (?–?). **5.** Rutland (1908–?); Worcester County. **6.** Sandisfield (1908–?); Berkshire County.

Michigan: **1.** Carp Lake (1882–?); Lazarus Silberman; Emmett County. **2.** Palestine/Bad Axe (1891–1899); Herman Lewenberg (funded by Detroit Reform Jewish Community and Baron de Hirsch Fund); Huron County. **3.** Sunrise (1933–1938); Joseph Cohen (funded by Jewish Agricultural Society). **4.** Twelve Corners (1890–?); Isaac Berliner (funded by Jewish Agriculturalists' Aid Society of Chicago); Berrien County.

Nebraska: **1.** Cherry County (1910–?); Cherry County. **2.** Lincoln County (1897–?); Lincoln County.

Nevada: Wellington/Occidental Land Company (1897–?); Daniel Schwartz.

New Jersey: **1.** Alberton/Halberton; (1891–?). **2.** Alliance/New Jerusalem (1882–1906); A. C. Sternberger (funded by Alliance Israelite Universelle, Hebrew Emigrant Aid Society, Alliance Land Trust, and Mansion House Committee of London); Salem County. **3.** Brotmanville (1880s–?); Abraham Brotman (funded by Jewish Agricultural and Industrial Aid Society); Cumberland County. **4.** Carmel (1882–?); Michael Heilbrin (funded by Baron de Hirsch Fund and Montefiore Agricultural Aid Society); Cumberland County. **5.** Estelleville (1882–1883); General Burbridge (funded by Hebrew Emigrant Aid Society). **6.** Farmingdale (1927–?); Monmouth County. **7.** Flemington (1906–?) (funded by Jewish Agricultural and Industrial Aid Society); Hunterdon County. **8.** Ganton Road (1888–?); Cumberland County. **9.** Hebron (1891–?). **10.** Hightstown (?–?); Mercer County. **11.** Mays Landing (?–?); Cape May County. **12.** Mitzpah (1891–?); J. D. Einstein; Daniel Blumenthal (funded by Mitzpah Agricultural and Industrial Company). **13.** Montefiore (?–?); Cape May County. **14.** Norma (ca. 1880s) (funded by Jewish Agricultural and Industrial Aid Society); Cumberland County. **15.** Riga/Reega (?–?). **16.** Rosenhayn (1882–?) (funded by Hebrew Emigrant Aid Society); Cumberland County. **17.** Six Points (1907–?) (funded by Jewish Agricultural and Industrial Aid Society); Salem County. **18.** Toms River (1908–?) (funded by Jewish Agricultural Society); Ocean County. **19.** Woodbine (1891–?); Hirsch L. Sabsovich (funded by Baron de Hirsch Fund); Cape May County. **20.** Zion/Ziontown (?–?).

New York: **1.** Ararat (1820–?); Mordecai Manuel Noah; Erie County. **2.** Rensselaer County (1904–?); Rensselaer County. **3.** Shalom (1837–1842); Moses Cohen; Ulster County. **4.** Syracuse (1904–?); Onondaga County.

North Dakota: **1.** Bowman (1908–?); Bowman County. **2.** Burleigh County (1901–?) (funded by Jewish Agriculturalists' Aid Society of Chicago and Jewish Agricultural and Industrial Aid Society); Burleigh County. **3.** Chananel (1887–beyond 1897); Ramsey County. **4.** Devils Lake (1882–?) (funded by Jewish Community of Minneapolis and Baron de Hirsch Fund); Ramsey County. **5.** Dogden (?–?); McLean County. **6.** Iola Settlement (1886–?) (funded by Baron de Hirsch Fund); Ramsey County. **7.** Lelpzig (?–?); Morton County. **8.** Painted Woods (1882–1887); Dr. Joseph Wechsler (funded by Baron de Hirsch Fund, Montefiore Agricultural Aid Society, and Jewish Community of St. Paul, Minnesota); Bismarck, Burleigh County. **9.** Stoud (1905/1906–?) (funded by Industrial Removal Office); McKenzie County.

10. Sulzberger (1904–?) (funded by Industrial Removal Office); McIntosh County.
11. Velva (?–?); Ward County.

Oregon: New Odessa (1882–1888); William Frey, William Heilprin, Paul Kaplan; Douglas County.

South Carolina: Happyville (1905–1908); Ebbie Julian Watson (funded by State Immigration Bureau); Aiken County.

South Dakota: **1.** Adler (1882–?); Davison County. **2.** Bethlehem-Yehudah (1882–1885); Saul Sokolofsky (funded by Alliance Israelite Universelle); Davison County. **3.** Cremieux (1882–1885); Herman Rosenthal; Mitchell, Davison County. **4.** Mendelsohn (1882–?); Davison County. **5.** Perkins County (1908–1910) (funded by Jewish Agricultural and Industrial Aid Society); Perkins County.

Tennessee: Williamson County (1913–?); Williamson County.

Texas: **1.** Ida Strauss Colony (1912–?) (funded by Jewish Farmers' Association of St. Louis). **2.** Tyler (1904–1905) (funded by Jewish Agricultural and Industrial Aid Society); Smith County.

Utah: Clarion (1911–1916); Benjamin Brown, Isaac Landman (funded by Jewish Agricultural and Colonial Association and Mormon Church); Sanpete County.

Virginia: **1.** Middlesex Settlement (1882–?); Middlesex County. **2.** Richmond (1897–?); Henrico County. **3.** Sunrise (1938–1940); Joseph Cohen. **4.** Waterview (1882–1886); Middlesex County.

Washington, D.C.: Washington (1883–?).

Washington: **1.** Lakebay (1906–?); Pierce County. **2.** Republic (1906–?) (funded by Jewish Agricultural and Industrial Aid Society); Ferry County.

Wisconsin: **1.** Arpin (1904–?); Adolph W. Rich, Henry F. Roehrig (funded by Milwaukee Jewish Agricultural Association); Wood County. **2.** Turtle Lake (1894–?) (funded by Jewish Agriculturalists' Aid Society of Chicago); Barron County.

Wyoming: **1.** Laramie County (1907–?) (funded by Jewish Agricultural and Industrial Aid Society); Laramie County. **2.** Platt Colony (1911–?) (funded by Hebrew Farmers' Colonization Society); Platt County.

Joyful (1844); Isaac B. and Sara Rumford; Kern County, California; vegetarian Christian.

Kansas Co-operative Farm/Prairie Home Colony. *See* Fourierist Movement

Kansas Vegetarian Company (ca. 1850s–ca. 1850s); Kansas.

Kaweah Co-operative Commonwealth (1885–1892); James J. Martin, Burnette Haskell; Tulare County, California; Socialist Marxist.

Keilite Movement (ca. 1840–1881); Dr. Wilhelm Keil; New York to Missouri, Washington, and Oregon; Christian Sectarian, Harmonist Secessionist. *See* Harmonist Movement

Missouri: **1.** Bethel (1844–1880); Wilhelm Keil; Shelby County. Three Out-Colonies: Elim, Hebron,Mamri. **2.** Nineveh (1850–1878); Adair County.

Oregon: Aurora (1856–1881); Wilhelm Keil; Marion County.

Washington: Willapa (1853–1855); Wilhelm Keil; inland from Willapa Bay.

Kiantone Community. *See* Domain

Kinderfarm. *See* Ozark Kinderfarm

Kinder Lou (1900–1901); Lowndes County, Georgia; Ruskinite.

Kingdom of Paradise (1736–1744); Christian Gottlieb Priber; Great Tellico (near present Knoxville, Tennessee); settlement for protection of Indian Rights (especially Catabaws, Cherokees, and Creeks). Cited sometimes as the earliest secular utopian community in North America.

Kingdom of St. James (1848–1856); James L. Strang; Manitou County, Michigan; schismatic Mormon.

King Ranch (1935–present); Montana.

King View. *See* Emissaries of Divine Light Movement

Kingwood (1949–?); Frenchtown, New Jersey.

Kirtland. *See* Mormon Movement

Kirtland Community (1830–1831); Sidney Rigdon; Lake County, Ohio; Baptist.

Koinonia (1951–present); Stevenson, Maryland; interdenominational, healing; New Age.

Koinonia Farm/Koinonia Partners (1942–present); Clarence Jordan; near Americus, Georgia; Evangelical Christian, Pacifist, interracial. Koinonia has inspired the following communities:

Idaho: Friendship House (1972–?); Boise.

Illinois: Laetare Partners (ca. 1970–?); Rockford.

Koreshan Unity Movement (1869–present); Cyrus Reed Teed ("Koresh"); New York, Illinois, California, Florida; Universology. *See* Order of Theocracy

California: Koreshan Unity—San Francisco (1890–1891); San Francisco.

Florida: Koreshan Unity—Estero/New Jerusalem (1894–1961); Cyrus Reed Teed, Hedwig Michel; Estero.

Illinois: Koreshan Unity—Chicago (1888–1903); Cyrus Teed; Chicago.

New York: **1.** Koreshan Unity—Moravia (1880–1886); Cyrus Teed; Moravia. **2.** Koreshan Unity—Syracuse (1880–ca. 1885); Cyrus Teed; Syracuse. **3.** Koreshan Unity—New York (ca. 1885–1886); Cyrus Teed; New York City.

Kristeen Community (1845–1846); Charles Mowland; Marshall County, Indiana.

Kriya Babaji Yoga Sangam (1953–present?); New York, New York; Hindu.

Krotona Community of Adyar Theosophists. *See* Theosophical Movement

Labadist Movement (ca. 1668–ca. 1727); Jean de Labadie; West Friesland and Cecil County, Maryland; Radical Pietist.

Maryland: Bohemia Manor (1683–1727); Pieter Slayter; Cecil County

Labor Exchange Colony. *See* Freedom Colony

Laetare Partners. *See* Koinonia Farm

La Grange Phalanx. *See* Fourierist Movement

Lake Rest. *See* Emissaries of Divine Light Movement

Lane's End Homestead. *See* School of Living Movement

La Reunion. *See* Fourierist Movement

Lawsonian (1943–?); Des Moines, Iowa.

League of Brotherhoods (1900); Syracuse, Onondaga County, New York.

Le Claire Village (1890–1918?); Edwardsville, Madison County, Illinois.

Le Mars (1881–?); Le Mars, Iowa; English colony.

Lemurian/Lemurian Fellowship (1941–?); Ramona, California.

LeRaysville Phalanx. *See* Fourierist Movement

Life Culture Society (1904); Los Angeles, California.

Lititz. *See* Moravian Movement

Little Landers Movement (1909–1916); William E. Smythe; California; land settlement. California: **1.** Little Landers Colony—Cupertino (?–?); Cupertino, near San Jose. **2.** Little Landers Colony—Hayward Heath (?–?); Hayward Heath, Alameda County. **3.** Little Landers Colony—Runnymede (?–?); Runnymede, near Palo Alto. **4.** Little Landers Colony—San Fernando Valley (?–?); San Fernando Valley. **5.** Little Landers Colony—San Ysidro (1909–1916); William E. Smythe; San Ysidro, San Diego County.

Llano del Rio. *See* Socialist Movement of Job Harriman

Llano del Rio Company of Nevada (1916–1918); C. V. Eggleston; Churchill County, Nevada.

Llewellyn Castle (1870–?); Kansas; English colony.

Longley Communities (1868–18??); Alcander Longley; Missouri; Communist, liberal reform.

   Missouri: **1.** Altruist Community (1907–1911); Sulfur Springs, Jefferson County. **2.** Friendship Community (1872–1877); near Buffalo, Dallas County. **3.** Mutual Aid Community (1883–1887); Bollinger County. **4.** Principia (1880–?); Polk County. **5.** Reunion/True Family Oronogo (1866–1870); Jasper County.

Lopez Community (1912–1920); San Juan County, Washington.

Lord's Farm (1889–1907); Paul Blandin Mason (formerly Mason T. Huntsman); Bergen County, New Jersey.

Los Angeles Fellowship Farm (1912–1927); Los Angeles County, California.

Lystra (1899–1902); Virginia.

Macedonia Cooperative Community (1937–?); Clarkesville, Georgia.

McKean County Association. *See* Teutonia

Magnolia (1896); Shepherd, Texas.

Mamri. *See* Keilite Movement

Mankind United (1943–?); California.

Marathon Colony. *See* Hugh MacRae's Immigrant Colonies

Marlboro Association (1843–1845); Stark County, Ohio.

Martha's Vineyard Co-operative Colony (1906?); Vineyard Haven, Massachusetts.

Massachusetts Bay Colony (1629–ca. 1636; not communal thereafter); Governor John Winthrop; Massachusetts; colonial settlement, Calvinist Christian. Massachusetts during this period of community of goods may be described as a "Bible-Commonwealth," and individual towns, such as Dedham, as "Christian Utopian Closed Corporate Communities."

May Valley. *See* School of Living Movement

May Valley Cooperative (1950s–?); Renton, Washington.

Memnonia Institute (1856–1857); Mary Grove Nichols, Thomas Low Nichols; Greene County, Ohio.

Mexican Communes: During the long reign of Porfirio Diaz known as the Porfiriato (1877–1910), the Mexican government encouraged the establishment of communal settlements for natives and immigrants. Some 60 colonies were started, 44 by private initiative and 16 by the government. Settlers from the United States formed 21 communities, the 10 listed below and the 11 by Mormon schismatics listed under Mormon Movement. **1.** Baja California Colonies: Colonia Romero Rubio at San Quintin and Colonia Carlos Pacheco (the latter including the towns of San Carlos, La Ensenada, and Punta Banda). *See also* Mormon schismatic communities in Mexico under Mormon Movement **2.** Blalock Mexico Colony (?); Tamaulipas. **3.** Metlaltoyuca (?); Puebla. **4.** Nacimiento (?); Coahuila; settlement for Kickapoo and Muskogee Indians from the United States. **5.** Navolato (?); Sinaloa. **6.** Ranchos Agricolos (?); Coahuila. **7.** Tapachula (?); Chiapas. **8.** Tihuatlan (Harrisburg) (?); Veracruz. **9.** Tlahualillo (Maipimi) (?); Durango. **10.** Topolobampo (1884–1899); Albert Kimsey Owen; Sinaloa west coast of Mexico; land settlement.

Millerite Adventist Movement (1830s–ca. 1900). Founded by William Miller in New York and spread to New England, the South, and Middle West. The Seventh-Day Adventist Church and Jehovah's Witnesses grew out of this movement. Second Advent of Christ.

   Massachusetts: Adonai Shomo Corporation/Community of Fullerites (1861–1897); Frederick T. Howland; Petersham, Worcester County.

Wisconsin: Germania Company (1856–1879); Benjamin Hall; Germania, Marquette County.

Missouri Preservation (?–?); Jefferson, Missouri.

Mixville Association. *See* Fourierist Movement

Model City Colony (1899?–?); St. Joseph, Berrien County, Michigan.

Model Farm Communities Movement. *See* Hugh MacRae's Immigrant Colonies

Modern Times (1851–1863); Josiah Warren; Long Island, Suffolk County, New York; Owenite influence. *See* Owenite Movement

Modjeska Colony (1877–1878); Helena Modjeska; Anaheim, Orange County, California.

Mohegan Colony (1923–1950); New York.

Molokan Community (1911–?); Glendale, Arizona.

Moravian Movement/Unitas Fratrum (early 1400s–present); Jan Hus, Count Nikolaus Ludwig von Zinzendorf; Moravia (Czechoslovakia) and worldwide; Protestant Christian, missions. Beginning in 1740 at Nazareth, Pennsylvania, Moravians operated new, usually frontier, communities for missionary activities and believers in America on a communal "Economy" or "General Economy" system in imitation of the communal plan initiated by Zinzendorf at the Moravian center at Herrnhut in Europe.

Indian Missions: Moravians opened the following Indian missions, of which Gnaden- hutten and Meniolagomeka are known to have lived communally. **1.** Gnadenhutten (1746–1755); Brother Martin Mack; village began near Mahoning Creek (Lehigh- ton), Pennsylvania, and moved to other side of Lehigh River, where a massacre oc- curred before a third village by the same name at the same place was occupied by white people. A fourth Gnadenhutten was located on the Tuscarawas River, Clay County, Ohio. **2.** Meniolagomeka (1749–1754); Brothers Cammerhof and Seidel; Monroe County, Pennsylvania. **3.** Pachatgoch (?–?); New Jersey. **4.** Shomoko (ca. 1747–1756); Brothers Joseph Powell and John Hagen; now Sunbury, Northumber- land County, Pennsylvania.

Indiana: Goshen/Hope (1830–ca. 1830s); Martin Hauser; Hope, Bartholomew County.

New Jersey: Hope/Greenland (1769; 1774–1807); Peter Worbass; Hope (near the Delaware River).

North Carolina: **1.** Bethabara (1753–ca. 1772); Bernard Adam Grube; Wachovia (now part of Winston-Salem), Forsyth County. **2.** Bethania (1759–?); Wachovia (later Forsyth County). **3.** Friedberg (1754–?); Adam Spach; Wachovia (now Forsyth County). **4.** Friedland (1770–?); Wachovia (now Forsyth County). **5.** Hope (1780–?); Wachovia (now Forsyth County). **6.** Salem (1766–ca. 1770s; not com- munal to present); Wachovia (later Salem, now Winston-Salem, Forsyth County).

Pennsylvania: **1.** Bethlehem (1741; 1744–1762; not communal to present); Bishop David Nitschmann; Bethlehem, Northampton County. **2.** Lititz (1754–?; not com- munal to present); Lancaster County. **3.** Nazareth (1740–?; not communal to pres- ent); Nazareth, Northampton County. The following farm and mill communities were attached to Nazareth: Christiansbrunn (1748–1752 or later), Friedensthal (1749–1752 or later), Gnadensthal (1745–1752 or later), and Rose Inn (1752–?). Rose Inn's associated settlement, Gnadenstadt, failed. **4.** Quittopehille (1723–1729); Lebanon County; settlement for Germans from the Palatinate.

South Carolina: Charleston (1760s?); Charleston, Charleston County.

Wisconsin: **1.** Ephraim (1849–1853); Nils Otto Tank; Green Bay, Brown County; Norwegian Moravians. **2.** Ephraim (1853–1864); Pastor Iverson; Ephraim, Door County.

Morehouse Union. *See* Fourierist Movement

Mormon Movement/Church of Jesus Christ of Latter-day Saints/United Order/United Order of Enoch (1829–present); Joseph Smith; New York and worldwide.

California: San Bernardino Colony (1851–1857); Amasa Lyman, Charles C. Rich; San Bernardino.

Illinois: Nauvoo (1839–1847); Joseph Smith; Nauvoo, Hancock County.

Missouri: **1.** Adam-ondi-Ahman (1838–1839); Joseph Smith, John Smith; near Gallatin, Daviess County. **2.** DeWitt (ca. 1836–1838); an out-community of Far West, Caldwell County. **3.** Far West/City of Enoch (1836–1838); Joseph Smith; near Kingston, Caldwell County. **4.** Haun's Mill (1838–1838); an out-community of Far West, Caldwell County. **5.** Independence (1831–1834); Joseph Smith; Independence, Jackson County.

Ohio: Kirtland (1831–1836); Sidney Rigdon, Joseph Smith; Kirtland, Ohio.

Utah: **1.** Brigham City (1864–?); Brigham Young; Brigham City, Box Elder County. **2.** Orderville (1875–1884); Brigham Young; Orderville, Kane County.

Mormon schismatics founded many communities based on the United Order in various forms and under various leaders, especially after the lynching death of Joseph Smith in 1844. Prominent among these are the following:

Mexico

1. Carlos Pacheco (?); Chihuahua. **2.** Fernandez Leal (?); Chihuahua. **3.** Garcia (?); Chihuahua. **4.** Guadalupe (?); Chihuahua. **5.** Hidalgo (?); Chihuahua. **6.** Juarez (?); Chihuahua. **7.** LeBaron Colony/Church of the Firstborn of the Fullness of Times (early 1900s–present); Alma Dayer LeBaron; Galeana, Chihuahua; other offshoots exist. **8.** Manuel Dublan (?); Chihuahua. **9.** Morelos (?); Sonora. **10.** Oaxaca (?); Sonora. **11.** Porfirio Diaz (?); Chihuahua.

United States

Arizona: **1.** Woolley Colony/United Order Effort Movement (1929–1951); Lorin C. Woolley; Short Creek; then with LeRoy Johnson to Colorado City (1951–?). **2.** Zion's Order Movement/Kilgore Colony (1951–present); Marl Kilgore; Phoenix; later moved to Mansfield, Missouri.

Iowa: **1.** Cutler Colony (1853–1864); Alpheus Cutler; Manti, Iowa; after Cutler's death in 1864, members moved to Clitherall, Minnesota, then on to Independence, Missouri, after 1900. **2.** Preparation/Thompson Colony (1853–1858); Charles B. Thompson; Preparation, Minona County.

Kansas: **1.** Bickerton Colony (1862–?); William Bickerton; St. Johns; later some followed William Cadman to Monongahela, Pennsylvania. **2.** Tickhill Colony/Church of Jesus Christ (1909–1928); Charles Tickhill, A. B. Cadman; Comanche County.

Michigan: Beaver Island Strangite Colony (1847–?); Beaver Island. *See* Voree Colony, Voree, Wisconsin.

Missouri: **1.** Peterson Colony/United Order of Equality Movement (ca. 1900–?); Ephraim Peterson; Independence. **2.** Zahnd Colony (ca. 1918–ca. 1928); John Zahnd; Kansas City.

Texas: **1.** Colonia/Brewster Colony (1850s–?); James C. Brewster; Rio Grande Valley. **2.** Zodiac Colony (1847–1853); Lyman Wight; Fredericksburg, Gillespie County.

Utah: **1.** Aaronic Order Movement/Levites (1843–present) and Partoun Colony (1949–present); Maurice and Helen Glendenning; Salt Lake City and other places. **2.** Gudmundsen Colony (1918–?); Moses Gudmundsen; West Tintic. **3.** Joseph Colony/Church of Jesus Christ of Solemn Assembly (1974–present); Alexander

Joseph; Big Water. **4.** Morris Colony/Morrisite Movement (1861–1862); Joseph Morris; near Salt Lake City.

Wisconsin: Voree Colony (ca. 1840–1856); James J. Strang; Voree. Some members moved from a colony at Beaver Island, Michigan (1847–?).

Mountain Cove Community. *See* Spiritualist Movement of Thomas Lake Harris

Mount Ariel (?–?); Cokesbury, South Carolina.

Mount Carmel. *See* Branch Davidian Movement

Mount Lebanon/New Lebanon. *See* Shaker Movement

Muellerite Movement (ca. 1829–1871); Bernhard Mueller (Count de Leon, "the Lion of Judah"); Pennsylvania and Louisiana; Adventist, Harmonist Secessionist. *See* Harmonist Movement

Louisiana: **1.** Germantown (1836–1871); Dr. John George Goentgen; Minden, Webster County. **2.** Grand Ecore (1834–1836); Bernhard Mueller; Natchitoches Parish.

Pennsylvania: New Philadelphia Society (1832–1853); Bernhard Mueller; Philippsburgh (later changed to New Philadelphia, Lionsburg, and Monaca), Beaver County.

Mutual Aid Community. *See* Longley Communities

Mutual Home Association/Home Colony (1896–1921); Pierce County, Washington. *See* Anarchist Movement

Narcoosee. *See* Shaker Movement

Nashoba. *See* Antislavery Movement and Owenite Movement

Nauvoo. *See* Mormon Movement and Icarian Movement

Nazareth. *See* Moravian Movement

Nehalem Valley Cooperative Colony (1886–1892); Mist, Oregon.

Nevada Colony (1916–1918); C. V. Eggleston; Fallon, Nevada; Socialist.

New Berlin Colony. *See* Hugh MacRae's Immigrant Colonies

New Clairvaux/New Clairvaux Village Shop Association (1900–?); Edward Pearson Pressey; Montague, Massachusetts.

New Deal Community Program (1933–1954). Federal Government program begun by Franklin D. Roosevelt administration in thirty-two states for unemployment relief and creation of idealistic garden cities. Farming, mining, industrial, and forestry communities and garden cities.

Alabama: **1.** Bankhead Farms; Jasper; industrial. **2.** Cahaba (Trussville Homesteads); near Birmingham; industrial. **3.** Gee's Bend Farms; Wilcox County; farm community. **4.** Greenwood Homesteads; near Birmingham; industrial. **5.** Palmerdale Homesteads; near Birmingham; industrial. **6.** Prairie Farms; Macon County; farm community. **7.** Skyline Farms; Jackson County; farm community.

Arizona: **1.** Arizona Part-Time Farms; Phoenix; industrial. **2.** Casa Grande Valley; Pinal County; cooperative farm. **3.** Phoenix Homesteads; Phoenix; industrial.

Arkansas: **1.** Biscoe Farms; Prairie County; farm community. **2.** Chicot Farms; Chicot and Drew Counties; farm community. **3.** Clover Bend Farms; Lawrence County; farm community. **4.** Desha Farms; Desha and Drew Counties; farm community. **5.** Dyess Colony; Mississippi County: farm community. **6.** Lake Dick; Jefferson and Arkansas Counties; cooperative farm. **7.** Lakeview Farms; Lee and Phillips Counties; farm community. **8.** Lanoke Farms; Lanoke County; farm community. **9.** Plum Bayou; Jefferson County; farm community. **10.** St. Francis River Farms; Poinsett County; farm community. **11.** Townes Farms; Crittenden County; farm community. **12.** Trumann Farms; Poinsett County; farm community.

California: **1.** El Monte Homesteads; El Monte; industrial. **2.** San Fernado Homesteads; Reseda; industrial.

Florida: **1.** Cherry Lake Farms; near Madison; farm and rural industrial. **2.** Escambia Farms; Okaloosa County; farm community.

Georgia: **1.** Flint River Farms; Macon County; farm community. **2.** Irwinville; Irwin County; farm community. **3.** Piedmont Homesteads; Jasper County; farm community. **4.** Pine Mountain Valley; Harris County; farm and rural industrial. **5.** Wolf Creek; Grady County; farm community.

Illinois: Lake County Homesteads; Chicago; industrial.

Indiana: **1.** Decatur Homesteads; Decatur; industrial. **2.** Wabash Farms Project; Loogootee. Deshee Unit; Vincennes; farm community. Scenic Hill Unit; Loogootee; farm community.

Iowa: Granger Homesteads; Granger; industrial.

Kentucky: **1.** Christian-Trigg Farms; Christian County; farm community. **2.** Sublimity Farms; Laurel County; forest homestead.

Louisiana: **1.** Mounds Farm; Madison and East Carroll Parishes; farm community. **2.** Terrebonne; Terrebonne Parish; cooperative plantation. **3.** Transylvania Farms; East Carroll Parish; farm community.

Maryland: Greenbelt; Berwyn; garden city.

Michigan: **1.** Ironwood Homesteads; Ironwood; small garden city. **2.** Mount Olive Homesteads; near Biyal Oak. **3.** Saginaw Valley Farms; Saginaw County; farm community.

Minnesota: **1.** Albert Lea Homesteads; Albert Lea; industrial. **2.** Austin Homesteads; Austin; industrial. **3.** Duluth Homesteads; Duluth; industrial.

Mississippi: **1.** Hattiesburg Homesteads; Hattiesburg; industrial. **2.** Hinds Farms; Hinds County; farm community. **3.** Lucedale Farms; George and Greene Counties; farm community. **4.** Magnolia Homesteads; Meridian; industrial. **5.** McComb Homesteads; McComb; industrial. **6.** Mileston Farms; Holmes County; farm community. **7.** Richton Homesteads; Richton; farm community. **8.** Tupelo Homesteads; Tupelo; industrial.

Missouri: **1.** La Forge Farms; New Madrid County; farm community. **2.** Osage Farms; Pettis County; farm community.

Montana: Kinsey Flats; Custer County; farm community.

Nebraska: **1.** Fairbury Farmsteads; Jefferson County; farm village. **2.** Fall City Farmsteads; Richardson County; farm village. **3.** Grand Island Farmsteads; Hall County; farm village. **4.** Kearney Homesteads; Buffalo County; farm village. **5.** Loup City Farmsteads; Sherman County; farm village. **6.** Scottsbluff Farmsteads; Scotts Bluff County; farm village. **7.** South Sioux City Farmsteads; Dakota County; farm village. **8.** Two Rivers Farmsteads; Douglas and Saunders Counties; farm village.

New Jersey: Jersey Homesteads; Hightstown; cooperative industrial.

New Mexico: Bosque Farms; Valencia County; farm community.

North Carolina: **1.** Penbroke Farms; Robeson County; farm community. **2.** Penderlea Homesteads; Pender County; farm community. **3.** Roanoke Farms; Halifax County; farm community. **4.** Scuppernong Farms; Tyrrell and Washington Counties; farm community.

North Dakota: Burlington Project; Burlington; miner community.

Ohio: **1.** Dayton Homesteads; Dayton; industrial. **2.** Greenhills; Cincinnati; garden city.

Pennsylvania: Westmoreland Homesteads; Greensburg; miner community.

South Carolina: **1.** Ashwood Plantation; Lee County; farm community. **2.** Orangeburg Farms; Orangeburg and Calhoun Counties; farm community. **3.** Tiverton Farms; Sumter County; farm community.

South Dakota: Sioux Falls Farms; Minnehaha County; farm village.

Tennessee: Cumberland Homesteads; Crossville; miner community.

Texas: 1. Beauxart Gardens; Beaumont; industrial. 2. Dalworthington Gardens; Arlington; industrial. 3. Houston Gardens; Houston; industrial. 4. McLennan Farms; McLennan County; farm community. 5. Ropesville Farms; Hockley County; farm community. 6. Sabine Farms; Harrison County; farm community. 7. Sam Houston Farms; Harris County; farm community. 8. Three Rivers Gardens; Three Rivers; industrial. 9. Wichita Gardens; Wichita Falls; industrial. 10. Woodlake Community; Wood County; farm village.

Virginia: 1. Aberdeen Gardens; Newport News; garden city. 2. Shenandoah Homesteads; five counties; resettlement communities.

Washington: Longview Homesteads; Longview; industrial.

West Virginia: 1. Arthurdale; Reedsville/Arthurdale; miner community. 2. Eleanor. *See* Red House 3. Red House/Eleanor; Red House; miner community. 4. Tygart Valley Homesteads; Elkins; miner community.

Wisconsin: 1. Drummond Project; Bayfield County; forest homestead. 2. Greendale; Milwaukee; garden city.

New Era Union Movement (1896–ca. 1912); Charles Willard Caryl; California, Colorado; model town planning, Spiritualism, eugenics. *See also* Brotherhood of Light Movement

California: Caryl Co-operative Industrial System (ca. 1907–1912); Charles W. Caryl; locations intentionally kept secret by Caryl.

Colorado: 1. Vril Society (1903–ca. 1904); Charles W. Caryl; place unknown. 2. Wall Street (1898–1899); Charles W. Caryl; Wall Street; mining town.

New Gloucester/Sabbathday Lake. *See* Shaker Movement

New Hanover Colony. *See* Hugh MacRae's Immigrant Colonies

New Harmony. *See* Harmonist Movement and Owenite Movement

New House of Israel (1895–1920); Texas.

New Jersey Co-operative Association (1901–1904); Campgaw, Bergen County, New Jersey.

New Lebanon/Mount Lebanon. *See* Shaker Movement

Newllano. *See* Socialist Movement of Job Harriman

New Meadow Run. *See* Society of Brothers Movement

New Odessa Community (1833–1887); William Frey; Douglas County, Oregon; Socialist.

New Philadelphia Society. *See* Muellerite Movement

Niksur Co-operative Association (1899–1900); Lawrence (now Wahkou), Mille Lacs County, Minnesota; Socialist.

Nineveh. *See* Keilite Movement

Niskeyuna/Watervliet. *See* Shaker Movement

North American Phalanx. *See* Fourierist Movement

Northampton Association of Education and Industry (1842–1846); Sojourner Truth a member; Broughton's Meadows (now Florence), Hampshire County, Massachusetts; Socialist, interracial, antislavery.

North Union. *See* Shaker Movement

Norwegian Settlement Movement of Ole Bull (1840s–1853); Ole Bull, Oleona (now Ole Bull State Park), Potter County, Pennsylvania; Norwegian Settlement.

Pennsylvania: 1. New Bergen (1852–1853); Potter County. 2. New Norway (1852–1853); Potter County. 3. Oleona/Ole Bull's Colony (1852–1853); Potter County. 4. Walhalla (1852–1853); Potter County.

100 Mile Lodge/100 Mile House. *See* Emissaries of Divine Light Movement

Oakwood Farm. *See* Emissaries of Divine Light Movement

Oberlin Colony (1833–1841); John Shipherd; Lorrain County, Ohio; Christian.

Ohio Phalanx. *See* Fourierist Movement

Oleona/New Norway. *See* Norwegian Settlement Movement of Ole Bull

Olivehain (1884–?); Encinitas, California.

Oneida Community. *See* Perfectionist Movement of John Humphrey Noyes

Ontario Union. *See* Fourierist Movement

Ora Labora Community (1862–1868); Emil Gottlob Baur; Bay Port, Huron County, Michigan; German Methodist.

Order Ecumenical (1954–present); Phoenix, Arizona. A community at the headquarters of the Institute of Cultural Affairs that is active in thirty-five countries through the Global Order Movement. *See* Global Order Movement

Order of Theocracy (1910–1931); Lee County, Florida. Secessionists from Koreshan Unity at Estero. *See* Koreshan Unity Movement

Orderville United Order (1875–1884); Kane County, Utah; Mormon.

Our Home on the Hillside (?–?); Dansville; Livingston County, New York.

Owenite Movement (1812–ca. 1860s); Robert Owen; originated in Scotland and England, spread to United States, Canada, Ireland, Wales; Communitarian Socialist.

Canada

Maxwell (1827–1829); Henry Jones; now Sarnia Township, Lambton County, Ontario; Owenite influence, Scottish settlement.

England

1. Cooperative and Economical Society (1821–1823); George Mudie; Spa Fields; Owenite. 2. Devon/Exeter (1826–1826?); Mr. Vesey; Exeter; Owenite. 3. Dowlands Devon Community (ca. 1826–ca. 1827); Honiton and Exeter; Owenite. 4. Harmony Hall/Queenwood (1839–1846); Robert Owen; East Tytherly, Hampshire; Owenite. 5. Manea Fen (1838–1841); William Hodson; Cambridgeshire; Owenite.

Ireland

Ralahine Agricultural and Manufacturing Cooperative Association (1831–1833); John Scott Vandeleur, Edward Thomas; County Clare; Owenite.

Mexico

Robert Owen made an unsuccessful attempt to secure land for communities in the Mexican provinces of Coahuila and Texas in 1829.

Scotland

Orbiston (1826–1827); Archibald James Hamilton, Abram Combe; Lanarkshire; Owenite.

United States

Illinois: Joint Stock Society (1825); William Hall (of Morris Birkbeck's English settlement in Edwards County near Albion, Illinois); Wanborough; Owenite inspired and had membership and constitution, but likely did not begin community life.

Indiana: 1. Blue Spring Community (1826–1827); near Bloomington, Van Buren Township, Monroe County; Owenite. 2. Coal Creek Community and Church of God (1825–1832); Jonathan Crane, Isaac Romine, William Ludlow; Stone Bluff, Fountain County; Owenite influence. 3. Goshen Community (1825–1826); led by Methodist Posey County farmers whose leader had been a member of Owenite New Harmony, three miles southwest of New Harmony, Posey County; Owenite influence. 4. New Harmony (1825–1827); Robert Owen, William Maclure; New Harmony, Posey County; Owenite.

New York: 1. Forestville Community (1825–1827); Coxsackie, Greene County;

America's Communal Utopias

481

Owenite. **2.** Franklin Community (May 1826–Oct. 1826); George Houston, Abner Kneeland, Henry A. Fay; Haverstraw, Rockland County; Owenite. **3.** Modern Times (1851–1863); Josiah Warren; Long Island, Suffolk County; Owenite influence. *See* Time Store Cooperative Movement **4.** Skaneateles Community (1843–1846); John A. Collins; Mottville, Onondaga County, New York; Owenite influence.

Ohio: **1.** Equity (1833–1835); Josiah Warren; Tuscarawas County; Owenite influence. *See* Time Store Cooperative Movement **2.** The Friendly Association for Mutual Interests at Kendall (1826–1829); Kendall (now Massillon), Perry Township, Stark County; Owenite. **3.** Nevilsville (ca. 1827); eighty New Harmony dissidents; thirty miles from Cincinnati, but no evidence of actual settlement; Owenite influence. **4.** Utopia (1847–1851); Josiah Warren; Clermont County; Owenite influence. *See* Time Store Cooperative Movement **5.** Yellow Springs Community (1825–1826); Daniel Roe; Yellow Springs; Owenite.

Pennsylvania: **1.** Friendly Association for Mutual Interests (Jan. 1826–Sept. 1826); Valley Forge, Chester County; Owenite. **2.** Goose Pond Community (1843–1844); Mr. Hudson; on site of former Fourierist phalanx, Pike County; Owenite influence. Seceders from Society of One-Mentians. **3.** Promisewell. *See* Society of One-Mentians **4.** Society of One-Mentians/Promisewell Community (1843–1844); J. M. Horner; Monroe County; Owenite influence.

Tennessee: Nashoba Community (1825–1830); Frances Wright; Shelby County; antislavery, Harmonist and Owenite influence. *See* Antislavery Movement

Wisconsin: **1.** Equality/Colony of Equality/Hunt's Colony (1843–1846); Thomas Hunt; Spring Lake, Mukwonago Township, Waukesha County; Owenite. **2.** Hunt's Colony. *See* Equality in Wisconsin **3.** Utilitarian Association of United Interests (1845–1848); Campbell Smith; south of Colony of Equality, near Mukwonago, Waukesha County; Owenite interest.

Wales: **1.** Leeds Redemption Society/Garnlwyd Community (1847–1855); David Green, James Hole; Garnlwyd, Carmarthenshire; Owenite. **2.** Pant Glas (1840–1840); John Moncas, James Spurr; Pant Glas, Merionethshire; Owenite.

Ozark Kinderfarm (1901?–1906?); Liking, Texas County, Missouri.

Painted Woods (1882–1887); Burleigh County, North Dakota; Russian Jewish.

Pantisocracy (1794); Community proposed near Cooper and Priestly on the Susquehanna River in Pennsylvania by Samuel Taylor Coleridge and Robert Southey in England, but never founded.

Paradise. *See* Kingdom of Paradise

Parishfield (1948–?); Brighton, Michigan.

Peace Mission Movement (1914–present); George Baker ("Father Divine"), Edna Rose Ritchings ("Mother Divine"); New York, nationwide, and worldwide; religious, humanitarian. No fewer than 203 "Kingdoms," "Extensions," and "Connections" in at least 29 states of the United States and the District of Columbia, and 38 in Australia, British West Indies, Canada, England, Panama, and Switzerland.

Peace Union (1843–1845); Andreas Bernardos Smolnikar; Warren County, Pennsylvania.

Pendle Hill (1930–present); Wallingford, Pennsylvania; Quaker.

Penn-Craft (1937–1943); Penn-Craft, Fayette County, Luzerne Township, Pennsylvania; land settlement project of American Friends Service Committee for unemployed miners.

People of the Living God (1932–?); New Orleans, Louisiana.

Peoples Temple Movement (1956–ca. 1978); Rev. Jim Jones; Indiana, California, and Guyana; religious, interracial, social reform.

Guyana

Peoples Temple Agricultural Project (1974–1978); Jim Jones; Jonestown. More than

900 people died in suicide-massacre, November 18, 1978.

United States

California: **1.** Peoples Temple—San Francisco (1970–ca. 1978); Jim Jones; San Francisco. **2.** Peoples Temple—Ukiah (1965–1970); Jim Jones; Ukiah.

Indiana: Peoples Temple—Indianapolis (1956–1965); Jim Jones; Indianapolis.

Perfectionist Movement of John Humphrey Noyes (1836–1881); John Humphrey Noyes; New England, New Jersey, and New York; Christian Perfectionist.

Connecticut: Wallingford Community (1851–1881); Wallingford, New Haven County.

New Jersey: Newark Branch (ca. 1851–ca. 1855); Newark.

New York: **1.** Brooklyn Branch (ca. 1851–ca. 1855); Brooklyn. **2.** Manilus Branch (ca. 1851–ca. 1855); Manilus. **3.** Oneida Community (1848–1881); John Humphrey Noyes; Kenwood, Oneida Township, Madison County.

Vermont: **1.** Cambridge Branch (ca. 1851–ca. 1855); Cambridge. **2.** Putney Society/Putney; Windham County.

Philadelphia Industrial Association. *See* Fourierist Movement

Pigeon River Fourier Colony. *See* Fourierist Movement

Pilgrims. *See* Pilgrims Adventist Movement

Pilgrims Adventist Movement (ca. 1817–1820s); Isaac Bullard; Canada and United States as far west as Missouri; Adventist.

Arkansas: Pilgrim Island (ca. 1819–ca. 1820s).

New York: Pilgrims were refused membership by Shakers.

Ohio: Ten Pilgrims admitted to Shaker Union Village, Warren County.

Vermont: Pilgrims (1817–1818); South Woodstock, Windsor County.

Pisgah Grande. *See* Pisgah Movement

Pisgah Movement (ca. 1910s–present); Dr. Finis E. Yoakum; California and Tennessee; Pentecostal Christian, humanitarian.

California: Pisgah Grande (1914–1921); Finis E. Yoakum; on ranch in Santa Susana Mountains along Los Angeles–Ventura County line; Pentecostal Christian, humanitarian.

Tennessee: Headquarters moved to Pikeville several years after death of Finis E. Yoakum in 1920, where they remain to the present.

Pleasant Hill. *See* Shaker Movement

Pleasant View. *See* Society of Brothers Movement

Plockhoy's Commonwealth (1663–1664); Pieter Cornelisz Plockhoy van Zierikzee; Sussex County, Delaware; Anabaptist.

Plymouth Colony (1620–1623; not communal thereafter); Governor William Bradford; Plymouth; colonial settlement, Calvinist Christian.

Point Hope (1860–1861); Ohio.

Point Loma. *See* Theosophical Movement

Port Royal Experiment of Edward Philbrick. *See* Antislavery Movement

Port Royal Experiment of the United States Government. *See* Antislavery Movement

Prairie Home Community (1844–?); John O. Wattles; Logan County, Ohio.

Preparation (1853–1858); Monona County, Iowa; schismatic Mormon.

Presbyterian Community (?); Westminster, California.

Principia. *See* Longley Communities

Progressive Community (1871–1878); William and Mary Frey, Dr. Stephen Briggs; near Cedar Vale, Chautauqua County, Kansas; Russian Materialist, American Spiritualist.

Promisewell Community. *See* Society of One-Mentians

Protestant Episcopal Benedictine Order; monastic communities.
Michigan: St. Gregory's Abbey (?–present); Three Rivers.

Puget Sound Co-operative Colony (1887–1904); George Venable Smith; Port Angeles, Challam County, Washington; Socialist.

Putney Society. *See* Perfectionist Movement of John Humphrey Noyes

Quest (1950–?); Royal Oak, Michigan.

Ramakrishna Movement. *See* Vedanta Movement

Raritan Bay Union. *See* Fourierist Movement

Reba Place Fellowship (1957–present); Evanston, Illinois; Mennonite, Anabaptist, Charismatic.

Refugee Home Society. *See* Antislavery Movement

Reorganized Church of Jesus Christ of Latter-day Saints. *See* Mormon Movement

Reunion. *See* Longley Communities

Rigdonite Mormon Farm (1845–1847); Sidney Rigdon; near Greencastle, Franklin County, Pennsylvania; Anti-Young, anti-polygamy Mormon. *See* Mormon Movement

Right Relationship League (?); Chicago, Illinois. *See* Christian Commonwealth Colony

Rising Star Association (1853–1857); John S. Patterson; Darke County, Ohio.

Rochdale Co-operative Association of Missouri (1900?–?); St. Louis, Missouri.

Roman Catholic Religious Orders. *See* Benedictine Monastic Movement; Cistercian Monastic Movement; Addendum

Rose Valley (1903–?); near Philadelphia, Pennsylvania.

Rosenhayn (1882–1889); Cumberland County, New Jersey; Russian Jewish.

Rosicrucian Colony (?); Oceanside, California.

Roycrofters/Roycroft Shop (1900–1915); Elbert Hubbard; East Aurora, Erie County, New York; semi-Communistic corporation.

Rudolf Steiner Movement. *See* Camphill Movement

Rugby Colony (1880–1887); Thomas Hughes; Rugby, Morgan County, Tennessee; secular education, English lifestyle.

Runnymede (1885–?); Harper County, Kansas.

Ruskin Colony (1899); near Hastings, British Columbia, Canada.

Ruskin Commonwealth. *See* Socialist Movement of Julius Wayland

Ruskin Cooperative Association. *See* Socialist Movement of Julius Wayland

Rys. *See* Bohemian Colonies

Sabbathday Lake/New Gloucester. *See* Shaker Movement

St. Benedict's Farm (1956–present); Waelder, Texas; lay Roman Catholic monastery.

St. Francis Acres. *See* Glen Gardner Cooperative Colony

St. Gregory's Abbey. *See* Protestant Episcopal Benedictine Order

St. Helena. *See* Hugh MacRae's Immigrant Colonies

St. Louis–Western Colony (1871–?); Greeley, Colorado.

St. Meinrad Archabbey. *See* Benedictine Monastic Movement

St. Nazianz Community (1854–1874; less communal to 1897); Fr. Ambrose Oschwald; St. Nazianz, Manitowoc County, Wisconsin; Roman Catholic.

St. Walburg Convent. *See* Benedictine Monastic Movement

Salem. *See* Moravian Movement

Saline Valley Farms (1932–?); Michigan.

Salvation Army Movement (1865–present); William Booth; England, United States, and worldwide; Christian, charity.
California: Fort Romie (1898–1910); Romie?; unemployment colony.
Colorado: Amity/Fort Amity (1898–1910); Frederick Booth Tucker; Holly, Prowers County; religious unemployment colony.

Ohio: Fort Herrick (1898–1910); Herrick?; unemployment colony.

San Fernando Farm (1943–?); near Los Angeles, California.

Saunders's Colony. *See* Antislavery Movement

Savoy. *See* Shaker Movement

School of Living Movement (1936–present); Ralph Borsodi, Mildred Loomis; Maryland, New York, Ohio, Pennsylvania, Washington, Virginia; cooperative homesteading and business, nonviolent, human-scale living.

Maryland: Heathcote (1965–present); Mildred Loomis; Freeland.

New York: **1.** Bayard Lane (1936–1940s); Ralph Borsodi; Suffern. **2.** Skyview Acres (1946–?); Pomona.

Ohio: Lane's End Homestead (1940–1968); Mildred and John Loomis; near Brookville.

Pennsylvania: **1.** Birthright Leasehold (?–present); Cochranville. **2.** School of Living—Deep Run Farm (ca. 1930s–present); York. **3.** School of Living—Sonnewald Homestead (?–present); Spring Grove.

Virginia: Common Ground (1980–present).

Washington: May Valley Cooperative (1950s–?); Renton.

Seventh Day Baptist Movement (1732–present); Johann Conrad Beissel; Pennsylvania, Virginia; Radical Pietist.

Pennsylvania: **1.** Antietam (1763–ca. 1770); Franklin County. **2.** Bermudian Creek (1758–1820); York County. **3.** Ephrata Community/Ephrata Cloister (1732–1786; non-communal to 1814); Johann Conrad Beissel; Ephrata, Lancaster County. **4.** Snow Hill/Snow Hill Nunnery/Seventh Day Baptist Church of Snow Hill (1798–1889); Snow Hill, Quincy Township, Franklin County.

Virginia: Shenandoah Valley Community (1754–1764); Ezechiel Sangmeister; Shenandoah Valley.

Shaker Movement/United Society of Believers in Christ's Second Appearing (ca. 1774–present); Ann Lee; England and United States; Adventist, Perfectionist.

Connecticut: Enfield (1790–1917); Hartford County.

Florida: Narcoosee (1894–1912); Narcoosee, Osceola County.

Georgia: White Oak (1898–1902); Camden County.

Indiana: West Union (1810–1827); Haddon Township, Sullivan County.

Kentucky: **1.** Pleasant Hill (1806–1910); Mercer County. **2.** South Union (1807–1922); Logan County.

Maine: **1.** Alfred (1793–1932); York County. **2.** Gorham (1808–1819); Cumberland County. **3.** Sabbathday Lake/New Gloucester (1794–present); New Gloucester, Cumberland.

Massachusetts: **1.** Hancock (1790–1960); Berkshire County. **2.** Harvard (1791–1918); Worcester County. **3.** Savoy (1817–1825); Berkshire County. **4.** Shirley (1793–1908); Middlesex County. **5.** Tyringham (1792–1875); Berkshire County.

New Hampshire: **1.** Canterbury (1792–present); Merrimack County. **2.** Enfield (1793–1932); Grafton County.

New York: **1.** Groveland (1836–1895); Groveland Township, Livingston County. **2.** Mount Lebanon/New Lebanon (1787–1947); New Lebanon Township, Columbia County. **3.** Sodus Bay (1826–1836); Sodus and Huron Townships, Wayne County. *See also* Fourierist Movement **4.** Watervliet/Niskeyuna (1787–1938); Colonie Township, Albany County.

Ohio: **1.** North Union (1822–1889); Cleveland, Cuyahoga County. **2.** Union Village (1805–1912); Turtle Creek Township, Warren County. **3.** Watervliet (1806–1910); Van Buren Township (now Dayton), Montgomery County. **4.** Whitewater (1824–1907); Crosby Township, Hamilton County.

Shalam (1884–1901); John Ballou Newbrough; near Dona Ana County, New Mexico; Spiritualist.

Shenandoah Valley Community. *See* Seventh Day Baptist Movement

Shiloh. *See* Shiloh Movement

Shiloh Communities (1942–present); founded and led by Rev. E. Crosby Monroe to 1961; New York and Arkansas; Christian.

Arkansas: Shiloh Community (1968–present); Sulphur Springs.

New York: Shiloh Community (1942–1968); Rev. E. Crosby Monroe; southwestern New York.

Shiloh Farms (1942–?), Sulphur Springs, Arkansas.

Shiloh Movement/Church of the Living God (1893–present); Frank and Hellen Sandford; Durham, Maine, and other American cities; England, Africa, and Jerusalem; Millennialist.

Maine: Shiloh (1895–1920); Frank and Helen Sandford, Durham.

Shirley. *See* Shaker Movement

Sicily Island Colony. *See* Jewish Agricultural Colonies

Silkville Colony. *See* Fourierist Movement

Silver Lake Community. *See* Antislavery Movement

Single Tax Movement (1879–present); Henry George; nationwide; single tax reform, poverty eradication.

Alabama: Fairhope Single Tax Corporation/Fairhope Industrial Association (1895–1908; incorporated as town in 1908, landholding cooperative to present); Fairhope, Baldwin County.

Delaware: **1**. Arden (1900–present); Arden, New Castle County. **2**. Ardencroft (1950–present); Arden, New Castle County; racial integration. **3**. Ardentown (1922–present); Arden, New Castle County.

Colorado: Colorado Cooperative Colony (1894–1910); E. L. Gallatin; Nucla, Montrose County.

Maine: Halidon (1911–1938); Fiske Warren; Westbrook, Cumberland County.

Maryland: Gilpen's Point (1926–?).

Massachusetts: **1**. Shakerton (1921–?). **2**. Tahanto (1909–1934); Fiske Warren; Harvard, Worcester County. **3**. Trapelo (1927–?).

Mississippi: Wall Hill (1932–?).

New Jersey: Free Acres Association (1910–1950); Bolton Hall, New Providence (now Berkeley Heights) Township, Union County.

Skaneateles Community (1843–1846); John A. Collins; Mottville, Onondaga County, New York. *See* Owenite Movement

Skyview Acres. *See* School of Living Movement

Snow Hill Nunnery. *See* Seventh Day Baptist Movement

Social Democracy of America Movement (1897–ca. 1913); Eugene V. Debs; Chicago, Illinois, and nationwide; labor unionist, Socialist.

Washington: Burley Colony/Co-operative Brotherhood/Co-operative Commonwealth Company (1898–1913); Richard J. Hinton, Cyrus Field Willard, Wilfred P. Borland; Burley, Kitsap County, Washington; Socialist.

Social Freedom Community (1874–1880); Chesterfield County, Virginia.

Socialist Movement of Job Harriman (1914–1938); Job Harriman; California and Louisiana; Socialist.

California: Llano del Rio (1914–1918); Job Harriman; Los Angeles County.

Louisiana: Newllano Co-operative Colony (1917–ca. 1938); Job Harriman, George T. Pickett; Leesville, Vernon Parish.

Socialist Movement of Julius Wayland (1893–1901); Julius Wayland; Nationwide; Socialist.

    Georgia: Ruskin Commonwealth (1899–1901); Ware County; secessionists from Ruskin Cooperative Association, Ruskin, Tennessee.

    Tennessee: Ruskin Cooperative Association (1894–1899); Julius Wayland; Tennessee City and Ruskin, Dickinson County, Tennessee.

Social Reformers Co-operative Emigration Society (1843–?).

Social Reform Unity. *See* Fourierist Movement

Societas Fraternia (1879–?); Dr. Schlesinger; Los Angeles County, California; vegetarian.

Society of Brothers Movement/Bruderhof/Hutterian Brethren/Bruderhof Communities (1920–present); founded by Eberhard and Emmy Arnold in Germany; emigrated to England, Paraguay, and United States; somewhat affiliated with certain Hutterites at times since 1950s; Christian. *See also* Hutterite Movement

    England

    Darvell Bruderhof (1972–present); Robertsbridge, East Sussex.

    United States

    Connecticut: Deer Spring Bruderhof/Evergreen (1958–present); Norfolk.

    New York: **1.** Catskill Bruderhof (1990–present); Elka Park. **2.** Pleasant View Bruderhof (1985–present); Ulster Park. **3.** Woodcrest Bruderhof (1954–present); Rifton.

    Pennsylvania: **1.** New Meadow Run (1956–present); Farmington. **2.** Spring Valley (1990–present); Farmington.

    West Germany

    Michaelshof (1988–1995); Auf der Hohe.

Society of Industry. *See* Teutonia

Society of One-Mentians (1843–1844).

    Pennsylvania: **1.** Goose Pond Community (1843–1844); Pike County. **2.** Promisewell Community (1843–1844); Monroe County.

Society of Separatists of Zoar (1817–1898); Joseph Bimeler; Zoar, Tuscarawas County, Ohio; Radical Pietist.

Society of the United Germans/United Germans at Teutonia/Teutonia (1827–1831); Peter Kaufmann; Columbiana County, Springfield Township, Ohio; Harmonist Secessionist, antislavery. *See* Harmonist Movement

Society of True Inspiration. *See* Inspirationist Movement

Society of Universal Friends. *See* Jerusalem

Sodus Bay Phalanx. *See* Fourierist Movement and/or Shaker Movement

Sonnewald Homestead. *See* School of Living Movement

Southern Co-operative Association of Apalachicola (1900–1904); Harry C. Vrooman; Franklin County, Florida; Swedenborgian.

South Union. *See* Shaker Movement

Southwestern & Western Co-operative Farm, Manufacturing, and Transportation Colony (1901?); Star, Nebraska.

Southwestern Colony (early 1870s–?); Green City, Colorado.

Spirit Fruit Society (1901–1930); Jacob Beilhart; Lisbon, Columbiana County, Ohio, until 1905, then Ingleside, Lake County, Illinois; Spiritualist, Theosophist. *See* Theosophical Movement

Spiritualist Movement of Thomas Lake Harris/Brotherhood of the New Life (1861–1900); Thomas Lake Harris; New York, California; Spiritualist.

    California: Fountain Grove (1876–1900); Santa Rosa, Sonoma County.

    New York: **1.** Amenia Community/Brotherhood of the New Life (1863–1867); Amenia, Dutchess County. **2.** Brocton/Salem-on-Erie Community (1867–1881); Brocton, Chautauqua County. **3.** Brotherhood of the New Life (1861–1892); Wassaic, Dutchess County.

West Virginia: Mountain Cove Community (1851–1853); Thomas Lake Harris; Fayette County.

Spring Farm Phalanx. *See* Fourierist Movement

Spring Valley. *See* Society of Brothers Movement

Steiner Movement/Rudolf Steiner Movement. *See* Camphill Movement

Still Meadow. *See* Emissaries of Divine Light Movement

Stonington Colony (1837–ca. 1841); Samuel Peabody; Christian County, Illinois; Baptist homestead.

Straight Edge Industrial Settlement (1899–1918); Wilbur F. Copeland; New York, New York.

Sunrise Community (1932–1936); Joseph Cohen; Saginaw, Michigan; Jewish anarchist.

Sunrise Cooperative Farm (1933–1937); Michigan.

Sunrise Cooperative Farm (1937–1939); Virginia.

Sunrise Cooperative Farms (early 1930s–?); Monmouth County, New Jersey.

Sunrise Ranch. *See* Emissaries of Divine Light Movement

Sylvania Association. *See* Fourierist Movement

Tahanto. *See* Single Tax Movement

Tanguy Homesteads (1945–present); Glen Mills, Pennsylvania; interracial cooperative housing.

Temple Home Association. *See* Theosophical Movement

Temple of the Gospel of the Kingdom (1900–?); New York, New York.

Temple of the People. *See* Theosophical Movement

Teutonia (Ohio). *See* Society of the United Germans

Teutonia/McKean County Association/Society of Industry (1842–1844); Henry Ginal; Ginalsburg (near present Smethport), McKean County, Pennsylvania; German Immigrant.

Thelemic Magic Community (1939–?); Pasadena, California.

Theosophical Movement/Theosophical Society (1875–present); Helena P. Blavatsky, Henry Steel Olcott, William Q. Judge, Katherine A. Tingley; United States and worldwide; Theosophy.

Canada

British Columbia: Aquarian Foundation/Cedar-by-the-Sea (1927–1933); Edward Arthur Wilson ("Brother XII"); Cedar-by-the-Sea, Vancouver Island.

United States

California: **1.** Krotona Community of Adyar Theosophists (1912–1924); Albert Powell Warrington; Ventura County. **2.** Krotona Institute of Theosophy (1912–1924); Hollywood. **3.** Krotona Institute of Theosophy (1924–present); Ojai (continuation of Krotona Institute, Hollywood). **4.** Point Loma/Universal Brotherhood and Theosophical Society (1897–1942); Katherine A. Tingley; Point Loma, San Diego. **5.** Temple of the People/Temple Home Association (1903–1913; noncommunal to present); William H. Dower; Halcyon, San Luis Obispo County (continuation of Temple of the People, Syracuse, New York). **6.** Theosophical Society International Headquarters Community (moved from Point Loma Community in 1942; moved to Pasadena beginning 1950 and completed 1951); Gottfried de Purucker to 1942, council leadership to 1945, Col. Arthur L. Conger to 1951; Covina. **7.** Theosophical Society International Headquarters Community (moved from Covina in 1950 and 1951–present); Col. Arthur L. Conger to 1951, James A. Long to 1971, Grace F. Knoche to present; Pasadena.

Illinois: Spirit Fruit Society (1901–1930); Jacob Beilhart; moved from Ohio in 1905 to Ingleside, Lake County; Spiritualist, Theosophist.

New York: Temple of the People (1897–1903); Syracuse.

North Carolina: Theosophical Community (1925–?); Asheville, Buncombe County.

Ohio: Spirit Fruit Society (1901–1930); Jacob Beilhart; Lisbon, Columbiana County, Ohio (in 1905 moved to Ingleside, Lake County, Illinois [see above]); Spiritualist, Theosophist.

Theosophical Society. *See* Theosophical Movement

Theosophical Society International Headquarters Community at Covina and Pasadena, California. *See* Theosophical Movement

Thompson Colony (1800–?); Saline County, Kansas 3HO. *See* Healthy, Happy, Holy Organization Movement

Time Store Cooperative Movement (1833–ca. 1863); Josiah Warren; Ohio and New York; anarchist, free love, Owenite influence. *See* Owenite Movement

New York: Modern Times (1851–1863); Josiah Warren, Stephen Pearl Andrews; Long Island, Suffolk County.

Ohio: **1.** Equity Community (1833–1835); Josiah Warren; Tuscarawas County.

2. Utopia (1847–1851); Josiah Warren; Clermont County.

Tivoli Farms (ca. 1940–present); New York; Roman Catholic.

Tobias Community. *See* Camphill Movement

Tolstoy Farm (1963–present); Davenport, Washington; organic farming.

Topolobampo Bay Colony (1884–1899); Albert Kimsey Owen; Sinaloa, Topolobampo Bay, Mexico; land settlement. *See* Mexican Communes

Trabuco College (1942–1949); Gerald Heard; Orange County, California; meditation, Vedanta influence.

Triform. *See* Camphill Movement

True Family. *See* Longley Communities

Trumbull Phalanx. *See* Fourierist Movement

Tuolumne Cooperative Farms (1945–?); Central California.

Twin Valleys Community. *See* Emissaries of Divine Light Movement

Tyringham. *See* Shaker Movement

The Union (1804–1810); north of Potsdam, St. Lawrence County, New York; nonsectarian.

Union Colony (1869–1872); Nathaniel C. Meeker; now Greeley, Weld County, Colorado; nonsectarian, land settlement, temperance.

Union Grove (1856–1858); Meeker County, Minnesota.

Union Home/The Free Community (1844–1846); John O. Wattles, Hiram Mendenhall; Randolph County, Indiana; Socialist.

Union Mill (1891–1897); Daniel and Catherine Cornen; Tillamook County, Oregon.

Union Village. *See* Shaker Movement

Unitarian Association (1844–1844); Wisconsin.

United Cooperative (1926–1939); California.

United Cooperative Industries (1923–?); Los Angeles, California.

United Family (1896?–?); Worcester, Worcester County, Massachusetts.

United Germans at Teutonia. *See* Society of the United Germans

United Order. *See* Mormon Movement

United Order of Enoch. *See* Mormon Movement

United Society of Believers in Christ's Second Appearing. *See* Shaker Movement

Universal Brotherhood. *See* Theosophical Movement

Utilitarian Association of United Interests (1845–1848); Campbell Smith; near

Mukwonago, Waukesha County, Wisconsin; secular, settlement, Owenite interest, sponsored by Utilitarian Association of United Interests in England. *See* Owenite Movement

Utopia. *See* Time Store Cooperative Movement and Owenite Movement

(The) Vale (1961–present); Griscom and Jane Morgan; Yellow Springs, Greene County, Ohio; family, peace, nature. Operates Community Service, Inc., begun in 1940 by engineer/educator Arthur E. Morgan to aid small communities.

Valley of the Swans. *See* Plockhoy's Commonwealth

VanEeden Colony. *See* Hugh MacRae's Immigrant Colonies

Vedanta Movement (1870s–present). The Vedanta Movement began in the 1870s in Bengal, India, where it was led by Sri Ramakrishna and was known as the Ramakrishna Movement. When Swami Vivekananda introduced it into the United States in 1893, the movement took the name Vedanta. The movement began establishing communal ashrams in major American cities by 1895. A rural commune was begun in California in 1900, and a monastic community was started in San Francisco in 1906 by Swami Trigunitita.

California: **1.** Vedantic Center (?–present); Harold Jones; Agoura. **2.** Vedantic Monastery (1906–?); Swami Trigunitita; San Francisco.

Illinois: Vivekananda Vedanta Society (1930–present); Chicago.

Michigan: Vivekananda Vedanta Society Monastery (?–?).

Vegetarian Colony (ca. 1901–?); Highland, New York.

Virginia Phalanx (1845–1850); Gilmer County, Virginia. *See* Fourierist Movement

Vivekananda Vedanta Society. *See* Vedanta Movement

Voree (1844–1849); James Jesse Strang; Spring Prairie Township, Walworth and Racine Counties, Wisconsin.

Vril Society. *See* New Era Union Movement

Wakefield, Kansas (late 1860s–?); English colony.

Wallingford Community. *See* Perfectionist Movement of John Humphrey Noyes

Wall Street. *See* New Era Union Movement

Warm Springs Colony (1871); Madison County, North Carolina.

Washington Colony (1881–1884); Bellingham, Whatcom County, Washington; land settlement.

Watervliet/Niskeyuna Shaker Village, New York. *See* Shaker Movement

Watervliet Shaker Village, Ohio. *See* Shaker Movement

Wayne Produce Association (1921–1939); McKinnon, Georgia.

Western New York Industrial Association (1844–1844); New York.

Westminster Colony (1869–?); Anaheim, California.

West Union. *See* Shaker Movement

WFLK Fountain of the World (late 1940s–?); Box Canyon, California.

Whitehall Co-op (1949–present); Austin, Texas; housing cooperative.

White Oak. *See* Shaker Movement

Whitewater. *See* Shaker Movement

Wilberforce Settlement. *See* Antislavery Movement

Willard Cooperative Colony (1895–1896); William C. Damon, Ralph Albertson; Cherokee County, North Carolina, and another branch in Tennessee; Prohibitionist.

Winters Island. *See* Co-operative Brotherhood of Winters Island

Wisconsin Phalanx. *See* Fourierist Movement

Woman in the Wilderness (1694–1708; movement continued to ca. 1748); Magister Kelp(ius); now Fairmont Park, Pennsylvania; Radical Pietist.

Women's Commonwealth/Sanctificationists (1874–1906); Martha McWhirter; Belton, Bell County, Texas, and Washington, D.C.; Sanctificationist.

Woodcrest. *See* Society of Brothers Movement

Yasodhara Ashram (1956–present); Swami Sivananda Radha; Kootenay Bay, British Columbia.

Yellow Springs Community. *See* Owenite Movement

Zion City (1893–1906); John Alexander Dowie; Chicago and Zion City, Lake County, Illinois; theocratic.

Zoarite Movement. *See* Society of Separatists of Zoar

Zodiac (1847–1853); Lyman Wright; Gillespie County, Texas; Mormon.

Addendum

Movements of Roman Catholic religious orders in addition to the Benedictine and Cistercian movements listed in detail above include the following (*see* Index for each in text):

Augustinian
Camaldolese
Carmelite
Capuchin
Carthusian
Christian Brothers
Citeaux
Daughters of Charity
Discalced Carmelite
Dominican
Franciscan
Jesuit
Marianist
Maryknoll
Mendicant
Paulist
Poor Clares
Recollects
Sacred Heart Daughters
Sisters of Charity
Sisters of Loretto
Sisters of Mercy
Sisters of Notre Dame de Manur
Sisters of Perpetual Adoration
Sisters of Providence
Sisters of St. Elizabeth
Sisters of St. Francis
Sisters of St. Joseph
Sisters of the Holy Cross
Sisters of the Holy Family
Sisters of the Holy Name
Sisters of the Precious Blood

Trappist
Ursuline
Vallambrosan
Vincentian
Visitandine

Principal Sources

Albertson, Ralph. "A Survey of Mutualistic Communities in America." *Iowa Journal of History and Politics* 34 (October 1936): 375–440.

Anderson, Lawrence C. Unpublished list of Hutterite colonies in the archives of the Center for Communal Studies, University of Southern Indiana, Evansville, Indiana, 1989.

Andrews, Edward Deming. *The People Called Shakers.* New York: Dover, 1963. Enlarged edition of 1953 original.

Arndt, Karl J. R. *George Rapp's Harmony Society, 1785–1847.* Rutherford, N.J.: Fairleigh Dickinson University Press, 1965. Rev. ed., 1972.

Arrington, Leonard J., Feramorz Y. Fox, and Dean L. May. *Building the City of God: Community and Cooperation among the Mormons,* 2d ed. Urbana: University of Illinois Press, 1992.

Bartelt, Pearl W. List of Jewish Agricultural Colonies prepared for this volume, in Center for Communal Studies, University of Southern Indiana, Evansville, Indiana, 1993.

Bestor, Arthur E., Jr. *Backwoods Utopias: The Sectarian Origins and the Owenite Phase of Communitarian Socialism in America, 1663–1829,* 2d ed. Philadelphia: University of Pennsylvania Press, 1970, 27, 277–285, listing 130 communities from 1663 to 1858.

Braden, Charles S. *These Also Believe: A Study of Modern American Cults and Minority Religious Movements.* New York: Macmillan, 1949.

Brewer, Priscilla J. *Shaker Communities, Shaker Lives.* Hanover, N.H.: University Press of New England, 1986, listing Shaker communities.

Calverton, Victor F. *Where Angels Dared to Tread.* Indianapolis: Bobbs-Merrill, 1941.

Conkin, Paul K. *Tomorrow a New World: The New Deal Community Program.* Ithaca, N.Y.: Cornell University Press, 1959.

Dare, Philip, ed. *American Communes to 1860: A Bibliography.* New York: Garland, 1990.

Fogarty, Robert S. *All Things New: American Communes and Utopian Movements, 1860–1914.* Chicago: University of Chicago Press, 1990.

———. "American Communes, 1865–1914." *Journal of American Studies* 9 (August 1975): 145–62.

———. *Dictionary of American Communal and Utopian History.* Westport, Conn.: Greenwood, 1980. Appendix A: "Annotated List of Communal and Utopian Societies, 1787–1919," by Otohiko Okugawa, 173–233, listing 270 communities.

Gold, David M. "Jewish Agriculture in the Catskills, 1900–1920." *Agricultural History* 55 (1981): 31–49.

Grant, H. Roger. "'One Who Dares to Plan': Charles W. Caryl and the New Era Union." *Colorado Magazine* 51 (Winter 1974): 13–27.

Guarneri, Carl J. *The Utopian Alternative: Fourierism in Nineteenth-Century America.* Ithaca, N.Y.: Cornell University Press, 1991.

Harrison, John F. C. *Quest for the New Moral World: Robert Owen and the Owenites in Britain and America.* New York: Scribner's, 1969.

Herscher, Uri D. *Jewish Agricultural Utopias in America, 1880–1910.* Detroit: Wayne State University Press, 1981.

Hine, Robert V. *California's Utopian Colonies*. New York: Norton, 1966.

Infield, Henrik F. *Cooperative Communities at Work*. New York: Dryden Press, 1945, p. 16, list of Jewish communal settlements.

Jackson, Dave, and Neta Jackson. *Glimpses of Glory: Thirty Years of Community, the Story of Reba Place Fellowship*. Elgin, Ill.: Brethren, 1987.

————. *Living Together in a World Falling Apart*. Carol Stream, Ill.: Creation House, 1974.

Kagan, Paul. *New World Utopias: A Photographic History of the Search for Community*. New York: Penguin, 1975.

Lee, Dallas. *The Cotton Patch Evidence: The Story of Clarence Jordan and the Koinonia Farm Experiment*. New York: Harper and Row, 1971.

LeWarne, Charles Pierce. *Utopias on Puget Sound, 1885–1915*. Seattle: University of Washington Press, 1975. Rev. ed., 1994.

Lockridge, Kenneth A. *A New England Town: The First Hundred Years*. New York: Norton, 1970.

Lowenthal, Bennett. "The Topolobampo Colony in the Context of Porfirian Mexico." *Communal Societies* 7 (1987): 47–66, listing 21 Mexican immigration communities founded by people from the United States.

McCrank, Lawrence J. Compilation of Roman Catholic religious orders, monasteries, and convents in America, in Center for Communal Studies, University of Southern Indiana, Evansville, Indiana, 1990.

McLaughlin, Corinne, and Gordon Davidson. *Builders of the Dawn: Community Lifestyles in a Changing World*. Shutesbury, Mass.: Sirius, 1986.

Melcher, Marguerite F. *The Shaker Adventure*. Cleveland, Ohio: Press of Case Western Reserve University, 1968.

Mellon, Knox, Jr. "Christian Priber's Cherokee 'Kingdom of Paradise.'" *Georgia Historical Quarterly* 52 (Fall 1973): 319–31.

Melton, J. Gordon. *Biographical Dictionary of American Cult and Sect Leaders*. New York: Garland, 1986.

————. *The Encyclopedia of American Religions*. Detroit: Gale Research, 1978–94 eds.

Miller, Timothy. *American Communalism, 1860–1960: A Bibliography*. New York: Garland, 1990.

The New Age Community Guidebook: Alternative Choices in Lifestyles. Middletown, Calif.: Harbin Springs, 1989.

The 1990/91 Directory of Intentional Communities: A Guide To Cooperative Living. Evansville, Ind.: Fellowship for Intentional Community, and Stelle, Illinois: Communities Publications Cooperative, 1990; updated, 1991; 2d ed., 1995.

Nordhoff, Charles. *The Communistic Societies of the United States: From Personal Visit and Observation*. New York: Dover, 1966.

Noyes, John Humphrey. *History of American Socialisms*. Philadelphia: Lippincott, 1870. Reprinted as *Strange Cults and Utopias of Nineteenth-Century America*. New York: Dover, 1966.

Oved, Yaacov. *Two Hundred Years of American Communes*. New Brunswick, N.J.: Transaction, 1988, 485–93, listing 277 communities founded from 1663 to 1937.

Pease, William H., and Jane H. Pease. *Black Utopia: Negro Communal Experiments in America*. Madison: State Historical Society of Wisconsin, 1963. Paperback ed., 1972.

Price, George M. "The Russian Jews in America." Translated by Leo Shpall. *American Jewish Historical Quarterly* 48 (1958): 26–62, 78–133.

Robinson, Leonard G. *Agricultural Activities of the Jews in America*. Reprint from the *American Jewish Year Book 5673*. New York: American Jewish Committee, 1912.

Shpall, Leo. "Jewish Agricultural Colonies in the United States." *Agricultural History* 24 (1950): 120–46.

Solis, Miguel J. *American Utopias, 1693–1900.* Bloomington: Indiana University Printing Services, 1984.

Spiritual Community Guide. San Rafael, Calif.: Spiritual Community, 1972–1985. Sixth edition, titled *The New Consciousness Sourcebook,* published by Arcline Publications, Pomona, Calif., 1985.

Stein, Stephen J. *The Shaker Experience in America: A History of the United Society of Believers.* New Haven: Yale University Press, 1992.

Veysey, Laurence. *The Communal Experience: Anarchist and Mystical Counter-Cultures in America.* New York: Harper and Row, 1973.

Weimer, Mark F. "The William A. Hinds *American Communities* Collection." *Communal Societies* 7 (1987): 99–103.

Wooster, Ernest S. *Communities of the Past and Present.* New York: AMS Press, 1974; reprint of 1924 first edition.

Bibliographical Essay

This book employs a new "developmental communalism" approach for interpreting communal history, but it stands in a two-centuries-old tradition of gathering, analyzing, and publicly presenting information on America's communal utopias.[1] Public curiosity always has demanded news about communitarian groups and the movements that spawn them. Their unorthodox beliefs and practices, isolated and sometimes mysterious or threatening character, potential solutions to societal and metaphysical problems, and the secrets of their economic strengths and weaknesses perpetually attract attention.

Travelers from Europe and America began satisfying the public's need to know about communal utopians as early as 1759, when Israel Acrelius published an account in Swedish of his visit to the Seventh Day Baptist Ephrata Cloister in Pennsylvania.[2] In the first three decades of the nineteenth century, most attention went to the Shaker communities in New England, New York, Ohio, Kentucky, and Indiana; the three towns of the Harmony Society in Pennsylvania and Indiana; and the communal phase of Owenism at New Harmony, Indiana. Yale president Timothy Dwight observed Shaker settlements several times after 1799, as did Yale chemistry and natural history professor Benjamin Silliman after 1819. Their thoughtful, if critical, assessments appeared in print early in the 1820s.[3] Authors Alexis de Tocqueville and Charles Dickens described visits with Shakers in New York—the first at Niskeyuna (near Albany), the second at Mount Lebanon, where the United Society first adopted communal organization in 1787.[4] Harriet Martineau became the most important of at least fifteen British travelers who penned their impressions of the Shakers before 1835.[5] Touring the United States between 1834 and 1836, Martineau sought to understand the practical application of the communal principles of both the Shakers and the Harmonists. In her *Society in America*, printed in London in 1837, she explored ways in which Shaker and Harmonist communal life might offer solutions to European problems.[6] John Melish's glowing report of the Harmonist village of Harmony, Pennsylvania, published first in 1812, helped attract Robert Owen to communal experimentation in America.[7] Naturalist Constantine Rafinesque and geologist Charles Lyell, respectively, consulted on herbs with the Harmonists and geology with former Owenites at New Harmony. By the 1830s numerous travelers were writing their findings not only of the Shakers, Harmonists, and Owenites but also of the German Separatists of Zoar in Ohio; Frances Wright's attempt to give the antislavery movement a communal dimension at Nashoba in Tennessee; and the Fourierist communities at the North American Phalanx in New Jersey and Brook Farm in Massachusetts.[8]

A secondary literature on communal utopias did not begin until the endeavors of Mary Hennell and John Finch of England and A. J. Macdonald of the United States. The first book devoted to communalism appeared in 1844 in London as Hennell's *Outline of the Various Social Systems & Communities Which Have Been Founded on the Principle of Cooperation*. Significant as the earliest general historical survey of the subject, this work nevertheless suffered from being based entirely on ancient and modern literary sources with no basis in personal investigation. The first comprehensive study of American communal societies resting on informed, on-site observation and comparison of many sectarian and nonsectarian communities resulted from the tour of John Finch in 1843. Having resigned his presidency of the central Owenite organization in Britain (the Rational Society) with the expressed purpose of examining America's communes, Finch published his descriptive evaluation of a wide variety of communal groups in 1844 as a series of twenty-two letters of "Notes on Travel in the United States" in the English Owenite *New Moral World*.[9] Scottish immigrant printer A. J. Macdonald conceived the grandest project for publicly revealing the nature of communities formed by movements in America before the mid-1800s. From 1842 until cholera cut his life and project short about 1854, Macdonald visited and studied American communal sites more thoroughly than anyone before. Through a form letter he circulated with carefully designed questions, he also gathered reminiscences from former communitarians in an effort to assemble and publish source material on all groups having lived communally in this country.[10]

Macdonald's invaluable materials and the manuscript for his unfinished book were not permanently lost, however. Rediscovered in 1865 by John Humphrey Noyes, founder of the Oneida community, Macdonald's "Manuscripts and Collections" (now in the Yale University Library) provided almost 600 pages of text for his *History of American Socialisms* (1870).[11] Noyes's volume is significant as the earliest of the first three major books treating communalism in America from the knowledge of firsthand investigation, all published in the 1870s. Noyes included most movements that used communal living except the Moravians, Mormons, and Icarians. An imbalance in the coverage occurred, though, because of Noyes's own interest in the socialistic aspect of communities. This resulted in his overexposing the Owenites and Fourierists and underexposing the religious communities to the point of nearly excluding the important German sectarians of Economy, Zoar, Ebenezer, and Amana. Although Noyes uncritically printed errors and biases from Macdonald's work, which were repeated by later writers, Noyes contributed the initial theories and interpretations of American communal usage from the perspective of a communitarian leader. He also inspired the book by William Alfred Hinds, who was a member of his Oneida community and editor of its organ *The Circular*, in which extracts of Macdonald's study had appeared for months in 1868 and 1869 before Noyes's book was published. Hinds gathered the reminiscences of communitarians who responded to Noyes's book and printed many in *The Circular* and its successor *The American Socialist*. Then he traveled to several communal sites before recording his information in *American Communities: Brief Sketches of Economy, Zoar, Bethel*, . . . published at Oneida in 1878. Hinds emphasized the religious movements slighted by Noyes. He also expanded his book in 1902 and 1908 editions, the last of which gave facts about communities of the late nineteenth century not available elsewhere.[12]

Another book in the 1870s based on direct observation was the most complete and objective. Its author, Charles Nordhoff, was an accomplished author and journalist with the New York *Evening Post* and New York *Herald*. He achieved his goal of visiting virtually all the existing communal societies, digesting the literature on each and writing descriptions of all aspects of their community life. His underlying purpose was to permit evidence from communal economic success to demonstrate the cooperative settlement as a viable alternative to urban labor problems and as a formula for efficient land settlement. Nordhoff offered *The Communistic Societies of the United States: From Personal Visit and Observation* (1875) as a suggested escape from labor unionism and the complexities of an increasingly industrial society.[13] Ironically, by limiting his survey to communities then in operation, he mostly witnessed movements that had already made fateful decisions freezing them into rigid communal forms and other set practices that produced the equilibrium of stagnation so characteristic of utopias. Although Nordhoff pronounced groups that had lived communally for many years such as the Shakers, Harmonists, and Zoarites "successful Communists," he did not recognize that their failure to adjust to changing realities both inside and outside their organizations signaled the doom of their larger movements along with their communities that would occur in the later nineteenth and twentieth centuries. Omitted from Nordhoff's study were the movements of the Seventh Day Baptists, Moravians, Mormons, and others that had developed beyond their communal stages by the time of his travels and that continue today. By not treating the nonsectarian Owenite and Fourierist movements, Nordhoff left the mistaken impression that these had died with their communal experiments and that all "successful" cooperative communities rested on a religious commitment.[14]

Seven decades passed before the next significant general study of the American communal tradition appeared in 1950 as *Backwoods Utopias: The Sectarian Origins and the Owenite Phase of Communitarian Socialism in America, 1663–1829* by historian Arthur Eugene Bestor Jr. The late 1960s arrived before Richard Fairfield and Consuelo Sandoval traveled to and reported on enough contemporary communes to rival Nordhoff's feat of the 1870s.[15] This lapse did not occur because scholars and the public lost interest in communalism or because communal methods ceased to attract new practitioners. Instead, by the 1880s communitarianism was being integrated into works on the ever more popular reforms of socialism and trade unionism.[16] By 1900, general histories of the United States included sections on the major communal utopias.[17] Specialization captivated the earliest generation of professional historians and social scientists. Their work focused narrowly and produced monographs on individual communal groups, biographies of leaders, and edited collections of sources rather than general surveys.[18] Furthermore, in the twentieth century, seminal writing in the fields of religious, economic, social, literary, and intellectual history deepened the understanding of communitarianism.[19] Novel interpretations of communalism were introduced without new factual information during the first half of the twentieth century in Lewis Mumford's *The Story of Utopias* (1922), V. F. Calverton's *Where Angels Dared to Tread* (1941), Alice Felt Tyler's *Freedom's Ferment: Phases of American Social History from the Colonial Period to the Outbreak of the Civil War* (1944), and Charles A. Madison's *Critics and Crusaders: A Century of American Protest* (1946).[20]

The publication of Bestor's *Backwoods Utopias* marked a watershed in communitarian scholarship as a new era began in the 1950s with several general histories. Bestor's thorough historical research, careful documentation, exhaustive bibliographical essay, and accurate list of 130 communities formed between 1663 and 1860 made his work a methodological model as the standard of scholarly excellence in this field.[21] *Backwoods Utopias* emphasizes the Owenites and terminates its narrative in 1829. These understandable, self-imposed limitations nevertheless left a void that subsequent publications still attempt to fill. Mark Holloway, an English writer engaged by a publisher to produce a book on American communes, brought the story up to 1880. His work went to press in London in 1951 without the benefit of his using the latest findings of Bestor. Holloway's survey, *Heavens on Earth: Utopian Communities in America, 1680–1880*, is more inclusive though far less penetrating and less understanding of utopian eccentricities than Bestor's.[22] In 1952 Donald D. Egbert and Stow Persons edited the outstanding scholarly work on communitarian socialism titled *Socialism and American Life*, with a complete bibliography by T. D. Seymour Bassett.

In 1953 historian Robert V. Hine gave the public its first composite glimpse of the variety of reform and religious movements that found communal organization attractive on the west coast during the late nineteenth and early twentieth centuries in his detailed study *California's Utopian Colonies*.[23] After visiting many of the historic communal sites discussed in Hine's book, Paul Kagan published his well-illustrated *New World Utopias: A Photographic History of the Search for Community* (1975). Everett Webber wrote *Escape to Utopia: The Communal Movement in America* (1959) as a literary and sometimes intentionally humorous treatment of the principal historic communitarian groups. The 1950s resurgence of incisive communal scholarship closed with Paul Conkin's *Tomorrow a New World: The New Deal Community Program* (1959), which added the dimension of government adoption of communal methods during a time of economic crisis.

Public and scholarly interest in communal phenomena increased dramatically as the youth movement of the 1960s sought the escape, security, and idealism of the perennially available communal utopia. General historical accounts of established merit such as those by Noyes, Nordhoff, Hinds, Bestor, and Hine were reprinted, some with new introductions and revisions. Standard accounts of individual historic communal societies from Amana to Zoar reappeared.[24] A body of literature rapidly came into existence trying to catalog and explain the unexpected revival of the use of communalism, but a comprehensive history of American communes since 1960 awaits an author.[25] National and international gatherings of social scientists, historians, and contemporary communitarians resulted in noteworthy published proceedings.[26] The latest utopian and communal scholarship also appeared in the journals of the Society for Utopian Studies and the National Historic Communal Societies Association (which changed its name to the Communal Studies Association in 1990). The former printed *Alternative Futures: The Journal of Utopian Studies* from 1978 to 1981 and *Utopian Studies* since 1990. *Communal Societies: Journal of the NHCSA* (CSA since 1990) has been published annually since 1981. Lyman Tower Sargent and Gregory Claeys edit the books in the Utopianism and Communitarianism Series begun by Syracuse University Press in 1991.

New sociological and historical studies and reference works dealing with communes past and present emerged after 1970.[27] In addition to volumes about individual communities mentioned in the essays and selected bibliographies in this book, several studies deserve mention here. Sociologists led the way into the new era with adventurous visitations, innovative interpretations, and useful findings. Rosabeth Moss Kanter's *Commitment and Community: Communes and Utopias in Sociological Perspective* (1972), suggested that commitment mechanisms found in varied degrees in communes begun between 1780 and 1860 determined their longevity, which she equated with their success. Kanter's thesis influenced studies of contemporary communes and assessments of previous communities. Hugh Gardner's *Children of Prosperity: Thirteen Modern American Communes* (1978) reviewed the first wave of youth communes in the western states and found certain commitment mechanisms Kanter identified as productive of solidarity in earlier communes, such as sacrifice, more dysfunctional to communal survival since 1965. Benjamin Zablocki used Kanter's notion as a model for his survey of 120 communes in *Alienation and Charisma: A Study of Contemporary American Communes* (1980). Zablocki identified length of communal existence with consensus decision making and lesser attachment between couples but, like Gardner, found no relationship between economic communism and survival in community. William M. Kephart put the communal aspects of the Shakers, Mormons, Hutterites, Oneidans, Father Divine's movement, and modern communalists into sociological perspective in *Extraordinary Groups: An Examination of Unconventional Life-Styles* (1971) (the fifth edition with William W. Zellner [1994] omits the Shakers and adds the Christian Scientists).

Important historical works since 1960 began as William and Jane Pease's *Black Utopia: Negro Communal Experiments in America* (1963) revealed efforts to aid black people who had recently escaped or been freed from slavery, through communal settlements in the United States and Canada. Paul Conkin's study *Two Paths to Utopia* (1964) compared the religious discipline of the Hutterites with the secular anarchism of the socialists of the Llano community of the 1910s. The roots and lives of two anarchist and two mystical communes of the early twentieth century were analyzed by Laurence Veysey in *The Communal Experience: Anarchist and Mystical Counter-Cultures in America* (1973).[28] *Utopias on Puget Sound, 1885–1915* (1975; rev. ed., 1995), is Charles P. LeWarne's fine documentation of the radical communes founded by the socialist movement in the Northwest. Dolores Hayden looked at historic communes through the eyes of an architectural historian in her *Seven American Utopias: The Architecture of Communitarian Socialism, 1790–1975* (1976). Carol Weisbrod's *The Boundaries of Utopia* (1980) was the first book to summarize the history of litigation by former members against communal groups. Edward K. Spann's *Brotherly Tomorrows: Movements for a Cooperative Society in America, 1820–1920* (1989) touched on several movements that adopted the communal method. Focusing on the millennialistic House of David are Robert Fogarty, *The Righteous Remnant* (1981), and Clare Adkin Jr., *Brother Benjamin: A History of the Israelite House of David* (1990). Important accounts of the Oneida perfectionists and Jewish communal settlers appeared as Spencer Klaw, *Without Sin: The Life and Death of the Oneida Community* (1993), and Ellen Eisenberg, *Jewish Agricultural Societies in New Jersey, 1882–1920* (1995).

Sex, marriage, and gender in communal life are examined in Raymond L. Muncy, *Sex and Marriage in Utopian Communities: Nineteenth-Century America* (1974); Lawrence Foster, *Religion and Sexuality: The Shakers, the Mormons, and the Oneida Community* (1984; originally published as *Religion and Sexuality: Three American Communal Experiments of the Nineteenth Century* [1981]); Jon Wagner, ed., *Sex Roles in Contemporary American Communes* (1982); Robert and Jeanette Lauer, *The Spirit in the Flesh: Sex in Utopian Communities* (1983); and Lynn Marie Oliver, *The "Natural Order": Gender Roles at Brook Farm and Oneida* (1992). Two works concentrated on Owenism. Barbara Taylor's *Eve and the New Jerusalem: Socialism and Feminism in the Nineteenth Century* (1983) opened new vistas on the relation of socialism and the ideal of gender equality in Owenite communes in Britain and America. Carol Kolmerten's *Women in Utopia: The Ideology of Gender in the American Owenite Communities* (1990) treated, from a recent feminist point of view, the residual conservative attitudes toward women, some of the middle-class women's reactions, and the resulting effects. Roger Wunderlich's *"Low Living and High Thinking" at Modern Times, New York, 1851–1864* (1986) deals with one of Josiah Warren's communities. Collections of essays in the 1990s on gender and marriage in historic utopian communities include Lawrence Foster's *Women, Family, and Utopia* (1991); Wendy E. Chmielewski, Louis J. Kern, and Marlyn Klee-Hartzell, eds., *Women in Spiritual and Communitarian Societies in the United States* (1993); and Jean M. Humez, ed., *Mother's First-Born Daughters: Early Shaker Writings on Women and Religion* (1993). Dealing with these and other themes in Shaker history, Stephen J. Stein's *The Shaker Experience in America* (1992) has become the standard work. Intimate insights into communal relationships are given in Seymour R. Kesten, *Utopian Episodes: Daily Life in Experimental Colonies Dedicated to Changing the World* (1993), and Robert S. Fogarty, ed., *Special Love/Special Sex: An Oneida Community Diary* (1994).

On the continuing question of the correlation, if any, between religious and economic cycles and the establishment of communes, the latest studies are Michael Barkun's "Communal Societies as Cyclical Phenomena," *Communal Societies* 4 (1984), and "The Awakening-Cycle Controversy," *Sociological Analysis* 46 (1985), and Brian J. L. Berry's *America's Utopian Experiments: Communal Havens from Long-Wave Crises* (1992). In his revealing historical survey of 141 communities, Robert Fogarty concludes in *All Things New: American Communes and Utopian Movements, 1860–1914* (1990) that in that period movements found communalism attractive in times of both boom and bust, and that for the communes he examined no generalizations can be made between economic distress and religious millennialism.

In addition to Berry's and Fogarty's books, three other works dealing broadly with American communal history, including the present anthology, complete the cycle of more than two centuries of gathering and writing the communal saga. Yaacov Oved's *Two Hundred Years of American Communes* in 1988 was the first comprehensive survey by a historian since Bestor's *Backwoods Utopias* in 1950. In his work written in Hebrew and translated into English, Oved, an Israeli kibbutz member, lists 277 communes founded by 1937, gives a sympathetic narrative of 70 of them, and uses one-fifth of the book for comparative analysis. In 1991 Carl Guarneri's extensively researched and historically detailed treatment of Fourierism appeared as *The Utopian Alternative: Fourierism in Nineteenth-Century America* and has become the standard account. The seventeen historians and social scientists who contributed essays to *America's Communal Utopias* offer a developmental interpretation to the ongoing scholarship in this engrossing field as we approach the new millennium. Reawakened adventist hopes already are producing new movements that can be expected to create new communal utopias as the third millennium since the birth of Jesus and the prophetically significant seventh, and final, millennium of Fundamentalist dispensationalism dawns on January 1, 2001.[29]

Notes

1. J. Gordon Melton, Philip N. Dare, and Timothy Miller, eds., *Bibliography of Communal Life in North America*, 3 vols. (New York: Garland, 1990–), is the most recent and most complete summary of works about America's communal utopias. Two of the three volumes appeared in 1990 as Philip N. Dare, ed., *American Communes to 1860: A Bibliography*, and Timothy Miller, ed., *American Communes, 1860–1960: A Bibliography*. Two critical summaries of the literature of communal and utopian movements and individual communities as well as the writings of communitarians themselves appeared in Robert Fogarty, *Dictionary of American Communal and Utopian History* (Westport, Conn.: Greenwood, 1980), 235–46, and his *All Things New: American Communes and Utopian Movements, 1860–1914* (Chicago: University of Chicago Press, 1990), 261–73. Arthur E. Bestor Jr., *Backwoods Utopias: The Sectarian Origins and the Owenite Phase of Communitarian Socialism in America, 1663–1829* (Philadelphia: University of Pennsylvania Press, 1970), 1, 2, 40–48, 287–310, surveys the historical writings about communal groups up to 1969. Communal bibliography from the 1960s to the early 1980s appears in Robert V. Hine, *California's Utopian Colonies* (Berkeley: University of California Press, 1983), xiii–xvii, 179–96, and Donald Pitzer, "The Uses of the American Communal Past," *Communal Societies* 4 (1984): 218–20. The above are the bases for this discussion unless otherwise indicated.

2. Acrelius's description appeared later in William M. Fahnestock, "An Historical Sketch of Ephrata," *Hazard's Register of Pennsylvania* 15 (March 14, 28, 1835): 161–67, 208, and in an English translation by William M. Reynolds in Acrelius, *A History of New Sweden; or,*

the Settlements on the River Delaware, in *Memoirs* (Philadelphia: Historical Society of Pennsylvania, 1874), 11:373–401. Ephrata became so well known it found a place in Voltaire's *Dictionnaire Philosophique* (Amsterdam, 1789), 1:81.

3. Timothy Dwight, *Travels in New-England and New-York*, 4 vols. (New Haven: T. Dwight, 1821–22), 1:149–69; [Benjamin Silliman], *Remarks Made on a Short Tour between Hartford and Quebec in the Autumn of 1819* (New Haven: S. Converse, 1820), 40–53. Silliman later published an entire book titled *Peculiarities of the Shakers, Described in a Series of Letters from Lebanon Springs* (New York: J. K. Porter, 1832). Harvard professor of Greek Edward Everett wrote an extensive article, "The Shakers," in the *North American Review* 16 (January 1823): 76–102, suggesting that economic benefits rather than religious beliefs attracted Shaker converts.

4. Alexis de Tocqueville's letter to his mother, Auburn, [New York], July 17, 1831, printed in his *Oeuvres completes*, 9 vols. (Paris: M. Levy Freres, 1864–67), 7:34–36, and Charles Dickens, *American Notes for General Circulation* (London: Everyman's Library, 1907), 211–15 (first published in 1842).

5. Bestor, *Backwoods Utopias*, 44.

6. Harriet Martineau, *Society in America*, 3 vols. (London: Saunders and Otley, 1837), 1:x–xiv, xvii–xviii, 1, 54–65, 57, 58.

7. John Melish, *Travels in the United States of America, in the Years 1806 & 1807, and 1809, 1810, & 1811* (Philadelphia: T. and G. Palmer, 1812), 2:64–83. Byron wrote twenty-four lines about the Harmony Society in *Don Juan*, canto 15.

8. The German duke of Saxe-Weimar-Eisenach described his visit with Robert Owen in New Harmony and George Rapp in Economy in *Travels in North America, during the Years 1825 and 1826*, 2 vols. (Philadelphia: Carey, Lea & Carey, 1828), 2:106–23, 159–66, and Mrs. Frances M. Trollope wrote of her time at Nashoba in *Domestic Manners of the Americans*, 2 vols. (London: Whittaker, Treacher, 1832), 1:38–42, 194–96. Swedish author Fredrika Bremer went to the North American Phalanx at least twice; Hungarian Sandor Farkas, to the Shakers and Economy, the last place also seen by economist Frederick List. Scientific interests brought German prince Maximilian of Wied-Neuwied to New Harmony, where he spoke to Owenites who continued the scientific and educational experiments beyond intentional community days in 1832–33, and he also visited Zoar, Ohio, as described in his *Travels in the Interior of North America* (London: Ackermann, 1843) and in Reuben Gold Thwaites, ed., *Early Western Travels, 1748–1846*, 32 vols. (Cleveland: A. H. Clark, 1904–7), 22:163–97, 24:154–56. John Silk Buckingham saw Economy and Zoar and the Shakers in Ohio, New York, and New Hampshire between 1837 and 1841. His descriptions were printed in London in 1841 and 1842. See Bestor, *Backwoods Utopias*, 1, 2, 45.

9. *New Moral World* (January 13–July 6, 1844), xii:232–xiii:10, 11.

10. Macdonald's letter is reprinted in John Humphrey Noyes, *Strange Cults and Utopias of Nineteenth-Century America* (New York: Dover, 1966), 3–6.

11. Noyes, *History of American Socialisms* (Philadelphia: Lippincott, 1870; reprint under same title, New York: Dover, 1960, and as *Strange Cults and Utopias of Nineteenth-Century America*, New York: Dover, 1966), see introduction by Mark Holloway, v–xviii.

12. William A. Hinds, *American Communities and Co-operative Colonies*, 2d ed. (actually 3d ed.) (Chicago: C. H. Kerr, 1908). Also during the 1870s, George Jacob Holyoake, a leader in the cooperative and rationalistic movements in Britain, wrote *The History of Co-operation in England: Its Literature and Its Advocates*, 2 vols. (London: Trubner, 1875–79), the first inclusive work on the communal utopias of Great Britain and also covering some of the American communes.

13. Charles Nordhoff, *The Communistic Societies of the United States: From Personal Visit and Observation* (New York: Harper and Bros., 1875; reprinted with introduction by Mark Holloway, New York: Dover, 1966).

14. Nordhoff, *Communistic Societies*, 19, 408. Nordhoff asserted that "Mr. [John Humphrey] Noyes believes that religion must be the base of a successful commune" (408). But he qualified his own view by stating, "If it is meant . . . that in order to [succeed] there must be some peculiar religious faith, fanatically held, I do not believe it at all" (408).

15. Fairfield edited and periodically published *The Modern Utopian* after 1966 to report the rising use of communes in the United States, Europe, Japan, and Israel. He and Consuelo Sandoval traveled 12,000 miles together contacting scores of groups that turned to communal living during the youth movement. Their observations appeared in *The Modern Utopian* and are summarized in Fairfield's *Communes USA: A Personal Tour* (Baltimore: Penguin, 1972.

16. Richard T. Ely, *French and German Socialism in Modern Times* (New York: Harper and Bros., 1883), put discussions of communitarian and socialist theories together. Ely, *The Labor Movement in America* (New York: T. Y. Crowell, 1886), and Morris Hillquit, *History of Socialism in the United States* (New York: Funk and Wagnalls, 1903), analyzed religious, Owenite, and Fourierist communes from the viewpoint of the history of organized labor.

17. For example, Edwin Erle Sparks, *Expansion of the American People* (Chicago: Scott, Foresman, 1900), 376–401, and John Bach McMaster, *A History of the People of the United States* (New York: D. Appleton, 1900), 5:88–108.

18. See Bestor, *Backwoods Utopias*, 295–310, and the selected bibliographies accompanying each essay in the present anthology.

19. For example, John R. Commons, ed., *History of Labour in the United States*, vol. 1 (New York: Macmillan, 1918); Norman J. Ware, *The Industrial Worker, 1840–1860* (Boston: Houghton Mifflin, 1924); Elmer T. Clark, *The Small Sects in America* (Nashville, Tenn.: Cokesbury, 1937); Carl Wittke, *We Who Built America: The Saga of the Immigrant* (New York: Prentice-Hall, 1939); Merle Curti, *Growth of American Thought* (New York: Harper and Bros., 1943); and Vernon L. Parrington Jr., *American Dreams: A Study of American Utopias* (Providence, R.I.: Brown University Press, 1947; rev. ed., New York: Russell and Russell, 1964).

20. Speculative interpretations were presented in Gilbert Seldes, *The Stammering Century* (New York: John Day, 1928), and Arthur E. Morgan, *Nowhere Was Somewhere: How History Makes Utopias and How Utopias Make History* (Chapel Hill: University of North Carolina Press, 1946).

21. The 1970 edition updated the bibliography and appended two of Bestor's later papers on the subject: "Patent-Office Models of the Good Society" and "The Transit of Communitarian Socialism to America." Bestor contributed significant specific works on Fourierism and Owenism to the field of communal studies, as noted in the essays dealing with these movements in the present book. Also see his "The Search for Utopia," in *The Heritage of the Middle West*, ed. John J. Murray (Norman: University of Oklahoma Press, 1958).

22. Mark Holloway, *Heavens on Earth: Utopian Communities in America, 1680–1880* (New York: Dover, 1966), rev. ed. Three other important books dealt exclusively with English communes: A. L. Morton, *The English Utopia* (London: Lawrence and Wishart, 1952); Walter H. G. Armytage, *Heavens Below: Utopian Experiments in England, 1560–1960* (Toronto: University of Toronto Press, 1961); and Dennis Hardy, *Alternative Communities in Nineteenth-Century England* (London: Longman Group, 1979).

23. Robert V. Hine, *California's Utopian Colonies* (San Marino, Calif.: Huntington Library, 1953; reprint, Berkeley: University of California Press, 1966; rev. ed. 1983). See also Hine's *Community on the American Frontier: Separate but Not Alone* (Norman: University of

Oklahoma Press, 1980) and *California Utopianism: Contemplations of Eden* (San Francisco: Boyd and Fraser, 1981).

24. Porcupine Press and AMS Press reprinted many of these recognized works. Dover Publications reprinted Noyes and Nordhoff.

25. Most literature on American communal groups formed since 1965 fits into two broad categories: (1) accounts by leaders, members, and early visitors and (2) studies by later, nonmember social scientists and historians, some of whom have done on-site research. Richard Fairfield began the first type of writing in 1966 with issues of *The Modern Utopian* describing his visits to many communes. Later he published his thoughtful reflections in *Communes USA*. Other works by leaders, members, and visitors include Donald Walters (Swami Kriyananda), *Cooperative Communities: How to Start Them and Why* (Nevada City, Calif.: Ananda, 1968; rev. ed., 1972); William Hedgepeth and Dennis Stock, eds., *The Alternative: Communal Life in New America* (New York: Macmillan, 1970); Roy Ald, *The Youth Communes* (New York: Tower, 1970); Stephen Diamond, *What the Trees Said: Life on a New Age Farm* (New York: Dell, 1971); Robert Houriet, *Getting Back Together* (New York: Coward, McCann & Geoghegan, 1971); Raymond Mungo, *Total Loss Farm* (New York: Bantam, 1971) and *Famous Long Ago* (New York: Citadel, 1990); Kathleen Kinkade, *A Walden Two Experiment: The First Five Years of Twin Oaks Community* (New York: William Morrow, 1973) and her sequel *Is It Utopia Yet?: An Insider's View of Twin Oaks Community in Its Twenty-Sixth Year* (Louisa, Va.: Twin Oaks, 1994); Stephen and The Farm, *Hey Beatnik!: This Is The Farm Book* (Summertown, Tenn.: Book Pub. Co., 1974); Dave Jackson and Neta Jackson, *Living Together in a World Falling Apart* (Carol Stream, Ill.: Creation House, 1974) and its sequel by the same author-members, *Glimpses of Glory: Thirty Years of Community, the Story of Reba Place Fellowship* (Elgin, Ill.: Brethren, 1987); Donald G. Bloesch, *Wellsprings of Renewal: Promise in Christian Communal Life* (Grand Rapids, Mich.: Eerdmans, 1974); Frances FitzGerald, *Cities on a Hill: A Journey through Contemporary American Cultures* (New York: Simon and Schuster, 1981) (treats Rajneeshpuram); Satsvarupa dasa Goswami, *Prabhupada: He Built a House in Which the Whole World Can Live* (Los Angeles: Bhaktivedanta Book Trust, 1983); Cris Popenoe and Oliver Popenoe, *Seeds of Tomorrow: New Age Communities That Work* (New York: Harper and Row, 1984); Hayagriva Dasa, *The Hare Krishna Explosion: The Birth of Krishna Consciousness in America, 1966–1969* (Singapore: Palace, 1984); Corinne McLaughlin and Gordon Davidson, *Builders of the Dawn: Community Lifestyles in a Changing World* (Walpole, N.H.: Stillpoint, 1985); and Daniel Wright, *Utopian Concepts for Social Revolution* (Williams, Ind.: Padanaram, 1987).

Many contemporary communal groups have printed booklets, books, and periodicals in addition to those listed above explaining their histories and philosophies. See, for example, *Living in Community, for the Time of Your Life* (n.d.) by the Federation of Egalitarian Communities headquartered at East Wind Community in Tecumseh, Mo., describing seven affiliated communes, and numerous magazines and books in the 1970s and 1980s by Kerista commune in San Francisco, including *Utopian Classroom, Utopian Eyes, Kerista,* and *Utopia 2*. In 1972 seven collectives formed the Community Publications Cooperative and combined their publications, *Alternatives* (formerly *The Modern Utopian*), *Communitarian,* and *Communitas,* into *Communities,* to be published at Twin Oaks in Louisa, Va. *Communities* rapidly fulfilled its purpose of becoming the single most representative organ giving a unified voice to nonsectarian advocates of communal alternatives to societal problems. With slight title changes from *Communities* to *Communities: Journal of Cooperative Living* and *Communities: Journal of Cooperation,* this source continues under the auspices of the Fellowship for Intentional Community. Directories of current communes have appeared in this journal from its first appearance in December 1972 to its special directory issues in 1990, 1991, and 1994. Other listings of communes, cooperatives, and communities have appeared in the *Spiritual Community Guide*, printed annually since the early 1970s by Spiritual Community Publications, San Rafael, Calif.; *The New Consciousness Sourcebook*, Berkeley, Calif.; *New England Network of Light Directory* (1983, etc.), edited by Corinne McLaughlin and Gordon Davidson for Sirius Community, Amherst, Mass.; *A Guide to Co-operative Alternatives* (New Haven, Conn., and Louisa, Va.: Community Publications Co-operative, 1979); J. Lipnack and J. Stamps, *Networking: The First Report and Directory* (Garden City, N.Y.: Doubleday, 1982); *Unity in Diversity Directory* (Los Angeles: World Trade Center, n.d.); *Community Service Newsletter*, printed by Community Service, Inc., Yellow Springs, Ohio, since 1943; and *The Whole Again Resource Guide* (Santa Barbara, Calif.: Capra, 1982). The most recent publications from inside communal utopian ranks focus on the newest forms of communal sharing through cohousing, land trusts, and electronic communities. Such works include Carolyn Shaffer and Kristin Anundsen, *Creating Community Anywhere* (New York: Putnam, 1993), and Claude Whitmyer, ed., *In the Company of Others: Making Community in the Modern World* (New York: Putnam, 1993).

The second category of literature on communal utopias founded since 1965 is composed of studies by nonmember social scientists, historians, and other scholars. Beyond those mentioned in the text, these include Lewis Yablonsky, *The Hippie Trip* (New York: Western Pub. Co., 1968); Ron E. Roberts, *The New Communes: Coming Together in America* (Englewood Cliffs, N.J.: Prentice-Hall, 1971); George Fitzgerald, *Communes: Their Goals, Hopes, Problems* (New York: Paulist Press, 1971) (gives a Catholic view); Sallie Teselle, ed., *The Family, Communes, and Utopian Societies* (New York: Harper and Row, 1972); Ronald M. Enroth, *The Jesus People: Old-Time Religion in the Age of Aquarius* (Grand Rapids, Mich.: Eerdmans, 1972) (uses an evangelical perspective); Keith Melville, *Communes in the Counter Culture: Origins, Theories, Styles of Life* (New York: William Morrow, 1972); Judson Jerome, *Families of Eden: Communes and the New Anarchism* (New York: Seabury, 1974); Marguerite Bouvard, *The Intentional Community Movement: Building a New Moral World* (Port Washington, N.Y.: Kennikat, 1975); David French and Elena French, *Working Communally: Patterns and Possibilities* (New York: Russell Sage Foundation, 1975); John Rothchild and Susan Wolf, *The Children of the Counter Culture* (Garden City, N.Y.: Doubleday, 1976); John R. Hall, *The Ways Out: Utopian Communal Groups in an Age of Babylon* (London: Routledge and Kegan Paul, 1978); Eric Raimy, *Shared Houses, Shared Lives* (Los Angeles: J. P. Tarcher 1979); James T. Richardson, *Organized Miracles: A Study of a Contemporary, Youth, Communal, Fundamentalist Organization* (New Brunswick, N.J.: Transaction, 1978) (on the Shiloh movement); Bennett Berger, *Survival of a Counterculture: Ideological Work and Everyday Life among Rural Communards* (Berkeley: University of California Press, 1981); J. Gordon Melton and Robert L. Moore, *The Cult Experience: Responding to the New Religious Pluralism* (New York: Pilgrim, 1982); Burke Rochford, *Hare Krishna in America* (New Brunswick, N.J.: Rutgers University Press, 1985); John R. Hall, *Gone from the Promised Land: Jonestown in American Cultural History* (New Brunswick, N.J.: Transaction, 1985); Timothy Miller, *The Hippies and American Values* (Knoxville: University of Tennessee Press, 1991); and David Pepper, *Communes and the Green Vision: Counterculture, Lifestyle, and the New Age* (London: Green Print, 1991).

The newest form of communal literature is being produced by former members of communal groups—usually from the communes of strict, sectarian movements—who left voluntarily or were expelled. These writers attempt to give one another mutual assistance in understanding their experiences, adjusting to their new lives, confronting communal leaders, and informing the public of the realities of communal life as they knew them. Most prominent in this group are former members of the Hutterites and Society of Brothers who, since 1991, have published the *KIT* (Keep in Touch) *Newsletter*. Yaacov Oved takes this evidence into account in his *The Witness of the Brothers: A History of the Bruderhof* (New

Brunswick, N.J.: Transaction, 1996). In its Women from Utopia Series, edited by Gertrude Enders Huntington, Carrier Pigeon Press of San Francisco printed Elizabeth Bohlken-Zumpe's *Torches Extinguished: Memories of a Communal Bruderhof Childhood in Paraguay, Europe, and the USA* (1993) and Nadine Moonje Pleil's *Free from Bondage after Forty Years in Bruderhof Communities on Three Continents* (1994).

26. Papers from the Conference on Communes: Historical and Contemporary conducted in April 1975 at Northern Illinois University were printed in a special issue of the *International Review of Modern Sociology* 6 (Spring 1976), guest edited by noted sociologist Ruth Shonle Cavan. The Colston Symposium on Utopia held in May 1983 at the University of Bristol, England, produced Peter Alexander and Roger Gill, eds., *Utopias* (London: Duckworth, 1984). Yosef Gorni, Yaacov Oved, and Idit Paz, eds., *Communal Life: An International Perspective* (New Brunswick, N.J.: Transaction, 1986), contains lectures delivered during the International Conference on Kibbutz and Communes at Yad Tabenkin, Efal, Israel, in May 1985. The eight plenary session addresses and abstracts of sixty-one other papers of the July 1988 international conference on utopian thought and communal experience at New Lanark, Scotland, sponsored by the International Communal Studies Association and the National Historic Communal Societies Association, were edited by Dennis Hardy and Lorna Davidson as *Utopian Thought and Communal Experience* (Enfield, England: Middlesex Polytechnic, 1989).

27. Documents from communal history not previously readily available appeared in Robert S. Fogarty, *American Utopianism* (Itasca, Ill.: F. E. Peacock, 1972). Fogarty's *Dictionary of American Communal and Utopian History* (Westport, Conn.: Greenwood, 1980) describes 147 leaders and 59 major historic communes and contains the invaluable list of 270 communal societies between 1787 and 1919 compiled by Otohiko Okugawa. J. Gordon Melton's groundbreaking reference works in this field began with the 1978 edition of his *Encyclopedia of American Religions* (Detroit: Gale Research). His other contributions include the *Biographical Dictionary of American Cult and Sect Leaders* (New York: Garland, 1986), *Encyclopedic Handbook of Cults in America* (New York: Garland, 1986), and *The New Age Encyclopedia* (Detroit: Gale Research, 1990).

General accounts during the 1960s and 1970s included Donna Lawson, *Brothers and Sisters All over This Land: America's First Communes* (New York: Praeger, 1972); Michael Fellman, *The Unbounded Frame: Freedom and Community in Nineteenth-Century American Utopianism* (Westport, Conn.: Greenwood, 1973); and Kenneth Roemer, *The Obsolete Necessity: America in Utopian Writings, 1888–1900* (Kent, Ohio: Kent State University Press, 1976).

28. See Kenneth Rexroth, *Communalism: From Its Origins to the Twentieth Century* (New York: Seabury, 1974), for a broad, interpretive account but with little documentation.

29. Three hundred and twenty North American groups were described but many more asked not to be given public notice in *The 1990/1991 Directory of Intentional Communities: A Guide to Cooperative Living* printed by the Fellowship for Intentional Community and the Communities Publications Cooperative in the special double issue of *Communities: Journal of Cooperation* 77–78 (October 1990; updated, 1991). The 1995 edition, titled *Communities Directory: A Guide to Cooperative Living*, lists over 500 intentional communities. Geoph Kozeny, one of the compilers of these directories, far exceeded his predecessors such as Macdonald and Nordhoff by visiting more than 350 contemporary communal groups during the late 1980s and 1990s.

Jonathan G. Andelson, professor of anthropology at Grinnell College, Grinnell, Iowa, earned his Ph.D. from the University of Michigan. He has been studying the Amana Colonies since 1971. In addition to his work on intentional communities he is interested in the interface between ecology and religion. He is past president of the Communal Studies Association and, since 1994, has served as book review editor for its journal *Communal Societies*.

Karl J. R. Arndt, now deceased, was emeritus professor of German at Clark University, having received his Ph.D. from Johns Hopkins University. Arndt's exhaustive studies of the Harmony Society of George Rapp for more than half a century resulted in narrative and documentary histories with translations and abstracts of the original German. Among these are *George Rapp's Harmony Society, 1785–1847* (1965; 1972); *George Rapp's Successors and Material Heirs, 1847–1916* (1971; 1972); *Harmonie on the Connoquenessing, 1803–1815: George Rapp's First American Harmony* (1980); *A Documentary History of the Indiana Decade of the Harmony Society, 1814–1824* (vol. 1, 1975; vol. 2, 1978); *Harmony on the Wabash in Transition, 1824–1826* (1982); *George Rapp's Re-established Harmony Society, 1848–1868* (1993); and *George Rapp's Disciples, Pioneers, and Heirs: A Register of the Harmonists in America* (1994).

Pearl W. Bartelt, dean of liberal arts and sciences and professor of sociology at Rowan University, received her Ph.D. from Ohio State University. She is past president and a founding board member of the International Communal Studies Association and former treasurer and board member of the Communal Studies Association. Her research on ethnicity and gender in American communal groups has been presented at meetings of those organizations, the American Sociological Association, and the Society for the Study of Social Problems. Her work on gender roles in historical and contemporary American communal societies has been published in *Communal Life: An International Perspective* (1987). As a visiting senior research fellow at the University of Surrey, she conducted field research and presented material on the Society of Dependents (The Cokelers). Her other publications are in the areas of writing in the disciplines, symbolic interactionism, and the sociology of gender.

Priscilla J. Brewer, associate professor of American studies at the University of South Florida in Tampa, received her Ph.D. in American civilization from Brown University in 1987. Her research has focused on communal societies, material culture, and women's history. Brewer's publications on the Shakers include *Shaker Communities, Shaker Lives* (1986) and "'Tho' of the Weaker Sex': A Reassessment of Gender Equality among the Shakers," *Signs: Journal of Women in Culture and Society* (1992). Her other articles have appeared in the *New England Quarterly*, *Communal Societies*, *Journal of Interdisciplinary History*, *Journal of American Culture*, and *Winterthur Portfolio*.

Donald F. Durnbaugh, archivist of Juniata College and formerly Carl W. Zeigler Professor of Religion and History at Elizabethtown College and professor of church history at Bethany Theological Seminary, earned his Ph.D. from the University of Pennsylvania. He is a board member of the Communal Studies Association, the Brethren Journal Association, and the Pennsylvania German Society. Durnbaugh is editor of *Communal Societies* and author or editor of ten books and more than one hundred scholarly articles. He was editor in chief of *The Brethren Encyclopedia* (3 vols., 1983–84). His works on religious movements in Europe and colonial America include *European Origins of the Brethren* (1958; 1986); *The Brethren in Colonial America* (1967; 1974); *The Believers' Church: The History and Character of Radical Protestantism* (1968; 1985); and *Every Need Supplied: Mutual Aid and Christian Community in the Free Churches, 1525–1675* (1974).

Lawrence Foster, professor of American history at Georgia Tech in Atlanta, earned his Ph.D. from the University of Chicago. He is a past president of the Communal Studies Association. A former Woodrow Wilson, Ford Foundation, National Endowment for the Humanities, and Fulbright fellow, he has written extensively on American religious and social history. His *Religion and Sexuality* (1981; 1984), a comparative study of alternative forms of sexuality and family life in Shaker, Oneida, and Mormon communities, won the Mormon History Association's "Best Book" award. His *Women, Family, and Utopia* (1991) further explores how women reacted to the alternative systems in the same three groups. Foster has contributed articles on communalism to many edited volumes and encyclopedias and to *Journal of the Early Republic, Church History, Communal Societies, Communities: Journal of Cooperative Living, Utah Historical Quarterly, Dialogue: A Journal of Mormon Thought, Sunstone, Journal of Mormon History,* and *Australasian Journal of American Studies*.

Carl J. Guarneri, professor of history at Saint Mary's College of California, received his Ph.D. at Johns Hopkins University. His writings on American communal movements include *The Utopian Alternative: Fourierism in Nineteenth-Century America* (1991) and articles in *Journal of the History of Ideas, Church History, Journal of the Early Republic, Communal Societies,* and *Utopian Studies*. Since 1984 he has been an associate editor of *Communal Societies*.

Robert V. Hine, professor emeritus of history at the University of California at Riverside and Irvine, received his Ph.D. from Yale University. He has been honored with two Guggenheim Fellowships, a National Endowment Senior Fellowship, the E. Harris Haribson Award for Distinguished Teaching, the Communal Studies Association's Distinguished Scholar Award, and the Western History Association's Honorary Lifetime Membership. Among his books related to communal studies are *California's Utopian Colonies* (1953; 1983); *Community on the American Frontier: Separate but Not Alone* (1980); *The American West: An Interpretive History* (2d ed., 1984); and *Josiah Royce: From Grass Valley to Harvard* (1992).

Gertrude E. Huntington, lecturer in anthropology and environmental studies at the University of Michigan, received her Ph.D. from Yale University. With John A. Hostetler she coauthored *Hutterites in North America* (3d ed., 1996) and "Communal Socialization Patterns in Hutterite Society," *Ethnology* (1968). Her many articles on the Hutterites include "Children of the Hutterites," *Natural History* (1981), and "History, Ideology, and Agriculture in Contemporary North America," *Culture and Agriculture* (1993). She is editor of the series *Women from Utopia,* in which two books by women who left the Society of Brothers were published in 1993 and 1994. Her "Age, Gender, and Influence in Hutterite Colonies" appeared in *Communities* (Spring 1996). She is a recipient of the Distinguished Scholar Award of the Communal Studies Association.

James E. Landing, associate professor of geography at the University of Illinois at Chicago, received his Ph.D. from Pennsylvania State University. His research has centered on the allocation of resources among small minority groups, such as the Old Order Amish, the Old Order Mennonites, and the Old Order German Baptist Brethren; small communal groups; and the many urban groups of Eastern Christians and Black Jews. His articles have appeared in *Professional Geographer, Geographical Bulletin, Journal of Geography, International Geography, Mennonite Quarterly Review, Illinois Audubon,* and many others. He is currently involved in large-scale environmental projects.

Dean L. May, professor of history at the University of Utah, earned his Ph.D. at Brown University. He is past editor of the *Journal of Mormon History* and author, with Leonard J. Arrington and Feramorz Y. Fox, of *Building the City of God: Community and Cooperation among the Mormons* (1976). A social and cultural historian of the American West, his *Three Frontiers: Family, Land, and Society in the American West, 1850–1900* is a prize-winning recent title in the distinguished series *Interdisciplinary Perspectives on Modern History,* edited by Stephen Thernstron and Robert Fogel. May also wrote *Utah: A People's History* (1987), edited *A Dependent Commonwealth: Utah's Economy from Statehood to the Great Depression* (1974), and has chapters in *Utah's History* (1978) and *New Views of Mormon History* (1987). His articles have appeared in *Church History, Journal of Family History, Journal of Mormon History* and *Utah Historical Quarterly.* In 1988 May produced the twenty-part video series *A People's History of Utah.*

Lawrence J. McCrank, who holds his Ph.D. from the University of Virginia, was formerly dean and university librarian at Auburn University at Montgomery and at Ferris State University, and is now with ITT Corporation's Education Services. He has authored and edited twenty monographs and published over sixty articles. He is senior editor for Haworth Press, for which he edits the series *Primary Sources and Original Works.* The connection between frontier monasticism in the Old and New Worlds is made in a collection of essays focusing on the twelfth-century Cistercian abbeys of Poblet and Santes Creus and the see of Tarragona appearing as *Frontier History in Medieval Catalonia.* In a forthcoming book, *Conversions: Information and Transformation in the Catholic Mission to Oregon, 1835–1885,* missionary efforts among the Pacific Northwest's Native Americans are explored.

J. Gordon Melton, founder and director of the Institute for the Study of American Religion in Santa Barbara, California, and research specialist in the Department of Religious Studies at the University of California at Santa Barbara, has his Ph.D. from Northwestern University. He has been president of the Communal Studies Association and of its Pacific Coast Chapter. A specialist in the history of new religions in America, Melton has published more than twenty-five books, including *Directory of Religious Bodies in the United States* (2d ed., 1992); *Encyclopedia of American Religions* (4th ed., 1992); *The Cult Experience* (1982); *Biographical Dictionary of American Cult and Sect Leaders* (1986); *The Encyclopedia Handbook of Cults in America* (1986); *New Age Encyclopedia* (1990); and *Encyclopedia of African American Religion* (1993). Melton is a member of the committee for the New Religions Study Area of the American Academy of Religion and of the Society for the Scientific Study of Religion.

Donald E. Pitzer, professor of history and director of the Center for Communal Studies at the University of Southern Indiana, received his Ph.D. from Ohio State University. He served as the first president of the Communal Studies Association (then the National Historic Communal Societies Association) in 1975 and 1976 and was its executive director from 1977 to 1993. He was the first president of the International Communal Studies

Association, 1988–1991. He edited *Robert Owen's American Legacy* (1972) and, with Josephine Elliott, wrote *New Harmony's First Utopians* (1979). His developmental communalism approach to communal studies is used as the conceptual framework for the essays in this volume. Dr. Pitzer has stated this developmental perspective at scholarly meetings and published it in *Communal Societies, Contemporary Education*, and "Developmental Communalism: An Alternative Approach to Communal Studies," in *Utopian Thought and Communal Experience* (1989), edited by Dennis Hardy and Lorna Davidson. Pitzer's work on American communities, especially Harmonist and Owenite New Harmony, also appears as articles and chapters in *Indiana Magazine of History, Historic Preservation, Ohio Journal of Science, Utopias* (1984), *Built in the U.S.A.* (1985), *Communal Life: An International Perspective* (1987), *The History of Education in the Middle West* (1978), and a special issue of *Communities: Journal of Cooperation* (1985) which he guest edited.

Robert P. Sutton, professor of history and director of the Center for Icarian Studies at Western Illinois University, received his Ph.D. from the University of Virginia. Sutton edits the *Newsletter* of the Communal Studies Association and has translated and written the introduction of the only English edition of the entire version of Etienne Cabet's *Travels in Icaria* (1985). In 1994 the University of Illinois Press published his *Les Icariens: The Utopian Dream in Europe and America*, which was nominated for the Theodore Saloutos Memorial Book Award in American Immigration History. Sutton's work on Icarian and other communal history has appeared as articles in *Gateway Heritage: Quarterly Magazine of the Missouri Historical Society, Western Illinois Regional Studies, Communities: Journal of Cooperation*, and *Illinois Magazine*; as chapters in *Human Values of the Icarian Movement* (1981), *Illinois: Its Heritage and Legacy* (1984), *Adaptation of the Icarians to America* (1993), and *Icaria-Speranza: Final Utopian Experiment of Icarians in America* (1995); and in his *The Prairie State: A Documentary History of Illinois* (2 vols., 1976). In 1989 the University Press of Virginia published his *From Revolution to Secession: Constitution Making in the Old Dominion*, which was nominated for the Merle Curti Award in American Intellectual History. His *Rivers, Railways, and Roads: A History of Henderson County, Illinois* (1988) received the Certificate of Excellence award by the Illinois State Historical Society. He is coauthor with Leslie Roberts of a new translation of part 1 of *Travels of Icaria* from Syracuse University Press. Sutton is coeditor of Michel Cordillot's *Dictionnaire biographique des Emigrés politiques et des Militants ouvriers et socialistes Français aux Etats-Unis, 1848–1917*. He is currently preparing a book on the full history of communal societies in America for Syracuse University Press.

Jon Wagner, professor of anthropology at Knox College, holds his Ph.D. from Indiana University. A student of both historic and contemporary utopian communal groups, Wagner edited *Sex Roles in Contemporary American Communes* (1982) and has published his research in *The International Review of Modern Sociology, Essays in Humanistic Anthropology, Communes: Historical and Contemporary, Prairie Journal*, and *Communal Societies*. The fall 1989 issue of *Western Illinois Regional Studies* carried his article on the historic community of Bishop Hill, Illinois.

Robert S. Weisbrot, the Christian A. Johnson Distinguished Teaching Professor of History at Colby College, earned his Ph.D. at Harvard University. He is the author of *Father Divine and the Struggle for Racial Equality* (1983) and *Freedom Bound: A History of America's Civil Rights Movement* (1990). He won the *Choice* citation for outstanding works of biography. In the field of ethnic history, Weisbrot prepared the entry on Father Divine in *American Reformers: An H. W. Wilson Biographical Dictionary* (1985).

INDEX

Apostates: Shaker, 46–48, 50; Harmonist, 76–78; Inspirationist, 195; writings and networking of, 504–5 (n. 25)

Aquarian Foundation, 411–13; developmental communal process of, 411–13; Edward Arthur Wilson, founder of, 411–13; as an initiative within Theosophy, 411–13; monetary gifts to, 412; and rejection of Jiddu Krishnamurti, 412; sexual practices of, to produce "sixth rootrace," 412; and Wilson's articles in *The Occult Review*, 412; and Wilson's *The Three Truths* and *Foundation Letters and Teachings*, 412; Cedar-by-the-Sea community of, 412–13; and the Masters of Wisdom, as inspirational sources of, 412–13; occult beliefs of, 412–13; Wilson's attempt to produce new world teacher, 412–13; and end of Cedar-by-the-Sea community, 413; chronology, 415

Ararat Jewish colony, 354

Architecture: of Ephrata Cloister, 23; of Harmonists, 66–67, 73; of Inspirationists in Amana, 181–82; of monasteries, 243; of Bishop Hill, 304–5, 307, 311–12; *Seven American Utopias*, 499

Arkwright, Richard, 90

Army of Industry, 422–23

Arnold, Eberhard, 336, 343, 349

Arnold, Emmy, 336

Arpin Jewish colony, 364

Art: Shaker, 53 (n. 30), 55; monastic, 243

Artisans: in communal utopias. *See names of communes, groups, and movements*

Asceticism: of Labadists, 18; of Seventh Day Baptists, 24; of Roman Catholic religious orders, 204–6, 211, 216. *See also* Monasticism; Mysticism

Associationists. *See* Fourierist movement

Atwood Jewish colony, 354

Augustinians, 219–21

Aurora, Ore.: Keilite colony of, 78, 473

Austin, Alice Constance, 428

Ayres, George D., 397

Bacon, Sir Francis, 4

Bad Axe Jewish colony, 363, 368

Bainbridge, William Sims, 46–47

Baker, John L., 66

Baker, Romelius L., 79–80

Baptism, 58; of infants, 60; among Hutterites, 321–22, 325, 330, 347

Barclay, Robert, 19

Barlow, Joel, 108

Baron de Hirsch Agricultural School, 363–64. *See also* Hirsch, Maurice de, Baron

Baron de Hirsch Fund, 362–64, 366. *See also* Hirsch, Maurice de, Baron

Baumgartner, Myrtle, 412–13

Baxter, Sylvester, 397

Becker, Peter, 22

Bée, Emile, 286, 420

Beersheba Jewish colony, 361

Behaviorism, 100

Beissel, Conrad, 22–27, 30

Bellah, Robert N., 135

Bellamy, Edward, 146, 396–401, 413, 420, 423–24. *See also* Theosophical movement

Bender, Peter, 392

Benedictine movement, 210–13, 217, 221–23, 226–27, 244; developmental communal process of, 205–38 *passim*; gender roles in, 210; daily regimen of, 210–11; St. Benedict, founder of, 211–12; American map of, 214–15; chronology, 239–41; selected bibliography, 250–52

Benson, Ezra Taft, 155

Bentham, Jeremy, 94, 99, 100

Bermudian Creek community. *See* Seventh Day Baptist movement

Besant, Annie, 398, 401–2, 409, 411

Bestor, Arthur E., Jr., x, xx–xxi, 161; *Backwoods Utopias*, 125 (n. 1), 497

Bethabara community. *See* Moravian movement

Bethel, Mo.: Keilite colony of, 78, 473

Bethlehem community. *See* Moravian movement

Beth-Ophra: Koreshan commune, 381, 383, 394

Beuron abbey, 217

Biblicalism, Protestant, 204

Biedermann, Ludwig, 20

Bigelow, Jo, 392–93

BILU ("House of Jacob, Let Us Go") Jewish colony, 354

Birth control: advocated by Robert Owen, 119; as urged in Robert Dale Owen's *Moral Physiology*, 119, 273 (n. 13); and male continence in Perfectionist movement of John Henry Noyes, 257–59, 271, 273 (n. 13)

Bishop Hill, Ill.: communal economy of, 300, 309–13; gender roles and family in, 304; architecture of, 304–5, 307, 311–12; tourism and restoration of, 314. *See also* Janssonist movement

Black monks. *See* Benedictine movement

Black Utopia (W. and J. Pease), 499

Blackwell, Elizabeth, 172

Blanchet, Archbishop Francis, 222

Blaurock, George, 321, 342

Blavatsky, Madame Helena Petrovna, 396–402, 413

Blooming Grove colony: Dr. Frederick C. Haller, founder of, 62–63; Harmonist origins of, 62–63. *See also* Harmonist movement

Blossius, Abbot, 213

Blue Cloud abbey, 223

Boatload of Knowledge, 92, 114

Boehme, Jakob, 19–21, 24, 60; *Aurora*, 21

Bohemia Manor, 7, 17–19, 30

Bon Homme Hutterite colony, 334, 343

Book of Mormon (J. Smith), 137

Book of the New Moral World (R. Owen), 100, 125 (n. 3)

Boston Globe, 397

Boston Herald, 397

Bourg, Pierre, 290

Bowman, Samuel, 19

Branching: as a developmental communal process of Hutterite colonies, 329–30, 335, 349

Brigham City, Utah: influence of Owenite Rochdale cooperative upon, 146; Mormon cooperative of, 146; Mercantile and Manufacturing Association of, 148; United Order in, 148

Brisbane, Albert, 160–62, 164–65, 167–68, 170–72, 174, 175 (n. 3); *Social Destiny of Man*, 164

Brook Farm, ix, 165–66, 168–69, 172, 176 (n. 9), 496, 499

Brotherhood of Humanity, 397. *See also* Theosophical movement

Brothers, monastic, 207, 242. See also *Conversi*, Catholic

Brown, Benjamin, 365–66

Brown, Paul, 108, 113; *Twelve Months in New Harmony*, 130 (n. 68)

Bruderhof Communities. *See* Society of Brothers

Bruderhofs, 8. *See also* Hutterite movement; Society of Brothers movement

Bubbett, Laurence W., 391–93

Burned-Over District, 167, 176 (n. 13)

Bursfield abbey, 213, 217

Butzel, Marin, 363

Byzantine. *See* Orthodoxy

Cabet, Etienne, 9, 109, 279–96, 420

Calhoun, John C., 108

California's Utopian Colonies (R. Hine), 498

Calligraphy, 25

Calvinism, 17, 110

Camaldolese movement, 212

Campbell, Alexander, 107, 139

Canon law, 208, 210, 225

Capuchin order, 24, 218, 239

Carden, Maren Lockwood, 260

Carinthia, 332, 342

Carmelite movement, 219, 227; chronology, 240

Carmel Jewish colony, 359

Carrol, Bishop John, 219

Carthusian movement, 212

Cassian, John, 212

Cassinese American Congregation, 223, 226. *See also* Benedictine movement

Cassiodorus of Vivarium, 212

Catholicism, 17, 24, 26–28, 204–52 *passim*; and Indian mission villages, 14; orthodoxy of, 205, 210, 243; Evangelical Counsels of, 206, 209; ordination in, 206, 210, 237; laity of, 207–8, 213, 226; canon law of, 208, 210, 225; bishops of, 208, 219, 243; clergy of, 208–9, 218, 243; patrons of, 209, 243–44; priests of, 210, 232, 237; Black vs. White clergy in, 210, 243; and Council of Baltimore, 219; persecution of, in America, 219, 236–37, 245; parishes of, 224, 227; and Vatican Council II,

63, 167–68, 170–74; of Inspirationist movement, 183, 185, 187–89, 193–201; of Roman Catholic religious orders, 205–23 passim, 224–38; of Perfectionist moevement of John Henry Noyes, 256, 261, 264–71; of Icarian movement, 279–94; of Janssonist movement, 300, 302–3; of Hutterite movement, 319–41; of Jewish agricultural colony movement, 352–69; of Koreshan movement, 378–92; of Theosophical movement, 396, 402–15; of Peace Mission movement, 437–38; neglect of in Nordhoff's *The Communistic Societies of the United States*, 497; and earlier interpretation of success/failure based on communal longevity, 498; of New Deal community program, 498

Devil's Lake Jewish colony, 362

Dickens, Charles, 495

Directories: of current communal utopias since 1972, 503–4 (n. 25), 505 (n. 29)

Discalced Carmelites, 227

Disciples of Christ movement, 139–40

Divorce: and remarriage in Owenite New Harmony, 119

Doktor Faustus (T. Mann), 25

Dominican movement, 212, 219, 221, 227

Dower, William H., 407

Drama: at Oneida, 266; at Point Loma, 404–5. *See also* Theater

Dress: for women, in Owenite New Harmony, 119; in Amana colonies, 182, 195; of Roman Catholic religious orders, 208, 217; in Oneida Community, 262, 263 (ill.); in Point Loma Theosophical community, 405

Durant, Thomas J., 174

Duss, John, 81

Dutch Reformed Church, 17

Dwight, John, 172

Dwight, Timothy, 495

Dystopia, 4

Eames, Benjamin, 140–41

East Wind Community, 503 (n. 25)

Ebenezer Society, 188–90. *See* Inspirationist movement

Eckensberger, Frederick, 70

Eckerlin, Isaac, 26

Economy, Pa. *See* Harmonist movement

Ecumenism, 27

Edmunds Act of 1882, 150

Education. *See* Schools

Egalitarianism, 96, 103, 503 (n. 25)

Ehrenpreis, Andreas, 325, 342

Eichstatt abbey, 223–24

Einseldeln abbey, 217

Electronic communities, 504

Elmspring Hutterite colony, 334, 343

Emerson, Ralph Waldo, ix, 165

Emigration. *See names of groups and movements*

Emmanuel, Charles "Daddy Grace," 435

Enfield Shaker community, Conn., 43

Enfield Shaker community, N.H., 43, 51, 53

Engelberg abbey, 217

Engels, Friedrich, 103, 123, 161

England, 15, 20. *See also* Owenite movement; Shaker movement

Enlightenment, 100, 108

Environmental determinism, 94, 100

Environmentalism, 11

Ephrata Cloister, 7, 22–27, 30, 31; *Chronicon Ephratense*, 23, 26, 31; music of, 25; *Fraktur*, printing and publications of, 25–26, 31. *See also* Seventh Day Baptist movement

Eremiticism. *See* Monasticism

Essenes, 3

Estelleville Jewish colony, 359

Estero Koreshan community. *See* Koreshan Unity movement

Eugen, Duke Karl of Württemberg, 57–59

Eugenics (stirpiculture): experiment at Oneida Community, 9, 253, 267, 271

Evangelical Lutheran Church, 57

Evans, Frederick W., 48, 51

Faber, Gustav, 390

Falckner, Daniel, 20

The Farm: as New Age community, 415; publications of, 503 (n. 25)

Farmers' Alliance, 422

Farming. *See* Agriculture

Father Divine, 10, 432–46; birth of, 432; religious values of, 432, 434, 438, 441–43; early career of, 432–34; and black churches, 432–35; leadership of, 432,

Index

Hutterite movement, 112, 319–51; age-sex hierarchy in, 319; communalism and community of goods of, 319–20, 322, 325, 328, 330–31, 334, 342, 344; submission and individualism in, 319–20, 322–23, 325, 328, 330, 333, 335, 341, 345; economics of, 319–20, 324, 328, 330, 338–40, 346, 350; developmental communal process of, 319–41; as oldest family communal group in Western World, 320; demography of, 320, 324, 328, 335, 337, 342, 349; in Russian Ukraine, 320, 327, 329, 330, 332, 342–43, 347–48; and Roman Catholicism, 320, 329, 332, 342; in Transylvania, 320, 332, 342–43; and hardships in Peasant War, 321; as radical Anabaptists, 321, 322; cultural persistence of, 321, 325, 328, 340, 344; and separation from the world, 321, 327–29, 331, 333, 336–38; as separatists, 321–22; baptismal beliefs and practices of, 321–22, 325, 330, 347; process of institutionalization in, 321–26; origins of, 321–32; pacificism of, 322, 325, 337, 340, 350 (n. 94); and spiritual Ark of Noah, 322, 333; religious beliefs of, 322–24, 329, 333, 336–37, 341, 344 (n. 1), 347 (n. 45); in Moravia, 323, 325, 328, 338, 342; missionizing of, 323, 325, 328–29, 344 (n. 1); sermons of, 323, 325–26, 331, 348; Jakob Hutter, founder of, 323, 336, 342, 344; *Confession of Faith*, 323, 341–42, 345; writings of, 323–25, 331, 347–48; *Das grosse Geschichtsbuch* (the Great Chronicle), 324, 341–42, 344; persecution of, 324–25, 328, 330, 332, 337, 340, 342, 344; schools and education of, 325, 327, 332, 346 (n. 37); *Great Article Book*, 325, 342; children and child rearing of, 325–27, 331–32, 338, 346 (n. 37), 347 (n. 41); *Klein-Geschichtsbuch der Hutterischen Bruder* (The Small Chronicle of the Hutterian Brethren), 326, 342, 347; hymns of, 327, 331, 349; in South Dakota, 327, 334, 337, 340, 343; hardships for in Thirty Years' War, 329; branching as a developmental process of, 329–30, 335, 349; flight to Romania, 332, 342; and Lutherans, 332, 342; and Mennonites, 332, 343; migrations of, 333–35, 337, 340; first American bruderhof of, at Bon Homme, 334, 343; leadership and gender roles, 335–36; and Owa Community in Japan, 336; as law-abiding citizens, 337; treatment as conscientious objectors in WWI and WWII, 337, 340, 350 (n. 94); and agricultural contribution to Manitoba, 338; discrimination against, in Alberta, 340, 343; in Slovakia, 342; chronology, 342–43; and relations with Society of Brothers, 343, 344 (n. 7), 347 (n. 43), 348 (n. 47), 349 (n. 88); early inability of to form *bruderhof* communities in Germany, 348 (n. 74); selected bibliography, 350–51; compared to Llano del Rio socialists, 499

Hymns. *See* Music

Icarian movement, 9, 161, 420; Etienne Cabet, founder of, 109, 279–96, 420; and *Le Populaire*, 279, 281; Texas Icaria, 279, 281, 283, 294; Nauvoo Icaria, 279, 282–85, 289, 293; Corning Icaria, 279, 285–86, 289, 291, 293–94; at Cloverdale, 279, 293–94; communal utopianism of, 279–81, 294; developmental communal process of, 279–94; influence of Cabet's *Voyage en Icarie* (Travels in Icaria) on, 280, 282–83, 287, 289; advance guard of comes to America, 281, 287; communities of described, 281–94; and Temple Square in Nauvoo, 282, 294; and dissidents and Cabetists at Nauvoo, 284; Cheltenham Icaria, 284, 290, 293–94; progressives and conservatives, at Corning, 285, 289, 293; and Young Icaria, 286; New Icaria, 286–87; Icaria Speranza, 286–87, 420; music and dancing of, 290–91; chronology, 294–95; selected bibliography, 296
Icaria Speranza, 286–87, 420. *See also* Icarian movement
Immaculate Conception abbey, 227
Incorporative Farming Association, 365
Individualism, x, xi, 14, 264; of Josiah

ence of secularism upon, 205, 208, 231; chastity and celibacy of, 205, 209, 226, 234–35, 237, 242 (n. 10); developmental communal process of, 205–23 *passim*, 224–38; collectivism of, 206; solitude in, 206; poverty of, 206, 209, 233; vows in, 206, 209–10, 226, 232; perfectionism of, 206, 212; vocations of, 206, 224, 226, 232, 248; business of, 207; cloisters of, 207; husbandry of, 207; refectories of, 207; sororities of, 207; fraternities of, 207, 210, 242; and friars, 207, 212, 221, 242; nuns of, 207, 220–22, 227–28, 230; brothers of, 207, 242 (n. 11); facilities of, 207, 243; economy of, 207–8; customs of, 207–8, 210–11; conformity in, 208; spirituality of, 208, 210, 237–38; ministry of, 208, 213, 224–25, 227, 234; habits, 208, 217; novices of, 209; schools of, 209, 211, 219, 224, 227; choirs and music of, 209, 217, 231; sexuality in, 209, 235–36, 242 (n. 9); *conversi* of, 209, 243; children in, 209–10; gender roles in, 210, 219, 237; meditation in, 210, 238; daily regimen of, 210–11; Rules of, 210–12, 244; scriptoria in, 211; missionaries of, 211–12, 228; abolition of, in Europe, 213; American map of, 214–15; dissolution of, in England, 216; colleges of, 224, 227; hospitals of, 224, 227; orphanages of, 224, 227; Americanism and modernism as threats to, 226, 247; nursing homes of, 227, 229; witnessing of, 233, 250; and homosexuality, 235–36; and AIDS, 236; chronology, 239–41; segregation by sex, 242 (n. 9); architecture of, 243; oblates of, 244 (n. 17); liturgy of, 244, 249; selected bibliography, 250–52
Monasticism: of Society of the Woman in the Wilderness, 20–21; of Seventh Day Baptists at Ephrata, 23–24; historiography of, 204–5, 241; of Roman Catholic religious orders, 204–52; ideals of, 205, 237–38, 250; terminology of, 205–8, 241–42; desert fathers of, 206, 211; historicism of, 208, 211–12; history of, 211–19, 220–22, 239–41, 245; and immigration, 216, 220–21. *See*

also Catholicism; Monasteries, Roman Catholic
Monastics (Brothers, Monks, Nuns, Sisters), 204–52; defined, 205
Montmartre abbey, 213
Monroe, James, 106, 108
Montana: Hutterite colonies in, 337, 340, 343–44
Monte Cassino abbey, 213, 217
Montefiore Agricultural Aid Society, 362, 366
Moravia: Hutterites in, 323, 325, 328, 338, 342
Moravian Brethren, 7, 27–30. *See also* Moravian movement
Moravian movement, 27–30, 60, 91, 112; congregation towns of, 7; "General Economy" communalism of, 7, 28, 31; Count Nicholas Ludwig von Zinzendorf, founder of modern renewal of, 27–28, 30; developmental communal process of, 27–28, 30–31; education in, 28; in Lititz, Pa., 28; music of, 28; industries and businesses of, 28–29; in Bethlehem, Pa., 28–29, 31; in Salem, Wachovia, N.C., 29–30; in Bethabara, Wachovia, N.C., 30; in Nazareth, Pa., 30; chronology, 30–31; selected bibliography, 36
More, Thomas, 4, 280, 281
Mormon movement (Church of Jesus Christ of Latter-day Saints; Reorganized Church of Jesus Christ of Latter Day Saints), 9, 69, 135–58, 161, 167, 376, 393, 419; polygamy of, 9, 68; in Orderville, Utah, 135, 136 (ill.), 149; concept and practice of United Order of Enoch, 135–36, 147–49; Joseph Smith, founder of, 135–56 *passim*; practice of Consecration and Stewardship, 136, 140, 146; founding of, 137; integrative tendency of, 137; teachings of, 137; City of Zion concept, 139; and prophet Enoch, 139; communalism of, 139–41; developmental communal process of, 139–55; and Christian primitivists of Disciples of Christ, 140; communalism of as revealed to Joseph Smith, 140; in Ohio, 140; and Shakers, 140; terms of Deed of Consecration, 140; Plat of City

of Zion, 141; terms of Deed of Stewardship, 141; urban planning of, 141; at
Nauvoo, Ill., 142; persecution of, 142;
Consecration and Stewardship replaced
by tithing, 143; millennialism of, 143;
and millennial significance of Jackson
County, Mo., 143; Council of Fifty, 144;
at Independence, Mo., 144; migration
to west, 144; and Reorganized Church
of Jesus Christ of Latter Day Saints, 144;
and Utah War (1857–58), 146; and
Panic of 1873, 147; Zion's Cooperative
Mercantile Institution, 147; and
Edmunds Act of 1882, 150; Study of
Values in Five Cultures Project, 151;
Church Welfare Plan of, 152; effects of
Great Depression on, in Utah, 152;
women in, 152; work of women's relief
society, 152; communal values of, 153;
contemporary vestiges of communalism
in, 154; chronology, 155–56; selected
bibliography, 158
Morrow, U. G., 385, 392, 394
Most Holy Rosary abbey, 228
Mother Ann (Lee). *See* Lee, Ann; Shaker
movement
Mother Superior, 208
Mount Angel abbey, 217, 222, 226, 229
(ill.)
Mt. Carmel, Utah: Mormon United Order
at, 149
Mount St. Benedict abbey, 227
Mount St. Joseph abbey, 228
Mueller, Bernhard: claims to have Philoso-
pher's Stone and knowledge of second
advent of Christ, 76; leads seceding
Harmonists from Economy, Pa. (1832),
76–78. *See also* Muellerite movement
Mueller, Dr. Christopher (Johann
Christoph), 62, 65, 70–71
Muellerite movement, 76–78; Bernard
Mueller (Count de Leon, the "Lion of
Judah"), founder of, 76–78; Grand
Ecore and Germantown, La., communi-
ties of, 78; New Philadelphia Society of,
78
Mumford, Lewis, 497
Music: of Shakers, ix, 37, 53 (n. 30),
55; mystical hymns of Society of the
Woman in the Wilderness, 20, 21; of

Ephrata Cloister, 25; of Moravians, 28;
of Harmonists, 72–74, 81; of Owenites,
88–89, 118; of Mormons, 154; Fourierist John Dwight becomes leading music
critic, 172; of Inspirationists, 183; of
Roman Catholic religious orders, 209,
217, 231; of Icarians, 290–91; of Hutterites, 327, 331, 349; of Jewish colonies, 361; of Koreshan Estero colony,
388–89; of Peace Mission movement,
436
Mutschler, Hildegard, 75
Mutual criticism: at Oneida, 259–60, 262
Mysticism: of Labadists, 17–19; of Seventh
Day Baptists, 23; of Roman Catholic
religious orders, 204–6, 248–49 (n. 62)

Napoleon (emperor of France), 61
Napoleonic era: effects of, 95, 104
Nashoba community, 10, 118, 496;
Frances Wright, founder of, 10, 108,
118–19, 495
National Association for Mental Health,
380, 392
National Farm School, 364–65, 368
National Historic Communal Societies
Association, xi, xv. *See also* Communal
Studies Association
Nationalism, 422, 424. *See also* Bellamy,
Edward; Nationalist movement; Theo-
sophical movement
Nationalist clubs. *See* Nationalist move-
ment; Theosophical movement
Nationalist movement/Nationalist clubs,
396–401; and Theosophical movement,
396–401; Boston Theosophists begin,
397
Nativism, American, 219, 236, 245
Nauvoo, Ill. *See* Icarian movement; Mor-
mon movement
Nauvoo Icaria, 279, 282–85, 289, 293–94
Neef, Eloisa Buss, 114, 115
Neef, Joseph, 114, 115
Netherlands, 16–18
Networking: among modern communal
utopias, 503–4 (n. 25)
New Age movement, 4, 414–15; communities of, 414–15; use of occult,
414–15. *See also* Theosophical move-
ment

204–38; congregations of, 207–8, 217, 223–24; affiliations with, 209. *See also* Monasteries, Roman Catholic; Monasticism

Orderville, Utah, 135, 136 (ill.); Mormon United Order in, 149

Ordway, Anne G. (Victoria Gratia), 388–90

Orthodoxy, 205, 210, 243

Orvis, John, 172

Osiris, 413

Otis, Harrison Gray, 424, 427

Ottilien Benedictine movement, 226

Oved, Yaacov, xvi, 500

Owa Community: as Anabaptists in Japan, 336

Owen, Ann Caroline (Dale), 91, 92

Owen, David Dale, 117

Owen, Jane Dale, 92

Owen, Richard, 92, 117

Owen, Robert, ix, 9, 74, 88–133 *passim*, 159, 281, 355, 419; boyhood, 89; Declaration of Mental Independence, 89; on religion, 89, 90, 107; secular millennialism, spiritualism, and phrenology of, 89, 91, 100; on marriage and divorce, 89, 119; views on God, 90; use of developmental communal process, 90–92, 95, 100–107, 112–13, 121–23, 125 (n. 1), 127 (n. 36), 128 (n. 38), 129 (n. 54); community-building ideas of, 91, 92, 102; marriage of, 91, 92, 105; derives communal models, 91, 103, 111; invents silent monitor, 92; advocates a science of society, 92, 100; precedes Jacksonian reform movements to America, 92, 106, 107; pioneers infant schools, 92–94, 114; starts Institution for the Formation of Character, 92–95, 102; pictured, 93; on negative influence of families, 94; character formation idea of, 94, 100, 101; and concern for poor, 95; low opinion of uneducated masses, 95, 96; paternalism of, 95, 96, 104; seeks reform legislation in Britain, 95, 101, 102, 108; seeks philanthropists, 95, 108; New Moral World utopianism of, 95–99, 104, 113, 121; proposes Agricultural and Manufacturing Villages of Unity and Mutual Coop-

eration, 96, 97 (ill.), 97–99, 103, 104; as philanthropist, 96, 105; sources of ideas, 99, 100; *A New View of Society*, 99, 100, 101; and behaviorism, 100; *Book of the New Moral World*, 100; economic theories stated in *Report to the County of Lanark*, 103; on equality, 103; nonviolence of, 103; urges common property based on surplus production, 103; advocates class divisions, 104; denounces bankers, merchants, military leaders, and aristocracy, 104; flexibility of, 104; bans Bible from New Lanark, 105; strained relations with New Lanark mill workers, 105; suspects electoral processes, 106; brings communitarian socialism to United States, 106–7; debates religion with Alexander Campbell, 107; speaks in Hall of Congress, 108; underestimates need to inspire commitment among communitarians, 112; relies on progressive education, 112, 116; purchases New Harmony, 113; and recruitment of educators and scientists, 114; controversy over New Harmony schools with partner William Maclure, 115, 116; economic and governing failures of in New Harmony, 118–20; on birth control, divorce, and remarriage, 119; avoidance of democracy, 121; Friedrich Engels and Harriet Martineau note reform contributions of, 123. *See also* Owenite movement

Owen, Robert Dale: in New Harmony, 92; reforms of, as Indiana state legislator, 117; influences public educational purpose of Smithsonian Institution, as U.S. Congressman, 117–18; urges President Lincoln to issue Emancipation Proclamation, 118; *Moral Physiology* of advocates birth control, 119, 273 (n. 13)

Owen, William, 92

Owenite movement, 88–134, 161, 174, 481–82; influenced by Harmonists, 82; *The New-Harmony Gazette*, 88, 122; music of, 88; Preliminary Society of, 88; Robert Owen, founder of, 88–125 *passim*; urges rational mental independence, 89; millennialism of, 89, 91,

100; character formation idea central to, 89, 94, 100, 101; human happiness goal of, 89, 99; education in, 89, 111; developmental communal process of, 90–92, 100–107, 112–13, 121–23, 125 (n. 1), 127 (n. 36), 128 (n. 38), 129 (n. 54); New Lanark as a community model for, 91; and birth control, 92; and emancipation, 92; women's rights in, 92, 118–19; and tax-supported public schools, 92–94; children in, 93–94, 113–16; infant education of, 93–94, 114–15; avoidance of negative influence of family, 94; adult education of, 94–95; coining of term "socialist," 95; New Moral World utopianism of, 95–99, 104, 113, 121; architectual model of ideal town, 96, 97 (ill.), 126 (n. 21); attempt at Agricultural and Manufacturing Village of Unity and Mutual Cooperation, 96–99, 103; sources of Owen's ideas, 99–100; Marx and Engels's views on, 103; Shaker and Harmonist influence on, 103; helps form cooperative and trade union movements in England, 104; communitarian socialism of, 107; failure of to adjust to common people on frontier, 110–11; lack of membership requirements at New Harmony, 111; official dress of for women of New Harmony, 111, 119; compared to Shaker and Harmonist communalism, 112–13; and English settlement of Morris Birkbeck, 113; schools of in New Harmony, 114–16; traditional gender roles of, 115, 118–19, 499; and flaws in New Harmony communalism, 117; bars African Americans from New Harmony, 118; dances and concerts of, 118; and liberal legacy of New Harmony, 118; and charges of sexual infidelity in New Harmony, 119; divorce and remarriage ideas of, 119; and use of labor notes as time money, 120, 121 (ill.); and difficulties governing New Harmony, 120–21; former members of print *The Free Enquirer* and support Working Men's Party of New York, 122; summary of importance of, 122–23; Friedrich Engels and Harriet Martineau on, 123;

and New Lanark and New Harmony restorations and tourism, 123; starts workers' cooperatives and trade unions in Britain, 123; chronology, 124–25; selected bibliography, 133; Charles Lyell confers with former Owenites at New Harmony on geology, 495. *See also* New Harmony, Ind.; Owen, Robert

Pacifism, 8, 65; of Harmonists, 65, 69; of Hutterites, 322, 325, 337, 340, 350 (n. 94). *See also* Nonviolence
Paine, Thomas, 108
Painted Woods Jewish colony, 361–62
Palestine Jewish colony, 362–63, 368
Palmer, Elihu, 108
Papacy, 208, 214–17, 225–26, 247
Partridge, Edward, 140
Paulist movement, 221, 226, 230
Payne, Edward Biron, 422
Peace Mission movement, 10, 435–47, 482; Father Divine, founder of, 432–45; benefit of emotional display of, 434; economic collapse of 1929 as stimulant to, 434; growth of related to giving food and finding jobs for destitute, 434; developmental communal process of, 434–35, 437–40; as blend of communal idealism and charismatic evangelism, 435; communal centers of known collectively as Peace Mission, 435, 437–38; emphasis on racial harmony, nonviolence, and inner serenity, 435; white legal action against, 435; white people in, 435; banquets of, 436; celibacy of, 436; membership of, 436; operations in Skid Road and ghettoes, 437, 445; promotion of racial equality, 438; purchase of "Krum Elbow," 438; expansion into white neighborhoods, 438–39; social reform efforts of, 438–41; "Promised Land" rural cooperatives of, 439; cooperative economics of, 439–40; antilynching campaigns of, 440; Righteous Government Platform of, 440–41; bureaucratization of, 441; conservative shift of, 441; incorporation of, 441–42; chaste religious orders of, 443; leadership of Mother Divine (Edna Rose Ritchings), 443, 444; decline of, 443–

munalism of, 405; A. P. Spaulding as resident of, 406; economy of, 406; government of, 406; number of residents, 406; effects of Tingley's death on, 406–7; Geoffrey de Purucker as leader, 406–7; sale and operations of moved to Covina and Pasadena, Ca., 407; chronology, 415. *See also* Theosophical movement

Polygamy: of Mormons, 9, 68

Poor Clares movement, 219, 227

Popes. *See* Papacy

Popular Culture Association, xvi

Populist Party, 422

Pordage, John, 20

Porter, Francis L., 135–36, 150

Powell, Adam Clayton, Sr., 434

Prairieleut: as non-colony Hutterites, 63, 464. *See also* Hutterite movement

Pratt, Parley P., 142

Price, Hannah Fisher, 118

Priory. *See* Monasteries, Roman Catholic

Profession. *See* Monasteries, Roman Catholic: vows in

Protective Union (cooperative stores), 173–74

Protestant Reformation. *See* Reformation

Puritans: character of villages, 6–7; commonwealths of, 14

Putney Community, 256–57, 259–60, 271. *See also* Perfectionist movement of John Humphrey Noyes

Quakerism, 18–20, 38, 184

Race relations: African Americans barred from Owenite New Harmony, 118; racial equality, harmony, and anti-lynching efforts in Peace Mission movement, 438, 440

Radical pietism. *See* Pietism

Rafinesque, Constantine, 495

Ramah Mormon community, 151

Rapp, Christina Benzinger, 58, 60, 62

Rapp, Frederick (Reichert), 62–79 *passim*, 113

Rapp, George (Johann Georg; "Father Rapp"), 8, 57–82, 111–12; *Thoughts on the Destiny of Man*, 71. *See also* Harmonist movement

Rapp, Gertrude, 66, 70, 78

Rapp, Johannes, 58, 62, 65

Rapp, Rosina, 58

Rappites. *See* Harmonist movement

Raritan Bay Union, 168

Recollect movement, 218

Reformation, 212–13; Renewal, 212, 226; English, 213; Protestant, 213

Relativism, 233

Religious liberty, 15, 22

Religious orders. *See* Monasteries, Roman Catholic; Monasticism

Religious Union of Associationists, 173

Renewed Moravian Church, 27–30

Reorganized Church of Jesus Christ of Latter Day Saints. *See* Mormon movement

The Republic (Plato), 4, 100

Republican Party: in 1820 election, 106; Fourierists active in antislavery crusade of, 172

Restoration. *See names of historic communal groups and movements*

Reunion colony, 171, 177 (n. 23)

Revivalism, 167

Riasnovsky, Nicholas, 173

Ricardo, David, 95

Rich, Adolph W., 364

Riedmann (Rideman), Peter, 324, 336, 338, 342, 346

Riepp, Mother Benedicta, 223

Rigdon, Sidney, 139

The Righteous Remnant (R. Fogarty), 499

Ripley, George, 165, 170, 172

Ritchings, Edna Rose (Mother Divine), 443–44

Robertson, Constance Noyes, 266–67

Rochdale cooperative system, Owenite, 146

Rock, Johann Friedrich, 184

Roman Catholicism. *See* Catholicism

Romania: Hutterites flee to, 332, 342

Romney, Marion C., 153

Rosenhayn Jewish colony, 359

Rosenthal, Herman, 358

Rosicrucianism, 21

Ross, Marie Marchand, 287, 291

Rousseau, Jean Jacques, 99, 280

Rugby community, 356–57

Rules, monastic, 210–12, 244; Rule of

in Fourierist phalanxes, 169; in Roman
Catholic religious orders, 205, 209,
226, 234–37; at Oneida and Putney
perfectionist communities, 253, 257–
59, 261–62, 271, 273 (n. 13); in New
Odessa Jewish colony, 359; in theosophical Aquarian Foundation community,
412–13; in Peace Mission movement,
436; in communal utopias, works on,
499. *See also* Celibacy
Shaker movement, ix, 7, 9, 37–56, 90, 91,
101, 103, 108, 109, 111–12, 140, 161,
167, 378–79, 388, 390; music of, ix, 37,
53 (n. 30), 55; furniture of, 37; present
influence of, 37; membership of, 37, 44,
48–49, 50–52; basic tenets of, 38; perfectionism of, 38, 40, 42; celibacy of,
38, 40, 111; developmental communal
process of, 38, 41–52; separation from
Anglican Church, 38, 50–51; Ann Lee
(Mother Ann), founder of, 38–52
passim, 52 (n. 12), 90, 111–12, 378;
millennialism of, 39, 40–42, 45–46,
50–51; worship of, 39, 42; persecution
of Ann Lee, 40; economy of, 40, 43–
44, 46; at Niskeyuna/Watervliet, N.Y.,
40–43, 46–47, 50, 55; utopianism of,
41–42; at New Lebanon, N.Y., 41–44,
46–48, 50–52, 52 (n. 15), 53 (n. 22);
dancing of, 42; historical dispensations
of, 42; publications of, 42–43, 45, 48,
50–51; at Hancock near Pittsfield,
Mass., 42–43, 51, 55; communal organization of, 42–44; communities of,
42–52, 485; geographic expansion of,
43, 44; at Sabbathday Lake, Maine, 43,
49, 52; at Canterbury, N.H., 43, 52;
rules of, 43–44, 46, 51; gender roles in,
44; industries of, 44; relations between
sexes of, 44, 47; children and education
among, 44, 48; missionary work of, 44,
50, 485; at Pleasant Hill, Ky., 44–45,
49, 56; architecture of, 45; demographic
characteristics of, 45; apostasy among,
46–48, 50; revivals among ("Mother's
Work"), 47; vegetarianism of, 47; and
Spiritualism, 48; crafts of, 49; chronology, 50–52; gift drawings of, 53 (n. 30),
55; songs of, 53 (n. 30), 55; selected
bibliography, 54–56; and Harmonists,

60, 80, 82; and influence on Jansson-
ists, 309, 312
Shakers (United Society of Believers in
Christ's Second Appearing). *See* Shaker
movement
Shalom Jewish colony, 354
Shenandoah Valley: Seventh Day Baptists
settlement in, 26
Shirley Shaker community, 43, 47
Sicily Island Jewish colony, 358
Silkville Phalanx, 171, 175
Silliman, Benjamin, 115, 495
Sinclair, Upton: EPIC program, 429
Sisters of Charity movement, 221–22,
228–29; Mother Elizabeth Seton,
founder of, 221
Sisters of Loretto movement, 221
Sisters of Mercy movement, 221, 230
Sisters of Notre Dame de Namur move-
ment, 221–22
Sisters of Perpetual Adoration movement,
224
Sisters of Providence movement, 221–22,
229
Sisters of St. Elizabeth movement, 228
Sisters of St. Francis movement, 228
Sisters of St. Joseph movement, 221, 230
Sisters of the Holy Cross movement, 229
Sisters of the Holy Family movement, 221
Sisters of the Holy Name movement, 222
Sisters of the Precious Blood movement,
221
Skottowe, Mabel (Madame Zee), 413
Slovakia: Hutterites in, 342
Sluyter, Pieter, 18–19
Smith, Adam, 95
Smith, Hyrum, 144
Smith, Joseph, 9, 137, 138 (ill.), 144, 153,
282, 378, 393. *See* Mormon movement
Smith, Joseph, III, 144
Snow, Erastus, 150, 151
Snow, Lorenzo, 146–47
Snowberger family, 26–27
Snow Hill Society. *See* Seventh Day Baptist
movement
Social Destiny of Man (A. Brisbane),
160–62, 164
Social Gospel, 204
Socialism, 88, 95, 204, 419–31; of Robert
Owen, 95–99; of Owenism, 106–7; of

Fourierism, 150–74; Saint-Simonian, 159–60, 286, 419; of Theosophy, 396–400, 407; Progressive, 421; of Job Harriman, 423

Socialist Labor Party, 420, 423

Social science: Robert Owen's advocacy of, 100; Fourierist promotion of, 164, 169–70, 172

Society for Utopian Studies, xv, xvi, 498

Society of Brothers movement (Bruderhof Communities): origins and development of, 343, 349 (nn. 88, 89); and relations with Hutterites in America, 344 (n. 7), 347 (n. 43), 348 (n. 47), 349 (n. 88); as seen by former members, 349 (n. 88); Eberhard and Emmy Arnold, founders of, 487

Society of Friends. See Quakerism

Society of Separatists of Zoar. See Zoarite movement

Society of the Woman in the Wilderness, 7, 19–22, 30; Johannes Kelpius, founder of, 19–22; developmental communal process of, 20–22; art, science, and literature of, 21; millennialism of, 21; semi-monasticism of, 21; school of, 21; celibacy of, 22; Theosophy of, 22; chronology, 30

Society of True Inspiration. See Inspirationist movement

Sodus Bay Phalanx, 167

Sodus Bay Shaker community, 44, 49, 51

Solesmes abbey, 217

Songs. See Music

Soule, Eldress Gertrude, 52

Sovereigns of Industry, 172

Speakman, John, 109, 114

Spener, Philip Jakob, 20, 183

Spiritual Community Guide, 503 (n. 25)

Spiritualism, 378; Shaker interest in, 48; Robert Owen's interest in, 91

Stanton, Edwin M., 118

Stirpiculture. See Eugenics

Stony Creek community. See Seventh Day Baptist movement

Subiaco abbey, 223

Success/Failure interpretation: in contrast to developmental communalism interpretation, xviii; based on communal

longevity of communes and movements, 498

Sulpician movement, 218

Sunrise Jewish colony, 366

Swedenborg, Emmanuel, 61, 172

Swift, Lindsay, 165

Swiss American Congregation, 223. See also Benedictine movement

Sylvestrine Benedictines, 226

Symmes, Captain John C., 379

Tannenberg, David, 28

Tauler, Johannes, 61

Teed, Dr. Cyrus Reed, 11; as founder of Koreshan Unity movement, 375–95; alchemy of, 376; millennialism of, 376–79; celibacy of, 378, 381; use of pseudonyms, 378, 393; and developmental communal process of, 378–92; cellular cosmogony of, 379–80, 386, 393–94; as social reformer, 387–91

Teed, Delia M. (Row), 376, 389

Teed, Douglas, 376, 392

Temple Home Association. See Temple of the People

Temple of the People: alcoholic clinic of, 407; Frances LaDue and William H. Dower, founders of, 407; utopian and socialistic reform ideas of, 407; communal arrangement at Halcyon, 407–8; guidance of Masters, 407–8; developmental communalism of, 407–9; as Theosophical community at Halcyon, Ca., 407–9; as an initiative within Theosophical movement, 407–9, 414; economy of, in Halcyon, 408–9; flaws in Masters' Plan of communal enterprise, 408–9; publishes The Temple Artisan, 408–9; builds temple at Halcyon, 409; creates Temple Home Association, 409; survives non-communally to present, 409; chronology, 415

Texas Icaria, 279, 281, 283, 294

Theater: Mormon activity in, 154; first American outdoor Greek-style at Point Loma, 404; Greek at Krotona, 410. See also Drama

Theosophical Masters. See Masters

Theosophical movement, 396–415; developmental communal process of, 396,

402–15; utopianism of, 396, 405, 409; universal brotherhood ideal of, 396–97, 400, 402, 404, 412–13; influence of Edward Bellamy and *Looking Backward: 2000–1887* upon, 396–401, 413; Madame Helena Petrovna Blavatsky, founder of, 396–402, 413; Theosophical Society of, 396–415; members of initiate Nationalist movement and Nationalist clubs, 397–401; Blavatsky approves Nationalist principles in *The Key to Theosophy*, 398; Blavatsky reviews *Looking Backward* in *Lucifer*, 398; Blavatsky's agreement with non-Darwinian evolution and "divinity within" ideas in *Looking Backward*, 398; leaders' attraction to women's liberation, as depicted in *Looking Backward*, 398; William Q. Judge reviews *Looking Backward* in *The Path*, 398; Blavatsky and Bellamy compared, 399; shrinks from Nationalist movement, 399; Blavatsky, Judge, and Henry S. Olcott found Theosophical Society of, 400; official objectives of Theosophical Society, 400; occult teachings of based on wisdom of Masters, 400–402; Masters of Wisdom as sources of plans and guidance, 400–402, 407–8, 411–12, 414; Esoteric Section of Theosophical Society, 401; formation of Theosophical Society in America and American Section of the Theosophical Society (Adyar), 401; schism in, 401; leadership of Annie Besant, 401–2; leadership of E. T. Hargrove, 401–2; leadership of Katherine A. Tingley, 401–7; formation of Temple of the People and United Lodge of Theosophy, 402; *The Key to Thesophy* as inspiration for experimental communities of, 402; Point Loma community of, 402–7; creation of Universal Brotherhood organization, 404; Temple of the People (Halcyon) community, 407–9; Krotona community, 409–11; Aquarian Foundation community, 411–13; summary of communal impulse of, 413–15; individualism of occult at odds with communal impulse of, 414; New Age occultist communities and their com-munications with Masters of Wisdom, 414; revival of in New Age movement of 1970s, 414; Findhorn in Scotland and The Farm in Tennessee as New Age communities, 414–15; chronology, 415; selected bibliography, 417–18. *See also* Aquarian Foundation; Krotona Institute of Theosophy; Point Loma Theosophical community; Temple of the People

Theosophical Society, 396–415; founding of, 400. *See also* Thesophical movement

Theosophy, 11; of Society of the Woman in the Wilderness, 19, 22; of Ephrata Cloister, 24; of Theosophical Society, 396–415. *See also* Theosophical movement

Thirty Years' War: hardships for Hutterites during, 329

Thomas, Robert David, 260–61, 272 (n. 3), 275 (n. 29), 275–76 (n. 36)

Thompson, Jeremiah, 108

Thompson, William, 103

Time Store Cooperative movement, 120, 123; Josiah Warren, founder of, 120, 121; use of labor notes as time money in Equity, Utopia, and Modern Times communities, 120, 121 (ill.); Modern Times closing of, 123

Tingley, Katherine, 11, 398, 401–7; *The God's Await*, 402

Tithe: Mormon use of, 143

Tocqueville, Alexis de, x, 154, 495

Tomorrow a New World: The New Deal Community Program (P. Conkin), 498

Transcendentalists: of Brook Farm, 165

Transylvania: Hutterites in, 320, 332, 342–43

Trappist movement, 218, 221, 246

A Traveler from Altruria (W. D. Howells), 422

Troost, Dr. Gerard, 109, 114

True Church of Brotherly Love. *See* Irenia community

Twain, Mark, x

Twelve Corners Jewish colony, 362

Tyler, Alice Felt, ix, x, 497

Tyringham Shaker community, 43, 49, 51

The Union, 125 (n. 1)
Union Village Shaker community, 44, 53 (n. 22)
Unitarians, 422
Unitary Household, 173
United Cooperative Industries, 429
United Lodge of Theosophy, 402
United Order/United Order of Enoch. *See* Mormon movement
United Society of Believers in Christ's Second Appearing. *See* Shaker movement
United States Geological Survey, 117
Unity of Czech Brethren, 27–28, 30
Universal brotherhood. *See* Theosophical movement
Ursuline movement, 230
Utah Poultry Producers Cooperative Association, 366
Utah War (1857–58), 146
Utopia (T. More), 4
Utopianism, xi, 204; classic works on, 4; of Shakers, 41–42; of Owenites, 95–99, 104, 113, 121; of Fourierists, 160–61, 163–64, 169, 172–73; of Roman Catholic religious orders, 204, 242–43 (n. 12); of Theosophical movement, 396, 402–3, 405, 409; of Edward Bellamy, 397; of youth movement of 1960s, 498
Utopian Socialism/Communitarian socialism, x, 4, 5; of Pieter Plockhoy, 17; of Robert Owen, 95–99; of Fourierism, 161, 163
Utopian Studies (Journal of Society for Utopian Studies), 498
Utopias on Puget Sound (C. LeWarne), 499

Valladolid congregation, 213
Vallambrosan movement, 212
Vallet, Emile, 289
Valley of the Swans community (Plockhoy's Commonwealth), 7, 15–17, 30; developmental communal process of, 15–17, 30; Pieter C. Plockhoy, founder of, 15–17, 30; destroyed by English in Anglo-Dutch War, 16; as first utopian settlement in America, 17; and utopian socialism, 17; chronology, 30; selected bibliography, 35

Vatican. *See* Papacy
Vatican Congregation for Religious and Secular Institutes, 225
Vatican Council II, 224–25, 231, 234, 247
Vegetarianism: of Shakers, 47; of Theosophists, 410
Vincentian movement, 220
Violence: by leaders against members of Aquarian Foundation community, 413
Visitandines, 219, 221
Visitation. *See* Communal visitation
Voyage en Icarie (Travels in Icaria, E. Cabet), 280, 282–83, 287, 289

Waldner, Johannes, 326, 342, 347
Waldner, Michel, 333
Wallachia (in Romania): Hutterites flee to, 332, 342
Wallingford community, 483. *See also* Perfectionist movement of John Humphrey Noyes
Walter, Jacob, 330
Walter, Zacarias, 342
Wardley, James and Jane, 38–40, 50
Ware, Norman F., x
Warren, Josiah, 120, 123, 130 (n. 68). *See also* Time Store Cooperative movement
Warrington, Albert P., 409–10
Watervliet Shaker community, N.Y. *See* Niskeyuna
Watervliet Shaker community, Ohio, 44, 49
Watson, Ebbie Julian, 364
Weingartner, Wallrath, 67
Weintraub, Charles, 365
Werkzeuge (inspired instruments), 184–86, 192, 198
Western Comrade, 425, 427
West Friesland, 17–18
West Union Shaker community, 44
White Monks. *See* Cistercian movement
Whitewater Shaker community, 44, 49
Whittaker, James, 42, 50
Whittier, John Greenleaf, 21
Whitwell, Stedman, 97 (ill.), 126 (n. 21)
Wiewerd, 17–18
Willard, Cyrus Field, 397
Wilson, Edward A., 411–13
Wimmer, Boniface S., 222–23

Index